Lecture Notes in Artificial Intelligence 1574

Subseries of Lecture Notes in Computer Science
Edited by J. G. Carbonell and J. Siekmann

Lecture Notes in Computer Science

Edited by G. Goos, J. Hartmanis and J. van Leeuwen

Springer

Berlin
Heidelberg
New York
Barcelona
Hong Kong
London
Milan
Paris
Singapore
Tokyo

Ning Zhong   Lizhu Zhou (Eds.)

Methodologies for Knowledge Discovery and Data Mining

Third Pacific-Asia Conference, PAKDD-99
Beijing, China, April 26-28, 1999
Proceedings

 Springer

Series Editors

Jaime G. Carbonell, Carnegie Mellon University, Pittsburgh, PA, USA
Jörg Siekmann, University of Saarland, Saarbrücken, Germany

Volume Editors

Ning Zhong
Yamaguchi University
Department of Computer Science and Systems Engineering
Tokiwa-Dai, 2557, Ube 755, Japan
E-mail: zhong@ai.csse.yamaguchi-u.ac.jp

Lizhu Zhou
Tsinghua University
Department of Computer Science and Technology
Beijing, China
E-mail: dcszlz@mail.tsinghua.edu.cn

Cataloging-in-Publication data applied for

Die Deutsche Bibliothek – CIP-Einheitsaufnahme

Methodologies for knowledge discovery and data mining : third Pacific Asia
conference ; proceedings / PAKDD-99, Beijing, China, April 26 - 28, 1999. Ning
Zhong ; Lizhu Zhou (ed.). - Berlin ; Heidelberg ; New York ; Barcelona ;
Budapest ; Hong Kong ; London ; Milan ; Paris ; Singapore ; Tokyo : Springer,
1999
(Lecture notes in computer science ; Vol. 1574 : Lecture notes in artificial
intelligence)
ISBN 3-540-65866-1

CR Subject Classification (1998): I.2, H.3, H.5.1, G.3, J.1

ISBN 3-540-65866-1 Springer-Verlag Berlin Heidelberg New York

© Springer-Verlag Berlin Heidelberg 1999
Printed in Germany

Typesetting: Camera-ready by author
SPIN 10703058   06/3142 – 5 4 3 2 1 0   Printed on acid-free paper

Preface

This volume contains the papers selected for presentation at the Third Pacific-Asia Conference on Knowledge Discovery and Data Mining (PAKDD-99) held in the Xiangshan Hotel, Beijing, China, April 26-28, 1999. The conference was sponsored by Tsinghua University, National Science Foundation of China, Chinese Computer Federation, Toshiba Corporation, and NEC Software Chugoku, Ltd. PAKDD-99 provided an international forum for the sharing of original research results and practical development experiences among researchers and application developers from different KDD-related areas such as machine learning, databases, statistics, knowledge acquisition, data visualization, knowledge-based systems, soft computing, and high performance computing. It followed the success of PAKDD-97 held in Singapore in 1997 and PAKDD-98 held in Australia in 1998 by bringing together participants from universities, industry, and government.

PAKDD-99 encouraged both new theory/methodologies and real world applications, and covered broad and diverse topics in data mining and knowledge discovery. The technical sessions included: Association Rules Mining; Feature Selection and Generation; Mining in Semi, Un-structured Data; Interestingness, Surprisingness, and Exceptions; Rough Sets, Fuzzy Logic, and Neural Networks; Induction, Classification, and Clustering; Causal Model and Graph-Based Methods; Visualization; Agent-Based, and Distributed Data Mining; Advanced Topics and New Methodologies.

Of the 158 submissions, we accepted 29 regular papers and 37 short papers for presentation at the conference and for publication in this volume. In addition, over 20 papers were accepted for poster presentation.

The PAKDD-99 program was further supplemented by two invited speakers: Won Kim and Hiroshi Motoda, a special session on Emerging KDD Technology (Speakers: Zdzislaw Pawlak, Philip Yu, T.Y. Lin, Hiroshi Tsukimoto), and a panel session on Knowledge Management in Data Mining (Chair: Xindong Wu; Panelists: Rao Kotagiri, Zhongzhi Shi, Jan M. Żytkow).

Two tutorials: Automated Discovery - Combining AI, Statistics and Theory of Knowledge by Jan M. Żytkow, Quality Data and Effective Mining by Hongjun Lu, and a workshop on Knowledge Discovery from Advanced Databases organized by Mohamed Quafafou and Philip Yu, were also offered to all conference participants on April 26.

A conference such as this can only succeed as a team effort. We would like to acknowledge the contribution of the program committee members and thank the reviewers for their reviewing efforts, the PAKDD steering committee members for their invaluable input and advice, and the conference chairs: Bo Zhang and Setsuo Ohsuga whose involvement and support have added greatly to the quality of the conference. Our sincere gratitude goes to all of the authors who submitted papers. We are grateful to our sponsors for their generous support. Special thanks are due to Alfred Hofmann of Springer-Verlag for his help and cooperation.

April 1999   Ning Zhong and Lizhu Zhou

PAKDD-99 Conference Committee

Conference Chairs:

Bo Zhang   Tsinghua University, China
Setsuo Ohsuga   Waseda University, Japan

Program Chairs:

Ning Zhong   Yamaguchi University, Japan
Lizhu Zhou   Tsinghua University, China

Organizing Committee Chairs:

Zhongzhi Shi   Chinese Academy of Sciences
Shan Wang   People's University of China

Publicity Chair:

Lianhua Xiao   The National Science Foundation of China

Local Chair:

Zengqi Sun   Tsinghua University, China

PAKDD Steering Committee:

Xindong Wu   Colorado School of Mines, USA (Chair)
Hongjun Lu   Hong Kong Univ. of Science & Technology
Rao Kotagiri   (Co-Chair)
Huan Liu   University of Melbourne, Australia
Hiroshi Motoda   National University of Singapore
Ning Zhong   Osaka University, Japan
                     Yamaguchi University, Japan

Program Committee

Contents

Invited Talks

Emerging KDD Technology

Association Rules

Feature Selection and Generation

Mining in Semi, Un-structured Data

Interestingness, Surprisingness, and Exceptions

Rough Sets, Fuzzy Logic, and Neural Networks

Induction, Classification, and Clustering

Visualization

Causal Model and Graph-Based Methods

Agent-Based, and Distributed Data Mining

Advanced Topics and New Methodologies

KDD as an Enterprise IT Tool: Reality and Agenda

Won Kim

Cyber Database Solutions, USA
E-mail: won.kim@cyberdb.com

KDD is a key technology for harnessing the "business intelligence" IT infrastructure. Although KDD has been a longstanding field of research, it is in its infancy in commercial endeavors. Commercial KDD products have many major weaknesses that have slowed KDD's becoming an enterprise IT tool. In this presentation, I will review the technological and business reality of KDD, and discuss what needs to happen before KDD can attain the status that other enterprise IT tools have reached, including database servers, data warehouses, decision support and OLAP tools, etc.

Computer Assisted Discovery of First Principle Equations from Numeric Data

Hiroshi Motoda

Institute of Scientific and Industrial Research,
Osaka University
Mihogaoka, Ibaraki, Osaka 567-0047, JAPAN
motoda@ar.sanken.osaka-u.ac.jp

Just like physicists have tried for many years to find the truth that is hidden in the observed data by the deep insight and understood the phenomena, computer can assist in analyzing huge amount of data that is beyond the capability of human cognition and derive equations that explain the phenomena. Being able to reproduce the observed data does not necessarily mean that the derived equations represent the first principle. We show that there is a method that ensures to derive the first principle. Notion of scale types of the observed data and interesting properties that are deduced by the scale type constraints and dimensional analysis are the basis of the method. These two together with simple mathematics can constrain the form of admissible relations among the variables in great depth. A complete equation that describes the system behavior can be represented by a set of dimensionless variables whose cardinality is smaller than that of the original variables. Each dimensionless number is related to a subset of the original variables and forms a chunk called a regime whose form is constrained by the scale types of the variables. An algorithm is developed to construct possible regimes in a bottom up way making the best use of the constraints. A number of different statistical tests are performed to ensure that the correct relations are identified. The method works for phenomena for which nothing is known about the number of equations that are needed to describe them and no knowledge of dimensions of the variables involved is available. Thus, the method can be applied to discover models of less-well-understood domains such as biology, psychology, economics and social science. Many of the known first principles that involve several tens of variables and a few tens of equations have been re-discovered by numerical experiments with noisy data. The talk covers our recent advancement in this research. This is a joint work with Takashi Washio.

References

[1] T. Washio and H. Motoda. Discovering Admissible Models of Complex Systems Based on Scale-Types and Identity Constraints. In *Proc. of IJCAI97*, pp. 810–817, 1997.
[2] T. Washio and H. Motoda. Discovering Admissible Simultaneous Equations of Large Scale Systems. In *Proc. of AAAI98*, pp. 189–196, 1998.
[3] T. Washio and H. Motoda. Development of SDS2: Smart Discovery System for Simultaneous Equation Systems. In *Discovery Science, Lecture Notes in Artificial Intelligence 1532*, Springer, pp. 352-363, 1998.

Data Mining – a Rough Set Perspective

Zdzisław Pawlak

Institute for Theoretical and Applied Informatics
Polish Academy of Sciences
Bałtycka 5, 44 000 Gliwice, Poland

1 Introduction

Data mining (DM) can be perceived as a methodology for discovering hidden patterns in data. DM is a relatively new area of research and applications, stretching, over many domains like statistics, machine learning, fuzzy sets, rough sets, cluster analysis, genetics algorithms, neural networks and others. Despite many various techniques employed in DM yet it can be seen as a distinct discipline with its own problems and aims.

Reasoning methods associated with discovering knowledge from data attracted attention of philosophers for many years. Particularly some ideas of B. Russell and K. Popper about data, induction and experimental knowledge can be viewed as precursory ones for DM.

Many valuable papers and books have been published on data mining recently. In this paper we will focus our attention on some problems pertinent to rough sets and DM [2, 3, 5, 6, 7, 8, 9, 11, 14, 15, 16, 19, 24, 32, 33, 36, 37].

Rough set theory has proved to be useful in DM, and it "... constitutes a sound basis for data mining applications" [4]. The theory offers mathematical tools to discover hidden patterns in data. It identifies partial or total dependencies (i.e. cause-effect relations) in databases, eliminates redundant data, gives approach to null values, missing data, dynamic data and others. The methods of data mining in large databases using rough sets have recently been proposed and investigated [5, 14, 16].

The theory is based on sound mathematical foundation. It can easily be understood and applied. Several software systems based on rough set theory have been implemented and many nontrivial applications of this methodology for knowledge discovery have been reported. More about rough sets and their applications can be found in [19].

The theory is not competitive but complementary to other methods and can also be often used jointly with other approaches (e.g. fuzzy sets, genetic algorithms, statistical methods, neural networks etc.).

The main objective of this talk is to give basic ideas of rough sets in the context of DM. The starting point of rough set theory is a data set. The theory can also be formulated in more general terms, however for the sake of intuition we will refrain from general formulation. Data are usually organized in the form of a table, columns of which are labeled by attributes, rows – by objects and entries of the table are attribute values. Such a table will be called a database. Next, basic operations on sets in rough set theory, the lower and the upper approximation of a set will be defined. These operations will be used to define the basic concepts of the theory (from the DM point of view) – total and partial dependency of attributes in a database. The concept of dependency of attributes is used to describe cause-effect relations hidden in the data. Further, a very important issue, reduction of data, will be introduced. Finally certain and possible decision rules determined by total and partial dependencies will be defined and analyzed. Besides, certainty and coverage factors of a decision rule will be defined and reasoning methods based on the idea outlined.

2 Database

An example of a simple database is presented in Table 1.

Table 1. An example of a database

Store	E	Q	L	P
1	high	good	no	profit
2	med.	good	no	loss
3	med.	good	no	profit
4	no	avg.	no	loss
5	med.	avg.	yes	loss
6	high	avg.	yes	profit

In the database six stores are characterized by four attributes:

E – empowerment of sales personnel,
Q – perceived quality of merchandise,
L – high traffic location,
P – store profit or loss.

Each store is described in terms of attributes E, Q, L and P.

Each subset of attributes determines a partition (classification) of all objects into classes having the same description in terms of these attributes. For example, attributes Q and L aggregate all stores into the following classes $\{1, 2, 3\}, \{4\}, \{5, 6\}$. Thus, each database determines a family of classification patterns which are used as a basis of further considerations.

Formally a database will be defined as follows.

By a *database* we will understand a pair $S = (U, A)$, where U and A are finite, nonempty sets called the *universe* and a set of *attributes* respectively.

With every attribute $a \in A$ we associate a set V_a of its *values*, called the *domain* of a. Any subset B of A determines a binary relation $I(B)$ on U, which will be called an *indiscernibility relation* and is defined as follows:

$(x, y) \in I(B)$ if and only if $a(x) = a(y)$ for every $a \in A$, where $a(x)$ denotes the value of attribute a for element x.

It can easily be seen that $I(B)$ is an equivalence relation. The family of all equivalence classes of $I(B)$, i.e. partition determined by B will be denoted by $U/I(B)$ or simple U/B; an equivalence class of $I(B)$, i.e. block of the partition U/B containing x will be denoted by $B(x)$.

If (x, y) belongs to $I(B)$ we will say that x and y are *B-indiscernible*. Equivalence classes of the relation $I(B)$ (or blocks of the partition U/B) are referred to as *B-elementary sets* or *B-granules*.

Equivalence relation as a basis for rough set theory for many applications is not sufficient. Therefore other relations e.g. a tolerance relation, an ordering relations and others, have been proposed, e.g. [21, 23, 31]. But for the sake of simplicity in this paper we will stick to the equivalence relation as a basis for rough set theory.

3 Approximations of Sets

First let us consider the following exmaple: what are the characteristic features of stores having profit (or loss) in view of information available in Table 1. It can easily be seen that this question cannot be answered uniquely since stores 2 and 3 display the same features in terms of attributes E, Q and L, but store 2 makes a profit, whereas store 3 has a loss. In view of information contained in Table 1, we can say for sure that stores 1 and 6 make a profit, stores 4 and 5 have a loss, whereas stores 2 and 3 cannot be classified as making a profit or having a loss. Employing attributes E, Q and L, we can say that stores 1 and 6 *surely* make a profit, i.e. *surely* belong to the set {1, 3, 6}, whereas stores 1, 2, 3 and 6 *possibly* make a profit, i.e. *possibly* belong to the set {1, 3, 6 }. We will say that the set {1, 6} is the *lower approximation* of the set (concept) {1, 3, 6} and the set {1, 2, 3, 6} is the *upper approximation* of the set {1, 3, 6}. The set {2, 3}, being the difference between the upper approximation, and the lower approximation, is referred to as the *boundary region* of the set {1, 3, 6}.

Approximations can be defined formally as operations assigning to every $X \subseteq U$ two sets $B_*(X)$ and $B^*(X)$ called the *B-lower* and the *B-upper approximation* of X, respectively and defined as follows:

$$B_*(X) = \bigcup_{x \in U} \{B(x) : B(x) \subseteq X\},$$

$$B^*(X) = \bigcup_{x \in U} \{B(x) : B(x) \cap X \neq \emptyset\}.$$

Hence, the B-lower approximation of a concept is the union of all B-granules that are included in the concept, whereas the B-*upper* approximation of a concept is the union of all B-granules that have a nonempty intersection with the concept. The set

$$BN_B(X) = B^*(X) - B_*(X)$$

will be referred to as the B-*boundary region* of X.

If the boundary region of X is the empty set, i.e., $BN_B(X) = \emptyset$, then X is *crisp* (*exact*) with respect to B; in the opposite case, i.e., if $BN_B(X) \neq \emptyset$, X is referred to as *rough* (*inexact*) with respect to B.

"Roughness" of a set can be also characterized numerically as

$$\alpha_B(X) = \frac{card(B_*(X))}{card(B^*(X))},$$

where $0 \leq \alpha_B(X) \leq 1$ and if $\alpha_B(X) = 1$, X is crisp with respect to B, whereas if $\alpha_B(X) < 1$, X is rough with respect to B.

Rough sets can be also defined using a *rough membership function* [17], defined as

$$\mu_X^B(x) = \frac{card(B(x) \cap X)}{card(B(x))}.$$

Obviously

$$0 \leq \mu_X^B(x) \leq 1.$$

Value of the membership function $\mu_X^B(x)$ is a conditional probability $\pi(X|B(x))$, and can be interpreted as a degree of *certainty* to which x belongs to X (or $1 - \mu_X^B(x)$, as a degree of *uncertainty*).

4 Dependency of Attributes

Another important issue in data analysis is discovering dependencies between attributes. Suppose that the set of attributes A in a database $S = (U, A)$ is divided into two subsets C and D, called *condition* and *decision* attributes respectively, such that $C \cup D = A$ and $C \cap D = \emptyset$. Such databases are called *decision tables*.

Intuitively, a set of attributes D *depends totally* on a set of attributes C, denoted $C \Rightarrow D$, if all values of attributes from D are uniquely determined by values of attributes from C. In other words, D depends totally on C, if there exists a functional dependency between values of C and D.

We would need also a more general concept of dependency, called a *partial dependency* of attributes. Intuitively, the partial dependency means that only some values of D are determined by values of C.

Dependency is strictly related with approximations and is the basic issue in data mining, because it reveals relationships in a database.

Formally, dependency can be defined in the following way. Let C and D be subsets of A.

We will say that D *depends on* C to a *degree k* $(0 \leq k \leq 1)$, denoted $C \Rightarrow_k D$, if

$$k = \gamma(C, D) = \sum_{X \in U/D} \frac{card(C_*(X))}{card(U)}.$$

If $k = 1$ we say that D *depends totally* on C, and if $k < 1$, we say that D *depends partially* (to a *degree k*) on C, and if $k = 0$, then D *does not depend on C*.

The coefficient k expresses the ratio of all elements of the universe, which can be properly classified to blocks of the partition U/D, employing attributes C and will be called the *degree of the dependency*.

For example in Table 1 the degree of dependency between the attribute P and the set of attributes $\{E, Q, L\}$ is 2/3.

Obviously if D depends totally on C then $I(C) \subseteq I(D)$. That means that the partition generated by C is finer than the partition generated by D.

5 Reduction of Attributes

A reduct is the minimal set of condition attributes that preserves the degree of dependency. It means that a reduct is a minimal subset of condition attributes that enables to make the same decisions as the whole set of condition attributes.

Formally if $C \Rightarrow_k D$ then a minimal subset C' of C, such that $\gamma(C, D) = \gamma(C', D)$ is called a *D-reduct* of C.

For example, in Table 1 we have two reducts $\{E, Q\}$ and $\{E, L\}$ of condition attributes $\{E, Q, L\}$.

Reduction of attributes is the fundamental issue in rough set theory.

In large databases computation of reducts on the basis of the given definition is not a simple task and therefore many more effective methods have been proposed. For references see [19].

6 Significance of Attributes

The concept of a reduct enables us to remove some attributes in the database in such a way that the basic relationships in the database are preserved. Some attributes, however, cannot be removed from the database without changing their properties. To express this idea more precisely we will need the notion of *significance of an attribute*, which is defined next.

Let C and D be sets of condition and decision attributes respectively and let a be a condition attribute, i.e. $a \in C$. We can ask how the coefficient $\gamma(C, D)$ changes when removing the attribute a, i.e. what is the difference between $\gamma(C, D)$ and $\gamma(C - \{a\}, D)$. We can normalize the difference and define the significance of an attribute a as:

$$\sigma_{(C,D)}(a) = \frac{(\gamma(C, D) - \gamma(C - \{a\}, D))}{\gamma(C, D)} = 1 - \frac{\gamma(C - \{a\}, D)}{\gamma(C, D)},$$

and denote simply by $\sigma(a)$, when C and D are understood.

Thus the coefficient $\sigma(a)$ can be understood as an error which occurs when attribute a is dropped. The significance coefficient can be extended to set of attributes as follows:

$$\sigma_{(C,D)}(B) = \frac{(\gamma(C, D) - \gamma(C - B, D))}{\gamma(C, D)} = 1 - \frac{\gamma(C - B, D)}{(\gamma C, D)},$$

denoted by $\sigma(B)$, if C and D are understood, where B is a subset of C.

If B is a reduct of C, then $\sigma(B) = 1$, i.e. after removing any reduct from the set of decision rules one cannot make sure decisions, whatsoever.

7 Decision Rules

Dependences between attributes are usually symbolized as a set of decision rules. For example, decision rules describing the dependency $\{E, Q\} \Rightarrow \{P\}$ in Table 1 are the following:

$(E,\ high)\ and\ (good) \rightarrow (profit)$,
$(E,\ med.)\ and\ (good) \rightarrow (loss)$,
$(E,\ med.)\ and\ (good) \rightarrow (profit)$,
$(E,\ no)\ and\ (avg.) \rightarrow (loss)$,
$(E,\ med.)\ and\ (avg.) \rightarrow (loss)$,
$(E,\ high)\ and\ (avg.) \rightarrow (profit)$.

A set of decision rules is usually referred as a *knowledge base*.

Usually we are interested in the optimal set of decision rules associated with the dependency, but we will not consider this issue here. Instead we will analyze some probabilistic properties of decision rules.

Let S be a decision table and let C and D be condition and decision attributes, respectively.

By Φ, Ψ etc. we will denote logical formulas built up from attributes, attribute-values and logical connectives (*and, or, not*) in a standard way. We will denote by $|\Phi|_S$ the set of all objects $x \in U$ satisfying Φ and refer to as the *meaning* of Φ in S.

The expression $\pi_S(\Phi) = \frac{card(|\Phi|_S)}{card(U)}$ will denote the probability that the formula Φ is true in S.

A *decision rule* is an expression in the form "*if...then...*", written $\Phi \rightarrow \Psi$; Φ and Ψ are referred to as *condition* and *decision* of the rule, respectively.

A decision rule $\Phi \to \Psi$ is *admissible* in S if $|\Phi|_S$ is the union of some C-elementary sets, $|\Psi|_S$ is the union of some D-elementary sets and $|\Phi \wedge \Psi|_S \neq \emptyset$. In what follows we will consider admissible decision rules only.

With every decision rule $\Phi \to \Psi$ we associate a *certainty factor*

$$\pi_S(\Psi|\Phi) = \frac{card(|\Phi \wedge \Psi|_S)}{card(|\Phi|_S)},$$

which is the conditional probability that Ψ is true in S, given Φ is true in S with the probability $\pi_S(\Phi)$.

Besides, we will also need a *coverage factor* [26]

$$\pi_S(\Phi|\Psi) = \frac{card(|\Phi \wedge \Psi|_S)}{card(|\Psi|_S)},$$

which is the conditional probability that Φ is true in S, given Ψ is true in S with the probability $\pi_S(\Psi)$.

Let $\{\Phi_i \to \Psi\}_n$ be a set of decision rules such that all conditions Φ_i are pairwise mutually exclusive, i.e. $|\Phi_i \wedge \Phi_j|_S = \emptyset$, for any $1 \leq i, j \leq n$, $i \neq j$, and

$$\sum_{i=1}^{n} \pi_S(\Phi_i|\Psi) = 1. \tag{1}$$

Then the following properties hold:

$$\pi_S(\Psi) = \sum_{i=1}^{n} \pi_S(\Psi|\Phi_i) \cdot \pi_S(\Phi_i), \tag{2}$$

$$\pi_S(\Phi|\Psi) = \frac{\pi_S(\Psi|\Phi) \cdot \pi_S(\Phi)}{\sum_{i=1}^{n} \pi_S(\Psi|\Phi_i) \cdot \pi_S(\Phi_i)}. \tag{3}$$

It can be easily seen that the relationship between the certainty factor and the coverage factor, expressed by the formula (3) is the Bayes' theorem [1]. The theorem enables us to discover relationships in the databases.

8 Conclusions

Data mining is the quest for knowledge in databases. Many methods have been proposed for knowledge discovery in databases. No doubt rough sets proved to be a valuable methodology for data mining. Some advantages of rough set theory in this context are listed below:

- provides efficient algorithms for finding hidden patterns in data
- finds minimal sets of data (data reduction)
- evaluates significance of data
- generates minimal sets of decision rules from data
- it is easy to understand and offers straightforward interpretation of results

The rough set approach to data mining is not competitive to other methods but rather complementary and can be also used jointly with other approaches.

References

1. Borkowski L. (Ed.) (1970) Jan Lukasiewicz – Selected Works, North Holland Publishing Company, Amsterdam, London, Polish Scientific Publishers, Warszawa
2. Cercone N., Ziarko W. (1997) GRS: A Generalized Rough Set Model for Data Mining Applications. In: Wang P.P. (Ed.) Joint Conference of Information Sciences, March 1-5, Duke University 3, 181–186
3. Cios J., Pedrycz H., Swiniarski R. (1998) Data Mining for Knowledge Discovery, Kluwer Academic Publishers
4. Deogun J.S., Raghavan V.V., Sarkar A., Sever H. (1997) Data Mining: Trends in Research and Development. In: Lin T.Y., Cercone N. (Eds.) Rough Sets and Data Mining, Kluwer Academic Publishers, 9–45
5. Fernandes-Baizan M.C., Menasalvas Ruiz E., Castano M. (1996) Integrating RDMS and Data Mining Capabilities using Rough Sets. In: Proceedings of the Sixth International Conference, Information Processing and Management of Uncertainty in Knowledge Based Systems (IPMU'96) 2, July 1-5, Granada, Spain, 1439–1445.
6. Grzymała-Busse J. (1986) On the Reduction of Knowledge Representation Systems. In: Proc. of the 6th International Workshop on Expert Systems and their Applications 1, Avignon, France, April 28–30, 463–478
7. Hu X., Cercone N., Ziarko W. (1997) Generation of Multiple Knowledge from Databases Based on Rough Set Theory. In: Lin T.Y., Cercone N. (Eds.) Rough Sets and Data Mining. Analysis of Imprecise Data. Kluwer Academic Publishers, Boston, Dordrecht, 109–121
8. Hu X., Shan N., Cercone N., Ziarko W. (1994) DBROUGH: A Rough Set Based Knowledge Discovery System. In: Ras Z. W., Zemankova M. (Eds.) Proceedings of the Eighth International Symposium on Methodologies for Intelligent Systems (ISMIS'94), Charlotte, NC, October 16–19, 1994, Lecture Notes in Artificial Intelligence 869, Springer-Verlag, 386–395
9. Kowalczyk W., Piasta Z. (1998) Rough Sets-Inspired Approach to Knowledge Discovery in Business Databases. In: The Second Pacific–Asian Conference on Knowledge Discovery and Data Mining, (PAKDD'98), Melbourne, Australia, April 15–17 (accepted)
10. Lin T. Y. (Ed.) (1994) Proceedings of the Third International Workshop on Rough Sets and Soft Computing (RSSC'94). San Jose State University, San Jose, California, USA, November 10–12
11. Lin T. Y. (Ed.) (1995) Proceedings of the Workshop on Rough Sets and Data Mining at 23rd Annual Computer Science Conference. Nashville, Tennessee, March 2
12. Lin T. Y. (Ed.) (1996) Journal of the Intelligent Automation and Soft Computing 2/2 (special issue)
13. Lin T. Y. (Ed.) (1996) International Journal of Approximate Reasoning 15/4(special issue)
14. Lin T. Y. (1996) Rough Set Theory in very Large Databases. In: Borne P., Dauphin-Tanguy G., Suer C., Khattabi S. El., (Eds.) Proceedings of IMACS Multiconference: Computational Engineering in Systems Applications (CESA'96) 3/4, July 9-12. Lille, France, Gerf EC Lille-Cite Scientifique, 936–941.

15. Lin T. Y., Cercone N. (Eds.) (1997) Rough Sets and Data Mining. Kluwer Academic Publishers

16. Millan M., Machuca F. (1997) Using Rough Set Theory to Exploit the Data Mining Potential in Relational Databases Systems. In: Wang P. P. (Ed.) Joint Conference of Information Sciences 3, March 1-5, Duke University, 344–347

17. Pawlak, Z., Skowron, A. (1994) Rough Membership Functions. In: Yaeger R. R., Fedrizzi M., Kacprzyk J. (Eds.) Advances in the Dempster Shafer Theory of Evidence, John Wiley & Sons, Inc., New York 251–271

18. Pawlak, Z. (1998) Reasoning about Data – a Rough Set Perspective. In: Polkowski L., Skowron A. (Eds.) Rough Sets and Current Trends in Computing, Lecture Notes in Artificial Intelligence 1424 Springer, First International Conference, RSCTC'98, Warsaw, Poland, June, Proceedings, 25–34

19. Polkowski L., Skowron A., (Eds.) Rough Sets in Knowledge Discovery, Methodology and Applications, Vol. 1,2, Physica -Verlag, A Springer Verlag Company

20. Polkowski L., Skowron A. (Eds.) (1998) Rough Sets and Current Trends. In Computing, Lecture Notes in Artificial Intelligence 1424 Springer, First International Conference, RSCTC'98, Warsaw, Poland, June, Proceedings,

21. Skowron A., Stepaniuk J. (1994) Generalized Approximations Spaces. Proceedings of the Third International Workshop on Rough Sets and Soft Computing, San Jose, November 10–12, 156–163

22. Słowiński R. (Ed.) (1992) Intelligent Decision Support – Handbook of Applications and Advances of the Rough Sets Theory. Kluwer Academic Publishers, Boston, Dordrecht

23. Słowiński R. (1992) A generalization of the indiscernibility relation for rough set analysis of quantitative information. Rivista di Matematica per le Scienze Economiche e Sociali 15/1: 65–78

24. Swiniarski R., Berzins A. (1996) Rough Sets for Intelligent Data Mining, Knowledge Discovering and Designing of an Expert Systems for on–line Prediction of Volleyball Game Progress. In: Tsumoto S., Kobayashi S., Yokomori T., Tanaka H., Nakamura A. (Eds.) Proceedings of the Fourth International Workshop on Rough Sets, Fuzzy Sets, and Machine Discovery (RSFD'96). The University of Tokyo, November 6–8, 413–418

25. Tsumoto S., Kobayashi S., Yokomori T., Tanaka H., Nakamura A. (Eds.) (1996) Proceedings of the Fourth International Workshop on Rough Sets, Fuzzy Sets, and Machine Discovery (RSFD'96). The University of Tokyo, November 6–8

26. Tsumoto, S. (1998) Modelling Medical Diagnostic Rules Based on Rough Sets. In: Polkowski L., Skowron A. (Eds.) Rough Sets and Current Trends in Computing, Lecture Notes in Artificial Intelligence 1424, Springer, First International Conference, RSCTC'98, Warsaw, Poland, June, Proceedings, 475–482

27. Wang P. P. (Ed.) (1995) Proceedings of the International Workshop on Rough Sets and Soft Computing at Second Annual Joint Conference on Information Sciences (JCIS'95), Wrightsville Beach, North Carolina, 28 September - 1 October

28. Wang P. P. (ed.) (1997) Proceedings of the Fifth International Workshop on Rough Sets and Soft Computing (RSSC'97) at Third Annual Joint Conference on Information Sciences (JCIS'97). Duke University, Durham, NC, USA, Rough Set & Computer Science 3, March 1–5

29. Ziarko, W. (1987) On reduction of knowledge representation. In: Proc. 2nd International Symp. on Methodologies of Intelligent Systems, Charlotte, NC, North Holland, 99–113

30. Ziarko W. (Ed.) (1993) Proceedings of the Second International Workshop on Rough Sets and Knowledge Discovery (RSKD'93). Banff, Alberta, Canada, October 12–15

31. Ziarko W. (1993) Variable Precision Rough Set Model. Journal of Computer and System Sciences 46/1:39–59

32. Ziarko W. (1994) Rough Sets and Knowledge Discovery: An overview. In: Ziarko W. (Ed.) Rough Sets, Fuzzy Sets and Knowledge Discovery (RSKD'93). Workshops in Computing, Springer-Verlag & British Computer Society, London, Berlin, 11–15

33. Ziarko W. (Ed.) (1994) Rough Sets, Fuzzy Sets and Knowledge Discovery (RSKD'93). Workshops in Computing, Springer-Verlag & British Computer Society, London, Berlin

34. Ziarko W. (1995) Introduction to the Special Sssue on Rough Sets and Knowledge Discovery. In: Ziarko W. (Ed.) Computational Intelligence: An International Journal 11/2:223–226 (special issue)

35. Ziarko W., Shan N. (1995) Knowledge Discovery as a Search for Classifications. In: Lin T. Y. (Ed.) Proceedings of the Workshop on Rough Sets and Data Mining at 23rd Annual Computer Science Conference. Nashville, Tennessee, March 2 23–29

36. Ziarko W., Shan N. (1996) Rough Sets and Knowledge Discovery. Encyclopedia of Computer Science and Technology, Marcell Dekker Inc. 35, supplement 20:369–379

37. Ziarko W. (1996) Review of the Basics of Rough Sets in the Context of Data Mining. The Fourth Intl. Workshop on Rough Sets, Fuzzy Sets and Machine Discovery, Tokyo, 447–457

Data Mining Techniques for Associations, Clustering and Classification

Charu C. Aggarwal and Philip S. Yu

IBM T. J. Watson Research Center, Yorktown Heights, NY 10598

Abstract. This paper provides a survey of various data mining techniques for advanced database applications. These include association rule generation, clustering and classification. With the recent increase in large online repositories of information, such techniques have great importance. The focus is on high dimensional data spaces with large volumes of data. The paper discusses past research on the topic and also studies the corresponding algorithms and applications.

1 Introduction

Data mining has recently become an important area of research. The reason for this recent interest in the data mining area arises from its applicability to a wide variety of problems, including not only databases containing consumer and transaction information, but also advanced databases on multimedia, spatial and temporal information. In this paper, we will concentrate on discussing a few of the important problems in the topic of data mining. These problems include those of finding associations, clustering and classification. In this section, we will provide a brief introduction to each of these problems and elaborate on them in greater detail in later sections.

(1) **Associations:** This problem often occurs in the process of finding relationships between different attributes in large customer databases. These attributes may either be 0-1 literals, or they may be quantitative. The idea in the association rule problem is to find the nature of the causalities between the values of the different attributes. Consider a supermarket example in which the information maintained for the different transactions is the sets of items bought by each consumer. In this case, it may be desirable to find how the purchase behavior of one item affects the purchase behavior of another. Association Rules help in finding such relationships accurately. Such information may be used in order to make target marketing decisions. It can also be generalized to do classification of high dimensional data [21].

(2) **Clustering:** In the clustering problem, we group similar records together in a large database of multidimensional records. This creates segments of the data which have considerable similarity within a group of points. Depending upon the application, each of these segments may be treated differently. For example, in image and video databases, clustering can be used to detect interesting spatial patterns and features and support content based retrievals

of images and videos using low-level features such as texture, color histogram, shape descriptions, etc. In insurance applications, the different partitions may represent the different demographic segments of the population each of which have different risk characteristics, and may be analyzed separately.

(3) **Classification:** The classification problem is very closely related to the clustering problem, and is referred to as *supervised learning*, as opposed to the clustering problem which is referred to as *unsupervised learning*. In the classification problem, the attributes are divided into two categories: a multiplicity of feature attributes, and a single class label. The training data is used in order to model the relationship between the feature attributes and the class label. This model is used in order to predict the class label of a test example in which only the feature attributes are known. Consider for example, the previous insurance application in which we have a large training data set in which the different records represent the feature values corresponding to the demographic behavior of the population, and a class label which represents the insurance risk for each such example. The training data is used in order to predict the risk for a given set of feature attributes.

In this paper we will discuss each of the above data mining techniques and their applications. In section 2, we will discuss the association rule problem, and its application and generalizations for many real problems. In section 3, we will discuss the clustering problem. We will also discuss the difficulties in clustering for very high dimensional problems, and show how such difficulties may be surmounted by using a generalization of the clustering problem, which we refer to as *projected clustering*. In section 4, we discuss the various techniques for classification, and its applications. Finally, the conclusion and summary is presented in section 5.

2 Association Rules

Association rules find the relationships between the different items in a database of sales transactions. Such rules track the buying patterns in consumer behavior eg. finding how the presence of one item in the transaction affects the presence of another and so forth. The problem of association rule generation has recently gained considerable importance in the data mining community because of the capability of its being used as an important tool for knowledge discovery. Consequently, there has been a spurt of research activity in the recent years surrounding this problem.

Let $I = \{i_1, i_2, \ldots, i_m\}$ be a set of binary literals called items. Each transaction T is a set of items, such that $T \subseteq I$. This corresponds to the set of items which a consumer may buy in a basket transaction.

An *association rule* is a condition of the form $X \Rightarrow Y$ where $X \subseteq I$ and $Y \subseteq I$ are two sets of items. The idea of an association rule is to develop a systematic method by which a user can figure out how to infer the presence of some sets of items, given the presence of other items in a transaction. Such information is useful in making decisions such as customer targeting, shelving, and sales promotions.

The *support* of a rule $X \Rightarrow Y$ is the fraction of transactions which contain both X and Y.

The *confidence* of a rule $X \Rightarrow Y$ is the fraction of transactions containing X, which also contain Y. Thus, if we say that a rule has 90% confidence then it means that 90% of the tuples containing X also contain Y.

The process of mining association rules is a two phase technique in which all *large itemsets* are determined, and then these large itemsets are used in order to find the rules [5]. The large itemset approach is as follows. Generate all combinations of items that have fractional transaction support above a certain user-defined threshold called *minsupport*. We call all such combinations *large itemsets*. Given an itemset $S = \{i_1, i_2, \ldots, i_k\}$, we can use it to generate at most k rules of the type $[S - \{i_r\}] \Rightarrow \{i_r\}$ for each $r \in \{1, \ldots, k\}$. Once these rules have been generated, only those rules above a certain user defined threshold called *minconfidence* may be retained.

In order to generate the large itemsets, an iterative approach is used to first generate the set of large 1-itemsets L_1, then the set of large itemsets L_2, and so on until for some value of r the set L_r is empty. At this stage, the algorithm can be terminated. During the kth iteration of this procedure a set of candidates C_k is generated by performing a $(k-2)$-join on the large itemsets L_{k-1}. The itemsets in this set C_k are *candidates* for large itemsets, and the final set of large itemsets L_k must be a subset of C_k. Each element of C_k needs to be validated against the transaction database to see if it indeed belongs to L_k. The validation of the candidate itemset C_k against the transaction database seems to be bottleneck operation for the algorithm. This method requires multiple passes over a transaction database which may potentially be quite time consuming. Subsequent work on the large itemset method has concentrated on the following aspects:

(1) **Improving the I/O costs:** Brin et. al. proposed a method for large itemset generation which reduces the number of passes over the transaction database by counting some $(k+1)$-itemsets in parallel with counting k-itemsets. In most previously proposed algorithms for finding large itemsets, the support for a $(k+1)$-itemset was counted after k-itemsets have already been generated. In this work, it was proposed that one could start counting a $(k+1)$-itemset as soon as it was suspected that this itemset might be large. Thus, the algorithm could start counting for $(k+1)$-itemsets much earlier than completing the counting of k-itemsets. The total number of passes required by this algorithm is usually much smaller than the maximum size of a large itemset. A partitioning algorithm was proposed by Savasere et. al. [26] for finding large itemsets by dividing the database into n partitions. The size of each partition is such that the set of transactions can be maintained in main memory. Then, large itemsets are generated separately for each partition. Let LP_i be the set of large itemsets associated with the ith partition. Then, if an itemset is large, then it must be the case that it must belong to

at least one of LP_i for $i \in \{1, \ldots, k\}$. Now, the support of the candidates $\cup_{i=1}^{k} LP_i$ can be counted in order to find the large itemsets. This method requires just two passes over the transaction database in order to find the large itemsets.

(2) **Improving the computational efficiency of the large itemset procedure:** A hash-based algorithm for efficiently finding large itemsets was proposed by Park et. al. in [24]. It was observed that most of the time in the was spent in evaluating and finding large 2-itemsets. The algorithm in Park et. al.[24] attempts to improve this approach by providing a hash based algorithm for quickly finding large 2-itemsets. When augmented with the process of transaction-trimming, this technique results in considerable computational advantages.

A common feature of most of the algorithms proposed in the literature is that most such research is are variations on the "bottom-up theme" proposed by the *Apriori* algorithm[5, 6]. For databases in which the itemsets may be long, these algorithms may require substantial computational effort. Consider for example a database in which the length of the longest itemset is 40. In this case, there are 2^{40} subsets of this single itemset, each of which would need to be validated against the transaction database. Thus, the success of the above algorithms critically relies on the fact that the length of the frequent patterns in the database are typically short. An interesting algorithm for itemset generation has been proposed very recently by Bayardo [7]. This algorithm uses clever "look-ahead" techniques in order to identify longer patterns earlier on. The subsets of these patterns can then be pruned from further consideration. Computational results in [7] indicate that the algorithm can lead to substantial performance improvements over the *Apriori* method.

(3) **Extensions of the large itemset method beyond binary data:** Initially, the association rule problem was proposed in the context of supermarket data. The motivation was to find how the items bought in a consumer basket related to each other. A number of interesting extensions and applications have been proposed. The problem of mining quantitative association rules in relational tables was proposed in [30]. In such cases association rules are discovered in relational tables which have both categorical and quantitative attributes. Thus, it is possible to find rules which indicate how a given range of quantitative and categorical attributes may affect the values of other attributes in the data. The algorithm for the quantitative association rule problem discretizes the quantitative data into disjoint ranges and then constructs an item corresponding to each such range. Once these pseudo-items have been constructed, a large itemset procedure can be applied in order to find the association rules. Often a large number of rules may be produced by such partitioning methods, many of which may not be interesting. An interest measure was defined and used in [30] in order to generate the association rules. Variations of the quantitative association rule technique may be used in order to generate profile association rules [3]. Such rules relate the consumer profile information to their buying behavior.

An interesting issue is that of handling taxonomies of items. For example, in a store, there may be several kinds of cereal, and for each individual kind of cereal, there may be multiple brands. Rules which handle such taxonomies are called *generalized associations*. The motivation is to generate rules which are as general and non-redundant as possible while taking such taxonomies into account. Algorithms for finding such rules were presented in [28].

(4) **Algorithms for online generation of association rules:** Since the size of the transaction database may be very large, the algorithms for finding association rules are both compute-intensive and require substantial I/O. Thus it is difficult to provide quick responses to user queries. Methods for online generation of association rules have been discussed by Aggarwal and Yu[2]. This algorithm uses the preprocess-once-query-many paradigm of OLAP in order to generate association rules quickly by using an adjacency lattice to prestore itemsets. The interesting feature of this work is that the rules which are generated are independent of both the size of the transaction data and the number of itemsets prestored. In fact, the running time of the algorithm is completely proportional to the size of the output. It is also possible to generate queries for rules with specific items in them. In the same work, redundancy in association rule generation has been discussed. A rule is said to be redundant at a given level of support and confidence if its existence is implied by some other rule in the set. For example, consider the following pair of rules: {Milk} $\Rightarrow$ {Bread, Butter} and {Milk, Bread} $\Rightarrow$ {Butter}. In this example, the second rule is redundant since its existence is implied by the first. Algorithms were proposed to generate a minimal set of essential rules for a given set of data.

(5) **Alternatives to the large itemset model:** The large itemset model is a useful tool for mining the relationships among the items when the data is sparse. Unfortunately, the method is often difficult to generalize to other scenarios because of its lack of statistical robustness. Several models have been developed in order to take these statistical considerations into account. Among these models are included the correlation model [9] and the collective strength model [4].

3 Clustering

The clustering problem has been discussed extensively in the database literature as a tool for similarity search, customer segmentation, pattern recognition, trend analysis and classification. The method has been studied in considerable detail by both the statistics and database communities [8, 12, 13, 15, 18, 19]. Detailed studies on clustering methods may be found in [16].

The problem of clustering data points can be defined as follows: Given a set of points in multidimensional space, find a partition of the points into *clusters* so that the points within each cluster are close to one another. (There may also be a group of outlier points.) Some algorithms assume that the number of clusters is prespecified as a user parameter.

Most clustering algorithms do not work efficiently in higher dimensional spaces because of the inherent sparsity of the data[14]. In high dimensional applications, it is likely that at least a few dimensions exist for which a given pair of points are far apart from one another. So a clustering algorithm is often preceded by feature selection (See, for example [20]). The goal is to find the particular dimensions for which the points in the data are correlated. Pruning away irrelevant dimensions reduces the noise in the data. The problem of using traditional feature selection algorithms is that picking certain dimensions in advance can lead to a loss of information. Furthermore, in many real data examples, some points are correlated with respect to a given set of dimensions and others are correlated with respect to different dimensions. Thus it may not always be feasible to prune off too many dimensions without at the same time incurring a substantial loss of information. We demonstrate this with the help of an example.

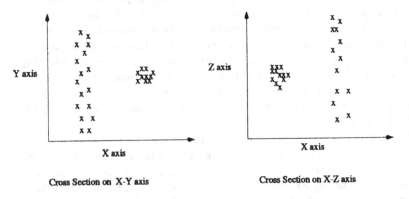

Fig. 1. Difficulties Associated with Feature Preselection

In Figure 1, we have illustrated two different projected cross sections for a set of points in 3-dimensional space. There are two patterns to the data. The first pattern corresponds to a set of points in the x-y plane, which are close in distance to one another. The second pattern corresponds to a set of points in the x-z plane, which are also close in distance. We would like to have some way of discovering such patterns. Feature preselection is not a viable option here, since each dimension is relevant to at least one of the clusters.

In this context, we shall now define what we call a projected cluster. Consider a set of data points in some (possibly large) dimensional space. A *projected cluster* is a subset D of dimensions together with a subset C of data points such that the points in C are closely clustered in the projected subspace of dimensions D. In Figure 1, two clusters exist in two different projected subpaces. Cluster 1 exists in projected x-y space, while cluster 2 exists in projected x-z space.

We assume that the number k of clusters to be found is an input parameter. The output of the algorithm will be twofold:

- a $(k + 1)$-way partition $\{C_1, ..., C_k, \mathcal{O}\}$ of the data, such that the points in each partition element except the last form a cluster. (The points in the last partition element are the *outliers*, which by definition do not cluster well.)
- a possibly different subset D_i of dimensions for each cluster C_i, $1 \leq i \leq k$, such that the points in the ith cluster are correlated with respect to these dimensions. (The dimensions for the outlier set $\mathcal{O}$ can be assumed to be empty.) The cardinality of each set D_i for the different clusters can be different.

Techniques for performing projected clustering have been discussed in [1]. One advantage of this technique is that since its output is two-fold in terms of reporting both the points and the dimensions, it gives the user a very good idea of both the identity and nature of the similarity of the different points in each cluster. For example, consider similarity searches in image and video databases using precomputed features. The number of features captured can potentially be very large. In a marketing application, the information available in the database can contain thousands of attributes on customer profile and product purchased. In either case, it is very unlikely that similarity can be found for each and every feature or attribute in the high dimensional space. However, it is possible to segment the data into groups, such that each group is defined by its similarity based on a specific set of attributes. Clearly the representative dimensions for each cluster is useful information, since it may directly be used for analyzing the behavior of that cluster.

4 Classification

The problem of *classification* has been studied extensively by the database and Artificial Intelligence communities. The problem of classification is defined as follows:

The input data is referred to as the *training set*, which contains a plurality of records, each of which contains multiple attributes or features. Each example in the training set is tagged with a *class label*. The class label may either be categorical or quantitative. The problem of classification in the context of a quantitative class label is referred to as the *regression modeling* problem. The training set is used in order to build a *model* of the classification attribute based upon the other attributes. This model is used in order to predict the value of the class label for the *test set*.

Some well known techniques for classification include the following:

(1) *Decision Tree Techniques:* The idea in decision trees is to recursively partition the data set until each partition contains mostly of examples from a particular class [23, 27]. Each non-leaf node of the tree contains a *split point* which uses some condition to decide how the data set should be partitioned.

For each example in the training data, the split point is used in order to find how to best partition the data. The performance of the decision tree depends critically upon how how the split point is chosen. The condition which describes the split point is described as a *predicate*. Predicates with high inference power are desirable for building decision trees with better accuracy. Most decision trees in the literature are based on single attribute predicates. Recent work by Chen and Yu [11] has discussed how to use multi-attribute predicates in building decision trees.

(2) *k-Nearest Neighbor Techniques:* In this case, we find the nearest neighbors of the test example and assign its class label based on the majority labels of the nearest neighbors. The distributions of the class labels in the nearest neighbors may also be used in order to find the relative probabilities for the test example to take on different values. Thus, nearest neighbor techniques assume that locality in the feature space may often imply strong relationships among the class labels. This technique may often lose robustness in very high dimensional space, since the data tends to be sparse, and the concept of locality is no longer well defined. (In other words, well defined clusters do not exist in the original feature space.)

(3) *DNF Rules:* The left hand side of the DNF rules consist of a union of a set of possible non-disjoint regions in the feature space. The right hand side of the rule corresponds to the class label. For each test example, we find the rules whose left hand side may contain the particular instance of the example. More than one rule may be discovered which contain the test example. These rules may be used in order to predict the final class label. In general, it is desirable to provide a minimality property while building DNF rules. For a given test example, it desirable to decide the label based on a few of the DNF rules. Thus, it is desirable to cover the feature space with as few rules as possible without losing the universality of coverage. More details on past work done on DNF rules may be found in RAMP [10].

(4) *Neural Networks:* A variety of other methods are known to exist for classification. These include neural networks [22] and genetic algorithms among others. A neural network is a data structure constructed of a network of *neurons* which are functions taking in one or more values and returning an output, which is the class label. The functions in the neurons are defined based on the weights of the nodes connecting the links. During the training phase, the data is fed to the neural network one by one, and the functions in the neurons are modified based on the error rates of the resulting outputs. Multiple passes are required over the data in order to train the network. As a result, the training times are quite large even for small datasets.

(5) *Bayesian Classifiers:* Bayesian Classifiers [17] fall into a category of classifiers, which are *parametric* in nature. Parametric classifiers are desirable for those applications in which the number of feature variables are very large. For example, text classification is best handled by such classifiers. The training data is assumed to fit a certain probability distribution in terms of the values of the features for the different classes. This is used in order

to estimate the parameters of this probability distribution. For a given test document, the features in it are used in order to determine its class label. In order to simplify the process of model building, it is often assumed that the features are statistically independent from one another. This assumption is far from accurate, and hence such a classifier is referred to as the *naive* Bayes Classifier. Such classifiers have been demonstrated to perform surprisingly well in a very wide variety of problems in spite of the simplistic nature of the model.

4.1 Applications of classification

The classification problem has several direct applications in target marketing, and electronic commerce. A prototypical application of classification is that of mass mailing for marketing. For example, credit card companies often mail solicitations to consumers. Naturally, they would like to target those consumers who are most likely to respond to a mailer. Often demographic information is available for those people who have responded before to such solicitations, and this information may be used in order to target the most likely respondents. Other applications of classification include risk estimation and analysis, fraud detection, and credit scoring.

Another area of exploration includes medical diagnosis, in which large sets of features containing the medical history of a subject is used in order to make the diagnosis of a patient regarding his medical condition, weather prediction based on satellite image, etc.

Algorithms for text classification have considerable application in automated library organization. Also, many e-commerce applications may be handled using text classification, since the subject material from a web page may be inferred from the text on it. This subject material may be used in order to make product and marketing recommendations. Text databases pose a special challenge to classifiers because of the huge number of features in terms of which the data is represented.

5 Conclusions and Summary

This paper discussed a survey of some of the important techniques for data mining including association rule mining, clustering, and classification. We provided an overview of the algorithms which for each of these techniques, and their applications to high dimensional data space.

References

1. Aggarwal C. C., Procopiuc C., Wolf J. L., Yu P. S. Park J.-S.: A Framework for Finding Projected Clusters in High Dimensional Spaces. IBM Research Report RC 21286.

2. Aggarwal C. C., Yu P. S.: Online Generation of Association Rules. International Conference on Data Engineering. Orlando, Florida, (1998).

3. Aggarwal C. C., Sun Z., Yu P. S.: Online Algorithms for Finding Profile Association Rules. Knowledge Discovery and Data Mining, (1998).

4. Aggarwal C. C., Yu P. S.: A New Framework for Itemset Generation. Proceedings of the ACM Symposium on PODS, (1998).

5. Agrawal R., Imielinski T., Swami A.: Mining Association Rules between Sets of Items in Very Large Databases. Proceedings of the ACM SIGMOD Conference (1993) pages 207-216.

6. Agrawal R., Srikant R.: Fast Algorithms for Mining Association Rules in Large Databases. Proceedings of the 20th VLDB Conference (1994) pages 478-499.

7. Bayardo R. J.: Efficiently Mining Long Patterns from Databases. Proceedings of the ACM SIGMOD (1998).

8. Berger M., Rigoutsos I.: An Algorithm for Point Clustering and Grid Generation. IEEE Transactions on Systems, Man and Cybernetics, Vol. 21, No. 5:1278-1286, (1991).

9. Brin S., Motwani R., Silverstein C.: Beyond Market Baskets: Generalizing Association Rules to Correlations. Proceedings of the ACM SIGMOD (1997) pages 265-276.

10. Apte C, Hong S. J., Lepre J., Prasad S., Rosen B.: RAMP: Rules Abstraction for Modeling and Prediction. *IBM Research Report.*

11. Chen M.-S., Yu P. S.: Using Multi-Attribute Predicates for Mining Classification Rules. *IBM Research Report 20562*, (1996).

12. Ester M., Kriegel H.-P., Xu X.: A Database Interface for Clustering in Large Spatial Databases. Knowledge Discovery and Data Mining (1995).

13. Ester M., Kriegel H.-P., Xu X.: Knowledge Discovery in Large Spatial Databases: Focusing Techniques for Efficient Class Identification. International Symposium on Large Spatial Databases (1995).

14. Keim D., Berchtold S., Bohm C., Kriegel, H.-P.: A Cost Model for Nearest Neighbor Search in High-dimensional Data Space. International Symposium on Principles of Database Systems (PODS). (1997), pages 78-86.

15. Ester M., Kriegel H.-P., Sander J., Xu X.: A Density Based Algorithm for Discovering Clusters in Large Spatial Databases with Noise. International Conference on Knowledge Discovery in Databases and Data Mining (1995).

16. Jain A., Dubes R.: Algorithms for Clustering Data. Prentice Hall, Englewood Cliffs, New Jersey, (1998).

17. Langley P., Iba W., Thompson K.: An analysis of Bayesian classifiers. AAAI, (1990), 223-228.

18. Ng R., Han J.: Efficient and Effective Clustering Methods for Spatial Data Mining. Proceedings of the 20th VLDB Conference (1994) pages 144-155.

19. Zhang T., Ramakrishnan R., Livny M.: BIRCH: An Efficient Data Clustering Method for Very Large Databases. Proceedings of the ACM SIGMOD Conference (1996).

20. Kohavi R., Sommerfield D.: Feature Subset Selection Using the Wrapper Method: Overfitting and Dynamic Search Space Topology. Knowledge Discovery and Data Mining (1995).

21. Liu B., Hsu W., Ma Y.: Integrating Classification and Association Rule Mining. Knowledge Discovery and Data Mining, pages 80-86, (1998).

22. Lu H., Setiono R., Liu H.: NeuroRule: A Connectionist Approach to Data Mining. Proceedings of the 21st VLDB Conference (1995).

23. Mehta M., Agrawal R., Rissanen J.: SLIQ: A Fast Scalable Classifier for Data Mining. IBM Research Report.

24. Park J. S., Chen M. S., Yu P. S.: Using a Hash-based Method with Transaction Trimming for Mining Association Rules. IEEE Transactions on Knowledge and Data Engineering, Volume 9, no 5, (1997), pages 813-825.

25. Quinlan J. R.: Induction of Decision Trees, Machine Learning, Volume 1, Number 1, (1986).

26. Savasere A., Omiecinski E., Navathe S. B: An efficient algorithm for mining association rules in large databases. Proceedings of the 21st VLDB Conference (1995).

27. Shafer J., Agrawal R., Mehta M.: SPRINT: A Scalable Parallel Classifier for Data Mining. Proceedings of the 22nd VLDB Conference (1996).

28. Srikant R., and Agrawal R.: Mining Generalized Association Rules. Proceedings of the 21st VLDB Conference (1995) pages 407-419.

29. Weiss S. M., Kulikowski C. A.: Computer Systems That Learn: Classification and Prediction Methods from Statistics, Neural Nets, Machine Learning, and Expert Systems. Morgan Kaufman, (1991).

30. Srikant R., Agrawal R.: Mining quantitative association rules in large relational tables. Proceedings of the ACM SIGMOD Conference, (1996) pages 1-12.

Data Mining: Granular Computing Appraoch

T.Y. Lin[1,2]

[1] Department of Mathematics and Computer Science
San Jose State University, San Jose, California 95192
[2] Berkeley Initiative in Soft Computing
Department of Electrical Engineering and Computer Science
University of California, Berkeley, California 94720
tylin@cs.sjsu.edu, tylin@cs.berkely.edu

Abstract. In the relational database theory, it is assumed that the universe U to be represented is a set. The classical data mining took such assumption. In real life applications, the entities are often related. A "new" data mining theory is explored with such additional semantics.

1 Introduction

In relational database theory, the universe of entities is represented as a set of tuples, and each attribute domain is tactically assumed to be a set [6]. In other words, we assume there are no relationships among the entities or the attribute values of each domain respectively. All data are sets. However, in real life, the universe, in stead of being a set of entities, is a class of objects. These objects are naturally partitioned (clustered) into clumps of objects which are drawn together by indistinguishability, similarity or functionality [21]. Briefly, data are clustered together by some relationships. What is the mathematical structure of such relationships? In formal logic, a relational structure is assumed [7]; Intuitively, a clump is a neighborhood (e.g., the nearest neighborhood)of an object or objects. These relationships can be formulated in terms of binary relations or neighborhood systems [9].

Rougly speaking, data mining is just the opposite of database processing. Database processing is to organize and to store data according to the given semantics, such as functional dependencies and etc., while data mining is to discover the semantics of data from the stored bits and bytes. One should point out that the actual meaning of bits and bytes are to human only, it plays no role in the processings. The term "knowledge discovering" or "data mining" means *a derivation of properties*, which are interested to human, from and only from the *formal structures* of the stored data. From this aspect, data mining of relational theory is to derive set theoretical properties of stored data. In this paper, however, our interests are beyond that; the data mining that we are pursuing is to derive, in addition, the properties of stored clumps, mathematically an additional structures imposed by previously mentioned binary relations. To process these additional semantics, we use the notion of granular computing [9].

The idea of granulation is very natural, it is almost everywhere in computer science and mathematics. In the context of formal theory, it may be traced back to [22] and is outlined in [20] recently. For convenience, this author proposed the term "granular computing" to label the computational theory of information granulation.

2 Data Mining on Discrete Data

Discrete data, mathematically, is a set. This section is a pure set theoretical approach to the extensional relational model ([6], pp.90) and its data mining. A relation is a knowledge representation of a set of entities. A "column" of a relation induces a partition on the set of entities; an attribute value, then, is a label of an equivalence class.

2.1 Single Attribute Tables and Partitions

Let U be a set of entities, and C be an attribute domain that consists of meaningful labels. In database theory, elements in C are the primitive data (attribute values). However, from data mining aspect, each element represents a common property of some entities. As the example given below, the restaurants ID_1, ID_2, ID_3 have a common property, namely, they are all located in West Wood. We will call C concept space and its elements elementary concepts. Note that adjective "meaningful" is to human, as far as computer systems are concerned, "meaningful" or not, a label is bits and bytes. We will be interested in a very simple type of knowledge representations. A map from the entities to the labels, $P : U \longrightarrow C$, is called *a single attribute representation* or simply a representation. We will assume P is onto, that is, every elementary concept has an entity mapped onto it; this is reasonable, since there is no point to consider labels that refer to nothing. Its graph $(u, P(u))$ is called a single attribute table; "physically" the table has two columns. Since the map and its graph determine each other, we will use the two terms interchangeable.

The representation P induces a partition, denoted by P again, on U. It is clear that P can be factored through the quotient sets:

$$P : U \longrightarrow U/P \longrightarrow C,$$

The first map is called the *natural projection*, the second the *naming map*. An elementary set plays two roles: one as an element of the quotient set, another as a subset of U. We can regard the first role as the **canonical name** of the second.

Conversely, suppose we are given an equivalence relation P and each elementary set is given its canonical name. Then, we have a map from the entities to the canonical names

$$u \longrightarrow [u] \longrightarrow NAME([u]),$$

where, as usual, [u] denote the elementary set that contains u. The map and its graph is called a *canonical single attribute representation or canonical single attribute table*.

Propositon 1.

1. There is a one-to-one correspondence between canonical single attribute tables and partitions (equivalence relations).
2. The relationships among attribute values (elementary concepts) are defined by the corresponding elementary sets.

In the following example, we can see from the meaningful labels that some restaurants are located in West Wood, West LA, and Brent Wood (these symbols means something to human), but no information for human when canonical names are used. For computer systems either choice gives rise to the same mathematical structures of the stored data.

Example. Let $U = \{ID_1, ID_2, ...ID_7\}$ be a set of 7 restaurants. Assume U is partitioned into elementary sets by their location. We give these elementary sets meaningful names (locations) and canonical names. For comparison, we combine two single attribute representations into Table 1.

Restaurants	Locations	...	Restaurants	Canonical names
ID_1	West Wood	...	ID_1	$\{ID_1, ID_2, ID_3\}$
ID_2	West Wood	...	ID_2	$\{ID_1, ID_2, ID_3\}$
ID_3	West Wood	...	ID_3	$\{ID_1, ID_2, ID_3\}$
ID_4	West LA	...	ID_4	$\{ID_4, ID_5\}$
ID_5	West LA	...	ID_5	$\{ID_4, ID_5\}$
ID_6	Brent Wood	...	ID_6	$\{ID_6, ID_7\}$
ID_7	Brent Wood	...	ID_7	$\{ID_6, ID_7\}$

Table 1. Two Single Attribute Tables

2.2 Multiple Attributes and Multiple Partitions

Now, it is easy to generalize the idea to multiple attributes. A multiple attribute representation is simply a join of single attribute representations. Its graph is called a multiple attribute table or simply table. It is easy to see table is equivalent to *information table* [10]. We will use these terms interchangeably. Pawlak [18] called the pair, the universe and a multiple partition, *a knowledge base*. We have called it rough structure; see Section 3.1.

Proposition 2

1. There is a one-to-one correspondence between tables and multiple partitions (knowledge bases;rough structure).

2. The relationships among attribute values (elementary concepts) of a table are defined by the elementary sets of a multiple partition.

For example, inclusion of an elementary set in another elementary set is an inference on the corresponding elementary concepts; a functional dependency of two columns is a refinement of two corresponding partitions.

2.3 Partition Coarsening and Concept Hierarchy

Consider a sequence PN of coarsening partitions:

$$PN^n, n = 1, 2, \ldots; PN^1 = P, \text{and } PN^h \prec P^{(h+1)}$$

where $\prec$ is a refinement of partitions. In other words, each elementary set of PN^h is contained in some elementary set of $P^{(h+1)}$, or conversely each elementary set of $P^{(h+1)}$ is a union of elementary sets of PN^h. Note that the latter property (but not the former) will be generalized to clustered data below.

We would like to stress that, if two elementary sets are identical, then their names should be the same. The universe and the total collection of the nested partitions, $(U; PN, QN, RN, \ldots)$, is called a *high level knowledge base or high level rough structure*; see Section 3.1. The concept spaces, such as $NAME(PN)$, $NAME(QN) \ldots$, are called concept hierarchies.

2.4 Data Mining on Multiple Partitions

It is easy to see a relation in a relational database is a multiple attribute representation,

$$\bigwedge_i P^i : U \longrightarrow \times_i NAME(P^i),$$

where U is the set of entities, and $P^i, i = 1, 2, \ldots$ are the attributes. Let E_j^i be elementary sets of P^i and $C_j^i = NAME(E_j^i)$. For readability, we rename the partitions by $P = P^1, Q = P^2, C = C^1, D = C^2 \ldots$, and elementary sets and concepts by $P_j = E_j^1, Q^h = E_h^2, C_j = C_j^1$ and $D_h = C_h^2$. From *Proposition 2* we have the following "theorem."

"**Theorem**" 1 Automated data mining of a given relation is to derive interesting properties of elementary sets of the corresponding high level rough structure (knowledge base).

Corollary.

1. Association rules: A pair (C_j, D_h) is an association rules, if $\mid P_j \cap Q_h \mid \geq$ *threshhold*. [1]
2. Inference rules: A formula $C_j \rightarrow D_h$ is an inference rule, if $P_j \subseteq Q_h$ [18]
3. Robust inference rules: A formula $C_j \rightarrow D_h$ is an inference rule, if $P_j \subseteq Q_h$ and $\mid P_j \cap Q_h \mid \geq$ *threshhold* [12]

4. High level (robust) inference rules: Write $P = PN^i$ and $Q = QN^k$, where $k \geq i$. A formula $C_j \rightarrow D_h$ is a high level inference rule, if $P_j \subseteq Q_h$ (and $| P_j \cap Q_h | \geq threshhold$) [3, 9]

5. Soft (robust) inference rules: Write $P = PN^1$ and $Q = QN^k$ where and $k \geq 1$. A formula $C_j \rightarrow D_h$ is a soft (robust)inference rule, if $P_j \subseteq Q_h$ (and $| P_j \cap Q_h | \geq threshhold$) [16, 9]

3 Granulations and Mining Clustered Data

We have shown that data mining in relational theory is deriving properties from a set of partitions (equivalence relations). Now we will show that data mining (of real life data) is deriving properties of from a set of granulations (binary relations).

3.1 Granular Structures for Clustered Data

An equivalence relation partitions the universe into disjoints elementary sets. A binary relation decomposes the universe into elementary neighborhoods that are not necessarily disjoint. The decomposition is called a binary granulation and the collection of the granules a binary neighborhood system [9, 10]. We will recall few relevant notions.

1. *Binary relations*: B is a binary relation on U, if $B \subseteq U \times U$. It defines a

2. *Binary neighborhood system*, namely, a map

$$N : p \longrightarrow B_p \equiv \{u \mid (p, u) \in B\},$$

where B_p is called an elementary neighborhood. We will use B to denote the collection $\{B_p \mid \forall p \in U\}$, the map N or the binary relation B and refer to every one of them as a binary neighborhood system. If the binary relation is an equivalence relation, elementary neighborhoods are elementary sets. Conversely, we can define a binary relation by elementary neighborhoods:

$$B = \{(p, u) \mid p \in U \text{ and } u \in B_p\}$$

3. A subset $X \subseteq U$ is a definable neighborhood/set, if X is a union of elementary neighborhoods/sets.

4. A space with a neighborhood system is called a NS-space; it is a mild generalization of Frechet(U) space [19].

5. A *binary granular structure* or simply *granular structure* consists of 3-tuple (U, B, C), where (1) U is an NS-space imposed by B; see Item 4. (2) B is a set of binary neighborhood systems $B^i, i = 1, 2, \ldots$ and (3) C is a set of concept spaces $C^i = NAME(B^i), i = 1, 2, \ldots$; each C^i is an NS-space; see next Item. If B is an equivalence relation, the granular structure is called a rough structure. Rough structure is equivalent to knowledge base and granular structure is equivalent to binary knowledge base [9, 10].

6. B^i induces a binary relation on the concept space C^i as follows: We will suppress the index i by writing $C = C^i$ and $B = B^i$. Two concepts, C_h and C_k, are B-related iff there exist $e_h \in C_h$ and $e_k \in C_k$ such that $(e_h, e_k) \in B$.

3.2 Table Representations of Granular Structures

Let $(U, \{B^i, C^i, i = 1, 2, \ldots, n\})$ be a binary granular structure. For a fixed i, we write $B = B^i, C = C^i$. We should note here that U and C are NS-spaces. Let us consider the following map

$$GT : p \longrightarrow B_p \longrightarrow NAME(B_p).$$

This map is continuos in the sense of NS-spaces [11]; we will call it a *single attribute granular representation*. Its graph (p, GT(p)) is a single attribute granular table. As before, we will call it canonical single attribute granular table or simply *canonical granular table*, if we use the canonical names. A join of such single column table forms a *multiple attribute granular representation*. Its graph of the map will be called *granular table*; it is equivalent to extended information table [10]. If the binary granular structure is a rough structure, then the granular table reduces to information table. We would like to caution readers that unlike the case of discrete data, the entries in the granular table are not semantically independent; there are relationships among elementary concepts (attribute values).

Proposition 3.

1. There is an one to one correspondence between canonical granular tables and granular structures (binary knowledge bases [10]).
2. The relationships among attribute values (elementary concepts) of a multiple attribute granular table are defined by the elementary neighborhoods of the corresponding granular structure.

Examples
Example. Let U be the restaurants as given in Table 1. U has granular structures described below.

We will suppress the ID from ID_i, so the set of restaurant is $U = \{1, 2, 3, 4, 5, 6, 7\}$.

1. B is a binary neighborhood system defined by

$$B_1 = \{3, 4, 5, 6, 7\}, \ B_2 = \{3, 4, 5, 6, 7\}; \ B_3 = \{1, 2, 3\}; \ B_4 = B_5 = B_6 = B_7 = \{4, 5, 6, 7\}$$

Elementary concepts of B are:

$$NAME(B_1) =$$
$$NAME(B_2) = \ heavy, NAME(B_3) = \ middle, NAME(B_4) =$$
$$NAME(B_5) = NAME(B_6) = NAME(B_7) = \ light.$$

B-concept space is an NS-space whose binary relation is described in Table 3

2. E is an equivalence relation defined by

$$E_1 = E_2 = E_3 = \{1, 2, 3\}; \ E_4 = E_5 = E_6 = E_7 = \{4, 5, 6, 7\}$$

Elementary concepts of E are:

$$NAME(E_1) = NAME(E_2) = NAME(E_3) = low; \quad NAME(E_4) =$$
$$NAME(E_5) = NAME(E_6) = NAME(E_7) = high.$$

E-concept space is discrete; there is no binary relation on it.

Objects	(U, B, C)-attribute	(U, E, C)-attribute
ID_1	heavy	low
ID_2	heavy	low
ID_3	middle	low
ID_4	light	high
ID_5	light	high
ID_6	light	high
ID_7	light	high

Table 2. Binary Granulations; entries are semantically interrelated

(U, B, C)-attribute	(U, B, C)-attribute
heavy	light
heavy	middle
middle	heavy
middle	middle
light	light

Table 3. Semantic Relation on (U, B, C)-attribute

3.3 Nested Granulations and Concept Hierarchies

The concepts of nested partitions (equivalence relations) form a concept hierarchy. In this section, we relax the equivalence relation to a general binary relation [15].

Let (U, B^2, C^2) and (U, B^1, C^1) be two binary granular structures.

1. B^2 is *strongly depended* on B^1, denoted by $B^1 \Longrightarrow B^2$, iff every B^2-neighborhood is a definable B^1-neighborhood that is, every B^2-neighborhood is a union of B^1-neighborhood. If $B^1 \Longrightarrow B^2$, we will say B^1 is *definably finer* than B^2 or B^2 is *definably coarser* than B^1.

2. C^2 is *definably more general than* on C^1, denoted by $C^1 \prec C^2$,

A *concept hierarchy* is a nested sequence $(U; BN^i, CN^i, i = 0, 1, 2 \ldots)$ of strongly depended binary granular structures, more precisely,

1. BN_j^i is a ith level elementary neighborhood, $j = 1, 2, \ldots$
2. $CN_j^i = NAME(BN_j^i)$ is a ith level elementary concept, $j = 1, 2, \ldots$
3. $BN^i \Longrightarrow BN^{(i+1)}$
4. $CN^i \prec CN^{(i+1)}$.

Such a nested granular structure, $(U; BN^i, CN^i, i = 0, 1, 2 \ldots)$, is called a *nested high level knowledge base or nested high level granular structure*. The sequence of concept spaces, $CN^i = NAME(BN^i), i = 0, 1, 2 \ldots$, is also called a concept hierarchy.

3.4 Mining on Multiple Granular Structures

A relation in real life databases is a granular table.

"**Theorem**" **2** Automated data mining of a relation (in a real life database) is to derive interesting properties among the elementary neighborhoods of the corresponding high level granular structure (high level binary knowledge base).

$(U; B^i, C^i, i = 0, 1, 2 \ldots)$ be a collection of granular structures. Let B_j^i be elementary neighborhoods. and $C_j^i = NAME(B_j^i)$ be elementary concepts. For readability, we rename the granulations by $P = B^1, Q = P^2, C = C^1, D = C^2 \ldots$, and elementary neighborhoods and concepts by $P_j = B_j^1$, $Q_h = E_h^2$, $C_j = C_j^1$ and $D_h = C_h^2$. We have used N_p to denote a neighborhood of p, we will use $NEIGH(p)$ in this section.

Main Theorem.

1. Soft association rules: A pair (C_j, D_h) is a soft association rule, if $| NEUGH(P_j) \cap NEIGH(Q_h) | \geq threshhold$.
2. Continuous inference rules: A formula $C_j \rightarrow D_h$ is a continuous inference rule, if $NEIGH(P_j) \subseteq NEIGH(Q_h)$
3. Softly robust continuous inference rules: A formula $C_j \rightarrow D_h$ is a softly robust continuous inference rule, if $NEIGH(P_j) \subseteq NEIGH(Q_h)$ and $| NEIGH(P_j) \cap NEIGH(Q_h) | \geq threshhold$ [12]
4. (Softly robust)High level continuous inference rules: Suppose $PN = B^i$, $QN = B^j$, and $j \neq i$ are two nested granular structures, that is, $PN^i \prec PN^{(i+k)}$ and $QN^i \prec QN^{(i+k)}$. Write $P = PN^m$ and $Q = QN^n$, where $n \geq m$ and $k > 0$. A formula $C_j \rightarrow D_h$ is a (softly robust) high level continuous inference rule, if $NEIGH(P_j) \subseteq NEIGH(Q_h)$ (and $| NEIGH(P_j) \cap NEIGH(Q_h) | \geq threshhold$) [9]
5. Soft (softly robust) continuous inference rules: Write $P = PN^1$ and $Q = QN^k$, where $k > 1$. A formula $C_j \rightarrow D_h$ is a soft (softly robust) continuous inference rule, if $NEIGH(P_j) \subseteq NEIGH(Q_h)$ (and $| NEIGH(P_j) \cap NEIGH(Q_h) | \geq threshhold$) [9]

These results are immediate from definitions, we label it as a theorem to stress it is conceptually important. We can also easily define many variants; we shall not do so here.

4 Conclusion

Data mining is essentially a "reverse" engineering of database processing. The latter organizes and stores data according to the given semantics, while the former is "discovering" the semantics of stored data. So automated *data mining is a process of deriving interesting (to human) properties from the underlying mathematical structure of the stored bits and bytes.*

This paper focuses on relational databases that have additional semantics, e.g., [14, 13, 4, 8, 5, 17]. The underlying mathematical structure of such a relation is a set of binary relations or a granular structure. Data mining is, then, a processing of the granular structure-granular computing. If there is no additional semantics, then the binary relations are equivalence relations and granular computing reduces to rough set theory.

References

1. R. Agrawal, T. Imielinski, and A. Swami, Mining Association Rules Between Sets of Items in Large Databases. In Proceeding of ACM-SIGMOD international Conference on Management of Data, pp. 207-216, Washington, DC, June, 1993
2. S. Bairamian, *Goal Search in Relational Databases*, thesis, California State Univeristy-Northridge, 1989.
3. Y.D. Cai, N. Cercone, and J. Han. Attribute-oriented induction in relational databases. In *Knowledge Discovery in Databases*, pages 213–228. AAAI/MIT Press, Cambridge, MA, 1991.
4. W. Chu and Q. Chen, Neighborhood and associative query answering, *Journal of Intelligent Information Systems*, 1, 355-382, 1992.
5. W. Chu and Q. Chen, A structured approach for cooperative query answering, *IEEE Transactions on Knowledge and Data Engineering*, 6(5), 1994,738–749.
6. C. J. Date, *Introduction to Database Systems 3rd, 6th editions* Addision-Wesely, Reading, Massachusetts, 1981, 1995.
7. H. Enderton, *A Mathematical Introduction to Logic.* Academic Oress, Boston 1992.
8. T. Gaasterland, *Generating Cooperative Answers in Deductive Databases*, Ph.D. dissertation, University of Maryland, College Park, Maryland, 1992.
9. T. Y. Lin, Granular Computing of Binary relations I: Data Mining and Neighborhood Systems. In:Rough Sets and Knowledge Discovery Polkowski and Skowron (Editors), Springer-Verlag,1998,107-121.
10. T. Y. Lin, Granular Computing of Binary relations II: Rough Set Representations and Belief Functions. In:Rough Sets and Knowledge Discovery Polkowski and Skowron (Editors), Springer-Verlag,1998, 121-140.

11. T. Y. Lin, Neighborhood Systems -A Qualitative Theory for Fuzzy and Rough Sets. In: *Advances in Machine Intelligence and Soft Computing*, Volume IV. Ed. Paul Wang, 132-155, 1997.

12. T. Y. Lin, Rough Set Theory in Very Large Databases, Symposium on Modeling, Analysis and Simulation, IMACS Multi Conference (Computational Engineering in Systems Applications), Lille, France, July 9-12, 1996, Vol. 2 of 2, 936-941.

13. T. Y. Lin , Neighborhood Systems and Approximation in Database and Knowledge Base Systems. In:*Proceedings of the Fourth International Symposium on Methodologies of Intelligent Systems*, Poster Session, October 12-15, 1989, 75-86.

14. T. Y. Lin, Neighborhood Systems and Relational Database. In: *Proceedings of 1988 ACM Sixteen Annual Computer Science Conference*, February 23-25, 1988, 725

15. T. Y. Lin and M. Hadjimichael, Non-Classificatory Generalization in Data Mining. In: *Proceedings of The Fourth International Workshop on Rough Sets, Fuzzy Sets, and Machine Discovery*, November 6-8, 1996, Tokyo, Japan, 404-411

16. T. Y. Lin, and Y. Y. Yao, Mining Soft Rules Using Rough Sets and Neighborhoods. In: Symposium on Modeling, Analysis and Simulation, CESA'96 IMACS Multiconference (Computational Engineering in Systems Applications), Lille, France, 1996, Vol. 2 of 2, 1095-1100, 1996.

17. B. Michael and T. Y. Lin, Neighborhoods, Rough sets, and Query Relaxation, Rough Sets and Data Mining: Analysis of Imprecise Data, Kluwer Academic Publisher, 1997, 229 -238. (Final version of paper presented in Workshop on Rough Sets and Database Mining , March 2, 1995

18. Z. Pawlak, *Rough Sets (Theoretical Aspects of Reasoning about Data)*. Kluwer Academic, Dordrecht, 1991.

19. W. Sierpenski and C. Krieger, General Topology, University of Torranto Press Press 1952.

20. L.A. Zadeh, Toward a theory of fuzzy information granulation and its centrality in human reasoning and fuzzy logic, *Fuzzy Sets and Systems*, 90, 111-127, 1997.

21. Lotfi Zadeh, The Key Roles of Information Granulation and Fuzzy logic in Human Reasoning. In: *1996 IEEE International Conference on Fuzzy Systems*, September 8-11, 1, 1996.

22. L.A. Zadeh, Fuzzy Sets and Information Granularity, in: M. Gupta, R. Ragade, and R. Yager, (Eds), *Advances in Fuzzy Set Theory and Applications*, North-Holland, Amsterdam, 1979, 3-18.

Rule Extraction from Prediction Models

Hiroshi Tsukimoto

Research & Development Center, Toshiba Corporation
70, Yanagi-cho, Saiwai-ku, Kawasaki 210 Japan
tukimoto@ssel.toshiba.co.jp

Abstract. Knowledge Discovery in Databases(KDD) should provide not only predictions but also knowledge such as rules comprehensible to humans. That is, KDD has two requirements, accurate predictions and comprehensible rules. The major KDD techniques are neural networks, statistics, decision trees, and association rules. Prediction models such as neural networks and multiple regression formulas cannot provide comprehensible rules. Linguistic rules such as decision trees and association rules cannot work well when classes are continuous. Therefore, there is no perfect KDD technique. Rule extraction from prediction models is needed for perfect KDD techniques, which satisfy the two KDD requirements, accurate predictions and comprehensible rules. Several researchers have been developing techniques for rule extraction from neural networks. The author also has been developing techniques for rule extraction from prediction models. This paper briefly explains the techniques of rule extraction from prediction models.

1 Introduction

Knowledge Discovery in Databases(KDD) means the discovery of knowledge from (a large amount of) data, therefore, KDD should provide not only predictions but also knowledge such as rules comprehensible to humans. Therefore, KDD techniques should satisfy the two requirements, that is, **accurate predictions** and **comprehensible rules**.

KDD consists of several processes such as preprocessing, learning and so on. This paper deals with learning. The learning in KDD can be divided into supervised learning and unsupervised learning. This paper deals with supervised learning, that is, classification and regression.

The major KDD techniques are neural networks, statistics, decision trees, and association rules. When these techniques are applied to real data, which usually consist of discrete data and continuous data, they each have their own problems. In other words, there is no perfect technique, that is, a technique which can satisfy the two requirements, accurate predictions and comprehensible rules.

Neural networks are black boxes, that is, neural networks are incomprehensible. Multiple regression formulas, which are the typical statistical models, are black boxes too. Decision trees do not work well when classes are continuous

[11], that is, if accurate predictions are desired, comprehensibility should be sacrificed, and if comprehensibility is desired, accurate predictions should be sacrificed. Association rules, which are unsupervised learning techniques, do not work well when the right hand sides of rules, which can be regarded as classes, are continuous [14]. The reason is almost the same as that for decision trees.

Neural networks and multiple regression formulas are prediction models. Decision trees and association rules are linguistic rules. Prediction models can provide predictions but cannot provide comprehensible rules. On the other hand, linguistic rules can provide comprehensible rules but cannot provide accurate predictions in continuous classes.

How can we solve the above problem? The solution is rule extraction from prediction models. Rule extraction from prediction models is needed for developing the perfect KDD techniques, that is, satisfying the two KDD requirements, accurate predictions and comprehensible rules.

Several researchers have been developing rule extraction techniques from neural networks, therefore, neural networks can be used in KDD [7], whereas few researchers have studied rule extraction from linear formulas. We have developed rule extraction techniques from prediction models such as neural networks, linear formulas and so on.

Section 2 explains the problems in the major KDD techniques and how the problems can be solved by rule extraction from prediction models. Section 3 briefly surveys rule extraction from neural networks. Section 4 explains the techniques developed by the author. Section 5 briefly surveys open problems.

2 The problems of major KDD techniques

The major KDD techniques, that is, decision trees, neural networks, statistics and association rules are reviewed in terms of the two requirements for KDD techniques, accurate predictions and comprehensible rules.

2.1 Neural networks

Neural networks can provide accurate predictions in the discrete domain and the continuous domain. The problem is that the training results of neural networks are sets of mathematical formulas, that is, neural networks are incomprehensible black boxes.

2.2 Multiple regression analysis

There are a lot of statistical methods. The most typical method is multiple regression analysis, therefore, only multiple regression analysis is discussed here. Multiple regression analysis usually uses linear formulas, therefore, only linear regression analysis is possible and nonlinear regression analysis is impossible, while neural networks can perform nonlinear regression analysis. However, the linear regression analysis has the following advantages.

1. The optimal solution can be calculated.
2. The linear regression analysis is the most widely used in the world.
3. Several regression analysis techniques such as nonparametric regression analysis, multivariate autoregression analysis, and so on have been developed based on the linear regression analysis.

Linear regression analysis can provide appropriate predictions in the continuous domain and discrete domain. The problem is that multiple regression formulas are mathematical formulas, which are incomprehensible black boxes too. Therefore, rule extraction from linear regression formulas is important.

2.3 Decision trees

When a class is continuous, the class is discretized into several intervals. When the number of the intervals, that is, the number of the discretized classes, is small, comprehensible trees can be obtained, but the tree cannot provide accurate predictions. For example, the figure on the left side in Fig. 1 shows a tree where there are two continuous attributes and a continuous class. To improve the prediction accuracy, let the number of intervals be large. When the number of intervals is large, the trees obtained are too complicated to be comprehensible.

From the above simple discussion, we can conclude that it is impossible to obtain trees which can satisfy the two requirements for KDD techniques, accurate predictions and comprehensible rules at the same time. Therefore, decision trees cannot work well when classes are continuous [11].

As a solution for continuous classes, for example, Quinlan presented Cubist. Cubist generates piecewise-linear models [12], which are a kind of regression trees. The figure on the right side in Fig. 1 shows an example. As seen from this figure, the tree is an extension of linear formulas, so the tree is a prediction model, that is, incomprehensible. As a result, this solution has solved the inaccurate prediction problem but has generated the incomprehensibility problem.

2.4 Association rules

Association rules are described as $a \rightarrow b$, where b can be regarded as a class. Association rules do not work well when "classes" like b in the above rule are continuous. When there are many intervals, the rules are too complicated to be comprehensible, whereas there are few intervals, the rule cannot provide accurate predictions, therefore some concessions are needed [14]. Some techniques such as fuzzy techniques can be applied to the above problem [6], but while fuzzy techniques can improve predictions, they degrade the comprehensibility.

type	1	2	3	4
class	discrete	discrete	continuous	continuous
attribute	discrete	continuous	discrete	continuous
neural network	△	△	△	△
linear regression	△	△	△	△
regression tree	△	△	△	△
decision tree	o	o	△	△

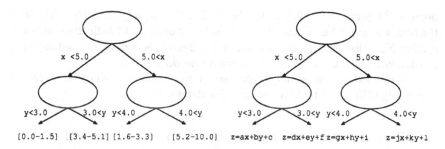

Fig. 1. Decision trees with a continuous class

The above table shows the summary.

△ in neural network means that training results are incomprehensible.

△ in linear regression means that training results are incomprehensible.

△ in regression tree means that training results are incomprehensible.

△ means that decision trees cannot work well in continuous classes.

Association rules are omitted in the above table, because association rules do not have classes. However the evaluations for association rules are the same as those for decision trees.

Thus, we conclude that there is no technique which can satisfy the two requirements for KDD techniques, that is, the technique which can provide accurate predictions and comprehensible rules in the discrete domain and the continuous domain.

2.5 The solution for the problem

The solution for the above problem is extracting comprehensible rules from prediction models such as neural networks, multiple regression formulas, and so on. When rules are extracted from prediction models, the rules are not used for predictions, but used for only humans comprehension. The prediction models are used to make the predictions. A set of a prediction model and a rule(rules) extracted from the prediction model is the perfect KDD technique.

How a rule extracted from a neural network is used is briefly explained. When a neural network predicts, the neural network outputs only a class or a figure. Humans cannot understand how or why the neural network outputs the class or the figure. A rule extracted from the neural network explains how or why the network outputs the class or the figure.

For example, let a network be trained using process data consisting of four attributes, that is, a temperature (t), a pressure (p), a humidity (h), and a class, the quality of a material (q). Let the rule extracted be as follows:

$(200 \leq t \leq 300) \vee (p \leq 2.5) \vee (70 \leq h \leq 90) \to q \leq 0.2$.

Assume that the network is used for a prediction, and the inputs for the network are $t = 310, p = 2.0$, and $h = 60$ and the output from the network is 0.1, which means low quality. The above rule shows that the network outputs 0.1, because the pressure is 2.0, which is below 2.5, that is, $p \leq 2.5$ holds. Without the rule, we cannot know how or why the network outputs 0.1 indicating the low quality. Note that the rule extracted from the neural network is not used for the predictions, which are made by the neural network.

The rule extraction technique has been implemented in a KDD tool KINO (Knowledge INference by Observation). For details, see [15].

3   The survey of rule extraction from neural networks

This section briefly surveys algorithms for rule extraction from neural networks. Some rule extraction algorithms are based on the structurization of neural networks [5], but the rule extraction algorithms cannot be applied to neural networks trained by another training method such as the back-propagation method. It is desired that rules can be extracted from any neural network trained by any training method. The rule extraction algorithms based on the structurization of neural networks are out of scope.

There are several algorithms for rule extraction from neural networks [1], [2]. The algorithms can be divided into decompositional algorithms and pedagogical algorithms. Decompositional algorithms extract rules from each unit in a neural network and aggregate them into a rule. For example, [3] is a decompositional algorithm. Pedagogical algorithms generate samples from a neural network and induce a rule from the samples. For example, [4] is a pedagogical algorithm. Decompositional algorithms can present training results of each unit in neural networks, so we can understand the training results by the unit, while pedagogical algorithms can present only the results of neural networks, so we cannot understand the training results by the unit. Therefore, decompositional algorithms are better than pedagogical algorithms in terms of understandability of the inner structures of neural networks.

Rule extraction algorithms are compared in several items such as network structures, training methods, computational complexity, and values.

network structures : This means the types of network structures the algorithm can be applied to. Several algorithms can be applied only to particular network structures. Most algorithms are applied to three-layer feedforward networks, while a few algorithms can be applied only to recurrent neural networks, where DFAs(Deterministic Finite-state Automata) are extracted [10].

training methods :This means the training methods the rule extraction algorithm can be applied to. Several rule extraction algorithms depend on training methods, that is, the rule extraction algorithms can extract rules only from the neural networks trained by a particular training method [13],[3]. The pedagogical algorithms basically do not depend on training methods.

computational complexity : Most algorithms are exponential in computational complexity. For example, in pedagogical algorithms, the total number of samples generated from a neural network is 2^n, where n is the number of inputs to the neural network. It is very difficult to generate many samples and induce a rule from many samples. Therefore, it is necessary to reduce the computational complexity to a polynomial. Most decompositional algorithms are also exponential in computational complexity.

values :Most algorithms can be applied only to discrete values and cannot be applied to continuous values.

The ideal algorithm can be applied to any neural network, can be applied to any training method, is polynomial in computational complexity, and can be applied to continuous values. So far, there are a few algorithms which satisfy the first and second items [4]. There has been no algorithm which satisfies all of the items above.

4 The rule extraction techniques of the author

4.1 The outline

We have developed rule extraction techniques for prediction models. We presented an algorithm for extracting rules from linear formulas and extended it for the continuous domain [16]. Afterwards, we presented efficient algorithms for extracting rules from linear formulas [18] and applied them to discover rules from numerical data [9]. Currently we are applying the algorithms to nonparametric regression formulas to discover rules from images [21].

We extended the algorithms for linear formulas to the algorithms for neural networks [19], and modified them to improve the accuracies and simplicities [20].

The rule extraction algorithm from a linear formula is almost the same as the rule extraction algorithm from a unit in a neural network. Therefore, hereinafter in this section, we focus on neural networks. For the rule extraction algorithms from neural networks, the algorithms basically satisfy the four items listed in the preceding section, that is, the algorithms can be applied to any neural network trained by any training method, are polynomial in computational complexity, and can be applied to continuous values. However, the algorithms have a constraint, that is, they can be applied only to neural networks whose units' output functions are monotone increasing. The algorithms are decompositional algorithms.

There are two kinds of domains, that is, discrete domains and continuous domains. The continuous domain will be discussed later. The discrete domains can be reduced to $\{0, 1\}$ domains by dummy variables. So only $\{0, 1\}$ domains have to be discussed. In the $\{0, 1\}$ domain, the units can be approximated to the nearest Boolean functions, which is the basic idea for the rule extraction algorithm. The approximation theory is based on multilinear function space. The space, which is an extension of Boolean algebra of Boolean functions, can be made into a Euclidean space and includes linear functions and neural networks. Due to space limitations, the details can be found in [22].

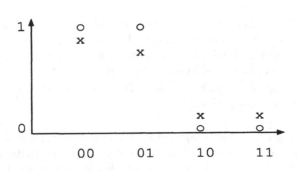

Fig. 2. Approximation

4.2 The outline of the rule extraction algorithms

The basic algorithm is that the units of neural networks are approximated by Boolean functions. The output functions are sigmoid functions, so the values of the units are [0,1]. Let (f_i) $(i = 1,..,2^n)$ be the values of a unit of a neural network. Let (g_i) be the values of Boolean functions, that is, $g_i = 0$ or 1. The basic algorithm is as follows:

$$g_i = \begin{cases} 1(f_i \geq 0.5), \\ 0(f_i < 0.5). \end{cases}$$

This algorithm minimizes Euclidean distance.

Fig. 2 shows a case of two variables. Crosses stand for the values of a unit of a neural network and circles stand for the values of a Boolean function. $00, 01, 10$ and 11 stand for the domains, for example, 00 stands for $x = 0, y = 0$. In this case, there are four domains as follows:

$(0,0), (0,1), (1,0), (1,1)$

The values of the Boolean function $g(x,y)$ are as follows:

$g(0,0) = 1, g(0,1) = 1, g(1,0) = 0, g(1,1) = 0$.

The Boolean functions corresponding to the points are as follows:

$(0,0) \Leftrightarrow \bar{x}\bar{y}, \quad (0,1) \Leftrightarrow \bar{x}y, \quad (1,0) \Leftrightarrow x\bar{y}, \quad (1,1) \Leftrightarrow xy$.

A Boolean function $g(x,y)$ of two variables are represented as follows:

$g(x,y) = g(0,0)\bar{x}\bar{y} \vee g(0,1)\bar{x}y \vee g(1,0)x\bar{y} \vee g(1,1)xy$.

Therefore, in the case of Fig. 2, the Boolean function is as follows:

$$\begin{aligned} g(x,y) &= g(0,0)\bar{x}\bar{y} \vee g(0,1)\bar{x}y \vee g(1,0)x\bar{y} \vee g(1,1)xy \\ &= 1\bar{x}\bar{y} \vee 1\bar{x}y \vee 0x\bar{y} \vee 0xy = \bar{x}\bar{y} \vee \bar{x}y = \bar{x}. \end{aligned}$$

The basic algorithm is exponential in computational complexity, therefore, polynomial algorithms are needed. The author has presented polynomial algorithms. The details are omitted due to space limitations. The outline of the polynomial algorithms follows.

1. Check if a term exists in the Boolean function after the approximation.
2. Connect the terms existing after the approximation by logical conjunction to make a DNF formula.

3. Execute the above procedures up to a certain (usually two or three) order.

After rules are extracted from all units, the rules are aggregated into a rule for the network.

If accurate rules are obtained, the rules are complicated, and if simple rules are obtained, the rules are not accurate. It is difficult to obtain rules which are simple and accurate at the same time. We have presented a few techniques to obtain simple and accurate rules. For example, attribute selection works well for obtaining simple rules [20].

4.3 The continuous domain

When classes are continuous, rule extraction from neural networks is important. However, in the continuous domain, few algorithms have been proposed. For example, algorithms for extracting fuzzy rules have been presented [8], but fuzzy rules are described by linear functions, and so fuzzy rules are incomprehensible.

Continuous domains can be normalized to [0,1] domains by some normalization method. The author presented a qualitative expression system corresponding to Boolean functions, in the [0,1] domain. The system consists of direct proportion($y = x$), reverse proportion($y = 1 - x$), conjunction and disjunction. The inverse proportion ($y = 1 - x$) is a little different from the conventional one ($y = -x$), because $y = 1 - x$ is the natural extension of the negation in Boolean functions. The conjunction and disjunction can also be obtained by a natural extension. The functions generated by direct proportion, reverse proportion, conjunction and disjunction are called continuous Boolean functions, because they satisfy the axioms of Boolean algebra[17].

In the [0,1] domain, the units in a neural network can be approximated to the nearest continuous Boolean functions. The basic algorithm and polynomial algorithms are almost the same as in the discrete domain. For example, a rule is described as follows.
$(t \wedge p) \vee \bar{h} \to q,$
where t stands for temperature, p stands for a pressure, h stands for humidity, and q stands for the quality of a material. The above rule means
"(temperature increases and pressure increases) or humidity decreases, then quality increases." or
"(temperature decreases and pressure decreases) or humidity increases, then quality decreases."

5   Open problems

1. When classes are continuous, other techniques such as decision tree do not work well as explained in Section 2. Therefore, rule extraction from prediction models with continuous classes are important. Continuous Boolean functions work well for linear formulas, but cannot express the detailed information on neural networks, because the neural networks are nonlinear. The

continuous Boolean functions are insufficient, therefore, extracting rules described by intervals such as
$(200 \leq t \leq 300) \vee (p \leq 2.5) \vee (70 \leq h \leq 90) \rightarrow q \leq 0.2$ from neural networks is needed.

2. Usual real data consist of discrete data and continuous data. Therefore, rule extraction from a mixture of discrete attributes and continuous attributes is needed.

3. Training domains are much smaller than prediction domains. For example, in the case of *voting-records*, which consist of 16 binary attributes, the number of possible training data is $2^{16}(= 65536)$, while the number of training data is about 500. The outputs of a neural network are almost 100% accurate for about 500 training data, and are predicted values for the other approximately 65000 data. These predicted values are probabilistic, because the parameters for the neural network are initialized probabilistically. Since 65000 is much greater than 400, that is, the probabilistic part is much larger than the non-probabilistic part. Therefore, when a rule is extracted from a neural network, the predicted values of the neural network has to be dealt with probabilistically.

We have developed two types of algorithms. The first one deals with the whole domain equally [19]. The second one deals with only the training domain and basically ignores the prediction domain [20]. Both algorithms can be regarded as opposite extremes. We also have developed an algorithm which deals with the prediction domains probabilistically[9]. Future work includes the development of algorithms dealing with the prediction domains appropriately.

4. There are several prediction models based on linear formulas. It is desired that rule extraction techniques from linear formulas be applied to nonparametric regression analysis[21], (multivariate) autoregression analysis, regression trees, differential equations (difference equations), and so on.

6 Conclusions

This paper has explained that rule extraction from prediction models is needed for perfect KDD techniques. This paper has briefly reviewed the rule extraction techniques for neural networks and has briefly explained the rule extraction algorithms developed by the author. There are a lot of open problems in the field of rule extraction from prediction models, therefore the author hopes that researchers will join this field.

References

1. Andrews,R., Diederich,J., and Tickle,A.B.: Survey and critique of techniques for extracting rules from trained artificial neural networks, *Knowledge-Based Systems*, Vol.8, No. 6, pp.373-189, 1995.

2. Andrews,R. and Diederich,J. eds: *Rules and Networks, Proceedings of the Rule Extraction from Trained Artificial Neural Networks Workshop, AISB'96*, Queensland University of Technology, 1996.
3. Craven,M.W. and Shavlik,J.W.: Learning symbolic rules using artificial neural networks, *Proceedings of the Tenth International Machine Learning Conference*, pp.73-80,1993.
4. Craven,M.W. and Shavlik,J.W.: Using sampling queries to extract rules from trained neural networks, *Proceedings of the Eleventh International Machine Learning Conference*, pp.37-45, 1994.
5. Ishikawa,M.: Structural Learning with Forgetting, *Neural Networks*, Vol.9, No.3, pp.509-521, 1996.
6. Kuok,C.M., Fu,A., and Wong,M.H.: Mining fuzzy association rules in databases, *ACM SIGMOD record*, Vol. 27, No.1, pp.1-12,1998.
7. Lu,H.J., Setiono,R., and Liu,H.:Effective data mining using neural networks. *IEEE Trans. on Knowledge and Data Engineering*, Vol.8, pp.957-961,1998.
8. Mascarilla,L.: Fuzzy rule extraction and redundancy elimination: an application to remote sensing image analysis, *Int. J. Intell. Syst.*, Vol.12, No.11-12, pp.793-817, 1997.
9. Morita,C. and Tsukimoto,H.: Knowledge discovery from numerical data, *Knowledge-based Systems*, Vol.10, No.7, pp.413-419, 1998.
10. Omlin,C.W. and C.L. Giles: Extraction of Rules from Discrete-time Recurrent Neural Networks, *Neural Networks*, Vol.9, No.1, pp.41-52, 1996.
11. Quinlan,J.R.: *C4.5: Programs for machine learning*, Morgan Kaufmann Pub., 1993.
12. Data Mining with Cubist: http://www.rulequest.com/cubist-info.html.
13. Setiono,R. and Liu, H.: Understanding Neural Networks via Rule Extraction, *Proceedings of The 14th International Joint Conference on Artificial Intelligence*, pp.480-485, 1995.
14. Srikant,S. and Agrawal,R.: Mining quantitative association rules in large relational tables, *ACM SIGMOD conf. on management of Data*, pp.41-46, 1996.
15. Data Mining Tool KINOsuite-PR: http://www2.toshiba.co.jp/datamining/index.htm.
16. Tsukimoto,H.: The discovery of logical propositions in numerical data, *AAAI'94 Workshop on Knowledge Discovery in Databases*, pp.205-216, 1994.
17. Tsukimoto,H.: On continuously valued logical functions satisfying all axioms of classical logic, *Systems and Computers in Japan*,Vol.25, No.12, pp.33-41, SCRIPTA TECHNICA, INC., 1994.
18. Tsukimoto,H. and Morita,C.: Efficient algorithms for inductive learning-An application of multi-linear functions to inductive learning, *Machine Intelligence 14*, pp.427-449, Oxford University Press, 1995.
19. Tsukimoto,H.: An Algorithm for Extracting Propositions from Trained Neural Networks Using Multilinear Functions, *Rules and Networks, Proceedings of the Rule Extraction from Trained Artificial Neural Networks Workshop, AISB'96*, pp.103-114, Queensland University of Technology, 1996.
20. Tsukimoto,H.:Extracting Propositions from Trained Neural Networks. *Proceedings of The 15th International Joint Conference on Artificial Intelligence*, pp.1098-1105, 1997.
21. Tsukimoto,H. and Morita,C.:The Discovery of Rules from Brain Images. *Discovery Science, Proceedings of the First International Conference DS'98*, pp.198-209, 1998.
22. Tsukimoto,H.:Symbol pattern integration using multilinear functions, in *Deep Fusion of Computational and Symbolic Processing*, (eds.) Furuhashi,T., Tano,.S., and Jacobsen,H.A. Springer Verlag, 1999.

Mining Association Rules on Related Numeric Attributes

Xiaoyong Du, Zhibin Liu, Naohiro Ishii

Department of Intelligence and Computer Science
Nagoya Institute of Technology, Nagoya, Japan
E-mail:{duyong, zhibin, ishii }@egg.ics.nitech.ac.jp

Abstract. In practical applications, some property is represented by a pair of related attributes. For example, blood pressure, temperature changes etc. The existing data mining approaches for association rules can not tackle those cases, because they treat every attribute independently. In this paper, as a special kind of correlation, we express the pair of attributes as a range-type attribute. We define a set of fuzzified relations between ranges and revise the definition of association rules. We also propose effective algorithms to evaluate the measures for ranking association rules on related numeric attributes.

keywords: Data mining, Association rules, Numeric attributes, Fuzzified relations

1 Introduction

In practical applications, there may exist correlation among attributes. In this paper, we pay attention to a special kind of correlation. that is, a property is represented by a pair of related attributes. For example, blood pressure, temperature changes, time interval etc. In this case, it is nature to treat a pair of values as a range. So an association rule on range-type attribute is expected.

Let us see an example. There are a collection of experimental data which record occurrence of an event, say Y, and the temperature changes, say X, in each fixed time interval. The temperature is a continual variable, which should be discreted in some way. Assume we record only the highest and lowest temperature in each interval, denoted as X_1 and X_2, respectively. Assume we also know according to practical experience that Y is related with not only the difference of temperature (distance between X_1 and X_2) but also the highest and lowest temperature (the values of X_1 and X_2). In this case, It is better to treat $[X_1, X_2]$ as a range than the three independent factors. Hence, an association rule, like $[X_1, X_2] \subseteq_f R \Rightarrow (Y = yes)$ is expected, where $\subseteq_f$ is a binary relation between two ranges, whose membership function is a value in [0,1]. If X is a true subset of R, the membership of $(X, R) \in \subseteq_f$ is 1. If X does not overlap with R, the membership is 0, Otherwise, it is a value between 0 and 1 determined by the percent of X covered by R . We call this relation fuzzified subset relation in this paper. The existing data mining approaches on numeric or interval data [3, 4, 6] can not tackle this case appropriately, because they treat each attribute independently. By their approaches, an association rule, like $X_1 \in [a_1, b_1] \wedge X_2 \in [a_2, b_2] \Rightarrow (Y = Yes)$ or $(X_1, X_2) \in P \Rightarrow (Y = Yes)$, where P is a rectangle, can be extracted. In this rule, X_1 and X_2 are treated as two independent attributes.

In this paper, we focus on mining the association rules on range-type attribute. For understanding the contribution of this study, we review briefly the work in the discovery of association rules. Given a huge database, an association rule is a relationship between two conditions C_1 and C_2 such that if a tuple meets the condition C_1, then it also satisfies the other condition C_2 with a probability (called confidence), denoted by $C_1 \Rightarrow C_2$. Agrawal et al.[1, 2] considered the Boolean-type data in their study of finding association rule from a huge database of sales transactions. An unordered attribute (also called categorical attribute) can be transformed into this case by treating each value v of the attribute A as a new attribute $A.v$. In this case, the membership of specified data to a given set is necessary in defining the measures of the patterns of interest. Srikant and Agrawal [7] studied a more complex case that the attribute may be a quantitative one. A quantitative attribute is an ordered discrete one, but the separation between two neighbor values has no meaning. In this case, whether a specified datum is in a given range need to be considered. Minker et. al. [6] and Fukuda et. al. [3] further considered more general case that the data are interval, that is, ordered data for which the separation between data points has meaning. In this case, the distance between data should be considered in addition.

From the above brief review, we see that the problem proposed in this paper is different with the existing ones. A pair of related numeric attributes can be viewed as a range. Hence this paper discusses mining association rules on range-type data. The concepts of association rules as well as measures of support and confidence should be revised. Especially, the overlapped part between two ranges should be considered in the definition of measures. Moreover, an efficient algorithm to extract optimized association rules is proposed.

The remainder of this paper is organized as follows. In section 2, we define three fuzzified relations on range data. In section 3, we revise the definitions of support and confidence for an association rule, and the concept of optimized association rules. We also propose a naive algorithm with time complexity $O(n^2)$ to extract the optimized rules, where n is the number of buckets. In section 4, we propose a set of iterative formulas for evaluation of the measures. Its time complexity is $O(n)$. It is much better than the naive one. In section 5, a set of experiments are designed for verifying the efficiency of our algorithm.

2 Fuzzified Relations on Ranges

The operations between ranges like $\cup$ (union), $\cap$ (intersection), and $-$ (difference) are defined as usual. For example, $[5, 10] \cap [2, 8] = [5, 8]$, $[5, 10] \cup [2, 8] = [2, 10]$, $[5, 10] - [2, 8] = [8, 10]$, and $[2, 8] - [5, 10] = [2, 5]$. However, the relations between ranges like $\subseteq$, $\supseteq$ and $=$ should be reconsidered as we showed in Introduction. Similar to the way in fuzzy set theory, we define a fuzzified relation between ranges by a membership function whose domain is [0,1].

Definition 1. Assume there are two comparable (closed) ranges $S = [s_1, s_2]$ and $T = [t_1, t_2]$. Let $\| \cdot \|$ denote the length of a range. A fuzzified subset relation between S and T, denoted by $(S, T) \in \subseteq_f$ or $S \subseteq_f T$, is defined by the following membership function:

$$d_{\subseteq_f}(S, T) = \frac{\|S \cap T\|}{\|S\|}.$$

Similarly, a fuzzified superset and equivalence relation between S and T, denoted by $S \supseteq_f T$ and $S =_f T$, is defined by the following membership function, respectively: $d_{\supseteq_f}(S, T) = \dfrac{\|S \cap T\|}{\|T\|}$ and $d_{=_f}(S, T) = \dfrac{\|S \cap T\|}{\|S \cup T\|}$.

Example 1. Consider the following two ranges $S = [5, 20]$ and $T = [10, 15]$.

$$d_{\subseteq_f}(S, T) = (\|[5, 20] \cap [10, 15]\|) / \|[5, 20]\| = 1/3$$
$$d_{\supseteq_f}(S, T) = (\|[5, 20] \cap [10, 15]\|) / \|[10, 15]\| = 1$$
$$d_{=_f}(S, T) = (\|[5, 20] \cap [10, 15]\|) / \|[5, 20] \cup [10, 15]\| = 1/3$$

As we mentioned in Introduction, which fuzzified relation is used depends on application. In the following discussion, a fuzzified relation is denoted as $\sim_f$ if there is no necessity to distinguish them.

3 Optimized Association Rules

3.1 Basic Definitions

In this paper, we are interested in a specific form of association rules on range-type attribute, $(X \sim_f [a, b]) \Rightarrow (Y = Yes)$, where $\sim_f$ is one of the fuzzified relation defined in Definition 1.

Association rules are typically ranked by a set of measures. Common measures are *support* and *confidence*[1, 2]. *support* of a rule is the frequency of the occurrence of the rule (or the premise of the rule) in the database. *confidence* is the strength of the rule implication. For example, for a database of sales transactions, one usually measures a buying pattern $A \Rightarrow B$ (it means that users who buy item A almost always buy item B) by the two measures[1, 2]. The measure *support* quantifies how often the users who buy both item A and B (or only A) as a fraction of the total number of users. The other measure *confidence* is the ratio of the users who buy item B to the users who buy the item A.

The measures for patterns of interest for categorical attribute[1], quantitative attribute (ordered discrete attribute)[7] or continuous attribute[6, 3] have been defined. However, their definitions can not be applied directly for range-type attributes, because their membership functions are not Boolean ones. Here, we define a set of measures for range-type attributes.

Assume there is a database $D = \{t_1, \cdots, t_n\}$, which contains a range-type attribute X and a Boolean attribute Y, $t_i.X (= [l_i, u_i])$ is the value of X in the tuple t_i. Let $R = [L, U]$ be a given range, C a Boolean condition on Y. We denote $D_c = \{t_i | t_i \in D \wedge C\}$, and $D_R = \{t_i | t_i \in D_c \wedge t_i.X \cap R \neq \phi\}$.

Definition 2 . The support of a rule $X \sim_f R \Rightarrow C$ is defined as below

$$\alpha(R) = |D_R|/|D| \tag{1}$$

where $|\cdot|$ represents the size of a set.

The support of a rule is the ratio of the number of tuples in the database that satisfies the given condition C and intersects with the given range R in the attribute X. Since the condition C is fixed in this study, the range R is the unique parameter in this definition.

However, the measure $\alpha(R)$ considers only if a range is intersected with the given range R. The bigger the R, the bigger the $\alpha(R)$ is. Hence $\alpha(R)$ is not enough to define an appropriate range R for the association rule. We have to consider how many percent of the R is covered on the average.

Definition 3 . The intensity of a rule $X \sim_f R \Rightarrow C$ is defined as below,

$$\beta(R) = \frac{\Sigma_{t_i \in D_c} d_{\sim_f}(R, t_i.X)}{|D_R|} \tag{2}$$

where $d_{\sim_f}(R, r_i)$ is one of the membership function defined in Definition 1 .

The measure $\beta(R)$ quantifies the percent of the given range R covered by all tuples in the database on the average. The smaller the R, the bigger the $\beta(R)$ is.

Example 2 . Assume there is a database D(X,Y) = { ([0,8],1), ([0,5],1), ([5,10],1), ([8,10], 0), ([7,15],1) }. Consider two rules with ranges $R_1 = [5, 10]$ and $R_2 = [0, 10]$, respectively. The values of $d_{\supseteq_f}(R_1, X)$ are 0.6, 0, 1, 0.4 and 0.6 respectively. The values of $d_{\supseteq_f}(R_2, X)$ are 0.8, 0.5, 0.5, 0.2 and 0.3 respectively. So, $\beta(R_1) = (0.6 + 1 + 0.6)/3 = 0.733$, and $\beta(R_2) = (0.8 + 0.5 + 0.5 + 0.3)/4 = 0.525$. Hence, the intensity of the rule with R_1 is larger than that with R_2.

Definition 4 . The confidence of a rule $(X \sim_f R) \Rightarrow C$ is defined as below,

$$\gamma(R) = \frac{\Sigma_{t_i \in D_c} d_{\sim_f}(R, t_i.X)}{\Sigma_{t_i \in D} d_{\sim_f}(R, t_i.X)} \tag{3}$$

$\gamma(R)$ reflects the ratio of the weighted number of ranges in D_c to that in D.

Example 3 . Consider the database and range R_1 and R_2 in Example 2 . We have $\Sigma_{t_i \in D_c} d_{\sim_f}(R_1, t_i.X) = 2.2$; $\Sigma_{t_i \in D} d_{\sim_f}(R_1, t_i.X) = 2.6$; $\Sigma_{t_i \in D_c} d_{\sim_f}(R_2, t_i.X) = 2.1$ and $\Sigma_{t_i \in D} d_{\sim_f}(R_2, t_i.X) = 2.3$. Then, $\gamma(R_1) = 2.2/2.6 = 0.85$, and $\gamma(R_2) = 2.1/2.3 = 0.91$. Hence, the confidence of the rule $X \supseteq_f R_2 \Rightarrow C$ is larger than that of the rule $X \supseteq_f R_1 \Rightarrow C$.

Definition 5 . A rule $X \sim_f R \Rightarrow C$ is called *interested* if its support $\alpha(R)$, intensity $\beta(R)$ and confidence $\gamma(R)$ are not less than the given minimum thresholds, respectively. Among interested rules, an *optimized rule* maximizes one of the measures in all interested rules.

For a given range, we can compute the three measures by scanning the database one time. However, when computing the optimized rules, we need to check possibly infinite candidate ranges and we may have to scan the whole database more than one time. These two points are not acceptable for a huge database in practice. Fortunately, an approximate solution is enough for practical applications. In the remainder of this section, we propose a naive algorithm to mine the optimized association rules based on bucketing techniques.

3.2 Bucketing

For processing a continue attribute, bucketing method is widely used. In existing algorithms, two kinds of buckets are used: equi-size and equi-volume. The former requires that the size of buckets are the same, but the number of data in the buckets are different. The later requires that the number of data in buckets are the same, but the size of buckets are different. Our algorithm has no special requirement for buckets. User can give a sequence of intervals, which divides the whole domain of the attribute, according to the requirement of application. We then construct a set of buckets from the intervals

Let MAX and MIN be the maximum and minimum bound of the continuous attribute X. Assume the range [MIN,MAX] is divided into a set of intervals $I_1, I_2, \cdots, I_m$, where $I_i = [x_{i-1}, x_i]$. From the interval set $\{I_1, \cdots, I_m\}$, we construct a set of buckets $B_{s,t} = \cup_{s \leq k \leq t}(I_k)$, where $1 \leq s, t \leq m$. We call $B = \{B_{1,1}, B_{1,2}, \cdots, B_{m,m}\}$ a bucket set. Let the number of bucket be n. Clearly, $n = m(m+1)/2$. The bucket set can be organized as a triangle (See Figure 1). The point with label ij represents the bucket $B_{i,j}$. A range $[l, u]$ is distributed to bucket $B_{s,t}$ if and only if $l_{s-1} < l \leq l_s$ and $u_{t-1} < u \leq u_t$, where $B_{s+1,t-1} = [l_{s+1}, u_{t-1}]$, $B_{s,t} = [l_s, u_t]$. Ranges in the same bucket are treated as the same. This procedure is called normalization of the data. The length of ranges in a bucket are equal to the length of the bucket. One tuple in the database belongs to one and only one bucket. Let $u_{s,t}$ denote the number of tuples in bucket $B_{s,t}$, and $v_{s,t}$ denote the number of tuples in bucket $B_{s,t}$ that satisfy the condition C. Moreover, let $I_{s,t}$ denote the interval obtained by combining a set of consecutive intervals $I_s, I_{s+1}, \cdots, I_t$. In this paper, we consider all $I_{s,t}$ as candidates of the optimized range. Obviously, the interval $I_{s,t}$ corresponds to the bucket $B_{s,t}$.

3.3 Naive Algorithm

Property 6. Let $U_{s,t} = \Sigma_{t_i \in D} d_{\sim_f}(I_{s,t}, t_i.X)$, $V_{s,t} = \Sigma_{t_i \in D_c} d_{\sim_f}(I_{s,t}, t_i.X)$, and $W_{s,t} = |D_{I_{s,t}}|$. $P = \{(k,l)|1 \leq k \leq t, max(s,k) \leq l \leq m\}$ Then,

$$\begin{cases} U_{s,t} = \Sigma_{(k,l) \in P}(d_{\sim_f}(I_{s,t}, I_{k,l}) * u_{k,l}) \\ V_{s,t} = \Sigma_{(k,l) \in P}(d_{\sim_f}(I_{s,t}, I_{k,l}) * v_{k,l}) \\ W_{s,t} = \Sigma_{(k,l) \in P} v_{k,l} \end{cases} \quad (4)$$

Proof. It can be proved from the fact that the ranges intersected with $I_{s,t}$ are exactly those in the buckets in polygon $B_{1,s}B_{s,s}B_{t,t}B_{t,m}B_{1,m}$ (Figure 1). That is, the buckets in $\{B_{k,l}|(k,l) \in P\}$.

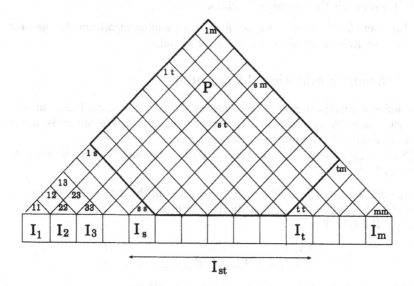

Fig. 1. Buckets intersected with $I_{s,t}$

Algorithm 7. (Evaluating the optimized rules)

    s1: evaluating $U_{s,t}, V_{s,t},$ and $W_{s,t}$ by the formula (4).

    s2: for $(1 \leq s \leq t \leq m)$ do {

        evaluating $\alpha(I_{s,t})$, $\beta(I_{s,t})$ and $\gamma(I_{s,t})$ according to their definitions.

        if $(\alpha(I_{s,t}) \geq \theta_s \wedge \beta(I_{s,t}) \geq \theta_i \wedge \gamma(I_{s,t}) \geq \theta_c$) then

            insert $(I_{s,t}, \alpha(I_{s,t}), \beta(I_{s,t}), \gamma(I_{s,t}))$ into table T;

    };

    s3: Evaluating I_{s^*,t^*} such that $\gamma(I_{s^*,t^*}) = max_{I_{s,t} \in T} \gamma(I_{s,t})$;

Although the algorithm evaluates only the optimized confidence association rule, it is similar to evaluate the other optimized rules.

Theorem 8. *The complexity of algorithm 7 is $O(n^2)$, where n is the number of the buckets.*

Proof. The most expensive step is obviously the step s1 of evaluation of $U_{s,t}$, $V_{s,t}$ and $W_{s,t}$. We count the number of arithmetical operations in the step s1. For an arbitrary interval $I_{s,t}$, the polygon P in Figure 1 contains $mt - t(t - 1)/2 - s(s - 1)/2$ buckets, where m is the number of the intervals. From their evaluation formulas, we know that the number of the arithmetical operations is the constant times of the number of the buckets in the polygon P. Hence, the complexity of the step s1 is, $O(\Sigma_{1 \leq s \leq t \leq m}(mt - \frac{t(t-1)}{2} - \frac{s(s-1)}{2})) = O(m^4) = O(n^2)$. where n is the number of buckets.

However, $O(n^2)$ is too complex for a data mining algorithm. In the next section, we derive a set of efficient iterative formulas.

4 Efficient Evaluation Algorithms

The naive algorithm computes the measures for each candidates independently. In fact, there are tight relationship between candidates. We can make use of them to reduce the complexity of the evaluation.

Since $W_{s,t}$ is independent with the fuzzified relations, we consider its evaluation at first.

Property 9 . Let $W'_{s,t}$ be the number of ranges in the database that are contained in the interval $I_{s,t}$ and satisfy the condition C. That is, $W'_{s,t} = |\{t_i.X \subseteq I_{s,t}|t_i \in D \wedge C\}|$. Then,

$$W'_{s,t} = \begin{cases} v_{s,s} & ,t = s \\ W'_{s,t-1} + W'_{s+1,t} - W'_{s+1,t-1} + v_{s,t} & ,t > s \end{cases}$$

This formula says that $W'_{s,t}$ can be evaluated iteratively.

Proof. Since the buckets are pairwise disjoint, we have

$$\begin{aligned} W'_{s,t} &= |\{t_i.X \subseteq I_{s,t}|t_i \in D \wedge C\}| \\ &= |\{t_i.X \subseteq I_{s,t}|t_i \in B_{k,l} \wedge (1 \leq k \leq l \leq m) \wedge C\}| \\ &= |\{t_i.X \subseteq I_{s,t}|t_i \in B_{k,l} \wedge (s \leq k \leq l \leq t) \wedge C\}| \\ &= \Sigma_{s \leq k \leq l \leq t}(|\{t_i.X \subseteq I_{s,t}|t_i \in B_{k,l} \wedge C\}|) \\ &= \Sigma_{s \leq k \leq l \leq t}(v_{k,l}) \\ &= \Sigma_{s \leq k \leq l \leq t-1}(v_{k,l}) + \Sigma_{s+1 \leq k \leq l \leq t}(v_{k,l}) - \Sigma_{s+1 \leq k \leq l \leq t-1}(v_{k,l}) + v_{s,t} \\ &= W'_{s,t-1} + W'_{s+1,t} - W'_{s+1,t-1} + v_{s,t} \end{aligned}$$

From this property, we can evaluate all $W_{s,t}$ by the following property

Property 10 . For arbitrary interval $I_{s,t}$, we have

$$W_{s,t} = (W'_{1,m} - W'_{1,s-1} - W'_{t+1,m}) \tag{5}$$

In the sequel, we consider the iterative formulas for the intensity and confidence which are dependent with the definition of fuzzified relation.

Property 11 . For the fuzzified relation $\supseteq_f$, we have

$$U_{s,t} = \begin{cases} \Sigma_{1 \leq k \leq s}\Sigma_{s \leq l \leq m}(u_{k,l}) & ,s = t \\ \Sigma_{i=s}^{t}\bar{U}_{i,i}/(t-s+1) & ,s \neq t \end{cases}$$

$$V_{s,t} = \begin{cases} \Sigma_{1 \leq k \leq s}\Sigma_{s \leq l \leq m}(v_{k,l}) & ,s = t \\ \Sigma_{i=s}^{t}\bar{V}_{i,i}/(t-s+1) & ,s \neq t \end{cases}$$

Proof. We prove the first formula only. The proof for the second one is similar.

1. (case $t = s$) Since the interval $I_{s,s}$ is a unit interval, every range intersected with $I_{s,s}$ covers $I_{s,s}$ also. Hence, $d_{\supseteq_f}(I_{s,s}, I_{k,l}) = 1$ if the range $I_{k,l}$ is intersected with $I_{s,s}$. From the formulas in Property 6, we have $U_{s,t} = \Sigma_{1 \leq k \leq s} \Sigma_{s \leq l \leq m}(u_{k,l})$.

2. (case $s \neq t$) Consider an arbitrary bucket $B_{k,l}$ in the polygon P in Figure 1. If it covers the interval $I_{s,t}$, it contributes to every $B_{i,i}(s \leq i \leq t)$. If it is intersected with $I_{s,t}$, it contributes to those $B_{i,i}$ which are contained in both $I_{s,t}$ and $I_{k,l}$. Hence, each bucket contributes $U_{s,t}$ as the same times as the $t - s + 1$, that is, the length of the interval $I_{s,t}$. Hence, $U_{s,t} = \Sigma_{s \leq k \leq t} U_{k,k}/(t - s + 1)$.

Evaluating $U_{s,t}$ and $V_{s,t}$ by these formulas is still too complex. We further construct a set of iterative formulas for them.

Property 12. For the fuzzified relation $\supseteq_f$, let $U'_{s,t} = \Sigma_{i=s}^{t} U_{i,i}$, $V'_{s,t} = \Sigma_{i=s}^{t} V_{i,i}$. Then,

$$
U'_{s,t} = \begin{cases} \Sigma_{1 \leq l \leq m}(u_{1,l}) & , s = t = 1 \\ U'_{i-1,i-1} - \Sigma_{j=1}^{i-1} u_{j,i-1} + \Sigma_{j=i}^{m} u_{i,j} & , s = t = i > 1 \\ U'_{s,t-1} + U'_{t,t} & , s \neq t \end{cases}
$$

$$
V'_{s,t} = \begin{cases} \Sigma_{1 \leq l \leq m}(v_{1,l}) & , s = t = 1 \\ V'_{i-1,i-1} - \Sigma_{j=1}^{i-1} v_{j,i-1} + \Sigma_{j=i}^{m} v_{i,j} & , s = t = i > 1 \\ V'_{s,t-1} + V'_{t,t} & , s \neq t \end{cases}
$$

Proof. Straightforward from Property 11.

Property 13. For the fuzzified relation $\supseteq_f$, we have

$$
\begin{cases} U_{s,t} = U'_{s,t}/(t - s + 1) \\ V_{s,t} = V'_{s,t}/(t - s + 1) \end{cases} \tag{6}
$$

Proof. Straightforward from Property 11 and Property 12.

We now consider the evaluation of measures for the fuzzified relation $\subseteq_f$.

Property 14. For the fuzzified relation $\subseteq_f$, we have

$$
U_{s,t} = \begin{cases} \Sigma_{j=1}^{m} u_{1,j}/j & , s = t = 1 \\ U_{i-1,i-1} - \Sigma_{j=1}^{i-1} u_{j,i-1}/(i - j) + \Sigma_{j=i}^{m} u_{i,j}/(j - i + 1) & , s = t = i \\ U_{s,t-1} + U_{t,t} & , s \neq t \end{cases} \tag{7}
$$

$$
V_{s,t} = \begin{cases} \Sigma_{j=1}^{m} v_{1,j}/j & , s = t = 1 \\ V_{i-1,i-1} - \Sigma_{j=1}^{i-1} v_{j,i-1}/(i - j) + \Sigma_{j=i}^{m} v_{i,j}/(j - i + 1) & , s = t = i \\ V_{s,t-1} + V_{t,t} & , s \neq t \end{cases} \tag{8}
$$

Proof. It is easy derived from their definitions and the fact that $d_{\subseteq_f}(I_{s,s}, I_{k,l}) = 1/\|I_{k,l}\|$ when $I_{k,l}$ covers $I_{s,s}$.

The algorithm for evaluating the optimized rules is similar to Algorithm 7, but replacing step s1 with the following one.

s1: evaluate $U_{s,t}$ and $V_{s,t}$ and $W_{s,t}$ by the iterative formulas (6) and (5) for $\supseteq_f$, or formulas (7),(8) and (5) for $\subseteq_f$;

Theorem 15 . *The time complexity of the new algorithm is* $O(n)$.

Proof. The complexity except step s1 is $O(m^2)$. Now we consider the step s1 for the case of $\supseteq_f$. For computing $U'_{1,1}$, it takes m arithmetical operations. For computing the other $U'_{i,i}(i = 2, \cdots, m)$, it takes $m + 1$ arithmetical operations. For computing $U'_{s,t}(s \neq t)$, it takes only 2 operations. Hence, the complexity is $m + (m + 1) * (m - 1) + 2 * m * (m - 1)/2 = 2m^2 - 1 = O(m^2)$ Hence, the total complexity is $O(m^2) = O(n)$.

For the third fuzzified relation, $=_f$, unfortunately, we can not find such an iterative formula now.

5 Experimental Results

The proposed algorithms are implemented in C language on the Sun Sparc Workstation 5/110 with SunOS 4.1.4. We design an experiment to test the effectiveness of the algorithm. We put a pattern into a data set, we expect our algorithm can extract the pattern accurately. Our approach is described in the following.

There is a data set which contains 10000 tuples generated randomly. The domain of the continue attribute is the integer in [0,1000]. We choose an arbitrary tuple, say ([914,941],1), as the pattern. Then we duplicate the tuple 10, 100, and 1000 times respectively into the data set to generate 3 new datasets, DS1, DS2 and DS3, respectively. By comparing the range in the optimized support rule that extracted from the various datasets by the algorithm with the given pattern, we see that the extracted optimized range becomes more and more closer to the given pattern when we increase the number of that pattern. Table 1 lists the test results.

Table 1: Effectiveness of the algorithm

No. Intervals	1000	500	200	100
DS1	(-845,-818)	(-846,-819)	(-839,-816)	(-694,-671)
DS2	(-26,-2)	(-24,1)	(-24,4)	(-24,-1)
DS3	(0, 0)	(0, 1)	(-4,-1)	(-4, -1)

where (a, b) in the table means the difference of the left and right bounds of the two ranges.

In the dataset DS1, there are only 10 tuples of ([914,941],1). The test showed that it is much different with the extracted one. While we increase the number of tuple ([914,941],1), the extracted optimized range becomes closer to the pattern. When we duplicate 1000 times of that pattern, the extracted optimized range is almost the same as the expected one in all bucket sets. This result shows that the iterative algorithm can find effectively the rule from the dataset.

We also test efficiency of our algorithm. It shows that the running time of the iterative algorithm is much better than the naive one. Both algorithms run on the same datasets with 10000 tuples and the same thresholds.

Table 2: Runing Time (in 1/60 seconds)

No. Intervals	100	200	500
Naive Algorithm	1959	30855	1673479
Iterative Algorithm	70	104	353

6 Conclusions and Future Research

The contribution of this paper is twofold. First, this paper defined three fuzzified relations between range-type data, and represented association rule on range attribute by using them. Furthermore, we revised the measures for ranking this kind of association rules. To our knowledge, it is the first time to discuss range-type data in data mining application. Second, we proposed a set of iterative formulas for evaluating the measures of association rules. It reduces the time complexity from $O(n^2)$ of the naive algorithm to $O(n)$, while the space complexity is as the same $O(n)$ as that of the naive one.

Correlation is an important relationship among attributes. To represent and catch correlation in the premise of an association rule in a general form is worthful to be investigated further.

References

1. Agrawal, R., Imielinski, T., Swami, A.: Mining Association Rules between Sets of Items in Large Databases, *Proc. SIGMOD*, pp.207–216 (1993)
2. Agrawal, R., Srikant, R. Fast Algorithms for Mining Association Rules, *Proc. VLDB*, pp.487–499 (1994)
3. Fukuda, T., Morimoto,Y., Morishita, S., Tokuyama, T.: Mining Optimized Association Rules for Numeric Attributes *Proc. PODS*, pp.182–191 (1996)
4. Fukuda, T., Morimoto,Y., Morishita, S., Tokuyama, T.: Data Mining Using Two-Dimensional Optimized Association Rules: Scheme, Algorithms, and Visualization *Proc. SIGMOD*, pp.13–23 (1996)
5. Fayyad,U., Piatetsky-Shapiro, G., Smyth, P., and Uthurusamy R.: Advances in Knowledge Discovery and Data Mining *AAAI press/MIT press* (1996)
6. Miller, R.J., Yang, Y.: Association Rules over Interval Data *Proc. SIGMOD*, pp. 452–461 (1997)
7. Srikant, R., Agrawal, R: Mining Quantitative Association Rules in Large Relational Tables, *Proc. SIGMOD*, pp.1–12 (1996)
8. Smyth, P., Fayyad,U., Burl, M., Perona, P.: Modeling Subjective Uncertainty in Image Annotation, *in "Advances in Knowledge Discovery and Data Mining", edited by Fayyad,U., et al* , AAAI press/MIT press (1996)

LGen — A Lattice-Based Candidate Set Generation Algorithm for I/O Efficient Association Rule Mining

Yip, Chi Lap   K. K. Loo   Ben Kao   David Cheung   C. K. Cheng

Department of Computer Science and Information Systems,
The University of Hong Kong, Hong Kong.
{*clyip, kkloo, kao, dcheung, ckcheng*}*@csis.hku.hk*

Abstract. Most algorithms for association rule mining are variants of the basic Apriori algorithm [2]. One characteristic of these Apriori-based algorithms is that candidate itemsets are generated in rounds, with the size of the itemsets incremented by one per round. The number of database scans required by Apriori-based algorithms thus depends on the size of the largest large itemsets. In this paper we devise a more general candidate set generation algorithm, LGen, which generates candidate itemsets of multiple sizes during each database scan. We show that, given a reasonable set of suggested large itemsets, LGen can significantly reduce the number of I/O passes required. In the best cases, only two passes are sufficient to discover all the large itemsets irrespective of the size of the largest ones.

Keywords: Data mining, association rules, lattice, Apriori, LGen

1 Introduction

Data mining has recently attracted considerable attention from database practitioners and researchers because of its applicability in many areas, such as decision support, market strategy and financial forecasts. Combining techniques from the fields of machine learning, statistics and databases, data mining enables us to find out useful and invaluable information from huge databases.

Mining of association rules is a research topic that has received much attention among the various data mining problems. Many interesting works have been published recently on this problem and its variations [1, 2, 4, 5, 7–9]. The retail industry provides a classic example application. Typically, a sales database of a supermarket keeps, for each transaction, all the items bought in that transaction and information such as transaction time, customer-id, etc. The association rule mining problem is to find out all inference rules such as: "A customer who buys item X and item Y is also *likely* to buy item Z in the same transaction", where X, Y and Z are not known beforehand. Such rules are very useful for marketers to develop and to implement customized marketing programs and strategies.

The problem of mining association rules was first introduced in [1]. In that paper, it was shown that the problem could be decomposed into two subproblems:

1. Find out all *large itemsets* and their support counts. A large itemset is a set of items which are contained in a sufficiently large number of transactions, with respect to a support threshold *minimum support*.
2. From the set of large itemsets found, find out all association rules that have a confidence value exceeding a confidence threshold *minimum confidence*.

Since the solution to the second subproblem is straightforward [2], major research efforts have been spent on the first subproblem. Most of the algorithms devised to find large itemsets are based on the `Apriori` algorithm [2]. The `Apriori` algorithm finds out the large itemsets iteratively. In the ith iteration, `Apriori` generates the candidate itemsets of size i [1] from the set of size $(i-1)$ large itemsets L_{i-1}, and scans the database to find the support count of each candidate itemset. `Apriori` terminates when no more candidate set can be generated.

The key of the `Apriori` algorithm is the `Apriori_Gen` function [2] which wisely generates only those candidate itemsets that may be large. However, at each database scan, only candidate itemsets of the same size are generated. So, the number of database scans required by Apriori-based algorithms depends on the size of the largest large itemsets. For example, if a database contains a size-10 large itemset, then at least 10 passes over the database are required. For large databases containing gigabytes of transactions, the I/O cost is dauntingly big.

The goal of this paper is to improve the I/O requirement of the `Apriori` algorithm. In particular, we generalize `Apriori_Gen` to a new candidate set generation algorithm, LGen, based on lattice theory. The main idea is to relax `Apriori`'s restriction that candidate itemsets generation must start from size one and that at each pass, only candidate itemsets of the same size are generated. Instead, LGen takes a (partial) set of multiple-sized large itemsets *as a hint* to generate a set of multiple-sized candidate itemsets. This approach allows us to take advantage of an educated guess, or a *suggestion*, of a set of large itemsets.

In this paper, we present the LGen candidate set generation function and the `FindLarge` algorithm which uses LGen to discover large itemsets in a database. We prove their correctness and show that replacing `Apriori` and `Apriori_Gen` by `FindLarge` and LGen allows us to significantly reduce the amount of I/O cost required for mining association rules. We study the various properties of the algorithms and address the following issues:

- `FindLarge` does not generate more candidate itemsets than `Apriori` does. In general, it generates them earlier and in fewer passes.
- The set of suggested large itemsets for `FindLarge` can be found in different ways. Although the suggested set is not mandatory to `FindLarge`, it significantly improves the preformance of the algorithm.
- The amount of I/O saved by `FindLarge` over `Apriori` depends on the *accuracy* of the suggested large itemsets. As an extreme case, if the suggested itemsets cover all the large itemsets, `FindLarge` requires only 2 passes.
- If sampling is used to obtain a set of suggested large itemsets, we observed that a small sample is usually sufficient. Sampling plus `FindLarge` is thus a viable option for fast association rule mining.

---

[1] The size of an itemset is the number of items the itemset contains.

```
1    function FindLarge(SuggestedLarge)
2        Set of large itemsets with associated counters, MaxLargeItemsets := ∅
3        Iteration := 1
4        CandidateSet := (all size-1 itemsets) ∪ (⋃_{s∈SuggestedLarge} ↓ s)
5        Scan database and count occurrence frequency of every set in CandidateSet
6        NewLargeItemsets := large itemsets in CandidateSet
7        while (NewLargeItemsets ≠ ∅)
8            Iteration := Iteration+1
9            MaxLargeItemsets := Max(MaxLargeItemsets ∪ NewLargeItemsets)
10           CandidateSet := LGen(MaxLargeItemsets, Iteration)
11           Count occurrence frequency of every set in CandidateSet
12           NewLargeItemsets := large itemsets in CandidateSet
13       end while
14       return all subsets of elements in MaxLargeItemsets
```

Fig. 1. Finding large itemsets

2 LGen

We generalize Apriori_Gen to a new candidate set generation function called LGen based on lattice theory. The main idea of LGen is to generate candidate itemsets of bigger sizes early using information provided by a set of suggested large itemsets. Before we describe our algorithm formally, let us first illustrate the idea with an example.

(**Example 1**) Consider a database whose large itemsets are $\{a, b, c, d, e, f\}$, $\{d, e, f, g\}$, $\{e, f, g, h\}$, $\{h, i, j\}$ and all their subsets. Assume that the itemsets $\{a, b, d, e, f\}$, $\{e, f, g, h\}$, and $\{d, g\}$ are suggested large. During the first iteration, we count the supports of the singletons as well as those of the suggested itemsets. Assume that the suggested itemsets are verified large in the first iteration. In the second iteration, since $\{a, b, d, e, f\}$ is large, we know that its subset $\{d, e\}$ is also large. Similarly, we can infer from $\{e, f, g, h\}$ that $\{e, g\}$ is also large. Since $\{d, g\}$ is also large, we can generate the candidate itemset $\{d, e, g\}$ and start counting it. Similarly, the candidate itemset $\{d, f, g\}$ can also be generated this way. Therefore, we have generated some size-3 candidate itemsets before we find out all size-two large itemsets.

Our algorithm for finding large itemsets, FindLarge, is shown in Figure 1. The method is similar to Apriori except that:

- it takes a set of suggested itemsets, *SuggestedLarge* as input and counts their supports during the first database scan, and
- it replaces the Apriori_Gen function by the more general LGen function which takes the set of maximal large itemsets (*MaxLargeItemsets*) as input.

The algorithm consists of two stages. The first stage consists of a single database scan (lines 4–6). Singletons, as well as the suggested large itemsets and their subsets ($\bigcup_{s\in SuggestedLarge} ↓ s$, where $↓ s = \{x \mid x \subseteq s\}$), are counted. Any itemset found to be large at this stage is put into the set of newly found large itemsets (*NewLargeItemsets*).

```
1    function LGen(MaxLargeItemsets,n)
2        CandidateSet:= ∅
3        repeat
4            NewCand:= LGFixedSize(MaxLargeItemsets,n)
5            CandidateSet:= CandidateSet ∪ NewCand
6            n := n + 1
7        until (NewCand = ∅)
8        return CandidateSet
```

Fig. 2. Generating candidate itemsets for a certain iteration

The second stage of FindLarge is iterative. The iteration continues until no more new large itemsets can be found. At each iteration, FindLarge generates a set of candidate itemsets based on the large itemsets it has already discovered. As discussed in [11], we could apply Apriori_Gen on the whole set of large itemsets already found. However, the drawback is that the set of large itemsets could be large, and that it would result in the generation of many redundant candidate itemsets. Instead, FindLarge first *canonicalizes* the set of large itemsets into a set of *maximal* large itemsets (*MaxLargeItemsets*), and passes the maximal set to LGen to generate candidate itemsets. The function Max() (line 9) performs the canonicalization.

We can consider canonicalization as a way of compressing the information contained in the set of large itemsets. Suppose we know that a set s is large, we immediately know that all of its subsets are also large. Considering the set of itemsets with the subset operator as a lattice, we borrow notations from lattice theory [3][6] and denote the set of all subsets of s by its downset $\downarrow s$. Defining the set of maximal elements of L as $\max(L) = \{x \in L \mid \forall y \in L \ [x \subseteq y \Rightarrow y \subseteq x]\}$, we can represent the set of all large itemsets L by a union of downsets: $L = \bigcup_{s \in \max(L)} \downarrow s$.

In Example 1 (page 3) where $\{a,b,c,d,e,f\}$, $\{d,e,f,g\}$, $\{e,f,g,h\}$, $\{h,i,j\}$ and all their subsets are large, $\max(L) = \{\{a,b,c,d,e,f\},\{d,e,f,g\},\{e,f,g,h\}, \{h,i,j\}\}$. Hence, only 4 itemsets are needed to represent L, which contains 86 large itemsets (including the null set).

The set of maximal large itemsets found is then passed to LGen to generate candidate itemsets (line 10). The crux is how to do the generation based on the compressed maximals only. We remark that the Apriori algorithm with Apriori_Gen is in fact displaying a special case of candidate generation with canonicalization. Recall that in Apriori, at the beginning of the the the n-th iteration, the set of large itemsets already discovered is $\bigcup_{k=1}^{n-1} L_k$. The set of elements with size $(n-1)$ in the canonicalized set $\max(\bigcup_{k=1}^{n-1} L_k)$ is L_{n-1}. Interestingly, Apriori_Gen generates the candidate set C_n based solely on L_{n-1}.

The function LGen is shown in Figure 2. By simple induction, one can show that at the beginning of the n-th iteration of FindLarge, all large itemsets whose sizes are smaller than n are known. Hence, when LGen is called at the n-th iteration of FindLarge, it only generates candidate itemsets that are of size n or larger. To generate fix-sized candidate itemsets, LGen calls the helper function,

```
1    function LGFixedSize(MaxLargeItemsets,n)
2        CandidateSet := ∅
3        foreach i, j ∈ MaxLargeItemsets, i ≠ j,
4            if (|(i ∩ j)| ≥ n − 2)
```

$$
\text{NewCand} := \left\{ \{a_1, a_2, ..., a_n\} \left| \begin{array}{l} a_1, a_2, ..., a_{n-2} \in i \cap j, \\ a_{n-1} \in i - j, \ a_n \in j - i, \\ \forall i \in [1, n] \ \exists t \in MaxLargeItemsets \\ \text{s.t.} \{a_1, a_2, ..., a_n\} - \{a_i\} \subseteq t \\ \nexists u \in MaxLargeItemsets \text{ s.t.} \\ \{a_1, a_2, ..., a_n\} \subseteq u \end{array} \right. \right\}
$$

```
6            CandidateSet := CandidateSet ∪ NewCand
7        end if
8    end foreach
9    return CandidateSet
```

Fig. 3. Generating candidate itemsets of a fixed size

LGFixedSize (Figure 3). Essentially, given a target candidate itemset size n, LGFixedSize examines every pair of maximal large itemsets i, j whose intersection is at least $n − 2$ in size (lines 3–4). It then generates candidate itemsets of size n by picking $n − 2$ items from the intersection between i and j, one item from the set difference $i − j$, and another item from $j − i$. A candidate itemset so generated is then checked to see if all of its size-$(n − 1)$ subsets are already known to be large. (That is, if all of them are subsets of certain maximal large itemsets.) If not, the candidate itemset is discarded. The candidate itemsets so generated are collected in the set *NewCand* as shown in line 5 of Figure 3.

2.1 Theorems

We summarize a few properties of LGen in the following theorems. For the proofs, please refer to [11]. We use the symbol S to represent the set of suggested large itemsets and $\downarrow y$ to represent the downset of any itemset y (i.e., $\downarrow y = \{x \mid x \subseteq y\}$). So $\bigcup_{s \in S} \downarrow s$ is the set of all itemsets suggested implicitly or explicitly by the suggested set S. Also, we use C_{LGen} to represent the set of all candidate itemsets generated by LGen in FindLarge and $C_{Apriori}$ to represent the set of all candidate itemsets generated by Apriori_Gen in the Apriori algorithm.

Theorem 1. *Given a set of suggested large itemsets S, $C_{Apriori} \subseteq C_{LGen} \cup (\bigcup_{s \in S} \downarrow s)$.*

Since FindLarge (which uses LGen) counts the supports of all itemsets in $C_{LGen} \cup (\bigcup_{s \in S} \downarrow s)$, Theorem 1 says that any candidate itemset that is generated by Apriori will have its support counted by FindLarge. Hence, if Apriori finds out all large itemsets in the database, FindLarge does too. In other words, FindLarge is correct.

Theorem 2. $C_{LGen} \subseteq C_{Apriori}$.

Theorem 2 says that the set of candidate itemsets generated by LGen is a subset of that generated by Apriori_Gen. LGen thus does not generate any unnecessary candidate itemsets and waste resources in counting bogus ones. However, recall that FindLarge counts the supports of the suggested large itemsets in the first database scan for verification. Therefore, if the suggested set contains itemsets that are actually small, FindLarge will count their supports superfluously. Fortunately, the number of large itemsets in a database is usually order-of-magnitude fewer than the number of candidate itemsets. The extra support counting is thus insignificant compared with the support counting of all the candidate itemsets. FindLarge using LGen thus requires similar counting effort as Apriori does.

Theorem 3. *If $S = \emptyset$ then $C_{LGen} = C_{Apriori}$.*

Theorem 3 says that without suggested large itemsets, FindLarge reduces to Apriori. In particular, they generate exactly the same set of candidate itemsets.

3 Experiments

To evaluate the performance of FindLarge using LGen as the candidate set generation algorithm, we performed extensive simulation experiments. Our goals are to study the I/O savings that can be achieved by FindLarge over Apriori, and how sampling can be used to obtain a good set of suggested large itemsets. In this section, we present some representative results from the experiments.

3.1 Synthetic Database Generation

In the experiments, we used the model of [8] to generate synthetic data as the test databases. Due to space limitations, readers are referred to [8] and [11] for details.

3.2 Coverages and I/O Savings

For each database instance generated, we first discovered the set of large itemsets, L, using Apriori. Our first set of experiments studies how the "coverage" of the suggested large itemsets affects the performance of FindLarge. By coverage, we mean the fraction of large itemsets in L that are suggested.[2] To model coverage, we drew a random sample from L to form a set of suggested large itemsets S. We define the *coverage* of a suggested set S over the set of large itemsets L by

$$coverage = \frac{|\bigcup_{s \in (S \cap L)} \downarrow s|}{|L|}.$$

Since in our first set of experiments, S was drawn from L, we have $S \cap L = S$. After we had constructed S, we ran FindLarge on the database using S as the

---

[2] If an itemset is suggested, then all of its subsets are also implicitly suggested.

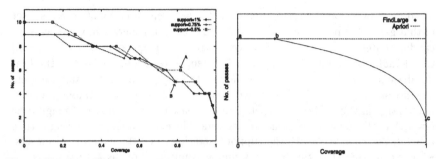

Fig. 4. Number of I/O passes vs. coverage under different support threshold.

Fig. 5. A representative I/O vs. coverage curve.

suggested set. Finally, we compared the number of I/O passes each algorithm had taken. Note that with the way we generated the suggested set S, no element in S was small. In practice, however, the suggested itemsets could contain small itemsets. Since small suggested itemsets are discarded in the first pass of FindLarge (see Figure 1), their presence does not affect the number of I/O passes required by FindLarge. So they were not modeled in this set of experiments.

We generated a number of database instances according to the model mentioned above. For each database instance, we applied Apriori to find the large itemsets under different support thresholds. Also, we generated a number of suggested sets of various coverages. We then applied FindLarge to the different database instances with different suggested sets under different support thresholds. The number of I/O passes that Apriori and FindLarge had taken were then compared. Figure 4 shows the result obtained from one typical database instance. In the following we refer to this particular database as $\mathcal{D}$.

In Figure 4, three sets of points ('◇', '+', '□') are shown corresponding to the support thresholds 1%, 0.75%, and 0.5% respectively. Each point shows the number of I/O passes FindLarge took when applied to $\mathcal{D}$ with a particular suggested set of a certain coverage. For example, the □ point labeled A shows that when FindLarge was applied with a suggested set whose coverage was 81.6%, 6 passes were required. Note that the points shown in Figure 4 take on discrete values. The lines connecting points of the same kind are there for legibility reason only and should not be interpreted as interpolation.

For the database $\mathcal{D}$, when the support threshold was set to either 1.0% or 0.75%, the size of the largest large itemsets was 9. Apriori took 9 I/O passes. This is shown in Figure 4 by the '◇' and '+' points when coverage equals 0. (Recall that FindLarge reduces to Apriori when the suggested set is null.) When the support threshold was lowered to 0.5%, the support counts of certain size-10 itemsets also exceeded the support threshold. In that case, the size of the largest large itemsets was 10. Apriori thus took 10 I/O passes, as shown by the '□' points when coverage equals 0.

One general observation from Figure 4 is that the higher the coverage of the suggested set has with respect to the set of large itemsets, the smaller the number of I/O passes FindLarge is required. In fact, all of the data points we obtained from our experiment exhibit a typical curve as shown in Figure 5.

In general, we can divide the curve into four stages:

At point a (coverage $= 0$). When the suggested set does not cover any large itemsets, FindLarge with LGen degenerates to Apriori. The number of I/O passes required by the two algorithms are thus the same.

Between points a and b. In this region, FindLarge takes the same number of passes as Apriori does. With a very small coverage, there are only few large itemsets suggested, and these itemsets usually consist of only a small number of items.[3] In this case, LGen is unable to provide the advantage of generating large-sized candidate itemsets early. Hence, no saving in I/O is obtained. The length of the line $\overline{ab}$, fortunately, is usually small. In our experiments, for example, the line $\overline{ab}$ in general spans only from coverage = 0% to 20%. As we will see later, a suggested set with a larger-than-20% coverage is easily obtainable by sampling techniques.

Between points b and c. The number of I/O passes required by FindLarge decreases gradually as the coverage of the suggested set increases. This is because as more large-sized itemsets are suggested, LGen is better able to generate large-sized candidate itemsets early. As an example, when mining the database instance $\mathcal{D}$ with the support threshold set at 1% using a suggested set whose coverage is 0.743 (point labeled B in Figure 4), LGen generated candidate itemsets of sizes ranging from 2 to 7 *early in pass number 2.*

We also observe that the amount of I/O saving increases more rapidly when the coverage is approaching 1. This is because with a very large coverage, the suggested set contains many *top-sized*, or maximal large itemsets. This greatly facilitates the generation of other not-yet-discovered maximal large itemsets as candidates early. Since FindLarge terminates once all the maximals are found, only very few passes are required.

At point c (coverage $= 100\%$). FindLarge only needs two passes over the database when the suggested set covers all large itemsets. The first pass counts the support of the suggested itemsets. Since they are the only large itemsets in the database, LGen will generate the negative border[4] [10] as candidates. In the second pass, FindLarge counts the supports of the candidate itemsets. Since none of the candidate is large, FindLarge terminates after only two passes.

3.3 Candidate Set Sizes

As discussed in Section 2, FindLarge checks the same number of candidate itemsets as Apriori does, but in fewer passes. As an example, we mined the database

---

[3] A size-k itemset suggested implicitly suggests $2^k - 1$ non-empty itemsets. So if the suggested set contains large-sized itemsets, it would possess a good coverage.

[4] The negative border is the set of itemsets which are small but all of their subsets are large.

Pass	Apriori	FindLarge with support=1%, coverage=8%	FindLarge with support=1%, coverage=74%	FindLarge with support=1%, coverage=98%
1	1,000	1,234	3,461	4,118
2	220,780	220,687	220,335	220,173
3	937	858	366	56
4	777	732	159	-
5	519	504	23	-
6	229	227	3	-
7	84	84	-	-
8	19	19	-	-
9	2	2	-	-
Total	224,347	224,347	224,347	224,347

Table 1. Candidate set size for each pass when database $\mathcal{D}$ is mined using Apriori and FindLarge.

$\mathcal{D}$ using Apriori and FindLarge with three suggested sets of different coverages (8%, 74%, and 98%). Note that the numbers shown in Table 1 equal the candidate sets' sizes except for those listed under the first pass of FindLarge. This is because FindLarge counts the supports of all subsets of the suggested itemsets in the first pass, besides those of the singletons. These support counts are also included in the table. For example, during the first pass when FindLarge mined the database $\mathcal{D}$ with a suggested set S of coverage 8%, it counted the supports of 1,000 singletons as well as 234 itemsets suggested (explicitly or implicitly) by S.

From the table, we observe that the candidate set size for the second pass dominates the others, and thus determines the memory requirement. FindLarge redistributes the counting work and, in general, generates fewer candidate itemsets in the second pass as Apriori does. Hence, the memory requirement of FindLarge is comparable to that of Apriori.

3.4 Sampling

We performed a set of simulation experiments to study how sampling should be done in order to obtain a good suggested set. In the experiments, a number of databases were generated. For each database, we extracted a fraction f of transactions as samples. We then mined the samples using Apriori. The resulting large itemsets discovered were then used as the suggested set for FindLarge.

We observed that even with a small set of samples (e.g. $f = 1/16$), the expected coverage of the suggested set derived exceeded 90%. Also, FindLarge saved 31% of I/O compared with Apriori. For details, please refer to [11].

4   Conclusion

This paper described a new algorithm FindLarge for finding large itemsets in a transaction database. FindLarge uses a new candidate set generation algorithm

LGen which takes a set of multiple-sized large itemsets to generate multiple-sized candidate itemsets. Given a reasonably accurate suggested set, LGen allows big-sized candidate itemsets to be generated and processed early. This results in significant I/O saving compared with traditional Apriori-based mining algorithms.

We stated a number of theorems about FindLarge and LGen. In particular, FindLarge is correct and LGen never generates redundant candidate itemsets. Hence the CPU requirement of FindLarge is compatible with Apriori. Detailed proof of the theorems can be found in [11].

In order to evaluate the I/O performance of FindLarge, we conducted extensive experiments. We showed that the better coverage the suggested set has, the fewer I/O passes FindLarge requires. In the best case, when the suggested set covers all large itemsets, FindLarge takes only two passes over the database.

To obtain a good suggested set, sampling techniques can be applied. We showed that a small sample is usually sufficient to generate a suggested set of high coverage. FindLarge is thus an efficient and practical algorithm for mining association rules.

References

1. R. Agrawal, T. Imielinski, and A. Swami. Mining association rules between sets of items in large databases. In *Proc. ACM SIGMOD*, Washington, D.C., May 1993.
2. R. Agrawal and R. Srikant. Fast algorithms for mining association rules in large databases. In *Proc. of the 20th VLDB Conference*, Santiago, Chile, 1994.
3. Garrett Birkhoff. *Lattice Theory*, volume 25 of *AMS Colloquium Publications*. AMS, 1984.
4. David W. Cheung, Jiawei Han, Vincent T. Ng, Ada Fu, and Yongjian Fu. A fast distributed algorithm for mining association rules. In *Proc. Fourth International Conference on Parallel and Distributed Information Systems*, Miami Beach, Florida, December 1996.
5. David W. Cheung, Jiawei Han, Vincent T. Ng, and C. Y. Wong. Maintenance of discovered association rules in large databases: An incremental updating technique. In *Proceedings of the Twelfth International Conference on Data Engineering*, New Orleans, Louisiana, 1996. IEEE computer Society.
6. B. A. Davey and H. A. Priestley. *Introduction to Lattices and Order*. Cambridge University Press, 1990. ISBN 0 521 36584 8.
7. Jiawei Han and Yongjian Fu. Discovery of multiple-level association rules from large databases. In *Proc. of the 21st VLDB Conference*, Zurich, Switzerland, 1995.
8. Jong Soo Park, Ming-Syan Chen, and Philip S. Yu. An effective hash-based algorithm for mining association rules. In *Proc. ACM SIGMOD*, San Jose, California, May 1995.
9. Ramakrishnan Srikant and Rakesh Agrawal. Mining quantitative association rules in large relational tables. In H. V. Jagadish and Inderpal singh Mumick, editors, *Proc. ACM SIGMOD*, Montreal, Canada, June 1996.
10. Hannu Toivonen. Sampling large databases for association rules. In *Proc. of the 22th VLDB Conference*, Bombay, India, September 1996.
11. C.L. Yip, K.K. Loo, B. Kao, D. Cheung, and C.K. Cheng. LGen - a lattice-based candidate set generation algorithm for I/O efficient association rule mining. Technical report TR-99-01, Dept. of CSIS, The University of Hong Kong, 1999.

Extending the Applicability of Association Rules

Karthick Rajamani[1], Sam Sung[2], and Alan Cox[3]

[1] Department of Electrical and Computer Engineering, Rice University
[2] School of Computing, National University of Singapore
[3] Department of Computer Science, Rice University
Email: {karthick,alc}@rice.edu, ssung@comp.nus.edu.sg

Abstract

An important issue that needs to be addressed when using association rules is the validity of the rules for new situations. Rules are typically derived from the patterns in a particular dataset. When the conditions under which the dataset has been obtained change, a new *situation* is said to have risen. Since the conditions existing at the time of observation could affect the observed data, a change in those conditions could imply a changed set of rules for a new situation. Using the set of rules derived from the dataset for an earlier situation could lead to wrong decisions. In this paper, we provide a model explaining the difference between the sets of rules for different situations. Our model is based on the concept of rule-generating groups that we call *caucuses*. Using this model, we provide a simple technique, called *Linear Combinations*, to get a good estimate of the set of rules for a new situation. Our approach is independent of the core mining process, and so can be easily implemented with any specific technique for association rule mining. In our experiments using controlled datasets, we found that we could get up to 98.3% accuracy with our techniques as opposed to 26.6% when directly using the results of the old situation.

Keywords: Extending association rules, Linear Combinations, rule-generating model.

1 Introduction

Association rule mining is a valuable data mining technique and researchers have studied many aspects of the technique. However, the issue of the validity of the rules for new situations has not been addressed so far. By a *new situation*, we mean a change in the circumstances that existed when the data was collected. In general, the rules are derived from patterns in a dataset that corresponds to a particular situation. However, a decision has to be made, based on the rules, at a later instance - which could be a new situation (under changed circumstances). When the rules are influenced by the existing set of conditions, direct application of the rules from the old situation (corresponding to a different set of conditions) could lead to wrong decisions.

Consider the following real-world example. A retail chain is planning to open a store in a new location. Decisions have to be made regarding the inventory and shop-space allocation for the new store – a job for which association rules between the items for sale would be very useful. However, the only available rules are from the sales information of already-operational stores. How dependable are the rules from these stores from locations different from the new store ? Is there a way to obtain a "correct" set of rules for the new store, without having to wait for the sales transactions from the new store?

We address the above issues in this paper, through the following contributions:

- We introduce the concept of a set of rule-generating groups, called *caucuses*, that are common to different situations. We provide a model for association rules for different situations based on the concept of caucuses. This model provides an analytical framework for explaining the differences between the sets of rules for different situations.

- We provide a simple technique, called Linear Combinations, that gives the estimated set of rules for a new situation. It can be used with any available association rule mining approach as it requires no modification to the core mining algorithm.

- We demonstrate the effectiveness of our technique over just using the rules from the available dataset for the new situation. Our experiments using controlled datasets (generated by a common synthetic-data generation approach for association rule mining) show that as the differences between the individual caucuses increased, the mismatches in the rules for the two different situations also increased. When just using the rules from the available (old) dataset directly the accuracy for correctly predicting rules for a new situation varied from 82.9% to 26.7% (from similar caucuses to totally different caucuses). While with our Linear Combinations approach, the accuracy varied between 96.7% and 98.3%.

The rest of the paper is organized as follows. Section 2 describes the general problem of association rule mining. Section 3 describes our problem in more detail and our Linear Combinations approach for solving it. Section 4 explains our experiments and results. In section 5, we discuss an alternative approach and explain why such an approach would not be feasible for our particular problem. Section 6 provides the conclusions.

2 Background on Association Rule Mining

This section is based largely on the description of association rule mining given by Agrawal et.al. [1, 2]. Let $\mathbf{I} = \{I_1, I_2, ..., I_n\}$ be the domain of literals called *items*. A record called a *transaction* contains a set of items $I_1, I_2, ..., I_k \subset \mathbf{I}$. The input to the association rule mining algorithm is a set of transactions, $\mathbf{T}$. We call any set of items $I_1, I_2, ..., I_m \subset \mathbf{I}$ collectively an *itemset*. An *association rule* is a relation of the form $A \Longrightarrow B$ in $\mathbf{T}$, where A, B are itemsets, and $A \cap B = \emptyset$. A is the antecedent of the rule and B is the consequent of the rule.

An itemset has a measure of statistical significance associated with it called *support*. Support for an itemset X in $\mathbf{T}$ ($support(X)$) is the number of transactions

in **T** containing X. For a rule, $A \implies B$, the associated support is *support($A \cup$
B)*. A *support fraction* is the ratio of the support value to the total number of
transactions. The strength of a rule is given by another measure called *confidence*.
The confidence of $A \implies B$ is the ratio *support($A \cup B$)/support(A)*.

The problem of association rule mining is to generate all rules that have support and confidence greater than some user-specified thresholds. Itemsets that
have support greater than the user-specified support (or have a corresponding
support fraction in the subset of the data under consideration) are called *large*
itemsets. For a large itemset S, if $A \subset S$ and *support(S)/support(A)* $\geq$ confidence
threshold, then $A \implies S - A$ is an association rule. The problem of association
rule mining is, thus, broken down into:

(a) The task of determining all large itemsets.

(b) The task of determining the rules with enough confidence, from the large
itemsets.

In association rule mining, the input data is used in the task of determining
the large itemsets. The process of determining the large itemsets captures all the
necessary information for association rules from the data. The rule-generation
portion is then dependent only on the large itemsets. This implies that in order
to obtain a correct estimate for a set of rules, a correct estimate for the large
itemsets (from which the rules are generated) is both necessary and sufficient.

3 Problem Description and Solution

3.1 Importance of background attributes

The importance of the rules identified by association rule mining (or for that
matter any rule mining technique) is often decided by the applicability of the
discovered rules. Consider the example depicted in Fig. 1. It shows association
rules discovered at two stores having the same inventory, but located in different
neighborhoods. The rule *diaper $\implies$ beer*, is valid in the first store but not in the
second, while *diaper $\implies$ ice cream* is valid only in the second store. However, the
price of beer, ice cream and diapers and the conditions for their purchases are
similar in both stores. Further study shows that 80% of the customers for store
1 are men and 70% of the customers for store 2 are women, and that the men
were found to have a strong preference for beer and the women had a preference
for ice cream. Only then do the discrepancies in the rules make sense.

Here, gender is a background attribute – an attribute not directly involved in
the association rule – and is a causative factor for the two rules. The distribution
of the different values of gender (male and female) was different among the
customers at the two stores, giving rise to different sets of association rules
for them. When applying association rules derived from one dataset to a new
situation, it is necessary to ensure that the background attributes, which are
factors giving rise to the rules, are consistent between the source of the rules
and the situation they are being applied to. When such factors can be identified
and are found to be different, that knowledge has to be incorporated into the
data mining procedure for providing a better set of rules for the new situation.

Parameters common for both stores :
Total transactions = 1000, Support threshold = 50, Confidence threshold = 40%.
Price: Diapers = $ 10, Beer = $ 4, ice-cream = $ 3.
STORE 1 : *diaper* $\Longrightarrow$ *beer* (confidence = 42%).
STORE 2
Proposed rule : *diaper* $\Longrightarrow$ *beer* (confidence = 28% < 40%, **not valid**).
Alternate rule : *diaper* $\Longrightarrow$ *ice cream* (confidence = 43%, **valid rule**).

Fig. 1. Example showing variation of rules for two stores

3.2 Problem definition

We first introduce and define a basic set of terms used in the rest of the paper. A background attribute whose value affects the relation between the items is called a *factor*. In general, a set of factors with specific values (or sets of values) together affect the relation between items. When the factors are demographic characteristics, they would identify a particular group of people having similar characteristics. For instance, gender would be a factor in the example considered above – male and female, would be the associated values that identify a group of people having similar characteristics, and affect the relation between diapers, beer and ice-cream. Members of a group have a similar behavior on their part producing the same relation for the items they are involved with e.g. men, in general, like beer. This causes them to buy beer when they buy diapers, rather than ice-cream.

A set of factors together with their associated values/value-ranges that cause specific sets of rules is called a *caucus*. Each caucus is always defined by distinct sets of values for the factors affecting the rules. Our model for the generation of association rules is as follows. Every caucus has a strong affinity for producing a certain set of association rules (or associated items). Independent of which situation a caucus is found in, the set of rules (or associated items) that it has affinity for does not change. Each situation has a mixture of different caucuses in some specific proportion. The difference in the proportions of the caucuses for different situations gives rise to the difference between the overall set of association rules for each situation. This is the fundamental idea in our approach. So far, we have used the conventional meaning for the term situation wherever we have used it. We could continue to use it in the same fashion. However, in addition to that, it would also refer to the specific combination of caucuses that are associated with it. Every situation is also associated with its own distinct dataset, the patterns in which are caused by the caucuses associated with that situation.

We now define the problem of estimating association rules as follows. Given,

1. the set of caucuses that make up two situations,
2. the proportions of the caucuses for the second situation, and
3. a *source* dataset – a database of transactions involving items with corresponding values for all the factors, for the first situation;

the task is to provide a good estimate of the association rules for the second situation, also referred to as the *target*.

Since the data-dependent portion of the rule mining process is just the phase when the large itemsets are determined (refer section 2), determining a good estimate of the large itemsets (including the right values for their support) for a new situation is equivalent to determining a good estimate of the rules for it. So we provide a method, Linear Combinations, to obtain a good estimate of the large itemsets for new situations.

3.3 Linear Combinations

Our approach to estimating the itemsets for the new situation is a straightforward application of the method of linear combinations. Every caucus for a situation defines a distinct region in the multi-dimensional factor-space. The values for the factors in every transaction are used to map that transaction to a particular caucus. For every caucus, the set of large itemsets (along with their fractional support in the caucus) is determined from the set of transactions associated with it. The union of the set of large itemsets in every caucus is a superset of the set of itemsets that are large in the entire dataset (that is because, an itemset that has adequate fractional support in a dataset, would need to have adequate fractional support in at least one of the caucuses). We call this union of the set of large itemsets of every caucus as the *union-set*. For any dataset whose transactions are composed of transactions of the same set of caucuses, this union-set could be treated as the candidate set for the dataset. Thus, only the support of all the sets in this union-set need to be estimated, when determining the large itemsets for the dataset of any situation that has the same set of caucuses.

Using the dataset for the first situation (*source*), the large itemset determination phase is performed for the transactions of every caucus separately. After this phase, the support of every potentially large itemset is available for each caucus. The support of a large itemset in the second situation (*target*) is estimated from its support in the different caucuses of the source and the relative proportion of these caucuses in the target. Given N caucuses, L_i – set of large itemsets for each caucus i, and N_i – strength (fraction) of each caucus in the target, with $S(L)_i$ as the notation for the support fraction of itemset L in caucus i, we have:

$$\text{Union-set } \mathbf{U} = \bigcup_{i=1,N} L_i. \tag{1}$$

$$\text{For each } L \in U, \text{ estimated support fraction in target } = \sum_{i=1}^{N} S(L)_i * N_i. \tag{2}$$

The large itemsets for the target are those that have the estimated support greater than the specified support threshold. The caveat in the above approach is the requirement of the availability of representative samples for each caucus (that can occur in a target) in the source situation. However, this is an understandable requirement, as one can hardly be expected to predict the behavior of a group without any information about the group. The simplicity of our approach is tied to its ability to be used independent of the core mining process. Thus, the approach can be applied to the vast number of association rule mining techniques [3–10], each of which is different in the nature of items it handles or the approach taken to identifying the large itemsets, with a little or no modification.

4 Experimental Results

The data-dependent (situation-dependent) phase of association rule mining is the one when large itemsets are determined. The quality of the estimated large itemsets directly determines the quality of the estimated rules for new situations. Hence, we demonstrate the efficiency of the techniques from the quality of large itemsets generated. Using the data generation procedure described below we generate two datasets, one for the source and another for the target. Both datasets are mined to obtain the correct set of large itemsets for them – L_s and L_t for the source and target, respectively. We then estimate the large itemsets for the target, L_{LC}, using our technique and the source dataset. The extent of matching of L_t with L_s determines the accuracy of using just the source dataset, and the extent of its matching with L_{LC} determines the accuracy of our approach.

4.1 Experiments

The comparison between the correct set of large itemsets and the estimated set of large itemsets is based on two factors:
- the actual items in the itemsets, and
- the support values associated with the matching itemsets.

Further, to detect any variation in the efficiency of the technique with the extent of differences between the caucuses for the situations, we study three conditions:

(a) All the caucuses involve the same set of items – similar caucuses,
(b) Half the items of each caucus are unique to it, the rest are common to all.
(c) All the items for a caucus are unique to it – the most dissimilar caucuses.

4.2 Data generation

To examine all three conditions we use synthetic datasets in our experiments. We use a popular method for generating transactions containing associations, first presented by Agrawal and Srikant [2]. We modify the method to include the presence of multiple caucuses in a single dataset. We generate separate datasets for the source and target situations. We generate a set of **G** caucuses that will be common for both situations – this involves the assignment of items to each caucus, and the generation of maximal and potentially large itemsets for each caucus from its items – these two together determine the difference between the large itemsets/rules of the different caucuses. Next we assign an independent set of weights as the relative proportions of the caucuses for each situation. This gives rise to the overall difference between the large itemsets/rules of the two datasets. For all three cases the total number of items for each caucus is set to 100 as indicated in Fig. 2. We use a support value of 0.5 % in our experiments

G	Number of caucuses	25
–	Number of items in a caucus	100
–	number of common items between caucuses	0, 50, 100
I	Average size of an itemset (Poisson distribution)	4
L	Number of itemsets for a caucus	500
T	Average size of a transaction (Poisson distribution)	10
N	Total Number of transactions in a dataset	100000

Fig. 2. Parameters for data generation

(a reasonable value for items in retail transactions). Figure 2 gives the various input parameters and the values used for them in our experiments.

4.3 Platform

We performed our experiments on a Dell workstation with a 300Mhz Pentium II processor and 128 MB of memory. Our datasets were stored as relational tables in a DB2 Universal Database system running on top of NT Server 4. We used the OR-extensions of DB2 [11] to build our data mining applications - for association rule mining (similar to the approach in [12]), and for caucus-wise rule mining - in an efficient manner.

4.4 Results

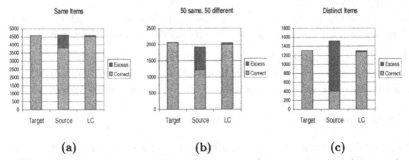

(a)　　　　　　　　(b)　　　　　　　　(c)

Fig. 3. Distribution of predicted large itemsets (correct and excess/incorrect)

Figure 3 presents the charts showing the relative accuracy of the different approaches in terms of the number of large itemsets that are correctly predicted by them. Figure 3(a) shows the results for the case when all caucuses involve the same set of 100 items, figure 3(b) shows the case when there are 50 distinct items per caucus with the other 50 items being common to all, and Fig. 3(c) shows the case when all the caucuses have their own distinct set of 100 items. The y-axis shows the number of large itemsets. Target represents the number of itemsets of the target for comparison with the other two bars. Source stands for the case when large itemsets of the source are used directly. LC stands for the case when estimates for the target are obtained using Linear Combination. For each case, the lower component of the corresponding bar indicates the number of correct large itemsets predicted with that technique and the higher component indicates the number of excess (incorrect) itemsets predicted by that technique.

The percentage of correct large itemsets captured with the linear combinations approach varies from 96.7% to 98.3% and the excess itemsets from 4% to 1.8%. In contrast, directly using the large itemsets of the source results in the percentage of correct itemsets varying from 82.9% to 26.6%, and the percentage of excess itemsets varying from 16.3% to 59.7%. The error with Source increases as we move from similar caucuses to more distinct caucuses ((a) to (c)).

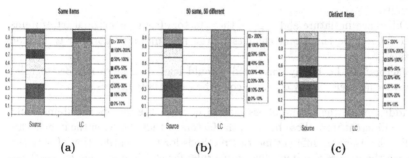

| (a) | (b) | (c) |

Fig. 4. Distribution of error in support values for correctly predicted large itemsets

Figure 4 shows the distribution of the percentage error in support values for the correctly predicted itemsets. The bars marked Source and LC are associated with the direct usage of source's large itemsets and the Linear Combinations approach, respectively. Each bar is broken down into many components, where each component is proportional to the number of itemsets with a particular error percentage (range) in the support value. The legend specifies each component that corresponds to a specific range in the support error percentage. It can be seen that for the Linear Combinations approach the percentage error in the support values is almost always less than 20% (and mostly less then 10%), while when using the large itemsets of the source there are plenty of itemsets with large errors in the support values.

The results indicate that, in the presence of different proportions of the caucuses for different situations, using Linear Combination improves the accuracy of estimated association rules quite dramatically. Our technique is not only quite accurate in capturing the correct set of itemsets, but even the values for their actual support. It also seems to be equally effective across the entire range of item-composition for the caucuses - from identical items to completely distinct sets of items for each caucus. In contrast, we see that the error on not using Linear Combinations increases as the item-compositions of the caucuses become more and more distinct from one another.

5 Alternative Approach

An alternative approach to that of using the notion of caucuses is one where the rule generating process is modified by including the causative factors in the core mining process. The idea behind this would be that one would obtain rules that are *qualified* by the values of the corresponding factors for those rules e.g. (*For Men*: Diaper $\Longrightarrow$ beer), and (*For Women*: Diaper $\Longrightarrow$ ice-cream). Since the rules are conditioned by the values for the factors, knowledge of any change in the distribution of these values for new situations can be used in conjunction with these qualifiers to identify the correct set of rules. The difficulties in realizing this approach are :

- Additional attributes could make the computational cost increase exponentially.
- Difference in nature and type of these factors from the original set of items could require significant changes to the rule mining algorithm to include them.
- Factors can be highly correlated - could lead to a large number of rules involving them, many of which could be potentially useless.

Additionally, the nature of association between the factors and items could be very different from those between the factors or those between the items. This implies the usage of different metrics/methods for the identification of patterns between the factors and items (causative rules for which quite different methods are used [13, 14]), and for patterns between the items alone. Further, the qualifications for a rule, in terms of values for the causative factors, might need to be simplified or eliminated (customized for the new situation) when trying to get the whole picture of the set of rules for a new situation. However, in the absence of any knowledge about the caucuses or any method to identify them, this alternate approach might be a reasonable method for obtaining a more informed set of rules (than the ones involving just the items).

6 Conclusions

Researchers in mining association rules have focused on aspects of the mining process related to the discovery of rules from a dataset corresponding to a particular situation. However, the ability to identify the association rules for new situations has an equally important role in knowledge discovery and decision support systems. In this paper, we provide a model that distinguishes between the rules for different situations using the concept of association-rule-generating groups or caucuses. Using this model, given the dataset for one situation, we provide a simple approach for estimating the set of rules for the second situation. Our approach, Linear Combinations, requires no modification to the core mining process, and can be used to extend the rules from all kinds of association rule mining techniques. We show the errors in directly applying association rules derived from the dataset of one situation to another different situation. We demonstrate the effectiveness of the Linear Combinations approach in deriving the rules for the second situation with a high degree of accuracy. We conclude that our approach provides a simple, but powerful, means for correctly extending the application of association rules from one situation to another.

We are currently working on getting access to real-world datasets that might exhibit additional complexities to fine-tune our technique. We are also looking at techniques for the automatic identification of the causative factors and the caucuses.

References

1. R. Agrawal, T. Imielinski, and A. Swami, "Mining association rules between sets of items in large databases," in *Proceedings of the 1993 ACM SIGMOD International Conference of Management of Data*, pp. 207–216, May 1993.
2. R. Agrawal and R. Srikant, "Fast algorithms for mining association rules," in *Proceedings of the 20th International Conference on Very Large Databases*, September 1994.
3. J. Park, M. Chen, and P. Yu, "An effective hash based algorithm for mining association rules," in *Proceedings of the 1995 ACM SIGMOD International Conference of Management of Data*, May 1995.
4. A. Savasere, E. Omiecinski, and S. Navathe, "An efficient algorithm for mining association rules in large databases," in *Proceedings of the 21st International Conference on Very Large Databases*, September 1995.
5. R. Srikant and R. Agrawal, "Mining generalized association rules," in *Proceedings of the 21st International Conference on Very Large Databases*, September 1995.
6. J. Han and Fu, "Discovery of multiple-level association rules from large databases," in *Proceedings of the 21st International Conference on Very Large Databases*, September 1995.
7. H. Toivonen, "Sampling large databases for association rules," in *Proceedings of the 22nd International Conference on Very Large Databases*, pp. 134–145, September 1996.
8. R. Srikant and R. Agrawal, "Mining quantitative association rules in large relational tables," in *Proceedings of the 1996 ACM SIGMOD International Conference of Management of Data*, 1996.
9. R. Miller and Y. Yang, "Association rules over interval data," in *Proceedings of the 1997 ACM SIGMOD International Conference of Management of Data*, 1997.
10. S. Brin, R. Motwani, and C. Silverstein, "Beyond market baskets: Generalizing association rules to correlations," in *Proceedings of the 1997 ACM SIGMOD International Conference of Management of Data*, 1997.
11. IBM Corporation, *IBM DB2 Universal Database SQL Reference Version 5.0.* 1997.
12. K. Rajamani, B. Iyer, and A. Chadha, "Using DB2's Object Relational Extensions for mining association rules," Tech. Rep. TR 03,690, Santa Teresa Laboratory, IBM Corporation, September 1997.
13. P. Sprites, C. Glymour, and R. Scheines, *Causation, Prediction and Search.* Springer-Verlag, New York, 1993.
14. C. Silverstein, S. Brin, R. Motwani, and J. Ullman, "Scalable techniques for mining causal structures," in *Proceedings of the 24th International Conference on Very Large Databases*, August 1998.

An Efficient Approach for Incremental Association Rule Mining

Pauray S.M. Tsai[1], Chih-Chong Lee[2], and Arbee L.P. Chen[2]

[1] Department of Information Management, Ming Hsin Institute of Technology, Hsin-Feng, Hsinchu 304, Taiwan
pauray@mis.mhit.edu.tw

[2] Department of Computer Science, National Tsing Hua University, Hsinchu 300, Taiwan,

alpchen@cs.nthu.edu.tw

Abstract. In this paper, we study the issue of maintaining association rules in a large database of sales transactions. The maintenance of association rules can be mapped into the problem of maintaining large itemsets in the database. Because the mining of association rules is time-consuming, we need an efficient approach to maintain the large itemsets when the database is updated. In this paper, we present efficient approaches to solve the problem. Our approaches store the itemsets that are not large at present but may become large itemsets after updating the database, so that the cost of processing the updated database can be reduced. Moreover, we discuss the cases where the large itemsets can be obtained without scanning the original database. Experimental results show that our algorithms outperform other algorithms, especially when the original database need not be scanned in our algorithms.

1 Introduction

Data mining has attracted much attention in database communities because of its wide applicability. One major application area of data mining is to discover potentially useful information from transaction databases. The problem of mining *association rules* from transactional data was introduced in [1]. A transaction in the database consists of a set of items (itemset). An example of such an association rule might be " 80% of customers who buy itemset X also buy itemset Y". The *support count* of an itemset is the number of transactions containing the itemset, and the *support* of the itemset is the fraction of those transactions. The itemset ($X \cup Y$ in the example) involved in an association rule must be contained in a predetermined number of transactions. The predetermined number of transactions is called the *minimum support count*, and the fraction of transactions is called the *minimum support threshold*. An itemset is called a *large itemset* if its support is no less than the minimum support threshold. Since the generation of association rules is straightforward after the large itemsets are discovered, finding large itemsets becomes the main work of mining association rules.

A database is "dynamic" in the sense that users may periodically or occasionally insert data to or remove data from the database. The update to the database may cause not only the generation of new rules but also the invalidation of some existing rules. Thus, the maintenance of the association rules is a significant problem. One possible approach to the problem is to rerun the mining algorithm on the updated database. This approach is simple but inefficient since it does not use the existing information such as the support counts of the current large itemsets. In [2], FUP algorithm is proposed for the maintenance of discovered association rules in large databases. If there are frequent itemsets in the increment database, which are not large itemsets of the original database, then the algorithm scans the original database to check whether they are large itemsets or not. FUP, FUP* [3] and FUP2 [4] all belong to the kind of generate-and-test algorithms, and are referred to as k-pass algorithms because they have to scan the database k times. Two algorithms DIUP and DDUP [5], extended from DLG [7], are proposed to handle the incremental update problem. An association graph and an information table are constructed to record whether a previously generated large itemset remains large in the updated database. With this information, these two algorithms can finish the update work in one database scan.

In this paper, we present efficient approaches to maintain large itemsets. Our approaches store the itemsets that are not large in the original database but may become large itemsets after the database is updated, so that the cost of processing the updated database can be reduced. Moreover, we discuss the cases where the large itemsets can be obtained without scanning the original database. Experimental results show that our algorithms outperform FUP and FUP2 algorithms, especially when the original database need not be scanned in our algorithms.

The remaining of the paper is organized as follows. The problem description is given in Section 2. In Section 3, our approaches are proposed for the maintenance of large itemsets. Performance results are presented in Section 4. Section 5 contains the conclusion.

2 Problem Description

Let L be the set of all the large itemsets in the original database DB, s be the minimum support threshold, and d the number of transactions in DB. Assume that the support count of each large itemset in the original database has been recorded. After some updates, the increment database DB^+ is added into the original database DB and the decrement database DB^- is removed from the original database, resulting in the updated database DB'. The numbers of transactions in DB^+, DB^-, and DB' are denoted d^+, d^-, and d', respectively, and the support counts of itemset X in DB, DB^+, DB^-, and DB' are X_{count}, X_{count}^+, X_{count}^-, and X_{count}', respectively. With the same minimum support threshold s, a large itemset X of DB remains a large itemset of DB' if and only if its support in DB' is no less than s, i.e. $X_{count}' \geq (d + d^+ - d^-) * s = d'*s$.

All the itemsets in DB can be divided into the following four groups:

Group 1: the itemsets which are large in both DB and DB'.
Group 2: the itemsets which are large in DB but not large in DB'.
Group 3: the itemsets which are not large in DB but large in DB'.
Group 4: the itemsets which are neither large in DB nor DB'.

The itemsets of group 4 can not be used to generate any rule because their supports are less than the minimum support threshold. Thus, these itemsets are indifferent. The itemsets in group 1 and group 2 can be obtained easily. For example, X is a large itemset of DB. The support count of X in DB' is $X'_{count} = X_{count} + X^+_{count} - X^-_{count}$, where X_{count} is known and X^+_{count} and X^-_{count} are available after scanning DB^+ and DB^-, respectively. However, the itemsets of group 3 need further consideration. The support counts of these itemsets in DB' can not be determined after scanning DB^+ and DB^- since their support counts in DB are unknown in advance. Thus, how to efficiently generate the itemsets of group 3 is an important problem for the maintenance of association rules. In the following section, we propose efficient approaches to solve the problem.

3 Our Approaches

Basically, the framework of our algorithm is similar to that of the FUP algorithm [3]. We store the large itemsets of DB and their support counts in the set L. Let t be the *tolerance degree*, $0 < t < s$. The degree is used to control the number of itemsets whose supports are less than the minimum support threshold s but no less than (s-t). We call these itemsets the *potential* large itemsets. The potential large itemsets and their support counts are stored in the set PL. It is easy to see that the more the number of the potential large itemsets is, the less the cost of processing the original database will be. Besides, we record the itemsets of the increment database, that are not in L and PL but may become large itemsets, in the set M.

3.1 Insertion

Let DB and DB^+ be the original database and the increment database, respectively. Assume that the size of DB and DB^+ are d and d^+, respectively, and sets L and PL are available before we update DB. When the increment database DB^+ is scanned, the support counts of the itemsets in $L \cup PL$ are accumulated. Then L and PL are updated according to the support count thresholds $s*(d+d^+)$ and $(s-t)*(d+d^+)$, respectively. Let X be an itemset of DB^+ and $X \notin L \cup PL$. By Theorem 1, if the support count of X in DB^+ is greater than $d^+*(s-t)$, then X may be a large or potential large itemset of the updated database DB'. In the case, the itemset X is stored in set M. Let *MS* be the maximal value of the support counts of itemsets in M. By Theorem 2, if $MS < d^+*s + d*t$, we need not scan DB. Namely, in this case all itemsets in M can not be large itemsets of the updated database. The Insert algorithm is shown in [6].

Theorem 1: Assume that the support counts of itemset X in the original database DB, the increment database DB^+, and the updated database DB' are X_{count}, X^+_{count}, and X'_{count}, respectively. If $X \notin L \cup PL$ and $X^+_{count} \leq d^+ * (s-t)$, then X is not a large or potential large itemset of DB'.

> [PROOF]
>
> $$X'_{count} = X_{count} + X^+_{count}$$
> $$< d * (s-t) + X^+_{count}$$
> $$\leq d * (s-t) + d^+ * (s-t)$$
> $$= (d + d^+) * (s-t)$$
>
> Therefore, X is not a large or potential large itemset of DB'.

Theorem 2: If $MS < d^+ * s + d * t$, then we need not scan the database DB.

> [PROOF]
>
> Assume that X is the itemset in M, which has the maximal support count.
>
> Since $X \notin L \cup PL$, $X_{count} < d * (s-t)$.
>
> Therefore, if $MS + d * (s-t) < (d + d^+) * s$
>
> (that is, $MS < (d^+ * s + d * t)$), then X is not a large itemset in the updated database DB'. In other words, all the itemsets in M can not be large itemsets of DB'.

3.2 Deletion

The user may remove out-of-date data from the database. In the following, we discuss the maintenance of association rules when deletions occur. Let DB and DB^- be the original database and the decrement database, respectively. Assume that the sizes of DB and DB^- are d and d^-, respectively, and sets L and PL are available before we update database DB. When the decrement database DB^- is scanned, the support count of the itemset in $L \cup PL$ lessens if this itemset appears in DB^-. Then L and PL are updated according to the support count thresholds $s * (d - d^-)$ and $(s-t) * (d - d^-)$, respectively. Let X be an itemset of DB and $X \notin L \cup PL$. By Theorem 3, if $d^- \leq d * t/s$, then we need not process the updated database $(DB - DB^-)$. Otherwise, we use DLG algorithm [7] to generate the large itemsets in the updated database. The Delete algorithm is shown in [6].

Theorem 3: If $d^- \leq d * \dfrac{t}{s}$, i.e., $t \geq s * \dfrac{d^-}{d}$, then we need not scan the updated database DB $^{'}$.

$\qquad$ [PROOF]

$\qquad\qquad$ Assume that X is an itemset of DB.

$\qquad$ $< 1 > X \in L \cup PL$

$\qquad\qquad$ Since $X^{'}_{count} = X_{count} - X^-_{count}$

$\qquad\qquad$ and X_{count} and X^-_{count} are available,

$\qquad\qquad$ we need not scan DB $^{'}$.

$\qquad$ $< 2 > X \notin L \cup PL$

$\qquad\qquad$ Since $X^{'}_{count} = X_{count} - X^-_{count}$

$\qquad\qquad\qquad$ $< d * (s - t) - X^-_{count}$

$\qquad\qquad\qquad$ $\leq d * s - d * t$

$\qquad\qquad\qquad$ $\leq d * s - d * s * \dfrac{d^-}{d}$

$\qquad\qquad\qquad$ $= d * s - d^- * s = d^{'} * s$

$\qquad\qquad$ $\Rightarrow$ X is not a large itemset of DB $^{'}$.

$\qquad\qquad$ $\Rightarrow$ We need not scan DB $^{'}$.

$\qquad$ By $< 1 >< 2 >$, the theorem is proved.

3.3 Update with Insertion and Deletion

In the following, we consider insertion and deletion at the same time. Let DB, DB^+, and DB^- be the original database, the increment database, and the decrement database, respectively. Assume that the sizes of DB, DB^+, and DB^- are d, d^+, and d^-, respectively. When DB^+ and DB^- are scanned, the support count of the itemset in $L \cup PL$ is updated. Consider the following two cases.

Case 1: $d^+ \geq d^-$

(1) Let X be an itemset of DB^+ and $X \notin L \cup PL$. If the support count of X in DB^+ is no less than $(d^+ - d^-) * (s-t)$, it may be a large or potential large itemset of the updated database. In this case, itemset X is stored in set M. It is proved as follows:

[PROOF]

Assume $X^+_{count} < (d^+ - d^-) * (s-t)$.

$X'_{count} = X_{count} + X^+_{count} - X^-_{count}$

$\qquad < d * (s-t) + (d^+ - d^-) * (s-t)$

$\qquad < (d + d^+ - d^-) * (s-t)$

Thus X is not a large or potential large itemset of the updated database.

(2) Let X be an itemset of DB but not an itemset of DB^+. Assume $X \notin L \cup PL$. Then X can not be a large itemset of the updated database. It is proved as follows:

[PROOF]

$X'_{count} = X_{count} + X^+_{count} - X^-_{count}$

$\qquad < d * (s-t)$

$\qquad \leq (d + d^+ - d^-) * (s-t)$

Thus X is not a large or potential large itemset in the updated database.

Case 2: $d^+ < d^-$

Let X be an itemset of DB but not an itemset of DB^+ or DB^-. Assume $X \notin L \cup PL$. Then X may be a large itemset in the updated database. It is proved as follows:

[PROOF].

$X'_{count} = X_{count} + X^+_{count} - X^-_{count}$

$\qquad < d * (s-t)$

Since $d * (s-t) > (d + d^+ - d^-) * (s-t)$, X may be a large itemset of the updated database. In the case, we use DLG algorithm [7] to process the updated database and generate the sets L and PL.

Let *MS* be the maximal value of the support counts of itemsets in M. By Theorem 4, if $MS \leq d * t + d^+ * s - d^- * s$, we need not process the updated database. The Update algorithm is shown in [6].

Theorem 4: If $MS \leq d*t + d^+*s - d^-*s$, we need not scan the updated database DB'.

[PROOF]

Assume that X is an itemset of $DB \cup DB^+$.

$<1> X \in L \cup PL$

Since $X'_{count} = X_{count} + X^+_{count} - X^-_{count}$

and $X_{count}, X^+_{count}, X^-_{count}$ are available, we need not scan DB'.

$<2> X \notin L \cup PL$

Since $X'_{count} = X_{count} + X^+_{count} - X^-_{count}$

$< d*(s-t) + X^+_{count} - X^-_{count}$

$\leq d*s - d*t + MS - X^-_{.count}$

$\leq d*s - d*t + MS$

$\leq d*s - d*t + (d*t + d^+*s - d^-*s)$

$= d*s + d^+*s - d^-*s = d'*s$

$\Rightarrow$ X is not a large itemset of DB'.

$\Rightarrow$ We need not scan DB'.

By $<1><2>$ the theorem is proved.

4 Experimental Results

To assess the performance of our algorithms for the maintenance of large itemsets, we perform several experiments on Sun SPARC/10 workstation.

4.1 Generation of Synthetic Data

In the experiments, we used synthetic databases to evaluate the performance of the algorithms. The data is generated using the same approach introduced in [2]. The parameters used to generate the database are described in Table 1.

Table1. The parameters

d	Number of transactions in the original database DB
d^+, d^-	Number of transactions in the increment/decrement databases (DB^+ / DB^-)
$|I|$	Average size of the potentially large itemsets
$|MI|$	Maximum size of potentially large itemsets
$|L|$	Number of the potentially large itemsets
$|T|$	Average size of the transactions
$|MT|$	Maximum size of the transactions

We generate the dataset by setting N=1000, d=100,000, $|L|$=2000, $|I|$=3, $|MI|$=5, $|T|$=5, and $|MT|$=10. The way we insert the increment database DB^+ is to put the d^+ transactions in the rear of the original database. And the way we delete the decrement database DB^- is to remove the first d^- transactions from the original database.

4.2 Comparison of Insert Algorithm with FUP

We perform an experiment on the dataset with minimum support 1%. The experiment run eight insertions of increment databases and the relative execution time of each insertion is recorded for Insert algorithm and FUP algorithm. A new database is generated for each insertion. Fig. 1 shows the relative execution times in the cases of t=0.1% and t=0.5%. The size of each increment database is 1% of the size of the original database. In this experiment, Insert algorithm takes much less time than FUP algorithm since Insert algorithm does not scan the original database.

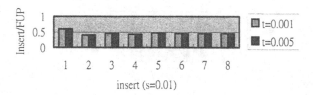

Fig. 1. Relative execution time for Insert and FUP (d^+ :d = 1:100)

4.3 Comparison of Delete Algorithm with FUP2

In the following, we compare Delete algorithm with FUP2 algorithm. The minimum support considered is also 1%. In Fig. 2, the size of each decrement database is 1% of the size of the original database and t=0.1% and t=0.5% are considered respectively. It can be seen that Delete algorithm take much less time than FUP2.

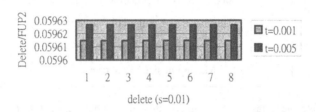

Fig. 2. Relative execution time for Delete and FUP2 (d $^-$:d = 1:100)

4.4 Comparison of Update Algorithm with FUP2

We assess the performance of Update algorithm considering insertion and deletion at the same time. In Fig. 3, the sizes of the increment database and the decrement database are 0.1% of the size of the original database. It can be seen that Update algorithm takes much less time than FUP2 algorithm since the size of the original database is much larger than that of the increment database and the decrement database.

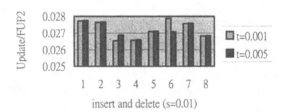

Fig. 3. Relative execution time for Update and FUP2 (d $^+$:d $^-$:d = 1:1:1000)

5 Conclusion

The database users may frequently or occasionally update the database. This behavior would change the characteristic of the database. To efficiently discover and maintain large itemsets in a large database, we present three algorithms to solve the problem:
1. Insert algorithm for the insertion of the increment database to the original database.
2. Delete algorithm for the deletion of the decrement database from the original database.
3. Update algorithm considering both the increment database and the decrement database at the same time.

In our algorithms, we store more information than other algorithms so that the cost of processing the original database can be reduced. Moreover, we discuss the cases where the large itemsets can be obtained without scanning the original database. Experimental results show that our algorithms outperform other algorithms, especially when the size of the original database is much larger than that of the increment database and the decrement database.

Acknowledgments

This work was partially supported by the Republic of China National Science Council under Contract No. NSC 88-2213-E-007-052 and NSC 88-2213-E-159-003.

References

1. Agrawal, R., Imielinski, T., Swami, A.: Mining Association Rules between Sets of Items in Large Databases, Proc. ACM SIGMOD, (1993) 207-216
2. Cheung, D.W., Han, J., Ng, V.T., Wong, C.Y.: Maintenance of Discovered Association Rules in Large Databases: An Incremental Updating Technique, Proc. the International Conference on Data Engineering, (1996) 106-114
3. Cheung, D.W., Ng, V.T., Tam, B.W.: Maintenance of Discovered Knowledge: A case in Multi-level Association Rules, Proc. 2nd International Conference on Knowledge Discovery and Data Mining, (1996) 307-310
4. Cheung, D.W., Lee, S.D., Kao, B.: A general Incremental Technique for Mining Discovered Association Rules, Proc. International Conference on Database System for Advanced Applications, (1997) 185-194
5. Lee, K.L., Efficient Graph-Based Algorithms for Discovering and Maintaining Knowledge in Large Databases, NTHU Master Thesis, (1997)
6. Tsai, P.S.M., Lee, C.C., Chen, A.L.P.: An Efficient Approach for Incremental Association Rule Mining, Technical Report, (1998)
7. Yen, S.J., Chen, A.L.P.: An Efficient Approach to Discovering Knowledge from Large Databases, Proc. the IEEE/ACM International Conference on Parallel and Distributed Information System, (1996) 8-18

Association Rules in Incomplete Databases

Marzena Kryszkiewicz

Institute of Computer Science, Warsaw University of Technology
Nowowiejska 15/19, 00-665 Warsaw, Poland
mkr@ii.pw.edu.pl

Abstract. Discovering association rules among items in large databases is recognized as an important database mining problem. The problem has been introduced originally for sales transaction database and did not relate to missing data. However, missing data often occur in relational databases, especially in business ones. It is not obvious how to compute association rules from such incomplete databases. It is provided and proved in the paper how to estimate support and confidence of an association rule induced from an incomplete relational database. We also introduce definitions of expected support and confidence of an association rule. The proposed definitions guarantee some required properties of itemsets and association rules. Eventually, we discuss another approach to missing values based on so called valid databases and compare both approaches.

1 Introduction

Discovering association rules among items in large databases is recognized as an important database mining problem. The problem was introduced in [1] for sales transaction database. The association rules identify sets of items that are purchased together with other sets of items. For example, an association rule may state that 80% of customers who buy fish buy also white wine. Several extensions and variations of the notion of an association rule were offered in the literature (see e.g. [5, 6 ,14, 15]). One of such extensions is a generalized rule that can be discovered from a taxonomic database [14]. It has been proposed languages (see e.g. [9] for an SQL-extension) for mining for associations rules satisfying user imposed constraints. Applications for association rules range from decision support to telecommunications alarm diagnosis and prediction.

Originally, missing values have not been considered for a transaction database. However, when one tries to discover associations between values of different attributes one may often face the problem of missing values. The problem is especially acute for business databases. Missing data may result from errors, measurement failures, changes in the database schema etc.

Several solutions to the problem of generating decision tree or decision rules from the training set of examples with unknown values have been proposed in the area of artificial intelligence. The simplest among them consist in removing examples with unknown values or replacing unknown values with the most common values. More complex approaches were presented in [4, 11]. A Bayesian formalism is used in [4] to determine the probability distribution of the unknown value over the possible values from the domain. This method could either choose the most likely value or divide the example into fractional examples, each with one possible value weighted according to the probabilities determined. It is suggested in [11] to predict the value of an attribute based on the value of other attributes of the example, and the class information. These and other approaches to missing values were proposed also in the area of rough sets (e.g. [7, 8]; see the overview in [3]).

In [12] it was proposed yet another treatment of missing values. The main idea was to cut a database into several valid databases without missing values. The notions of support and confidence of an association rule were redefined. It was shown how to modify efficient data mining algorithms [2] so that to compute association rules from incomplete databases.

In the paper we investigate properties of databases with missing attribute values. We provide and prove pessimistic and optimistic estimations of support and confidence of an association rule. Whatever are a real support and confidence of a rule they do not exceed the estimated thresholds. This part of the paper is an extension of the work [8] where classification rules generation from incomplete decision Fig.s was considered in the context of rough sets [10].

In the paper we offer also definitions of expected values of support and confidence based on known attribute values in the database. The proposed definitions guarantee some required properties of itemsets and association rules. Finally, we present in more detail the approach to missing values offered in [12] and point out its shortcomings.

2 Association Rules

2.1 Association Rules in Transaction Databases

The definition of a class of regularities called *association rules* and the problem of their discovering were introduced in [1]. Here, we describe this problem after [1, 2]. Let $I = \{i_1, i_2, ..., i_m\}$ be a set of distinct literals, called *items*. In general, any set of items is called an *itemset*. Let D be a set of transactions, where each transaction T is a set of items such that $T \subseteq I$. An *association rule* is an expression of the form: $X \Rightarrow Y$, where $\varnothing \neq X, Y \subset I$ and $X \cap Y = \varnothing$. X is called the *antecedent* and Y is called the *consequent* of the rule.

Statistical significance of an itemset X is called *support* and is denoted by $sup(X)$. $sup(X)$ is defined as the percentage (or the number) of transactions in D that contain X. Statistical significance (*support*) of a rule $X \Rightarrow Y$ is denoted by $sup(X \Rightarrow Y)$ and is defined as follows: $sup(X \Rightarrow Y) = sup(X \cup Y)$.

Additionally, an association rule is characterized by *confidence*, which expresses its strength. The confidence of an association rule $X \Rightarrow Y$ is denoted by $conf(X \Rightarrow Y)$ and is defined as follows: $conf(X \Rightarrow Y) = sup(X \Rightarrow Y) / sup(X)$.

The problem of mining association rules is to generate all rules that have support greater than some user specified minimum support and confidence not less than a user specified minimum confidence. Several efficient solutions applicable for large databases were proposed to solve this problem (see [2, 13]). The problem of generating association rules is usually decomposed into two subproblems:

1. Generate all itemsets whose support exceeds the minimum support *minSup*. The itemsets of this property are called *frequent (large)*.
2. Generate all association rules whose confidence is not less than the minimum confidence *minConf*. In the process of rules' generation only frequent itemsets are considered. Let X be a frequent itemset and $\varnothing \neq Y \subset X$. Then any candidate rule $X \setminus Y \Rightarrow Y$ is association one if $(sup(X) / sup(X \setminus Y)) \geq minConf$.

   In both subproblems the following properties of itemsets are exploited extensively:
   - If $X \subset Y$ then $sup(X) \geq sup(Y)$.
   - All subsets of a frequent itemset are frequent and all supersets of an infrequent itemset are infrequent.

   The properties above allow reducing considerably unnecessary (redundant) evaluations of candidate itemsets and candidate rules.

2.2 Association Rules in Relational Databases

Relational table is a pair $D = (O, AT)$, where O - is a non-empty finite set of *tuples* and AT is a non-empty finite set of *attributes*, such that $a: O \rightarrow V_a$ for any $a \in AT$, where V_a is called the *domain* of a. The notion of a tuple corresponds to the notion of a transaction, but the size of a tuple is fixed. A *relational item* is meant to be an *attribute-value pair* (a,v), where $a \in AT$ and $v \in V_a$. In the paper, we assume that a *relational itemset* is any set of relational items in which no attribute occurs more than once[1]. *Relational association rules* are constructed in usual way, but only from relational itemsets. The definitions of support and confidence are the same as for a transaction database.

Example 1. Let Fig. 1 present a database D under consideration.

Id	X1	X2	X3	X4
1	a	a	a	c
2	a	a	b	d
3	a	b	c	c
4	a	b	d	c
5	b	b	e	d
6	b	b	f	c
7	b	c	g	c
8	b	c	h	d

Fig. 1. Exemplary database

Fig. 2 contains exemplary association rules that hold in D:

$X \Rightarrow Y$	$sup(X \Rightarrow Y)$	$conf(X \Rightarrow Y)$
$\{(X1,a)\} \Rightarrow \{(X4,c)\}$	3/8	3/4
$\{(X4,c)\} \Rightarrow \{(X1,a)\}$	3/8	3/5
$\{(X1,a),(X2,b)\} \Rightarrow \{(X4,c)\}$	2/8	2/2
$\{(X2,b),(X4,c)\} \Rightarrow \{(X1,a)\}$	2/8	2/3

Fig. 2. Exemplary association rules with their support and confidence in D

$\square$

---

[1] In general, it may be useful to allow several items with the same attribute in an itemset. This is the case when association rules are to be discovered from groups of tuples (see e.g. [9]).

3 Incomplete Databases

3.1 Basic Notions

Computation of support and confidence of an association rule is not obvious in the case of databases with missing attribute values. Below, we introduce some notions that will be useful in investigating properties of such rules. Missing values will be denoted by "*".

We call an itemset X *regular* iff for every $(a,v) \in X$: $v \neq *$. Further on, we consider only regular itemsets. Sometimes X will play a role of a *pattern*:

The *maximal set of tuples that match the pattern X necessarily* is denoted by $n(X)$ and is defined as follows: $n(X) = \{x \in D | \forall (a,v) \in X: a(x)=v\}$.

By $m(X)$ we denote the *maximal set of tuples that may match the pattern X* in D, i.e. $m(X) = \{x \in D | \forall (a,v) \in X: a(x) \in \{v,*\}\}$.

The difference $m(X) - n(X)$ is denoted by $d(X)$, that is $d(X)$ is the set of tuples in D that are likely to match pattern X but this is not certain.

By $n(-X)$ we denote the *maximal set of tuples that certainly do not match the pattern X* in D, i.e. $n(-X) = D \setminus m(X)$.

By $m(-X)$ we denote the *maximal set of tuples that may not match the pattern X* in D, i.e. $m(-X) = D \setminus n(X)$.

The difference $m(-X) - n(-X)$ is denoted by $d(-X)$.

We may interpret $-X$ in the following way:

Let $F(X) = \{\{(a_1,v_1),...,(a_k,v_k)\} | a_i \in X, v_i \in V_a, a_i \neq a_j$, for $i,j = 1, ..., k\}$. Then, $-X$ may be understood as a generalized pattern that is an alternative of all patterns in $F(X)$ except X. Further on, $-X$ will be called *anti-pattern* of X.

Example 2. Given the incomplete database D presented in Fig. 3, we will illustrate the introduced notions of necessary and possible patterns and anti-patterns matching.

Id	X1	X2	X3	X4
1	*	a	a	c
2	a	a	b	*
3	a	b	c	c
4	a	b	d	c
5	*	b	e	d
6	b	b	f	*
7	b	c	g	*
8	b	c	h	*

Fig. 3. Exemplary database with missing values

Fig. 4 contains the respective sets of tuples that match exemplary itemsets-patterns.

Itemset X	$n(X)$	$m(X)$	$d(X)$	$n(-X)$	$m(-X)$	$d(-X)$
{(X1,a)}	{2,3,4}	{1,2,3,4,5}	{1,5}	{6,7,8}	{1,5,6,7,8}	{1,5}
{(X4,c)}	{1,3,4}	{1,2,3,4,6,7,8}	{2,6,7,8}	{5}	{2,5,6,7,8}	{2,6,7,8}
{(X1,a),(X4,c)}	{3,4}	{1,2,3,4}	{1,2}	{5,6,7,8}	{1,2,5,6,7,8}	{1,2}
{(X1,a),(X2,b)}	{3,4}	{3,4,5}	{5}	{1,2,6,7,8}	{1,2,5,6,7,8}	{5}
{(X2,b),(X4,c)}	{3,4}	{3,4,6}	{6}	{1,2,5,7,8}	{1,2,5,6,7,8}	{6}
{(X1,a),(X2,b),(X4,c)}	{3,4}	{3,4}	∅	{1,2,5,6,7,8}	{1,2,5,6,7,8}	∅

Fig. 4. Tuples matching (anti)pattern X

Let us note that e.g. tuple 5 in Fig. 3 does not match the pattern {(X1,a),(X4,c)} certainly, though the value of attribute X1 is missing. Nevertheless, the value of attribute X4 for tuple 5 is known and it is equal to d, which is different from the value c related to attribute X4 in the pattern $\{(X1,a),(X4,c)\}$. So, whatever is the real value of tuple 5 for attribute X1, the tuple will not match the pattern $\{(X1,a),(X4,c)\}$.

□

Below we provide several properties of the introduced notions of pattern matching.

Property 1. Let X be an itemset in D.

a) $n(-X) = \{x \in D | \exists (a,v) \in X: a(x) \notin \{v,*\}\}$

b) $m(-X) = \{x \in D | \exists (a,v) \in X: a(x) \neq v\}$

c) $d(X) = \{x \in D | \forall (a,v) \in X: a(x) \in \{v,*\}$ and $\exists (a,w) \in X: a(x) = *\}$

d) $n(X) \cap n(-X) = \varnothing$

e) $n(X) \cap m(-X) = \varnothing$

f) $m(X) \cap n(-X) = \varnothing$

g) $m(X) \cap m(-X) = d(X)$

h) $d(X) = d(-X)$

i) $n(X) \cup d(X) \cup n(-X) = D$

Property 2. Let X, Y be itemsets in D and $X \subset Y$. Then:

a) $n(X) \supseteq n(Y)$

b) $m(X) \supseteq m(Y)$

c) $m(X) \supseteq n(Y)$

d) $m(X) \supseteq d(Y)$

e) $m(X) \setminus n(Y) \supseteq d(Y)$

f) $d(X) \cap n(Y) = \varnothing$

Property 3. Let X, Y be itemsets in D. Then:

a) $m(X \cup Y) = m(X) \cap m(Y)$

b) $n(X \cup Y) = n(X) \cap n(Y)$

c) $d(X \cup Y) = [n(X) \cap d(Y)] \cup [d(X) \cap n(Y)] \cup [d(X) \cap d(Y)]$

3.2 Estimations of Support and Confidence

In the case of an incomplete information system one may not be able to compute support of an itemset X precisely. Nevertheless, one can estimate the actual support by the pair of two numbers meaning the *lowest possible support* (*pessimistic* case) and the *greatest possible support* (*optimistic* case). We will denote these two numbers by $pSup(X)$ and $oSup(X)$, respectively. Clearly,

$$pSup(X) = |n(X)| / |D| \quad \text{and} \quad oSup(X) = |m(X)| / |D|.$$

The difference $oSup(X) - pSup(X)$ will be denoted by $dSup(X)$.

Property 4. Let X, Y be itemsets in D and $X \subset Y$. Then:

a) $pSup(X) \geq pSup(Y)$

b) $oSup(X) \geq oSup(Y)$

Proof: Follows immediately from Property 2. □

A similar problem arises when one tries to compute the confidence of a rule in an incomplete database. Let $pConf(X \Rightarrow Y)$ and $oConf(X \Rightarrow Y)$ denote the *lowest possible confidence* and *greatest possible confidence* of $X \Rightarrow Y$, respectively. The property below shows how to compute these values.

Property 5. Let $X \Rightarrow Y$ be a rule in an incomplete database D.

a) $pConf(X \Rightarrow Y) = |n(X) \cap n(Y)| / (|n(X) \cap n(Y)| + |m(X) \cap m(-Y)|)$

b) $oConf(X \Rightarrow Y) = |m(X) \cap m(Y)| / (|m(X) \cap m(Y)| + |n(X) \cap n(-Y)|)$

Proof: Let us assume that there are k tuples which match both X and Y in reality, but not necessarily in D (i.e. these tuples belong to $d(X \cup Y)$). Let l be the number of tuples that in reality match X and do not match Y, but the contents of D is not sufficient to extract this information with certainty. Then in the real world, the confidence of the rule $X \Rightarrow Y$ is equal to $(|n(X) \cap n(Y)| + k) / (|n(X) \cap n(Y)| + k + |n(X) \cap n(-Y)| + l)$. However, if we have only the information from D, we should treat the confidence of $X \Rightarrow Y$ as a function $f(k,l) = (|n(X) \cap n(Y)| + k) / (|n(X) \cap n(Y)| + k + |n(X) \cap n(-Y)| + l)$, where $k \in [0, |m(X) \cap m(Y)| - |n(X) \cap n(Y)|]$, $l \in [0, |m(X) \cap m(-Y)| - |n(X) \cap n(-Y)|]$.

Ad. a) One can easily notice that the function $f(k,l)$ has infimum for minimal value of k and maximal value of l. Therefore, $pConf(X \Rightarrow Y) = f(0, |m(X) \cap m(-Y)| - |n(X) \cap n(-Y)|)$ $= |n(X) \cap n(Y)| / (|n(X) \cap n(Y)| + |m(X) \cap m(-Y)|)$.

Ad. b) It can be easily noticed that the function $f(k,l)$ has supremum for maximal value of k and minimal value of l. Therefore, $oConf(X \Rightarrow Y) = f(|m(X) \cap m(Y)| - |n(X) \cap n(Y)|, 0) = |m(X) \cap m(Y)| / (|m(X) \cap m(Y)| + |n(X) \cap n(-Y)|)$. $\square$

Estimations of how exemplary patterns are supported in the database from Fig. 3 are given in Fig. 5, while estimations of confidence of exemplary association rules are placed in Fig. 6.

3.3 Expected Values of Support and Confidence

Although we know already how to estimate support and confidence of rules it may be confusing how to treat rules for which the difference between optimistic and pessimistic estimations is high. It would be useful to be able to predict values of support and confidence close to real (though unknown) ones. Therefore, we provide definitions of expected support and confidence of an association rule.

The expected value of support for a pattern (or anti-pattern) X will be denoted by $eSup(X)$. A definition of the expected support we will propose is based on the following assumptions:

$$eSup(X) / eSup(-X) = pSup(X) / pSup(-X) \quad \text{and} \quad eSup(X) + eSup(-X) = 1.$$

According to the above constraints we obtain the following definition of *expected support* for an itemset X:

$$eSup(X) = pSup(X) / (pSup(X) + pSup(-X)).$$

Property 6. Let X be an itemset in D. Then, $eSup(X) = pSup(X) / (1 - dSup(X))$.

Proof: Follows immediately from the definition of expected support and Prop. 1(i). $\square$

Property 7. Let X be an itemset in D. Then, $pSup(X) \leq eSup(X) \leq oSup(X)$

Proof:

$pSup(X) / eSup(X) = 1 - dSup(X) \leq 1$. So, $pSup(X) \leq eSup(X)$.

$oSup(X) - eSup(X) = [pSup(X) + dSup(X)] - [pSup(X) / (1 - dSup(X))] =$

$= dSup(X) * [-pSup(X) + 1 - dSup(X)] / [1 - dSup(X)] \geq 0$. So, $oSup(X) \geq eSup(X)$. $\square$

Property 8. Let X, Y be itemsets in D and $X \subset Y$. Then: $eSup(X) \geq eSup(Y)$.

Proof: First, let us observe that the cardinality of $d(Y)$ is maximal if $d(Y) = m(X) \setminus n(Y)$ (see Property 2(e)). On the other hand, $m(X) \setminus n(Y) = (n(X) \cup d(Y)) \setminus n(Y) = (n(X) \setminus n(Y)) \cup (d(X) \setminus n(Y))$ and $(d(X) \setminus n(Y)) = d(X)$ (by Property 2(f)). So, $d(Y)$ is maximal for $d(Y) = (n(X) \setminus n(Y)) \cup d(X)$. By Property 6 we have:

$eSup(X) = (|n(X)| / |D|) / (|1 - |dSup(X)|)$ and $eSup(Y) = (|n(Y)| / |D|) / (1 - |dSup(Y)|)$.

Let $\alpha = |n(Y)| / |D|$, $\beta = |n(X) \setminus n(Y)| / |D|$ and $\chi = (1 - |dSup(X)|) * (|1 - (\beta + |dSup(X)|))$. Then: $eSup(X) - eSup(Y) = [(\alpha+\beta) / (1 - |dSup(X)|) - \alpha / (1 - |dSup(Y)|)] \geq$

$[(\alpha+\beta) / (1 - |dSup(X)|) - \alpha / (1 - (\beta + |dSup(X)|))] =$

$[(\alpha+\beta) * (1 - \beta - |dSup(X)|) - \alpha * (1 - |dSup(X)|)] / \chi =$

$[-\alpha\beta + \beta - \beta^2 - \beta|dSup(X)|] / \chi = \beta* [1 - (\alpha + \beta + |dSup(X)|)] / \chi =$

$\beta* [1 - |m(X)|] / \chi \geq 0$. Hence, $eSup(X) \geq eSup(Y)$. $\quad\square$

The *expected confidence* of a rule $X \Rightarrow Y$ will be denoted by $eConf(X \Rightarrow Y)$ and we define it in usual way: $eConf(X \Rightarrow Y) = eSup(X \cup Y) / eSup(X)$.

Property 9. Let $X \Rightarrow Y$ be a rule in an incomplete database D. Then:

$$pConf(X \Rightarrow Y) \leq eConf(X \Rightarrow Y) \leq oConf(X \Rightarrow Y)$$

Proof: Property 5 allow us to conclude that for any support of $X \Rightarrow Y$, which belongs to $[pSup(X \cup Y), oSup(X \cup Y)]$, and for any support of the antecedent of the rule $X \Rightarrow Y$, which belongs to $[pSup(X), oSup(X)]$, the confidence of $X \Rightarrow Y$ belongs to $[pConf(X \Rightarrow Y), oConf(X \Rightarrow Y)]$. By Property 7, both $eSup(X \Rightarrow Y) \in [pSup(X \cup Y), oSup(X \cup Y)]$ and $eSup(X) \in [pSup(X), oSup(X)]$. Hence, $eConf(X \Rightarrow Y) \in [pConf(X \Rightarrow Y), oConf(X \Rightarrow Y)]$. $\quad\square$

Example 3. Let us consider the database from Fig. 3. In Fig. 5, we place pessimistic, optimistic and expected supports for exemplary itemsets. The values can be quickly computed by applying extracted information on D that is contained in Fig. 4.

Itemset X	$pSup(X)$	$oSup(X)$	$dSup(X)$	$pSup(-X)$	$eSup(X)$
{(X1,a)}	3/8	5/8	2/8	3/8	3/6
{(X4,c)}	3/8	7/8	4/8	1/8	3/4
{(X1,a),(X4,c)}	2/8	4/8	2/8	4/8	2/6
{(X1,a),(X2,b)}	2/8	3/8	1/8	5/8	2/7
{(X2,b),(X4,c)}	2/8	3/8	1/8	5/8	2/7
{(X1,a),(X2,b),(X4,c)}	2/8	2/8	0	6/8	2/8

Fig. 5. Estimated and expected values of support of exemplary itemsets

Fig. 6 is filled with pessimistic, optimistic and expected values of confidence of rules from Example 1. One may use information in Figures 4-5 to derive respective supports of the rules and their antecedents.

$X \Rightarrow Y$	$pConf(X \Rightarrow Y)$	$oConf(X \Rightarrow Y)$	$eConf(X \Rightarrow Y)$
{(X1,a)} $\Rightarrow$ {(X4,c)}	2/3	4/4	2/3
{(X4,c)} $\Rightarrow$ {(X1,a)}	2/6	4/4	4/9
{(X1,a),(X2,b)} $\Rightarrow$ {(X4,c)}	2/3	2/2	7/8
{(X2,b),(X4,c)} $\Rightarrow$ {(X1,a)}	2/3	2/2	7/8

Fig. 6. Estimated and expected values of confidence of rules

$\square$

4 Another Approach Based on Valid Databases

In this section we remind briefly and analyse another approach to missing values presented recently in [12]. Let us start with the notations applied in this approach:

A tuple is disabled for X in D, if it contains missing values for at least one item in X. $Dis(X)$ denotes the subset of D disabled for X, i.e. $Dis(X) = \{\exists (a,v) \in X: a(x) = *\}$. The valid database (vdb) for an itemset X is defined as follows: $vdb(X) = D \setminus Dis(X)$.

Support $(vSup)$ of an itemset X is computed in $vdb(X)$ and is defined in the following way: $vSup(X) = |n(X)| / |vdb(X)| = |n(X)| / (|D| - |Dis(X)|)$.

Confidence $(vConf)$ of a rule $X \Rightarrow Y$ is computed in $vdb(X \cup Y)$ and is defined as follows: $vConf(X \Rightarrow Y) = |n(X \cup Y)| / [|n(X)| - (|n(X)| \cap |Dis(Y)|)]$.

Property 10. Let X, Y be itemsets in D and $X \subset Y$. Then:

a) $Dis(X) \subseteq Dis(Y)$

b) $d(X) \subseteq Dis(X)$

Proof: Ad. 10(b). Follows immediately from Prop. 1(c) and the definition of $Dis(X)$. $\square$

Example 3. Let us consider the incomplete database D presented in Fig. 3. In Fig. 7, we placed disabled tuples and support computed in valid databases for exemplary itemsets. For comparison purposes, it was added estimated and expected supports of these itemsets.

Itemset X	$Dis(X)$	$vSup(X)$	$pSup(X)$	$oSup(X)$	$eSup(X)$	$d(X)$
{(X1,a)}	{1,5}	3/6	3/8	5/8	3/6	{1,5}
{(X4,c)}	{2,6,7,8}	3/4	3/8	7/8	3/4	{2,6,7,8}
{(X1,a),(X4,c)}	{1,2,5,6,7,8}	2/2	2/8	4/8	2/6	{1,2}
{(X1,a),(X2,b)}	{1,5}	2/6	2/8	3/8	2/7	{5}
{(X2,b),(X4,c)}	{2,6,7,8}	2/4	2/8	3/8	2/7	{6}
{(X1,a),(X2,b),(X4,c)}	{1,2,5,6,7,8}	2/2	2/8	2/8	2/8	∅

Fig. 7. Estimated and expected values of support of exemplary itemsets

Let us compare differently computed supports for the itemset $X = \{(X1,a),(X4,c)\}$. Let us note that $vSup(X)$ does not belong to $[pSup(X), oSup(X)]$, which means that there is no substitution for missing values in the database that would produce such a support for X! Additionally, we may notice that $vSup(X)$, which is equal to 1, is higher than the supports of proper subsets of X, which are equal to 3/6 for {(X1,a)} and 3/4 for {(X4,c)}, respectively!

Let us also observe how quickly increases the difference between $Dis(X)$ and $d(X)$ when adding items to any itemset X.

In Fig. 8 we put confidence of rules computed in valid databases. Additionally, we placed estimated and expected values of confidence of the rules.

$X \Rightarrow Y$	$vConf(X \Rightarrow Y)$	$pConf(X \Rightarrow Y)$	$oConf(X \Rightarrow Y)$	$eConf(X \Rightarrow Y)$
{(X1,a)} ⇒ {(X4,c)}	1	2/3	1	2/3
{(X4,c)} ⇒ {(X1,a)}	1	1/3	1	4/9
{(X1,a),(X2,b)} ⇒ {(X4,c)}	1	2/3	1	7/8
{(X2,b),(X4,c)} ⇒ {(X1,a)}	1	2/3	1	7/8

Fig. 8. Exemplary association rules for the database from Fig. 3

$\square$

Let us conclude Example 3 with the property beneath:

Property 11. Let X, Y be itemsets in D. What follows does not hold in general:
a) $vSup(X) \in [pSup(X), oSup(X)]$
b) If $X \subset Y$ then $vSup(X) \geq vSup(Y)$

$\square$

Property 12. Let $X \Rightarrow Y$ be a rule in an incomplete database D.

$$pConf(X \Rightarrow Y) \leq vConf(X \Rightarrow Y)$$

Proof: In the proof we will apply the following equivalences:
- $|n(X)| = |n(X) \cap n(Y)| + |n(X) \cap Dis(Y)| + |n(X) \cap [D \setminus (Dis(Y) \cup n(Y))]|$,
- $n(X \cup Y) = n(X) \cap n(Y)$,
- $|m(\text{-}Y)| + |d(Y)| = |D|$.

Now, we may rewrite $vConf$ and $pConf$ as follows:
$vConf(X \Rightarrow Y) = |n(X) \cap (Y)| / [|n(X) \cap n(Y)| + |n(X) \cap [D \setminus (Dis(Y) \cup n(Y))]|$,
$pConf(X \Rightarrow Y) = |n(X) \cap n(Y)| / (|n(X) \cap n(Y)| + |m(X) \cap [D \setminus d(Y)]|$.

By Property 10(b) $d(Y) \subseteq Dis(Y)$, so $[D \setminus (Dis(Y) \cup n(Y)] \subseteq [D \setminus d(Y)]$. Additionally, $n(X) \subseteq m(X)$. Hence, $vConf(X \Rightarrow Y) \leq pConf(X \Rightarrow Y)$.

$\square$

Property 13. Let $X \Rightarrow Y$ be a rule in an incomplete database D. The following statement does not hold in general: $vConf(X \Rightarrow Y) \leq oConf(X \Rightarrow Y)$

Proof: We will proof Property 13 by showing an example of a database D and an association rule $X \Rightarrow Y$ such that $vConf(X \Rightarrow Y) > oConf(X \Rightarrow Y)$ in D. Let D be a database as in Fig. 9. Let $X = \{(X1,a)\}$ and $Y = \{(X2,a),(X3,a)\}$. Then, $vConf(X \Rightarrow Y) = 1$, whereas $oConf(X \Rightarrow Y) = 1/2$.

Id	X1	X2	X3
1	a	a	a
2	a	b	*
3	b	b	b

Fig. 9. Exemplary database with missing values

$\square$

5 Conclusions

Support and confidence of association rules induced from incomplete databases may not be computable but they can be precisely estimated. It was shown in the paper how to estimate them. Any real support and confidence of a rule belong to the estimated thresholds. Additionally, we offered definitions of expected values of support and confidence of a rule. Both pessimistic, optimistic as well as expected support of itemsets decrease when adding items. This is required and important feature of itemsets that speeds up rule mining process considerably. In the process of looking for association rules a user may decide whether constraints on support and confidence should be imposed on estimated or expected values.

We analysed also another approach to missing values that was presented in [12]. We proved that applying this approach does not guarantee that 1) the support of an itemset is not greater than the support of its subset, 2) the support of an itemset belongs to the estimated threshold, 3) the confidence of an association rule is less than the optimistic estimation.

References

[1] Agraval, R., Imielinski, T., Swami, A.: Mining Associations Rules between Sets of Items in Large Databases. In: Proc. of the ACM SIGMOD Conference on Management of Data. Washington, D.C. (1993) 207-216

[2] Agraval R., Mannila H., Srikant R., Toivonen H., Verkamo A.I.: Fast Discovery of Association Rules. In: Fayyad, U.M., Piatetsky-Shapiro, G. , Smyth, P. , Uthurusamy, R. (eds.): Advances in Knowledge Discovery and Data Mining. AAAI, CA (1996) 307-328

[3] Deogun J.S., Raghavan V.V., Sarkar A., Sever H.: Data Mining: Trends in Research and Development. In: Lin, T.Y., Cercone, N. (eds.): Rough Sets and Data Mining. Kluwer Academic Publishers (1997) 9-45

[4] Kononenko, I. , Bratko, I. , Roskar, E.: Experiments in Automatic Learning of Medical Diagnostic Rules. Technical Report. Jozef Stefan Institute, Ljubljana, Yugoslavia (1984)

[5] Kryszkiewicz, M.: Representative Association Rules. In: Proc. of PAKDD '98. Melbourne, Australia. LNAI 1394. Research and Development in Knowledge Discovery and Data Mining. Springer-Verlag (1998) 198-209

[6] Kryszkiewicz, M.: Fast Discovery of Representative Association Rules. In: Proc. of RSCTC '98. Warsaw, Poland. Rough Sets and Current Trends in Computing. Springer-Verlag. (1998) 214-221

[7] Kryszkiewicz M.: Properties of Incomplete Information Systems in the Framework of Rough Sets: In Polkowski, L. , Skowron, A. (eds.): Studies in Fuzziness and Soft Computing 18. Rough Sets in Knowledge Discovery 1. Physica-Verlag, Heidelberg (1998) 442-450

[8] Kryszkiewicz M., Rybinski H.: Incompleteness Aspects in the Rough Set Approach. In: Proc. of JCIS '98. Raleigh, USA. (1998) 371-374

[9] Meo, R., Psaila, G., Ceri, S.: A New SQL-like Operator for Mining Association Rules. In: Proc. of the 22nd VLDB Conference. Mumbai (Bombay), India (1996)

[10] Pawlak Z.: Rough Sets: Theoretical Aspects of Reasoning about Data. Kluwer Academic Publishers, Vol. 9 (1991)

[11] Quinlan J.R.: Induction of Decision Trees. In: Shavlik J. W., Dietterich T. G. (eds.): Readings in Machine Learning. Morgan Kaufmann Publishers (1990) 57-69

[12] Ragel A., Cremilleux B.: Treatment of Missing Values for Association Rules. In: Proc. of Second Pacific Asia Conference, PAKDD '98. Melbourne, Australia. LNAI 1394. Research and Development in Knowledge Discovery and Data Mining. Springer (1998) 258-270

[13] Savasere, A, Omiecinski, E., Navathe, S.: An Efficient Algorithm for Mining Association Rules in Large Databases. In: Proc. of the 21st VLDB Conference. Zurich, Swizerland (1995) 432-444

[14] Srikant, R., Agraval, R.: Mining Generalized Association Rules. In: Proc. of the 21st VLDB Conference. Zurich, Swizerland (1995) 407-419

[15] Washio, T., Matsuura, H., Motoda, H.: Mining Association Rules for Estimation and Prediction. In: Proc. of PAKDD '98. Melbourne, Australia. LNAI 1394. Research and Development in Knowledge Discovery and Data Mining. Springer-Verlag (1998) 417-419

Parallel SQL Based Association Rule Mining on Large Scale PC Cluster: Performance Comparison with Directly Coded C Implementation

Iko Pramudiono, Takahiko Shintani,
Takayuki Tamura*, Masaru Kitsuregawa

Institute of Industrial Science, The University of Tokyo
7-22-1 Roppongi, Minato-ku, Tokyo 106, Japan
{iko,shintani,tamura,kitsure}@tkl.iis.u-tokyo.ac.jp

Abstract. Data mining is becoming increasingly important since the size of databases grows even larger and the need to explore hidden rules from the databases becomes widely recognized. Currently database systems are dominated by relational database and the ability to perform data mining using standard SQL queries will definitely ease implementation of data mining. However the performance of SQL based data mining is known to fall behind specialized implementation. In this paper we present an evaluation of parallel SQL based data mining on large scale PC cluster. The performance achieved by parallelizing SQL query for mining association rule using 4 processing nodes is even with C based program. Keywords: data mining, parallel SQL, query optimization, PC cluster

1 Introduction

Extracting valuable rules from a set of data has attracted lots of attention from both researcher and business community. This is particularly driven by explosion of the information amount stored in databases during recent years.

One method of data mining is finding association rule that is a rule which implies certain association relationship such as "occur together" or "one implies the other" among a set of objects [1]. This kind of mining is known as CPU power demanding application. This fact has driven many initial researches in data mining to develop new efficient mining methods [1][2]. However they imply specialized systems separated from the database.

Therefore there are some efforts recently to perform data mining using relational database system which offer advantages such as seamless integration with existing system and high portability. Methods examined are ranging from directly using SQL to some extensions like user defined function (UDF) [4]. Unfortunately SQL approach is reported to have drawback in performance.

---

* Currently at Information & Communication System Development Center, Mitsubishi Electric, Ohfuna 5-1-1 Kamakura-shi Kanagawa-ken 247-8501, Japan

However the increasing computing power trend continues and more can be expected by utilizing parallel processing architecture. More important, most major commercial database systems have included capabilities to support parallelization although no report available about how the parallelization affects the performance of complex query required by data mining. This fact motivated us to examine how efficiently SQL based association rule mining can be parallelized using our shared-nothing large scale PC cluster pilot system. We have also compared it with well known Apriori algorithm based C program[2].

2 Association Rule Mining Based on SQL

An example of association rule mining is finding "if a customer buys A and B then 90% of them buy also C" in transaction databases of large retail organizations. This 90% value is called confidence of the rule. Another important parameter is support of an itemset, such as {A,B,C}, which is defined as the percentage of the itemset contained in the entire transactions. For above example, confidence can also be measured as support({A,B,C}) divided by support({A,B}).

A common strategy to mine association rule is:

1. Find all itemsets that have transaction support above minimum support, usually called large itemsets.
2. Generate the desired rules using large itemsets.

Since the first step consumes most of processing time, development of mining algorithm has been concentrated on this step.

In our experiment we employed ordinary standard SQL query that is similar to SETM algorithm [3].It is shown in figure 1.

```
CREATE TABLE SALES (id int, item int);              WHERE       p.id       = q.id
                                                    AND         p.item_1 = q.item_1
- PASS 1                                            AND         p.item_2 = q.item_2

CREATE TABLE C_1 (item_1 int, cnt int);                           .
CREATE TABLE R_1 (id int, item_1 int);                            .
                                                    AND         p.item_k-2 = q.item_k-2
INSERT INTO C_1                                     AND         p.item_k-1 < q.item_k-1;
    SELECT    item AS item_1, COUNT(*)
    FROM      SALES                                 INSERT INTO C_k
    GROUP BY  item                                      SELECT     item_1, item_2, ..., item_k,
    HAVING COUNT(*) >= :min_support;                               COUNT(*)
                                                    FROM       RTMP_k
INSERT INTO R_1                                     GROUP BY   item_1, item_2, ..., item_k
    SELECT    p.id, p.item AS item_1                HAVING COUNT(*) >= :min_support;
    FROM      SALES p, C_1 c
    WHERE     p.item = c.item_1;                    INSERT INTO R_k
                                                        SELECT    p.id, p.item_1, p.item_2, ...,
- PASS k                                                          p.item_k
CREATE TABLE RTMP_k (id int, item_1 int,            FROM      RTMP_k p, C_k c
    item_2 int, ... , item_k int)                   WHERE     p.item_1 = c.item_1
CREATE TABLE C_k       (item_1 int,                 AND       p.item_2 = c.item_2
    item_2 int, ... , item_k int, cnt int)
CREATE TABLE R_k       (id int, item_1 int,                        .
    item_2 int, ... , item_k int)                                  .
                                                    AND       p.item_k = c.item_k;
INSERT INTO RTMP_k
    SELECT    p.id, p.item_1, p.item_2, ... ,       DROP TABLE R_k-1;
              p.item_k-1, q.item_k-1               DROP TABLE RTMP_k;
    FROM      R_k-1 p, R_k-1 q
```

Fig.1. SQL query to mine association rule

Transaction data is normalized into the first normal form (transaction ID, item) . In the first pass we simply gather the count of each item. Items that satisfy the minimum support inserted into large itemsets table C_1 that takes form(it em, item count). Then transaction data that match large itemsets stored in R_1.

In other passes for example pass k, we first generate all lexicographically ordered candidate itemsets of length k into table RTMP_k by joining k-1 length transaction data. Then we generate the count for those itemsets that meet minimum support and included them into large itemset table C_k. Finally transaction data R_k of length k generated by matching items in candidate itemset table RTMP_k with items in large itemsets.

Original SETM algorithm assumes execution using sort-merge join. Inside database server on our system, relational joins are executed using hash joins and tables are partitioned over nodes by hashing. As the result, parallelization efficiency is much improved. This approach is very effective for large scale data mining.

Inside execution plan for this query, join to generate candidate itemsets is executed at each node independently. And then after counting itemsets locally, nodes exchange the local counts by applying hash function on the itemsets in order to determine overall support count of each itemset. Another data exchange occurs when large itemsets are distributed to every nodes. Finally each node independently execute join again to create the transaction data.

3 Performance Evaluation

3.1 Parallel Execution Environment

The experiment is conducted on a PC cluster developed at Institute of Industrial Science, The University of Tokyo. This pilot system consists of one hundred commodity PCs connected by ATM network named NEDO-100. We have also developed DBKernel database server for query processing on this system. Each PC has Intel Pentium Pro 200MHz CPU, 4.3GB SCSI hard disk and 64 MB RAM.

The performance evaluation using TPC-D benchmark on 100 nodes cluster is reported[7]. The results showed it can achieve significantly higher performance especially for join intensive query such as query 9 compared to the current commercially available high end systems.

3.2 Dataset

We use synthetic transaction data generated with program described in Apriori algorithm paper[2] for experiment. The parameters used are : number of transactions 200000, average transaction length 10 and number of items 2000. Transaction data is partitioned uniformly correspond to transaction ID among processing nodes' local hard disk.

3.3 Results

The execution times for several minimum support is shown in figure 2(left). The result is surprisingly well compared even with directly coded Apriori-based C program on single processing node. On average, we can achieve the same level of execution time by parallelizing SQL based mining with around 4 processing nodes. The speedup ratio shown in figure 2(right) is also reasonably good, although the speedup seems to be saturated as the number of processing nodes increased. As the size of the dataset asssigned to each node is getting smaller, processing overhead and also synchronizing cost that depends on the number of nodes cancel the gain.

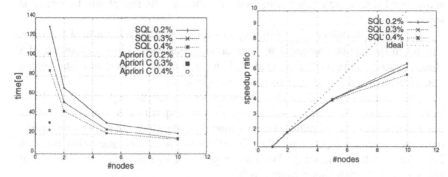

Fig. 2. Execution time(left) Speedup ratio(right)

Figure 3(left) shows the time percentage for each pass when the minimum support is 0.5%. Eight passes are necessary to process entire transaction database. It is well known that in most cases the second pass generates huge amount of candidate itemsets thus it is the most time consuming phase. Figure 3(right) shows the speedup ratio for each pass. The later passes, the smaller candidate itemsets. Thus non-negligible parallelization overhead become dominant especially in passes later than five. Depending on the size of candidate itemsets, we could change the degree of parallelization. That is, we should reduce the number of nodes on later passes. Such extensions will need further investigations.

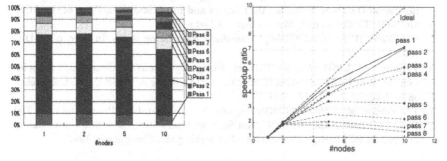

Fig.3. Pass analysis (minimum support 5%). Contribution of each pass in execution time(left) Speedup ratio of each pass(right)

4 Summary and Conclusion

In this paper, we have compared the parallel implementation of SQL based association rule mining with the directly coded C implementation. Since SQL is popular and it has already sophisticated optimizer, we believed that parallel SQL system could achieve reasonably sufficient performance.

Through real implementation, we have confirmed that parallization using 4 processing nodes for association rule mining can beat the performance of directly coded C implementation. We do not have to buy or write special data mining application codes, SQL query for association rule mining is extremely easy to implement. It is also very flexible, we have extended the SQL query to handle generalized association rule mining with taxonomy. The report will be available soon.

At present, parallel SQL is running on expensive massively parallel machines but not in the future. Instead it will run on inexpensive PC cluster system or WS cluster system. Thus we believe that SQL implementation based on sophisticated optimization would be one of reasonable approaches.

There remains lots of further investigations. Current SQL query could be more optimized. In addition we plan to do large experiments. Since our system has 100 nodes, we could handle larger transaction database. In such experiments, data skew become a problem. Skew handling is one of the interesting research issue for parallel processing. We have reported some mining algorithms that effectively deal with this problem in [6].

References

1. R. Agrawal, T. Imielinski, A. Swami. Mining Association Rules between Sets of Items in Large Databases. In Proc. of the ACM SIGMOD Conference on Management of Data, 1993.
2. R. Agrawal, R. Srikant. Fast Algorithms for Mining Association Rules. In Proc. of the VLDB Conference, 1994.
3. M. Houtsma, A. Swami. Set- oriented Mining of Association Rules. In Proc. of International Conference on Data Engineering, 1995.
4. S. Sarawagi, S. Thomas, R. Agrawal. Integrating Association Rule Mining with Relational Database Systems: Alternatives and Implications. In Proc. of the ACM SIGMOD Conference on Management of Data, 1998.
5. R. Srikant, R. Agrawal. Mining Generalized Association Rules. In Proc. of VLDB, 1995.
6. T. Shintani, M. Kitsuregawa. Parallel Mining Algorithms for Generalized Association Rules with Classification Hierarchy. In Proc. of the ACM SIGMOD Conference on Management of Data, 1998.
7. T. Tamura, M. Oguchi, M. Kitsuregawa. Parallel Database Processing on a 100 Node PC Cluster: Cases for Decision Support Query Processing and Data Mining. In Proc. of SC97: High Performance Networking and Computing, 1997.

H-Rule Mining in Heterogeneous Databases

Yuping Yang and Mukesh Singhal

Department of Computer and Information Science
The Ohio State University
Columbus, OH 43210
{yangy,singhal}@cis.ohio-state.edu

Abstract. We examined the problem of applying association rules in a heterogeneous database. Due to heterogeneity, we have to generalize the notion of association rule to define a new heterogeneous association rule (h-rule) which denotes data association between various types of data in different subsystems of a heterogeneous and multimedia database, such as music pieces vs. photo pictures, etc. Boolean association rule and quantitative association rule are special cases of h-rule. H-rule integrates previously defined rule concepts and expands association rule mining from single dataset mining to database mining.

1 Introduction

The essence of association rule mining problem is to find interesting data correlations between data items in different attributes. Boolean association rule (BAR) [6] is data association between pairs of data (or vector) values. Quantitative association rule [6] (QAR) and distance based association rule [7] are more general and represent set-oriented associations between data. However, they are still restricted to association between data in different attributes of a single tabular dataset. In a heterogeneous and multimedia database (HMD), the interest to find data associations should not be restricted to mining rules within a single relation. We propose a new and more general form of association rule, h-rule, to suit the knowledge discovery task in an HMD.

Section 2 defines heterogeneous association rule (h-rule). Sect. 3 shows that h-rule is a generalization of the BAR and QAR. Finally, Sect. 4 concludes the paper.

2 Heterogeneous Association Rules

The concept of "related" entries is simple in a relation: two entries are related if they are in the same tuple. However, in an HMD, in general, only pointers or IDs can exist as (logical and/or physical) connections between entities of different relations or data files [4, 5, 8]. This leads to the following definition:

Dfn 2.1: Related entries in an HMD Let d_1 be an entry in a relation (or object cluster) D_1, d_2 be an entry in another relation (or object cluster) D_2. D_1 and D_2 can be the same, or different relations (object clusters). d_1 and d_2 are related if one of the following is true:

- If both D_1 and D_2 are relations, then either d_1 and d_2 are in the same tuple of the same relation, or d_1 and d_2 are on tuples t_1 and t_2, respectively, and t_1 and t_2 are joinable.
- If at least one of D_1 and D_2 is an object cluster, a and b are connected by a (physical, logical, ID, etc) pointer.

Note the subtle difference between a value and an entry. A *value* is a pattern, such as a text string, a number, an image pattern, etc. An *entry* is a cell that can hold a value, or values, such as a relational table entry.

In the case of a single relation, the support of an association rule is simply the number of tuples that contain both antecedent and consequent. However, the notion "support" actually has two separate meanings, i.e., the data coupling strength and the usefulness of data implication. We call the first one the association support and the second one the implication support. Formally, we have:

Dfn 2.2: Heterogeneous Association Rule (h-rule) Let A_X be a set of attributes in a subsystem D_1 and A_Y be a set of attributes in a subsystem D_2. If $D_1 = D_2$, then condition $A_X \cap A_Y = \emptyset$ is added.

A heterogeneous association rule (h-rule) is a data association denoted as $X \Rightarrow^h Y$, where X is a value (if A_X is a set, then X is a vector), or a set of values (vectors) in A_X and Y is a value (if A_Y is a set, then Y is a vector), or a set of values (vectors) in A_Y.

- The association support of the rule is the number of pairs (d_1, d_2) in $D_1 \times D_2$, where d_1 is an entry in D_1 that contains a value in X and d_2 is an entry in D_2 that contains a value in Y; d_1 and d_2 are related. We call d_1 and d_2 the support nodes of the h-rule.
- The implication support of the rule is the number of entries d_2 in D_2 such that the pair (d_1, d_2) exists in $D_1 \times D_2$, and d_1 and d_2 are related support nodes.
- The association confidence of the rule is the ratio of the number of pairs (d_1, d_2) (related support nodes) in $D_1 \times D_2$ to the number of entries d (contains value in X) in D_1.
- The implication confidence of the rule is the ratio of the number of support nodes in D_2 to the number of entries d (contain values in X) in D_1.

s_1, s_2, c_1, and c_2 are related quantities as shown in Theorem 1.

Theorem 1. For a h-rule $X \Rightarrow^h Y$, its association support s_1, implication support s_2, association confidence c_1, and implication confidence c_2 satisfy $s_1/c_1 = s_2/c_2$.

Proof. Let n be the total of entires in D_1 contains values in X. Then, $c_1 = s_1/n$ and $c_2 = s_2/n$. From these equalities we obtain $n = s_1/c_1$ and $n = s_2/c_2$. Hence $s_1/c_1 = s_2/c_2$.

As an example of the supports and confidences in h-rules, suppose two relations R_1 and R_2 are joinable and these two relations have many-to-many relationship. Also suppose $a_i \in R_1$, $b_j \in R_2$, $i \in \{1,2,3\}$, $j \in \{1,2\}$, $(a_i, b_j) \in R_1 \bowtie R_2$ (join of R_1 and R_2), and $| (a_i, b_j) | = 6$. If $\{a_1, a_2, a_3\} \Rightarrow \{b_1, b_2\}$ is a h-rule, then its association support is 6, implication support is 2, association confidence is $6/3 = 2$, and implication confidence is $2/3 = 0.67$. Note that a confidence is no longer a measure of "probability" and may not be less than 1.

3 Integration of Association Rule Concepts

H-rules in a single relation are actually BARs or QARs. This theoretical integration of various rule concepts lays the foundation for a uniform association rule mining operation across the entire HMD. In the following, Dfn 3.3 is adopted from [6] and Dfn 3.1 is the definition of BAR [2] re-stated using the similar formal description as in Dfn 3.3.

Dfn 3.1: Boolean Association Rule (BAR) Let $L = \{i_1, i_2, ..., i_m\}$ be a set of literals, called attributes. Let P denote a set of values (text strings, numbers, etc.). For any $A \subseteq L \times P$, attribute(A) denotes the set $\{x \mid < x, v > \in A\}$. If restriction is added that each attribute occurs at most once in A, then A is called a record. Let D be a set of records.

A record R is said to support $X (\subseteq L \times P)$, if attribute($R \cap X$) = attribute(X).

A BAR $X \Rightarrow Y$ in D, where $X, Y \subseteq L \times P$, attribute($X$) $\cap$ attribute(Y) = $\emptyset$, is an implication from X to Y in set D. The rule has support s if s records in D support $X \cup Y$. The rule has confidence $c\%$ if $c\%$ of the records that support X also support Y.

Dfn 3.2: Tuple Pattern R is a relational schema. r is a relation under the schema R. $A_X \subseteq R$. T is called a tuple pattern in $r[A_X]$ means that if r is projected to A_X and all duplicates are eliminated, then $r[A_X]$ has a unique tuple T.

Theorem 2. R is a relational schema. r is a relation under the schema R. $A_X, A_Y \subseteq R$. $A_X \cap A_Y = \emptyset$. X is a tuple pattern in $r[A_X]$ and Y is a tuple pattern in $r[A_Y]$.

A h-rule $X \Rightarrow^h Y$ in r is the same as a BAR $X \Rightarrow Y$ [6]. Also, the association support s_1 and the implication support s_2 of the h-rule are equal to the support of the BAR; the association confidence c_1 and the implication confidence of the h-rule are the same as the confidence of the BAR.

Proof. Two entries are related in r means that they are in the same tuple. By Dfn 2.2, association support of the h-rule should be equal to the implication support of the h-rule. By theorem 1, association confidence of the h-rule is equal to the implication confidence of the h-rule.

Referring to Dfn 3.1, we can take $R = L$, $r = D$, $A_X = attribute(X)$, $A_Y = attribute(Y)$, a tuple in r is a record R in D, a value X in the antecedent of the h-rule is the antecedent value $X \in L \times P$ in BAR, and a value Y in the consequent of the h-rule is the consequent value $Y \in L \times P$ in BAR. So, in this case a h-rule is a BAR.

Dfn 3.3: Quantitative Association Rule (QAR) Let $L = \{i_1, i_2, ..., i_m\}$ be a set of literals, called attributes. Let P denote the set of positive integers. Let L_v denote the set $L \times P$.

Let L_R denote the set $\{< x, l, u > \in L \times P \times P \mid l \leq u$, if x is quantitative; $l = u$, if x is categorical$\}$. For any $X \subseteq L_R$, attribute(X) denotes the set $\{x \mid < x, l, u > \in X\}$.

Let D be a set of records R, where each $R \subseteq L_v$. Each attribute occurs at most once in a record.

A record R is said to support $X(\subseteq L_R)$, if $\forall < x, l, u > \in X (\exists < x, q > \in R$ such that $l \leq q \leq u)$.

A QAR $X \Rightarrow Y$, where $X, Y \subseteq L_R$, attribute$(X) \cap$ attribute$(Y) = \emptyset$, is an implication from X to Y in set D. The rule has support s if s records in D support $X \cup Y$. The rule has confidence $c\%$ if $c\%$ of the records that support X also support Y.

The intuition of this definition is that for quantitative data, the antecedent X and the consequent Y in a QAR are high dimensional "cubes". The meaning of "a record R supports X" is that for each interval $< x, l, u >$ in X, R has at least one $< x, v >$ which is contained in $< x, l, u >$. In reality, the antecedent and the consequent of the rule do not have to be in "cubic" shape. However, when h-rules are defined within a single relation and this "cubic" shape restriction is added, the h-rules are precisely QARs.

Dfn 3.4: Interval Pattern S is a relational schema. r is a relation under S. $A_X \subseteq S$. T is a tuple under A_X that each of its entry is an interval. T is called an interval pattern in $r[A_X]$ means that if r is projected to A_X and all duplicates are eliminated, then T contains at least one tuple in $r[A_X]$, i.e., at least one tuple t in $r[A_X]$ that each entry of t is contained in the interval of T at the same attribute.

Theorem 3. *S is a relational schema. r is a relation under S. $A_X, A_Y \subseteq S$. $A_X \cap A_Y = \emptyset$. X is an interval pattern in $r[A_X]$ and Y is an interval pattern in $r[A_Y]$.*

An h-rule $X \Rightarrow^h Y$ in r is the same as a QAR $X \Rightarrow Y$. Also, the association support s_1 and the implication support s_2 of the h-rule are equal to the support of the QAR; the association confidence c_1 and the implication confidence of the h-rule are the same as the confidence of the QAR.

Proof. In the definition of the h-rule, two relational table entries are related in r means that they are in the same tuple. By Dfn 2.2, association support of the h-rule should be equal to the implication support of the h-rule. By theorem 1, association confidence of the h-rule is equal to the implication confidence of the h-rule.

Referring to Dfn 3.2, we can take $S = L$, $r = D$, $A_X = attribute(X)$, $A_Y = attribute(Y)$, a tuple in r is a record R in D, a set X of values in the antecedent of the h-rule is the antecedent set $X \subseteq L \times P$ in QAR, and a set Y of values in the consequent of the h-rule is the consequent set $Y \subseteq L \times P$ in QAR. So, in this case, a h-rule is a QAR.

4 Summary Remarks

Mining association rules across an entire database, i.e., database mining, has a much stronger impact to business operations than simple dataset mining [1-3, 6, 7]. H-rule generalizes association rule mining and includes BARs and QARs as its special cases. This unifies data mining and database mining into a common theoretical framework and also allows many techniques developed in the data mining, such as the Apriori algorithm, to be applied in database mining.

Database mining is a very complex issue. By defining h-rule, we have only built a base for exploring this complex issue. Considerable amount of research need to be done for defining various special forms of h-rules in various special database structures, for designing new algorithms and strategies to mine h-rules, for designing new data structures to store and facilitate the search of mined h-rules, and for investigating strategies to use h-rule mining to best benefit business operations.

References

1. Piatetsky-Shapiro, G.: Discovery, Analysis, and Presentation of Strong Rules. In Knowledge Discovery in Databases. Editors G. P.-Shapiro and W. J. Frawley, AAAI Press/MIT Press, (1991) 229-238.
2. Agrawal, R., Imielinksi, T., Swami, A. Mining Association Rules between Sets of Items in Large Databases. In Proc. 1993 SIGMOD Conf., 207-216
3. Agrawal, R., Srikant, R.: Fast Algorithm for Mining Association Rules. In Proc. 20th VLDB (1994) 478-499.
4. Papakonstantinou, Y., Garcia-Molina, H., Widom, J.: Object Exchange Across Heterogeneous Information Sources. In Proc. 11th Int'l Conf. on Data Engineering, IEEE, (1995) 251-270.
5. Papakonstantinou, Y., Abiteboul, S., Garcia-Molina, H.: Object Fusion in Mediator Systems. In Proc. 22nd VLDB (1996) 413-424.
6. Srikant, R., Agrawal, R.: Mining Quantitative Association Rules in Large Relational Tables". In Proc. 1996 ACM-SIGMOD Conf., 1-12.
7. Miller, R. J., Yang, Y.: Association Rules over Interval Data. In Proc. 1997 ACM-SIGMOD Conf., 452-461.
8. Roth, M. T., Schwarz, P.: Don't Scrap It, Wrap It! A Wrapper Architecture for Legacy Data Sources. In Proc. of 23rd VLDB (1997) 266-275.

An Improved Definition of Multidimensional Inter-transaction Association Rule*

Aoying Zhou, Shuigeng Zhou, Wen Jin,   and Zengping Tian

Computer Science Department, Fudan University, 220 Handan Road, 200433,
Shanghai, China
{ayzhou, 970218, 970220, zptian}@fudan.edu.cn

Abstract. Association rule is an important contribution to the data
mining field from the database research community, and its mining has
become a promising research topic. Traditional association rule is limited to intra-transaction mining. Recently the concept of multidimensional inter-transaction association rule (MDITAR) is proposed by H.J.
Lu. Based on analysis of inadequencies of Lu's definition, this paper
introduces a modified and extended definition of MDITAR, which consequently makes MDITAR more general, practical and reasonable.
Keywords: Multidimensional Transaction Database, Data Mining, Multidimensional Inter-transaction Association Rule (MDITAR), Definition.

1 Introduction

Mining association rules in large databases is one of the top problems in the
data mining field, which has attracted great attention of the database research
community. First introduced by R. Argrawal *et al* for market basket analysis
[1], association rules imply the association among different items bought by customers. Nowadys association rules mining is no longer limited to transaction
databases, it is also applied to relational databases, spatial databases and multimedia databases *etc* [2], [3], [4]. However, the semantic of traditional association
rule introduced by R. Argrawal has not been changed, *i.e*, association rules imply
associations among attribute items within the same data record. Recently H.J.Lu
et al propose the multidimensional inter-transaction association rule (MDITAR)
while mining stock transaction data[5]. In Comparison with traditional association rules, MDITAR differs in two aspects:
1. It implyes associations among items within different transaction records;
2. It deals with data records having dimensional attributes.

Obviously, MDITAR is more general than traditional association rule both
semantically and formally, which makes the traditional association rule one special case of MDITAR. However, there are some limitations of the MDITAR
definition given by H.J.Lu.

---

* This work was supported by the National Natural Science Foundation of China and
the National Doctoral Subject Foundation of China.

In this paper, we first analyze the inadequencies of Lu's definition, then a modified and extended definition of MADITAR is introduced, which is more general, practicable and reasonable. The remaining of this paper is organized as follows. Section 2 presents an analysis of Lu's MDITAR definition, then in Section 3 our new definition of MDITAR is introduced. Section 4 is the conclusion remarks.

2 Inadequencies of Lu's definition of MDITAR

There are 3 major limitations in the definition of MDITAR given by Lu.

2.1 Only quantitative attributes are considered

According to Lu's definition of MDITAR, for an arbitrary transaction record $T_i = (d_1, d_2, \ldots, d_n, E_i), d_1, d_2, \ldots, d_n$ are treated as equal interval values in the N–dimensional attribute space. In such a case, relationship of transaction records can be represented by relative differences in dimensional attribute values. However, things in the real-life world are not always in such a way. For example, if we want to mine the commodity wholesale market data to predict price trends, then 2 dimensional attributes will be used, one is the trading *time*, another is the locations of the wholesale markets, let's say *cities*. So there is a dimensional attribute pair(*city*, *time*) for each transaction record, where the *city* attribute is categorical, can not be set with concrete quantitative values and involved in arithmetic operation. Therefore, while defining MDITAR, different types of dimensional attributes should be considered to make it more general and appliable.

2.2 Association rule is formulated too strictly

In [5], a MDITAR $X \Rightarrow Y$ (X, Y and $X \cup Y$ are frequent item-sets) is strictly formulated by the relative address $E\text{-}ADDR(X \cup Y)$. Such a rigid relative address constraint on MDITAR very possibly leads to failure of mining some MDITARs which are available if with a less strict constraint. For example, providing the mining goals are: $a(0) \Rightarrow b(1)$, $a(0) \Rightarrow b(2)$, and $a(0) \Rightarrow b(4)$. For a predefined *support* threshold, it's very possibly that we can not find the frequent event sets $\{a(0), b(1)\}$, $\{a(0), b(2)\}$ and $\{a(0), b(4)\}$. However, if we set the formal constraint a little loose, for example, put the mining goal as $a(0) \Rightarrow b(n)$ ($n \leq 4$), then it's greatly possible that we will discover such rules. Furthermore, if the mining goal is set to $a(n1) \Rightarrow b(n2)(\mid n1 - n2 \mid \leq 4)$, the success possibility of mining this rule is greater than that of the previous cases. On the other hand, relative address $E\text{-}ADDR$ is not suitable for dealing with categorical attributes. Consequently, in order to enhance the practicability of MDITARs, a more flexible formal constraint of MDITAR must be introduced.

2.3 The *support* and *confidence* definitions are not reasonable enough

Based on the *support* and *confidence* definitions of MDITAR in [5], the following results can be inferred.

1. *Support* $\leq$ *confidence*;

2. The implication of support for different frequent item sets or event sets is not consistent.

Here gives an example for demonstration. Supposed there is a transaction database $TD = \{T_1(0,a), T_2(3,b), T_3(3,c)\}$. Based on Lu's definintion, we can get *support* of $\{a(0), c(3)\}$ is 100%, and *support* of $\{a(0)\}$ is 33%. This is a very strange result for $\{a(0), c(3)\}$ and $\{a(0)\}$ all occur only one time in the database, and the later is a subset of the former, but their *support* is quite different. The cause lies in the definition of *support*. With such a *support* definition, the foundation of the Apriori algorithm can no longer be guaranteed. Nevertheless, [5] still applies an extended Apriori algorithm to mine one-dimensional stock data. Therefore, new definitions for *support* and *confidence* of MDITAR are necessary in order to eliminate the unreasonable aspect in the existing definition of MDITAR.

3 An improved definition of MDITAR

Based on above analysis of the inadequencies of the MDITAR definition, here we propose a new definition of MDITAR for strengthening its generality, practicability and reasonability. Modification and extension focuses on the following 3 aspects:

1. Introduce categorical attributes into MDITAR definition;

2. Adopt *association constraint mode* to formulate MDITAR;

3. Define new *support* and *confidence* formula.

Definition 1. Let $E = \{e_1, e_2, \ldots, e_u\}$ be literals set or events set, $\{C_1, C_2, \ldots, C_k, D_1, D_2, \ldots, D_l\}$ be attributes set, and $l + k = N$. A transaction database consists of a series of transaction records$(c_1, c_2, \ldots, c_k, d_1, d_2, \ldots, d_l, E_i)$, where $\forall i(1 \leq i \leq k)(c_i \in DOM(C_i))$, $\forall j(1 \leq j \leq l)(d_j \in DOM(D_j))$, $DOM(C_i)$ and $DOM(D_j)$ are domains of C_i and D_j respectively, and $E_i \in E$. $C_i(1 \leq i \leq k)$ is categorical attribute and $D_j(1 \leq j \leq l)$ is quantitative attribute with an infinite domain. A transaction database with N attributes is called N-dimensional transaction database, or multidimensional transaction database (for $N \geq 2$).

Here we introduce two types of attributes, C type is categorical attribute, and D type is quantitative attribute with an infinite domain. Just as in [5], we take D type attribute value as equal interval in its domain. In fact, when all attributes in database are categorical, MDITAR can also be treated as traditional association rule.

Definition 2. For any transaction record T_i or event e_i in a transaction record, correspondingly there is a set of attribute values $(c_{1i}, c_{2i}, \ldots, c_{ki}, d_{1i}, d_{2i}, \ldots, d_{li})$, which is called *status* of the transaction record T_i or event e_i, and abbreviated as s.

Definition 3. For any transaction set $\{T_1, T_2, \ldots, T_k\}$ or event set $\{e_1, e_2, \ldots, e_k\}$, there is a set of *status* $\{s_1, s_2, \ldots, s_k\}$ in which certain relationship must exist among all elements of the *status* set. This kind of relationship can be seen as constraint on the transaction set or event set. We define such a relationship as *status constraint mode* of the transaction set $\{T_1, T_2, \ldots, T_k\}$ or event set $\{e_1, e_2, \ldots, e_k\}$, and denote it by *SCM*.

Supposes there is a 2-dimension transaction database with attributes A_1 and A_2 which are C type and D type attributes respectively. Now there is a event set $e = \{a("A", 2), b("B", 4), and\, c("C", 5)\}$. Giving 3 *SCMs* as follows.
1. $a.A_1 = "A", b.A_1 = "B", c.A_1 = "C", b.A_2 - a.A_2 = 2, c.A_2 - b.A_2 = 1$;
2. $a.A_1 = "A", b.A_1 = "B", c.A_1 = "C", b.A_2 - a.A_2 \leq 3, c.A_2 - b.A_2 \leq 3$;
3. $max(a.A_2, b.A_2, c.A_2) - min(a.A_2, b.A_2, c.A_2) \leq 5$

Obviously, the event set e conforms with all the 3 *SCMs*. However, the constraint strength of the 3 *SCMs* is different. The advantage of *SCM* over *E-ADDR* is its flexibility and capability of coping with categorical attributes.

Definition 4. Given an event set $e = \{e_1, e_2, \ldots, e_k\}$ and its *SCM*, and a transaction set $T = \{T_1, T_2, \ldots, T_l\}$. If there is a minimum subset T_{min} of T, $T_{min} = \{T_{i1}, T_{i2}, \ldots, T_{ij}\}(1 \leq ij \leq l)$ that satisfies
1. for every event e_i in e, correspondingly there is a transaction T_j in T_{min} such that $e_i \in T_j.E_j$;
2. T_{min} conforms with *SCM* in the same way as e does, then we say T contains e in term of *SCM*, and T_{min} is one of T's minimum subset containing e.

Definition 5. If a set of events $e = \{e_1, e_2, \ldots, e_k\}$ is associative at certain frequency in the database, then we call e's *SCM* as *association-constraint mode*, and denote it by *ACM*.

Definition 6. Supposes there is a N-dimensional transaction database D_N from which MDITARs are mined. The minimum of *support* and *confidence* are predifined as sup_{min} and cof_{min} respectively. Then N-dimensional inter-transaction association rule $X \Rightarrow Y$ can be represented by a quadruple (X, Y, ACM, sup, cof), where
1. X, Y and $X \cup Y$ are frequent event-sets conforming with *association constraint mode ACM*. and $X \cap Y = \Phi$;
2. *sup* and *cof* are *support* and *confidence* of $X \cup Y$, and

$$sup = |X \cup Y| / |D_N| \geq sup_{min} \qquad (1)$$
$$cof = sup(X \cup Y)/sup(X) \geq cof_{min} \qquad (2)$$

Here $|D_N|$ is the cardinality of N-dimensional transaction database D_N, and $|X \cup Y|$ is the total number of minimum subsets containing $X \cup Y$ in D_N.

Clearly, the above definitions of *support* and *confidence* is similar to that of traditional association rule, which avoids the problems coming with Lu's definitions. And the introduction of *association constraint mode* makes MDITARs mining more flexible and practicable. The miner can choose freely a proper *ACM* according to his interest.

Based on definition 6, a lemma about MDITAR can be obtained, which forms the basis of mining MDITAR with A-priori algorithm.

Lemma 7. *If N-dimensional event-set $e = \{e_1, e_2, \ldots, e_k\}$ which conforms with ACM is a frequent event-set in the N-dimensional transaction database D_N, then any subset of e conforming with the same ACM is also frequent event-set in D_N.*

4   Conclusions

MDITAR is a generalization and extension form of traditional association rule. Meanwhile it's also a new challenge to the data mining community. This paper gives a modified and extended definition of MDITAR on the basis of the original definition introduced by Lu[5]. The improved definition makes MDITAR more general, practicable and reasonable than the old one. Future work will focus on developing efficient and effective mining algorithm for MDITARs.

References

1. R. Agrawal, T. Imielinski, and A. Swami. Mining Association Rules between Sets of Items in Large Databases. In: Proc. of the ACM SIGMOD Conference on Management of Data. Washington, D. C., May 1993.
2. Y. Fu and J. Han. Meta-rule-guided mining of association rules in relational databases. In Proc. 1st Int'l Workshop on Integration of Knowledge Discovery with Deductive and Object-Oriented Databases (KDOOD'95), pages 39-46, Singapore, Dec.1995.
3. K. Koperski and J. Han. Discovery of Spatial Association Rules in Geographic Information Databases. In Advances in Spatial Databases, Proceedings of 4th Symposium, SSD'95. (Aug.6-9, Portland, Maine). Springer-Verlag, Berlin, 1995, pp.47-66.
4. O.R.Za"iane, et al. Multimedia-miner: A system prototype for multimedia data mining. In Proc. 1998 ACM-SIGMOD Conf. On Management of Data, 581-583, Seattle, Washington, June 1998.
5. H. Lu, J. Han, and L. Feng. Stock Movement and N-Dimensional Inter- Transaction Association Rules. Proc. of 1998 SIGMOD'96 Workshop on Research Issues on Data Mining and Knowledge Discovery (DMKD'98), Seattle, Washington, June 1998.

Incremental Discovering Association Rules: A Concept Lattice Approach

Keyun Hu[1], Yuchang Lu[2] and Chunyi Shi[3]

Computer Science Deptartment, Tsinghua university,
Beijing 100084, P.R.China
[1]hky@s1000e.cs.tsinghua.edu.cn   {[2]lyc, [3]scy}@mail.tsinghua.edu.cn

Abstract Concept lattice is an efficient tool for data analysis. Mining association rules is a important subfield of data mining. In this paper we investigate the ability of concept lattice on associate rules and present an efficient algorithm which generate the large itemsets incrementally on the basis of Godin's work.

1 Introduction

Concept hierarchy has been shown to have many advantages in the field of knowledge discovery from large databases. It is convenient to model dependence and causality, and provides a vivid and concise account of the relations between the variables in the universe of discourse. Concept hierarchy is not necessarily a tree structure. Wille et al. propose to build corresponding concept lattice from binary relations [1, 2, 3]. This kind of special lattice and the corresponding Hasse diagram represent a concept hierarchy. Concept lattice reflects entity-attribute relationships between objects. In some practical applications such as information management and knowledge discovery, concept lattice has gained good results [1, 4]. R.Missaoui et al present algorithms for extracting rules from concept lattice [5], R.Godin et al propose a method to build concept lattice and the corresponding Hasse diagram incrementally and compare it with other concept lattice constructing methods [1].

Discovering association rules among items in large databases is recognized as an important database mining problem. The problem was introduced in [7] for sale transaction databases. The problem can be formally described as following [6].

Let I = {i_1, i_2,..., i_m} be a set of literals, called items. Let D be a set of transactions, where each transaction T is a set of items such that T⊆I. The quantities of items bought are not considered. Each transaction is assigned an identifier, called TID. Let X be a set of items, A transaction T is said to contain X if and only if X⊆T. An association rule is an expression of the form X⇒Y, where X≠∅, Y⊂I and X∩Y= ∅. The rule holds with confidence c if c% of transactions in D that contain X also contain Y. The rule has support s in D if s% of D contain X∪Y.

The problem of generating association rules is usually decomposed into two subproblems. We firstly generate all itemsets whose support exceeds the minimum support s, then each above itemset we generate association rules whose confidence is not less than the minimum confidence c. It's noted that the overall performance of mining association rules is determined by the first subproblem.

In this paper we address the first subproblem using concept lattice based on Godin's work [1]. We argue that our method has several advantages. Firstly, our method takes only one pass over the database; secondly, it is incremental; finally, it is efficient.

2 Basic Notions of Concept Lattice

In this section we recall necessary basic notions of concept lattice briefly, the detail description about concept lattice can be found in [1, 2, 3].

Suppose given the context (O, D, R) describing a set O of objects, a set D of descriptors and a binary relation R, there is a unique corresponding lattice structure, which is known as *concept lattice*. Each node in lattice L is a couple, noted (X', X), where $X' \in P(O)$ is called *extension* of the concept, $X \in P(D)$ is called *intension* of concept. Each couple must be complete with respect to R. A couple (X', X)$\in P(O) \times P(D)$ is complete with respect to relation R, if and only if the following properties are satisfied:

(1) $X' = \{x' \in O \mid \forall x \in X, xRx'\}$;

(2) $X = \{x \in D \mid \forall x' \in X', xRx'\}$.

Note that only maximal extended couple can appear in concept lattice.

A partial order relation can be built on all concept lattice nodes. Given $H_1 = (X', X)$ and $H_2 = (Y', Y)$, therefore $H_1 < H_2 \Leftrightarrow X \subset Y$, and the precedent order means H_1 is parent of H_2 or direct generalization in the lattice. In fact, there is a dual relationship between X' and X in the lattice. i.e., $X \subset Y \Leftrightarrow Y' \subset X'$, and therefore $H_1 < H_2 \Leftrightarrow Y' \subset X'$. So, concept lattice is two lattices connected together in essence. The Hasse diagram of the lattice can be generated by use of the partial order relation. if $H_1 < H_2$ and there is no other elements such that $H_1 < H_3 < H_2$, there is an edge from H_1 to H_2. It reveals the generalization/specialization relationship between the concepts and could be used as an efficient tool for data analysis and knowledge acquisition.

We would observe that the relationship between item sets can be well modelled by concept lattice. We look O as a set of TIDs, D as a set of items, R as every element of O having the same D. In fact, in our case the content of O doesn't matter. What matters is the cardinal of O. For efficiency's sake we use cardinal of O instead. Thus, a node in lattice is denoted by (C, X), where C is the cardinal of transaction set, X is their common item set.

Proposition 1 For every node(C, X) if C is bigger than threshold t, then X is one of the large item set we look for.

Because every node of the concept lattice is maximally extended, above proposition is obvious.

Now, we'll address the problem of generating lattice, that is, generating the large item sets incrementally.

3 Using Concept Lattice to generate large item sets

Some algorithms have been proposed for generating the concept lattice from a binary relation. R.Godin et al proposed an incremental concept formation algorithm based on Galois lattice [1]. Below, we'll present an improved version, and apply it to incremental large item set generation.

Suppose given a concept lattice L and a new transaction T to be inserted into the lattice. The new lattice after the insertion of T is L'. We say that there are three kinds of node in the new lattice L'. One kind remains intact, One kind is modified and One kind is new node, which is generated by the interaction of the inserted node and nodes in L. Then the questions which node should be modified and when should a new node be generated?

Proposition 2 If node H=(N, T) is to be inserted into lattice L, for each node N=(C, X) in L, if $X \subseteq T$, N is updated to N=(C+1, X).

It is easy to understand if we consider that a couple of the lattice must be maximal extended. Since T includes X', the number of Transactions including X' must be increased by 1.

Proposition 3 if (C, X) = inf {(D, Y) $\in$ L| X=Y$\cap$T)} and there is no node (E, X)$\in$L, then a new pair (C=D+1, X=Y$\cap$T) should be generated. (D, Y) is the child of the new node, called generator of new node.

The proposition says when a node's intension and new node's intersection result in a new set which doesn't exists in the lattice, and the node is the minimal one, a new node should be generated.

In addition, the edge in new lattice L' must be updated. The generator of new node is always a child of the new node, and the generator's original parent must be modified. New node may have another child, which should be another new node. The children and parents of intact nodes would not change. The key point is the search for parent nodes of new generated node that can help modify the edges. The proposition below embodies basic ideas of improvement we propose to the algorithm in [1].

Proposition 4 The parent of new node (C, X) is a new node or modified node (D, Y) such that (D, Y)= Sup{(D, Y)$\in$L'|Y$\subseteq$X}.

We know the parent of new node (C, X) must satisfy Y$\subseteq$X according to the property of concept lattice. It also should be the minimal one.

Now we introduce the algorithm. The lattice is initialized by elements (0, Sup(L)). Sup(L) includes all the items in the transaction database while Inf(L) includes all transactions. Sup(L) and Inf(L) stand for lowest upper bound and greatest lower bound of the lattice respectively. Note that Inf(L) is not explicitly given in the algorithm, as it is only for theoretical interestg.

Incremental concept and large item set generation algorithm
Input: Lattice L and item set Σ, transaction to be added X, threshold t
Output: Updated lattice L' and rule set Σ
BEGIN
    Mark$\leftarrow\varnothing$ /* Initialize set Mark */
    FOR each element H in lattice in ascending $\| Y(H) \|$ order **DO**
        /*Y(H) stands for intension of H**/

```
IF Y(H)⊆X THEN    /* modified node */
    Add C(H) by 1;
    IF C(H) >t
        IF there is no P in Σ such that X(P)=X(H)
            Add H to Σ
        ELSE
            Add C(P) by 1
        ENDIF
    ENDIF
    Add H to Mark
    IF Y(H)=X THEN exit FOR ENDIF
ELSE
    int←Y(H)∩X
    IF no such H_k∈Mark that Y(H_k)=int THEN        /* H is generator */
        Create new node N=(C(H)+1, int) and add it to Mark
        IF C(H)+1 >t   add N to Σ
        Add edge H←N
        FOR each node M of ancestor of H DO
            /* Search the parent node for new node and modify edges */
            IF there is M∈Mark such that Y(M)⊂int THEN /* M is parent node
of N */
                Add edge N←M
                IF M is parent of H THEN delete edge H←M ENDIF
                exit FOR
            ENDIF
        ENDFOR
        IF int=Y THEN exit FOR ENDIF
    ENDIF
ENDIF
ENDFOR
END
```

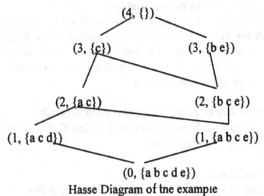

Hasse Diagram of the example

The complexity of the algorithm depends on how many new nodes will be generated when a new transaction is inserted. Suppose that transactions in average are consisting of k items, at most 2^k new node could be generated when a new transaction is inserted. The complexity of the algorithm is at most $O(2^k \bullet \|U\|)$, where $\|U\|$ is the cardinal of the database and k is a const. We observe that in fact new generated nodes are much less than 2^k at most time.

We use example [8] to illustrate our algorithms. Suppose $T_1=\{a, c, d\}$, $T_2=\{b, c, e\}$, $T_3=\{a, b , c, e\}$, $T_4=\{b, e\}$. The hasse diagram of the lattice after four node inserted is shown above. If the threshold is 2, we get large 3-itemset (2, {b, c, e}), 2-itemset {(2, {a, c}), (3, {b, e})}, 1-itemset (3, {c}).

4 Conclusion

Discovering association rules among items in large databases is an important database mining problem, and concept lattice is an convenient tool to data analysis and knowledge discovery. We use concept lattice approach to model the problem of generating large itemsets and present an incremental algorithm to build lattice and generate large itemsets. Our method has several advantages. Firstly, our method takes only one pass over the database; secondly, it is incremental; finally, it is efficient at most time.

REFERENCES

1   Godin, R., Missaoui, R., Alaui, H.: Incremental Concept Formation Algorithms Based on Galois (Concept) Lattices. Computational Intelligence, 1995, 11(2): 246-267

2   Wille, R.: Restructuring Lattice Theory: An Approach Based on Hierarchies of Concepts. In: Rival I (Ed.). Dordrecht Reidel (1982) 445-470

3   Wille, R: Knowledge Acquisition by Methods of Formal Concept Analysis. In: Diday E (Ed.). Data Analysis, Learning Symbolic and Numeric Knowledge. New York Nova Science Publisher (1989) 365-380

4   Oosthuizen, G. D.: Rough Sets and Concept Lattices. In: Ziarko W P(Ed.). Rough Sets, and Fuzzy Sets and Knowledge Discovery (RSKD'93). London Springer-Verlag (1994) 24-31

5   Missaoui, R., Godin, R: Search for Concepts and Dependencies in Databases. In: Ziarko W P(Ed.). Rough Sets, and Fuzzy Sets and Knowledge Discovery (RSKD'93). London: Springer-Verlag (1994) 16-23

6   Chen, M. S., Han, J., Yu, P. S.: Data Mining:An Overview from a Database Perspective. IEEE Trans. On Knowledge and Data Eng., 8(1996)

7   Agrawal, R., Imielinski, T., Swami, A.: Mining Association Rules between Sets of Items in Large Databases. Proc. ACM SIGMOD (1993) 490-501

8   Wang Z.: Research on Extended Rough Set Model, Doctoral dissertation. Hefei University of Technology. 1998

Induction as Pre-processing

Xindong Wu

Department of Mathematical and Computer Sciences
Colorado School of Mines
1500 Illinois Street, Golden, Colorado 80401, USA

Abstract. In most data mining applications where induction is used as the primary tool for knowledge extraction, it is difficult to precisely identify a complete set of relevant attributes. The real world database from which knowledge is to be extracted usually contains a combination of relevant, noisy and irrelevant attributes. Therefore, pre-processing the database to select relevant attributes becomes a very important task in knowledge discovery and data mining. This paper starts with two existing induction systems, C4.5 and HCV, and uses one of them to select relevant attributes for the other. Experimental results on 12 standard data sets show that using HCV induction for C4.5 attribute selection is generally useful.

1 Introduction

The pervasive use of sensor and information technology has resulted in the generation of vast amounts of digital data. Making use of this resource is of vital importance to the business, medical, manufacturing and many other sectors. Converting raw sensor data into useful information for human decision makers is one of the driving forces behind research into applications of data mining. Inductive learning is an area of research in data mining which describes the process of hypothesising a concept from a set of examples. It is the primary method for creating or discovering new knowledge from a data set by providing concept descriptions which are able to generalize. In order to generalize, a learning system needs to contain bias, assumptions without which learning would not be possible [1]. These biases can be incorporated in the structure of the model, the hypothesis representation language or in the workings of the model during hypothesis generation.

One major form of representation used in inductive learning is the decision tree (DT) in a process known as the top-down induction of decision trees. Example algorithms include C4.5 [11], its predecessor ID3 [10], and ITI [13]. The other major representation from is the "*if... then*" rule structure. Examples include the AQ series [7], CN2 [2], and HCV [15].

DT structures as induced by ID3-like algorithms are known to cause fragmentation of the data set whenever a high-arity attribute is tested at a node [9]. This diminishes the understandability of the induced concept hypotheses. Furthermore ID3-like DT structures have a tendency to repeat subtrees when expressing disjunctive concepts of the form (attribute 1 = A) or (attribute

2 = B). This is referred to as the replication problem. As a consequence of these two problems DT's tend to grow very large in most realistic problem domains.

Rule-like structures are a more convenient form to express knowledge. Rules are similar to the way human experts express their expertise and human users are comfortable with this way of expressing newly extracted knowledge [4]. This is an important consideration during expert validation of a large knowledge base (KB) which might well be equivalent to tens of decision trees, during debugging of the KB and in engendering user acceptance of a KB system. Therefore with DT algorithms there is often the added overhead of having to decompile the DT into a set of rules. Algorithms directly inducing a set of rules are therefore at a distinct advantage as they circumvent the creation of a DT and go directly to the creation of the rule set. It is also often the case that a direct rule inducer produces a more compact concept description than a DT inducer.

Hypothesis generation in induction involves searching through a vast (possibly infinite) space of concept descriptions. Practical systems constrain the search space through the use of bias [14]. Bias forces the search to prefer certain hypothesis spaces over others. One such bias, which has not been given much attention is to minimize the number of features in the concept description. This paper starts with C4.5 [11], which is commonly recognized as a state-of-the-art method for inducing decision trees [3], and HCV [16], which performs rule induction without generating decision trees. Experiments are carried out using one of these two systems to select relevant attributes for the other. In the next section we outline C4.5 and HCV and provide their baseline results on the 12 databases for our experiments. In the third section we present the results of our empirical investigation of using induction for attribute selection.

2   C4.5, HCV and Their Baseline Results

2.1   C4.5 – A Decision Tree Inducer & Rule Decompiler

The heart of the popular and robust C4.5 program is a decision tree inducer. It performs a depth-first, general to specific search for hypotheses by recessively partitioning the data set at each node of the tree.

C4.5 attempts to build a simple tree by using a measure of the information gain ratio of each feature and branching on the attribute which returns the maximum information gain ratio. At any point during the search a chosen attribute is considered to have the highest discriminating ability between the different concepts whose description is being generated. This bias constrains the search space by generating partial hypotheses using a subset of the dimensionality of the problem space. This is a depth-first search in which no alternative strategies are maintained and in which no back-tracking is allowed. The final DT built therefore, though simple is not guaranteed to be the simplest possible tree.

C4.5 uses a pruning mechanism wherein the tree construction process is stopped if an attribute is deemed to be irrelevant and should not be branched upon. A χ^2- test for statistical dependency between the attribute and the class label is carried out to test for this irrelevancy. The induced DT can be converted to a set of rules, by its rule decompiler C4.5rules, with some pruning and the generation of a default rule.

In the case of missing attribute values the unknown values are assumed to be distributed in proportion to the relative frequency of these values in the training set. Replacement of unknown values is therefore carried out according to this assumption. When classifying test data with missing attribute values C4.5 tests all branches of this attribute and works out the probability that each value is the correct choice. This probability is summed over all classes. This method performs well under conditions of increasing incidence of unknown values on the data sets used by Quinlan [6].

2.2   HCV (Version 2.0) – A Rule Induction Program

HCV avoids constructing a DT by using an extension matrix approach [9] to generate a set of conjunctive rules to cover each class in the training set relative to all other instances. The extension matrix approach was originally proposed by Hong [5] and then extended in HCV by Wu [15, 16]. In a revised version HCV (Version 2.0) has been extended to be able to deal with both noisy data and continuous attributes [17]. HCV (Version 2.0) is the version used in this study.

The HCV algorithm considers one class of instances in turn (termed the positive examples, PE) against all the other classes (termed the negative examples, NE). The matrix of NE is termed the negative example matrix (NEM). An extension matrix (EM) is constructed by taking a positive example and comparing it against each member in the NEM. Each attribute value in the NEM which is equal to the corresponding attribute value of the positive example is replaced by a flag denoting a dead element which is unable to distinguish between the positive example and the NE. Repeating this exercise for all positive examples results in a set of extension matrices. Superimposing a group of extension matrices results in the formation of a disjunction matrix (EMD). This superpositioning is governed by two rules: a dead element flag results where at least one EM has a dead element and the original NEM attribute value is retained where no EM has a dead element.

A path is defined as the set of attribute values in the NEM such that there is only one value per row and none of the attribute values are dead elements. An intersecting group of positive examples occurs when a disjunction matrix contains at least one valid path. Such a path corresponds to a conjunctive cover for all the positive examples in the EMD but none of the negative ones. Since the tasks of finding optimal partitions and extracting optimal conjunctive rules from the disjunction matrices are both NP-hard, HCV provides a set of heuristics to carry out these tasks.

HCV has been shown to induce compact rules in low order polynomial time. The rules are expressed in the form of variable-valued logic. On a battery of data sets from both artificial and real world domains HCV has been found to be highly accurate relative to results from ID3-like algorithms [17].

2.3 Baseline Results

The Data The data used in our experiments (see Table 1) throughout this paper can be divided into two groups. The first group is made up of data with 100% nominal attributes. The second group contains data of mixed nominal and continuous attributes. All these data sets were obtained from the University of California at Irvine machine learning database repository [8]. The majority of these data sets are obtained from real world domains and are noisy.

Table 1. Data Sets Characteristics

Data Set	# of Instances	Attributes	Classes	Majority Class (%)	Continuous Attributes (%)	Avg # of Values per Attributes	Unknown Values (%)
Audiology	226	69	24	21.00	0.00	2.23	2.00
Monk 1	556	6	2	50.00	0.00	2.80	0.00
Monk 3	554	6	2	52.00	0.00	2.80	0.00
Vote	435	16	2	61.40	0.00	3.00	5.00
Aus-Credit	690	15	2	56.00	40.00	4.56	0.65
Hungarian 2	294	13	2	64.00	36.00	3.00	20.46
Imports 85	205	25	7	32.70	60.00	6.00	1.15
Lab Neg	56	16	2	65.00	50.00	2.62	35.75
Swiss 5	123	13	5	39.00	38.00	3.00	17.00
Va 2	200	13	5	28.00	38.00	3.00	26.80
Va 5	200	13	5	28.00	38.00	3.00	26.80
Wine	178	13	3	40.00	100.00	n/a	0.00

These databases have been selected because each of them consists of two standard components when created or collected by the original providers: a training set and a test set. The standard deviation has been given in some by the original database providers. The databases have been used "as is". Example ordering has not been changed, neither have examples been moved between the sets. For each database, induction was performed on the training set, and the accuracies listed in the following tables are from the test set.

Test Conditions Table 2 presents the results generated by C4.5, C4.5rules and HCV on the databases in Table 1. The second column (#) shows the original number of attributes in each database. # (HCV), # (C4.5) and # (C4.5) indicate the number of attributes used in the induction results of HCV, C4.5 and C4.5rules respectively. % (HCV) is HCV's accuracy on the test set of each database, and Err (%, C4.5) and Err (%, C4.5rules) are C4.5 and C4.5rules' error rates.

Throughout the experiments the same default conditions were used for all the data sets. Obviously fine tuning different parameters in either C4.5 and HCV would have achieved higher accuracy rates. This however would have been at the expense of a loss in generality and applicability of the conclusions. Default conditions were adopted for the two other programs C4.5 and HCV (Version 2.0) as recommended by the respective authors.

Table 2. Baseline Results

Data Set	#	# (HCV)	% (HCV)	# (C4.5)	Err (%, C4.5)	# (C4.5rules)	Err (%, C4.5rules)
Audiology	69	42	73.08	14	15.4	15	19.2
Aus-Credit	15	14	82.50	9	20.0	9	19.5
Hungarian 2	13	11	86.25	10	20.0	7	15.0
Imports 85	25	21	62.71	10	32.2	10	32.2
Lab Neg	16	9	76.47	2	17.6	3	11.8
Monk 1	6	3	100.00	5	24.3	6	0.0
Monk 3	6	4	97.22	2	2.8	5	3.7
Swiss 5	13	10	28.13	6	68.8	5	71.9
Va 2	13	9	78.87	5	29.6	5	28.2
Va 5	13	12	26.76	7	73.2	8	71.8
Vote	16	14	97.04	2	3.0	7	4.4
Wine	13	9	90.38	4	17.3	4	17.3

3 Empirical Investigation

3.1 Experiment Design

This section carries out experiments of using one of C4.5 and HCV to select attribute for the other. The following is the experiment design for Section 3.1.

1. For each database in Table 1, run HCV on the training set of the database.
2. Extract the attributes ($\mathcal{A}$) HCV has used in its induction results.
3. For each attribute A in the original database, if $A \notin \mathcal{A}$, then
   - Comment it out from the dictionary file.
   - Take its values out from the training and test sets.
4. Run C4.5 and C4.5rules on the changed training and test sets and record the results.
5. Goto Step 1.

For Section 3.2, C4.5 and C4.5rules are used in Step 2 and HCV in Step 4. As in Section 2, default conditions were adopted for both HCV and C4.5, and the databases were used "as is" except the changes mentioned in the above design.

3.2 HCV Induction for C4.5 Arrtibute Selection

Table 3 provides numerical evaluation of the error rates of the decision trees produced by C4.5 and the rules produced by C4.5rules on the 12 databases, after using HCV induction for attribute selection. The baseline results (from Table 2) are given before the symbol →, and results after induction for attribute selection are given after →.

Table 3. C4.5/C4.5rules Accuracy after HCV

Data Set	#	# (HCV)	Errors (%, C4.5)	Errors (%, C4.5rules)
Audiology	69	42	15.4 → 15.4	19.2 → 19.2
Aus-Credit	15	14	20.0 → 20.0	19.5 → 19.5
Hungarian 2	13	11	20.0 → 20.0	15.0 → 13.8
Imports 85	25	21	32.2 → 32.2	32.2 → 32.2
Lab Neg	16	9	17.6 → 17.6	11.8 → 11.8
Monk 1	6	3	24.3 → 11.1	0.0 → 0.0
Monk 3	6	4	2.8 → 2.8	3.7 → 0.0
Swiss 5	13	10	68.8 → 68.8	71.9 → 75.0
Va 2	13	9	29.6 → 31.0	28.2 → 25.4
Va 5	13	12	73.2 → 73.2	71.8 → 71.8
Vote	16	14	3.0 → 3.0	4.4 → 3.0
Wine	13	9	17.3 → 17.3	17.3 → 17.3

Out of the 12 databases, C4.5's error rate decreases significantly on one database (Monk 1), increases slightly on another database (Va 2), and remains the same on the remaining 10 databases. In the meanwhile, C4.5rules has lower error rates on 4 databases (Hungarian 2, Monk 3, Va 2, and Vote), and a higher error rate on only one database (Swiss 5).

Table 4. C4.5/C4.5rules Sizes after HCV

Data Set	#	# (HCV)	# of Nodes (C4.5)	# of Rules (C4.5rules)	# of Tests (C4.5rules)
Audiology	69	42	52 → 52	23 → 23	65 → 65
Aus-Credit	15	14	44 → 44	14 → 14	42 → 42
Hungarian 2	13	11	37 → 37	7 → 9	14 → 16
Imports 85	25	21	67 → 67	14 → 14	34 → 34
Lab Neg	16	9	7 → 7	5 → 5	7 → 7
Monk 1	6	3	18 → 35	14 → 11	28 → 22
Monk 3	6	4	12 → 12	13 → 9	25 → 14
Swiss 5	13	10	25 → 25	7 → 8	15 → 18
Va 5	13	12	35 → 35	9 → 9	22 → 22
Va 2	13	9	19 → 12	6 → 7	11 → 18
Vote	16	14	7 → 7	7 → 7	10 → 10
Wine	13	9	9 → 9	6 → 6	10 → 10

Table 4 lists the number of nodes in C4.5 trees and the numbers of rules and tests (or conditions) in C4.5rules for each database. From this table, the number of nodes in C4.5 trees increases on one database (Monk 1) and decreases on another (Va 2). In the meanwhile, the complexity of the rules produced by C4.5rules decreases on 3 databases (Hungarian 2, Monk 1, and Monk 3) and increases on 2 databases (Swiss 5 and Va 2).

If we compare C4.5 and C4.5rules' error rates and description complexity before and after using HCV for attribute selection, the gains in Tables 3 and 4 do not seem to be very significant. However, since the numbers of attributes after HCV selection are significant less than that in the original databases, we can still claim that the attribute selection by HCV is useful, because it reduces the complexity of the original databases and subsequently C4.5 and C4.5rules' execution times.

3.3 C4.5 Induction for HCV Arrtibute Selection

Tables 5 and 6 detail the changes in HCV's accuracy and rule complexity after using C4.5 and C4.5rules for attribute selection.

Table 5. HCV Accuracy after C4.5 and C4.5rules

Data Set	#	# (HCV)	% (HCV)	# (C4.5)	% (HCV)	# (C4.5rules)	% (HCV)
Audiology	69	42	73.08	14	57.69	15	57.69
Aus-Credit	15	14	82.50	9	83.00	9	83.00
Hungarian 2	13	11	86.25	10	86.25	7	83.75
Imports 85	25	21	62.71	10	55.93	10	55.93
Lab Neg	16	9	76.47	2	64.71	3	64.71
Monk 1	6	3	100.00	5	100.00	6	100.00
Monk 3	6	4	97.22	2	97.22	5	97.22
Swiss 5	13	10	28.13	6	25.00	5	25.00
Va 2	13	9	78.87	5	78.87	5	78.87
Va 5	13	12	26.76	7	32.39	8	28.17
Vote	16	14	97.04	2	61.48	7	97.04
Wine	13	9	90.38	4	73.08	4	73.08

Apart from the Monk 1 database, on which HCV's results have not changed after C4.5 and C4.5rules' attribute selection, HCV's rule complexity in terms of the numbers of rules and tests decreases on all databases and in the meanwhile its accuracy also decreases on most of them.

If we look back at Table 2, HCV's baseline results have generally used more attributes than C4.5 and C4.5rules. When HCV does not have enough attributes to choose from during its induction, it is understandable that it has to sacrifice its accuracy, the most important criterion for many practical knowledge discovery applications. Therefore, it appears to be a reasonable conclusion that for those applications where accuracy is among the most important factors, C4.5 and C4.5rules are harmful for HCV's attribute selection.

Table 6. HCV Sizes after C4.5 and C4.5rules: Rules and Tests

Data Set	# (C4.5)	# of rules (HCV)	# of tests (HCV)	# (C4.5rules)	# of rules (HCV)	# of tests (HCV)
Audiology	69	14	59→ 37	124 → 98	15	→ 37	→ 101
Aus-Credit	15	9	99→ 25	223 → 91	9	→ 25	→ 91
Hungarian 2	13	10	22→ 17	64 → 46	7	→ 13	→ 25
Imports 85	25	10	76→ 32	104 → 62	10	→ 32	→ 62
Lab Neg	16	2	24→ 4	37 → 4	3	→ 4	→ 4
Monk 1	6	5	8→ 8	16 → 16	6	→ 8	→ 16
Monk 3	6	2	8→ 5	16 → 6	5	→ 7	→ 14
Swiss 5	13	6	32→ 18	85 → 55	5	→ 16	→ 36
Va 2	13	5	31→ 13	83 → 32	5	→ 13	→ 32
Va 5	13	7	50→ 30	151 →101	8	→ 33	→106
Vote	16	2	37→ 3	55 → 2	7	→ 12	→ 22
Wine	13	4	58→ 6	60 → 11	4	→ 6	→ 11

4 Conclusion

Induction always involves searching through a space of concept descriptions. Appropriate selection of attributes can constrain the search space through the use of pre-selected attributes. We have experimented in this paper the idea of using one induction system to select attributes for another induction system. The following conclusions appear to be supported by our experimental results.

- Attribute selection by a rule induction system like HCV is useful for decision tree construction. Even if the gains in predictive accuracy and description complexity are not significant, the selection can reduce the complexity of the original databases and subsequently the time for decision tree construction.
- Decision tree construction using C4.5 tends to use a minimal set of attributes. If the number of attributes in a decision tree is less than that required by a rule induction system, using a decision tree construction system to select attributes is harmful for the rule induction system.

References

1. Ali, K.M. & Passani, M.J., Reducing the small disjuncts problem by learning probabilistic concept descriptions, *Computational Learning Theory and Natural Learning Systems*, T. Petsche et al. (Eds.), Vol.3, 1992.
2. Clark, P.E. & Boswell, R., Rule induction with CN2: Some recent improvements. In Proceedings of the Fifth European Working Session on Learning, Porto, Portugal: Springer-Verlag, 1991, 151–163.
3. Dougherty *et al.*, Supervised and Unsupervised Discretization of Continuous Features, *Proceedings of the 12th International Conference on Machine Learning*, 194–202.

4. Gams, M., Drobnic, M. & Petkovsek,M. Learning from examples - a uniform view, *Int. J. Man-Machine Studies*, **34**(1991): 49–68.

5. Hong, J., AE1: An extension matrix approximate method for the general covering problem, *International Journal of Computer and Information Sciences*, **14**(1985), 6: 421–437.

6. Mahlen, P, Dealing with Continuous Attribute Domains in Inductive Learning, *Masters Thesis*, Dept. of Numerical Analysis and Computer Science, Royal Instit. Of Technology, Stockholm, Sweden, 1995.

7. Michalski, R.S., Mozetic, I., Hong, J., Lavrac, N., The multi-purpose incremental learning system AQ15 and its testing application to three medical domains, *Proceedings of the Fifth National Conference on Artificial Intelligence*, 1986, 1041–1045.

8. Murphe, P.M. & Aha, D.W., UCI Repository of Machine Learning Databases, Machine-Readable Data Repository, Irvine, CA, University of California, Department of Information and Computer Science, 1995.

9. Pagllo, G. & Haussler,D., Boolean feature discovery in empirical learning, *Machine Learning*, **5**(1990): 71-99.

10. Quinlan, J.R., Induction of decision trees, *Machine Learning*, **1**(1986).

11. Quinlan, J.R., *C4.5: Programs for Machine Learning*, CA: Morgan Kaufmann, 1993.

12. Shannon, C.E. & Weaver, W., *The Mathematical Theory of Communications*, The University of Illinois Press, Urbana, IL, 1949.

13. Utgoff, P.E., Incremental Induction of Decision Trees, *Machine Learning*, **4**(1989), 161–186.

14. Utgoff P.E., Shift of Bias for Inductive Concept Learning, *Machine Learning: An AI Approach*, Volume 2, Chapter 5, Morgan Kaufmann Pub., 1986, 107–148.

15. Wu, X., The HCV induction algorithm, *Proceedings of the 21st ACM Computer Science Conference*, S.C., Kwasny and J.Fuch (Eds.), ACM Press, USA, 1993, 168–175.

16. Wu, X., *Knowledge Acquisition from Data Bases*, Ablex Publishing Corp., U.S.A., 1995.

17. Wu, X., Krisar, J. & Mahlen, P., Noise Handling with Extension Matrices, *International Journal on Artificial Intelligence Tools*, **5**(1996), 1: 81–97.

Stochastic Attribute Selection Committees with Multiple Boosting: Learning More Accurate and More Stable Classifier Committees

Zijian Zheng and Geoffrey I. Webb

School of Computing and Mathematics
Deakin University, Geelong, Victoria 3217, Australia
{zijian,webb}@deakin.edu.au

Abstract. Classifier learning is a key technique for KDD. Approaches to learning classifier committees, including Boosting, Bagging, SASC, and SASCB, have demonstrated great success in increasing the prediction accuracy of decision trees. Boosting and Bagging create different classifiers by modifying the distribution of the training set. SASC adopts a different method. It generates committees by stochastic manipulation of the set of attributes considered at each node during tree induction, but keeping the distribution of the training set unchanged. SASCB, a combination of Boosting and SASC, has shown the ability to further increase, on average, the prediction accuracy of decision trees. It has been found that the performance of SASCB and Boosting is more variable than that of SASC, although SASCB is more accurate than the others on average. In this paper, we present a novel method to reduce variability of SASCB and Boosting, and further increase their average accuracy. It generates multiple committees by incorporating Bagging into SASCB. As well as improving stability and average accuracy, the resulting method is amenable to parallel or distributed processing, while Boosting and SASCB are not. This is an important characteristic for datamining in large datasets.

1 Introduction

To increase the prediction accuracy of classifiers, classifier committee[1] learning techniques have been developed with great success [2, 3, 4, 5, 6, 7, 8, 9, 10, 11]. This type of technique generates several classifiers to form a committee by using a single base learning algorithm. At the classification stage, the committee members vote to make the final decision.

Bagging [5] and Boosting [2, 3, 6, 10, 12], as two representative methods of this type, can significantly decrease the error rate of decision tree learning [3, 4, 11]. They repeatedly build different classifiers using a base learning algorithm, such as a decision tree generator, by changing the distribution of the training set. Bagging generates different classifiers using different bootstrap samples. Boosting builds different classifiers sequentially. The weights of training examples used for creating each classifier are modified based on the performance

---

[1] Committees are also referred to as ensembles [1].

of the previous classifiers. The objective is to make the generation of the next classifier concentrate on the training examples that are misclassified by the previous classifiers. The main difference between Bagging and Boosting is that the latter adaptively changes the distribution of the training set based on the performance of previously created classifiers and uses a function of the performance of a classifier as the weight for voting, while the former stochastically changes the distribution of the training set and uses equal weight voting. Although Boosting is generally more accurate than Bagging, the performance of Boosting is more variable than that of Bagging [4, 11].

As an alternative approach to generating different classifiers to form a committee, SASC (Stochastic Attribute Selection Committees) [13] builds different classifiers by modifying the set of attributes considered at each node, while the distribution of the training set is kept unchanged. Each attribute set is selected stochastically. Experiments show that SASC, like Boosting, can also significantly reduce the error rate of decision tree learning [13]. In addition, SASC is more stable than Boosting [13].

SASC [13] is a minor variant of a class of committee learning algorithm that learns a committee by randomizing the base learning process [1, 7, 8, 9]. While SASC has not been directly compared with these alternatives, comparisons of reported results suggest that its performance is comparable to that of others.

Base on the observation that both Boosting and SASC can significantly increase the prediction accuracy of decision trees but through different mechanisms, we developed another technique to further improve the accuracy of decision trees [14]. The new approach is called SASCB (Stochastic Attribute Selection Committees with Boosting), a combination of the Boosting and SASC techniques. SASCB has shown the ability to outperform, on average, either SASC or Boosting alone in terms of lower error rate. However, like Boosting, SASCB is more variable than SASC, as the Boosting component is the driving mechanism in the SASCB procedure. SASC and Bagging are amenable to parallel and distributed processing while SASCB and Boosting are not, since the generation of each committee member, a classifier, is independent for the former while it must occur sequentially for the latter.

In the light of the findings mentioned above from the previous studies on committee learning, in this paper, we present a novel approach, namely SASCMB (Stochastic Attribute Selection Committees with Multiple Boosting), to improving the stability and average accuracy of SASCB and Boosting. It generates multiple subcommittees by incorporating Bagging into SASCB using the multi-boosting technique [15]. We expect that splitting one committee into multiple subcommittees, with each subcommittee being created from a bootstrap sample of the training set, can reduce the variability of Boosting and SASCB, since the Boosting process is broken down into several small processes. In addition, we expect that introducing Bagging can further improve the accuracy, since it increases the diversity and independence of committee members. At the same time, the new algorithm is amenable to parallel and distributed processing.

2 Boosting, Bagging, SASC, and SASCB

Since the SASCMB technique is a combination of Bagging and SASCB which is, in turn, a combination of Boosting and SASC, we briefly discuss Boosting, Bagging, SASC, and SASCB in this section. The classification process of them is presented in Section 2.5, since it is the same for all of them.

2.1 Boosting

Boosting [4, 10, 11, 12] is a general framework for improving base learning algorithms. The key idea of Boosting was presented in Section 1. Here, we describe our implementation of the Boosting algorithm with decision tree learning, called BOOST. It follows the Boosted C4.5 algorithm (AdaBoost.M1) [4] but uses a new Boosting equation as shown in Equation 1, derived from [10].

Given a training set D consisting of m instances and an integer T, the number of trials, BOOST builds T pruned trees over T trials by repeatedly invoking C4.5 [16]. Let $w_t(x)$ denote the weight of instance x in D at trial t. At the first trial, each instance has weight 1; that is, $w_1(x) = 1$ for each x. At trial t, decision tree H_t is built using D under the distribution w_t. The error ϵ_t of H_t is, then, calculated by summing up the weights of the instances that H_t misclassifies and divided by m. If ϵ_t is greater than 0.5 or equal to 0, $w_t(x)$ is re-initialized using bootstrap sampling, and then the Boosting process continues. Note that the tree with $\epsilon_t > 0.5$ is discarded,[2] while the tree with $\epsilon_t = 0$ is accepted by the committee. Otherwise, the weight $w_{t+1}(x)$ of each instance x for the next trial is computed using Equation 1. These weights are, then, renormalized so that they sum to m.

$$w_{(t+1)}(x) = w_t(x)exp((-1)^{d(x)}\alpha_t), \tag{1}$$

where $\alpha_t = \frac{1}{2}ln((1 - \epsilon_t)/\epsilon_t)$; $d(x) = 1$ if H_t correctly classifies x and $d(x) = 0$ otherwise.

2.2 Bagging

The primary idea of Bagging [5] is to generate a committee of classifiers with each from a bootstrap sample of the original training set. Given a committee size T and a training set D consisting of m instances, BAG, our implementation of Bagging, generates $T-1$ bootstrap samples with each being created by uniformly sampling m instances from D with replacement. It, then, builds one decision tree using C4.5 from each bootstrap sample. Another tree is created from the original training set.

2.3 SASC

The key idea of SASC [13] is to vary the members of a decision tree committee by stochastic manipulation of the set of attributes available for selection at decision nodes. This creates decision trees that each partition the instance space differently. We use C4.5 [16] with the modifications described below as the base

---

[2] To make the algorithm efficient, this step is limited to $10 \times T$ times.

classifier learning algorithm in SASC. When building a decision node, by default C4.5 uses the information gain ratio to search for the best attribute to form a test [16]. To force C4.5 to generate different trees using the same training set, we modified C4.5 by stochastically restricting the set of attributes available for selection at a decision node. This is implemented by using a probability parameter P. At each decision node, an attribute subset is randomly selected with each available attribute having the probability P of being selected. The available attributes refer to those attributes that have positive gain values. After attribute subset selection, the algorithm chooses the attribute with the highest gain ratio to form a test for the decision node from the subset. The modified version of C4.5 is called **C4.5SAS** (**C4.5** Stochastic Attribute Selection). With $P = 1$, C4.5SAS generates the same tree as C4.5.

Having C4.5SAS, the design of SASC is very simple. C4.5SAS is invoked T times to generate T different decision trees to form a committee. As in Boosting, the first tree produced by SASC is the same as the tree generated by C4.5. The detailed description of C4.5SAS and SASC can be found in [13].

2.4 SASCB

The combination strategy adopted in SASCB [14] employs, when generating decision trees, both the stochastic selection of attribute subsets of SASC and the adaptive modification of the distribution of the training set of Boosting. SASCB uses the same Boosting procedure as BOOST except that C4.5SAS is used instead of C4.5 as the base tree generator. As in BOOST, the tree with an error rate greater than 0.5 is discarded,[3] while the tree with no errors on the training set is kept.

SASCB can be considered as introducing the stochastic attribute selection process into the generation of each tree in the Boosting process. It can also be thought of as adaptively modifying the distribution of the training set after the generation of each decision tree in the SASC process.

2.5 Decision Making in BOOST, BAG, SASC, and SASCB

At the classification stage, for a given example, all of BOOST, BAG, SASC, and SASCB make the final prediction through committee voting. In this paper, a voting method that uses the probabilistic predictions produced by all committee members without voting weights is adopted. With this method, each decision tree returns a distribution over classes that the example belongs to. This is performed by tracing the example down to a leaf of the tree. The class distribution for the example is estimated using the proportion of the training examples of each class at the leaf, if the leaf is not empty. When the leaf contains no training examples, the four committee learning algorithms estimate the class distribution using the training examples at the parent node of the empty leaf. The decision tree committee members vote by summing up the class distributions provided by all trees. The class with the highest score (sum of probabilities) wins the voting, and serves as the predicted class for this example.

---

[3] This step is also limited to $10 \times T$ times, where T is the number of Boosting trials.

SASCMB(*Att*, *D*, *P*, *S*, *N*)
    INPUT: *Att*: a set of attributes,
             D: a training set represented using *Att* and classes,
             P: a probability value,
             S: the size of each subcommittee,
             N: the number of subcommittees.
    OUTPUT: a committee, *H*, consisting of *N* subcommittees with each
             containing *S* trees.

Set *T*, the number of trials, $= S \times N$
Set instance weight $w_1(x) = 1$ for each x in D
$H_1 := $ **C4.5SAS**(*Att*, *D*, w_1, 1)
$t := 2$
WHILE ($t <= T$)
{ $D' :=$ training cases in D that are misclassified by $H_{(t-1)}$

$$\epsilon_{(t-1)} = \frac{1}{|D|} \sum_{x \in D'} w_{(t-1)}(x)$$

    IF ($\epsilon_{(t-1)} > 1/2$)
       $t := t - 1$
    ELSE IF (t modulus $S = 1$)
          Reset $w_t(x)$ using bootstrap sampling, i.e., $w_t(x)$ is set at 0 and
          incremented 1 unit every time instance x is selected during
          uniformly sampling $|D|$ instances from D with replacement
       ELSE IF ($\epsilon_{(t-1)} \neq 0$)
          Calculate $w_t(x)$, the weight of each x in D, from $w_{(t-1)}(x)$ using
          Equation 1 and renormalize these weights so that they sum to $|D|$
    $H_t := $ **C4.5SAS**(*Att*, *D*, w_t, *P*)
    $t := t + 1$
}
RETURN *H*

Fig. 1. The SASCMB learning algorithm

There are three other approaches to voting: The categorical predictions without voting weights, the probabilistic predictions with voting weights, and the categorical predictions with voting weights [13]. These three voting methods perform either worse than or similarly to the method that we use here [13, 14].

3 SASCMB: Incorporating Bagging into SASCB

Figure 1 presents the details of the SASCMB algorithm. It is resulted from incorporating Bagging into SASCB. SASCMB generates N subcommittees. This process can be parallelized. Each subcommittee contains S decision trees built using the SASCB procedure described in the previous section. The generation of the first subcommittee (or one of the subcommittees if using parallel or distributed processing) starts from the initial training set D with each training instance having the weight 1. The first tree in this subcommittee is the same one as that built by C4.5 using the entire training set. The generation of every other subcommittee starts from a bootstrap sample of D.

At the classification stage, all the members of all the subcommittees generated by SASCMB vote to predict a class for a given instance. SASCMB uses the same default voting method as BOOST, SASC, and SASCB, since it generally performs better than the other three voting approaches [13, 14] as mentioned in Section 2.5.

4 Experiments

In this section, we empirically evaluate SASCMB to examine whether incorporating Bagging into SASCB can increase stability and average accuracy of learned committees. It is compared with other committee learning algorithms: SASCB, BOOST, and SASC. In addition, a multiple Boosting algorithm MB [15] is also included in the comparison. C4.5, the base decision tree learning algorithm of all these committee learning algorithms, is used as the base line for the comparison. The results of BAG are not given in this paper due to the space limit. Note that the average error of BAG is higher than that of BOOST in our experiments.

MB is the same as SASCMB except that it does not include the stochastic attribute selection component. In other words, MB uses the same procedure as SASCMB for generating multiple decision tree committees, but the former uses C4.5 instead of C4.5SAS.

4.1 Experimental Domains and Methods

Forty natural domains from the UCI machine learning repository [17] are used. They include all the domains used by Quinlan [4] for studying Boosting.

In every domain, two stratified 10-fold cross-validations were carried out for each algorithm. The result reported for each algorithm in each domain is an average value over 20 trials. All the algorithms are run on the same training and test set partitions with their default option settings. Pruned trees are used for all the algorithms. All BOOST, SASC, SASCB, MB, and SASCMB use probabilistic predictions (without voting weights) for voting to decide the final classification. The number of trials (the parameter T) is set at 100 in the experiments for BOOST, SASC, and SASCB. The subcommittee size and the number of subcommittees are set at 5 and 20 respectively, resulting in 100 trees in total for MB and SASCMB. The probability of each attribute being selected into the subset (the parameter P) is set at the default, 33%, for SASC, SASCB, and SASCMB.

4.2 Results

Table 1 shows the error rates of the six algorithms. To facilitate pairwise comparisons among the six algorithms, error ratios are derived from Table 1 and presented in Table 2. An error ratio, for example for BOOST vs C4.5, presents a result for BOOST divided by the corresponding result for C4.5 – a value less than 1 indicates an improvement due to BOOST. To compare the error rates of two algorithms in a domain, a two-tailed pairwise t-test on the error rates of the 20 trials is carried out. The difference is considered as significant, if the significance level of the t-test is better than 0.05. In Table 2, **boldface** (*italic*) font, for example for BOOST vs C4.5, indicates that BOOST is significantly more (less)

Table 1. Error rates (%)

Domain	C4.5	Boost	Sasc	SascB	MB	SascMB
Annealing	7.40	4.90	5.85	4.12	4.67	5.06
Audiology	21.39	15.41	18.73	15.19	15.88	15.43
Automobile	16.31	13.42	14.35	15.88	16.10	16.82
Breast (W)	5.08	3.22	3.44	3.08	3.08	3.15
Chess (KR-KP)	0.72	0.36	0.67	0.36	0.39	0.39
Chess (KR-KN)	8.89	3.54	9.26	4.09	5.27	5.63
Credit (Aust)	14.49	13.91	14.71	14.20	12.82	12.61
Credit (Ger)	29.40	25.45	25.10	25.15	23.90	23.50
Echocardiogram	37.80	36.24	37.01	39.20	31.68	30.47
Glass	33.62	21.09	25.27	21.99	24.33	21.31
Heart (C)	22.07	18.80	16.65	18.63	18.13	18.29
Heart (H)	21.09	21.25	18.88	21.09	19.20	18.53
Hepatitis	20.63	17.67	18.40	15.79	17.12	17.12
Horse colic	15.76	19.84	17.39	19.43	15.90	16.04
House votes 84	5.62	4.82	4.59	4.25	3.90	4.25
Hypo	0.46	0.32	0.46	0.36	0.33	0.40
Hypothyroid	0.71	1.14	0.76	0.98	0.82	0.95
Image	2.97	1.58	2.06	1.58	1.77	1.93
Iris	4.33	5.67	5.00	5.67	5.00	5.00
Labor	23.67	10.83	18.83	9.83	12.33	10.50
LED 24	36.50	32.75	29.00	32.50	32.00	30.50
Letter	12.16	2.95	3.74	2.76	3.45	3.32
Liver disorders	35.36	28.88	29.90	29.47	26.73	27.29
Lung cancer	57.50	53.75	45.83	53.75	47.08	49.17
Lymphography	21.88	16.86	18.48	16.50	16.86	14.76
NetTalk(Letter)	25.88	22.14	21.98	19.91	21.37	20.12
NetTalk(Ph)	18.97	16.01	18.03	14.60	15.22	14.73
NetTalk(Stress)	17.25	11.91	12.44	11.30	12.26	10.54
Pima	23.97	26.57	23.76	26.43	23.31	23.18
Postoperative	29.44	38.89	28.89	38.89	32.22	34.44
Primary tumor	59.59	55.75	54.72	55.02	55.02	55.30
Promoters	17.50	4.68	7.09	4.73	5.64	5.64
Sick	1.30	0.92	1.42	1.04	1.10	1.33
Solar flare	15.62	17.57	15.70	17.57	16.31	15.95
Sonar	26.43	14.64	16.32	13.93	19.68	17.79
Soybean	8.49	6.22	5.42	5.64	6.66	5.49
Splice junction	5.81	4.80	4.50	3.65	4.23	3.81
Vehicle	28.50	22.40	25.12	22.40	24.00	23.52
Waveform-21	23.83	18.33	19.83	17.50	18.00	17.67
Wine	8.96	3.35	4.48	1.96	3.07	1.68
average	19.18	15.97	16.10	15.76	15.42	15.09

accurate than C4.5. The last two rows in Table 2 present the numbers of wins, ties, and losses between the error rates of the corresponding two algorithms in the 40 domains, and the significance levels of a one-tailed pairwise sign-test on these win/tie/loss records.

From Tables 1 and 2, we have the following observations.

(1) Incorporating Bagging into SascB can reduce variability of learned committees in terms of decreasing the frequency of producing significantly higher error rate than the base decision tree learning algorithm.

While both Boost and SascB obtain significantly higher error rates than C4.5 in five out of the 40 domains, SascMB only has significantly higher error rates than C4.5 in two domains. The highest relative error increase of Boost and SascB over C4.5 is 61% and 38% respectively. It is 34% for SascMB, the smallest one among the three algorithms. Note that Sasc and MB are more

Table 2. Error rate ratios

Domain	BOOST	SASC	SASCB	MB	SASCMB	SASCMB vs			
			vs C4.5			BOOST	SASC	SASCB	MB
Annealing	.66	.79	.56	.63	.68	1.03	.86	1.23	1.08
Audiology	.72	.88	.71	.74	.72	1.00	.82	1.02	.97
Automobile	.82	.88	.97	.99	1.03	1.25	1.17	1.06	1.04
Breast (W)	.63	.68	.61	.61	.62	.98	.92	1.02	1.02
KR-KP	.50	.93	.50	.54	.54	1.08	.58	1.08	1.00
KR-KN	.40	1.04	.46	.59	.63	1.59	.61	1.38	1.07
Credit(A)	.96	1.02	.98	.88	.87	.91	.86	.89	.98
Credit(G)	.87	.85	.86	.81	.80	.92	.94	.93	.98
Echo	.96	.98	1.04	.84	.81	.84	.82	.78	.96
Glass	.63	.75	.65	.72	.63	1.01	.84	.97	.88
Heart(C)	.85	.75	.84	.82	.83	.97	1.10	.98	1.01
Heart(H)	1.01	.90	1.00	.91	.88	.87	.98	.88	.97
Hepatitis	.86	.89	.77	.83	.83	.97	.93	1.08	1.00
Horse colic	1.26	1.10	1.23	1.01	1.02	.81	.92	.83	1.01
House votes	.86	.82	.76	.69	.76	.88	.93	1.00	1.09
Hypo	.70	1.00	.78	.72	.87	1.25	.87	1.11	1.21
Hypothyroid	1.61	1.07	1.38	1.15	1.34	.83	1.25	.97	1.16
Image	.53	.69	.53	.60	.65	1.22	.94	1.22	1.09
Iris	1.31	1.15	1.31	1.15	1.15	.88	1.00	.88	1.00
Labor	.46	.80	.42	.52	.44	.97	.56	1.07	.85
LED 24	.90	.79	.89	.88	.84	.93	1.05	.94	.95
Letter	.24	.31	.23	.28	.27	1.13	.89	1.20	.96
Liver	.82	.85	.83	.76	.77	.94	.91	.93	1.02
Lung cancer	.93	.80	.93	.82	.86	.91	1.07	.91	1.04
Lympho	.77	.84	.75	.77	.67	.88	.80	.89	.88
NetTalk(L)	.86	.85	.77	.83	.78	.91	.92	1.01	.94
NetTalk(P)	.84	.95	.77	.80	.78	.92	.82	1.01	.97
NetTalk(S)	.69	.72	.66	.71	.61	.88	.85	.93	.86
Pima	1.11	.99	1.10	.97	.97	.87	.98	.88	.99
Postoper	1.32	.98	1.32	1.09	1.17	.89	1.19	.89	1.07
Tumor	.94	.92	.92	.92	.93	.99	1.01	1.01	1.01
Promoters	.27	.41	.27	.32	.32	1.21	.80	1.19	1.00
Sick	.71	1.09	.80	.85	1.02	1.45	.94	1.28	1.21
Solar flare	1.12	1.01	1.12	1.04	1.02	.91	1.02	.91	.98
Sonar	.55	.62	.53	.74	.67	1.22	1.09	1.28	.90
Soybean	.73	.64	.66	.78	.65	.88	1.01	.97	.82
Splice	.83	.77	.63	.73	.66	.79	.85	1.04	.90
Vehicle	.79	.88	.79	.84	.83	1.05	.94	1.05	.98
Waveform	.77	.83	.73	.76	.74	.96	.89	1.01	.98
Wine	.37	.50	.22	.34	.19	.50	.37	.86	.55
average	.80	.84	.78	.78	.77	.99	.91	1.01	.98
w/t/l	33/0/7	32/1/7	32/1/7	35/0/5	33/0/7	27/0/13	29/1/10	19/1/20	21/4/15
p. of wtl	<.0001	<.0001	<.0001	<.0001	<.0001	.0192	.0017	.5000	.2025

stable than SASCMB, but they are less accurate than SASCMB on average (see below, for the discussion).

(2) Incorporating Bagging into SASCB can also reduce the average error rate of learned committees. SASCMB outperforms BOOST, SASC, SASCB, and MB in terms of lower error rate.

All the five committee learning algorithms achieve significant error rate reduction over C4.5 at a level better than 0.0001 using a one-tailed pairwise sign-test on the error rates of these algorithms in the 40 domains. Among them, SASCMB obtains the lowest average error rate 15.09%. The average error rate is 19.18%, 15.97%, 16.10%, 15.76%, and 15.42% for C4.5, BOOST, SASC, SASCB, and MB respectively. SASCMB also achieves the greatest average relative error reduction (23%) over C4.5 among these five committee learning algorithms.

A direct comparison shows that the average relative error reduction of SASCMB over BOOST and SASC is 1% and 9% respectively. A one-tailed sign-test suggests that SASCMB has significantly lower error rate than BOOST and SASC (p = 0.0192 and 0.0017 respectively). The average relative error reduction of SASCMB over MB is 2%, but a one-tailed sign-test fails to show that this reduction is significant at a level of 0.05. The average error ratio of SASCMB over SASCB is 1.01, although the average error rate of SASCMB is lower than that of SASCB. This is because SASCB performs better than SASCMB in domains in which they have relatively low error rates, and vice versa in domains in which they have relatively high error rates. It might be thought a disadvantage of SASCMB that the average error ratio compared to SASCB is greater than 1. However, we argue that this is a statistical anomaly, due to SASCB's superior performance when C4.5 has lower error rates. Increasing accuracy is as important as decreasing error. The average *accuracy ratio*, a measure that favors better performance at large error rates, of SASCMB against SASCB (an accuracy for SASCMB divided by the corresponding accuracy for SASCB) is also 1.01. Note that the average error rate of SASCMB is 0.67 percentage points lower, a considerable reduction, than that of SASCB.

5 Conclusions

We have presented a new classifier committee learning method, SASCMB, for decision tree learning. It generates multiple committees through incorporating Bagging into SASCB. In the new algorithm, the Boosting process is broken down into several small processes with each creating one subcommittee. The Bagging component of SASCMB further increases the diversity and independence of committee members. Our aim is to improve the stability and average accuracy of learned committees. Another advantage of SASCMB over SASCB and Boosting is that SASCMB is amenable to parallel and distributed processing, which is important for datamining in large datasets.

The results of experiments with a representative collection of natural domains suggest that SASCMB is more stable than SASCB and Boosting. It achieves the lowest error rate among the five committee learning algorithms on average in the 40 domains under investigation. It also achieves the greatest average relative error reduction over the base decision tree learning algorithm among the five committee learning algorithms. The experiments show that SASCMB can significantly outperform SASC and Boosting on average in terms of lower error rate. At the very least, SASCMB is as accurate as SASCB and MB, while demonstrating greater stability and amenability to parallel and distributed processing.

Acknowledgments

The authors are grateful to J. Ross Quinlan for providing C4.5.

References

1. Dietterich, T.G.: Machine learning research. *AI Magazine* **18** (1997) 97-136.
2. Freund, Y.: Boosting a weak learning algorithm by majority. *Information and Computation* **121** (1996) 256-285.
3. Freund, Y. and Schapire, R.E.: Experiments with a new Boosting algorithm. *Proceedings of the Thirteenth International Conference on Machine Learning*. San Francisco, CA: Morgan Kaufmann (1996) 148-156.
4. Quinlan, J.R.: Bagging, Boosting, and C4.5. *Proceedings of the Thirteenth National Conference on Artificial Intelligence*. Menlo Park, CA: AAAI Press (1996) 725-730.
5. Breiman, L.: Bagging predictors. *Machine Learning* **24** (1996a) 123-140.
6. Breiman, L.: Arcing classifiers. Technical Report (available at: http://www.stat. Berkeley.EDU/users/breiman/). Department of Statistics, University of California, Berkeley, CA (1996b).
7. Dietterich, T.G. and Kong, E.B.: Machine learning bias, statistical bias, and statistical variance of decision tree algorithms. Technical Report, Dept of Computer Science, Oregon State University, Corvallis, Oregon (1995) (available at ftp://ftp.cs.orst.edu/pub/tgd/papers/tr-bias.ps.gz).
8. Ali, K.M.: *Learning Probabilistic Relational Concept Descriptions*. PhD. Thesis, Dept of Info. and Computer Science, Univ. of California, Irvine (1996).
9. Chan, P., Stolfo, S., and Wolpert, D. (eds): *Working Notes of AAAI Workshop on Integrating Multiple Learned Models for Improving and Scaling Machine Learning Algorithms* (http://www.cs.fit.edu/~imlm/papers.html), Portland, Oregon (1996).
10. Schapire, R.E., Freund, Y., Bartlett, P., and Lee, W.S.: Boosting the margin: A new explanation for the effectiveness of voting methods. *Proceedings of the Fourteenth International Conference on Machine Learning*. Morgan Kaufmann (1997) 322-330.
11. Bauer, E. and Kohavi, R.: An empirical comparison of voting classification algorithms: Bagging, Boosting, and variants. *Machine Learning* (to appear) (available at: http://robotics.Stanford.EDU/~ronnyk/vote.ps.gz).
12. Schapire, R.E.: The strength of weak learnability. *Machine Learning* **5** (1990) 197-227.
13. Zheng, Z. and Webb, G.I.: Stochastic attribute selection committees. *Advanced Topics in Artificial Intelligence: Proceedings of the 11th Australian Joint Conference on Artificial Intelligence*. Berlin: Springer-Verlag (1998a).
14. Zheng, Z., Webb, G.I., and Ting, K.M.: Integrating Boosting and stochastic attribute selection committees for further improving the performance of decision tree learning. *Proceedings of the 10th IEEE International Conference on Tools with Artificial Intelligence*. IEEE Computer Society Press (1998) 216-223.
15. Zheng, Z. and Webb, G.I.: Multiple Boosting: A combination of Boosting and Bagging. *Proceedings of the 4th International Conference on Parallel and Distributed Processing Techniques and Applications*. CSREA Press (1998b) 1133-1140.
16. Quinlan, J.R.: *C4.5: Program for Machine Learning*. Morgan Kaufmann (1993).
17. Blake, C., Keogh, E. and Merz, C.J.: UCI Repository of Machine Learning Databases (http://www.ics.uci.edu/~mlearn/MLRepository.html). Irvine, CA: University of California, Dept of Information and Computer Science (1998).

On Information-Theoretic Measures of Attribute Importance

Y.Y. Yao, S.K.M. Wong, and C.J. Butz

Department of Computer Science, University of Regina
Regina, Saskatchewan, Canada S4S 0A2

Abstract. An attribute is deemed important in data mining if it partitions the database such that previously unknown regularities are observable. Many information-theoretic measures have been applied to quantify the importance of an attribute. In this paper, we summarize and critically analyze these measures.

1   Introduction

Watanabe [21] suggested that pattern recognition is essentially a conceptual adaptation to the empirical data in order to see a form in them. The form is interpreted as a structure which always entails small entropy values. Many of the algorithms in pattern recognition may be characterized as efforts to minimize entropy [20]. The philosophy of entropy minimization in pattern recognition can be applied to related fields, such as classification, data analysis, machine learning, and data mining, where one of the tasks is to discover patterns or regularities in a large data set. Regularities and structureness are characterized by small entropy values, whereas randomness is characterized by large entropy values.

One may partition the statistical population into smaller populations using the values taken by an attribute. Such an attribute is deemed important for data mining if regularities are observable in the smaller populations, while being unobservable in the statistical population. In other words, if an attribute is used for data mining, then the attribute should lead to entropy reduction. The well known ID3 inductive learning algorithm [16] uses exactly such a measure for attribute selection in a learning process. Based on the philosophy of entropy minimization, this paper examines information-theoretic measures [2, 18] for evaluating attribute importance in data mining.

2   Measuring Attribute Importance

Let X denote a discrete random variable and x_i a value in the domain of X. A joint probability distribution is a real-valued function P_X over X such that $0 \le P_X(x_i) \le 1$ and $\sum_{i=1}^n P_X(x_i) = 1$, where n denotes the number of elements in the domain of X. We write P_X as P if X is understood. Shannon's entropy function H is defined over P as:

$$H(P) = -\sum_{i=1}^{n} P(x_i) \log P(x_i),$$

where $P(x_i) \log P(x_i) = 0$ if $P(x_i) = 0$. We say Shannon's entropy is over X and write $H(P)$ as $H(X)$ when the distribution P over X is understood. Shannon's entropy is a nonnegative function, i.e., $H(X) \geq 0$. It reaches the maximum value $\log n$ when P is the *uniform* distribution, i.e., $P(x_1) = \ldots = P(x_n) = \frac{1}{n}$. The minimum entropy value 0 is obtained when the distribution P focuses on a particular value x_j, i.e., $P(x_j) = 1$ and $P(x_i) = 0$, $1 \leq i \leq n$, $i \neq j$.

The conditional entropy, i.e., the difference between joint and marginal entropies, is given by:

$$H(X \mid Y) = H(X, Y) - H(Y).$$

Mutual information can be defined as:

$$I(X;Y) = H(X) - H(X|Y) = H(Y) - H(Y|X) = H(X) + H(Y) - H(X,Y).$$

That is, the mutual information measures the decrease of uncertainty about X caused by the knowledge of Y, and vice versa. It is a measure of the amount of information about X contained in Y. This measure is the same as the amount of information about Y contained in X, namely, $I(X;Y) = I(Y;X)$. Furthermore, the amount of information contained in X about itself is obviously $H(X)$, namely, $I(X;X) = H(X)$.

One may view an attribute and a database as a statistical variable taking values from its domain and a statistical population, respectively [5, 14]. Information-theoretic measures quantify relationships between random variables. They can immediately be applied for the analysis of databases and the evaluation of the usefulness of attributes in data mining [14].

One of the main tasks in knowledge discovery and data mining (KDD) is to find important relationships, or associations, between attributes. In statistical terms, two attributes are associated if they are not independent [11]. Two attributes are independent if changing the value of one does not affect the value of the other. From this standpoint, we comment on the meaning of information-theoretic measures in the context of data mining.

For an attribute (or a set of attributes) X, the entropy value $H(X)$ indicates the information uncertainty associated with X. An attribute with a very large domain normally divides the database into more smaller classes than an attribute with a small domain. A regularity found in a very small portion of database may not necessarily be useful. On the other hand, an attribute with small domain usually divides the database into a few larger classes. One may not find regularities in such large subsets of the database. Entropy values may be used to control the selection of attributes. It is expected that an attribute with middle range entropy values may be more useful. Similar ideas have been used successfully in information retrieval [22]. A high frequency term tends to have a higher entropy value, and a lower frequency term tends to have a lower entropy value. Both may not be good index terms. The middle frequency terms tend to be useful in describing documents in a collection.

The conditional entropy $H(Y|X)$ measures the degree of one-way implication or functional dependency of the sets of attributes X and Y. If the functional dependency $X \rightarrow Y$ holds, we conclude that $P(y_j|x_i)$ is either 1 or 0. In term of conditional entropy, $X \rightarrow Y$ holds if and only if $H(Y|X) = 0$ [10, 14]. By the relationships between entropy, conditional entropy, and mutual information, the above condition can be equivalently stated as $H(X) = H(X,Y)$ or $I(X;Y) = H(Y)$ [10]. If Y is dependent on X, the partition of the database by X and Y is exactly the same as the one produced by X alone. The former condition reflects this observation. The latter condition shows that the mutual information between X and Y is the same as the self-information of Y. The conditional entropy function can be used to measure the importance of attributes for discovering one-way associations. For a fixed Y, one obvious disadvantage of using $H(Y|X)$ is that it favours attributes with large domains, namely, attributes with high entropy values [16].

Mutual information measures the degree of deviation of a joint distribution from the independence distribution [21]. It may be used to evaluate the usefulness of attributes in finding two-way associations. With a fixed Y, the use of $I(X;Y)$ for finding a two-way association is in fact the same as using $H(Y|X)$ for finding a one-way association [13, 19]. Two sets of attributes X and Y are statistically independent if $I(X;Y) = 0$. Equivalently, we can state this condition as $H(X) = H(X|Y)$, $H(Y) = H(Y|X)$, or $H(X,Y) = H(X) + H(Y)$. If X and Y are independent, one cannot use values of X to predicate the values of Y, and vice versa. In information-theoretic terms, knowing the value of Y does not reduce our uncertainty about X, and vice versa.

Conditional entropy and mutual information serve as the basic quantities for measuring attribute associations. By combination and normalization, one may obtain many information-theoretic measures of attribute importance. In summary, the following three groups can be obtained:

- Lee [10], Malvestuto [14], Pawlak *et al.* [15]: $H(X \mid Y), H(Y \mid X)$;
  Kvålseth [9], Malvestuto [14], Quinlan [16]: $I(X;Y)/H(X), I(X;Y)/H(Y)$.
- Knobbe and Adriaans [8], Linfoot [12], Quinlan [16]: $I(X;Y)$;
  Malvestuto [14]: $I(X;Y)/H(X,Y)$; Kvålseth [9]: $2I(X;Y)/(H(X) + H(Y))$;
  Horibe [4], Kvålseth [9]: $I(X;Y)/\max(H(X), H(Y))$;
  Kvålseth [9]: $I(X;Y)/\min(H(X), H(Y))$.
- López de Mántaras [13], Wan and Wong [19]: $H(X \mid Y) + H(Y \mid X)$;
  López de Mántaras [13], Rajski [17]: $(H(X \mid Y) + H(Y \mid X))/H(X,Y)$.

Measures in the first group are asymmetric while measures in the other two groups are symmetric. Measures in the third group are distance measures. One can obtain the following relationships between these measures:

(i)
$$\frac{I(X;Y)}{H(X)} = 1 - \frac{H(X|Y)}{H(X)},$$

(ii)
$$\frac{I(X;Y)}{\max(H(X), H(Y))} = \min\left(\frac{I(X;Y)}{H(X)}, \frac{I(X;Y)}{H(Y)}\right),$$

(ii)
$$\frac{I(X;Y)}{\min(H(X), H(Y))} = \max\left(\frac{I(X;Y)}{H(X)}, \frac{I(X;Y)}{H(Y)}\right),$$

(iv) $0 \leq \dfrac{I(X;Y)}{\max(H(X),H(Y))} \leq \dfrac{2I(X;Y)}{H(X)+H(Y)} \leq \dfrac{I(X;Y)}{\min(H(X),H(Y))},$

(v) $H(X|Y) + H(Y|X) = H(X,Y) - I(X;Y),$

(vi) $\dfrac{2I(X;Y)}{H(X)+H(Y)} = 2\left(1 - \dfrac{H(X,Y)}{H(X)+H(Y)}\right),$

(vii) $\dfrac{H(X\,|\,Y) + H(Y\,|\,X)}{H(X,Y)} = 1 - \dfrac{I(X;Y)}{H(X,Y)}.$

They provide additional support for various measures. Furthermore, measures of one-way association can be expressed in a general form as different normalizations of conditional entropy, while measures of two-way association as different normalizations of mutual information [9].

In studying main problems for KDD, Klösgen [7] discussed two types of problems, namely, *classification and predication* and *summary and description*. Kamber and Shinghal [6] referred to them as the discovery of discriminant and characteristic rules, respectively. The classification and predication problem deals with the discovery of a set of rules or similar patterns for predicting the values of a dependent variable. The ID3 algorithm [16] and the mining of associate rules [1] are examples for solving this type of problem. The summary and description problem involves the discovery of a dominant structure that derives a dependency. It is important to note that asymmetric measures may be suitable for former problem, while symmetric measures may be appropriate for the latter.

In the study of association of random variables using statistical measures, Liebetrau [11] pointed out that many symmetric measures do not tell us anything about causality. When two attributes are shown to be correlated, it is very tempting to infer a cause-and-effect relationship between them. It is very important to realize that the mere identification of association does not provide grounds to establish causality. Garner and McGill [3] showed that information analysis is very similar to analysis of variance. One may then extend the argument of Liebetrau [11] to information-theoretic measures. In order to establish causality, we need additional techniques in data mining.

3   Conclusion

This preliminary study has demonstrated that asymmetric measures quantify one-way association and are typically related to conditional entropy, while symmetric measures quantify two-way association and are typically related to mutual information. If information theory is to be used to develop a formal theory for knowledge discovery and data mining, then the principle of entropy reduction and models in which causality can be established [11] warrant more attention.

References

1. Agrawal, R., Imielinski, T., and Swami, A.: Mining association rules between sets of items in large databases. Proc. of the ACM SIGMOD International Conference on the Management of Data (1993) 207-216.

2. Cover, T. and Thomas, J.: Elements of Information Theory. John Wiley & Sons, Toronto (1991)

3. Garner, W.R. and McGill, W.J.: Relation between information and variance analyses. Psychometrika **21** (1956) 219-228.

4. Horibe, Y.: Entropy and correlation. IEEE Trans. Syst. Man Cybern. **SMC-15** (1985) 641-642.

5. Hou, W.: Extraction and applications of statistical relationships in relational databases. IEEE Trans. Knowl. Data Eng. **8** (1996) 939-945.

6. Kamber, M. and Shinghal, R.: Evaluating the interestingness of characteristic rules. Proc. of KDD-96 (1996) 263-266.

7. Klösgen, W.: Explora: a multipattern and multistrategy discovery assistant. in: Fayyad, U.M, Piatetsky-Shapiro, G., Smyth, P., and Uthurusamy, R. (Eds.), Advances in Knowledge Discovery and Data Mining. AAAI Press / MIT Press, California. (1996) 249-271.

8. Knobbe, A.J. and Adriaans P.W.: Analysis of binary association. Proc. of KDD-96 (1996) 311-314.

9. Kvålseth, T.O.: Entropy and correlation: some comments. IEEE Trans. Syst. Man Cybern. **SMC-17** (1987) 517-519.

10. Lee, T.T.: An information-theoretic analysis of relational databases – part I: data dependencies and information metric. IEEE Trans. Soft. Eng. **SE-13** (1987) 1049-1061.

11. Liebetrau, A.M.: Measures of Association. Sage Publications, Beverly Hills. (1983).

12. Linfoot, E.H.: An informational measure of correlation. Information and Control **1** (1957) 85-87.

13. López de Mántaras, R.: ID3 revisited: a distance-based criterion for attribute selection. in: Ras, Z.W. (Ed.), Methodologies for Intelligent Systems, 4. North-Holland, New York. (1989) 342-350.

14. Malvestuto, F.M.: Statistical treatment of the information content of a database. Inf. Syst. **11** (1986) 211-223.

15. Pawlak, Z., Wong, S.K.M., and Ziarko, W.: Rough sets: probabilistic versus deterministic approach. Int. J. Man-Machine Stud. **29** (1988) 81-95.

16. Quinlan, J.R.: Induction of decision trees. Machine Learning **1** (1986) 81-106.

17. Rajski, C.: A metric space of discrete probability distributions. Information and Control **4** (1961) 373-377.

18. Sheridan, T.B. and Ferrell, W.R.: Man-Machine Systems: Information, Control, and Decision Models of Human Performance. MIT Press, Cambridge. (1974).

19. Wan, S.J. and Wong, S.K.M.: A measure for attribute dissimilarity and its applications in machine learning. in: Janicki, R. and Koczkodaj, W.W. (Eds.), Computing and Information. North-Holland, Amsterdam. (1989) 267-273.

20. Wang, Q.R. and Suen, C.Y.: Analysis and design of a decision tree based on entropy reduction and its application to large character set recognition. IEEE Trans. Pattern Anal. Mach. Intell. **PAMI-6** (1984) 406-417.

21. Watanabe, S.: Pattern recognition as a quest for minimum entropy. Pattern Recognit. **13** (1981) 381-387.

22. Wong, S.K.M. and Yao, Y.Y.: A probability distribution model for information retrieval. Inf. Process. Manage. **25** (1989) 39-53.

A Technique of Dynamic Feature Selection Using the Feature Group Mutual Information

Kee-Cheol Lee

Dept. of Computer Science, HongIk University
Seoul, Korea 121-791
lee@cs.hongik.ac.kr

ABSTRACT

Knowledge discovery from raw data is very important to non-experts and even experts who feel difficulty in expressing their skills in machine interpretable forms. However, real world data often contain some redundant or unnecessary features, and if they are directly used, the quality of the seeking knowledge may be much degraded. Here, a new technique of dynamically selecting features is suggested. Contrary to the static feature selection, this scheme selects each new feature based on its correlation with the previously selected features. In addition, this scheme does not require setting any threshold, which would be too difficult to decide. Experiments have been conducted for some real world domains in terms of tree sizes and test data error rates. The results show the soundness of this scheme.

Keyword : machine learning, feature selection, mutual information, data mining

1. INTRODUCTION

In the past two decades, techniques of knowledge acquisition from raw data have been studied. The most notable ones are decision tree approaches like ID3[1] and C4.5[2], back propagation methods[3], INDUCE system[4], and logic minimization based approaches like R-MINI[5] and R-ESPRESSO[6]. However, the given data have been directly used by those systems without any preprocessing.

The raw data used for inductive learning often contain features irrelevant to the decision of the classes to which the data belong. Some features even worsen the process of learning in that they sometimes enormously increase the learning time, and produce more rules and less accurate recognition rates. For this reason, it is important to select the subset of the features of the given data such that the performance of the learning is optimal. The optimality may be judged by the combination of many factors including the learning time, the size of the final knowledge, and the recognition rates of data, especially of unseen data.

2. Previous Works

The problem FRn-k(Feature Reduction n-k) is to select the optimal k ($<n$) out of n features. However, the optimal subset selection time is on the order of nCk, which is practically impossible for large values of k and n.

Information-theoretic measures[7] may be applied for the selection of features. The mutual information $I(C; F)$ of C and F is measured by how much the uncertainty

This work was supported by Korea Science Foundation under contract 97-01-02-04-01-3.

decreases after the value of F gets known. Statically, k features may be selected with largest mutual information.

Battiti's algorithm[8], MIFS, calculates for each candidate feature F its mutual information with the class feature C, and the average of its mutual information with each of the already selected features. After scaling the average, the difference between the two values is used as the selection measure.

That is, for each candidate feature F, $\quad I\ (\ C\ ;\ F)\ -\beta\times\sum_{F'\in S}I(F;F')/\,|\,S\,|\quad$ is

calculated, and the feature with the maximum value is selected This corresponds to the balancing of static and dynamic characteristics. The problem is tha: the value of the balancing factor β is too hard to decide.

3. FGMIFS(Feature Group - Mutual Information based Feature Selection)

3.1 Flattened feature and Feature group mutual information

The values of the flattened feature (F, S) belong to $F\times S_1\times S_2\times ...\times S_K'$, where F is the feature the domain of which is F, and S is the set of k features the domains of which are $S_1, S_2, ... , S_k$, respectively.

For example, assume that a new feature (i.e., F) is length the values of which are long and short, and two features shape, and color are already selected. Assume further the values of shape are rectangle and triangle, and the values of color are red and yellow. Then, (rectangle, red, long), (triangle, yellow, short), (triangle, red, long) and so on are the values of the flattened feature. Only the values existing in the training data are used.

The new conditional entropy of the class C given the new flattened feature (F, S) is given by the equation 2. Here, S is the set of already selected features, and F is an unselected (or candidate) feature to be tested for a potential selection.

$$H(C) = -\sum_{c=1}^{Nc} P(c)\log P(c) \tag{1}$$

$$H(C\,|\,(F, S)) = -\sum_{S'\in S}P(s')(\sum_{c=1}^{Nc}P(c\,|\,s')\log P(c\,|\,s')) \tag{2}$$

$$S' = \text{the set of feature values of } (F, S)$$

Finally, the mutual information $GI(C; (F,S))$ of the flattened feature (F,S) is defined as the difference between $H(C)$ and $H(C|(F,S))$, and called the feature group mutual information between the feature F and the group S of features. Therefore, the feature F is selected among all candidate features such that $GI(C; (F,S))$ in equation 3 is maximum.

$$GI(C; (F, S)) = H(C) - H(C\,|\,(F,S)) \tag{3}$$

3.2 Selection of the first feature

The mutual information has a strong bias for the features with many values. For example, the resident id, not useful for the disease classification, has so many values that the feature will surely produce the maximum mutual information and be selected first. This will much degrade the quality of the feature selection, and tend to produce unnecessarily many rules. For that reason, the first feature is selected using the gain ratio[9] which is defined as the mutual information divided by the split information.

3.3 FGMIFS algorithm

FGMIFS selects the first feature as the one with the largest gain ratio. Afterwards, the next feature to select is decided as the one with the maximum group information in that the group information is judged between the flattened feature and a candidate feature. The process is repeated until k features are selected. This dynamic feature selection based on the flattened feature concept does not try to balance the static and dynamic characteristics because it already considers the relation with all the selected features. The concrete algorithm is as follows.

Step 1: $FS \leftarrow$ initial set of n features;
  $\quad S \leftarrow \{ \}$;
Step 2: for each feature $F \in FS$,
  $\quad$ Compute $I(C;F) / SI(F)$;
Step 3: Choose F from FS
  $\quad$ That maximize $I(C;F) / SI(F)$;
  $\quad FS \leftarrow FS - \{F\}$;
  $\quad S \leftarrow S \cup \{F\}$;
Step 4: Repeat until $|S| = k$
  $\quad$ Choose F from FS
  $\quad$ That maximize $GI(C; (F,S))$;
  $\quad FS \leftarrow FS - \{F\}$;
  $\quad S \leftarrow S \cup \{F\}$;

FGMIFS Algorithm

4. Experiments

The FGMIFS algorithm was compared with the Battiti's MIFS algorithm and static algorithm, based on the error rates by C4.5rules system and the tree sizes by C4.5 system. The MIFS algorithm was applied with the threshhold $\beta = 1$. The static algorithm corresponds to the MIFS with $\beta = 0$. Some results are below.

4.1 LED display data

The 2,000 training data with 10% error for each feature(i.e., bit) and 1,000 test data were used in the 10-class LED display domain[10]. 17 out of 24 features are irrelevant ones filled with random numbers. <Fig. 1> shows that the set of about 7 features with small tree sizes and small error rates can be successfully selected.

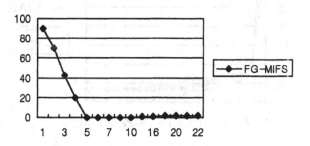

Fig. 1 Error rates by C4.5 rules for LED display test data

4.2 Mushroom data

In the 24-feature/2-class mushroom domain[10], the 2,822 training data and 2,822 test data without any missing features were used. FGMIFS results look steadily best.

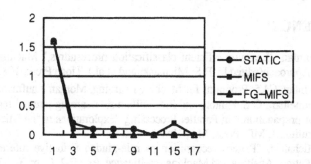

Fig.2 Error rates by C4.5 for mushroom test data after each algorithm is used.

4.3 KRKPA7 data

KRKPA7 data[10] contain 36 features and two classes, *win* and *nowin*. For this experiment, 2,338 training data and 584 test data were used.

In this domain, FGMIFS works better than MIFS in terms of the recognition rates. However, FGMIFS produces the bigger trees. The reason may be that MIFS could prune even the necessary branches, resulting in the lower recognition rates.

5. Conclusion and Future research

Through experiments, FGMIFS has been shown to be a very effective feature selection scheme compared with the static algorithm or Battiti's dynamic algorithm.

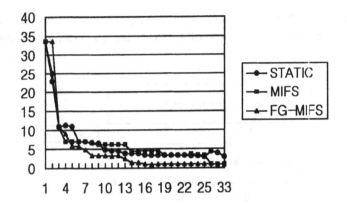

Fig.3 Error rates by C4.5rules for krkpa7 test data after each algorithm is used.

This scheme utilizes the concept of the flattened attribute and eliminates setting the threshold, resulting in a stable performance.

The automatic selection of an optimal k may be applied on top of this scheme, and preliminary results already show the usefulness of FGMIFS. Flattening all the selected features may be somewhat loosened such that some subset of selected features may be applied or grouping selected features may be used.

REFERENCES

[1] J.R. Quinlan, "Learning efficient classification procesudres," Machine Learning: An AI Approach(edited by R.S. Michalski and et al.), Tioga Press, 1983.

[2] J.R. Quinlan, C4.5: Programs for Machine Learning, Morgan Kaufmann, 1993.

[3] D.E. Rumelhart, G.E. Hinton, and R.J. Williams, "Learning internal representation by error propagation," In Parallel Processing: Explorations in the Microstructures of Cognition, 1, MIT Press, MA, 1986.

[4] R.S. Michalski, "Pattern recognition as rule-guided inductive inference," IEEE Trans. Pattern Analysis and Machine Intelligence, PAMI-2(4), pp.349-361, 1980.

[5] S.J. Hong, "R-MINI: An Iterative Approach for Generating Minimal Rules from Examples," IEEE Trans. Knowledge and Engineering, 9(5), pp.709-717, 1997.

[6] K.C. Lee and J.B. Kim, "A Rule Generation Technique Utilizing a Parallel Expansion Method," Korea Information Proc. Society, 5(4), pp.942-950, 1998.

[7] C.E. Shannon and W. Weaver, "A Mathematical Theory of Communication," Urbana, IL: University of Illinois Press, 1949.

[8] R. Battiti "Using Mutual Information for Selecting Features in Supervised Neural Net Learning," IEEE Trans. on Neural Networks, 5(4), pp537-550, July 1994.

[9] UCI ML Repository Content Summary, http://www.ics.uci.edu/~mlearn/MLSummary.html

A Data Pre-processing Method Using Association Rules of Attributes for Improving Decision Tree

Masahiro Terabe[1], Osamu Katai[2] Tetsuo Sawaragi[3],
Takashi Washio[4], and Hiroshi Motoda[4]

[1] Mitsubishi Research Institute,Inc.
2-3-6 Ohtemachi,Chiyoda,100-8141 Tokyo,Japan
terabe@mri.co.jp
[2] Graduate School of Informatics, Kyoto University
Yoshida-Honmachi,Sakyo,606-8501 Kyoto,Japan
katai@prec.kyoto-u.ac.jp
[3] Graduate School of Engineering, Kyoto University
Yoshida-Honmachi,Sakyo,606-8501 Kyoto,Japan
sawaragi@prec.kyoto-u.ac.jp
[4] Institute for the Scientfic and Industrial Research,Osaka University
8-7 Mihogaoka.Ibaraki,567-0047 Osaka,Japan
{washio,motoda}@sanken.osaka-u.ac.jp

Abstract. One of the approaches to generate a good decision tree is pre-processing the data to improve its description. There are many researches on data pre-processing such as attributes generation and attributes selection methods. However, most of them are based on logic programming so that it takes much run time. Additionally, some of them need a priori knowledge. These are disadvantage for the data mining. We propose a novel data driven approach that knowledge on the relevance of attributes are generated as association rules from the data, so a priori knowledge is not necessary. In this paper, we present the method and clarify its feature. The effectiveness of our method as data mining one is evaluated through experiments.

1 Introduction

In general, it is difficult to generate a good decision tree that is small size and high prediction accuracy. The reason is that the data always don't include the adequate attributes and their values. This is why it is necessary to pre-processing the data, i.e., adding new attributes to the data and improving its description. Many of researches have done on such data pre-processing for decision tree. Nevertheless, many of the proposed pre-processing methods are based on logic programming. Moreover they need a priori knowledge on the attributes and their relevance[Lavrăc]. These features are disadvantage as a data mining method.

In this paper, we propose a novel data pre-processing method for decision tree. In this method, the knowledge on attributes is generated from the data so that the analysts need no a priori knowledge on data and its attributes. Additionally, the method employs the apriori algorithm that works fast even if the data size is large[Agrawal], and succeeds to make the run time short.

2　The Proposed Method

Our proposed method is composed by five parts: (1) data transformation, (2) generating association rules of attributes, (3)generating the candidates of new attribute, (4) evaluation of the candidates, and (5) improving data description.

Data transformation: First, we transform the data description of training data $\mathcal{D}$ to transaction data $\mathcal{DN}$. Each of the data $data_i$ in $\mathcal{D}$ consists of a set of attribute values $v_{i,1}, \ldots, v_{i,n}$ for explanation attributes $A_1, \ldots, A_n$ and a class c_i for the class attribute C as follows.

$$data_i = <v_{i,1}, \ldots, v_{i,n}, c_i> \tag{1}$$

A transaction data $trans_i$ in $\mathcal{DN}$ is composed by items such as "$A_j = v_{i,j}$" and "$C = c_i$", and each item is a pair of an attribute and its value in $\mathcal{D}$ as follows.

$$trans_i = <A_1 = v_{i,1}, \ldots, A_n = v_{i,n}, C = c_i> \tag{2}$$

Generating association rules of attributes: Second, the knowledge of relevance of attributes and class is generated as association rules from the transaction data. In this method, we need the association rules that satisfy the next two conditions: (1)the condition part doesn't include item corresponding to class attribute and (2) the consequent part includes unique item corresponding to class. Such association rule described as follows.

Rule R_i : **if** $A_{i_1} = v_{i_1}, \ldots, A_{i_n} = v_{i_n}$ **then** $C = c_i$

$$support\ value : sup(R_i), confidence\ value : conf(R_i) \tag{3}$$

The support value of an association rule is that the ratio of the number of data that condition part of the rule matches to the number of data in the data set $\mathcal{DN}$. The confidence value of an association rule is that the ratio of the number of data that both of the condition part of the rule matches to the number of data that condition and consequent part of the rule matches. This association rule R_i implies that the class of a data is the consequent part's one if the data includes the same attribute set in the condition part in many cases. For the association rule generation process, proposed method employs apriori algorithm that can generates fast even if the data size is large. This makes the run time of proposed method enough short as data mining method.

Generating candidates of new attributes: Third, the candidates of new attributes and their attribute values are generated from the set of association rules $\mathcal{R} = \{R_1, \ldots, R_m\}$. At first, each of the rule R_i is a candidate of the new attribute. The candidate generated from the rule R_i is defined as follows.

Candidate of New Attribute : AN_i

Attribute : $\mathcal{A} = < A_{i_1}, \ldots, A_{i_n} >$

Attribute Value : $\mathcal{V} = \{V_1, V_2\}$

$$V_1 = < v_{i_1}, \ldots, v_{i_1} >$$

$$V_2 = \overline{V_1} \tag{4}$$

The attribute value V_1 is defined as the vector pattern of attribute values in the condition part of the association rule such as $V_1 = < v_{i_1}, \ldots, v_{i_n} >$. Additionally, the attribute value V_2 is add for the attribute value pattern that doesn't match any attribute values V_1 from the association rules. The candidates AN_i and AN_j that includes the same attributes $\mathcal{A}$ are merged into one candidate of new attribute. The attribute value of the merged candidate is the union set of the attribute values $\mathcal{V}$ for AN_i and AN_j. By this way, the set of candidates of new attribute $\mathcal{AN} = \{AN_1, \ldots, AN_k\}$ is generated from the $\mathcal{R}$.

Evaluation of the candidates: Fourth, the usefulness of new attributes candidates $AN_j \in \mathcal{AN}$ in the decision tree are evaluated. We use the information gain criterion, which is used in decision tree algorithm such as ID3[Quinlan]. The information gain $Gain(AN_j)$ for each candidate of a new attribute candidate AN_j is defined as follows.

$$
Gain(AN_j)
$$

$$
= -\sum_{i=1}^{|C|} \frac{n(c_i)}{N} \log_2 \frac{n(c_i)}{N}
$$

$$
- \sum_{i=1}^{|V|-1} \{-conf_i \log_2 conf_i - (1.0 - conf_i) \log_2 (1.0 - conf_i)/(|C|-1)\}
$$

$$
- \left\{ 1.0 - \sum_{i=1}^{|V|-1} sup_i \right\} \log_2 |C|
$$

where

N : number of data

$n(c_i)$: number of training data that the class is c_i

$sup_i, conf_i$: support and confidence value of $\mathcal{R}$ that are merget into AN_j(5)

This information gain estimated approximately in the case that the AN_j splits to the top node. You should mention that only indexes calculated in apriori algorithm are used in this evaluation, and it enable to evaluate the candidates in the short time.

Improving the description of data: Finally, if the $Gain(AN_j)$ bigger than 0, the candidate is added to the original data $\mathcal{D}$. By such pre-processing, the description of the data for decision tree is improved.

3   Experiments and Discussion

We present the effectiveness of our proposed method as data-preprocessing method in data mining domain through some experiments. The features of the data set used in experiments are summarized in table 1. They are picked up from UCI ML depository[ML]. As decision tree algorithm, we adopt C4.5 that is one of the famous decision tree algorithms[Quinlan]. We evaluate the effectiveness of the proposed method from two point of views. One is the improvement of decision tree on size and prediction accuracy. Another is run time when the method is applied to the large volume data. They are important points for the applicability to data mining.

3.1   Improvement of Decision Tree by Proposed Method

To confirm the effect of improving decision tree of the proposed method, we generate decision trees from two data. One is original data, and another is pre-processed data by proposed method. We compare the size and the prediction accuracy of the two decision trees. The results are summarized in table 1.

By applying proposed method to the data, the generated decision tree is improved in the size and prediction accuracy in many cases. However, the proposed method sometimes can't improve the decision tree. This may be because that there are too many attribute values and noisy data so that the association of attribute had not extracted as association rules appropriately. We need more researches on this problem as future work.

Table 1. The effectiveness of proposed method in improving decision tree

data	# of data	# of cls.	decision tree original data			decision tree pre-processed data		
			size	err. rate(%)	# of att.	size	err. rate(%)	# of attr.
census-data	32562	2	221	16.9	8	221	16.9	31
car	1728	4	173.2	6.8	6	88.7	4.5	18
monk1	124	2	18	24.3	6	8	0.0	22
monk2	169	2	31	35.0	6	35	24.5	19
monk3	122	2	12	2.8	6	11	7.2	27
mushroom	8124	2	32.0	0.0	22	32.6	0.0	42
nursery	12690	5	508.3	2.9	8	571.8	3.0	18
tic-tac-toe	958	2	139.3	15.2	9	23.7	0.3	25
votes	435	2	15.4	3.7	16	13.8	3.9	186
average			115.0	10.8	8.7	100.6	6.0	38.8

3.2 The Performance of Proposed Method to the Large Volume Data

Next, we investigate the performance of proposed method to the large volume data. To make the test data set, we use Monk1 data set. A data is picked up at random as a source of new data, and add noise to the class of the data with 5% probability. The process repeated as the same time as the required number of the test data. In this experiment, we use the PC(OS:Linux,CPU:Pentium 133MHz,memory:128MB). The experimental results are summarized in table 2.

Table 2. The run time for pre-processing in the large data

# of data	decision tree original data		decision tree pre-processed data		pre-processing run time (sec)
	size	err. rate(%)	size	err. rate(%)	
10,000	90	5.0	9	5.0	4
50,000	79	4.9	12	4.9	13
100,000	79	5.0	12	5.0	22
500,000	90	5.0	13	5.0	114

Even if the volume of data becomes larger the run time is increasing at most linearly. The calculation cost is much smaller than that of logic programming based methods. Furthermore, the effectiveness in improving decision tree is not decreased even if the data size is large. These features of proposed method are advantage as data mining one.

4 Conclusion

We proposed the new data pre-processing method for decision tree using association rules of attributes, and confirmed the effectiveness of improving decision tree and applicability to the data mining.

References

[Agrawal] Agrawal,R. et al.: Fast Algorithms for mining association rules. Proc. of the 20th VLDB Conference. (1994) 487–499.
[Berry] Berry,M.J.A. et al.: Data Mining Techniques For Marketing, Sales, and Customer Support. Wiley.(1997)
[Lavrăc] Lavrac, N. et al.: A relevancy filter for constructive induction, IEEE Intelligent Systems & their applications 13 2 (1998) 50–56
[ML] Merz,C.J. et al.: UCI Repository of machine learning databases. (1998) [http://www.ics.uci.edu/ mlearn/MLRepository.html]
[Quinlan] Quinlan,R.: C4.5: Programs for Machine Learning.Morgan Kaufmann.(1993)

An Algorithm for Constrained Association Rule Mining in Semi-structured Data

Lisa Singh[1], Bin Chen[1], Rebecca Haight[2], Peter Scheuermann[1]

[1] Northwestern University, Evanston, IL 60208, USA
{lsingh, bchen, peters @ ece.nwu.edu}
[2] Data Harbor, Inc., Chicago, IL 60610, USA
{rlh@dataharbor.com}

Abstract. The need for sophisticated analysis of textual documents is becoming more apparent as data is being placed on the Web and digital libraries are surfacing. This paper presents an algorithm for generating constrained association rules from textual documents. The user specifies a set of constraints, concepts and/or structured values. Our algorithm creates matrices and lists based on these prespecified constraints and uses them to generate large itemsets. Because these matrices are small and sparse, we are able to quickly generate higher order large itemsets. Further, since we maintain concept relationship information in a concept library, we can also generate rulesets involving concepts related to the initial set of constraints.

1 Introduction

Finding global patterns or generalizations can provide insight into subsets of a textual data set. However, because of the large number of patterns that typically exist in a textual database, preconstraining the data space and searching for targeted patterns can at times be more fruitful. This paper presents an algorithm for constrained association rule discovery. The main contributions of our algorithm are as follows. First, our algorithm creates matrices and lists based on prespecified user constraints and uses them to generate large itemsets. Because these matrices are sparse, we are able to quickly generate higher order large itemsets. Further, it incorporates knowledge from both the structured components and the unstructured components of the textual data set. Finally, since we maintain concept relationship information in a concept library, we can also generate rulesets involving concepts related to the initial set of constraints.

The remainder of this paper is organized as follows. Section 2 presents a motivating example from a business document collection. Section 3 describes our conceptual framework for generating rulesets from semi-structured data. Section 4 details our constrained association rule algorithm. Finally, Section 5 presents experimental results and conclusions.

2 Motivating Example

Magazine articles, research papers, and World Wide Web HTML pages are traditionally considered semi-structured information. Each of these examples contains some clearly identifiable features, including author, date, publisher and/or WWW address. In this paper, we refer to these identifiable features as *structured attributes*. Each document also includes blocks of text that are considered unstructured components of the document, e.g. abstract, headings, and paragraphs. We define a *concept* to be any meaningful word, phrase, acronym, or name that has been extracted from these components.

The problem with text data is that limited insight about documents can be attained using only the structured document components. A digital library system only provides limited knowledge about the document collection as a whole. For example, suppose a user is interested in answering the following question:

> *During the past year, how have articles in a particular journal been broken down in my research area?*

If the user is attempting to answer this question using a typical information retrieval system, he will enter the research area of interest (*organizational theory*) and a journal name (*Academy of Management*). When the list of articles is returned, he will need to find groupings of articles from the previous year and semi-automatically categorize them.

We propose an algorithm that not only answers this question, but also attempts to provide the user with some additional insight. We define a *constraint* to be any concept or structured value input by the user. For example, if the user specifies the following constraints (*1998, Academy of Management* and *organizational theory*), then our algorithm might return the following ruleset:

(*A*)   Academy of Management, 1998 → organizational theory : 20%

(*B*)   Academy of Management, organizational theory, 1998
                              → population ecology : 20%
                              → bureaucracy : 30%

Rule *A* involves the constraints specified by the user. This rule states that 20% of the articles in the *Academy of Management* in the *1998* journal are *organizational theory* articles. Rule *B* involves concepts related to the concept constraints (e.g. *organizational theory*). According to Rule *B*, in *1998, organizational theory* articles published in the *Academy of Management* journal were about *population ecology* 20% of the time and *bureaucracy* 30% of the time. We refer to these rules as *constrained association rules* since they are based on a set of prespecified constraints. In order for Rule B to be generated, we must maintain information about relationships that exist between the concepts, both the strength of the relationship and the type of relationship (e.g. synonym, broad-narrow, etc). By maintaining concept and structured value data, we can quickly extract patterns from a large document space.

3 Definitions and Conceptual Model

3.1 Association Rules

Formally, [1] defines an association rule in transactional databases to be an expression of the form $X \to Y$, where X and Y are sets of items or *itemsets*. The *support* of itemset XY is the probability of joint occurrence of X and Y, $P(XY)$. A *large itemset* is one in which $P(XY)$ is above the minimum support, *min_sup*. We will use large itemsets and *strong sets* interchangeably throughout the paper. The *confidence* of $X \to Y$ is defined as the conditional probability of Y given X, $P(Y|X)$, where *min_conf* represents the minimum confidence.

The definition of association rules in a transaction database can be extended to a semi-structured domain. Specifically, each document can be viewed as a transaction and each structured value or concept as an item. Even though we can model semi-structured data as a set of transactions, we choose to reformulate this model because text mining has different requirements than traditional transaction database mining. First, the number of distinct items is very large, and, therefore, interesting rules may have a very low support. Also, documents (transactions) are typically long and must be parsed offline to determine the meaningful set of concepts and structured values. Finally, online ontologies or dictionaries identify semantic relationships between concepts. This additional knowledge can be used to efficiently focus and add semantic knowledge to the final ruleset. Because of these distinctions, current structured value association rule algorithms that scan through all the items in all the transactions are not ideal for mining document data. Instead, it can be more advantageous to generate rules based on a set of constraints. For preconstrained textual mining, this structure facilitates the rule discovery process.

3.2 Conceptual Model

In our previous work [5], we proposed a system architecture that attempts to provide an infrastructure robust enough to facilitate the discovery of rules from semi-structured data sets. In this architecture, concepts are stored in the concept library, while structured values are stored in the database. Figure 1 shows some example structured value data and a mapping to the documents containing each structured value. We choose to associate each document name with a document id since storing varying length document names with each structured value uses more disk space. The concept library consists of two logical components. One is a mapping between concepts and documents containing each concept. Figure 2 shows examples of this. The other is a graph structure that maintains the relationships each concept has to other concepts in the domain, as well as the weight of each relationship. Figure 3 shows a portion of the concept library, where each concept, C_i, is a node and each relationship a weighted edge. Single directional edges point from broader to narrower concepts, while bidirectional arrows exist between similar sibling concepts. For every pair of concepts C_a and C_b, the *relationship weight* $rw(C_aC_b)$ identifies the strength of the relationship. There are

Structured Values (SV)	SV IDs	#. Docs	Document ID List
Joe Smith	S1	8	1, 3, 6, 8, 12, 16, 18, 20
... ...			
Administrative Science Quarterly	S5	6	1, 3, 8, 12, 15, 17
Academy of Management	S6	7	2, 4, 6, 9, 10, 16, 19
... ...			
1998	S8	10	1, 3, 4, 5, 6, 8, 10, 16, 18, 19

Fig. 1. Structured Value Document Mapping

different techniques for determining relationship weight. It can be manually determined by assigning a weight based on a defined relationship in a dictionary or ontology. Another approach uses information retrieval techniques to determine the weight based on the frequency of appearance of C_a and C_b in the same document. If $rw(C_a C_b)$ is greater than a minimum specified relationship weight, then we say that C_a and C_b have a *strong bond*. The notion of 'bonds' is derived from the bond-energy algorithm used in cluster analysis to derive similarities among attributes [7]. We use the bond to represent the relationship between two items. *Bond energy* or bond denotes the relationship weight. Document data can be

ConceptID	#. Docs	Document ID List
C1	10	1, 3, 4, 6, 7, 8, 11, 16, 18, 20
C2	2	2, 5
C3	8	1, 3, 6, 8, 11, 16, 18, 20
C4	8	5, 7, 8, 10, 12, 15, 16, 18
C5	4	2, 9, 13, 19
C6	3	5, 6, 10
C7	4	2, 3, 8, 10
C8	6	5, 10, 12, 15, 17, 19

Fig. 2. Concept Document Mapping

stored as traditional transaction systems, where the document id corresponds to the transaction id and the concepts or structured values map to transaction items. Our model differs from this traditional approach. Instead of storing each document transaction in the database, we choose to associate transaction ids with each item. In other words, for a given item (concept or structured value), we maintain a mapping to transaction (document) ids in the concept library and the database. Specifically, the problem of discovering large itemsets reduces to

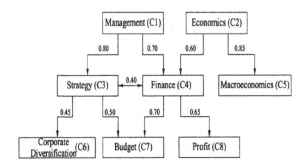

Fig. 3. Concept Library Data

the problem of traversing sparse matrices.

A small amount of literature exists about semi-structured text mining algorithms [2, 3, 6]. Of those, [6] is the only algorithm that uses prespecified constraints in it. The other works propose unsupervised procedures. As previously mentioned, for semi-structured data sets, unconstrained mining is very slow and leads to large numbers of rulesets.

Our previous work in [6] also identified associations among concepts and a single structured value. The user specifies one concept C_1, one structured value S_1, a minimum support min_sup, and a minimum confidence min_conf. The algorithm begins by obtaining the document ids of each constraint. The support for the potential large itemset $P(C_1 S_1)$ is calculated. If it is above min_sup, we search for large itemsets containing *concept_relatives* C_r of constraint C_1. For each concept C_r, if $rw(C_1 C_r)$ is larger than a minimum specified relationship weight, $P(C_1 S_1 C_r)$ is calculated. Rules are generated for all $P(C_1 S_1 C_r)$ above min_sup. Rules above min_conf are returned to the user.

To extend this algorithm to allow users to specify multiple constraints, it is necessary to introduce new data structures so as to avoid the computation of $P(C_i S_j C_r)$ for all combinations of concept constraints, C_i, structured value constraints, S_j, and *concept_relative*, C_r.

4 Constrained Association Rule Algorithm

We have extended our previous algorithm in the following ways:

1. We allow users to specify an unlimited number of constraints.
2. We use two sparse matrices to help us avoid comparing document lists for every subset of structured data values and concepts.
3. When determining large itemsets involving *concept_relatives*, we do not need to calculate the probability of joint occurrence for every *concept_relative* and the current large itemset. Instead we eliminate *concept_relatives* that clearly cannot be a member of a new large itemset.

4. Our concept library stores not only parent-child-sibling relationships, but others as well, synonym, part-to-whole and is-a. This in turn implies that a semantically more accurate set of rules can be generated. It should be noted that our concept library is a compilation of multiple extended concept hierarchies (ECHs) as proposed in [6].

During the development of our proposed algorithm, we will make use of the user inputs in Figure 4. Figure 5 highlights the main features of our algorithm.

STRUCTURED VALUES	CONCEPTS
AUTHOR:	strategy
Joe Smith	finance
PUBLICATION NAME:	management
Administrative Science Quarterly	profit
Academy of Management	
PUBLICATION DATE:	
1998	
MINIMUM SUPPORT:	0.1%
MINIMUM CONFIDENCE:	60%
MINIMUM RELATIONSHIP WEIGHT:	30%

Fig. 4. User Inputs

The algorithm begins by obtaining the document ids of all the structured values and all the concepts originally requested by the user, where N_c and N_s are the number of concepts and structured values specified by the user, respectively. The structured value information is obtained from the database, while the concept information is obtained from the concept library. For our example query illustrated in Figure 4, $N_s = 4$ and $N_c = 4$.

For all the specified constraints, C_i and S_j, Step 2 verifies that they are large 1-itemsets by checking the count of the document lists. The concept constraints above min_sup are placed in the *C-List*, a list containing all the large concept itemsets. Similarly, the structured value constraints above min_sup, 0.1% for our example, are placed in the *SV-List*, a list containing all the large structured value itemsets.

In Step 3, we generate a structured value matrix, *SV-Bond Matrix*, that will be used to determine higher order large itemsets. In order to create the matrix, we use the items in the SV-List to generate large 2-itemsets. We determine if $P(S_aS_b)$ is above min_sup for all pairs (a, b) in the list. If so, the pair (a, b) is added to the SV-List and a 1 is added to the SV-Bond Matrix to indicate a strong bond between two structured values. If pair (a, b) is less than min_sup a 0 is added.

Notice that we only populate the lower triangle of the matrix. At this stage, the sum of each column is calculated. This *pair count* identifies the number of

---

Algorithm: Generalized Constrained Association Rules

Input: C_i - concept constraints, (i: 1 to N_c)

  S_j - structured value constraints, (j: 1 to N_s)

Output: RS - ruleset containing constraints and related concepts

1. Get document ids for all C_i and S_j
2A. for every C_i
    if $support(C_i) > $ min_sup add to C-List
2B. for every S_j
    if $support(S_j) > $ min_sup, add to SV-List
3. Create structured value matrix, SV-Bond Matrix
4. Determine structured value large item sets, put in SV-List
5. Create concept matrix, C-Bond Matrix
6. Determine concept large itemsets, put in C-List
7. Identify large itemsets using lists
8. for each large itemset, determine *concept_relatives*
    generate additional large itemsets using *concept_relatives*
9. Calculate RS

Fig. 5. Pseudo-code for Constrained Association Rule Alg.

strong bonds existing in the column. Figure 6 shows the SV-Bond Matrix for our example. Column S_1 has the largest pair count. Just based on these counts alone, we know that the maximum large itemset size cannot exceed 3 and that it must include column S_1.

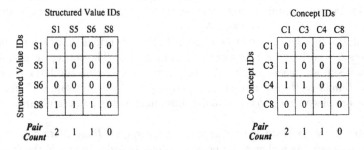

Fig. 6. Example SV-Bond Matrix   **Fig. 7.** Example C-Bond Matrix

The matrix can now be used to generate higher order large itemsets (Step 4 of algorithm) without first determining the intersections of every subset of structured values. Since all subsets of a large itemset must have strong bonds, we can use the information in the SV-Bond Matrix to find these larger sets. There are three criteria for determining the large itemsets of size N, where N is larger than 2:

1. The pair count for one of the N columns containing the data values is at least N - 1.
2. Each pair in the set must have a strong bond.
3. The set must have support above the min_sup.

We determine large 3-itemsets by using the strong bonds in the SV-Bond Matrix. For each set of size 2, we check the pair count for the first item in the set. If it is at least 2, we test whether it can be expanded by adding a structured value that has a strong bond to all of the elements in the current set. This new 3-itemset is a *potential large itemset*. Once all the potential large itemset of size 3 have been found, the joint probability of each potential large itemset is calculated. Those sets with a joint probability above min_sup are added to the SV-List. This continues until either no new set is found or the pair count for all the columns in the matrix is less than N - 1. Usually, the SV-Bond Matrix is not dense. Therefore, much work is saved by not testing every combination of the input set.

Based on the SV-Bond Matrix in Figure 6, $(S_1 S_5 S_8)$ is the only potential large 3-itemset. Notice that it is unnecessary to check for any potential large 3-itemsets beginning with S_5 since the pair count for the column is 1. If we assume the document collection contains 3000 documents, then $P(S_1 S_5 S_8) = 3 \div 3000 = 0.1\%$ and $(S_1 S_5 S_8)$ is a large itemset. Because no column has a pair count of 3, we know that there are no large 4-itemsets.

A similar matrix called the *C-Bond Matrix* is used to identify large itemsets involving concepts (Step 5 of algorithm). However, the process is less costly because intersections of document id lists is avoided when creating the matrix. This results because we have relationship information in the concept library.

In order to create the matrix, we determine if the relationship weight between every pair of concepts in the C-List is above the minimum specified relationship weight. If so, a 1 is added to the C-Bond Matrix. Figure 7 shows the C-Bond Matrix generated from our example data assuming the minimum relationship weight is 0.30.

Once the C-Bond Matrix is generated, Step 6 finds higher order large itemsets using the same approach as that presented in Step 4. One difference is that the potential large itemsets do not need to be verified. Each potential large itemset is an actual large itemset. Recall that in Step 4 the supports of all the potential large itemsets needed to be verified at every level by intersecting the document lists.

This is avoided because relationship weight overrides support. It is a more general weight that holds across individual databases within a particular domain. Therefore, if every pair of concepts in a set has a strong relationship, the set is a large itemset. Because we will be generating *mixed rulesets* that contain both structured values and concepts, we perform a union of the document lists associated with the large concept itemset. Therefore, the support for the large concept itemset is 1. In this manner, we ensure that the concept component of any mixed ruleset is large in and of itself. All concept large itemsets are added to the C-List.

Based on the C-Bond Matrix in Figure 7, $(C_1 C_3 C_4)$ is the only large 3-itemset. It should be noted, that in order to have a large N-itemset containing concepts, all the concepts in the large itemset must form a fully connected subgraph. Returning to Figure 3, we see that C_1, C_3 and C_4 is a fully connected subgraph.

At this stage in the algorithm, we have two lists, one consisting of structured value strong itemsets and the other of concept strong itemsets. These lists are used to generate mixed large itemsets. We calculate the support by intersecting the document lists of the structured value large itemset and the concept large itemset and keep the potential large itemset if it is above min_sup. This large itemset can now be used in rules. For example, the following large itemsets can be generated: $C_3 C_4 S_1 S_5 S_8$.

To generate large itemsets including related concepts or themes not prespecified by the user, *concept_relatives* with strong bonds must be determined (Step 8 of algorithm). The purpose of generating these itemsets is to facilitate the discovery of new concept sets that might otherwise have been overlooked by the user. We generate sets involving *concept_relatives* by taking the relatives of one concept in a large mixed set and checking whether or not all the other concepts in the large itemset are related to the *concept_relative*. If all the concepts in the large itemset are related to the *concept_relative*, a new large itemset composed of the current large itemset and the relative is created. This step is repeated for each mixed large itemset.

For our example, suppose we are attempting to find the *concepts_relatives* of the large itemset $C_3 C_4 S_5 S_8$. Concepts C_6 and C_7 are *concept_relatives* of concept C_3, but only C_7 is also a relative of C_4. Therefore, the large itemset $C_3 C_4 C_7 S_5 S_8$ is created.

The final step involves generating the actual rules. Similar to other works, we specify rules by finding antecedents and consequents above min_conf. An additional step we include involves checking the relationship type information to attempt to identify a rule with a meaningful semantic relationship. One of the rules generated from the large itemset $C_3 C_4 C_7 S_5 S_8$ is the following: 67% : C_3, C_4, S_5, $S_8 \rightarrow C_7$. Strategy and finance related articles written in Administrative Science Quarterly in 1998 focus on budgets 67% of the time.

5 Results

5.1 Data Set

Our data set consists of over 50,000 documents from the ABI/Inform Information Retrieval System. ABI/Inform maintains bibliographic information, abstracts, and documents from over 800 business related journals. We only use a small subset of the documents in the ABI/Inform IR System. The structured data values associated with each article are stored in an Oracle 7 relational database on an HP 700 series workstation over an NFS file system. Examples of structured value tables include author, publication, and location.

5.2 Experiments

During our experiments, both the C-Bond Matrix and the SV-Bond matrix were not very full: on average the S-Bond Matrix was 7% full and the C-Bond Matrix 10% full. We were interested in determining if a bound existed on the average number of relationships a concept has. Therefore, we sampled concepts in Word-Net, a general online ontology [4] and found that concepts had an average of 25 relationships. This implies that most columns in the C-Bond Matrix are sparse.

Likewise, the sparse nature of the SV-Bond Matrix is also a result of a textual data set. For example, multiple publication values cannot ever occur in the same document. Further, a typical author publishes with a small number of co-authors (150 in a lifetime) in a small number of journals (100 or so). Since a user will typically enter a mix of all different types of structured values, a relationship bound will exist.

Our experimental results for execution time of our algorithm averaged over 10 runs are shown in Figures 8, 9, 10. Figures 8 and 9 show that the overall time is quasi-linear with respect to the number of concepts entered and the number of structured values entered, respectively. For Figure 8, the number of structured values was held constant at 5. Similarly, in Figure 9, the number of concepts was also held constant at 5. Figure 10 shows the total running time with respect to the total number of

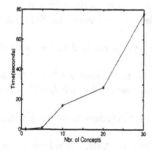 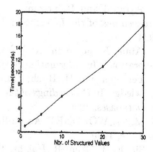

Fig. 8. Time vs. Nbr. of concepts

Fig. 9. Time vs. Nbr. of structured values

5.3 Conclusions

We have introduced an algorithm for generating constrained association rules. It incorporates knowledge from both the structured and unstructured components

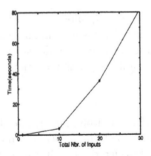

Fig. 10. Total running time

of the data set and generates rulesets using concepts related to the original set of constraints. It also uses some simple data structures that reduce the overall complexity of the algorithm.

This algorithm has only been tested on one semi-structured data set. We hope to continue our testing on other semi-structured data sets. At this stage we have not compared this algorithm against those proposed for structured transaction databases. We need to determine the sparsity of structured data sets to evaluate whether or not our approach is a good option in that domain. Finally, the rulesets presented here are fully constrained rulesets. We are also interested in partially constraining the document space and evaluating performance under those circumstances.

References

1. R. Agrawal and R. Srikant, "Fast algorithms for mining association rules," In *Proceedings of the International Conference of Very Large Databases*, September 1994.
2. A. Amir, R. Feldman, R. Kashi, "A new and versatile method for association generation," In *Information Systems*, Vol 22, 1997.
3. R. Feldman and H. Hirsh, "Mining associations in the presence of background knowledge. In *Proceedings of the International Conference on Knowledge Discovery in Databases*, 1996.
4. G. Miller. WORDNET: An on-line lexical database. *International Journal of Lexography*, 1990.
5. L. Singh, B. Chen, R. Haight, P. Scheuermann, and K. Aoki, "A robust system architecture for mining semi-structured data," In *Proceedings of International Conference on Knowledge Discovery and Data Mining*, 1998.
6. L. Singh, P. Scheuermann, and B. Chen. "Generating association rules from semi-structured documents using an extended concept hierarchy," In *Proceedings of the International Conference on Information and Knowledge Management*, November 1997.
7. T. Teorey and J. Fry. *Design of Database Structures*, Prentice Hall, 1982.

Incremental Mining of Schema for Semistructured Data[1]

Aoying Zhou   Jinwen   Shuigeng Zhou   Zenping Tian

Department of Computer Science
Fudan University, 200433, P.R.China
{ayzhou,970220,970218,zptian}@fudan.edu.cn

Abstract. Semistructured data is specified by the lack of any fixed and rigid schema, even though typically some implicit structure appears in the data. The huge amounts of on-line applications make it important and imperative to mine schema of semistructured data, both for the users (e.g., to gather useful information and facilitate querying) and for the systems (e.g., to optimize access). The critical problem is to discover the implicit structure in the semistructured data. Current methods in extracting Web data structure are either in a general way independent of application background [8], [9], or bound in some concrete environment such as HTML etc [13], [14], [15]. But both face the burden of expensive cost and difficulty in keeping along with the frequent and complicated variances of Web data. In this paper, we first deal with the problem of incremental mining of schema for semistructured data after the update of the raw data. An algorithm for incrementally mining schema of semistructured data is provided, and some experimental results are also given, which shows that our incremental mining for semistructured data is more efficient than non-incremental mining.

Keywords: Data Mining, Incremental Mining, Semistructured Data, Schema, Algorithm.

1 Introduction

As the more and more applications working successfully, Data Mining in very large databases has recently been focused greatly by many database research communities because of its promising future in many areas, such as OLAP in insurance safety, decision support, market strategy and financial forecast [1], [2]. In the early years, much research energy has targeted in the mining of transaction databases, relational databases, and spatial databases etc, which generally hold structured data [3], [4], [5], [6], [7]. However, as the maturity of Internet develops fast nowadays, the volume of data available on-line grows much rapidly too. Generally, data on network or in the digital library has no absolute schema fixed in advance, and the structure of data may be fairly irregular or incomplete. This kind of data is termed as semistructured data.

---

[1] This work was supported by the National Natural Science Foundation of China and the National Doctoral Subject Foundation of China.

Semistructured data is self-describing data that has some structure but which is neither regular nor known a-priori to the system. In order to facilitate querying and optimizing access the Web, mining certain common structure or schema from the semistructured data is particularly important.

The large amount of interesting data in the Web encourages people to try solving the problem above. Several effective work such as [8], [9] has made to extract the schema of semistructured data in a general way which is independent of the application environment, while [13], [14], [15] reached the same goal through different paths. S.Nestorov's work in [8] refers to approximately classifying the semistructured objects into a hierarchical collection of types to extract the implicit structure in large sets of semistructured data. K.Wang in [9] at the first time directly raises the problem of discovering schema for semistructured data, a framework and the corresponding algorithm for it are proposed. But their efforts in [8], [9] both are of the drawback of redundant computation work whose cost is expensive when the variances in Web data are so often. The work of Mendelzon's group in Toronto University tried to start their step from some applications field such as HTML etc. and with the help of cost locality, range expression bounds, finally getting the web data structure through the calculus based on virtual graph in [13], [14], [15]. Their idea is easy in implementation but is limited in the application field they applied first. As the data on the Internet/Web increasing continuously with the time moves on, mining data on Internet/Web cannot be done once and for all. The mined results need to be recast as the raw data grows. In the course of this period, a useful way to update the mined results is to take advantage of the already discovered results rather than do the whole work from scratch. So naturally, an incremental mining philosophy must be adopted. However, to our best knowledge, we still found no literature on incremental mining of schema for semistructured data up to now.

This paper solves the problem of incremental mining of schema for semistructured data, and an algorithm for this purpose is also presented. The other parts of this paper are organized as follows. We first introduce and describe some basic concepts in section 2, including the object exchange model (OEM) used for representing semistructured data, schema mining for semistructured data, and incremental mining problem. In section 3, the algorithm for incrementally mining semistructured data is given in detail. Section 4 provides some experimental results that show the advantage of incremental mining method. Finally, we summarize the paper in Section 5.

2 Defining the Problem

In this section, we assume that one description model, say OEM, is applied and the corresponding concepts or pre-definitions of schema and incremental mining on semistructured data are also introduced.

2.1 Object Exchange Model (OEM)

We represent semistructured data by object exchange model (OEM), which has been proposed for modeling semistructured data in [10]. In OEM, semistructured data is represented as a rooted, labeled, directed graph with the objects as vertices and labels on edges. Every object in OEM consists of an identifier and a set of outgoing edges with labels. The identifier uniquely identifies the object; the labels connect the object to its subobjects, which describes the meaning of the relationship between the object and the subobjects. OEM can be treated as a graph where the nodes are objects and the labels are on the edges (object references). If the graph is acyclic, that is to say, a tree, then the OEM is acyclic. In this paper, we assume that OEM is acyclic without additional explanation. Fig.1 illustrates an example of semistructured data modeled in OEM.

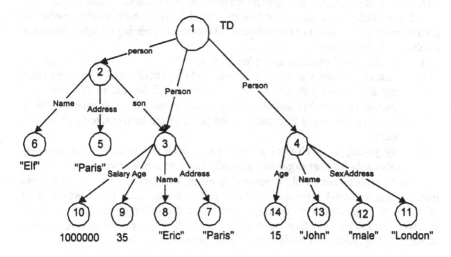

Fig. 1. Example semistructured database TD in OEM

2.2 Schema Mining for Semistructured Data

For the sake of convenience in discussing the mining schema from semistructured data, a transaction database as a collection of semistructured data objects has been defined, which are called transactions, i.e., each transaction represents an object which consists of a series of subobjects and labels.

A schema mined from semistructured data is to find a typical structure which could match most of the targeted objects in the transaction database. In OEM environment, a schema of data object can be represented by a *tree*, which is called *schema tree* or *st*. In [9] it is described as *tree expression*. A *Schema tree* is made of one or more tree branches. Each tree branch is defined as a path from the root object node to any subobject node in the tree. We say two branches are *distinct* if they are not contained or covered by each other. A *schema tree* with only one branch is called size-1 *schema tree*; and a size-k *schema tree* consists of k *distinct* tree branches.

A transaction database is supposed to exist, and *st* is a *schema tree* of some transactions. The support of *st* is the number of transactions *t* such that *st* is a *schema tree* of *t* versus the total number of transactions in the database. As to the user-specified minimum support MINSUP, *st* is frequent if the support of *st* is not less than MINSUP, and *st* is maximally frequent if it is frequent and is not covered or contained by any other frequent *trees*. *St* is a schema or simply pattern if *st* is maximally frequent. To discover mining schema is to find all patterns in the database.

Example 1: In figure 1, choose "person", as the targeted objects, its total number is 3. Let MINSUP=2%, then st1={name}, st2={address}, st3={age}, st4={name, address}, st5={name, age}, st6={address, age}, and st7={name, address, age} are all frequent *schema tree* of object "person", st7 is the only maximally frequent *schema tree*. St1, st2, st3 are size-1 tree, st4 and st5 are size-2 tree, and st7 is size-3 tree.

For a database (a collection of semistructured data), an A-Priori alike method is used to mining the schema of the database. The process of mining all schemata in the database is just as follow.

1. Discover all frequent size-1 *schema trees*;
2. Find all frequent size-k *schema trees* (k>1) repeatedly until there is no more any size of frequent *schema trees* can be found. Similar to the mining of association rules[11], before finding size-k *schema trees*, a candidate set of size-k *schema trees* is created on the basis of the found size-(k-1) *schema trees*;
3. By getting rid of all weak *schema trees* which are covered or contained by other *schema trees to get* all maximally frequent *schema trees*.

One or more consecutively connected labels may be included in a size-1 *schema tree*. Finding the size-1 *schema trees* is the most time-consuming phase because a lot of cases of combination of different labels and the different numbers of labels involved in the combination must be considered. The key of mining schema efficiently is to construct a minimum candidate set of *schema trees*.

2.3 Incremental Mining Problem

Within the network environment, especially the Web background, all kinds of data are growing continuously and rapidly. How to update the already mined results is an unavoidable problem challenging the data mining community. One possible way to the update problem is to re-run the schema-mining algorithm on the whole updated data from scratch. However this approach is not efficient for it does not utilize the already mined results. On the contrary, incremental mining approach makes use of the mined results, and at the same time, focuses on mining the newly added data. In this paper, we adopt a method similar to that in [12], but which is used for incremental maintenance of association rules, to mine schema of semistructured data efficiently.

Suppose *TDB* be a transaction database on which data mining is operated, and *TE* be the set of maximally frequent *schema trees* in *TDB*, *D* be the number of transactions in *TDB*. After some update activities, an increment *tdb* of new transactions is added to the original database *TDB*. The size of *tdb* is *d*. The essence of incremental mining problem is to find *TE*, that is, the set of maximally frequent *schema trees* in *TDB*∪*tdb*.

Those notations will be used in the remaining of this paper as follows. F_k is the set of all size-k frequent *schema trees* in *TDB*, and F_k' is the set of all size-k frequent *schema trees* in *TDB*∪*tdb*. C_k is the set of size-k candidate *schema trees*. Moreover, X.support$_D$, X.support$_d$, and X.support$_{Dd}$ represent the support counts of a *schema trees* X in *TDB*, *tdb* and *TDB*∪*tdb*, respectively.

3 The Incremental Mining Algorithm for Semistructured Data

After the database update activities have finished, two consequences may be triggered. Some frequent *schema trees* in *TDB* may become not frequent any more in *TDB*∪*tdb* because of the increasing of the total number of transactions. Thus, these *schema trees* are called losers; On the other hand, some *schema trees* which are not frequent in TDB may turn to being frequent in *TDB*∪*tdb*. These *schema trees* are called winners.

Consequently, the incremental mining process is composed of two major phases:
1. Getting rid of the losers from *TE* by scanning the incremental *tdb* ;
2. Discovering the winners from *TDB*∪*tdb* by checking *TDB*.

We present three lemmas which are useful in improving the efficiency of mining the frequent *schema trees* for the updated database. According to the definition of frequent *schema trees*, it is very easy to prove these lemma. So we leave out any further proofs of them here.

Lemma 1 A frequent size-k *schema tree* in F_k containing this *schema tree* can not be a winner in the k-th iteration, if a size-(k-1) *schema tree* is a loser at the (k-1)-th iteration.

Lemma 2 A size-k *schema tree* in the original size-k frequent *schema trees* set F_k is a loser in the updated database *TDB*∪*tdb* if and only if X.support$_{Dd}$ < st * (D+d).

Lemma 3 A size-k *schema tree* not in the original size-k frequent *schema trees* set F_k can become a winner in the updated database *TDB*∪*tdb* if and only if X.support$_{Dd}$ ≥ st * (D+d).

A detailed description of the incremental mining algorithm is as follows.

3.1 The First Step: To Discover Size-1 Schema Trees Set F₁' in TDB∪tdb

We divide into 4 steps which are outlined as follows to find frequent size-1 *schema trees* set F_1' in *TDB*∪*tdb*
1. For all *schema trees* X ∈ F_1 , scanning the incremental data *tdb* , updating its support count X.suuport$_{Dd}$. Once the scan is completed, all the losers in F_1 are found by checking the condition X.support$_{Dd}$ < st * (D+d) on all X∈ F_1

(based on Lemma 2). After pruning the losers, the *schema trees* in F_l which remain frequent after the update are identified.

2. For each $T \in tdb$, all size-1 *schema trees* $X \subseteq T$ which is not in F_l, a set C_l is created to store, in the same scan of step 1. This becomes the set of candidate *schema trees* and their support in *tdb* can also be found in the scan. Furthermore, according to Lemma 3, if $X \in C_l$ and X.support$_d$ < st * d, X can never be frequent in *TDB*∪*tdb*. Because of this, all the *schema trees* in C_l, whose support counts are less than st * d, are pruned off. In such a way, a very small candidate set for finding the new size-1 frequent *schema trees* is obtained.

3. One scan is then carried out on *TDB* to update the support count X.support$_{Dd}$ for each $X \in C_l$. By checking their support count, new frequent *schema trees* from C_l are found.

4. The set of all size-1 frequent *schema trees*, F_l', is generated by combining the results from step 1 and 3.

3.2 The Second Step and Beyond: To discover size-k(k>1) schema trees set F_k' in TDB∪tdb

We summarize the process of finding frequent size-2 *schema trees* F_2' in *TDB*∪*tdb* as follows similar to finding F_l'.

Like the first iteration, losers in F_2 will be pruned out in a scan on *tdb*. The pruning is done in two steps. At first, according to Lemma 1, some losers in F_2 can be filtered out without validating them against *tdb*. The set of losers $F_l - F_l'$ have been identified in the first iteration. Therefore, any *schema tree* $X \in F_2$, which has a sub- *schema tree* Y such that $Y \in F_l - F_l'$, cannot be frequent and are filtered out from F_2 without checking against *tdb*, Secondly, a scan is done on *tdb* and the support count of the remaining *schema trees* in F_2 are updated and the frequent *schema trees* from F_2 are identified.

As in the first iteration, the second part at this iteration is to find the new size-2 frequent *schema trees*. The key point is to construct a small set of candidate *schema trees*. The candidate set, C_2 is generated, before the above scan on *tdb* starts, by applying theorem 1 in [9] on F_l'. The *schema trees* in F_2 are not considered when creating C_2 because they have already been treated in step 1. The support count of the *schema trees* in C_2 is added up in the same scan of *tdb*. Then the *schema trees* in C_2 can now be pruned by checking their support count. For all $X \in C_2$, if X.support$_d$ < st * d, X is eliminated from C_2. Based on Lemma 3, all the eliminated *schema trees* cannot be frequent in *TDB*∪*tdb*.

The third step is to scan *TDB* to update the support count for all the *schema trees* in C_2. At the end of the scan, the entire *schema trees* $X \in C_2$, whose support count X.support$_{Dd}$ ≥ st * (D+d), are identified as the new frequent *schema trees*.

The set F_2', which contains all the frequent *schema trees* identified from F_2 and C_2 above, are the set of all size-2 frequent *schema trees* .

The same process with size-2 *schema trees* is applied to the k>2 iterations until no frequent *schema trees* can be found. Then all frequent *schema trees* sets { F_1', F_2',... , F_k' }are obtained.

3.3 The Final Step: To discover the maximally frequent schema trees

From all frequent *schema trees* sets { F_1', F_2',... , F_k' },by eliminating these *schema trees* which are contained or covered by other frequent *schema trees*, the remaining frequent *schema trees* make up of the maximally frequent *schema trees* set *TE*.

3.4 The Description of Incremental Algorithm

Finally, the incremental mining algorithm is presented as follows.
Algorithm 1: An incremental schema mining algorithm for semistructured data.
Input: (1) Original and incremental database: *TDB and tdb*;
       (2) The already mined schema trees set from *TDB*: { F_1, F_2,... , F_k };
       (3)The minimum support threshold: st.
Output: The maximally frequent schema trees set mined from *TDB∪tdb:TE*.
Method:
The 1-st iteration:
    W = F_1; C=φ; F_1'=φ;   /* W: winners, C: candidate set */
      for all T∈ *tdb* do   /* scan *tdb* */
       for all size-1 *schema tree* X⊆ T do {
       if X∈ W then X.support$_d$++; else {
       if X∉C then { C=C∪ {X}; X.support$_d$=0;} /* Initialize count, add X into C */
       X.support$_d$++;} };
      for all X∈ W do {   /* put winners into F_1' */
      if X.support$_{Dd}$ ≥ st * (D+d) then F_1'= F_1'∪{ X};
      for all X∈ C do /* prune candidates in C */
      if X.support$_d$ < st * d then { C=C-{ X};
      for all T ∈ *TDB* do { /* scan *TDB* */
       for all size-1 *schema trees* X⊆ T do if X∈ C then X.support$_D$++;
      for all X∈ C do   /* put winners into F_1' */
      if X.support$_{Dd}$ ≥ st * (D+d) then F_1'= F_1'∪{ X};
      return F_1'.   /* end of the first iteration */

The k-th iteration(k>1):
   /* This program segment is repeated till no frequent schema trees can be found */
   loop:
   k=2; W= F_k; F_k' =φ;   /* W:winners */
   /* create the k-size candidates */
   C=schema_tree_candidate_gen(F_{k-1}')-F_k ;   /* Implementing the function schema_tree_candidate_gen() according to theorem 1 in [9] */
    for all k-size *schema trees* X∈ W do /* prune the losers from W */

for all size-(k-1) *schema trees* $Y \in F_{k-1} - F_{k-1}'$ do
  if $Y \subseteq X$ then { W=W-{ X};break;}
  for all $T \in tdb$ do{ /* scan *tdb* and calculate support counts */
    for all $X \in W$ such that is contained in T do X.support$_d$++;
    for all $X \in C$ such that contained in T do X.support$_d$++;
}
for all $X \in W$ do /* add the winners into F_k' */
  if X.support$_{Dd} \geq$ st * (D+d) then $F_k' = F_k' \cup \{X\}$;
for all $X \in C$ do
  if X.support$_d <$ st * d then C=C-{ X}; /* prune the candidate sets */
for all $T \in TDB$ do
  for all $X \in C$ such that contained in T do X.support$_D$++;
for all $X \in C$ do /* add the winners into into F_k' */
  if X.support$_{Dd} \geq$ st * (D+d) then $F_k' = F_k' \cup \{ X \}$;
if F_k' have at least 2 frequent schema trees then {k++;continue};
  else break;
return {F_k' (k>1)}. /* end of the second step */

The last step: /* finding all maximally frequent schema trees */
  $TE = \{ F_1', F_2', \ldots, F_k' \}$;
  for all $X \in TE$ do
  for all $Y \in TE$ and X≠Y do {
  if X contains Y then do $TE = TE$-Y;
  if X is contained by Y then do $TE = TE$-X;
  } □

4 Experimental Results

In this section we present some preliminary experimental results. While the performance (in terms of time) is an important consideration in our work, the main focus of the experiments is the quality of the results. To test the efficiency of the proposed incremental mining algorithm, we have some experiments with the real-life data downloaded from the Web. Similar to [9], we choose the Internet Movies Database (IMDb) at http://us.imdb.com on the Web as our experimental data source. Our experiments are conducted on a PC platform with a Pentium II 200M CPU, 64M RAM, and Window NT OS. The results are illustrated in Fig. 2 and Fig.3. Here, speedup ratio means the time ratio of our new incremental method to the non-incremental A-Priori methods as K.Wang 's algorithm in [9]. Fig.2 shows the relation between speedup ratio and incremental data size. It's obvious that as the incremental size grows, the speedup ratio decreases. The effect of support threshold on speedup ratio is illustrated in Fig.3 which tells us that the increasing of support threshold will cause efficiency degradation of the incremental mining algorithm. Overall, the incremental mining approach outperforms the non-incremental mining method. From our best experimental results, the speedup ratio of incremental mining approach can reach over one order in magnitude.

5 Conclusions

In this paper, we present a method for extracting schema from semistructured data. Clearly, statically mining the semistructured data is not enough, for generally the on-line data (e.g. on the Web or in the digital library) is dynamically updated. Such a situation needs an incremental mining solution. An efficient algorithm for incremental mining of schema for semistructured data is developed, some experimental results are given. The experimental results show that incremental mining approach outperforms the non-incremental method considerably.

Mining complex-structured data is still an immature field compared to other fields due to the complexity and irregularity of data structure. Mining schema for the semistructured data is only a little step in this direction. There are a lot of open problems, such as mining Internet documents, mining Web multimedia etc, are waiting for sophisticated solutions.

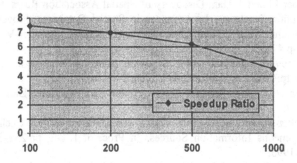

Fig.2. Speedup Ratio vs. Incremental Size (Original Data Size is 10000,minsup=15%)

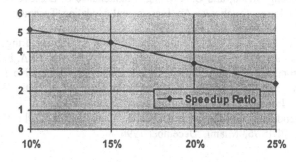

Fig. 3. Speedup Ratio vs. Support (Original data size is 10000,increment=1000)

References

1. U.M Fayyad, G.Piatetsky-Shapiro, P. Smyth, and R. Uthurusamy, Advances in Knowledge Discovery and Data Mining. AAAI/MIT Press, 1996.
2. M. S. Chen, J.H.Han, and P. S. Yu, Data Mining: An Overview from a Database Perspective. IEEE Trans. KDE, vol.8, No.6, pp866-883, December 1996.
3. R. Agrawal,T. Imielinski,and A.Swami. Mining Association Rules between Sets of Items in Large Databases. In Proc. of the ACM SIGMOD Conference on Management of Data. Washington,D.C.,May 1993.
4. R.Agrawal, R.Srikant. Fast Algorithms for Mining Association Rules. In Proc. of the 20th Int'l Conference on Very Large Databases. Santiago, Chile, Sept., 1994.
5. R.Srikant, R.Agrawal. Mining Generalized Association Rules. In Proc. of the 21st Int'l Conference on Very Large Databases. Zurich, Switzerland, Sept., 1995.
6. Y.Fu and J. Han. Meta-rule-guided mining of association rules in relational databases. In Proc. of 1st Int'l Workshop on Integration of Knowledge Discovery with Deductive and Object-Oriented Databases (KDOOD'95), pp.39-46, Singapore, Dec., 1995.
7. K. Koperski and J. Han. Discovery of Spatial Association Rules in Geographic Information Databases. In Advances in Spatial Databases, Proceedings of 4th Symposium, SSD'95. (Aug.6-9, Portland, Maine). Springer-Verlag, Berlin, 1995, pp.47-66.
8. S.Nestorov, S.Abiteboul, and R. Motwani, Inferring Structure in Semistructured data. (http://www.cs.stanford.edu/~rajeev)
9. K.Wang, H.Q. Liu, Schema Discovery for Semistructured Data. In Proc. of KDD '97.
10. Y.Papakonstantinow, H.Garcia-Marlia, and J.Widom, Object Exchange Across Heterogeneous Information Sources. In Proc. of ICDE, pp.251-260, Taiwan, March 1995.
11. R.Agrawal, R.Srikant, Fast Algorithms for Mining Association Rules. In Proc. of the 20th Int'l Conference on Very Large Databases, Santiago, Chile, Sept., 1994.
12. D.W.Cheung, J.Han, and C.Y. Wong, Maintenance of Discovered Association Rules in Large Databases: An Incremental Updating Technique, In Proc. of ICDE, New Orleans, LA., Feb., 1996.
13. G.O. Arocena and A.O. Mendelzon. "WebOQL: Restructuring Documents, Databases and Webs", In Proc. of ICDE, Orlando, Florida, USA, February 1998
14. L. Lakshmanan, F. Sadri, and I. Subramanian. "A Declarative Language for Querying and Restructuring the Web", In Proc. of 6th Int'l Workshop on Research Issues in Data Engineering, New Orleans, 1996.
15. A.O. Mendelzon, G. Mihaila, and T. Milo. "Querying the World Wide Web", In Proc. of PDIS'96, Miami, December 1996

Discovering Structure from Document Databases

Mon-Fong Jiang, Shian-Shyong Tseng*, Chang-Jiun Tsai

Department of Computer and Information Science
National Chiao Tung University
Hsinchu, Taiwan
E-mail: sstseng@cis.nctu.edu.tw

Abstract. Querying a database for document retrieval is often a process close to querying an answering expert system. In this work, we apply the knowledge discovery techniques to build an information retrieval system by regarding the structural document database as the expertise of the knowledge discovery. In order to elicit the knowledge embedded in the document structure, a new knowledge representation, named $StructuralDocuments(SD)$, is defined and a transformation process which can transform the documents into a set of SDs is proposed. To evaluate the performance of our idea, we developed an intelligent information retrieval system which can help users to retrieve the required personnel regulations in Taiwan. In our experiments, it can be easily seen that the retrieval results using SD are better than traditional approaches.

1 Introduction

Nowadays, database systems are useful in business and industrial environments due to their multiple applications. A lot of database systems are built for storing documents, say document databases, and be deserving more attention. Especially in the professional field, the reference manuals are usually preserved as the document databases in order to increase the convenience for query. A document database consists of a large number of electronic books. In addition to the electronic form of content stored in the database, some structural information, i.e., the chapter/section/paragraph hierarchy, may be also embedded in database. Classical information retrieval usually allows little structuring[3] since it retrieves information only on data. Therefore, the structural information could not be retrieved by classical information retrieval method. However, the structural information sometimes is useful in querying document database; for instance, most people usually read books with chapter-oriented concept. To build up an intelligent information retrieval system, our idea is regarding the document structure, including the index and the table of content, as the expertise of the knowledge discovery. In order to elicit the knowledge embedded in the document structure, we first propose a new knowledge representation, named $StructuralDocuments(SD)$, to be the basis of our system. Second, we

---

* Corresponding author.

design a knowledge discovery process of transforming the documents into a set of structural documents by merging two documents with similarity greater than the given threshold into one structural document. To evaluate the performance of our idea, we developed an system, named $CPRCS$, for Chinese personnel regulations in Taiwan. Our system may help users to retrieve the required personnel regulations. As mentioned above, a transformation process from the raw data to the format of a database is first applied. The embedded knowledge of the resulting data are then elicited by applying clustering techniques. By this way, the semantic indices of the raw data can be established, and the suitable results may be obtained. In our experiments, the structural information of the documents can be acquired from the database using the knowledge extraction module. By observing the operating process of users, we found the query process of users are simplified by using SD.

2 Knowledge discovery for structural documents

In this section, we will describe the flow of the knowledge discovery for structural documents $(KDSD)$ as shown in Figure 1. Two kinds of existing resources including the index and table of content for the books are used to be the knowledge source in the $KDSD$. The content of the document database is first transformed into the sets of words by the partition and transformation process. By computing each pair of documents, the similarity matrix for documents is computed which can be used to find the similar pair of documents by some clustering method. After clustering, the hierarchy of structural documents can be obtained.

In the followings, all of the three procedures in the $KDSD$ are described in detail.

(1) Partition and transformation

$KDSD$ is capable of processing English or Chinese document database. Since there is no obvious word boundary in Chinese text, an identification process for identifying each possible disyllabic word from target database is needed. After the disyllabic words are identified from the sentence by applying the association measure[2, 4], each document can be transferred to a set of keywords. It should be noted here that there is no need to identify words in English text, so the segmented method should be skipped for English text. In our approach, the indexes of the book are also used to identify the set of keywords for each document. Therefore, the size of both set are varying because the words are identified by association measure and the keywords are identified by comparing with index of the reference books.

(2) Similarity measure

To measure the similarity between two documents, we use the following heuristics: The similarity between two documents in the same chapter is higher than that in two different chapters, and the similarity between two documents in the same section is higher than that in two different sections. Without loss of generality, assume the whole reference book is divided into three-tier hierarchy, including chapter, section, and paragraph. Based upon the above heuristics, the

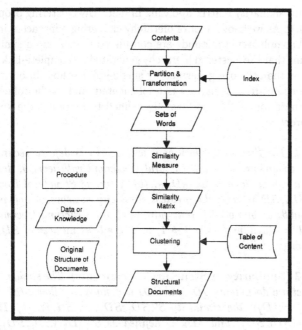

Fig. 1. Flowchart of the knowledge discovery for structural documents.

$HierarchyDependence(\dot{H}D)$ between two documents can be easily computed. Let the two documents be denoted as D_i and D_j. In $KDSD$, the similarity of D_i and D_j, denoted by $S(i,j)$, is computed by the following formula:

$$S(i,j) = (1-\delta) * same(i,j) + \delta * HD(i,j), \qquad (1)$$

where:

- $same(i,j)$ means the number of the words and keywords which appear both in documents D_i and D_j. The value is normalized by dividing the total number of keywords in documents D_i and D_j.
- $HD(i,j)$ means the hierarchy dependence of documents D_i and D_j.
- δ is an adaptive weight value, and $0 \le \delta \le 1$.

The default value of δ is 0.5, which can be adjusted by the number of chapters for a given book. For example, if n documents are obtained after partitioning step, we set δ as the value close to 0 when the number of chapters is near to 1 or n. This is because the structure of the book contains little meaning. By computing the similarity measure of all two different documents D_i and D_j, a similarity matrix $[S_{ij}], S_{ij} = S(i,j)$ can be formed. To simplify our further discussion, let the matrix be an upper triangular matrix and let the diagonal elements be 0's by assigning $S_{ij} = 0$ for $i \ge j$.

(3) Clustering and structuring documents

Clustering is an important step in the $KDSD$ for the purpose in structuring documents. To transfer the documents into a set of structural documents, we modify the algorithm for similarity matrix updating in hierarchy clustering proposed by Johnson(1967)[1]. As we know, a lot of hierarchy clustering approaches including single-link and complete-link methods are considered in measuring similarity of clusters. It seems that the clustered hierarchy generated by complete-link method is more balanced than the one generated by single-link method. In our modified algorithm, the complete-link method is implemented, and in the following the definition and notation of SD are formally defined to represent the knowledge in clustering process:

Definition 2.1 *The Structural Document with level l is defined recursively as follows: (a) A document D_i is a Structural Document with level 0, denoted as SD_i which also can be denoted as $(_0D_i)_0$. (b) A pair of Structural Documents, denoted as $(_lSD_i, SD_j)_l$, with the greatest similarity measure, which is greater than a threshold θ, among all different pairs is also a Structural Document with level l, where $l = Maximum(\ m, n\ ) + 1$, m is the level number of SD_i, and n is the level number of SD_j.*

Definition 2.2 (Similarity of Structural Documents) *The similarity S' between the structural documents SD_i and SD_j is defined as follows: (a) If $SD_i = (D_i)$ and $SD_j = (D_j)$, the similarity $S'(SD_i, SD_j) = S(i, j)$. (b) The similarity between (SD_i, SD_j) and SD_k is defined as $S'(SD_k, (SD_i, SD_j)) = \odot \{S'(SD_k, SD_i), S'(SD_k, SD_j)\}$, where the operator $\odot$ means 'minimum' for complete-link method, or 'maximum' for single-link method.*

Assume we have n documents, and then an $n \times n$ similarity matrix can be generated by our method. Firstly, each document is assigned to be a structural document, i.e. $SD_i = (D_i)$ for document D_i. Moreover, the similarity matrix for documents is transferred to the initial similarity matrix for structural documents. The elements of the similarity matrix $[S'_{ij}]$ is the similarity measure of structural documents SD_i and SD_j, that is, $S'_{ij} = S_{ij}$. Let $\Psi = \{SD_i\}$ be the set of all SD_i. Based upon the Johnson's algorithms (1967) for hierarchy clustering[1], we propose the following procedure for similarity matrix updating:

Step 1: Find the most similar pair of structural documents in the current similarity matrix, say pair $\{p, q\}$, where, $S'_{p,q} = \text{Maximum} \{S'_{i,j}, \text{ for any } i, j\}$.

Step 2: Merge structural documents SD_p and SD_q into a new structural document (SD_p, SD_q).

Step 3: Delete the structural documents SD_p and SD_q from the set Ψ, and insert the new structural document (SD_p, SD_q) into the set, i.e., $\Psi \leftarrow \Psi - \{SD_p\} - \{SD_q\} + \{(_lSD_p, SD_q)_l\}$, where $l = \text{Maximum}(\ m, n\ ) + 1$, m is the level number of SD_p, and n is the level number of SD_q.

Step 4: Update the similarity matrix by deleting the rows and columns related to structural documents SD_p and SD_q and adding a row and a column corresponding to the new structural document (SD_p, SD_q).

Step 5: If there are no two structural documents with similarity greater than θ, stop. Otherwise, go to Step 1.

After clustering, the hierarchy of structural documents can be obtained according to the set Ψ.

3 Experiments

As we know, a sound legal system and complete regulations are usually of most importance for a government by law. Right now, the personnel regulations (PR) for civil servant in Taiwan seem to be very sophisticated. Although several kinds of reference books about personnel regulations have been provided for general public to inquiry, they are not easy to use and a lot of access time is required. Therefore, how to improve the methods of inquiry and annotation of the personnel regulations have become an important issue. In the past two years, we implemented a prototype of database based on SD, named $CPRCS$ (Chinese Personnel Regulations Consultation System), to assist the querying process for PR documents. In $CPRCS$, users access the system through the web pages interface. Two different modes, with or without SD, are provided for users as they prefer. Eight groups, each including two or three users, are testing to evaluate the performance of the SD. Let the average rate of accuracy for each group be the ratio of dividing the amount of the documents conformed user's demand by the amount of total retrieval results. Table 1 shows the rate of accuracy for retrieval results with or without SD. It can be easily seen that the retrieval results using SD are better than traditional approaches.

Table 1. Accurate rate for retrieval results with or without SD.

Group's ID	1	2	3	4	5	6	7	8	Average
With SD	.87	.73	.84	.82	.91	.78	.89	.83	.834
Without SD	.78	.65	.81	.58	.52	.67	.85	.76	.703

References

1. A. K. Jain, and R. C. Dubes, *Algorithms for Clustering Data*, Prentice Hall Inc., pp. 58-86, 1988.
2. M. F. Jiang, S. S. Tseng, C. J. Tsai, and J. F. Liu, 'Building a Chinese Personnel Regulations Consultation System on WWW,' 1996 Taiwan Area Internet Conference, TANET'96 , Hsinchu, Taiwan, October 1996.
3. G. Navarro and R. Baeza-Yates, 'Proximal nodes: a model to query document database by content and structure,' *ACM Transactions on Information Systems*, Vol. 15, No. 4, pp. 400-435, October 1997.
4. R. Sproat and C. Shih, 'A Statistical Method for Finding Word Boundaries in Chinese Text,' *Computer Proceedings of Chinese and Oriental Languages*, Vol. 4, No. 4, pp. 336-351, 1990.

Combining Forecasts from Multiple Textual Data Sources

Vincent Cho and Beat Wüthrich

The Hong Kong University of Science and Technology

Clear Water Bay, Hong Kong

{wscho,beat}@cs.ust.hk

Abstract. These days more and more crucial and commercially valuable information becomes available on the World Wide Web. Also financial services companies are making their products increasingly available on the Web. This paper suggests and investigates six methods to combine multiple categorical predictions that are generated from distributed information available on the World Wide Web.

1   Introduction

There are various types of financial information sources on the Web (www.wsj.com, www.ft.com, www.bloomberg.com, etc) providing real-time news and quotations of stocks, bonds and currencies. We make use of these distributed textual sources to generate predictions about the world's major stock market indices [2]. Probably the most important factor influencing the prediction accuracy is the selection of the data sources. If the quality of the data source or information is low then no meaningful predictions can be expected. This comes as no surprise: analyzing bad data leads to bad results (i.e., GIGO, Garbage In Garbage Out). In this paper, we investigate the natural approach of trying to exploit *all* relevant data sources. From each data source a forecast is produced and finally a consensus prediction is generated.

Our application is to predict the Hang Seng Index (HSI), Hong Kong's major stock market index. If the closing value of HSI versus the previous day's closing value moves up at least $x\%$, then the classification is *up*. If the closing value of HSI versus the previous day's closing value slides down by at least $x\%$, then the classification is *down*. Finally, when HSI neither goes up nor down then it is *steady*. For the chosen training and test period, we set x to be 0.5 as this makes each of the possible outcomes up, down and steady about equally likely.

2   Framework

Suppose a set of training examples or time points $T=\{t_1, t_2, ..., t_m\}$. Each tuple t_i belongs to exactly one of the classes $C=\{c_1, c_2, ..., c_k\}$. This actual classification of tuple t_i is denoted a_i such that $a_i \in C$. There is a set $S=\{s_1, s_2, ..., s_n\}$ of data sources. From each source s_j we generate the classification s_{ij}, where $s_{ij} \in C$, for tuple t_i. The problem is to generate the consensus prediction p_i, where $p_i \in C$, for t_i. The overall situation is depicted in Fig. 1.

t_i	s_1	$\dots$	s_j	$\dots$	s_n		consensus prediction	actual class
t_i	S_{i1}		s_{ij}		s_{in}	$\Rightarrow$	p_i	a_i

Fig. 1. Individual and consensus classification for the tuples $\{t_1, t_2, , t_m\}$.

The generation of the consensus forecast p_i takes into account all individual forecast s_{ij} plus three kinds of meta information about each data source and classifier pair: the quality of the data source (this may be an objective or a subjective measurement), the historic classification accuracy, and prior probability information.

Zhang et al. [3] introduced a notion of *data quality* which is objective. That is, the quality of a data source is computed from the content of the source alone without human interaction. Data quality could also be a subjectively obtained measurement. In our experiments the mentioned objective data quality notion is used. Let q_j denote the quality of a data source s_j. The quality is a real number within the range of zero to one, one meaning highest quality.

The *accuracy* of a source is the percentage of correct predictions over a period of time. For a set of training examples T, the accuracy $a(s_j)$ of a source s_j is as follows.

$$a(s_j) = \frac{\sum_i \delta(s_{ij}, a_i)}{m} \tag{1}$$

$$\text{where } \delta(s_{ij}, c) = \begin{cases} 1 & \text{if } s_{ij} = c \\ 0 & \text{otherwise} \end{cases}$$

Prior probability information contains the historic prediction details of a source s_j. It is a $k{\times}k$ matrix of conditional probabilities derived from the training examples. Let $Pr_j(c_h|c_l)$ denote the probability that source s_j classifies into c_l and the actual outcome is c_h.

We predict daily movements of Hang Seng Index. From each data source a prediction is generated: it moves *up*, remains *steady* or goes *down*. In our experiments we take a training set of one hundred days. The data quality, accuracy and prior probability information of a source s_1 is provided in Fig. 2.

Source 1 Quality = 0.3		Prediction		
		Up	Steady	Down
Actual outcome	Up	30	1	3
	Steady	11	10	9
	Down	4	4	28
Sum		45	15	40
$a(s_1)$ = (30+10+28) / 100 = 0.68				

Fig. 2. Meta information about source s_1

Our objective is to combine predictions from individual sources to form an overall categorical prediction.

3 Consensus Prediction

3.1 Best Quality

Select the prediction s_{ij} if the source s_j has the highest quality among all sources.

$$p_i = s_{ij} \text{ iff } q_j = max \{q_1, q_2, ..., q_n\} \tag{2}$$

3.2 Majority Voting

Select as consensus prediction c_h if it has largest number of sources predicting it.

3.3 Voting Weighted by Quality

This is a refinement of the majority voting. Sources with higher quality have more importance in the vote. Let $v_i(c)$ denote the votes for class c when classifying case t_i:

$$v_i(c) = \Sigma_j \, q_j \times \delta(s_{ij}, c) \tag{3}$$

The consensus forecast p_i is class c exactly when c gets the highest vote among all possible outcomes.

3.4 Conditional Probability Selection

Recall that $Pr_{j.}(c_h|c_l)$ denotes the probability that when source s_j classifies into c_l, the actual outcome is c_h. The probability $P_i(c)$ of each class is computed using these conditional probabilities. The class with highest such probability is then the consensus classification for example t_i.

$$P_i(c) = \Sigma_j \, Pr_{j.}(c \mid s_{ij}) / n \tag{4}$$

3.5 Accuracy Selection

The accuracy $a(s_j)$ of a source s_j reflects the average historic prediction accuracy over all categories and is used to estimate k^2 parameters in the $k \times k$ prior conditional probability matrix.

$$Pr_j(c|s_{ij}) = \begin{cases} a(s_j) & \text{if } s_{ij} = c \\ \dfrac{1 - a(s_j)}{k-1} & \text{otherwise} \end{cases} \tag{5}$$

If a source s_j predicts a class c, then the likelihood for the final outcome to be c is estimated by taking its accuracy $a(s_j)$. On the other hand, the likelihood of the final outcome to be any other class than c is estimated to be $(1 - a(s_j))/(k-1)$, where k is the total number of categories. That is, suppose up is predicted by a source with accuracy 40%, then the likelihood that it is *down* or *steady* is both set to 30% ((100%-40%)/2).

The probability $P_i(c)$ of each class is computed using these conditional probabilities. The class with highest such cumulative likelihood is then the consensus.

$$P_i(c) = \Sigma_j \, Pr_{j.}(c \mid s_{ij}) / n \tag{6}$$

3.6 Meta Classifier

From the training examples the prediction matrix shown in Fig. 3 is produced. Consider the tuple t_i, the number of sources predicting class c_l is $v_{il} = \Sigma_i \, \delta(s_{ij}, c_l)$.

	c_1	...	c_l	...	c_k	outcome
t_i			v_{il}		v_{ik}	a_i

Fig. 3. Prediction matrix

This matrix is considered as training data itself. Each row constitutes one example where a_i is the classification. This data is used to again generate decision rules. Upon receiving new predictions from individual sources, the decision rules then conclude the overall or consensus prediction.

4 Experiments

There are thousands of pages updated each day. Each page contains valuable information about stock markets. The address of certain information is usually fixed. For example, the page www.wsj.com/edition.current/articles/hongkong.htm contains news about Hong Kong's stock market. This page will be considered as one data source on the Internet. However, some news page addresses change from time to time, usually these pages are under a content page. For example, the page www.ft.com/hippocampus/ftstats.htm is the content page for various regional financial news pages. But the individual news pages under this content page have changing URL addresses. So the fixed content page together with its underlying news pages is considered as one identifiable information source. Among numerous financial news Web sites on the Internet, we restricted ourselves to five financial information networks, the ones named above. These networks provide fast and accurate information. From those networks we selected forty one Web sources which we consider - using our common sense and understanding of stock markets - to be already relevant to the task of predicting Hong Kong's stock market index, the Hang Seng Index. We collected these data in the period 14 Feb. 1997 to 6 Nov. 1997. This provides a total of 179 stock trading days. The forecasting is done as described in Wüthrich et al. [2] and Cho et al. [1]. The first 100 trading days are used for training and estimation of the quality, accuracy and conditional probabilities. The remaining 79 days are used to test the performance of the six consensus forecasting methods.

A good yardstick of the consensus forecasting is the accuracy, i.e. what percentage of the predictions is correct. For instance, if the system predicts up and the index moves indeed up then it is correct. The accuracy is shown in the second column of Table 1. The third column in Table 1 indicates how many times the system predicts up or down and it was actually steady; or, the system predicts steady and it was actually up or down. The last column indicates the percentage of totally wrong predictions. That is, the system expects the index to go up and it moves down, or vice versa.

Table 1. Performance on the 79 trading days

	accuracy	Slightly wrong	wrong
Best Quality Source	30.4%	62.0%	7.6%
Majority Voting	51.9%	29.1%	19.0%
Weighted Majority	38.0%	22.8%	39.2%
Cond. Prob. Selection	39.2%	60.0%	3.8%
Accuracy Selection	44.3%	36.7%	19.0%
Meta Classifier	44.3%	22.8%	32.9%

Among the six consensus schemes, majority voting with an accuracy of above 50% is outperforming the others. Moreover, the percentage on wrong classifications is rather low, 19%. The second best method is accuracy selection with 44.3% accuracy and 19% wrong classifications. The other methods, except probabilistic rules, are clearly lagging behind. There is 99.9% probability that an accuracy of 51.9% on 79 test cases can not be achieved by random guessing.

Fig. 4 confirms the conjecture that the prediction accuracy of individual sources is less than the accuracy achieved by taking more complete information into account and combining it appropriately.

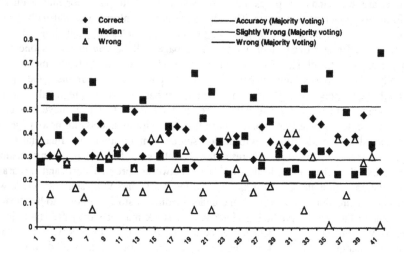

Fig. 4. Performance of individual sources compared with majority voting

5 Conclusions

We investigate six methods for making consensus predictions from individual predictions of classifiers. We showed that consensus decisions lead to higher accuracy as compared to the accuracy achieved even from the best quality source. In particular, majority voting is proved to be a simple but amazingly convincing way to produce the consensus.

References

1. Cho V., Wüthrich B., Zhang J.: Text Processing for Classification. Journal of Computational Intelligence in Finance (to appear, 1999).

2. Wüthrich B., Peramunetilleke D., Leung S., Cho V., Zhang J., Lam W.: Daily Prediction of Stock Market Indices from Textual WWW Data. 4th Int Conf on Knowledge Discovery and Data Mining - KDD98. New York (1998). (also invited for IEEE Int. Conf. on SMC, San Diego, 1998) 264-268

3. Zhang J., Wüthrich B., Cho V.: Distributed Data Source Selection. WS on Parallel and Distributed Data Mining. part of PAKDD97 (1998).

Domain Knowledge Extracting in a Chinese Natural Language Interface to Databases: NChiql*

Xiaofeng Meng[1,2], Yong Zhou[1], and Shan Wang[1]

[1]College of Information, Renmin University of China, Beijing 100872
[2]Institute of Computing Technology, The Chinese Academy of Sciences
xfmeng@public.bta.net.cn , swang@mail.ruc.edu.cn

Abstract. This paper presents the method of domain knowledge extracting in NChiql, a Chinese natural language interface to databases. After describing the overall extracting strategy in NChiql, we mainly discuss the basic semantic information extracting method, called DSE. A semantic conceptual graph is employed to specify two types of modification and three types of verbal relationship among the entities, relationships and attributes. Compared with related works, DSE has more strongly extracting ability.

1 Introduction

Natural language interfaces to databases (NLIDBs) is a system that allows the user to access information stored in a database by typing requests expressed in some natural language (e.g. Chinese, English). Since the early 1960s, much of the research on NLIDB has been motivated by its potential use for communicating with DBMS. Now two main issues hinder NLIDBs to gain the rapid and wide commercial acceptance: *portability* and *usability*[1]. These problems are resulted from the system poor ability to cover the domain knowledge in a given application.

Each application domain has different vocabulary and domain knowledge. Such uncertainty of domain-dependent knowledge reduces the usability of NLIDBs in different application domain. Therefore when a system is transported from one domain to another, it must be able to obtain new words and new knowledge. So in order to solve the problem of portability, it must enable the system to extract domain knowledge automatically or semi-automatically at least, in order to build the domain dictionaries for the next step of natural language processing.

Domain knowledge extraction is the process of acquisition of sufficient domain knowledge and reconstruction of domain information especially the semantic and usage of words in order to extend the ability of language processing. Nowadays widely attentions have been paid to studies on knowledge extraction. Researches on computing linguistics proposed some corpus based extracting methods. Technique of domain knowledge extracting from the aspect of NLIDBs is mainly based on database schema. These methods focused on simple extraction of database structure

* This paper is supported by the National Natural Science Foundation of China.

information whereas the potential extraction of semantic knowledge is not fully considered.

We think that extraction of domain knowledge in NLIDBs must not only reconstruct the information framework of the database and extract the semantic and usage information in the database schema, but also extract semantic and usage information based on user conceptual schema. Because most part of these information is not reflected in existing database schema and they are one part of user's own knowledge, it requires to be extracted by means of suitable learning mechanism.

2 Domain Knowledge's Classification and Extracting Strategies

Generally, the domain knowledge of NLIDBs can be classified into two types:
• *Domain-Independent Knowledge*, e.g. the usage of some common words, such as conjunction, preposition, all of which are independent on specific database application domain; and
• *Domain-Dependent Knowledge*, which is dependent on specific application domains.

Extraction of domain knowledge means to make up the gap between the realistic world knowledge model and database schema. Its goal is to provide necessary grammar and semantic information for the language processing in NChiql. Generally, domain-dependent knowledge falls into two catalogs:

1) Basic semantic information, which is contained in the database schema. The database logical model conveys some basic semantic information: entity and relation are expressed by tables, their names is expressed by symbol names; the primary key and foreign key describe the mutual reference relationship between entities, while relationship embodies what interplay relation of these entities and what positions these entities are; the constraint information depicts the restraint when an attribute is assigned a value.

2) Deductive semantic information, which is the extension to basic one and exists in domain application but is omitted when creates the database schema. Generally, such knowledge can be computed and deducted based on the basic information. For example, if the database stores the latitude and longitude information of different cities, then the distance between each city is the deductive information.

Because basic semantic information is dependent on relatively static database schema, the first phase of our extraction is DSE --- *Database Schema Extraction*. Generally, DSE can extract the following grammar and semantic information: entity, attribute, relationship (the verb usage of entity's names).

However, the design of database schema can not be controlled, some of which are non-normal (for example, they lack basic primary key constrain), so the database schemas maybe conform to different normalization. Because our extracting method is mainly based on heuristic rules, the above characteristic of non-normal gives rise to great difficulties.

Deductive semantic information exists beyond the database scheme of an application. For the complication of deductive information, the extracting of deductive information must employ different techniques to grasp the deductive concepts as more as possible. We propose the following hybrid-extractor for deductive information:

• *Corpus based extracting*: acquire more grammar and semantic information, by collecting relevant query corpus and process of analyzing. For example, "live" is a verb that is not contained in basic semantic information, it is the verb connecting the entity "student" and the attribute "address", such potential word can be obtained only by plenty of corpus;

• *Data mining based extracting*: the database contains abundant semantic knowledge, which can be acquired by data mining.

• *Learn-by-query extracting*: while communicating with the user, the system learns new knowledge continually and enriches its domain knowledge.

3 Database Schema Based Extracting in NChiql

NChiql is a Natural Chinese Query Language interface to database. In process of extraction, NChiql extracts the essential information of entities, relationships and attributes in databases by analyzing the relationship among these database objects. The procedure of DSE in NChiql is listed as following steps:

(1) Get database scheme information through data dictionary;
(2) Check whether every object is Entity or Relationship.
(3) If it is Entity then extracting the semantics of entity;
(4) If it is Relationship then extracting the semantics of relationship;
(5) Extract the information of attributes of entity or relationship.

The extracting is mainly based on some heuristic rules. For example our judgement of entities and relationship is based on the following rules:

In a database schema $R(R_1, R_2, \ldots R_n)$, if in Ri there exists the primary key k_i (A_1, $A_2, \ldots, A_m$), m>0,

(1) If m=1, R_i is an entity.
(2) If m>1, and primary key of R_j is k_j, $k_i \cap k_j \neq \varnothing$, then R_i is relationship; otherwise R_i is an entity.

All the results of extracting are stored in dictionaries. NChiql divides dictionaries into two types, which are independent on domain and dependent on domain, namely general dictionary and specific dictionary.

• General dictionary is independent on application and is the core of the system, it records the semantic of words which are most commonly used, e.g. pronoun, conjunction, quantifier, interrogative, routine words, etc.

• Specific dictionary records the semantics and usage of words, which are usually used in a specific application domain. When the system is being transported to another domain, it must be reconstructed. The specific dictionary includes:

(1) Dictionary of entity's semantics, which records the names of tables, synonyms and the semantics of the modifying attributes.
(2) Dictionary of the attribute's semantics, which records the attribute's names, synonyms, hints, modifiers and the semantics of constraints.
(3) Dictionary of the verb's semantics, which records the semantics and usage of the verb.
(4) Domain knowledge rules.

We call the results of DSE as *semantic conceptual model*, which reflects not only the semantics of words, but also, combination relationship among different words. So it's more powerful than the E-R model in term of semantics expression. The Figure 1 illustrates the conceptual model.

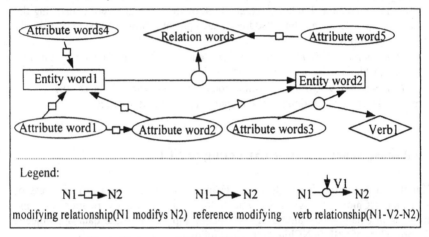

Fig. 1. Illustration of the semantic conceptual graph

The semantic conceptual graph regards semantic concept (words) as its main core, emphasizes on reflecting the semantic relationship among words. Generally, there are two types of modifying relationship and three types of verb relationship. To be specific, the types of modifying relationship are:
  (1) The Direct modifying relationship among entities, including the attribute-modify-entity and the entity-modify-entity.
  (2) Reference modifying among entities, which is engendered by foreign key reference relationship among entities.

The three types of verb relationship mean the verb combinations of relationships and entities, attributes and entities, entities and entities.

Modifying relationship can mainly determine the combination relationship of noun phrase(NP), while verb relationship presents the usage of verb phrase(VP). It is extremely useful to be provided with these semantic relationships in the analyzing process of natural language queries.

When NLIDB is transforming natural language into database language, it needs not only natural language knowledge, but also relevant database semantic knowledge, i.e. the mapping information from natural language to database semantic. NChiql is different from other.extracting methods in that the usage of words is represented by the database semantic, namely the composition of words in a sentence and the relationship of each word are directly mapped to the table and column in database logical model. Such extracting method is word-driven and it is based on the semantic and functional characteristic of word.

In reality, because of the differences in the quality of the designers, there are so many database schemas that are difficult to suit the pre-assumption of DSE. To overcome these non-formal cases and alleviate the burden of the user as far as possible, we propose some solutions, such as determining the primary key by reverse engineering [2], processing of non-normalization by building views, etc.

4 Related Works

TED[3] is one of the earliest prototype systems that dedicating to the problem of transportability of NLIDB. An important characteristic of TED is that it provided an automatic extracting interface--Automated Interface Expert, through which the user could guide the system to learn language and logical knowledge of the specific domain. The extracting ability of TED is very limited. Compared with TED, the extracting technology of TEAM [4] is relatively mature and complete. At first the extracting method of TEAM is menu driven and aided by interaction. In TEAM all the database objects to be extracted as well as the words extracted are listed in the menu, thus the whole extracting structure is very clear.

However, none of the above systems are able to take advantage of the information contained in the database schema sufficiently. Although TEAM includes extracting of the primary key and foreign key, it hasn't analyzed the relationship among entities and attributes, therefore it biased on extracting the general grammar of the words in a natural language category, thus increasing the complexity of extracting and leading to the complexity of language processing.

5 Conclusion

The semantic extracting is an indispensable part of natural language processing and the method of semantic extracting reflects the characteristic of the natural language processing. By extracting sufficiently the all sorts of information hidden in the domain, we could reduce the ambiguity of the words as far as possible and improve the efficacy of the natural language processing.

Now the difficult problem is the extracting of deductive semantic information. NChiql has a perfect mechanism of extracting the basic semantic information, but lots of work should be done further on the extracting of deductive semantic information.

References

1. Copestake, A., Jones, S. K.: Natural Language Interfaces to Databases. The Knowledge Engineering Review 4 (1990) 225-249.
2. Andersson, M.: Extracting an Entity Relationship Schema from a Relational Database through Reverse Engineering, *http://hypatia.dcs.qmw.ac.uk/SEL-HPC/Articles/DBAchive. html*
3. Hendrix, G.G., Lewis, W.H.: Transportable Natural Language Interface to Database. American Journal of Computational Linguistic 2 (1981) 159-165.
4. Grosz, B., et al.: Team: An Experiment in the Design of Transportable Natural-Language Interfaces, *Artificial Intelligence* 32 (1987) 173-243.

Evolutionary Hot Spots Data Mining
An Architecture for Exploring for Interesting Discoveries

Graham J Williams

CRC for Advanced Computational Systems,
CSIRO Mathematical and Information Sciences,
GPO Box 664, Canberra, ACT 2601, Australia,
Graham.Williams@cmis.csiro.au,
http://www.cmis.csiro.au/Graham.Williams

Abstract. Data Mining delivers novel and useful knowledge from very large collections of data. The task is often characterised as identifying key areas within a very large dataset which have some importance or are otherwise interesting to the data owners. We call this hot spots data mining. Data mining projects usually begin with ill-defined goals expressed vaguely in terms of making interesting discoveries. The actual goals are refined and clarified as the process proceeds. Data mining is an exploratory process where the goals may change and such changes may impact the data space being explored. In this paper we introduce an approach to data mining where the development of the goal itself is part of the problem solving process. We propose an evolutionary approach to hot spots data mining where both the measure of interestingness and the descriptions of groups in the data are evolved under the influence of a user guiding the system towards significant discoveries.

1 Introduction

Data mining is an inherently iterative and interactive process. A fundamental concern is the discovery of useful and actionable knowledge that might be contained in the vast collections of data that most organisations today collect but usually can not effectively analyse. In applying data mining techniques in a number of case studies with industrial collaborators (in health care, taxation, and insurance) we have developed the hot spots methodology for assisting in the task of identifying interesting discoveries (Williams and Huang 1997).

The hot spots methodology originally entailed the use of clustering and rule induction techniques to identify candidate groups of interesting entities in very large datasets. These groups were evaluated to assess their interestingness (i.e., whether they represented useful and actionable discoveries for the particular domain of application). In dealing with very large datasets the number of identified candidate groups becomes very large and is no longer amenable to simple nor manual evaluation. The groups, described by symbolic rules, serve as a reasonable starting point for the discovery of useful knowledge. However, it has been found empirically that an exploration of other but related areas of the data (e.g., nearby regions within the dataset), in concert with the domain user, leads to further interesting (and sometimes much more interesting) discoveries.

The focus of our data mining work is to *support* the domain user (fraud investigators, auditors, market analysts) in the task of focusing on *interesting* groups of a very large collection of data (many millions of records). The emphasis on support is important for data mining as our experience suggests that domain expertise will remain crucial for successful data mining. While the hot spots methodology established a useful starting point, it provided only little support to proceed further in identifying the most interesting discoveries from amongst the many thousands that were being made and others that lay nearby in the vast search space.

In this paper we develop an architecture for an evolutionary hot spots data mining system that is under development. The starting point is the many discoveries that the current hot spots methodology identifies. An evolutionary approach is employed to evolve nuggets using a fitness measure that captures aspects of interestingness. Since "interestingness" is itself hard to capture we closely couple with the nugget evolution a measure of interestingness that is itself evolved in concert with the domain user. We describe an architecture where a number of measures of interestingness compete to evolve alternative nugget sets from which the best nuggets are presented to the domain user for their ranking. This ranking is fed back into the system for further evolution of both the measure of interestingness and of the nuggets.

2 The Search for Interesting Nuggets

Padmanabhan and Tuzhilin (1998) demonstrate the need for a better grasp on the concept of interestingness for data mining with an example from marketing. Applying a traditional apriori association algorithm to the analysis of 87,437 records of consumer purchase data, over 40,000 association rules were generated, "many of which were irrelevant or obvious." Identifying the important and actionable discoveries from amongst these 40,000 "nuggets" is itself a key task for data mining.

The concept of *interestingness* is difficult to formalise and varies considerably across different domains. A growing literature in data mining is beginning to address the question. Early work attempted to identify objective measures of interestingness, and the confidence and support measures used in association algorithms are examples of objective measures. One of the earliest efforts to address the explosion of discoveries by identifying interestingness was through the use of rule templates with attribute hierarchies and visualisation (Klemettinen, Mannila, Ronkainen, Toivonen and Verkamo 1994). Silbershatz and Tuzhilin (1996) partition interestingness measures into objective and subjective measures, and further partition subjective measures into those that capture unexpectedness and those that capture actionability.

Many authors have focussed on capturing unexpectedness as a useful measure, particularly in the context of discovering associations (Silbershatz and

Tuzhilin 1995) and classifications (Liu, Hsu and Chen 1997). Most recently Padmanabhan and Tuzhilin (1998) develop an unexpectedness algorithm based on logical contradiction in the context of expectations or beliefs formally expressed for an application domain.

Capturing actionability is a difficult and less studied proposition. Matheus, Piatetsky-Shapiro and McNeill (1996) discuss the concept of payoff as a measure of interestingness, where they attempt to capture the expected payoff from the actions that follow from their discoveries (deviations). There is little other work specifically addressing actionability.

3   The Hot Spots Methodology

We characterise our concept of interestingness in terms of attempting to identify areas within very large, multi-dimensional, datasets which exhibit surprising (and perhaps unexpected) characteristics that may lead to some actions being taken to modify the business processes of the data owners. At this stage, rather than specifically formalising how interestingness can be expressed we are exploring how we can facilitate the domain user in their search for interesting discoveries in their data using the hot spots methodology.

We now introduce some terminology to describe the hot spots methodology, following Williams and Huang (1997). A *dataset* $\mathcal{D}$ consists of a set of real world *entities* (such as a set of policy holders in an insurance company or a set of Medicare patients). Generally $\mathcal{D}$ is relational with only one universal relation $\mathbf{R}(A_1, A_2, \ldots, A_m)$ where the A_i are the *attributes* of the entities. The dataset consists of a set of entities: $\mathcal{D} = \{e_1, e_2, \ldots, e_n\}$, where each entity is a tuple $\langle v_1, v_2, \ldots, v_m \rangle$ of values, one value for each attribute. For real world problems the number of attributes m and the number of tuples n are typically "large" (m may be anywhere from 20 to 1000 and n typically greater than 1,000,000).

The hot spots methodology uses a data-driven approach to generate a set of rules $\mathcal{R} = \{r_1, r_2, \ldots, r_p\}$, where each rule describes a *group* or set of entities $g_i = \{e_j | r_i(e_j)\}$, $g_i \subset \mathcal{D}$. (The Boolean function $r_i(e_j)$ is true when entity e_j is described by rule r_j.) We will find it convenient to refer to the set of groups described by $\mathcal{R}$ as $\mathcal{G} = \{g_1, g_2, \ldots, g_p\}$ but regard $\mathcal{R}$ and $\mathcal{G}$ to be essentially synonymous and call each element of $\mathcal{R}$ (or as the purpose suits, each element of $\mathcal{G}$) a *nugget*. The set of nuggets is synonymously $\mathcal{N} = \{r_1, r_2, \ldots, r_p\}$ or $\mathcal{N} = \{g_1, g_2, \ldots, g_p\}$. We note that p is generally much smaller than n but can still be substantial (perhaps one or two thousand for n in the millions). A rule consists of a conjunction of conditions, each condition being either: $A_i \in [v_1, v_2]$ for numeric attributes or $A_i \in \{v_1, v_2, \ldots, v_q\}$ for categorical attributes. While we have reduced the dimensionality of the problem (from n down to p) for real world applications p generally remains too large for manual consideration.

We identify a *hot spot* as a set of entities which are of some particular interest to the domain user (e.g., loyal customer groups or regular high insurance claimers). Simple techniques such as clustering or segmentation can help with the task of identifying nuggets that are candidate hot spots, but are often computationally expensive and/or build groups that are not well described. A heuristic approach to this segmentation task that we have empirically found to be effective in many real world problems involves the combination of clustering and rule induction, followed by an exploration of the discovered groups (Williams and Huang 1997), which we call the hot spots methodology.

The hot spots methodology is a three step process:

Step 1: Cluster $\mathcal{D}$ into p complete and disjoint clusters $\mathcal{C} = \{C_1, C_2, \ldots, C_p\}$ where $\mathcal{D} = \bigcup C_i$ and $C_i \cap C_j = \emptyset, i \neq j$. We generally use a mixed data-type k-means based clustering algorithm (Huang 1998).

Step 2: By associating with each record its cluster membership we use rule induction to build discriminatory descriptions of each cluster, leading to the rule set $\mathcal{R} = \{r_1, r_2, \ldots, r_q\}$. Usually $q \geq p$ and usually much greater (for each clusters multiple rules may be induced). We will refer to a rule as a description of a nugget (or simply as a nugget). Each nugget describes a subset of the original dataset $\mathcal{D}$ and r_i represents both the nugget description and the nugget subset. Note that $r_i \cap r_j$ is not necessarily empty.

Step 3: The third step is to evaluate each nugget in the nugget set to find those of particular interest. We define the function $Eval(r)$ as a mapping from nuggets to a measure of the interestingness of nugget r. Such a function is domain dependent and is the key to effectively mining the knowledge mine. The nuggets may be evaluated in the context of all discovered nuggets or evaluated for their action-ability, unexpectedness, and validity in the context of the application domain. This is the heart of the problem of interestingness.

An empirically effective approach to evaluating nuggets is based on building statistical summaries of the nugget subsets. Key variables that play an important role in the business problem at hand are characterised for each nugget and filters are developed to pick out those nuggets with profiles that are out of the ordinary. As the data mining exercise proceeds, the filters are refined and further developed.

A visualisation of the summaries provides further and rapid insights to aid the identification of hot spots using a simple yet effective matrix-based graphic display of the data. This facilitates the task of working towards a small (manageable) collection of nuggets towards which further resources can be devoted.

Domain users provide the most effective form of evaluation of discovered nuggets. Visualisation tools are also effective. However, as the nugget sets become large, such manual approaches become less effective.

4 Hot Spots Applications

We illustrate the hot spots methodology in the context of two case studies involving data from commercial collaborators. These relate to actual data mining exercises carried out on very large collections of data. While the actual results and data remain confidential we present indicative results in the following sections.

4.1   Hot Spots for Insurance Premium Setting

NRMA Insurance Limited is one of Australia's largest general insurers. A major task faced by any insurer is to ensure profitability, which, to oversimplify, requires that the total sum of premiums charged for insurance must be sufficient to cover all claims made against the policies, while keeping the premiums competitive. Our approach has been to identify, describe, and explore customer groups that have significant impact on the insurance portfolio—using the hot spots methodology for risk assessment by better understanding and characterising customers. After preprocessing the dataset the three step hot spot methodology was used: clustering; rule induction; nugget evaluation.

We present an example here consisting of a dataset of just some 72,000 records with 20 attributes, clustered into some 40 clusters, ranging in size from tens of records to thousands of records. Treating each cluster as a class we can build a decision tree to describe the clusters and prune the tree through rule generation. This leads to some 60 nuggets. An example is:

No Claim Bonus < 60 and Address is Urban and
Age ≤ 24 and Vehicle ∈ {Utility, Station Wagon}

An evaluation function was developed to identify interesting nuggets (groups of customers that exhibited some important characteristics in the context of the business problem). This began by deriving for each nugget a collection of indicators, such as the number and proportion of claims lodged by clients and the average and total cost of a claim for each nugget subset.

This summary information is presented in Table 1 for some nuggets. Over the whole dataset (the final row of the table) there were 3800 claims, representing a proportion of some 5% of all clients (a typical figure). The overall average claim cost is $3000 with a total of some $12 million of claims. Particular values that are out of the ordinary in the context of the whole dataset are italicised and nuggets that are above a certain threshold for interestingness based on these values are highlighted.

Our evaluation function identifies nuggets of reasonable size containing a high proportion of claims (greater than 10%) and having large average costs. This exploration and the refinement of the measure of interestingness is performed by the domain user.

4.2   Hot Spots for Fraud Detection in Health

The Australian Government's public health care system, Medicare, is managed by the Health Insurance Commission (HIC) who maintain one of the largest data holdings world wide recording information relating to all payments to doctors and patients made by Medicare since 1975. Like any large and complex payment system, Medicare is open to fraud. The hot spots methodology has been used to identify areas which may require investigation.

A subset of 40,000 of the many millions of patients is used for illustration here. The data consists of over 30 raw attributes (e.g., age, sex, etc.) and some

Table 1. Summary motor vehicle insurance nugget data.

Nugget	Size	Claims	Proportion	Average Cost	Total Cost
1	1400	150	*11*	3700	545,000
2	2300	140	6	3800	535,000
3	25	5	*20*	4400	13,000
4	120	10	8	*7900*	79,100
5	340	20	6	*5300*	116,000
6	520	65	*13*	4400	280,700
7	5	5	100	*6800*	20,300
...	...	...	...	...	...
60	800	1400	5.9	*3500*	2,800,000
All	3800	72000	5.0	3000	12,000,000

20 derived attributes (e.g., number of times a patient visited a doctor over a year, number of different doctors visited, etc.).

Nuggets were generated from clusters leading to over 280 nuggets. An example is:

$$\text{Age} \in [18, 25] \quad \text{and} \quad \text{Weeks Claimed} \geq 10 \quad \text{and}$$
$$\text{Hoarding Index} \geq 15 \quad \text{and} \quad \text{Benefit} > \$1000$$

Table 2 lists some nuggets, with cells of particular interest italicised and rows above a threshold for interestingness highlighted.

Table 2. Summary Medicare nugget data.

Nugget	Size	Age	Gender	Services	Benefits	Weeks	Hoard	Regular
1	9000	30	F	10	30	2	1	1
2	150	30	F	*24*	*841*	4	*2*	*4*
3	1200	65	M	7	220	20	1	1
4	80	45	F	*30*	*750*	*10*	1	1
5	90	10	M	12	*1125*	10	5	2
6	800	55	M	8	550	7	1	*9*
...								
280	30	25	F	15	450	15	2	6
All	40,000	45		8	30	3	1	1

With 280 nuggets it becomes difficult to manually scan for those that are interesting. For larger Medicare datasets several thousand nuggets are identified. The evaluation function takes account of the average number of services, the average total benefit paid to patients, etc.

The approach has successfully identified interesting groups in the data that were investigated and found to be fraudulent. A pattern of behaviour identified by this process was claim hoarding where patients tended to collect together many services and lodge a single claim. While not itself indicative of fraud a particularly regular subgroup was found to be fraudulent.

5 Evolving Interesting Groups

5.1 Background

The hot spots methodology was found to be a useful starting point for an exploration for interesting areas within very large datasets. It provides some summary information and visualisations of that information. However, as the datasets become larger (typically we deal with many millions of entities) the number of nuggets becomes too large to manually explore in this way. The simple expression for interestingness based on comparisons of summary data to dataset averages is of limited use.

To address this we propose an evolutionary approach that builds on the framework provided by the hot spots methodology. The aim is to allow domain users to explore nuggets and to allow the nuggets themselves to evolve according to some measure of interestingness. At a high level the two significant problems to be addressed are:

1. How to *construct* nuggets?
2. How to define the *interestingness* of a nugget?

In a perfect world where we could define interestingness precisely there would be no problem. The definition would be used directly to identify relevant nuggets. The nature of the domains and problems we consider in data mining though is such that both the data and the goals are very dynamic and usually ill-defined. It is very much an exploratory process requiring the sophisticated interaction of domain users with the data to refine the goals. Tools which can better facilitate this sophisticated interaction are needed.

We employ evolutionary ideas to evolve nuggets (described using rules). Previous work on *classifier systems* in Evolutionary Computation has also considered the evolution of rules, and there is a limited literature on using evolutionary ideas in data mining (Freitas 1997; Radcliffe and Surry 1994; Teller and Velosa 1995; Turney 1995; Venturini, Slimane, Morin and de Beauville 1997).

The hot spots methodology begins to address both of the high level problems identified above: constructing nuggets and measuring interestingness. For constructing nuggets a data driven approach is used: employing clustering and then rule induction. For measuring interestingness we define a measure based initially on the simple statistics of a group (e.g., a group is interesting if the average value of attribute A in the group is greater than 2 standard deviations from the average value of the attribute over the whole dataset). This may be augmented with tests on the size of the group (we generally don't want too large groups as they tend to exhibit "expected" behaviour) and meta conditions that limit the number of hot spots to 10 or fewer.

Assessing true interestingness, relying on human resources to carry out actual investigations, can be a time consuming task. As we proceed, working closely with the domain user, our ideas of what is interesting amongst the nuggets being discovered becomes refined and often more complex. This requires constant refinement of the measure and further loops through the nugget construction process to further explore the search space. An evolutionary approach which attempts to tackle both the construction of nuggets and the measure of interestingness is developed.

5.2 Proposed Architecture

We describe an evolutionary architecture to refine the set of nuggets $\mathcal{N}$ derived through either a hot spots analysis, random generation, or in some other manner. A small subset of $\mathcal{N}$ is presented to the domain user who provides insights into their interestingness.

A *measure of interestingness* of a nugget is to be determined. The aim is to develop an explicit function $\mathbf{I}(g)$ (or $Eval(r)$) that captures this. An initial random measure of interestingness will set the process going, or else we can employ the simple measures used in the current hot spots methodology.

The measure of interestingness can then be used as a fitness measure in an evolutionary process to construct a collection of nuggets. By using an evolutionary process we can explore more of the search space. Having evolved a fit population of nuggets we present some small subset of these to the domain user for their evaluation (to express whether they believe these to be interesting nuggets). We are working towards capturing the user's view on the interestingness of the nuggets and to feed this directly into the data mining process. An interesting twist is that the population of measures of interestingness is also evolved, based on the user feedback. The top level architecture of the evolutionary hot spots data mining system is presented in Fig. 1.

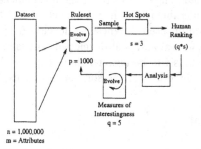

Fig. 1. The basic model for an evolutionary hot spots data miner with indicative sizes.

At any time in the process we will have some number, q, of measures of interestingness: $\mathcal{I} = \{\mathbf{I}_1, \mathbf{I}_2, \ldots, \mathbf{I}_q\}$. The rules in the ruleset $\mathcal{R}$ will be evolved independently in each cycle through the process, leading to q independent rule sets, each being fit as measured by one of the measures of interestingness I_k. Typically, a population of rules will consist of some thousand rules and it is not practical to present all rules in a "fit" population to the user. Instead a small subset of s rules is chosen from each population. Thus, for each cycle through the process, q (typically 5) independent sets of s (typically 3) rules will be presented to the user for ranking. The user ranks all of these $q \times s$ rules in terms of their assessment of the interestingness of the rules and the entities associated with the rules. This ranking is then used to evolve the interestingness measures through another generation to obtain a new population of q measures.

The analysis of the ranking might, for example, find in the top rules some commonality in conditions. These could be identified as atoms to genetically engineer the next generation of the rule set $\mathcal{R}$ (retaining these atoms in any rules that are modified). Alternatively we increase the fitness of other rules that contain the commonality. Indeed, under this scheme we can identify conditions that either increase or decrease the fitness of other rules in $\mathcal{R}$. A tuning parameter is used to indicate the degree to which fitness can be modified. The evolutionary process then takes over to generate the next population $\mathcal{R}'$ using these new fitness measures.

At each stage the domain users are involved in the process, and as interesting discoveries are brought to their attention, they assess whether further investigation is required.

6   Summary

We present an architecture that is being implemented and tested in actual data mining exercises. At this stage we can not make any claims about its usefulness although early feedback indicates that it does provide a useful expansion of the search space under the control of a domain user, allowing a focus on relevant discoveries to be established. The expression of the formulae capturing interestingness still requires considerable research. We expect to adopt various approaches to the actual expression of interestingness as developed by our experience and that of others. With a formal and well developed language the evolution of the measures of interestingness will be better able to capture the user's insights, as well as providing some direction setting suggestions for exploration.

Acknowledgements

The author acknowledges the support provided by the Cooperative Research Centre for Advanced Computational Systems (ACSys) established under the Australian Government's Cooperative Research Centres Program. Dr. Xin Yao (Australian Defence Forces Academy) has contributed tremendously in discussion of the evolutionary aspects and Reehaz Soobhany (Australian National University) has implemented much of the rule evolution code.

References

Freitas, A. A.: 1997, A genetic programming framework for two data mining tasks: classification and generalized rule induction, *in* J. R. Koza, K. Deb, M. Dorigo, D. B. Fogel, M. Garzon, H. Iba and R. L. Riolo (eds), *Proceedings of the Second Annual Conference on Genetic Programming*, Morgan Kaufmann, San Francisco, CA, pp. 96–101.

Huang, Z.: 1998, Extensions to the k-means algorithm for clustering large data sets with categorical values, *Data Mining and Knowledge Discovery* **2**(3), 283–304.

Klemettinen, M., Mannila, H., Ronkainen, P., Toivonen, H. and Verkamo, A. I.: 1994, Finding interesting rules from large sets of discovered association rules, *in* N. R. Adam, B. K. Bhargava and Y. Yesha (eds), *Proceedings of the Third International Conference on Information and Knowledge Management*, ACM Press, pp. 401–407.

Liu, B., Hsu, W. and Chen, S.: 1997, Using general impressions to analyse discovered classification rules, *KDD97: Proceedings of the Third International Conference on Knowledge Discovery and Data Mining*, AAAI Press, pp. 31–36.

Matheus, C. J., Piatetsky-Shapiro, G. and McNeill, D.: 1996, Selecting and reporting what is interesting, *in* U. M. Fayyad, G. Piatetsky-Shapiro, P. Smyth and R. Uthurusamy (eds), *Advances in Knowledge Discovery and Data Mining*, AAAI Press, pp. 465–515.

Padmanabhan, B. and Tuzhilin, A.: 1998, A belief-driven method for discovering unexpected patterns, *KDD98: Proceedings of the Fourth International Conference on Knowledge Discovery and Data Mining*, AAAI Press.

Radcliffe, N. J. and Surry, P. D.: 1994, Cooperation through hierarchical competition in genetic data mining, *Technical Report EPCC-TR94-09*, University of Edinburgh, Edinburgh Parallel Computing Centre, King's Buildings, University of Edinburgh, Scotland, EH9 3JZ.

Silbershatz, A. and Tuzhilin, A.: 1995, On subjective measures of interestingness in knowledge discovery, *in* U. M. Fayyad and R. Uthurusamy (eds), *KDD95: Proceedings of the First International Conference on Knowledge Discovery and Data Mining*, AAAI Press, pp. 275–281.

Silbershatz, A. and Tuzhilin, A.: 1996, What makes patterns interesting in knowledge discovery systems, *IEEE Transactions on Knowledge and Data Engineering* **8**(6), 970–974.

Teller, A. and Velosa, M.: 1995, Program evolution for data mining, *The International Journal of Expert Systems* **8**(3), 216–236.

Turney, P. D.: 1995, Cost-sensitive classification: Empirical evaluation of a hybrid genetic decision tree induction algorithm, *Journal of Artificial Intelligence Research* **2**, 369–409.

Venturini, G., Slimane, M., Morin, F. and de Beauville, J.-P. A.: 1997, On using interactive genetic algorithms for knowledge discovery in databases, *in* T. Bäck (ed.), *Proceedings of the Seventh International Conference on Genetic Algorithms*, Morgan Kaufmann, pp. 696–703.

Williams, G. J. and Huang, Z.: 1997, Mining the knowledge mine: The Hot Spots methodology for mining large, real world databases, *in* A. Sattar (ed.), *Advanced Topics in Artificial Intelligence*, Vol. 1342 of *Lecture Notes in Computer Science*, Springer-Verlag, pp. 340–348.

Efficient Search of Reliable Exceptions

Huan Liu[1], Hongjun Lu[2], Ling Feng[3] and Farhad Hussain[1]

[1]School of Computing, National University of Singapore, Singapore, 117599
{liuh, farhad}@comp.nus.edu.sg
[2]Department of Computer Science, Hong Kong University of Science and Technology[*]
[3]Department of Computing, Hong Kong Polytechnic University
luhj@cs.ust.hk, cslfeng@comp.polyu.edu.hk

Abstract. Finding patterns from data sets is a fundamental task of data mining. If we categorize all patterns into *strong, weak,* and *random*, conventional data mining techniques are designed only to find strong patterns, which hold for numerous objects and are usually consistent with the expectations of experts. While such strong patterns are helpful in prediction, the unexpectedness and contradiction exhibited by weak patterns are also very useful although they represent a relatively small number of objects. In this paper, we address the problem of finding weak patterns (i.e., reliable exceptions) from databases. A simple and efficient approach is proposed which uses deviation analysis to identify interesting exceptions and explore reliable ones. Besides, it is flexible in handling both subjective and objective exceptions. We demonstrate the effectiveness of the proposed approach through a set of real-life data sets, and present interesting findings.

1 Introduction

Data mining has attracted much attention from practitioners and researchers in recent years. Combining techniques from the fields of machine learning, statistics and database, data mining works towards finding patterns from huge databases and using them for improved decision making. If we categorize patterns into

- strong patterns - regularities for numerous objects;
- weak patterns - reliable exceptions representing a relatively small number of objects; and
- random patterns - random and unreliable exceptions.

Conventional data mining techniques are only designed to find the strong patterns which have high predictive accuracy or correlation. This is because we normally want to find such kinds of patterns that can help the prediction task. However, in certain tasks of data mining, we may seek more than predicting: as strong patterns are usually consistent with the expectations of experts, we want to know what is in the data that we do not know yet. Therefore, in some cases, we are more interested in finding out those weak patterns outside the strong

---

[*] on leave from School of Computing, National University of Singapore.

ones. Usually, such patterns (reliable exceptions) are unknown, unexpected, or contradictory to what the user believes. Hence, they are novel and potentially more interesting than strong patterns to the user. For example, if we are told that "some kind of jobless applicants are granted credit", that will be more novel and interesting, as compared to "jobless applicants are not granted credit". Moreover, an exception rule is often beneficial since it differs from a common sense rule which is often a basis for people's daily activity [16].

1.1 Insufficient support from current data mining techniques

Most current data mining techniques cannot effectively support weak pattern mining. Taking association rule mining as an example, all association rules $X \Rightarrow Y$ with *support* s and *confidence* c in a database are found in two phases. In the first expensive phase, the database is searched for all frequent itemsets, i.e., sets of items that occur together in at least $s\%$ of instances (records) in the database. A fast level-wise algorithm Apriori [1, 2] was developed to address the nature of this problem. It derives the frequent k-itemsets from frequent $(k - 1)$-itemsets. Apriori constructs a candidate set C_k from frequent itemset L_{k-1}, counts the number of occurrences of each candidate itemset, and then determines the set L_k of frequent itemsets based on pre-determined support s.

With the nice *downward* closure property (i.e., if a $(k + 1)$-itemset has support s, all its k-subsets also have support s), Apriori can efficiently cross out some $(k + 1)$-itemsets which cannot have s, and only check the remaining $(k + 1)$-itemsets. For instance, suppose $Sup(\{jobless, not\_granted\}) = .70$ and $Sup(\{jobless, granted\}) = .30$. By setting support threshold as .50, the strong frequent itemset $\{jobless, not\_granted\}$ is kept while the latter is pruned right away, and no further itemset like $\{jobless, female, granted\}$ will be explored. The search space is thus reduced greatly.

After obtaining all frequent itemsets, the second phase will generate association rules from each frequent itemset so that more than $c\%$ of records that contain X also contain Y. Since relatively infrequent itemsets like {jobless, female, granted} are omitted, some reliable exception rules such as *jobless* $\land$ *female* $\Rightarrow$ *granted* cannot be discovered although they show high confidence.

1.2 Intuitive extensions cannot help either

There are some intuitive ways we can think of to generate these weak patterns using traditional data mining techniques. To find exception association rules, for example, we can introduce two support thresholds $[s_1, s_2]$ as delimiters instead of only one $[s_1, 100\%]$, and search those itemsets whose support values fall into this range of $[s_1, s_2]$. However, in such case, the efficient pruning property - downward closure no longer exists, which may lead to an intolerable mining performance.

Another straightforward method is generate-and-remove: for a data set D, select the favorite induction algorithm, say C4.5 [12]; generate rules R on D; remove D' from D that are covered correctly by R; then generate rules R' on $D - D'$, repeat the process until no data is left. We can be sure that this procedure can find us many weak patterns. However, it is obvious that these weak patterns are induced independently of the strong patterns. An immediate problem is that there could be too many of weak rules. Although there are many, some interesting exceptions may be missed due to the bias of a chosen induction algorithm.

Generating all possible rules R_{all} is also a possible approach. It is certain that R_{all} will contain any interesting weak rules. However, there could be too many rules - it could be much more than the number of instances of data.

1.3 Related work

Generally, there are two schools in finding interesting and unexpected patterns: subjective vs. objective. The major objective factors used to measure the interestingness of discovered patterns include strength, confidence, coverage and simplicity [10, 3, 13].

Not all strong rules with high confidence and support are interesting as they may correspond to some prior knowledge or expectations. The importance of prior knowledge cannot be over-stressed [4]. [14, 9] propose two subjective measurements: unexpectedness and actionability, and define the unexpected measure of interestingness in terms of a belief system. [5] uses rule templates to find interesting rules from the set of all discovered association rules. [6] analyze the discovered classification rules against a set of general impressions that are specified using a representation language. Only those patterns conforming to these impressions are regarded as unexpected. The issue on interesting deviations is also discussed in [11].

As the interestingness of a pattern itself is subjective, a rule could be interesting to one user but not interesting to another. Thus, most of the previous work so far rely on users to distinguish those reliable exception patterns based on the existing concepts. One potential problem raised is that users' subjective judgments may be unreliable and uncertain in case the discovered rules are numerous. Recently, [16] proposes an autonomous probabilistic estimation approach which can discover all rule pairs (i.e., an exception rule associated with a common sense rule) with high confidence. Neither users' evaluation nor domain knowledge is required.

1.4 Our work

In this paper, we address the problem of finding weak patterns, i.e., reliable exceptions, from datasets. A simple yet flexible approach is proposed which works around the strong patterns and uses deviation analysis to find reliable exceptions. Different from previous work [16], we shun searching for strong common sense patterns; instead, we directly identify those exceptional instances and mine weak patterns from them. Besides the promised efficiency for weak pattern mining, the proposed method can also handle both subjective and objective exceptions. To demonstrate the effectiveness of this novel method, we apply it to a set of real-life data sets [8], and indeed find out some interesting exception patterns. From the mushroom data set, we can achieve more reliable exceptions, compared to the results from [16]. The remainder of the paper is organized as follows: section 2 gives a detailed description of the proposed approach. Experiments are conducted and some interesting exceptions are presented in section 3. Section 4 concludes this work.

2 A Focused Approach

Our approach is based on the following observations: (1) Any exception would have a low support [2] found in the data, otherwise it might be a strong pattern. (2) A reasonable induction algorithm can summarize data and learn rules. (3) Attributes in the rules are salient features. Observation (1) suggests that exceptions cannot be discovered from the data by applying standard machine learning techniques. Observations (2) and (3) allow us to focus on the important features so that we are more focused and an efficient method is possible for finding reliable exceptions. Our approach consists of the four phases below:

1. Rule induction and focusing.

This phase obtains the strong patterns. Normally, a user can stop here for his preliminary data mining probing. If the number of rules is too many, the user can choose to focus on the strongest rules or follow the suggestions in [6]. Let's assume that a few rules have caught our attention and we are curious to know any reliable exceptions with respect to these strong patterns. This is a filtering step that helps us focus on a few attributes quickly. If we are confident about what we want to investigate, i.e., we know the relevant attributes, then this step can be replaced by user specification of relevant attributes.

2. Contingency table and deviation.

Now we focus on some attribute in a rule. we can use these attributes and the class attribute to build a two-way contingency table that allows us to calculate deviations [15][1].

Class	Attribute			R-Total
	V_1	V_2	...V_c	
C_1	$(n_{11})x_{11}$	$(n_{12})x_{12}$	...$(n_{1c})x_{1c}$	$n_1.$
C_2	$(n_{21})x_{21}$	$(n_{22})x_{22}$	...$(n_{2c})x_{2c}$	$n_2.$
...	...	...	....	
C_r	$(n_{r1})x_{r1}$	$(n_{r2})x_{r2}$	...$(n_{rc})x_{rc}$	$n_r.$
C-Total	$n_{.1}$	$n_{.2}$	...$n_{.c}$	n

In the table, x_{ij} are the frequencies of occurrence found in the data. $n_{ij} = n_{i.}n_{.j}/n$ which are the expected frequencies of occurrence, $n = \sum_{i=1}^{r}\sum_{j=1}^{c}x_{ij}$ - total, $n_{.j} = \sum_{i=1}^{r}x_{ij}$ is a column total (C-Total), and $n_{i.} = \sum_{j=1}^{c}x_{ij}$ is a row total (R-Total). Using the expected frequency as the norm, we can define the deviation as

$$\delta_{ij} = \frac{x_{ij} - nij}{n_{ij}}.$$

---

[1] For more than one attribute, we need to resort to multi-way contingency tables.

3. Positive, negative, and outstanding deviations

Using the above definition to calculate deviations, we can expect to have three types: positive, zero, or negative. If the deviation is positive, it suggests that what is concerned is consistent with the strong patterns; if it is zero, it is the norm; and if it is negative, what's concerned is inconsistent with the strong patterns. The value of δ displays the magnitude of deviation. A large value means the deviation could be caused by chance. Since we are concerned about reliable exceptions and reliability is subject to the user's need, we specify a threshold δ_t to define how reliable is reliable. If $\delta_t > 0$, any deviation $\delta > \delta_t$ is positively outstanding; if $\delta_t < 0$, any deviation $\delta < \delta_t$ is negatively outstanding. Deviations are powerful and useful in this case as they provide a simple way of identifying interesting patterns in the data. This has been shown in the *KEFIR* [7] application.

4. Reliable exceptions

After we have identified outstanding, negative deviations of attribute-values with respect to the class label, we can get all the instances that contain these attribute-value and class pairs, and perform further mining on the focused dataset - a window, using any data mining techniques we prefer. For example, we can continue searching for frequent itemsets to investigate the above exceptional combinations. As the number of instances is much smaller now than the original one, the mining performance should improve greatly. Reliable exceptions can be those longest frequent itemsets with high support in the window.

A strong association rule found in the window may itself be a strong rule that can be found in the whole data set. We need to make sure what we find are weak patterns - low support but high confidence. In other words, any sub-itemsets found in a reliable exception should be excluded if they hold high support in the whole data. A simple method is like this: assuming that X is a sub-itemset that does not include the negatively deviated attribute in a strong association rule found in the window, we can compare the support sup_{win} of X in the window and its counterpart sup_{who} in the whole data. Note that what we really want to check is $P(X, c)$ for the window and $P(X)$ for the whole data with respect to $X \to c$. If we consider their ratio, they are actually the confidence values. Therefore, if the difference $conf_{win} - conf_{who}$ is sufficiently large (as $conf_{win}$ is always 1, the large difference means a low $conf_{who}$), we should be satisfied that $X's$ high confidence is unique to the window, otherwise, X does not have sufficient evidence to be included in the final reliable exception.

From exception rules to common sense and reference rules

Before we verify the proposed approach, we would like to say a few words about the exceptions found by our approach and those defined in [16]. Briefly, Suzuki suggested that for an exception rule, we should also be able to find its corresponding common sense rule and reference rule. A reference rule should hold low support and low confidence. Due to the nature of negative deviations, it is obvious that every exception rule found by our approach has a corresponding common sense rule (with positive deviation). A reference rule can also be found in our effort as we remove high confidence sub-itemsets mentioned in the previous paragraph. In summary, common sense and reference rules can be obtained based on exception rules.

3 Searching for Exceptions from Data Sets

In this section, we give detailed accounts of applying our approach to bench mark data sets [8].

3.1 Experiment 1 - the credit data set

The first data set used is the credit database which includes 10 attributes and 125 instances, recording situations where people are or aren't granted credit.

Step 1. Identifying relevant attributes

We ran C4.5rules on the data and obtained 5 rules in which the condition part of 3 rules contains attribute "Jobless". We thus consider it as relevant, and the class attribute is "Credit". As we can see, this step could be objective - the relevant attributes are obtained from an algorithm, or subjective - the relevant attributes are specified by an expert or user.

Step 2. Building contingency tables

Table 1 is a contingency table about "Jobless" and "Credit". For continuous attributes, the different range groups are drawn directly from the discretized results generated by the standard equal width method. The objective of the table is to determine whether the two directions of the pairings of "Jobless" and "Credit" are independent (as in the χ^2 test). Each cell of the table represents one of the $k = 2 \times 2 = 4$ categories of a two-directional classification of the $n = 125$ observations. The row-totals are $n_1 = 40$ for "Credit = No" and $n_2 = 85$ for "Credit = Yes", while the column-totals are $n_{.1} = 111$ for "Jobless = No" and $n_{.2} = 14$ for "Jobless = Yes". For example, x_{12} represents the (observed counts) number of applicants that are jobless and not granted a credit, while n_{12} represents the corresponding expected counts.

Table 1. (Expected) and observed cell counts for the "jobless" classification

Class	Attribute=Jobless		
grant	No	Yes	R-Total
No	(35.5) 28	(4.5) 12	40
Yes	(75.5) 83	(9.5) 02	85
C-Total	111	14	125

In contingency table analysis, if the two attributes are independent, the probability that an item is classified in any particular cell is given by the product of the corresponding marginal probabilities. This is because in a statistical sense, we know that independence of events A and B implies $P(A \wedge B) = P(A)P(B)$. It can be shown that the null hypothesis that the directions of classification are independent (in Table 1) is equivalent to the hypothesis that every cell probability is equal to the product of its respective row and column marginal probabilities.

Step 3. Identifying outstanding negative deviations

In Table 1, under the assumption of independence, we can compute the deviation δ_{ij} of the observed counts from the expected counts as $(\frac{x_{ij}-n_{ij}}{n_{ij}})$. Table 2 shows the deviations, sorted by their magnitudes.

Table 2. Deviation analysis of the jobless classification.

Jobless	Class	x_{ij}	n_{ij}	δ
Yes	No	12	4.5	* +1.68
Yes	Yes	02	9.5	* -.79
No	No	28	35.5	-.21
No	Yes	83	75.5	+.10

If the default threshold is $\delta_t = -.30$, we have two outstanding deviations denoted by "*" in Table 2. The large positive deviation is consistent with the trend suggested by the "norm". It is the large negative deviation that can lead to a reliable exception. The pattern "a jobless applicant is not given a credit grant" exhibits the most significant "positive deviation" at $\delta=+1.68$. Such patterns are always statistically significant, intuitive and represented by strong patterns. For example, the association below has a very high confidence.

Jobless="Yes", ... → class="No" [confidence = .857]

The outstanding negative deviation ($\delta = -.79$) says that "Jobless" applicants are given "Credit". This is intuitively wrong, or unexpected, and naturally worthy of probing.

Step 4. Finding reliable exceptions

Following the findings suggested by the outstanding negative deviation, we gather the instances that satisfy Jobless = "Yes" and Credit = "Yes", or "the jobless being granted a credit". The satisfied instances form a window, the number of instances defines the window size. Applying Apriori, for this application, we obtain the weak pattern "A female jobless with little working experience is given credit" after removing those items with high overall confidence (> 0.70) such as Area = "Good" (0.72) and Married = "Yes" (0.71).

The number of exception candidates is determined by δ_t - the higher the threshold, the fewer the candidates. Although there may not be exceptions for every individual attribute, the more attributes, the more likely that we can find more exceptions.

3.2 Experiment 2 - the mushroom data set

This data set is obtained from [8]. It has 22 attributes, each has 2 to 12 possible values, and 8124 instances with binary class. The two types (classes) of mushrooms are *poisonous* or *edible*. For this data set, we want to verify if our approach can find the exceptions found in [16].

Step 1. Identifying relevant attributes
Since all the four rules in [16] contain *Stalk-root* = ?, we select *Stalk-root* and the class for the experiment.

Step 2. Building contingency tables
This step is routine and results are shown in the table below. We only include expected frequencies for "Stalk-root = ?".

Contingency table for the "Stalk-root" classification.

Type	Attribute=Stalk-root					R-Total
	b	c	e	r	?	
p	1856	44	256	0	(1195) 1760	3916
e	1920	512	864	192	(1285) 720	4208
C-Total	3776	556	1120	192	2480	8124

Step 3. Identifying outstanding negative deviations
In the table below, we show the deviations for "Stalk-root = ?" and omit others. The outstanding negative deviation is -.44 for "Type = e".

Deviation analysis of the "Stalk-root = ?" classification.

Stalk-root	Type	x_{ij}	n_{ij}	δ
?	p	1760	1195	+.47
?	e	720	1285	-.44
...				

Step 4. Finding reliable exceptions
Using "Stalk-root = ?" and "Type = e", we find a window with 720 instances. If we simply run Apriori on the window to find frequent itemsets, we obtain two itemsets (recall that confidence for the window is always 1). For exception candidate number 1, we have the following itemset. "Chosen" below indicates whether an item is chosen to remain in the itemset.

Attribute-Value	Overall Conf	Chosen
stalk-root = ?	.29	Y
veil-type = p	.52	Y
stalk-shape = e	.46	Y
gill-size = b	.70	Y
bruises = f	.31	Y
ring-type = p	.79	N

After removing those with high overall confidence ($> .70$), we have rule 1 as found in [16] repeated here.

#1
      CS: bruises=f, g-size=b, stalk-shape=e $\rightarrow$ class=p
      RE: C, stalk-root=? $\rightarrow$ class=e
      RR: stalk-root=? $\rightarrow$ class=e

where CS is a common sense rule, RE is a reliable exception, C in RE is the conditional part of CS, and RR is a reference rule.

For exception candidate number 2, after removing items with high overall confidence. We obtain a *super-itemset* for exception rules 2, 3, and 4 in [16] as follows. We repeat the three rules below.

Attribute-Value	Overall Conf	Chosen
stalk-root = ?	.29	Y
spore-print-color = w	.24	Y
veil-color = w	.51	Y
veil-type = p	.52	Y
stalk-shape = e	.46	Y
gill-size = b	.70	Y
gill-attachment = f	.51	Y
ring-number = t	.88	N
odor = n	.97	N

#2	CS: g-attachment=f, stalk-root=? $\rightarrow$ class=p RE: C, g-size=b, stalk-shape=3, veil-color=w $\rightarrow$ class=e RR: g-size=b, stalk-shape=3, veil-color=w $\rightarrow$ class=e
#3	CS: stalk-root=?, sp-color=w $\rightarrow$ class=p RE: C, g-attachment=f, g-size=b, stalk-shape=e $\rightarrow$ class=e RR: g-attachment=f, g-size=b, stalk-shape=e $\rightarrow$ class=e
#4	CS: stalk-root=?, sp-color=w $\rightarrow$ class=p RE: C, g-size=b, stalk-shape=3, veil-color=w $\rightarrow$ class=e RR: stalk-root=? $\rightarrow$ class=e

4 Conclusion

We propose here a simple approach that enables us to study reliable exceptions with respect to a rule of our interest or attributes specified by a user. The major techniques are deviation analysis, windowing, and conventional mining tools (e.g., Apriori for association rule mining). For the concerned attributes, we first find their negative deviations which determine the window, and then search reliable patterns from the window using any data mining tools we want. Reliable exceptions are those patterns that are only valid in the window.

This approach is efficient because (1) it works around focused attributes, thus avoiding search all attributes in the database; (2) we are only concerned about negative deviations; (3) it only scan the data once to create the window; and (4) the window size (i.e., number of instances) is usually much smaller than the number of instances in the data. Besides, such approach is also flexible to handle both subjective and objective prior knowledge. Weak pattern finding is an important area for effective, actionable, and focused data mining.

Acknowledgments

We would like thank Gurmit Singh, Danny Oh, and Soh Seng Guan for implementing some of the programs used for this project. Special thanks go to Kian Sing Ng for his work in the beginning of this project.

References

1. R. Agrawal, T. Imielinski, and A. Swami. Mining association rules between sets of items in large databases. In *Proc. of the ACM SIGMOD Conference on Management of Data*, pages 207–216, Washington D.C., USA, May 1993.

2. R. Agrawal and R. Srikant. Fast algorithms for mining association rules. In *Proc. of the 20th Conference on Very Large Data Bases*, pages 478–499, Santiago, Chile, September 1994.

3. W. Frawely, G. Piatesky-Shapiro, and C. Matheus. *Knowledge Discovery in database: an overview.* G. Piatesky-Shapiro and W. Frawley (eds.) Knowledge Discovery in Database, AAAI/MIT Press, 1991.

4. B.R. Gaines. An ounce of knowledge is worth a ton of data. In A.M. Segre, editor, *Proceedings of The Sixth International Workshop on Machine Learning*, pages 156 – 159. Morgan Kaufmann Publishers, Inc., 1989.

5. M. Klemettinen, H. Mannila, P. Ronkainen, H. Toivonen, and I. Verkamo. Finding interesting rules from large sets of discovered association rules. In *Proc. of the Third International Conference on Information and Knowledge Management*, pages 401–407, November 1994.

6. B. Liu, W. Hsu, and S. Chen. Using general impression to analyze discovered classification rules. In *Proc. of the Third International Conference on Knowledge Discovery and Data Mining*, pages 31–36, Newport Beach, California, USA, 1997.

7. C. Matheus, G. Piatetsky-Shapiro, and D. McNeil. An application of KEFIR to the analysis of healthcare information. In *Proc. of the Eleventh International Conference on Artificial Intelligence, Workshop on Knowledge Discovery in Databases*, pages 25–36, ., 1994.

8. C. Merz and P. Murphy. UCI repository of machine learning databases. Technical Report http://www.ics.uci.edu/ mlearn/MLRepository.html.Irvine, CA: University of California, Department of Information and Computer Science, 1996.

9. B. Padmanabhan and A. Tuzhilin. A belief-driven method for discovering unexpected patterns. In *Proc. of the Fourth International Conference on Knowledge Discovery and Data Mining*, pages 27–31, April 1998.

10. G. Piatetsky-Shapiro. *Discovery, analysis, and presentation of strong rules.* G. Piatesky-Shapiro and W. Frawley (eds.) Knowledge Discovery in Database, AAAI/MIT Press, 1991.

11. G. Piatetsky-Shapiro and C. Matheus. The interestingness of deviations. In *AAAI Workshop on Knowledge Discovery in Database*, pages 25–36, Seattle, Washington, July 1994.

12. J. Quinlan. *C4.5: Programs for Machine Learning.* Morgan Kauffmann Publishers, Inc., 1993.

13. A. Silberschatz and A. Tuzhilin. On subjective measures of interestingness in knowledge discovery. In *Proc. of the First International Conference on Knowledge Discovery and Data Mining*, pages 275–281, Montreal, 1995.

14. A. Silberschatz and A. Tuzhilin. What makes patterns interesting in knowledge discovery systems. *IEEE Trans. on Knoweldge and Data Engineering*, 8(6):970–974, 1996.

15. P. Smith. *Into Statistics.* Springer-Verlag, Singapore, 1998.

16. E. Suzuki. Autonomous discovery of reliable exception rules. In *Proc. of the 3rd International Conference on Knowledge Discovery and Data Mining*, pages 259–263, Newport Beach, CA, USA., August 1997.

Heuristics for Ranking the Interestingness of Discovered Knowledge

Robert J. Hilderman and Howard J. Hamilton

Department of Computer Science
University of Regina
Regina, Saskatchewan, Canada S4S 0A2
{hilder,hamilton}@cs.uregina.ca

Abstract. We describe heuristics, based upon information theory and statistics, for ranking the interestingness of summaries generated from databases. The tuples in a summary are unique, and therefore, can be considered to be a population described by some probability distribution. The four interestingness measures presented here are based upon common measures of diversity of a population: variance, the Simpson index, and the Shannon index. Using each of the proposed measures, we assign a single real value to a summary that describes its interestingness. Our experimental results show that the ranks assigned by the four interestingness measures are highly correlated.

1 Introduction

Knowledge discovery from databases (KDD) is the nontrivial process of identifying valid, previously unknown, potentially useful patterns in data [3, 4]. However, the volume of data contained in a database often exceeds the ability to analyze it efficiently, resulting in a gap between the collection of data and its understanding [4]. A number of successful algorithms for KDD have previously been developed. One particular summarization algorithm, *attribute-oriented generalization* (AOG), has been shown to be among the most efficient of methods for KDD [1]. AOG summarizes in a database by replacing specific attribute values with more general concepts according to user-defined *concept hierarchies* (CHs).

Until recently, AOG methods were limited in their ability to efficiently generate summaries when multiple CHs were associated with an attribute. To resolve this problem, we previously introduced new serial and parallel AOG algorithms [8] and a data structure called a *domain generalization graph* (DGG) [5, 8, 10]. A DGG defines a partial order representing the set of all possible summaries that can be generated from a set of attributes and their associated CHs. However, when the number of attributes to be generalized is large, or the DGG associated with a set of attributes is complex, many summaries may be generated, requiring the user to manually evaluate each one to determine whether it contains an interesting result. In this paper, we describe heuristics, based upon information theory and statistics, for ranking the interestingness of summaries generated from databases. Our objective is to assign a single real value to a summary that describes its interestingness.

Although our measures were developed and utilized for ranking the interestingness of generalized relations, they are more generally applicable to other problem domains, such as ranking *views* (i.e., precomputed, virtual tables derived from a relational database) or *summary tables* (i.e., materialized, aggregate views derived from a data cube). However, we do not dwell here on the technical aspects of deriving generalized relations, views, or summary tables. Instead, we simply refer collectively to these objects as summaries, and assume that some collection of them is available for ranking.

The remainder of this paper is organized as follows. In the next section, we describe heuristics for ranking the interestingness of summaries and provide a detailed example for each heuristic. In the third section, we present a summary overview of the experimental results. In the last section, we conclude with a summary of our work and suggestions for future research.

2 Interestingness

We formally define the problem of ranking the interestingness of summaries, as follows. Let a *summary* S be a relation defined on the columns $\{(A_1, D_1), (A_2, D_2), \ldots, (A_n, D_n)\}$, where each (A_i, D_i) is an attribute-domain pair. Also, let $\{(A_1, v_{i1}), (A_2, v_{i2}), \ldots, (A_n, v_{in})\}$, $i = 1, 2, \ldots, m$, be a set of m unique tuples, where each (A_j, v_{ij}) is an attribute-value pair and each v_{ij} is a value from the domain D_j associated with attribute A_j. One attribute A_n is a derived attribute, called *Count*, whose domain D_n is the set of positive integers, and whose value v_{in} for each attribute-value pair (A_n, v_{in}) is equal to the number of tuples which have been aggregated from the base relation (i.e., the unconditioned data present in the original relational database). The *interestingness* I of a summary S is given by $I = f(S)$, where f is typically a function of the cardinality and degree of S, the complexity of its associated CHs, or the probability distributions of the tuples in S.

A sample summary is shown below in Table 1. In Table 1, there are $n = 3$ attribute-domain pairs and $m = 4$ sets of unique attribute-value pairs. A *Tuple ID* attribute is being shown for demonstration purposes only and is not actually part of the summary. Table 1 will be used as the basis for all calculations in the examples that follow.

Table 1. A sample summary

Tuple ID	Colour	Shape	Count
t_1	red	round	3
t_2	red	square	1
t_3	blue	square	1
t_4	green	round	2

We now describe four heuristics for ranking the interestingness of summaries and provide a detailed example for each heuristic. The tuples in a summary are unique, and therefore, can be considered to be a population described by some probability distribution (derived from the *Count* attribute). The well-known, domain-independent formulae, upon which these heuristics are based, have been selected for evaluation as interestingness measures because they are common measures of diversity of a population, and have previously seen extensive application in several areas of the physical, social, management, and computer sciences. The I_{var} measure is based upon variance, which is the most common measure of variability used in statistics [11]. The I_{avg} and I_{tot} measures, based upon a relative entropy measure (also known as the Shannon index) from information theory [12], measure the average information content in a single tuple in a summary, and the total information content in a summary, respectively. The I_{con} measure, a variance-like measure based upon the Simpson index [13], measures the extent to which the counts are distributed over the tuples in a summary, rather than being concentrated in any single one of them.

In the discussion that follows, the probabiltiy of each t_i occurring in the actual probability distribution of S is given by:

$$p(t_i) = \frac{v_{in}}{(v_{1n} + v_{2n} + \ldots + v_{mn})},$$

and the probability of each t_i occurring in a summary where the tuples have a uniform probability distribution is given by:

$$q(t_i) = \frac{\frac{(v_{1n}+v_{2n}+\ldots+v_{mn})}{m}}{(v_{1n} + v_{2n} + \ldots + v_{mn})} = \frac{1}{m},$$

where v_{in} is the value associated with the *Count* attribute A_n in tuple t_i.

2.1 The I_{var} Measure

Given a summary S, we can measure how far the actual probability distribution (hereafter called simply a distribution) of the counts for the t_i's in S varies from that of a uniform distribution. The *variance* of the distribution in S from that of a uniform distribution is given by:

$$I_{var} = \frac{\sum_{i=1}^{m}(p(t_i) - q(t_i))^2}{m-1},$$

where higher values of I_{var} are considered more interesting. For example, from the actual distribution of the tuples in Table 1, we have $p(t_1) = 0.429$, $p(t_2) = 0.143$, $p(t_3) = 0.143$, $p(t_4) = 0.286$, and from a uniform distribution of the tuples, we have $q(t_i) = 0.25$, for all i. So, the interestingness of the summary using the I_{var} measure is:

$$I_{var} = ((0.429 - 0.25)^2 + (0.143 - 0.25)^2 +$$
$$(0.143 - 0.25)^2 + (0.286 - 0.25)^2)/3$$
$$= 0.018.$$

Note that we use $m - 1$ in the denominator of our calculation for variance because we assume the summary may not contain all possible combinations of attributes, meaning we are not observing all of the possible tuples.

2.2 The I_{avg} Measure

Given a summary S, we can determine the average information content in each tuple. The *average information content*, in bits per tuple, is given by:

$$I_{avg} = -\sum_{i=1}^{m} p(t_i) \log_2 p(t_i),$$

where lower values of I_{avg} are considered more interesting. For example, the actual distribution for p is given in Example 1. So, the interestingness of the summary using the I_{avg} measure is:

$$I_{avg} = -(0.429 \log_2 0.429 + 0.143 \log_2 0.143 +$$
$$0.143 \log_2 0.143 + 0.286 \log_2 0.286)$$
$$= 1.842 \ bits.$$

2.3 The I_{tot} Measure

Given a summary S, we can determine its total information content. The *total information content*, in bits, is given by:

$$I_{tot} = m * I_{avg},$$

where lower values of I_{tot} are considered more interesting. For example, the average information content for the summary is given in Example 2. So, the interestingness of the summary using the I_{tot} measure is:

$$I_{tot} = 4 * 1.842$$
$$= 7.368 \ bits.$$

2.4 The I_{con} Measure

Given a summary S, we can measure the extent to which the counts are distributed over the tuples in the summary. The *concentration* of the distribution in S is given by:

$$I_{con} = \sum_{i=1}^{m} p(t_i)^2,$$

where higher values of I_{con} are considered more interesting. For example, the actual distribution for p is given in Example 1. So, the interestingness of the summary using the I_{con} measure is:

$$I_{con} = 0.429^2 + 0.143^2 + 0.143^2 + 0.286^2$$
$$= 0.306.$$

3 Experimental Results

In this section, we present a summary overview of the experimental results. All summaries in our experiments were generated using DB-Discover [1, 2], a software tool which uses AOG for KDD. To generate summaries, series of discovery tasks were run on the NSERC Research Awards Database (available in the public domain) and the Customer Database (confidential database supplied by an industrial partner). Both have been frequently used in previous data mining research [9, 2, 6, 8]. Similar results were obtained from both the NSERC and Customer discovery tasks, however, we restrict our discussion to those obtained from the NSERC discovery tasks.

Our experiments show some similarities in how the four interestingness measures rank summaries [7]. To determine the extent of the ranking similarities, we can calculate the Gamma correlation coefficient for each pair of interestingness measures. The Gamma statistic assumes that the summaries under consideration are assigned ranks according to an ordinal (i.e., rank order) scale, and is a probability computed as the difference between the probability that the rank ordering of two interestingness measures agree minus the probability that they disagree, divided by 1 minus the probability of ties. The value of the Gamma statistic varies in the interval $[-1, 1]$, where values near 1, 0, and -1 represent significant positive, no, and significant negative correlation, respectively.

The Gamma correlation coefficients (hereafter called the coefficients) for the two-, three-, and four-attribute discovery tasks are shown in Table 2. In Table 2, the *Interestingness Measures* column describes the pairs of interestingness measures being compared, and the *N-2*, *N-3*, and *N-4* columns describe the coefficients corresponding to the pairs of interestingness measures in the two-, three-, and four-attribute NSERC discovery tasks, respectively.

Table 2. Comparison of ranking similarities

Interestingness	Gamma Correlation Coefficient			
Measures	N-2	N-3	N-4	Average
I_{var} & I_{avg}	0.94737	0.95670	0.96076	0.95494
I_{var} & I_{tot}	0.92983	0.86428	0.91904	0.90438
I_{var} & I_{con}	0.91228	0.93172	0.94929	0.93110
I_{avg} & I_{tot}	0.91228	0.86356	0.90947	0.89510
I_{avg} & I_{con}	0.94737	0.96506	0.94516	0.95253
I_{tot} & I_{con}	0.85965	0.82862	0.86957	0.85261
Average		0.91813	0.90166	0.92555	0.91511

The coefficients vary from a low of 0.82862 for the pair containing the I_{tot} and I_{con} measures in the three-attribute discovery task, to a high of 0.96506 for the pair containing the I_{avg} and I_{con} measures in the same discovery task. The ranks assigned by the pair containing the I_{var} and I_{avg} measures are most similar, as indicated by the average coefficient of 0.95494 for the two-, three-, and four-attribute discovery tasks, followed closely by the ranks assigned to the pair containing the I_{avg} and I_{con} measures, as indicated by the average coefficient of 0.95253. The ranks assigned by the pairs of interestingness measures in the three-attribute discovery task have the least similarity, as indicated by the average coefficient of 0.90166, although this is not significantly lower than the two- and four-attribute average coefficients of 0.91813 and 0.92555, respectively. Given the overall average coefficient is 0.91511, we conclude that the ranks assigned by the four interestingness measures are highly correlated.

4 Conclusion and Future Research

We described heuristics for ranking the interestingness of summaries generated from databases. The hueristics are simple, easy to use, and have the potential to provide a reasonable starting point for further analysis of discovered knowledge. Future research will focus on further experimental evaluation of the measures proposed here, and other measures of diversity [7].

References

1. C.L. Carter and H.J. Hamilton. Efficient attribute-oriented algorithms for knowledge discovery from large databases. *IEEE Transactions on Knowledge and Data Engineering*, 10(2):193–208, March/April 1998.
2. C.L. Carter, H.J. Hamilton, and N. Cercone. Share-based measures for itemsets. In J. Komorowski and J. Zytkow, editors, *Proceedings of the First European Conference on the Principles of Data Mining and Knowledge Discovery (PKDD'97)*, pages 14–24, Trondheim, Norway, June 1997.
3. U.M. Fayyad, G. Piatetsky-Shapiro, and P. Smyth. From data mining to knowledge discovery. In U.M. Fayyad, G. Piatetsky-Shapiro, P. Smyth, and R. Uthurusamy, editors, *Adavances in Knowledge Discovery and Data Mining*, pages 1–34. AAAI/MIT Press, 1996.
4. W.J. Frawley, G. Piatetsky-Shapiro, and C.J. Matheus. Knowledge discovery in databases: An overview. In *Knowledge Discovery in Databases*, pages 1–27. AAAI/MIT Press, 1991.
5. H.J. Hamilton, R.J. Hilderman, L. Li, and D.J. Randall. Generalization lattices. In J. Zytkow and M. Quafafou, editors, *Proceedings of the Second European Conference on the Principles of Data Mining and Knowledge Discovery (PKDD'98)*, pages 328–336, Nantes,France, September 1998.
6. R.J. Hilderman, C.L. Carter, H.J. Hamilton, and N. Cercone. Mining market basket data using share measures and characterized itemsets. In X. Wu, R. Kotagiri, and K. Korb, editors, *Proceedings of the Second Pacific-Asia Conference on Knowledge Discovery and Data Mining (PAKDD'98)*, pages 159–173, Melbourne, Australia, April 1998.
7. R.J. Hilderman, H.J. Hamilton, and B. Barber. Ranking the interestingness of summaries from data mining systems. In *Proceedings of the 12th Annual Florida Artificial Intelligence Research Symposium (FLAIRS'99)*. To appear.
8. R.J. Hilderman, H.J. Hamilton, R.J. Kowalchuk, and N. Cercone. Parallel knowledge discovery using domain generalization graphs. In J. Komorowski and J. Zytkow, editors, *Proceedings of the First European Conference on the Principles of Data Mining and Knowledge Discovery (PKDD'97)*, pages 25–35, Trondheim, Norway, June 1997.
9. H. Liu, H. Lu, and J. Yao. Identifying relevant databases for multidatabase mining. In X. Wu, R. Kotagiri, and K. Korb, editors, *Proceedings of the Second Pacific-Asia Conference on Knowledge Discovery and Data Mining (PAKDD'98)*, pages 210–221, Melbourne, Australia, April 1998.
10. D.J. Randall, H.J. Hamilton, and R.J. Hilderman. Temporal generalization with domain generalization graphs. *International Journal of Pattern Recognition and Artificial Intelligence*. To appear.
11. W.A. Rosenkrantz. *Introduction to Probability and Statistics for Scientists and Engineers*. McGraw-Hill, 1997.
12. C.E. Shannon and W. Weaver. *The mathematical theory of communication*. University of Illinois Press, 1949.
13. E.H. Simpson. Measurement of diversity. *Nature*, 163:688, 1949.

Automated Discovery of Plausible Rules Based on Rough Sets and Rough Inclusion

Shusaku Tsumoto

Department of Information Medicine, Medical Research Institute,
Tokyo Medical and Dental University
1-5-45 Yushima, Bunkyo-ku Tokyo 113 Japan
E-mail: tsumoto@computer.org

Abstract. *One of the most important problems on rule induction methods is that they cannot extract rules, which plausibly represent experts' decision processes. On one hand, rule induction methods induce probabilistic rules, the description length of which is too short, compared with the experts' rules. On the other hand, construction of Bayesian networks generates too lengthy rules. In this paper, the characteristics of experts' rules are closely examined and a new approach to extract plausible rules is introduced, which consists of the following three procedures. First, the characterization of decision attributes (given classes) is extracted from databases and the classes are classified into several groups with respect to the characterization. Then, two kinds of sub-rules, characterization rules for each group and discrimination rules for each class in the group are induced. Finally, those two parts are integrated into one rule for each decision attribute. The proposed method was evaluated on medical databases, the experimental results of which show that induced rules correctly represent experts' decision processes.*

1 Introduction

One of the most important problems in developing expert systems is knowledge acquisition from experts[4]. In order to automate this problem, many inductive learning methods, such as induction of decision trees[3, 12], rule induction methods[7, 9, 12, 13] and rough set theory[10, 15, 19], are introduced and applied to extract knowledge from databases, and the results show that these methods are appropriate.

However, it has been pointed out that conventional rule induction methods cannot extract rules, which plausibly represent experts' decision processes[15, 16]: the description length of induced rules is too short, compared with the experts' rules. For example, rule induction methods, including AQ15[9] and PRIMEROSE[15], induce the following common rule for muscle contraction headache from databases on differential diagnosis of headache[16]:

$$[location = whole] \wedge [\text{Jolt Headache} = no] \wedge [\text{Tenderness of M1} = yes]$$
$$\rightarrow \text{muscle contraction headache.}$$

This rule is shorter than the following rule given by medical experts.

[Jolt Headache = no] $\wedge$[Tenderness of M1 = yes]
$$\wedge[\text{Tenderness of B1} = no] \wedge [\text{Tenderness of C1} = no]$$
$$\rightarrow \text{muscle contraction headache,}$$

where [Tenderness of B1 = no] and [Tenderness of C1 = no] are added.

These results suggest that conventional rule induction methods do not reflect a mechanism of knowledge acquisition of medical experts.

In this paper, the characteristics of experts' rules are closely examined and a new approach to extract plausible rules is introduced, which consists of the following three procedures. First, the characterization of each decision attribute (a given class), a list of attribute-value pairs the supporting set of which covers all the samples of the class, is extracted from databases and the classes are classified into several groups with respect to the characterization. Then, two kinds of sub-rules, rules discriminating between each group and rules classifying each class in the group are induced. Finally, those two parts are integrated into one rule for each decision attribute. The proposed method is evaluated on medical databases, the experimental results of which show that induced rules correctly represent experts' decision processes.

2 Rough Set Theory and Probabilistic Rules

In this section, a probabilistic rule is defined by the use of the following three notations of rough set theory[10]. The main ideas of these rules are illustrated by a small database shown in Table 1.

First, a combination of attribute-value pairs, corresponding to a complex in AQ terminology[9], is denoted by a formula R.

Secondly, a set of samples which satisfy R is denoted by $[x]_R$, corresponding to a star in AQ terminology. For example, when $\{2, 3, 4, 5\}$ is a set of samples which satisfy [$age = 40...49$], $[x]_{[age=40...49]}$ is equal to $\{2, 3, 4, 5\}$. [1]

Finally, U, which stands for "Universe", denotes all training samples.

Using these notations, we can define several characteristics of classification in the set-theoretic framework, such as classification accuracy and coverage. Classification accuracy and coverage(true positive rate) is defined as:

$$\alpha_R(D) = \frac{|[x]_R \cap D|}{|[x]_R|} (= P(D|R)), \text{ and}$$

$$\kappa_R(D) = \frac{|[x]_R \cap D|}{|D|} (= P(R|D)),$$

where $|A|$ denotes the cardinality of a set A, $\alpha_R(D)$ denotes a classification accuracy of R as to classification of D, and $\kappa_R(D)$ denotes a coverage, or a true positive rate of R to D, respectively.[2] It is notable that these two measures are equal to conditional probabilities: accuracy is a probability of D under the condition of R, coverage is one of R under the condition of D.

---

[1] In this notation, "n" denotes the nth sample in a dataset (Table 1).

[2] Those measures are equivalent to confidence and support defined by Agrawal[1].

Table 1. An Example of Database

	age	loc	nat	prod	nau	M1	class
1	50...59	occ	per	no	no	yes	m.c.h.
2	40...49	who	per	no	no	yes	m.c.h.
3	40...49	lat	thr	yes	yes	no	migra
4	40...49	who	thr	yes	yes	no	migra
5	40...49	who	rad	no	no	yes	m.c.h.
6	50...59	who	per	no	yes	yes	psycho

DEFINITIONS: loc: location, nat: nature, prod: prodrome, nau: nausea, M1: tenderness of M1, who: whole, occ: occular, lat: lateral, per: persistent, thr: throbbing, rad: radiating, m.c.h.: muscle contraction headache, migra: migraine, psycho: psychological pain,

According to the definitions, probabilistic rules with high accuracy and coverage are defined as:

$$R \xrightarrow{\alpha,\kappa} d \text{ s.t. } \quad R = \vee_i R_i = \vee \wedge_j [a_j = v_k],$$
$$\alpha_{R_i}(D) \geq \delta_\alpha \text{ and } \kappa_{R_i}(D) \geq \delta_\kappa,$$

where δ_α and δ_κ denote given thresholds for accuracy and coverage, respectively. For the above example shown in Table 1, probabilistic rules for m.c.h. are given as follows:

$$[M1 = yes] \rightarrow m.c.h. \ \alpha = 3/4 = 0.75, \ \kappa = 1.0,$$
$$[nau = no] \rightarrow m.c.h. \ \alpha = 3/3 = 1.0, \ \kappa = 1.0,$$

where δ_α and δ_κ are set to 0.75 and 0.5, respectively.

Rough Inclusion

In order to measure the similarity between classes with respect to characterization, we introduce a rough inclusion measure μ, which is defined as follows.

$$\mu(S,T) = \frac{|S \bigcap T|}{|S|}.$$

It is notable that if $S \subseteq T$, then $\mu(S,T) = 1.0$, which shows that this relation extends subset and superset relations. This measure is introduced by Polkowski and Skowron in their study on rough mereology[11]. Whereas rough mereology firstly applies to distributed information systems, its essential idea is rough inclusion: Rough inclusion focuses on set-inclusion to characterize a hierarchical structure based on a relation between a subset and superset. Thus, application of rough inclusion to capturing the relations between classes is equivalent to constructing rough hierarchical structure between classes, which is also closely related with information granulation proposed by Zadeh[18].

3 Interpretation of Medical Experts' Rules

As shown in Section 1, rules acquired from medical experts are much longer than those induced from databases the decision attributes of which are given by the same experts.[3]

Those characteristics of medical experts' rules are fully examined not by comparing between those rules for the same class, but by comparing experts' rules with those for another class. For example, a classification rule for muscle contraction headache is given by:

[Jolt Headache = *no*]
$\wedge$([Tenderness of M0 = *yes*] $\vee$ [Tenderness of M1 = *yes*] $\vee$ [Tenderness of M2 = *yes*])
$\wedge$[Tenderness of B1 = *no*] $\wedge$ [Tenderness of B2 = *no*] $\wedge$ [Tenderness of B3 = *no*]
$\wedge$[Tenderness of C1 = *no*] $\wedge$ [Tenderness of C2 = *no*] $\wedge$ [Tenderness of C3 = *no*]
$\wedge$[Tenderness of C4 = *no*]
$\rightarrow$ muscle contraction headache

This rule is very similar to the following classification rule for disease of cervical spine:

[Jolt Headache = *no*]
$\wedge$([Tenderness of M0 = *yes*] $\vee$ [Tenderness of M1 = *yes*] $\vee$ [Tenderness of M2 = *yes*])
$\wedge$([Tenderness of B1 = *yes*] $\vee$ [Tenderness of B2 = *yes*] $\vee$ [Tenderness of B3 = *yes*]
$\vee$[Tenderness of C1 = *yes*] $\vee$ [Tenderness of C2 = *yes*] $\vee$ [Tenderness of C3 = *yes*]
$\vee$[Tenderness of C4 = *yes*])
$\rightarrow$ disease of cervical spine

The differences between these two rules are attribute-value pairs, from tenderness of B1 to C4. Thus, these two rules can be simplified into the following form:

$$a_1 \wedge A_2 \wedge \neg A_3 \rightarrow \textit{muscle contraction headache}$$
$$a_1 \wedge A_2 \wedge A_3 \rightarrow \textit{disease of cervical spine}$$

The first two terms and the third one represent different reasoning. The first and second term a_1 and A_2 are used to differentiate muscle contraction headache and disease of cervical spine from other diseases. The third term A_3 is used to make a differential diagnosis between these two diseases. Thus, medical experts firstly selects several diagnostic candidates, which are very similar to each other, from many diseases and then make a final diagnosis from those candidates.

In the next section, a new approach for inducing the above rules is introduced.

---

[3] This is because rule induction methods generally search for shorter rules, compared with decision tree induction. In the latter cases, the induced trees are sometimes too deep and in order for the trees to be learningful, pruning and examination by experts are required. One of the main reasons why rules are short and decision trees are sometimes long is that these patterns are generated only by one criteria, such as high accuracy or high information gain. The comparative study in this section suggests that experts should acquire rules not only by one criteria but by the usage of several measures.

4 Rule Induction

Rule induction(Fig 1.) consists of the following three procedures. First, the characterization of each given class, a list of attribute-value pairs the supporting set of which covers all the samples of the class, is extracted from databases and the classes are classified into several groups with respect to the characterization. Then, two kinds of sub-rules, rules discriminating between each group and rules classifying each class in the group are induced(Fig 2). Finally, those two parts are integrated into one rule for each decision attribute(Fig 3).[4]

procedure *Rule Induction (Total Process)*;
  var
    $i : integer$; $M, L, R : List$;
    $L_D : List$; /* A list of all classes */
  begin
    Calculate $\alpha_R(D_i)$ and $\kappa_R(D_i)$ for each elementary relation R and each class D_i;
    Make a list $L(D_i) = \{R|\kappa_R(D) = 1.0\}$) for each class D_i;
    while $(L_D \neq \phi)$ **do**
      begin
        $D_i := first(L_D)$; $M := L_D - D_i$;
        while $(M \neq \phi)$ **do**
          begin
            $D_j := first(M)$;
            if $(\mu(L(D_j), L(D_i)) \leq \delta_\mu)$ **then** $L_2(D_i) := L_2(D_i) + \{D_j\}$;
            $M := M - D_j$;
          end
        Make a new decision attribute D_i' for $L_2(D_i)$;
        $L_D := L_D - D_i$;
      end
    Construct a new table $(T_2(D_i))$for $L_2(D_i)$.
    Construct a new table$(T(D_i'))$ for each decision attribute D_i';
      Induce classification rules R_2 for each $L_2(D)$; /* Fig.2 */
      Store Rules into a List $R(D)$
      Induce classification rules R_d for each D' in $T(D')$; /* Fig.2 */
      Store Rules into a List $R(D')(= R(L_2(D_i)))$
    Integrate R_2 and R_d into a rule R_D; /* Fig.3 */
  end {*Rule Induction* };

Fig. 1. An Algorithm for Rule Induction

---

[4] This method is an extension of PRIMEROSE4 reported in [17]. In the former paper, only rigid set-inclusion relations are considered for grouping; on the other hand, rough-inclusion relations are introduced in this approach. Recent empirical comparison between set-inclusion method and rough-inclusion method shows that the latter approach outperforms the former one.

procedure *Induction of Classification Rules*;
  var
    i : *integer*; M, L_i : *List*;
  begin
    $L_1 := L_{er}$; /* L_{er}: List of Elementary Relations */
    $i := 1$; $M := \{\}$;
    for $i := 1$ **to** n **do**   /* n: Total number of attributes */
      begin
        while ($L_i \neq \{\}$) **do**
          begin
            Select one pair $R = \wedge[a_i = v_j]$ from L_i;
            $L_i := L_i - \{R\}$;
            if $(\alpha_R(D) \geq \delta_\alpha)$ and $(\kappa_R(D) \geq \delta_\kappa)$
              then **do** $S_{ir} := S_{ir} + \{R\}$; /* Include R as Inclusive Rule */
              else $M := M + \{R\}$;
          end
        $L_{i+1} :=$ (A list of the whole combination of the conjunction formulae in M);
      end
  end {*Induction of Classification Rules* };

Fig. 2. An Algorithm for Classification Rules

Example

Let us illustrate how the introduced algorithm works by using a small database in Table 1. For simplicity, two thresholds δ_α and δ_μ are set to 1.0, which means that only deterministic rules should be induced and that only subset and superset relations should be considered for grouping classes.

After the first and second step, the following three sets will be obtained: $L(m.c.h.) = \{[prod = no], [M1 = yes]\}$, $L(migra) = \{[age = 40...49], [nat = who], [prod = yes], [nau = yes], [M1 = no]\}$, and $L(psycho) = \{[age = 50...59], [loc = who], [nat = per], [prod = no], [nau = no], [M1 = yes]\}$. Thus, since a relation $L(psycho) \subset L(m.c.h.)$ holds (i.e., $\mu(L(m.c.h.), L(psycho)) = 1.0$), a new decision attribute is $D_1 = \{m.c.h., psycho\}$ and $D_2 = \{migra\}$, and a partition $P = \{D_1, D_2\}$ is obtained. From this partition, two decision tables will be generated, as shown in Table 2 and Table 3 in the fifth step.

In the sixth step, classification rules for D_1 and D_2 are induced from Table 2. For example, the following rules are obtained for D_1.

$$[M1 = yes] \quad \rightarrow D_1 \ \alpha = 1.0, \ \kappa = 1.0, \ \text{supported by } \{1,2,5,6\}$$
$$[prod = no] \quad \rightarrow D_1 \ \alpha = 1.0, \ \kappa = 1.0, \ \text{supported by } \{1,2,5,6\}$$
$$[nau = no] \quad \rightarrow D_1 \ \alpha = 1.0, \ \kappa = 0.75, \ \text{supported by } \{1,2,5\}$$
$$[nat = per] \quad \rightarrow D_1 \ \alpha = 1.0, \ \kappa = 0.75, \ \text{supported by } \{1,2,6\}$$
$$[loc = who] \quad \rightarrow D_1 \ \alpha = 1.0, \ \kappa = 0.75, \ \text{supported by } \{2,5,6\}$$
$$[age = 50...59] \rightarrow D_1 \ \alpha = 1.0, \ \kappa = 0.5, \ \text{supported by } \{2,6\}$$

```
procedure Rule Integration;
  var
    i : integer;   M, L₂ : List; R(Dᵢ) : List; /* A list of rules for Dᵢ */
    L_D : List; /* A list of all classes */
  begin
    while(L_D ≠ φ) do
      begin
        Dᵢ := first(L_D); M := L₂(Dᵢ);
        Select one rule R' → D'ᵢ from R(L₂(Dᵢ)).
        while (M ≠ φ) do
          begin
            Dⱼ := first(M);
              Select one rule R → dⱼ for Dⱼ;
              Integrate two rules: R ∧ R' → dⱼ.
            M := M - {Dⱼ};
          end
        L_D := L_D - Dᵢ;
      end
  end {Rule Combination}
```

Fig. 3. An Algorithm for Rule Integration

Table 2. A Table for a New Partition P

	age	loc	nat	prod	nau	M1	class
1	50...59	occ	per	0	0	1	D_1
2	40...49	who	per	0	0	1	D_1
3	40...49	lat	thr	1	1	0	D_2
4	40...49	who	thr	1	1	0	D_2
5	40...49	who	rad	0	0	1	D_1
6	50...59	who	per	0	1	1	D_1

In the seventh step, classification rules for $m.c.h.$ and $psycho$ are induced from Table 3. For example, the following rules are obtained from $m.c.h.$.

$$[nau = no] \quad → m.c.h. \; \alpha = 1.0, \; \kappa = 1.0, \; \text{supported by } \{1,2,5\}$$
$$[age = 40...49] → m.c.h. \; \alpha = 1.0, \; \kappa = 0.67, \text{supported by } \{2,5\}$$

In the eighth step, these two kinds of rules are integrated in the following way. Rule $[M1 = yes] → D_1$, $[nau = no] → m.c.h.$ and $[age = 40...49] → m.c.h.$ have a supporting set which is a subset of $\{1,2,5,6\}$. Thus, the following rules are obtained:

$$[M1 = yes] \; \& \; [nau=no] \quad → m.c.h. \; \alpha = 1.0, \; \kappa = 1.0, \; \text{supported by } \{1,2,5\}$$
$$[M1 = yes] \; \& \; [age=40...49] → m.c.h. \; \alpha = 1.0, \; \kappa = 0.67, \text{supported by } \{2,5\}$$

Table 3. A Table for D_1

	age	loc	nat	prod	nau	M1	class
1	50...59	occ	per	0	0	1	m.c.h.
2	40...49	who	per	0	0	1	m.c.h.
5	40...49	who	rad	0	0	1	m.c.h.
6	50...59	who	per	0	1	1	psycho

5 Experimental Results

The above rule induction algorithm is implemented in PRIMEROSE4.5 (Probabilistic Rule Induction Method based on Rough Sets Ver 4.5), [5] and was applied to databases on differential diagnosis of headache, whose training samples consist of 1477 samples, 20 classes and 20 attributes.

This system was compared with PRIMEROSE4[17], PRIMEROSE[15], C4.5[12], CN2[5], AQ15[9] and k-NN[2] [6] with respect to the following points: length of rules, similarities between induced rules and expert's rules and performance of rules.

In this experiment, length was measured by the number of attribute-value pairs used in an induced rule and Jaccard's coefficient was adopted as a similarity measure[6]. Concerning the performance of rules, ten-fold cross-validation was applied to estimate classification accuracy.

Table 4 shows the experimental results, which suggest that PRIMEROSE4.5 outperforms PRIMEROSE4(set-inclusion approach) and the other four rule induction methods and induces rules very similar to medical experts' ones.

Table 4. Experimental Results

Method	Length	Similarity	Accuracy
		Headache	
PRIMEROSE4.5	8.8 ± 0.27	0.95 ± 0.08	$95.2 \pm 2.7\%$
PRIMEROSE4.0	8.6 ± 0.27	0.93 ± 0.08	$93.3 \pm 2.7\%$
Experts	9.1 ± 0.33	1.00 ± 0.00	$98.0 \pm 1.9\%$
PRIMEROSE	5.3 ± 0.35	0.54 ± 0.05	$88.3 \pm 3.6\%$
C4.5	4.9 ± 0.39	0.53 ± 0.10	$85.8 \pm 1.9\%$
CN2	4.8 ± 0.34	0.51 ± 0.08	$87.0 \pm 3.1\%$
AQ15	4.7 ± 0.35	0.51 ± 0.09	$86.2 \pm 2.9\%$
k-NN (7)	6.7 ± 0.25	0.61 ± 0.09	$88.2 \pm 1.5\%$

k-NN (i) shows the value of i which gives the highest performance in k ($1 \leq k \leq 20$).

---

[5] The program is implemented by using SWI-prolog [14] on Sparc Station 20.
[6] The most optimal k for each domain is attached to Table 4.

6 Discussion: Granular Fuzzy Partition

6.1 Granular Fuzzy Partition

Coverage is also closely related with granular fuzzy partition, which is introduced by Lin[8] in the context of granular computing.

Since coverage $\kappa_R(D)$ is equivalent to a conditional probability, $P(R|D)$, this measure will satisfy the condition on partition of unity, called BH-partition (If we select a suitable partition of universe, then this partition will satisfy $\sum_\kappa \kappa_R(D) = 1.0.$) Also, from the definition of coverage, it is also equivalent to the counting measure for $|[x]_R \bigcap D|$, since $|D|$ is constant in a given universe U. Thus, this measure satisfies a "nice context", which holds:

$$|[x]_{R_1} \bigcap D| + |[x]_{R_2} \bigcap D| \leq |D|.$$

Hence, all these features show that a partition generated by coverage is a kind of granular fuzzy partition[8]. This result also shows that the characterization by coverage is closely related with information granulation.

From this point of view, the usage of coverage for characterization and grouping of classes means that we focus on some specific partition generated by attribute-value pairs, the coverage of which are equal to 1.0 and that we consider the second-order relations between these pairs. It is also notable that if the second-order relation makes partition, as shown in the example above, then this structure can also be viewed as granular fuzzy partition.

However, rough inclusion and accuracy do not always hold the nice context. It would be our future work to examine the formal characteristics of coverage (and also accuracy) and rough inclusion from the viewpoint of granular fuzzy sets.

7 Conclusion

In this paper, the characteristics of experts' rules are closely examined, whose empirical results suggest that grouping of diseases are very important to realize automated acquisition of medical knowledge from clinical databases. Thus, we focus on the role of coverage in focusing mechanisms and propose an algorithm on grouping of diseases by using this measure. The above experiments show that rule induction with this grouping generates rules, which are similar to medical experts' rules and they suggest that our proposed method should capture medical experts' reasoning. Interestingly, the idea of this proposed procedure is very similar to rough mereology. The proposed method was evaluated on three medical databases, the experimental results of which show that induced rules correctly represent experts' decision processes and also suggests that rough mereology may be useful to capture medical experts' decision process.

References

1. Agrawal, R., Imielinski, T., and Swami, A., Mining association rules between sets of items in large databases, in *Proceedings of the 1993 International Conference on Management of Data (SIGMOD 93)*, pp. 207-216, 1993.
2. Aha, D. W., Kibler, D., and Albert, M. K., Instance-based learning algorithm. *Machine Learning*, 6, 37-66, 1991.
3. Breiman, L., Freidman, J., Olshen, R., and Stone, C., *Classification And Regression Trees*, Wadsworth International Group, Belmont, 1984.
4. Buchnan, B. G. and Shortliffe, E. H., *Rule-Based Expert Systems*, Addison-Wesley, New York, 1984.
5. Clark, P. and Niblett, T., The CN2 Induction Algorithm. *Machine Learning*, 3, 261-283, 1989.
6. Everitt, B. S., *Cluster Analysis*, 3rd Edition, John Wiley & Son, London, 1996.
7. Langley, P. *Elements of Machine Learning*, Morgan Kaufmann, CA, 1996.
8. Lin, T.Y. Fuzzy Partitions: Rough Set Theory, in *Proceedings of Seventh International Conference on Information Processing and Management of Uncertainty in Knowledge-based Systems(IPMU'98)*, Paris, pp. 1167-1174, 1998.
9. Michalski, R. S., Mozetic, I., Hong, J., and Lavrac, N., The Multi-Purpose Incremental Learning System AQ15 and its Testing Application to Three Medical Domains, in *Proceedings of the fifth National Conference on Artificial Intelligence*, 1041-1045, AAAI Press, Menlo Park, 1986.
10. Pawlak, Z., *Rough Sets*. Kluwer Academic Publishers, Dordrecht, 1991.
11. Polkowski, L. and Skowron, A.: Rough mereology: a new paradigm for approximate reasoning. Intern. J. Approx. Reasoning **15**, 333–365, 1996.
12. Quinlan, J.R., *C4.5 - Programs for Machine Learning*, Morgan Kaufmann, Palo Alto, 1993.
13. *Readings in Machine Learning*, (Shavlik, J. W. and Dietterich, T.G., eds.) Morgan Kaufmann, Palo Alto, 1990.
14. SWI-Prolog Version 2.0.9 Manual, University of Amsterdam, 1995.
15. Tsumoto, S. and Tanaka, H., PRIMEROSE: Probabilistic Rule Induction Method based on Rough Sets and Resampling Methods. *Computational Intelligence*, **11**, 389-405, 1995.
16. Tsumoto, S., Empirical Induction of Medical Expert System Rules based on Rough Set Model. PhD dissertation, 1997(in Japanese).
17. Tsumoto, S. Extraction of Experts' Decision Rules from Clinical Databases using Rough Set Model Journal of Intelligent Data Analysis, 2(3), 1998.
18. Zadeh, L.A., Toward a theory of fuzzy information granulation and its certainty in human reasoning and fuzzy logic. *Fuzzy Sets and Systems* **90**, 111-127, 1997.
19. Ziarko, W., Variable Precision Rough Set Model. *Journal of Computer and System Sciences*. 46, 39-59, 1993.

Discernibility System in Rough Sets

Liu Zongtian and Xie Zhipeng

Research Institute of Microcomputer
Hefei University of Technology, Hefei, Anhui, 230009, China.
E-Mail: ztliu@hfut.edu.cn or marihfut@mail.hf.ah.cn

Abstract: In the classic rough set theory [1], two important concepts (reduct of information system and relative reduct of decision table) are defined. They play important roles in the KDD system based on rough sets, and can be used to remove the irrelevant or redundant attributes from practical database to improve the efficiency of rule extraction and the performance of the rules mined. Many researchers have provided some reduct-computing algorithms. But most of them are designed for static database; hence they don't have the incremental learning capability. The paper first proposes the idea of discernibility system and gives out its formal definition, then presents the concept of reduct in discernibility system, which can be viewed as a generalization of the relative reduct of decision table and the reduct of information system. At last, based on the concept of discernibility system, an incremental algorithm, ASRAI, for computing relative reduct of decision table is presented.

Key word: Rough sets, information system, decision table, reduct, relative reduct, discernibility system, incremental learning.

1 Introduction

With the rapid development of computer technique, the data-collecting ability of mankind has been increasing rapidly and various kinds of databases have been becoming larger and larger. By contrary, man's data-dealing ability has fallen behind; a lot of data not handled is put away as rubbish in various fields of society. How to extract useful model from large amount of business data for making correct decision? How to handling scientific data for discovering underlying scientific laws? How to mine large number of clinic cases for constructing medical expert system? All of these have become the potential impetus for KDD research.

Practical database is always too huge, which may contain many redundant, irrelevant, or miscellaneous attributes. The existence of such attributes will decrease greatly the efficiency of rule-extraction process and the performance of rules mined. Performing attribute reduction to remove such redundant or irrelevant attributes has become an important phase in KDD process [2].

In the early 80s, Professor Pawlak Z presented the theory of Rough Sets, which can be used as a formal framework for attribute reduction. In the rough set theory, knowledge is considered as classification ability, and the essence of attribute reduction is thought as preserving the invariant of some kind of discerning ability through a minimal set of attributes. We think that the discerning should refer to two objects, and discernible relation should be symmetric, so we can use the concept of non-ordered pair as the basic element of discernible relation. Based on it, we present the concept of discernibility system as a formal framework for reducing the set of attributes. This can be regarded as an extension of classic Rough Sets.

This paper is organized as follows:

Section 2 gives some basic concepts of classic Rough Sets. In section 3, based on the concept of non-order pair, we give out the definitions of discernibility system and the reduct of it. In section 4, the problem of computing reduct set in information system or relative reduct set in decision table is transformed into the problem of computing the reduct set of a specific discernibility system. An incremental algorithm is developed in section 5. At the end of this paper, an example is used to illustrate the idea of this algorithm.

2 Basic Concept in Classic Rough Sets

In the theory of the classic Rough Sets [1], we have the following definitions:

Definition2.1. An information system is a pair $A=(U, A)$, where U is a non-empty, finite set called the universe and A is a non-empty, finite set of attributes, i.e. $a: U \rightarrow V_a$ for $a \in A$, where V_a is called the value set of attribute a. The elements of U are called objects.

Every information system $A=(U, A)$ and a non-empty set $B \subseteq A$ define a B-information function by $Inf_B(x)=\{(a, a(x)): a \in B\}$ for $x \in U$. The set $\{Inf_A(x): x \in U\}$ is called the A-information set and it is denoted by $INF(A)$.

Definition2.2. Let $A=(U, A)$ be an information system. For every subset of attributes $B \subseteq A$, an equivalence relation, denoted by $IND(B)$ called the B-indiscernible relation, is associated and defined by $IND(B) = \{(s, s'): s, s' \in U, b(s)=b(s')$ for every $b \in B\}$.

In this paper, indiscernible relation is also thought as a set of some non-ordered pairs on U. (As for the definition of non-ordered pair, you can refer to the definition3.1.)

For $(x, x') \in IND(B)$, object x and object x' can't be discerned by the attributes in B. The minimal subset B of A that satisfies $IND(A)=IND(B)$ is called a reduct of A. That is, if $B \subseteq A$ is a reduct of A, then $IND(A)=IND(B)$ and $\forall C \subset B(IND(C) \supset IND(A))$. The family set of all reducts of A is called the reduct set of A. In the paper, $(x, x') \in IND(B)$ is also written as $x\ IND(B)\ x'$.

Definition 2.3. If $A=(U, A)$ is a information system, $B \subseteq A$ is a set of attributes and $X \subseteq U$ is a set of objects, then set $B_*X=\{s \in U: [s]_B \subseteq X\}$ and set $B^*X=\{s \in U: [s]_B \cap X \neq \varnothing\}$ are called B-lower and B-upper approximation of X in A respectively.

Definition 2.4. A decision table is an information system of the form $A=(U, A \cup\{d\})$, where $d \notin A$ is a distinguishable attribute called the decision. The elements of A are called conditions.

For simplicity of notation we assume that the set V_d of values of the decision d is equal to $\{1, 2, ..., r(d)\}$. We can observe that the decision d determines the partition $\{X_1, X_2, ..., X_{r(d)}\}$ of the universe U, where $X_k = \{x \in U: d(x)=k\}$ for $1 \leq k \leq r(d)$.

Definition 2.5. Given a decision table $A=(U, A \cup\{d\})$, $B \subseteq A$, if $V_d=\{1, 2, ..., r(d)\}$ and $X_1, X_2, ..., X_{r(d)}$ are decision classes of A, then the set $B_*X_1 \cup B_*X_2 \cup ... \cup B_*X_{r(d)}$ is called B-positive region of A, denoted by $POS(B, \{d\})$.

Definition 2.6. Given a decision table $A=(U, A \cup\{d\})$, $B \subseteq A$, if $POS(B, \{d\})=POS(A, \{d\})$, and $\forall C \subset B\ POS(C, \{d\}) \subset POS(A, \{d\})$, then B is called a relative reduct of A. The family set of all relative reducts of A is called the relative reduct set of A.

Definition 2.7. If $A=(U, A \cup\{d\})$ is a decision table, then we define a function ∂_A: $U \rightarrow \rho(\{1, 2, ..., r(d)\})$, called generalized decision in A, by $\partial_A(x) = \{i|\ x'IND(A)\ x$ and $d(x')=i\}$.

Definition 2.8. A decision table A is called consistent if $|\partial_A(x)|=1$ for any $x \in U$; otherwise A is inconsistent.

NOTE: The decision table that appears in this paper is assumed to be consistent.

3 DISCERNIBILITY SYSTEM

Definition 3.1. Given a set X of objects, if $x \in X$, $y \in X$ then two-element set $\{x, y\}$ is called a non-ordered pair (NOP) on X, which can be denoted by (x, y). It is apparent that $(x, y)=(y, x)$. We use $ANO(X)$ to denote the set of all the non-ordered pairs on X, that is, $ANO(X)=\{ (x, y) \mid x \in X, y \in X \}$.

Definition3.2.   Given a non-empty, finite set X of objects and a non-empty, finite set A of attributes, we call (x, y) an A-discernible NOP on X if $x, y \in X$ and $\exists\ a \in A$ $(a(x) \neq a(y))$. The set of all the A-discernible NOP on X is denoted by $ADNO(X, A)$, that is, $ADNO(X, A) = \{ (x, y) \mid x, y \in X, \exists\ a \in A (a(x) \neq a(y)) \}$.

Definition3.3.   A triple $D = (X, A, D)$ is called a discernibility system, where X is a non-empty, finite set of objects, A is a non-empty, finite set of attributes and D is a subset of $ADNO(X, A)$.

Definition3.4.   Given a discernibility system $D = (X, A, D)$, if $B \subseteq A$ satisfies

$$\forall (x, y) \in D\ (\exists\ b \in B (b(x) \neq b(y))) \tag{1}$$

then we say that B is a distinction of D.

Property3.1.   Given a discernibility system $D = (X, A, D)$, if B is a distinction of D and $B \subset C \subseteq A$ then C is a distinction of D.
Proof: omitted.

Property3.2.   Give two discernibility systems $D1 = (X, A, D1)$ and $D2 = (X, A, D2)$, if $D1 \subseteq D2$ and $B \subseteq A$ is a distinction of $D2$ then B is also a distinction of $D1$.
Proof: omitted.

Definition3.5.   Given a discernibility system $D = (X, A, D)$, if B is a distinction of D and any $C \subset B$ is not a distinction of D, then B is called a reduct of D. The family set of all the reducts of D is called reduct set of D and it is denoted by RED(D).

Given a discernibility system $D = (X, A, D)$, if $B \subseteq A$ is a distinction of D, then we can get a reduct of D through the following algorithm:

```
for b∈B do
          begin
          if B-{b} is a distinction of D, then B:=B-{b};
          end;
B':=B;
```

It is apparent that B' is a minimum distinction of D, so B' is a reduct of D according to definition 3.5. We have the following theorem:

Theorem3.1.   Given a discernibility system $D = (X, A, D)$, if $B \subseteq A$ is a distinction of D, S is the reduct set of D, then there must exist a reduct $S \in S$ that satisfies $S \subseteq B$.
Proof: omitted.

Definition3.6. Given a family $B=\{B1, B2, ..., Bn\}$, we can define C=MIN_RED(B) as the minimum of B:

$$\text{MIN\_RED}(B)=\{B \in B \mid \forall Bi \in B \ (Bi \not\subset B)\}. \tag{2}$$

Theorem3.2. Given two discernibility system $D1=(X, A, D1)$ and $D2=(X, A, D2)$, if $S1$, $S2$ are the reduct sets of $D1$ and $D2$ respectively, $S'=\{S1 \cup S2 \mid S1 \in S1, S2 \in S2\}$, then S=MIN_RED(S') is the reduct set of the discernibility system $D=(X, A, D1 \cup D2)$.
Proof:
1. At first we prove that any $S \in S$ is a reduct of D.
   For any $S \in S$, $(x', y') \in D1 \cup D2$, we have $S \in S'$, so there exist $S1 \in S1, S2 \in S2$ that satisfy $S1 \subseteq S$ and $S2 \subseteq S$. If $(x', y') \in D1$, then there exists $s \in S1 \subseteq S$ that satisfies $s(x') \neq s(y')$. If $(x', y') \in D2$, then there exists $s \in S2 \subseteq S$ that satisfies $s(x') \neq s(y')$. Clearly we have: for any $S \in S$, $(x', y') \in D1 \cup D2$, there exists $s \in S$ satisfies $s(x') \neq s(y')$, that is, S is a distinction of D.
   Assume that S is not a reduct of D, then there exists $S_o \subset S$ is a distinction of D (Definition3.5), then there exists $SS \subseteq S_0$ is a reduct of D (Theorem 3.1). According to property3.2, SS is also a distinction of $D1$ and $D2$. So there exist $SS1 \in S1, SS2 \in S2$ that satisfy $SS1 \subseteq SS$ and $SS2 \subseteq SS$ according to theorem3.1. Therefore $(SS1 \cup SS2) \subseteq SS \subset S$ and $(SS1 \cup SS2) \in S'$. According to definition 3.6, we have $S \notin S$, which is a contradiction. So S is a reduct of D.
2. Then we prove that any reduct of D belongs to S.
   The process of the proof is similar to above proof, so it is omitted.

4 DISCERNIBILITY INVARIANT

Given an information system, we think that there exist two kinds of NOP (non-ordered pair): one kind includes the discernible pairs; the other kind includes the pairs expected to be discernible. For example, in classic rough sets, if we are given a decision table $A=(U, A \cup \{d\})$, then the first kind of pair is referring to $(x, y) \in ANO(U)$ that can be discerned by the set A of conditional attributes, that is, $\exists a \in A (a(x) \neq a(y))$. On the other hand, if $(x, y) \in ANO(U)$ and $d(x) \neq d(y)$ then we think that (x, y) is expected to be discernible, that is, we expect to discern between two elements of different decision values. If we are given an information system $A=(U, A)$ then the $(x, y) \in ANO(U)$ that satisfies $\exists a \in A (a(x) \neq a(y))$ is considered to be discerned by A, while any $(x, y) \in ANO(U)$ is considered to be expected to be discernible.

So we can think that:
reducing attributes in an information system is to search a minimal set of attributes that preserves an invariant——the discernibility of all the NOPs that are expected to be discernible and can be discerned.

Based on the above idea, we have the followings:

Theorem4.1. Given an information system $A=(X, A)$, then $ADNO(X, A)=ANO(X)-IND(A)$。

Proof: omitted.

Theorem4.2. Given an information system $A=(X, A)$, $B \subseteq A$ is a reduct of A if and only if B is a reduct of discernibility system $D=(X, A, ADNO(X, A))$.

Proof:

1. At first, we prove that if $B \subseteq A$ is a reduct of A then B is a reduct of D. For any $(x, y) \in ADNO(X, A)$, then $(x, y) \notin IND(A)$. If B is a reduct of A, then there exists $b \in B$ that satisfies $b(x) \neq b(y)$. So B is a distinction of D. For any $C \subset B$, because B is a reduct of A, there exists $x, y \in X$ that $(x, y) \notin IND(A)$ and $(x, y) \in IND(C)$, that is, $(x, y) \in ADNO(X, A)$ and $(x, y) \notin ADNO(X, C)$. (*Note:* we have $IND(A) \subseteq IND(C)$ because $A \supset C$.) So C is not a distinction of D. Followed by the above, we have: if B is a reduct of A then B is a reduct of D.
2. Similarly, we can prove that if B is a reduct of D then B is a reduct of A.

Theorem4.3. Given a decision table $A=(X, A \cup \{d\})$, $B \subseteq A$ is a relative reduct of A if and only if B is a reduct of discernibility system $D=(X, A, RD(X, A))$, where $RD(X, A) = \{(x, y) \in ADNO(X, A) \mid d(x) \neq d(y)\} = \{(x, y) \in ANO(X) \mid d(x) \neq d(y)$ and $\exists b \in A \ (b(x) \neq b(y))\}$.

Proof:

1. At first we prove that if B is a relative reduct of A then B is a reduct of discernibility system $D=(U, RD(X, A), A)$.
   For any $(x, y) \in RD(X, A)$, we have $d(x) \neq d(y)$ and $(x, y) \notin IND(A)$. Because B is a relative reduct of A, we have $POS(B, \{d\})=POS(A, \{d\})$. Decision table A being consistent, we have $x, y \in POS(A, \{d\})$ and $x, y \in POS(B, \{d\})$. Because $d(x) \neq d(y) \Rightarrow (x, y) \notin IND(B)$ (otherwise we have $x, y \notin POS(B, \{d\})$, which is a contradiction.), there must exists $b \in B$ that $b(x) \neq b(y)$. So B is a distinction of D. For any $C \subset B$, if B is a relative reduct of A, then $POS(A, \{d\}) \supset POS(C, \{d\})$, that is, there exists $x \in X$ that $x \in POS(A, \{d\})$ and $x \notin POS(C, \{d\})$. So there exists $y \in POS(A, \{d\})$ that $d(x) \neq d(y)$, $(x, y) \notin IND(A)$ and $(x, y) \in IND(C)$. That is, there doesn't exist $c \in C$ that $c(x) \neq c(y)$. So C is not a distinction of D. According to definition 3.5, we know that B is a reduct of D.
2. Analogically, we can also prove: if B is a reduct of $D=(X, A, D(X, A))$, then B is a relative reduct of A.

Based on the theorems above, we can easily transform the problems of computing reduct set in information system and computing relative reduct set in decision table into the problem of computing the reduct set of a specific discernibility system.

5 AN INCREMENTAL ALGORITHM FOR COMPUTING THE RELATIVE REDUCT SET OF DECISION TABLE

Theorem5.1. Given a decision table $A=(X, A\cup\{d\})$, $(x, x')\in RD(X, A)$, if $b=\{b|b\in A, b(x)\neq b(x')\}$, then $\{\{b\}|b\in b\}$ is the reduct set of $D=(X, A, \{(x, x')\})$. **Proof:** omitted.

In a decision table $A=(X, A\cup\{d\})$, S is the relative reduct set, that is, S is the reduct set of discernibility system $D=(X, A, RD(X, A))$. If a new object x is added to X, then we have $RD_x(X)=\{(x, x')|x'\in X, \exists a\in A(a(x)\neq a(x'))$ and $d(x)\neq d(x')\}$. Because $RD(X\cup\{x\}, A)= RD(X, A)\cup RD_x(X)$, the problem of computing the relative reduct set in decision table $A'=(X\cup\{x\}, A)$ can be transformed into the problem of computing the reduct set of discernibility system $D'=(X\cup\{x\}, A, RD(X\cup\{x\}, A))$.

Now, we present an incremental algorithm, ASRAI, as follows:

```
Input: the relative reduct set S of a decision table A=(X,
AU{d});
           an object x that is newly added;
Output: the relative reduct set S' of the decision table
A'=(XU{x}, AU{d});
Begin
    S' := S;
    For any x'∈X do
        Begin
            If  not(xIND(A)x') and (d(x)≠d(x'))   then
                Begin
                    b :={b|b∈A, b(x)≠b(x')};
                    S' :=minimize({BU{b}|B∈S',b∈b});
                End;
        End;
End.
```

The correctness of this algorithm can be proved easily through the theorem 3.2, theorem 4.3 and theorem 5.1. The minimize() in this algorithm is a function that computing the minimum of a family set (refer to definition 3.6). In its practical implementation, we can use the fact that $\{b\}$ is one-element set, in order to shorten the running time of this algorithm.

6 EXAMPLE

Example: To illustrate the idea of algorithm ASRAI, we consider the following decision table $A=(U, A\cup\{d\})$, which is extracted from [3]. Assume object 6 is the object newly added.

	H	W	R	E	d
1	Short	Light	Dark	Blue	1
2	Tall	Heavy	Dark	Blue	1
3	Tall	Heavy	Dark	Brown	1
4	Tall	Heavy	Red	Blue	2
5	Short	Light	Blond	Blue	2
6	Tall	Heavy	Blond	Brown	1

For $X=\{1, 2, 3, 4, 5\}$, $RD(X, A) = \{(1, 4), (1, 5), (2, 4), (2, 5), (3, 4), (3, 5)\}$, the relative reduct set of decision table $(X, A \cup \{d\})$ is $\{\{R\}\}$ which is also a reduct of discernibility system $(X, A, RD(X, A))$.

If object $x=6$ is newly added, then $RD_x(X)=\{(4, 6), (5, 6)\}$.

First we can compute the reduct set of reduct set of discernibility system $(X \cup \{6\}, A, RD(X, A) \cup \{(4, 6)\})$, which is equal to minimize($\{\{R\}, \{R, E\}\}$)= $\{\{R\}\}$. Then we compute the reduct set of discernibility system $(X \cup \{6\}, A, RD(X, A) \cup \{(4, 6)\} \cup \{(5, 6)\}) = (X \cup \{6\}, A, RD(X, A) \cup RD_x(X)\}) = (X \cup \{6\}, A, RD(X \cup \{6\}, A))$ which is equal to minimize($\{\{R,H\}, \{R, W\}, \{R, E\}\}$) = $\{\{R,H\}, \{R, W\}, \{R, E\}\}$.

Thus we have got the relative reduct set of decision table $A = (U, A \cup \{d\}) = (X \cup \{6\}, A \cup \{d\})$.

7   CONCLUSION

In this paper, we first present the definitions of discernibility system (definition3.3) and reduct in it (definition3.5), which can be used as a formal framework for attribute reduction based on Rough sets.

Then we develop an incremental algorithm for computing the relative reduct set of decision table. The algorithm has been implemented by authors and runs correctly. However, practical databases always contain a lot of noise; so approximate invariant should be defined to make our method be noise-proof, which is our next researched content.

8   REFERENCES

[1] **Pawlak Z.**: Rough Sets: Theoretical Aspects of Reasoning about Data. Kluwer Academic Publishers, Dordrecht, 1991

[2] **Fayyad U M, Piatetsky-Shapiro G, Smyth P.**: From data mining to knowledge discovery: an overview. In: Fayyad U M, Piatetsky-Shapiro G, Smyth P, Uthurusamy R ed. Advances in Knowledge Discovery and Data Mining. Menlo Park, California: AAAI Press / The MIT Press, 1996, 1-35

[3] **Skowron A, Stepaniuk J.**: Generalized approximation spaces. In: Lin T Y ed. Conference Proceedings of the Third International Workshop on Rough Sets and Soft Computing (RSSC'94). San Jose, Caifornia, USA, 1994, 156-163

Automatic Labeling of Self-Organizing Maps: Making a Treasure–Map Reveal Its Secrets

Andreas Rauber and Dieter Merkl

Institut für Softwaretechnik, Technische Universität Wien
Resselgasse 3/188, A–1040 Wien, Austria
{andi, dieter}@ifs.tuwien.ac.at

Abstract. Self-organizing maps are an unsupervised neural network model which lends itself to the cluster analysis of high-dimensional input data. However, interpreting a trained map proves to be difficult because the features responsible for a specific cluster assignment are not evident from the resulting map representation. In this paper we present our *LabelSOM* approach for automatically labeling a trained self-organizing map with the features of the input data that are the most relevant ones for the assignment of a set of input data to a particular cluster. The resulting labeled map allows the user to better understand the structure and the information available in the map and the reason for a specific map organization, especially when only little prior information on the data set and its characteristics is available.

1 Introduction

The self-organizing map (SOM) [2, 3] is a prominent unsupervised neural network model for cluster analysis. Data from a high-dimensional input space is mapped onto a usually two-dimensional output space with the structure of the input data being preserved as faithfully as possible. This characteristic is the reason why the SOM found large attraction for its utilization in a wide range of application arenas. However, its use in the knowledge discovery domain has been limited due to some drawbacks in the interpretability of a trained SOM. As one of the shortcomings we have to mention the difficulties in detecting the cluster boundaries within the map. This problem has been addressed intensively and led to a number of enhanced visualization techniques allowing an intuitive interpretation of the self-organizing map, e.g. the *U-Matrix* [10], *Adaptive Coordinates* [6] and *Cluster Connection* techniques [5].

However, it still remains a challenging task to label the map, i.e. to determine the features that are characteristic for a particular cluster. Given an unknown data set that is mapped onto a self-organizing map, even with the visualization of clear cluster boundaries it remains a non-trivial task to elicit the features that are the most relevant and determining ones for a group of input data to form a cluster of its own, which features they share and which features distinguish them from other clusters. We are looking for a method that allows the automatic assignment of labels describing every node in the map. A method addressing this problem using component planes for visualizing the contribution of each variable in the organization of a map has been presented recently [1]. This method, however, requires heavy manual interaction by examining each dimension separately and does thus not offer itself to automatic labeling of SOMs trained with high-dimensional input data.

In this paper we present our novel *LabelSOM* approach to the automatic labeling of trained self-organizing maps. In a nutshell, every unit of the map is labeled with the features that best characterize all the data points which are mapped onto that particular node. This is achieved by using a combination of the mean quantization error of every feature and the relative importance of that feature in the weight vector of the node.

We demonstrate the benefits of this approach by labeling a SOM that was trained with a widely used reference data set describing animals by various attributes. The resulting labeled SOM gives a description of the animals mapped onto nodes and characterizes the various (sub)clusters present in the data set. We further provide a real-world example in the field of text mining based on a digital library SOM trained with the abstracts of scientific publications. This SOM represents a map of the scientific publications with the labels serving as a description of their topics and thus the various research fields.

The remainder of the paper is organized as follows. In Section 2 we present a brief review of the self-organizing map, its architecture and training process as well as the *LabelSOM* method to assign a set of labels for every node in a trained SOM and provide results from a well known reference data set. In Section 3 we provide the results of applying the *LabelSOM* method to a real world data set labeling a map representing the abstracts of scientific publications. We further demonstrate how additional information on the cluster structure can be derived from the information provided by the labeling. A discussion of the presented *LabelSOM* method as well as its importance for the area of knowledge discovery and data mining is provided in Section 4. Finally, our conclusions are presented in Section 5.

2 SOM and LabelSOM

The self-organizing map is an unsupervised neural network providing a mapping from a high-dimensional input space to a usually two-dimensional output space while preserving topological relations as faithfully as possible. The SOM consists of a set of i nodes arranged in a two-dimensional grid, with a weight vector $m_i \in \Re^n$ attached to each node. Elements from the high dimensional input space, referred to as input vectors $x \in \Re^n$, are presented to the SOM and the activation of each node for the presented input vector is calculated using an activation function. Commonly, the Euclidean distance between the weight vector of the node and the input vector serves as the activation function. In the next step, the weight vector of the node showing the highest activation (i.e. the smallest Euclidean distance) is selected as the 'winner' c and is modified as to more closely resemble the presented input vector. Pragmatically speaking, the weight vector of the winner is moved towards the presented input signal by a certain fraction of the Euclidean distance as indicated by a time-decreasing learning rate α. Thus this node's activation will be even higher the next time the same input signal is presented. Furthermore, the weight vectors of nodes in the neighborhood of the winner are modified accordingly, yet to a less strong amount as compared to the winner. This learning procedure finally leads to a topologically ordered mapping of the presented input signals, i.e. similar input signals are mapped onto neighboring regions of the map.

Still, the characteristics of each node are not detectable from the map representation itself. With no a priori knowledge on the data, even providing information on the cluster boundaries does not reveal information on the relevance of single attributes for the clustering and classification process. In the *LabelSOM* approach we determine those vector elements (i.e. features of the input space) that are most relevant for the mapping of an input vector onto a specific node. This is basically done by determining the contribution of every element in the vector towards the overall Euclidean distance between an input vector and the winners' weight vector. The *LabelSOM* method is built upon the observation that after SOM training the weight vector elements resemble as far as possible the corresponding input vector elements of all input signals that are mapped onto this particular node as well as to some extent those of the input signals mapped onto neighboring nodes. Vector elements having about the same value within the set of input vectors mapped onto a certain node describe the node in so far as they denominate a common feature of all data signals of this node. If a majority of input signals mapped onto a particular node exhibit a highly similar input vector value for a particular feature, the corresponding weight vector value will be highly similar as well. Thus the quantization error for all individual features serves as a guide for their relevance as a class label.

However, in real world text mining application scenarios we are usually faced with a high number of attributes which are not existent and thus have a value of 0 for a certain class of input signals. These attributes frequently yield a quantization error of almost 0 for certain nodes but are nevertheless not suitable for labeling the node. The reason is, that we want to describe the present features that are responsible for a certain clustering rather than describe a cluster via the features that are not present in the data forming that cluster.

Hence, we need to determine those vector elements from each weight vector which, on the one hand, exhibit about the same value for all input signals mapped onto that specific node as well as, on the other hand, have a high overall value indicating its importance. Formally this is done as follows: Let C_i be the set of input patterns x_j mapped onto node i. Summing up the distances for each vector element over all the vectors x_j ($x_j \in C_i$) yields a quantization error vector q_i for every node (Equation 1).

$$q_{i_k} = \sum_{x_j \in C_i} \sqrt{(m_{i_k} - x_{j_k})^2}, \qquad k = 1..n \tag{1}$$

To create a set of p labels for every node i we take the p smallest vector elements from the quantization error vector q_i. In order to get rid of labels describing non-existent features we define a threshold τ and take only features having corresponding weight vector entries above τ. The threshold is typically set to very small values slightly above 0.

Attribute		Dove	Hen	Duck	Goose	Owl	Hawk	Eagle	Fox	Dog	Wolf	Cat	Tiger	Lion	Horse	Zebra	Cow
is	small	1	1	1	1	1	1	0	0	0	0	1	0	0	0	0	0
	medium	0	0	0	0	0	0	1	1	1	1	0	0	0	0	0	0
	big	0	0	0	0	0	0	0	0	0	0	0	1	1	1	1	1
has	2 legs	1	1	1	1	1	1	1	0	0	0	0	0	0	0	0	0
	4 legs	0	0	0	0	0	0	0	1	1	1	1	1	1	1	1	1
	hair	0	0	0	0	0	0	0	1	1	1	1	1	1	1	1	1
	hooves	0	0	0	0	0	0	0	0	0	0	0	0	0	1	1	1
	mane	0	0	0	0	0	0	0	0	0	1	0	0	1	1	1	0
	feathers	1	1	1	1	1	1	1	0	0	0	0	0	0	0	0	0
likes to	hunt	0	0	0	0	1	1	1	1	0	1	1	1	1	0	0	0
	run	0	0	0	0	0	0	0	0	1	1	0	1	1	1	1	0
	fly	1	0	0	1	1	1	1	0	0	0	0	0	0	0	0	0
	swim	0	0	1	1	0	0	0	0	0	0	0	0	0	0	0	0

Table 1. Input Data Set: Animals

Figure 1 shows the result of labeling a 6 × 6 SOM trained with the animals data set [8] given in Table 1. (Please note that the input vectors have been normalized to unit length prior to the training process.) The standard representation of the resulting SOM is given in Figure 1a, where each node is assigned the name of the input vectors that were mapped onto it. In the resulting map we find a clear separation of the *birds* in the upper part of the map from the *mammals* in the lower area. However, this conclusion can only be drawn if one has prior knowledge about the data and can thus infer the characteristic features of sets of input data from their name.

In Figure 1b, each node is assigned a set of 5 labels based on the quantization error vector and the value of the vector element. We find that each animal is labeled with its characteristic attributes. In addition to the information to be drawn from the characterization of the data points mapped onto the nodes, further information on the cluster boundaries can be derived, such as the fact that the *birds* are distinguished from the *mammals* by the fact that the all have *2 legs* and *feathers* instead of *4 legs* and *hair*. Further subclusters are identified by the size of the animals and their preferences for /em hunting, flying, swimming, etc. For example, the *big mammals* being located in the lower right corner of the map as a subcluster of the *mammals*. As another subcluster consider the distinction of *hunting* vs. *non-hunting* animals – irrespective of their belonging to the group of *birds* or group of *mammals*. The hunting animals may be found on the left side of the map whereas the non-hunting animals are located on the right side. Thus we can not only identify the decisive attributes for the assignment of every input signal to a specific node but also detect the cluster boundaries between nodes that are not winner for any specific input signal and tell the characteristics and extents of subclusters within the map. Mind that not

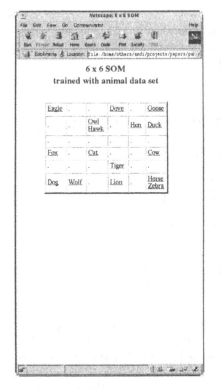
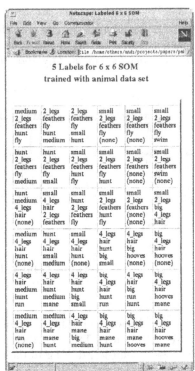

Fig. 1. Labeling of a 6 × 6 SOM trained with the animals data set. a.) Standard Representation of SOM b.) 5 labels assigned to each node of the SOM

all nodes have the full set of 5 labels assigned, i.e. one or more labels are empty *(none)* like the node representing the *dog* in the lower right corner. This is due to the fact that less than 5 vector elements have a weight vector value m_{i_k} greater than τ.

3 A Labeled Library SOM

For the following larger example we used 48 publications from the Department of Software Technology which are available via our department web server (www.ifs.tuwien.ac.at/ifs/). We used full-text indexing to represent the various documents. The indexing process identified 482 content terms, i.e. terms used for document representation. During indexing we omitted terms that appear in less than 10% or more than 90% of all documents and applied some basic stemming rules. The terms are weighted according to a simple $tf \times idf$ weighting scheme [9].

In the area of digital libraries we are faced with a tremendous amount of 'noise' in the input data resulting from the indexing of free-form documents. In the example presented thereafter another problem originates in the fact that abstracts contain little to no redundancy in terms of the information presented in the abstracts as well as in the choice of words. Due to their limited length and condensed structure, word repetition and clarification of the most important aspects within the text usually are not present, resulting in less specific vector representations of the documents. Thus using only the abstracts provides a somewhat more challenging task than using the complete documents. For some deeper discussion on the utilization of SOMs in text data mining we refer to [7, 4].

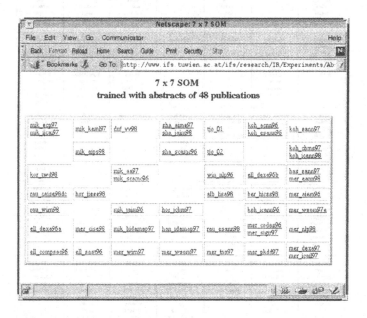

Fig. 2. Standard Representation of a 7 × 7 SOM trained with paper abstracts

Figure 2 depicts a 7 × 7 SOM trained with the 48 abstracts. The various nodes again list the input vectors, i.e. the abstracts, that were mapped onto the nodes. The naming convention for the abstracts is such as to give the name of the first author of a paper as the first three characters, followed by the short form label of the respective conference.

Without any additional knowledge on the underlying documents, the resulting mapping of the SOM given in Figure 2 is hard to interpret, although the names of the authors may give some hints towards the cluster structure of the map (at least if you know the authors and have some knowledge concerning their research areas). However, no information on the contents of the papers,

plan agent skeletal durative asbru design real world domain	skeletal plan task execution agent phase durative instantiate	all identify clinical practice guideline last present plan provide three	guideline record clinical provider ontology	enterprise propose access mechanism administration department	gait april novel pattern define biomechanic malfunction collect	hand gait malfunction ground force
skeletal plan asbru limitation	define domain skeletal plan different time physician visualize consequent	guideline patient	guideline intention automate provider states	enterprise key main applied public keep administration	gait	gait pattern platform aiming bio-feedback effects diseases active compensation employ
easy allow changing means clinical present plan asbru overcome	patient	provide designe interact interest health care internet patient	patient health care	concept relation document legal natural main space existing	concept first database automation semantic view specific large tool	evaluate growth sample indicate normay set networks conventional individual
available information provide interactive allowing distribute	changing system integrate experience ieee intensive work needs built	patient	validation	discover literature data define relation feature containing numerical find current	continuous learning management order changing organization means enterprise propose	neural network management organization goal temporal conventional standard challending technique
library system retrieval specific combination needs digital combined basic	qualitative	validation description therapy planning qualitative vie-vent applicability	data validation monitoring high frequency methods applied essential	dimension	high input dimension	literature document text hierarchical argue favor natural organize take built
process classify propose software product description definition promising projects	current library component reuse practice software precise retrieval relying large	current arrive description values high frequency qualitative illustrate useful time	identify models improvement on-line patient ventilation equipment benefits values	text provide technology cluster aiming visualize dimension prominent	hierarchy text retrieval challenging document feature mining	discover processing document text take built archive libraries
process hand organization reuse software often problem product concept	process practice software quality key improvement tool investigate function provide	cluster connection input item extension boundaries	relation allow cluster necessity input visualize grid intuitive movement weight	semantic input rule training similarity algorithm intuitive straight vector extension	discover document text result novel european algorithm libraries increase	case archive document legal public

Fig. 3. Labeling of a 7 × 7 SOM trained with paper abstracts

i.e. the keywords, can be drawn from the resulting map. With a weight vector dimensionality of 482, manual inspection of the importance of the single vector elements simply is not feasible.

Having a set of 10 labels automatically assigned to the the single nodes in Figure 3 leaves us with a somewhat clearer picture of the underlying text archive and allows us to understand the reasons for a certain cluster assignment as well as identify overlapping topics and areas of interest within the document collection. For example, in the upper left corner we find a group of nodes sharing labels like *skeletal plans, clinical, guideline, patient, health* which deal with the development and representation of skeletal plans for medical applications. Another homogeneous cluster can be found in the upper right corner which is identified by labels like *gait, pattern, malfunction* and deals with the analysis of human gait patterns to identify malfunctions and supporting diagnosis and therapy. A set of nodes in the lower left corner of the map is identified by a group of labels containing among others *software, process, reuse* and identifies a group of papers dealing with software process models and software reuse. This is followed by a large cluster to the right labeled with *cluster, intuitive, document, archive, text, input* containing papers on cluster visualization and its application in the context of document archives. Further clusters can be identified in the center of the map on plan validation, and quality analysis, neural networks, etc.

To present a more detailed example, the node representing the abstract *koh_icann98* (node (7/2) in the upper right part of the map) is labeled with the following keywords:*gait, pattern, platform, aiming, bio-feedback, effects, diseases, active, compensation, employ*. The full text of the abstract is given in Figure 4. It is obvious, that the labels derived from the *LabelSOM* approach describe the contents of the paper to a sufficient degree.

Experiments in Gait Pattern Classification with Neural Networks of Adaptive Architecture
Monika Köhle, Dieter Merkl

Abstract:
Clinical gait analysis is an area aiming at the provision of support for diagnoses and therapy considerations, the development of bio-feedback systems, and the recognition of effects of multiple diseases and still active compensation patterns during the healing process. The data recorded with ground reaction force measurement platforms is a convenient starting point for gait analysis. We discuss the usage of raw data from such measurement platforms for gait analysis and show how unsupervised artificial neural networks may be employed for gait malfunction identification. In this paper we provide our latest results in this line of research by using Incremental Grid Growing and Growing Grid networks for gait pattern classification.

Proceedings of the 8th Int'l Conference on Artificial Neural Networks (ICANN'98),
Skövde. Sweden. Sept 2-4. 1998.

Fig. 4. Abstract of koh_icann98

Using these labels as class identifiers clear cluster boundaries can be defined by combining nodes sharing a set of labels. This results in a total of 8 different clusters as shown in Figure 5.

4 Discussion

While the labels identified by our *LabelSOM* method in the text data mining example can probably not serve directly as a kind of class labeling in the con-

plan agent skeletal durative asbru design	skeletal plan agent durative	clinical guideline plan	guideline clinical provider	enterprise administration	gait pattern malfunction	gait malfunction
skeletal plan asbru	skeletal plan	guideline patient	guideline provider	enterprise administration	gait	gait pattern
plan asbru	patient	health care patient	patient health care	concept relation	concept	networks conventional
		patient	validation	relation	management organization	network management organization conventional
library retrieval	qualitative	validation description qualitative	validation high frequency	dimension	dimension	document text hierarchical take built
process software product	current library reuse software retrieval	current description values high frequency qualitative	values	text cluster dimension	hierarchy text document	document text take built archive libraries
process reuse software product	process software	cluster input	cluster input intuitive	input algorithm intuitive	document text algorithm libraries	archive document

Fig. 5. Cluster identification based on labels

ventional sense, they reveal a wealth of information about the underlying map and the structures learned during the self-organizing training process. Groups of nodes having a set of labels in common help to determine the cluster structure within the map. This can be used to provide an improved way of cluster boundary and map structure analysis and visualization by grouping and coloring nodes according to the common set of labels. The benefit of determining cluster boundaries with the *LabelSOM* method lies with the fact that in addition to the mere cluster structure, the user gets a justification for the clustering as well as information on the sub-structure within clusters by the very attributes.

The labels themselves aid in identifying the most important features within every node and thus help to understand the information represented by a particular node. In spite of the little redundancy present in abstracts, the labels turn out to be informative in so far as they help the user to understand the map and the data set as such. Especially in cases where little to no knowledge on the data set itself is available, the resulting representation can lead to tremendous benefits in understanding the characteristics of the data set.

It is important to mention that the information used for the labeling originates entirely from the self-organizing process of the SOM without the use of sophisticated machine learning techniques which might provide further improved labeling capabilities. Still, with the increasing use of self-organizing maps in the data mining area, the automatic labeling of resulting maps to identify the features of certain clusters based on the training process itself becomes an important aid in correctly applying the process and interpreting the results. Being based on a neural network approach with high noise tolerance allows the application of the *LabelSOM* approach in a wide range of domains, especially in the analysis of very high-dimensional input spaces.

5 Conclusion

We have presented the *LabelSOM* method to automatically assign labels to the nodes of a trained self-organizing map. This is achieved by determining those features from the high-dimensional feature space that are the most relevant ones for a certain input data to be assigned to a particular cluster. The resulting benefits are twofold: First, assigning labels to each node helps with the interpretation of single clusters by making the common features of a set of data signals that are mapped onto the same node explicit. This serves as a description for each set of data mapped onto a node. Second, by taking a look at groups of (neighboring) nodes sharing common labels it is possible to determine sets of nodes forming larger clusters, to identify cluster and sub-cluster boundaries and to provide specific information on the differences between clusters. Finally, labeling the map allows it to be actually *read*.

References

1. S. Kaski, J. Nikkilä, and T. Kohonen. Methods for interpreting a self-organized map in data analysis. In *Proc. 6th European Symposium on Artificial Neural Networks (ESANN98)*. D-Facto, Brugfes, Belgium, 1998.
2. T. Kohonen. Self-organized formation of topologically correct feature maps. *Biological Cybernetics*, 43, 1982. Springer Verlag, Berlin, Heidelberg, New York.
3. T. Kohonen. *Self-Organizing Maps*. Springer Verlag, Berlin, Germany, 1995.
4. D. Merkl. Text classification with self-organizing maps: Some lessons learned. *Neurocomputing*, 21(1-3), 1998.
5. D. Merkl and A. Rauber. Cluster connections – a visualization technique to reveal cluster boundaries in self-organizing maps. In *Proc 9th Italian Workshop on Neural Nets (WIRN97)*, Vietri sul Mare, Italy, 1997.
6. D. Merkl and A. Rauber. On the similarity of eagles, hawks, and cows – Visualization of similarity in self-organizing maps. In *Proc. of the Int'l. Workshop on Fuzzy-Neuro-Systems '97 (FNS97)*, Soest, Germany, 1997.
7. A. Rauber and D. Merkl. Creating an order in distributed digital libraries by integrating independent self-organizing maps. In *Proc. Int'l Conf. on Artificial Neural Networks (ICANN'98)*, Skövde, Sweden, 1998.
8. H. Ritter and T. Kohonen. Self-organizing semantic maps. *Biological Cybernetics*, 61:241 – 254, 1989. Springer Verlag.
9. G. Salton. *Automatic Text Processing: The Transformation, Analysis, and Retrieval of Information by Computer*. Addison-Wesley, Reading, MA, 1989.
10. A. Ultsch. Self-organizing neural networks for visualization and classification. In *Information and Classification. Concepts, Methods and Application*. Springer Verlag, 1993.

Neural Network Based Classifiers for a Vast Amount of Data[*]

Ling Zhang   Bo Zhang*

The State Key Lab of Intelligent Technology and Systems
Artificial Intelligence Institute   *Dept. of Computer Science
Anhui University, Anhui, China   Tsinghua University, Beijing, China

Abstract   When using neural networks to train a large number of data for classification, there generally exists a learning complexity problem. In this paper, a new geometrical interpretation of McCulloch-Pitts (M-P) neural model is presented. Based on the interpretation, a new constructive learning approach is discussed. Experimental results show that the new algorithm can greatly reduce the learning complexity and can be applied to real classification problems with a vast amount of data.

1   Introduction

A basic M-P neural model [1] is an element with n inputs and one output. The general form of its function is

$$y = \text{sgn}(wx - \varphi)$$

Where

$$x = (x_1, x_2, \cdots, x_n)^T \text{ - input vector}$$

$$w = (w_1, w_2, \cdots, w_n) \text{ - weight vector}$$

$$\varphi - \text{ threshold}$$

The node function above can be regarded as a function of two functions: a linear function $wx - \varphi$ and a sign (or characteristic) function. Generally, there are two ways to reduce the learning complexity in well-known feedforward neural networks. One is to replace the linear function by a quadratic function [2]-[9]. Although the learning capacity of a neural network can be improved by making the node functions more complex, the improvement of the learning complexity would be limited due to the complexity of quadratic functions. The second way to enhance the learning capacity is changing the topological structure of the network. For example, the number of hidden layers and the number of connections between layers are increased [10]-[12]. Similarly, the learning capacity is improved at the price of increasing the complexity of the network.

The proposed algorithm below can reduce the learning complexity and still maintain the simplicity of the M-P model and its corresponding network.

Note $wx - \varphi = 0$ can be interpreted as a hyper-plane P in an n-dimensional space.

---

[*] Supported by National Nature Science Foundation & National Basic Research Program of China

When $(wx - \varphi) > 0$, input vector x falls into the positive half-space of the hyper-plane P. Meanwhile, $y = \text{sgn}(wx - \varphi) = 1$. When $(wx - \varphi) < 0$, input vector x falls into the negative half-space of P, and $y=-1$. In summary, the function of an M-P neuron can geometrically be regarded as a spatial discriminator of an n-dimensional space divided by the hyper-plane P.

Define a transformation $T : D \rightarrow S^n, x \in D$, such that

$$T(x) = (x, \sqrt{d^2 - |x|^2})$$

where $d \geq \max \{|x| | x \in D\}$.

Thus, each point of D is projected upward on the S^n by transformation T. Obviously, each neuron represents a hyper-plane and divides the space into two halves. The intersection between the positive half-space and S^n is called "sphere neighborhood" (Fig. 1). When input x falls into the region, output $y=1$, otherwise, $y=-1$. Therefore, each neuron corresponds to a sphere neighborhood on S^n with w as its center and $r(\varphi)$ as its radius, a monotonically decreasing function of φ.

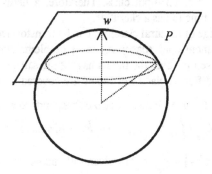

Fig. 1 A sphere neighborhood

2   A Constructive Algorithm of Neural Networks

Based on the above geometrical interpretation of neurons, a framework of the proposed constructive algorithm of neural classifiers can be stated as follows.

A set $K = \{l^t = (x^t, y^t), t = 0,1,2,\cdots, s\}$ of training samples is given. Assume that output y^t in K has only k different values, i.e., the training samples will be classified into k classes. There is no loss of generality in assuming that the first k outputs have mutually different values. Let $I(t)$ be the set of indices of samples with the same output y^t, $t = 0,1,\cdots,k-1, i.e., I(t) = \{i | y^i = y^t\}$, the input set corresponding to $I(t)$ be

$p(t) = \{x^i | i \in I(t)\} t = 0,1,\cdots,k-1.$

The design of a neural classifier can be divided into two stages: the input covering stage and the forward propagation algorithm stage.

2.1 Input Covering Stage

As a classifier (or an associative memory), the function of a neural network can be stated as follows. Given a set $K = \{l^t = (x^t, y^t), t = 0,1,\cdots,s\}$ of training samples, after learning, the network should store the input-pairs (x^t, y^t). Moreover, when the input becomes $x^t + \Delta^t$, the output y^t still remains the same, where Δ^t is regarded as a noise or an error. For an M-P neuron $(w - \varphi)$, when $w = x^t$ and $r(\varphi) = \Delta^t$, as mentioned before, it geometrically corresponds to a sphere neighborhood on S^n with x^t as its center and Δ^t as its radius. An M-P neuron acts as a discriminator of an input class. Therefore, a network consisting of these neurons has the same function as a classifier.

The first design stage of a neural classifier can be transformed to an input vectors (a point set of an n-dimensional space) covering problem. Namely, a set of sphere neighborhoods is chosen to cover the inputs having the same output, i.e., belonging to the same class. And different classes of inputs are covered by different sets of sphere neighborhoods. Namely, an M-P neuron also corresponds to a covering on S^n.

It means that a set $\{C_j(t), j = 1,2,\cdots,k_t\}$ of sphere neighborhoods (coverings) is chosen such that $C(t) = \bigcup c_j(t)$ covers all inputs $x^i \in p(t)$ and does not cover any input $x^i \notin p(t)$, and $C(t)'s, t = 0,1,\cdots,k-1$, are mutually disjoint.

2.2 Forward Propagation Algorithm

Given a set of training samples $K = \{l^{(t)} = (x^t, y^t), t = 0,1,\cdots,p-1\}$, by a covering approach, the input vectors have been covered by a set of coverings based on their classification. Assume that a set C of p-1 coverings is obtained as follows.

$$C=\{C(i), i=1, 2, \cdots, p\text{-}1\}.$$

Assuming that x^i is the center of covering $C(i)$ and y^t is its corresponding output, $i=1, 2, \cdots, p$-1. For simplicity, x^i's are assumed to be mutually different, i.e., one class only corresponds to one covering (When one class corresponds to a set of coverings, the constructive approach is almost the same). The domain of each component of x^i (y^t) is assumed to be {1, -1}. Then a three-layer neural network, i.e., two layer elements, can be constructed (Fig. 2) by the following Forward Propagation (FP) algorithm.

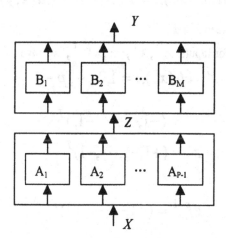

Fig. 2. A three-layer feedforward neural network

The network is constructed from its first layer.

Let the relationship between the input vector x and output vector z of the first layer network A be F. The number of elements in A is $p-1$. Element A_i in A is an M-P neuron with n inputs and one output, $i=1,2,\cdots,p-1$, thus z is an $(p-1)$-dimensional vector. We have.

$$z = F(x) = \text{sgn}(Wx - \varphi) \tag{1}$$

where W is an $(p-1) \times n$-weight matrix, φ-an $(p-1)$-threshold vector. And

$$W = \begin{pmatrix} w^1 \\ w^2 \\ \vdots \\ w^{p-1} \end{pmatrix}, \varphi = (\varphi_1, \varphi_2, \cdots, \varphi_{p-1})T,$$

Where w^i-the weight vector of element A_i, φ_i-its threshold.

Let
$$\begin{cases} w^i = (x^i)^T, i = 1,2,\cdots,p-1 \\ \varphi_i = \begin{cases} n - d_i + 1, \text{if } d_i \text{ is even} \\ n - d_i, \text{if } d_i \text{ is } odd, i = 1,2,\cdots,p-1 \end{cases} \end{cases} \tag{2}$$

Where $d_i = \min_{j \neq i} d(x^i, x^j), i = 1,2,\cdots,p-1, d(x,y)$ denotes the Hamming distance between x and y.

It is easy to prove that for inputs $x^0, x^1, \cdots, x^{p-1}$, we have

$$z^i = F(x^i), i = 1,2,\cdots,p-1$$

Where

$$z^0 = (-1,-1,\cdots,-1,)^T$$
$$z^1 = (+1,-1,\cdots,-1)^T$$
$$\vdots$$
$$z^{p-1} = (-1,-1,\cdots,+1)^T$$

Let

$$C(0) = \left\{ x \middle| d(x^i, x) \geq \frac{d_i}{2}, i = 1,2,\cdots,p-1 \right\}$$

Since $x^0 \notin C(i), i = 1,2,\cdots,p-1, x^0 \in C(0)$.

Obviously, for $x^0 \in C(0), F(x) = z^0 = F(x^0)$.

We now design the second layer B.

Let the relationship between the input z and output y of the second layer network B be G. The number of elements in B is m. Each element B_i in B is an M-P neuron with (p-1) inputs and one output, i=1, 2, $\cdots$, m. We have.

$$y = G(z) = \text{sgn}(Uz - \zeta) \tag{3}$$

where U is an $m \times (p$-1)-weight matrix, ζ-an m-threshold vector. And

$$U = \left\{ \begin{matrix} u^1 \\ u^2 \\ \vdots \\ u^m \end{matrix} \right\}, \zeta = (\zeta_1, \zeta_2, \cdots, \zeta_m)^T,$$

Where u^i the weight vector of element
B_i, ζ_i-its threshold.

Let
$$\begin{cases} u^i_j = 0, & if\ y^0_i = y^j_i \\ u^i_j = y^j_i, & otherwise \\ \zeta_i = -(y^0_i + u^i_1 + \cdots + u^i_{p-1}), i = 1,2,\cdots,m, j = 0,1,\cdots,p-1 \end{cases} \qquad (4)$$

We can prove that when formula (4) is satisfied, for p given output vectors $\left\{y^0, y^1, \cdots, y^{p-1}\right\}$ and $\left\{z^0, z^1, \cdots, z^{p-1}\right\}$, formula (3) holds, i.e.,

$$y^j = G(z^j), j = 1,2,\cdots,p-1$$

In contrast to the well-known BP algorithm, the constructive algorithm above starts from the first layer to the last one, so it is called forward propagation. When the components of input and output vectors are real-valued rather than {-1, 1}, by making small changes, the FP algorithm is still available.

3. Performances Analysis

Conventional neural network approaches, generally, have the following shortages. There is no general theorem about the convergence of a neural network and the learning complexity is very high. It's difficult to choose a proper number of hidden nodes. Now we discuss the performances of the proposed algorithm.

Hidden Nodes

Since the number of the first layer elements (hidden nodes) is decided by the number of the input coverings, if a (quasi-) minimum coverings can be found, then we have a (quasi-) minimal number of hidden nodes.

Learning Complexity

The proposed algorithm is a constructive one, so it does not have any convergence problem. Its 'learning' time consists mainly of the time needed for implementing the input covering.

Since the minimum coverings problems are known to be NP-hard, the key point in the design of the proposed neural network is to find a feasible covering approach such that a satisfactory result can generally be obtained. A new covering method called covering-deletion algorithm and its computer simulation results are given below to show the potential to use the proposed neural network in practice.

3.1. Covering-Deletion Algorithm

The input covering problem is actually a point set covering problem [15]. It's known that the covering problem is generally NP-hard. Although there are many well-known algorithms dealing the problem, an efficient algorithm is needed. Now we present a new covering approach called covering-deletion algorithm below. From the experimental results, it can be seen that the algorithm is quite efficient.

Assume that K={ $x_1, x_2, ..., x_k$ } is an input set, a point set in an n-dimensional space, $K_1 = \{x_1, x_2, ..., x_{m_1}\}, ...,$ and $K_s = \{x_{m_{s-1}+1}, x_{m_{s-1}+2}, ..., x_k\}$ are s subsets of K. Design a three-layer neural network such that for all $x_i \in K_i$, its output is always y_i, where $y_i = (0, ..., 1, 0, ..., 0)$, i.e., the i-th component is 1, otherwise 0. For simplicity, in the following discussion, let s=2, y_1=1 and $y_2 = -1$.

The general idea of the covering-deletion algorithm is as follows. Find a sphere neighborhood (or cover) C_1 which only covers the points belonging to K_1. Then delete the points covered by C_1. For all points left, find a neighborhood C_2, which only covers the points belonging to K_2. Then delete the points covered by C_2, ..., until the points belonging to K_s are covered. Then going back to the first class, the same procedure continues class-by-class, ... until all points are deleted.

In order to have less number of coverings as possible, each neighborhood C_i should cover as many points as possible. We alternatively use "finding the center of cover C_i "and "translating the center of the cover to a proper position to enlarge its covering area" for solving the problem above. A more detailed procedure will be discussed in another paper.

3.2. A Design Approach Based on Covering-Deletion Algorithm

A design approach, consisting of the covering-deletion algorithm and FP algorithm, can be presented below.

Project all points of K_1 and K_2 on sphere S^n, S^n is in an $(n+1)$-dimensional space, and its radius $R > \max|x_i|$. These points are still denoted by K_1 and K_2.

Step1: Find a neighborhood $C(i)$ (initially, i=1) which only covers the points belonging to K_1. The points covered by $C(i)$ are denoted by a subset K_{1i}.

Let $K_2 \leftarrow K_1 \backslash K_{1i}$, $K_2 \leftarrow K_1$, where $A \backslash B$ means that $x \in A$ and $x \notin B$,

$A \leftarrow B$ means that A is replaced by B. If K_1 or K_2 is empty, stop. Otherwise, i=$i+1$, go to step 1.

Finally, a set C={ $C_1, C_2, ..., C_p$ } of coverings is found.

Step 2: For the first layer, there are p elements, $A_1, A_2, ..., A_p$. Each element A_i corresponds to a covering C_i.

For the second layer, there is only one element B with p inputs. Assume that its weight and threshold are (u, a). Each u_i and a can be obtained as follows. Assume that finally K_1 is empty and K_2 is non-empty, K_1 corresponds to output 1, and K_2 corresponds to output -1.

$$-a < 0 \qquad \text{(for the final remainder points of } K_2 \text{)}$$

$$u_p - a > 0 \qquad \text{(for the points of } K_1 \text{ covered by } C_p \text{)}$$

$$u_{p-1} + u_p - a < 0 \qquad \text{(for the points of } K_2 \text{ covered by } C_{p-1} \text{)}$$

$$u_1 + b_2 u_2 + b_3 u_3 + ... + b_p u_p - a > 0,$$

where b_i is chosen from $\{0,1\}$. It is easy to see that, no matter what b_i is a solution of the set of inequalities above always exists.

Note: The design algorithm can be extended to $s>2$ (more than two classes). From the set of inequalities above, it can be seen that when the number of hidden nodes increase, the weight u_i will increase rapidly. Therefore, if the number of hidden nodes is very large, in order to reduce the weights, one more layer can be added. A more detailed discussion will be in another paper.

3.2. Simulation Results

By using the design procedure above, a set of classification problems is tested. Some computer simulation results are shown in Table 1. Compared to the results presented in [9][13][14][15], we can see that the classification of two-spirals based on BP fails [15], and takes 3,000 iterations and only has 89.6% correct classification rate by using the generating-shrinking algorithm presented in [14]. Fahlman[9] uses a cascade network with more than ten layers to treat the same two-spirals problem, and a part of his results was presented in [11]. The results shown in Table 1 are much better than those results.

Table 1. Computer simulation results

Problems	Number of Training Samples	Learning Time	Number of Coverings	Number of Testing Samples	Correct Rate (for testing samples)
Two-spirals	156	0.05s	10	10,000	98.245%
	20,000	35.49s	10	10,000	99.995%
Three-spirals	234	0.22s	24	10,000	91.11%
	30,000	90.46s	26	10,000	99.067%
Three Spatial Spirals	183	0.22s	28	10,000	96.293%
	30,000	81.56s	37	10,000	99.653%

Note: * All correct classification rates for training samples are 100%
*The program was implemented in 486/66 PC under DOS(Window 95) by Mr. Ling Li.

References

1. McCulloch, W. S. and Pitts, W.: A logical calculus of the ideas immanent in neurons activity, *Bulletin of Mathematical Biophysics*, 5 (1943) 115-133

2. Cooper, P. W.: A note on adaptive hypersphere decision boundary, *IEEE Transactions on Electronic Computers* (1996) 948-949

3. Roy, A. and Mukhopadhyay, S.: Pattern classification using linear programming, *ORSA Journal on Computer*, 3(1) (1991) 66-80

4. Mukhopadhyay, S., Roy, A., Kim, L. S. and Govil, S.: A polynomial time algorithm for generating neural networks for pattern classification: Its stability properties and some test results, *Neural Computation*, 5(2) (1993) 317-330

5. Musavi, M. T. M., Ahmed, W., Chan, K. H., Faris, K. B. and Hummels, D. M.: On the training of radial basis function classifiers, *Neural Networks*, vol.5 (1992) 593-603

6. Lee, S. and Kil, R.: Multilayer feedforward potential function network," *in Proc. of the IEEE Second International Conference on Neural Networks*, San Diego IEEE, New York (1988) 161-171

7. Reilly, D. L. and Cooper, L. N.: An overview of neural networks: early models to real world systems, in An Introduction to Neural and Electronic Networks, Zornetzer, S. F., Davis, J. L. and Lau, C. (eds.) Academic Press San Diego (1990) 227-246

8. Abe, S and Lan, M. S.: A method for fuzzy rules extraction directly from numerical data and its application to pattern classification, *IEEE Transactions on Fuzzy Systems*, vol.3 no.1 (1995) 18-28.

9. Abe, S. and Thawonmas, R.: A fuzzy classifier with ellipsoidal regions, *IEEE Trans. on Fuzzy Systems*, vol.5 no.3 (1997) 358-368

10. Fahlman, S. E. and Lebiere, C.: The cascade-correlation learning architecture, In Tourdtzhy, D. S. (ed.), *Advances in Neural Information Processing Systems*, 2, San Mateo, CA, Morgan Kaufmann, (1990) 524-532

11. Lang, K. J. and Witbrock, M. L.: Learning to tell two spirals apart, *in Proc. of the 1988 Connectionists Models Summer Schools* (Pittsburgh, 1988), Touretzky, D., Hinton, G. and Sejnowski, T. (eds.) Morgan Kaufmann, San Mateo, CA (1988) 52-59

12. Hassoun, M. H.: *Fundamentals of Artificial Neural Networks*, MIT Press, Cambridge, Massachusetts (1995)

13. Baum, E. B. and Lang, K. J.: Constructing hidden units using examples and queries, In Lippman, R. P., et al (eds.): *Neural Information Processing Systems*, 3 San Mateo, CA: Morgan Kaufmann (1991) 904-910

14. Chen, Q. C., et. al.: Generating-shrinking algorithm for learning arbitrary classification, *Neural Networks*, 7 (1994) 1477-1489

15. Roberts, F. S.: *Applied Combinatorics*, Prentice-Hall, Inc. (1984)

16. Hong, J. R.: AE1, An extension matrix approximate method for the general covering problem, *Int. J. of Computer and Information Science*, 14(6) (1985) 421-437

Accuracy Tuning on Combinatorial Neural Model

Hércules A. Prado *, Karla F. Machado **, Sandra R. Frigeri * * *, Paulo M. Engel [†]

Universidade Federal do Rio Grande do Sul
Instituto de Informática
Av. Bento Gonçalves, 9500 - Bairro Agronomia
Porto Alegre / RS - Brasil
Caixa Postal 15.064 - CEP 91.501-970
Fone: +55(051)316-6829
Fax: +55(051)319-1576
{prado, karla, rovena, engel}@inf.ufrgs.br

Abstract. The Combinatorial Neural Model (CNM) ([8] and [9]) is a hybrid architecture for intelligent systems that integrates symbolic and connectionist computational paradigms. This model has shown to be a good alternative to be used on data mining; in this sense some works have been presented in order to deal with scalability of the core algorithm to large databases ([2], [1] and [10]). Another important issue is the prunning of the network, after the training phase. In the original proposal this prunning is done on the basis of accumulators values. However, this criterion does not give a precise notion of the classification accuracy that results after the prunning. In this paper we present an implementation of the CNM with a feature based on the wrapper method ([6] and [12]) to prune the network by using the accuracy level, instead of the value of accumulators as in the original approach.

1 Introduction

Classification systems based on symbolic-connectionist hybrid architectures have been proposed ([5], [7], [4] and [11]) as a way to obtain benefits from the specific characteristics of both models. The associative characteristics of artificial neural networks (ANN) and the logical nature of symbolic systems have led to easier learning and the explanation of the acquired knowledge.

This work addresses one of such architectures, the Combinatorial Neural Model ([8] and [9]). In this model, the criterion to prune the network, after training, is based on values of accumulators. However, it does not express directly its accuracy level. To adjust this accuracy level it is necessary to set a value to an accumulator and observe the corresponding accuracy level. After some tryings the user may choose the accumulator that leads to the desired accuracy. In this paper we face this problem providing a way to avoid this boring task by means of an automatic process to reach the most accurate model without numerous manual tryings.

---

* Researcher at EMBRAPA — Brazilian Enterprise for Agricultural Research and lecturer at Catholic University of Brasìlia
** Research Assistant at Federal University of Rio Grande do Sul
* * * Lecturer at University of Caxias do Sul
[†] Professor at Federal University of Rio Grande do Sul

2 Description of the CNM

The CNM is a hybrid architecture for intelligent systems that integrates symbolic and connectionist computational paradigms. It has some significant features, such as the ability to build a neural network from background knowledge; incremental learning by examples, ability to solve the plasticity-stability dilemma [3]; a way to cope with the diversity of knowledge; knowledge extraction of an ANN; and the ability to deal with uncertainty. The CNM is able to recognize regularities from high-dimensional symbolic data, performing mappings from this input space to a lower dimensional output space.

The CNM uses supervised learning and a feedforward topology with: one input layer, one hidden layer - here called combinatorial - and one output layer (Figure 1). Each neuron in the input layer corresponds to a concept - a complete idea about an object of the domain, expressed in an object-attribute-value form. They represent the evidences of the domain application. On the combinatorial layer there are aggregative fuzzy AND neurons, each one connected to one or more neurons of the input layer by arcs with adjustable weights. The output layer contains one aggregative fuzzy OR neuron for each possible class (also called hypothesis), linked to one or more neurons on the combinatorial layer. The synapses may be excitatory or inhibitory and they are characterized by a strength value (weight) between zero (not connected) to one (fully connected synapses). For the sake of simplicity, we will work with the learning of crisp relations, thus with strenght value of synapses equal to one, when the concept is present, and zero, when the concept is not present. However, the same approach can be easily extended to fuzzy relations.

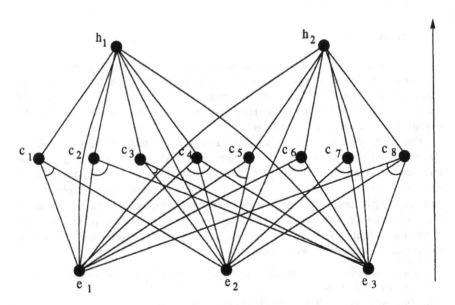

Fig. 1. The complete version of the combinatorial network for 3 input evidences and 2 hypotheses [8]

The network is created completely uncommited, according to the following steps: (a) one neuron in the input layer for each evidence in the training set; (b) a neuron in the output layer for each class in the training set; and (c) for each neuron in the output layer, there is a complete set of hidden neurons in the combinatorial layer which corresponds to all possible combinations (lenght between two and nine) of connections with the input layer. There is no neuron in the combinatorial layer for single connections. In this case, input neurons are connected directly to the hypotheses.

The learning mechanism works in only one iteration, and it is described bellow:
PUNISHMENT_AND_REWARD_LEARNING_RULE
- **Set** to each arc of the network an accumulator with initial value zero;
- **For each** example case from the training data base, **do:**
  - *Propagate* the evidence beliefs from input nodes until the hypotheses layer;
  - **For each** arc reaching a hypothesis node, **do:**
    * **If** the reached hypothesis node corresponds to the correct class of the case
    * **Then** *backpropagate* from this node until input nodes, increasing the accumulator of each traversed arc by its evidencial flow (Reward)
    * **Else** *backpropagate* from the hypothesis node until input nodes, decreasing the accumulator of each traversed arc by its evidencial flow (Punishment).

After training, the value of accumulators associated to each arc arriving to the output layer will be between [-T, T], where T is the number of cases present in the training set. The last step is the prunning of network; it is performed by the following actions: (a) remove all arcs whose accumulator is lower than a threshold (specified by a specialist); (b) remove all neurons from the input and combinatorial layers that became disconnected from all hypotheses in the output layer; and (c) make weights of the arcs arriving at the output layer equal to the value obtained by dividing the arc accumulators by the largest arc accumulator value in the network. After this prunning, the network becomes operational for classification tasks.

3 Accuracy Tuning

As described above, the prunning of the generated network is done by means of the accumulators values, what does not give a precise idea of the resulting classification accuracy of the trained network. To achieve a specific classification accuracy one has to repeatedly modify the prunning threshold, by trial and error. In this section we present a model that uses an implementation of a wrapper algorithm for accuracy tuning of CNM without this tryings. Examples of successful use of wrapper methods are the attribute subset selection algorithm presented by John [6] and the algorithm for parameter selection on ISAAC system [12]. In our application the algorithm involves the trained network and uses an off training dataset as input for test different values of accumulators for prunning. This model may be easily extended to incorporate more interesting validation methods, as n-fold cross validation. Figure 2 shows how the model carries out the accuracy tuning. Considering that the values of the accumulators vary from -T to T, being T the number of cases present in the training set, the user have to specify the step to be used on the first function of the wrapper: the generation of prunning points. For this purpose, the system shows the boundary values of the accumulators.

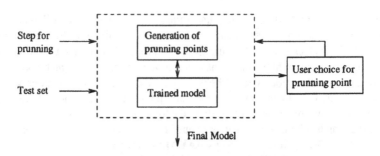

Fig. 2. The wrapper method for accuracy tuning on CNM

Using the specified step, the algorithm divides the interval defined between minimum and maximum accumulators in equal parts (with a possible exception on the last part); after this definition the user submit the test set to the trained network. It is repeated for each step and the results are reported in a graphical form, as depicted in Figure 3. One additional feature is the possibility to focus the attention on a particular interval (like a zoom effect), specifying a shorter step to refine the accuracy tuning.

On the x axis it is the prunning points and on the y axis it is shown the results on each prunning point. The user may choose one prunning point according to the values on the bottom of the screen. In the example, it is selected the prunning point eight. Having decided where to prune the network the user orders the prunning, obtaining the final network with the desired accuracy.

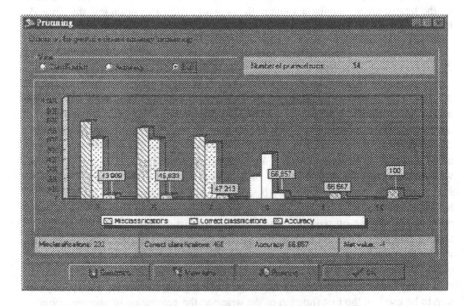

Fig. 3. Prunning points with corresponding accuracy

4 Conclusions and Future Work

CNM has received important improvements in order to be more adequate to data mining. This improvements has focussed on optimizations of processing time [1] and scalability of the algorithm to larger databases [10]. Another important issue is the development of tools to help one in accuracy tuning.

The wrapper method has shown to be useful to set parameters of a model using its own learning algorithm. Our contribution with the present work is the use of wrapper to help the user to overcome the laborious task of determining the prunning point of the combinatorial neural model. By this approach the search for the most accurate model has become easier than by trying many alternatives of prunning.

Although the effectiveness of this way of prunning, we believe that this approach must be improved by allowing the use of better methods for validation as n-fold cross validation. By using such validation methods, one can search for an optimum trade-off between the number of remaining rules after prunning and the accuracy level of the model.

References

1. Beckenkamp, F. G., Feldens, M. A., Pree, W.: Optimizations of the Combinatorial Neural Model. IN: Vth Brazilian Symposium on Neural Networks. (SBRN'98), Belo Horizonte, Brazil.
2. Feldens, M. A.: Engenharia da Descoberta de Conhecimento em Bases de Dados: Estudo e Aplicação na Área de Saúde. Porto Alegre: CPGCC da UFRGS, Brasil, 1997. Dissertação de mestrado.
3. Freeman, J. A., Skapura, D. M.: Neural Networks, Algorithms, Applications, and Program Techniques. [S.l.]: Addison-Wesley, 1992. p.292-339.
4. Guazzelli, A.: Aprendizagem em Sistemas Híbridos. Porto Alegre: CPGCC da UFRGS, Brasil, 1994. Dissertação de mestrado.
5. Hudson, D. L. et al.: Medical diagnosis and treatment plans derived from a hybrid expert system. In: Kandel, A. & Langholz, G. Hybrid architectures for intelligent systems, Boca Raton, FL: CRC Press, 1992.
6. John, G. H.: Enhancements to the Data Mining Process. Stanford, EUA: Stanford University, 1997. Ph.D. Thesis.
7. Knaus, R.: Representing expert knowledge in neural nets. In: Kandel, A. & Langholz G. Hybrids Architectures for Intelligent Systems, Boca Raton, FL: CRC Press, 1992.
8. Machado, R. J., Rocha, A. F.: Handling knowledge in high order neural networks: the combinatorial neural network. Rio de Janeiro: IBM Rio Scientific Center, Brazil, 1989. (Technical Report CCR076).
9. Machado, R. J., Carneiro, W., Neves, P. A.: Learning in the combinatorial neural model, IEEE Transactions on Neural Networks, v.9, p.831-847. Sep.1998.
10. Prado, H. A., Frigeri, S. R., Engel, P. M.: A Parsimonious Generation of Combinatorial Neural Model. IN: IV Congreso Argentino de Ciencias de la Computación (CACIC'98), Neuquén, Argentina, 1998.
11. Towell, G.G., Shavlik, J.W.: Knowledge-based artificial neural networks. Artificial Intelligence 70(1994) 119-165.
12. Talavera, L.: Exploring Efficient Attribute Prediction in Hierarchical Clustering. IN: VII Congreso Iberoamericano de Inteligencia Artificial, IBERAMIA'98, Lisbon, Portugal, 1998.

A Situated Information Articulation Neural Network: VSF Network

Y. Kakemoto and S. Nakasuka

Dpt. of engineering, The university of Tokyo
Komaba 4-6-1 Meguro-ku Tokyo, 153 Japan

Abstract. When a system will recognize the world around one, system requires segmenting or articulating information of the world. In this paper, we introduce a neural network model called VSF network for situated articulation. At first, we discuss situation and its relation to information coding. Next, we introduce the architecture and main procedure of the VSF network. Finally, we examine the validity of VSF-network model through the experiment which applies the VSF-network to a path planning task of a rover.

1 Situated articulation

A system working in some environment recognizes its surroundings environments and it modifies its knowledge to reduce the difference between required action and its own action. Extracting a part of information from environment and constructing knowledge is major part of learning. There are many ways how to extract a part of information from incoming information, and so working system in real world should discover most suitable one. We deal with these complex task by direction its attention to a most important part of them from the point of view of its task and situation[3].

Neural network model is an effective way in discovering knowledge from unorganized data. From the view of the neural network model, this type of articulation is thought as a kind of dynamical symbol generation. The key issues of dynamical symbol generation are summarized into following three points.

1. Timing of articulation.
   When do a system articulating outside information and take in it?
2. Form of information coding.
   The result of articulation is coded in a certain form.
3. Relation between timing and the form of information coding.

2 Relation between Timing and Form

2.1 Combination

Information Articulation is an action that a system extracts only worth parts of information based on their prior experiences. In this study, we direct our attention to the situation where conflict between system's recognition and a hindrance for it was occurred. The conflict can be thought as a difference between system's knowledge and result of action based on it. Several system have utilized this type of conflict for information articulation[6].

The result of articulation is not a lump of external information but structured one. Those structure of articulate information are summarized as the following primitive forms.

- AND type combination.
  Some information are valid when they are appeared at the same time.
- OR type combination.
  Some information are valid when only a part of them is appeared.

We define that occurrence of the conflict between a system's recognition and required action in a situation as the timing of articulation. This type of conflict becomes a cue of knowledge reconstruction. On neural network model, this difference is defined by a difference between an output of network and teacher signal. On neural network model, the output for an input is computed through internal connections between neurons. Those connections depend on global or local minimum on an error definition function for weigh update functions. An change of the coding form of information depending on the difference will affect the coded information structure. The difference between output and teacher signal for it determines the coding form of articulated information. The AND type combination and the OR type combination depend on the timing that sub-pattern of information are co-occurred. If a difference between an output of system and teacher signal for it is large, system will search for other solutions to minimize the difference. If this is small, system will elaborate their internal connection to improve their ability.

Another prerequisite to develop dynamical symbol system are the representation way of sub-patterns of a pattern obtained by neural network and combination of way of them. To realize the first requirement, we employed the oscillator neural model[1] and a chaotic oscillator lattice model to realize the second requirements. In the weights update process, each neuron in hidden layer is grouped into group expressing sub-structure of articulated information. This dynamics is controlled by the difference between input and output and attractors on it. This scheme is thought as a kind of the intermittent chaos[5].

3 The VSF network

The overview of the VSF network shown in the figure 1. The VSF network is a kind of hybrid neural network that is consisted of two modules called the BP module and the LF module. The BP module is a hierarchical neural network trained with back propagation process[4], so weights on each layer are thought as a result of articulation based on an external evaluation. The LF module is two layer network like the Boltzmann-completion network. The purpose of the

LF module is that to detect local features on inputs. The knowledge reconstruction on the VSF network is the result of two different kinds of process, namely bottom-up process and top-down process. The bottom-up process is based on local feature of input signals. The top-down process is a propagation process based on differences between inputs and teacher's signal for them. As a result, the interaction between the local feature layer and the hidden layer become output of the VSF network.

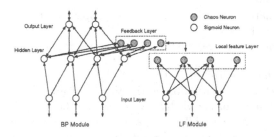

Fig. 1. The VSF Network

In the VSF network, neurons at the feedback layer and the local feature layer have chaotic behavior so it can be expected that the form of attractor is changed by some changes of inputs for the neuron. Dynamics on the feedback layer and the local feature layer are thought as a kind of CML(Coupled Mapping Lattice)[2]. From recent researches on CML, interaction between chaotic elements generates various forms of element group.

3.1 Processing on VSF network

The main purpose the VSF-network is the reconstruction of pre-learned knowledge based on experiences. By the VSF network, pre-learned knowledge is reconstructed according to the difference between system's action and its results.

The following procedure is the main procedure of the VSF-network. In our model, internal status of chaotic neuron is defined by the logistic mapping, and output of all neuron is defined by the sigmoid function.

1. The weights obtained in pre-learning phase are used as initial weights at each layers on the BP module.
2. The weights obtained in pre-learning phase are used as initial weights at layers on the LF module.
3. Apply following procedures for each input pattern.
   (a) Inputs a pattern to the input layer of BP module.
   (b) Inputs the same pattern to the input layer of LF module.

(c) The forward process is carried out in the BP module and the error between output of BP module and teacher signal is computed.

(d) The procedure based on the Kohonen-mapping algorithm is submitted for the LF module. At first, the winner is determined. Each weights between input layer and output layer is updated.

(e) Internal status of each neurons at hidden layer in the BP module and neurons at local feature layer in the LF modules is mixtured and internal status of feedback layer layer is determined.

(f) Effect of chaotic factors on the feedback layer depends on the difference between output and the teacher signals. Status of the neurons in the feedback layer is updated.

(g) The steps from (3a) to (3d) will be carry out until each member of neuron group become stable.

(h) Base on the correlation each neurons, transmition factor value is updated.

(i) Each mean status value of hidden layer in period is computed.

(j) Using the mean status value of hidden layer, the forward process at the BP model is submitted again. Each weights on the BP module is updates.

4 Experiment

Through an experiment which applies the VSF network to a path planning task of a rover, we examine the validity of VSF network model. Each environments of the experiment is shown in the figure 2. The input data for the experiment is data from a distance sensor on the rover. The teacher signals for the network are possibility of cornering of the rover at a T-junction or an obstacle. The basic specification of the rover is,

- the rover has n distance sensor directed to the head direction of the rover,
- the length and width of the rover can be variable.
- All weighs prior to the experiments were computed by hierarchical neural network with back propagation.

4.1 Task and results

This task was designed for conform the VSF network's learning performance when the additional situation and subtractional situation is provided for the rover. The training and verification of network's performance were generated under the following two kinds of condition.

- Additional condition : The task (1) in the figure 2. This task is designed for verifying the performance of the VSF network for the AND type information processing.
- Subtractional condition : The task (2) in the figure 2. This task is designed for verifying the performance of the VSF network for the OR type information processing.

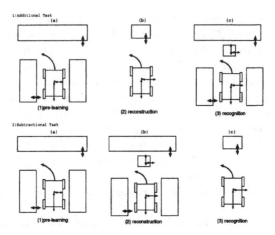

Fig. 2. Task of the experiment

The task for pre-learning is shown in the figure 2 (a-1) and the figure 2 (b-1). After the pre-learning, hidden-input weights and hidden-outputs weight which obtained at pre-learning phase are provided for both the VSF-network and the back-propagation network.

In the figure 3, each error rate in recognition phase of an additional sequence task and a subtractional task is shown.

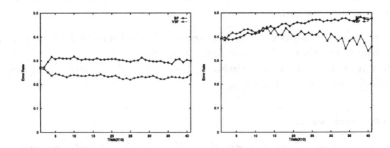

Fig. 3. Error rates on the additional and subtractional task

Form these results, we can see following properties of the VSF network.

- In both condition, an additional task and subtractional task, our network shows better performance than traditional hierarchical network trained with back-propagation.

- In subtractional task, the VSF shows worse results in initial 100 learning steps but it improve gradually.
- Variance of error rates in the subtractional task is higher than all other task sequence. Conditions in the recognition phase can be divided into better conditions and worse conditions.

5 Conclusion

In this paper, we show only result of subtractional combination task. In the additional combination task experiment, the VSF-network shows same tendencies as above results. Now, we are analyzing fire pattern at the hidden layer to verify hierarchical structure of obtained pattern and trying to apply the VSF-network to real-world rover.

References

1. Von der Malsburg. *Am I thinking assemblies ? in Brain Theory (eds by G.Palm and A.Aertsen.* Springer–Verlag(Berlin), 1986.
2. K. Kaneko. Chaotic but regular posi–nega switch among coded attractor by cluster size variation. *Phys. Rev. Lett.*, 63, 1989.
3. Hitoshi Matsubara. The role of robots in artificial intelligence. *Journal of Japan Society of Robots*, 14(4):478–481, 1996.
4. D. E. Rumelhart, J. L. MaClelland, and PDP Research Group. *Parallel Distributed Processing.* MIT Press, 1986.
5. I. Tsuda. Dynamic link of memory – chaotic memory map in nonequilibrium neural networks. *Neural Networks*, 5, 1991.
6. A. Zelinsky, Y. Kuniyoshi, and H. Tsukune. Monitoring and co-ordination behaviors for purposive robot navigation. In *Proc. IEEE Int. Conf. Intelligent Robots and Systems*, pages 894–901, 1994.

Neural Method for Detection of Complex Patterns in Databases[*]

Chao Deng,   Fanlun Xiong

University of Science and Technology of China
The Institute of Intelligent Machines, Academia Sinica, Hefei 230027, P. R. China
E-mail: cdeng@mail.ustc.edu.cn   flxiong@public.ustc.edu.cn

Abstract. Databases storing real data contain complex patterns, such as chaotic pattern which generally are characteristics of greatly random fluctuation that often appear between deterministic and stochastic patterns of knowledge discovery in database. Chaotic patterns are always treated as random fluctuation distributions and ignored in literature so far. A novel network approach to discover and predict chaotic pattern in databases is proposed in this paper, which together with Zytkow's Forty-Niner can not only discover the chaotic pattern but also predict it efficiently. In addition, this approach is very suitable to deal with large databases and has extensive applicable prospects in the vivid research fields of KDD.

1 Introduction

Automated knowledge discovery in large databases (KDD) has been extensively concerned in recent years. There exist many large databases that are constructed by the kind of data recording various natural and social phenomena. Relational data within one attribute or between different attributes of these databases usually lay out to be greatly random fluctuation and disordered. Researchers showed that many natural and social recordings (such as the rise and fall of stock price and the change of the weather) are all disordered and mixed[1]. However they can be almost described by chaos yet. The seemingly disordered and mixed relations can be easily confused with random relations since they share many similar characteristics. In fact, among these random relations there might exist chaotic patterns that result from simple nonlinear systems.

Concept, digital logic pattern, elementary pattern, statistical pattern and regularity are all the types of relations representing the knowledge in KDD. These relations are all deterministic patterns whatever they are expressed in what manner. Besides, other relations are all treated as completely irrelevant ones that are called random fluctuation relations. Yet in the random fluctuations there obviously exist a baffling range of relations that are different from pure noisy relations. Are there any useful patterns in these relations? You may ask. Theories for chaos reveal an evident that between deterministic patterns and random relations there exists a middle pattern relation, which is referred to as chaotic patterns by authors in this paper. So-called chaotic pattern is a

---

[*] This project was supported by the Natural Science Foundation of China, P. R. China

time sequence or an attribute relation that can be rebuilt by a low-order nonlinear dynamics' system. Since it distinguishes from both deterministic pattern and pure random relations, chaotic pattern, which can be understood as a generalization to the existing deterministic patterns in KDD, is an important class of patterns in the nature.

The establishment and development of the chaotic and fractal theories have provided with solid basis and sufficient tools for finding and understanding the disordered law (i.e., chaotic relation). If a disordered relation is judged as chaotic relation, it could be also predicted within short time in high accuracy by nonlinear techniques. Evolution of laws hidden in the chaotic pattern can be dug out and reconstructed by discovering chaotic pattern. Moreover discovery of chaotic patterns can find laws according to the character of chaos and recast the existing data into some expressible frame. Thus it provides a completely new approach and train of thought for the researches of the intra- and inter-attribute relations in KDD.

Since the available methods are hard to deal with chaotic patterns, they are all treated as random relations. It is well known that statistic technique is one of the important types of methods to estimate the attribute relations. Statistics in KDD has developed many methods for pattern searching and evaluating which are efficient in analyzing various relations [2]. Nevertheless it can not efficiently depict the chaotic attribute relations. Rather it usually disposes of chaotic patterns as random relations. 49er (Forty-Niner) proposed by J. Zytkow[3] is one of the most famous methods to find useful patterns in databases based on statistics. Analyses and experiments show that 49er is inefficient to find and depict the chaotic patterns and treat them as random relations as well. In this paper, a chaotic pattern discovery net (CPDN) is proposed for our purpose. Based on the relevant work [4], CPDN has many distinguishing advantages as given below. Combined with 49er, it can not only discover chaotic patterns but also predicate the future trend of the patterns.

2 Chaotic Pattern and Neural Network Approach

The chaotic pattern can be found both within an attribute and between different attributes in databases. Chaotic pattern is a special kind of dynamic relation that behaves between deterministic and random relations. For better comprehension of the chaotic pattern, we here discuss them in three aspects: correlativity, prediction length and Lyapunov exponent. It is well demonstrated that deterministic patterns are characterized by strong correlativity, very long prediction length and negative Lyapunov exponent. Whereas, pure random relations along with infinite value of Lyapunov exponent, do not have any correlation so that it can not be predicted. However, Chaotic patterns are just between them, which is characterized by weak correlation, short prediction length and finite positive Lyapunov exponents.

It has been proved that the approaches of statistic correlation analysis are efficient in discovery of non-chaotic patterns in databases in KDD field. It is pointed out in [3] that 49er has a good recognition capability for 2-D patterns. One hundred random fluctuation patterns were tested by 49er and only one was mistaken as deterministic pattern. But there might exist some chaotic patterns in the 99 patterns that can not be picked up by 49er. In this paper, we intent to preliminarily distinguish deterministic patterns from random relations by 49er and then search for chaotic patterns among the

3 Simulation and Analysis

To reveal the capability of detecting chaotic patterns among complex patterns in databases, we generate the following four kinds of relations for simulation test.

(1) A_1, A_2 is in random relationship (where A_1 is generated randomly in uniform distribution. A_2 is generated similar as A_1 but independently)

(2) A_1, A_3 is in simple functional relationship, $A_3 = a + bA_1^2$, where a and b are real and constant number respectively (generated in similar manner as [3])

(3) A_1, A_4 is in complex functional relationship that is in the form of $A_4 = a + bA_1^3 * \exp(A_1^2)$.

(4) Chaotic relation between attributes which are generated by Mackey-Glass sequence.

First, we calculate significance Q and Cramer's V coefficient [3] of the above four patterns, which are illustrated in Fig. 1 and Fig. 2, respectively.

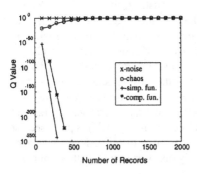
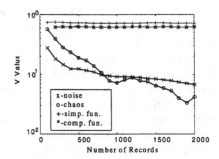

Fig. 1. Curves of Q versus record number   **Fig. 2.** Curves of V versus record number

With regard to random relationship, Q value is always much larger than a threshold of 10^{-5}, and V value always near to zero. For deterministic patterns, Q is below the threshold and V is close to 1 all the time. However, Q and V of chaotic pattern, for its complexity, change with record number, which behave in similar manner of deterministic patterns for small records while behave gradually as random relationship as record numbers increase. It can also be seen from Fig 1 and Fig 2 that chaotic pattern indeed locates between deterministic pattern and random fluctuation. Nevertheless, 49er can not discover the chaotic pattern and classify it into a random relationship.

Next, we apply CPDN to discover the three kinds of patterns (such as deterministic pattern of A_1 and A_3, random relationship of A_1 and A_2 and chaotic pattern). In the learning process, each pair of attribute values in databases is used as input and output of the net, respectively and the samples are sequentially presented in the input-end. The change of hidden nodes of the network during the learning process is plotted in Fig. 3.

In Fig. 3, there show three curves reflecting the change of hidden nodes when the CPDN is used to learn the three kinds of patterns. The curve in dashed line denotes the change of hidden nodes of CPDN in learning deterministic pattern of A_1 and A_3, while the curve in solid line the random relationship between A_1 and A_2. The hidden node change for chaotic pattern between two attributes of attri-1 and attri-2 is also drawn by thick solid line. It is shown that for the random relationship the hidden nodes increase as the input records increase all the time and the curve changes acutely and irregularly.

random relations by a connectionist model if there exist chaotic patterns.

Chaotic patterns always appear to be disordered and are shown to be similar to random patterns to some extent in statistic research. As a result, chaotic patterns usually were classified into and treated as random fluctuations in the past. Thus other approaches are needed to be invented to discover and forecast chaotic patterns efficiently. Non-linear is the fundamental reason to generate chaotic patterns. Though they are seemingly disordered, chaotic patterns obey certain laws and behave some correlation in the time delayed state space which gives some memory ability in intra- and inter-attributes. However, this correlation is difficult to be expressed by relation logic, symbolic processing and analytical methods. Neural network just possesses such ability of information processing.

This paper proposes a chaotic pattern discovery net (CPDN), which belongs to a kind of RBF-based neural network approach. This kind of chaotic pattern can occur both intra- and inter-attributes. CPDN can find and learn the chaotic relationship between attributes.

Conventional RBF network approach adopts a predetermined network structure (e.g., number of basis functions) according to the given problems. This approach is not able to deal with the problem of discovering useful patterns in databases because there are two basic problems in KDD: Is there a pattern? What is the pattern in database? But further this approach is not also suitable to large-scale database.

The proposed CPDN is a two-layer feedforward neural network. The activation function of the hidden layer is of the radical basis function, such as Gaussian function. The network output is the linearly weighted sum of all of the output of hidden nodes.

The main features of the proposed CPDN algorithm can be given as follows

(1) The hidden node of CPDN is dynamically allocated during the learning process. Three rules, which are learning error, the nearest distance between input and the existing pattern and the change of belief degree, respectively, are used here to determine whether the network need adding a new hidden node. Only when the three rules are satisfied can the network be added a new hidden node. The former two rules control the case when there is novel information in the coming data and the network unable to contain it. The third rule indicates that the newly arrived data must contain some interesting patterns we concern if degree of belief changes. These three rules together with the following pruning mechanism is very useful to determine whether there exists a pattern or not.

(2) CPDN is of pruning mechanism of basis function. Because the RBF neural network has local properties, the added hidden nodes only response to the local space and ignore the equilibrium of the whole space and sometimes result in redundant hidden nodes. Here we add a punishment factor ζ $(0<\zeta<1)$ to the weight between hidden nodes and output nodes when the weight is small enough, since very small weight means that corresponding synaptic connection contributes little to the net's output. Hence pruning is conducted when the weight is smaller than a preset threshold.

(3) CPDN also has good prediction ability to many complex patterns due to its good generalization performance.

Because there is short of correlation between data of random relationship, and each new comer is novel to the system, the CPDN must allocate additional hidden node to adapt them. For deterministic relationship, the number of hidden node changes steadily and gradually reaches a stable state. As there exists a strong correlation for the deterministic pattern, the pattern character must be limited. Therefore, CPDN can express the pattern efficiently by finite number of hidden nodes, and to filter out such patterns from random fluctuation. For chaotic pattern, the hidden nodes of CPDN become unchanged at 1300 observation samples during the learning process, which means it is enough to express the chaotic pattern by 24 hidden nodes in this simulation.

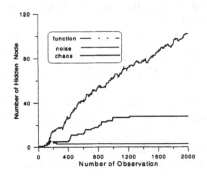

Fig. 3. Curves of hidden nodes versus number of observation

4 Concluding Remarks

The chaotic pattern is a class of useful patterns existing in databases but was ignored before, which is the embodiment of the natural complexity. This paper proposed a chaotic pattern discovery net based on neural network methodology to detect and discover the chaotic pattern together with static method from complex patterns in databases.

Acknowledgment
The authors would like to thank Prof. Jan M. Zytkow from Department of Computer Science, North Carolina University, USA, for his technical supports and materials.

References

1. M. Casdagli, "Nonlinear prediction of chaotic time series," Physica D, vol. 35, pp. 335-356, 1989.
2. J.F. Elder IV, Daryl Pregibon, "A Statistical Perspective on Knowledge Discovery in Databases," in Advances in Knowledge Discovery and Data Mining, U. Fayyad, G. Piatetsky-Shapiro, P. Smyth & R. Uthurusamy eds. AAAI press, 1996.
3. Jan M. Zytkow, "Database Exploration in Search of Regularities," Journal of Intelligent Information Systems, 2, 39-81, 1993.
4. Y. Lu, N, etc., "A Sequential Learning Scheme for Function Approximation Using Minimal Radial Basis Function Neural Networks," Neural Computation 9, pp. 461-478, 1997.

Preserve Discovered Linguistic Patterns
Valid in Volatility Data Environment

Xuemei SHI [1], CHAN Man-chung[1] , Deyi LI [2]
[1] Department of Computing,
Hong Kong Polytechnic University, Kolwoon, Hong Kong
{csxshi, csmcchan}@comp.polyu.edu.hk
[2] Institute of China Electronic System Engineering,
No.6 Wanshou Road, Bejing, 100036, China
ziqin@public2.bta.net.cn

Abstract. Many data mining techniques have been developed and shown to be successful in financial domains. A further aim is to make sense of numerical data through a human-friendly way, by which general patterns are extracted in terms of linguistic concepts. Problems associated with the linguistic mining approach are the effective representation and the validity preservation of the linguistic patterns. The volatile data may vary linguistic concepts and make previously discovered patterns invalid. This paper aims to solve the problem. Based on the cloud model proposed in our previous works, linguistic patterns can be represented effectively. Outdated linguistic patterns can be valid by a GA-based validity preservation technique in line with current data set. An example of Hong Kong stock market is given to illustrate how the technique works.

1 Introduction

Applying data mining technology to finance industry, the area dominated by traditional analytic techniques, have been considered as a practical and powerful way to exploit the huge resources [1],[2]. As reviewed in [3], many data mining techniques have been developed over the past few years. While they are shown to be successful in many applications, some difficulties are still emerged.

One of the difficulties is to make sense of financial data through a human-friendly approach, by which the general patterns can be mined from numerical data in terms of linguistic concepts. This linguistic mining approach is very welcomed by finance analysts since most of the financial data are meticulous numbers. For example, a linguistic predictive pattern mined from stock data might like this:

Linguistic Pattern (P1). If 3-days accumulated change of index is positive and volume maintains heavy, then the short-term market tendency is up. Meanwhile a potential drop is implied when the accumulated gain becomes big positive and the volume reduces from heavy to weak.

In the prediction, some linguistic concepts, e.g. *"positive"*, *"heavy"* and *"up"*, are used to describe the changes of stock index, the market volumes and the tendency instead of the accurate numbers. The advantages of linguistic patterns are that they can carry more information then numerical patterns, and easily understood by users.

There are two problems associated with the linguistic mining approach. The basic one is to represent linguistic concept effectively. This problem is solved by so-called *cloud model* proposed in our previous works [4],[5].

The other problem dues to the volatility of financial data. Rapidly changing data can make linguistic concepts outdated in different time periods and further invalid previously discovered linguistic patterns. The mapping of data→linguistic concept become invalid even the linguistic concept→pattern still correct. This is the problem the paper arms to solve.

2. Linguistic Representation Based on the Cloud Model

Three kinds of linguistic items, individual linguistic term, linguistic variable and linguistic pattern, need to be represented. For instance, the example P1 is a linguistic pattern with linguistic variables of *a-change*, *volume* and *tendency*, and each variable associates with several linguistic terms, such as *positive* and *big positive* for *a-change*. *heavy* and *weak* with *volume*.

Represent Linguistic Term. The cloud model has been defined in [4]. It can quantify a linguistic term by three numerical parameters: expected value Ex, entropy En and deviation D, e.g. *heavy (24,3,0.01) with Ex = 24, En = 3, D = 0.01*. Ex gives the position at U corresponding to the gravity center of the cloud. En measures how many elements in U are accepted by a linguistic term. D measures the randomness of membership degrees in the cloud. The *mathematically expected curve* (MEC) of a cloud is defined as:

$$MEC(u) = e^{-\frac{(u-Ex)^2}{2En^2}}$$ (1)

Given Ex, En and D, a so-called cloud generator can generate *drops(ui, μi)*, where *ui* is a value in U, and *μi* is the membership degree of *ui* belongs to the linguistic term. A specific *drop(u, μ)* is generated if either a value *u* or a degree *μ* is given.

Represent Linguistic Variable. A general format, $v \{T_1(Ex_1, En_1, D_1), ..., T_m (Ex_m, En_m, D_m)\}$, is used to represent a linguistic variable v contains m linguistic terms. For example, three linguistic variables used in stock data analysis are defined as: *a-change {big-negative(-450,50,0.03),negative(-200,90,0.04),neutral(0,60,0.02), positive(200,90,0.04), big-positive(450,50,0.03)};volume{weak(15,2,0.02),moderate(19,4,0.04),heavy(25,4,0.05)}; and tendency {down(-200,100,0.04), neutral(0,60,0.02), up(250,80,0.04)}.*

Represent Linguistic Pattern. A linguistic pattern is represented based on the linguistic variables and their relationships.

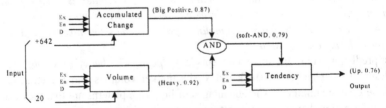

Fig. 1 Linguistic Pattern P1 Represented by Cloud Generators

Fig.1 shows the representation of the above example P1, where cloud generators of *a-change* and *volume* are used for the two inputs of *3-day accumulated change* and *market volume* respectively. The output of the pattern is the prediction of market tendency, which is represented by the generator of *tendency*. The operator is "soft-and" is defined as Eq. 2, where z is the result of x "soft-and" y.

$$z = \left(\frac{x+y}{2}\right)^2 - \left(\frac{x-y}{2}\right)^2 \qquad (2)$$

When a new pair of input, say <+642, 20> for *a-change* and *volume* respectively, is given, the linguistic terms triggered by the inputs and their associated compatibility degrees, are produced by the cloud generator, they are *(big-positive, 0.87)* and *(heavy, 0.92)* in Fig.1. The operation of *"x soft-and y"* is preformed obtaining *(soft-and, 0.79)*. The final output of the market tendency is *(up, 0.76)*.

3. Outdated Linguistic Variable and Invalid Linguistic Pattern

Data from Hong Kong Stock Exchange (HKSE) is given to be the example data set and shown in Fig.2. It is a combined chart of 3-day a-changes of Hang Seng Index (HSI) and market volumes during time period from January 1996 to December 1997.

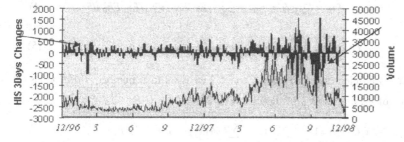

Fig. 2 Combined chart of 3Days HSI Accumulated Changes and Volume of HKSE

The historical data in a time period, e.g. in 1997, can be used to test the validity of linguistic patterns. For P1, the prediction is considered to be correct if the market moves to the same direction of the predicted tendency. Fig.3 (a) is the result when applying P1 to the data set in 1997, which indicates a big rising market with 92% *"up"* and 4% *"down"*. However, a distinct real behavior, shown in Fig.2, is that the stock market rises generally in the first half year but drops sharply in the second half year. Obviously, the linguistic pattern is invalid with respect to the data in 1997.

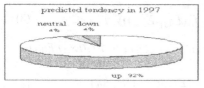 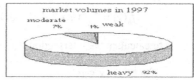

Fig. 3 Outdated linguistic variable invalid the linguistic pattern

The reason can be found if we look at performances of linguistic variables. Fig.3 (b) shows the linguistic variable *"volume"* with respect to the same data set, where *"heavy"* is dominated and *"weak"* is almost zero. This result obviously conflicts with the real situations shown in Fig.2. Since the linguistic terms do not refresh their mathematical definitions accordingly and become outdated in current data set, the linguistic pattern will be invalid and result in distorted conclusions.

4. Refresh Linguistic Variables

Outdated linguistic variable can be refreshed by adapting its numerical parameters to the current data set. The statistical characteristics of the data distribution in are used to optimize the parameters. Since parameter D does not influence whether an element belongs to a linguistic term or not, only Ex and En are needed to be considered.

The function f is synthesized by three sub-functions of f_a, f_b and f_c to evaluates individual terms, the relation of two neighbor terms and the data percentage covered in each term. The function f is defined as Eq.3 where m is the number of terms in the linguistic variable.

$$f = (\sum_{i=1}^{m} f_a(Ex_i, En_i) + f_b(v) + f_c(v))/3 \tag{3}$$

Function $f_a(Ex, En)$. Function $f_a(Ex, En)$ is a combination of f_{a1}, f_{a2} and f_{a3}, which are defined to evaluate the symmetry, the concentration of its kernel and the sparseness of its margin.

$$f_a(Ex, En) = (2f_{a1}(Ex, En) + 2f_{a2}(Ex, En) + f_{a3}(Ex, En))/5 \tag{4}$$

$$f_{a1}(Ex, En) = \sum_{i=1}^{n} Vote(x_i) / \sum_{j=1}^{n} Vote(x_j), x_i \in L, x_j \in R \tag{5}$$

where x_i is an element of data set $\{x_1..x_n\}$, n is its total number, $Vote(x_i)$ is the frequency of x_i, $L= [C\text{-}Ex - 3C\text{-}En/2, C\text{-}Ex], R=[C\text{-}Ex, C\text{-}Ex + 3C\text{-}En/2]$.

$$f_{a2}(C\text{-}Ex, C\text{-}En) = 1 - \left| \left(\sum_{i=1}^{n} Vote(x_i) / \sum_{j=1}^{n} Vote(x_j) \right) - 0.68 \right|, x_i \in B, x_j \in A \tag{6}$$

where, $B=C\text{-}Ex - \sqrt{\pi/2}En, C - Ex + \sqrt{\pi/2}En], A=[C\text{-}Ex - 3C\text{-}En/2, C\text{-}Ex + 3C\text{-}En/2]$

$$f_{a3}(C\text{-}Ex, C\text{-}En) = 1 - \left| \left(\left(\sum_{i=1}^{n} Vote(x_i) + \sum_{j=1}^{n} Vote(x_j) \right) / \sum_{k=1}^{n} Vote(x_k) \right) - 0.4 \right|, \tag{7}$$

$$x_i \in PR, x_j \in PL, x_k \in A$$

where $PR = [C\text{-}Ex + C\text{-}En, C\text{-}Ex + 3C\text{-}En/2], PL= [C\text{-}Ex - 3C\text{-}En/2, C\text{-}Ex - C\text{-}En]$

Function $f_b(v)$. The function f_b calculates the redundancy between two neighbor terms, which is measured by the intersection of their clouds.

$$f_b(v) = \sum_{i=1}^{m} (Max(f_{bb}(Ex_i, En_i), f_{bb}(Ex_{i+1}, En_{i+1})))/m \tag{8}$$

Where f_{bb} is to calculate the intersection between $T_i(Ex_i, En_i)$ and $T_{i+1}(Ex_{i+1}, En_{i+1})$.

$$f_{bb}(Ex_i, En_i) = \begin{cases} 0, x \in basic group_i \\ \dfrac{2x - 2Ex_i - En_i}{En_i}, x \in periphery_i \\ 1, x \in weak periphery_i \end{cases} \qquad x = \dfrac{(Ex_i En_{i+1}) - (Ex_{i+1} En_i)}{En_{i+1} - En_i} \tag{9}$$

Function $f_c(v)$. The f_c measures the data percentage covered by linguistic variable v. it is defined as the sum of the data percentages covered by all linguistic terms.

$$f_c(v) = \frac{\sum_{k=1}^{n} Vote(x_k)}{\sum_{t=1}^{n} Vote(x_t)}, x_k \in S_i - \bigcup_{j=1}^{i-1} S_j, i = 1..m \qquad (10)$$

where $S_i = [C-Ex_i - 3En_i/2,\ Ex_i + 3En_i/2]$.

5. Experiment and Discussions

Applying the algorithm to data from January to December 1997, the Ex and En of *volume {(weak(12,6,0.03), moderate(15,8,0.04), heavy(18,10,0.05)}* in 1996 is refreshed in line with the data set of July, August and November 1997 respectively (Fig.4-Left), i.e. *{(weak(16,8),moderate(19,10),heavy(22,16)},{(weak(22,10),moderate(27,18),heavy(35,20)}*, and *{(weak(7,3),moderate(8.2,6), heavy(10.6,7)}*.

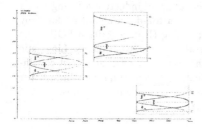 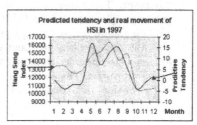

Fig. 4-Left. Linguistic Variable *volume* in July, August and November 1997
Fig. 4-Right The comparison between the predictive tendency and real movement of HSI

The prediction obtained by the refreshed pattern is shown in Fig. 4-Right, together with the real movement of HIS. It is shown that the market slide in the first quarter and soar during the middle and fall sharply in the last quarter, which generally matches the real stock market. It shows that the validity of linguistic pattern is preserved.

References

1. U. M. Fayyad, G. Piatetsky-Shapiro, P. Smyth, R. Uthurusamy, "From Data Mining To Knowledge Discovery: An Overview", Advances in Knowledge Discovery and Data Mining, P1-34, AAAI Press/The MIT Press, 1996.
2. G. Deboeck, "Trading on the Edge, Neural, Genetic, and Systems for Chaotic Financial Markets", John Wiley & Sons, Inc, 1994.
3. M.S. Cen, J. Han, P. Yu, "Data Mining: An Overview from a Database Perspective", IEEE Trans. On Knowledge and Data Engineering, Vol. 8, No.6, Dec. 1996.
4. D. Li, X. Shi, P. Ward, M.Gupta, "Soft Inference Mechanism Based n Cloud Models", Logic Programming and Soft Computing, 163-188, Research Studies Press Ltd., 1998.
5. D. Li, J. Han, X. Shi, M. Chan, "Knowledge Representation and Discovery Based on Linguistic Atoms", the Journal of Knowledge Based System, forthcoming, 1997.
6. J. Han, Y. Fu, "Dynamic Generation and refinement of Concept Hierarchies for Knowledge Discovery in databases", Proc. of AAAI'94 workshop on Knowledge Discovery in Databases, p157-168, July 1994.

An Induction Algorithm Based on Fuzzy Logic Programming

Daisuke Shibata†, Nobuhiro Inuzuka†,
Shohei Kato‡, Tohgoroh Matsui† and Hidenori Itoh†

†Nagoya Institute of Technology, Gokiso-cho, Showa-ku, Nagoya 466-8555, Japan
{dshiba, inuzuka, tohgoroh, itoh}@ics.nitech.ac.jp
‡Toyota National College of Technology, 2-1 Eisei-cho, Toyota 471-8525, Japan
shohey@tctcc.cc.toyota-ct.ac.jp

Abstract. This paper gives a formulation of inductive learning based on fuzzy logic programming (FLP) and a top-down algorithm for it by extending an inductive logic programming (ILP) algorithm FOIL. The algorithm was implemented and evaluated by experiments. Linguistic hedges, which modifies truth, are shown to have effect to adjust classification properties. The algorithm deals with structural domain as other ILP algorithms do and also works well with numeric attributes.

1 Introduction

Inductive logic programming (ILP) gathers attention from KDD researchers. It has been successfully evidenced to work for classification problems with structural domains, such as problems in natural language processing and mutagenicity of chemical compounds[1]. In spite of the success, ILP has less applicability for domains with numeric data. Several methods to handle numbers are proposed. [2] classifies real numbers by tolerance ranges. [3] and [4] inherit a method from propositional decision tree learning. [5] is based on constraint logic programming.

The algorithm given here handles numeric data and other structural data based on fuzzy logic programming (FLP). Although a membership function fixes a treatment of numbers, combining linguistic hedges has effect to supply several membership functions, or several ways classifying examples.

2 Inductive Fuzzy Logic Programming

Several frameworks of FLP has been proposed (e.g. [6,7]). Here, we define a framework of *inductive fuzzy logic programming (IFLP)* mainly obeying [7].

Fuzzy sets extend the true/false membership to continuous membership in $[0,1]$. When μ_A and μ_B denote the membership functions of fuzzy sets A and B, $A \cup B$, $A \cap B$ and $\overline{A}$ are defined by $\mu_{A \cup B}(x) = \max(\mu_A(x), \mu_B(x))$, $\mu_{A \cap B}(x) = \min(\mu_A(x), \mu_B(x))$ and $\mu_{\overline{A}}(x) = 1 - \mu_A(x)$, respectively. We write an element a in A as a/μ_0 when $\mu(A) = \mu_0$. The difference $A - B$ is $A \cap \overline{B}$. $\mathrm{sp}(A)$, the support set of A, is $\{a \mid a/\mu \in A, \ \mu > 0\}$.

A *fuzzy logic program* P is a fuzzy set of horn clauses. The semantics of a program is given by a fuzzy Herbrand interpretation (FHI), a fuzzy subset of the Herbrand base. For an FHI I, $I(A)$, called the truth of A in I, denotes the membership of the ground atom A in I. Truth of a ground clause is given by

$$I(A \leftarrow B_1 \wedge \cdots \wedge B_n) = \min\{n + I(A) - I(B_1) - \cdots - I(B_n), 1\}^1. \quad (1)$$

Then, the truth of a clause c is defined by $I(c) = \min_{\theta \text{ s.t. } c\theta \text{ is ground}} I(c\theta)^2$.

An FHI I is a *fuzzy Herbrand model (FHM)* of a program P (denoted by $I \models P$), if $\forall c \in \mathrm{sp}(P), \mu_P(c) \leq I(c)$. The least[3] FHM (LFHM) of P, denoted by M_P, can be characterized by almost the same procedure in [8] for LP. For a ground fact A/μ and a program P, we can see that $I \models A/\mu$ for every FHM I of P iff $M_P \models A/\mu$, for LFHM M_P of P. $P_1 \models P_2$ if $I_{P_1} \models P_2$ for every FHM I_{P_1} of P_1, equally $M_{P_1} \models P_2$.

A problem of *inductive fuzzy logic programming (IFLP)* is to give a fuzzy logic program H, called a hypothesis, satisfying

$$(a) \forall e^+ \in E^+, \ B \cup H \models e^+/\mu^+, \text{ and } (b) \forall e^- \in E^-, \ B \cup H \not\models e^-/\mu^-, \quad (2)$$

when a fuzzy logic program B, called background knowledge, a pair (E^+, E^-) of sets of (crisp) ground facts of a target predicate R, and constants $\mu^+, \mu^- \in [0, 1]$ are provided. Facts in $E^+(E^-)$ are called positive (negative) examples of R.

3   A Top-down IFLP Algorithm

By raising up operations in FOIL[3] to a fuzzy version, we propose an algorithm (Fig. 1) for IFLP problems with restrictions: (1) B does not include R, (2) H includes only clauses whose heads have R, (3) H does not include clauses defined recursively, and (4) all membership of clauses in H are 1.

The algorithm greedily finds clauses that do not cover negative examples with the membership more than μ_- until every positive example is covered by a clause more than μ_+. To find such a clause the inner loop keeps adding a literal to the body of clause while the condition in Line 6 satisfies.

For a crisp clause c covered(c) defines a fuzzy set

$$\mathsf{covered}(c) = \{e/\mu \mid e \in E^+ \cup E^-, \mu = M_{B \cup \{c/1\}}(e)\}, \quad (3)$$

which updates remain in Line 11 to check the condition (2-a) in Line 4.

The condition for the inner loop is also expressed by covered(clause) in Line 6. The algorithm keeps to add literals to clause while it holds. By the conditions in Lines 4 and 6 theory satisfies the conditions (2-a) and (2-b) obviously.

To extend *gain*, heuristics to evaluate literals in FOIL, we define fuzzy sets corresponding to sets of assignments of variables in clause. An assignment is a sequence $(a_1, a_2, \cdots)$ of values assigned to variables $x_1, x_2, \cdots$ occurred in clause in

---

[1] This rule is based on Lukasiewicz's conjunction and Lukasiewicz's implication[7].

[2] θ is a ground substitution. Application of θ to c is denoted by $c\theta$.

[3] in the sense of fuzzy set inclusion, i.e. $A \leq B$ if $A \subseteq B$ or $\mu_A(x) \leq \mu_B(x)$ for all x.

```
1   Initialization
2      theory := a null program
3      remain := {e⁺/1 | e⁺ is a positive examples of R}
4   While μ_remain(e⁺) > 1 − μ₊ for some e⁺ ∈ sp(remain)
5      clause := 'R(x₁,···,xₙ₀) ← /1'
6      While μ_covered(clause)(e⁻) > μ⁻ for some negative example e⁻
7         Find an atom l by using gain
8         Add l to the body of clause
9      EndWhile
10     Add clause to theory
11     remain := remain − covered(clause)
12  EndWhile
```

Fig. 1. An outline of an IFLP algorithm

this order. For the initial body-less clause, fuzzy sets $\widehat{A}_0^+$ and $\widehat{A}_0^-$ of assignments for positive and negative examples are

$$\widehat{A}_0^+ = \{\langle a_1,\cdots,a_{n_0}\rangle/1 \mid R(a_1,\cdots,a_{n_0})\in E^+\} \,,\, \widehat{A}_0^- = \{\langle a_1,\cdots,a_{n_0}\rangle/1 \mid R(a_1,\cdots,a_{n_0})\in E^-\} \,.$$

For $\widehat{A}_i^+$, assignments after adding an atom[4] $l = P(x_{i_1},\cdots,x_{i_k})$ are:

$$\widehat{A}_{i+1}^+ = \left\{ \begin{matrix} \langle a_1,\cdots,a_{n+m}\rangle \\ /\mu * M_B(l\theta) \end{matrix} \left| \begin{matrix} \langle a_1,\cdots,a_n\rangle/\mu \ \in \ \widehat{A}_i^+ \text{ and } \theta \text{ is a ground substitution} \\ \{x_{i_1}/a_{i_1},\cdots,x_{i_k}/a_{i_k}\} \text{ which is consistent with } \langle a_1,\cdots,a_n\rangle \end{matrix} \right. \right\}, \quad (4)$$

where $x_1,\cdots,x_n$ are variables in clause before adding l and $x_{n+1},\cdots,x_{n+m}$ are new ones introduced by l. $\widehat{A}_{i+1}^-$ is similarly defined by replacing all $+$ by $-$.

For sets $\widehat{A}^+$ and $\widehat{A}^-$, the information for finding an assignment is in $\widehat{A}^+$ is

$$\widehat{info}(\widehat{A}^+,\widehat{A}^-) = -log_2(\widehat{T}^+/(\widehat{T}^+ + \widehat{T}^-)), \quad (5)$$

where

$$\widehat{T}^+ = \sum_{\langle a_1,\cdots,a_n\rangle \in sp(\widehat{A}^+)} \max\left\{0, \mu_{\widehat{A}^+}(\langle a_1,\cdots,a_n\rangle) - \mu_{\overline{remain}}(\langle a_1,\cdots,a_{n_0}\rangle)\right\},$$

$$\widehat{T}^- = \sum_{\langle a_1,\cdots,a_n\rangle \in sp(\widehat{A}^-)} \mu_{\widehat{A}^-}(\langle a_1,\cdots,a_n\rangle).$$

Intuitively $\widehat{T}^+$ is the total of membership of assignments for positive examples covered by clause but not by theory. For $\widehat{T}^-$, all covered assignments are considered. The first n_0 of $a_1,\cdots,a_n$ are the assignments for variables in the head.

Then $\widehat{gain}$, a fuzzy version of $gain$, expressing the information gained by l is

$$\widehat{gain}(l) = \hat{k} \times \left\{ \widehat{info}(\widehat{A}^+,\widehat{A}^-) - \widehat{info}(\widehat{A}'^+,\widehat{A}'^-) \right\}, \quad (6)$$

when $\widehat{A}^+$ and $\widehat{A}^-$ become $\widehat{A}'^+$ and $\widehat{A}'^-$ by adding l, where $\hat{k}$ is calculated by

$$\hat{k} = \sum_{\substack{\langle a_1,\cdots,a_n\rangle \in sp(\widehat{A}_+^+) \\ \langle a_1,\cdots,a_n,\cdots\rangle \in sp(\widehat{A}'^+)}} \max\left\{0, maxtruth_{\widehat{A}'^+}(\langle a_1,\cdots,a_n\rangle) - \mu_{\overline{remain}}(\langle a_1,\cdots,a_{n_0}\rangle)\right\},$$

where $maxtruth_{\widehat{A}'^+}(\langle a_1,\cdots,a_n\rangle) = \max_{a=\langle a_1,\cdots,a_n,\cdots\rangle} \mu_{\widehat{A}'^+}(a)$ and $\langle a_1,\cdots,a_n,\cdots\rangle$ represents an assignment also for new variables introduced in l.

[4] Our algorithm for IFLP allows only positive literals or atoms.

Positive examples

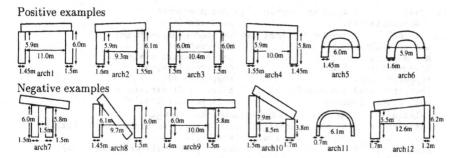

Fig. 2. Positive and negative examples for good-arch.

4 Implementation and an example problem

The algorithm is implemented as a system FCI. It combines top-down ways like SLD-resolution for background knowledge and and bottom-up fixpoint calculation for hypotheses in order to calculate LFHM.

FCI allows use of linguistic hedges very and more-or-less, only in hypotheses, but not in background knowledge. They modify the truth as $I(\text{very}\,l) = I(l)^2$ and $I(\text{more-or-less}\,l) = \sqrt{I(l)}$.

Fig. 2 illustrates an example IFLP problem to learn a predicate good-arch to specify well-constructed arches. For this problem FCI induced the following hypotheses with an input file (Fig. 3).

good-arch(A) ← has-archblk(A, B) ∧ well-proportioned(B).

good-arch(A) ← has-roofblk(A, B) ∧ has-supportblks(A, C, D) ∧ well-proportioned(D)

∧verybalanced-distance(C, D) ∧ support(D, B) ∧ support(C, B).

In the file, {very} in the balanced-distance line allows to combine the linguistic hedge very with this predicate. truth defines membership for the clauses including it. They are of the form 'truth(m)' for truth m, or 'truth($V, x_1, y_1, \cdots, x_k, y_k, n$)' for a membership function of a variable V, constituted by linking the points $(x_1, y_1), \cdots, (x_k, y_k)$ and by calculating the n-th power.

5 Experiments

We conducted three experiments with datasets *Animal* from examples of Progol[10] and *Iris* and *Labor Negotiations* from UCI machine learning databases[9].

Animal dataset successfully evidenced FCI to work as an ILP algorithm. Table 1 summarizes the results of two others. Results of FCI and FOIL-6.4 consists of ten complete five-fold cross-validations. The result of C4.5 was taken from [11]. For the induction with FCI we gave three different μ_+ and μ_-. For the test of unseen cases with FCI, we used the threshold 0.5 for classifying truth of cases. FCI classified both datasets with better accuracy than others.

Table 1 also shows complexity results. The numbers of atoms for FCI and FOIL correspond to nodes of C4.5. FCI induced smaller programs than others.

```
[target]        % type and mode of target predicate
   good-arch(arch).                      good-arch(+).
[prototype]     % predicates that can be used in hypotheses
   has-roofblk(arch,bl).                 has-roofblk(+,-).
   has-supportblks(arch,bl,bl).          has-supportblks(+,-,-).
   has-archblk(arch,bl).                 has-archblk(+,-).
   support(bl,bl).                       support(+,+).
   {very}balanced-distance(bl,bl).       balanced-distance(+,+).
   well-proportioned(bl).                well-proportioned(+).
[knowledge]     % definition of background knowledge
   has-archblk(arch5,a5). has-archblk(arch6,a6). has-archblk(arch11,a11).
   has-roofblk(arch1,r1). has-roofblk(arch2,r2). ...
   has-supportblks(arch1,bl1a,bl1b). has-supportblks(arch2,bl2a,bl2b). ...
   support(bl1a,r1). support(bl1b,r1). ...
   distance(bl1a,bl1b,11.0). distance(bl2a,bl2b,9.3). ...
   length(bl1a,5.9). length(bl1b,6.0). ...
   thickness(bl1a,1.45). thickness(bl1b,1.5). ...
   balanced-distance(BL1,BL2):-distance(BL1,BL2,D),truth(D,0,0,10,1,30,0,1).
   well-proportioned(BL):-medium-length(BL),medium-thickness(BL).
   medium-length(BL):-length(BL,H),truth(H,0,0,3,0,6,1,10,0,1).
   medium-thickness(BL):-thickness(BL,TH),truth(TH,0,0,0.8,0,1.5,1,2.5,0,2).
[positive]      % positive examples
   good-arch(arch1). good-arch(arch2). ... good-arch(arch6).
[negative]      % negative examples
   good-arch(arch7). good-arch(arch8). ... good-arch(arch12).
```

Fig. 3. An input file for learning good-arch.

6 Concluding remarks

We proposed a framework IFLP of inductive learning based on FLP and an algorithm to solve IFLP problems. The algorithm was implemented as a system FCI and it is evaluated with three datasets. The system provides a description framework of background knowledge in FLP. This can be expected to work for learning problems in complex domains.

The power of linguistic hedges is remarkably strong for induction. They are, however, important in representation complexity. When we describe a constraint for a value, we normally need two steps (literals) : the first literal picks a value in a variable and the other makes a restriction for it, e.g. length(Obj, Len)∧Len < 3. On the other hand we can describe this with only a literal, e.g. small-length(Obj), in fuzzy logic. The importance is that we need a variable to write a condition and have a variation of the condition, e.g. Len < 5, in normal logic, but we do not need any variable for this in FLP. We can use linguistic hedges like very small-length(Obj), and more-or-less small-length(Obj) for variations of the condition. Of course we can prepare a predicate for small-length(Obj) in normal logic, but the condition subjected by this predicate can not be modified.

Unnecessary for introduction of variables to deal with values keeps a hypothetic clause short and also keeps the number of variables small. Literals introducing variables for values are gain-less literal in many cases and are hard to be treated. Consequently this is a large advantage for ILP.

Table 1. Error rates (%) and complexities of hypotheses induced.

abbrev	error rates FCI (μ_+,μ_-)	C4.5	FOIL	complexities FCI clauses	atoms	C4.5 nodes	FOIL clauses	atoms
	(0.7, 0.3) 4.73±.15			2.20±.08	3.52±.16			
iris	(0.6, 0.4) 5.33±.0	4.87	6.13	1.46±.06	2.00±.01	8.50	3.6	6.96
	(0.5, 0.5) 5.33±.0	±.17	±.39	1.00±.00	1.00±.00	±.00	±.09	±.20
	(0.7, 0.3) 18.4±1.2			2.54±.05	6.04±.19			
labor	(0.6, 0.4) 16.0±1.0	19.1	20.2	2.48±.08	5.74±.19	7.00	3.02	5.46
	(0.5, 0.5) 14.7±1.0	±1.0	±1.3	2.42±.05	5.86±.14	±.30	±.06	±.11

Clauses, atoms and nodes means the numbers of clause, atoms and nodes induced.

Other attempts to extend ILP with fuzzy characteristic include [12] in which a system is developed and used for a control problems. It introduces linguistic variables which is an extension of normal variables and express vagueness. We doubt that linguistic variables spoil the advantage of FLP. Our system express vagueness by giving membership. We have already emphasized unnecessary of explicit use of variables in our system.

References

1. Bratko, I., Muggleton, S. and Karalič, A: "Application of Inductive Logic Programming", in *Machine Learning and Data Mining*, Wiley, pp. 131–143, (1998).
2. Muggleton, S., Page, D. and Srinivasan, A.: "An Initial Experiment into Stereo-chemistry-Based Drug Design Using Inductive Logic Programming", LNAI, No.1314, Springer, pp.25–40, (1996).
3. Quinlan, J.R.: "Learning logical definitions from relations", Machine Learning, **5**, pp.239–266 (1990).
4. De Raedt, L. and Blockeel, H.: "Using Logical Decision Trees for Clustering", LNAI, No.1297, Springer, pp.133–140, (1997).
5. Anthony, S. and Frish, A.M.: "Generating Numerical Literals During Refinement", LNAI, No.1297, Springer, pp.61–76, (1997).
6. Lee, R.C.T.: "Fuzzy Logic and the Resolution Principle", Journal of the Association for Computing Machinery, Vol.19, No.1, pp.109–119 (1972).
7. Yasui, H. and Mukaidono, M.: "A Consideration of Fuzzy Logic Programming Based on Lukasiewicz's Implication", Japanese Journal of Society for Fuzzy Theory and Systems, Vol.8, No.5, pp.863-878 (1996).
8. Lloyd, J.W.: "Foundation of Logic Programming, 2nd Ed.", Springer (1987).
9. Blake, C., Keogh, E. and Merz, C.J.: "UCI Repository of machine learning databases [http://www.ics.uci.edu/ mlearn/MLRepository.html]", Irvine, CA: U. California, Dept. of Information and Computer Science (1998).
10. Muggleton, S.: "Inverse entailment and progol", *New Generation Computing*, Vol.13, Nos.3+4, pp.245–286 (1995).
11. Quinlan, J.R.: "Improved Use of Continuous Attributes in C4.5", *Journal of Artificial Intelligence Research* Vol.4, pp.77–90 (1996).
12. Chen, G.: "Fuzzy Foil: A Fuzzy Logic Based Inductive Logic Programming Systems", Master Theses, School of Information Tech. and Eng., U. Ottawa (1996).

Rule Discovery in Databases with Missing Values Based on Rough Set Model

Shusaku Tsumoto

Department of Information Medicine, Medical Research Institute,
Tokyo Medical and Dental University
1-5-45 Yushima, Bunkyo-ku Tokyo 113 Japan
E-mail: tsumoto@computer.org

Abstract. *One of the most important problems on rule induction methods is that measures used for rule search will be influenced by missing values. In this paper, a new approach to missing values is introduced, called rough estimation of conditional probabilities. This technique uses three estimation strategies, ground mean, lower and upper methods. Attributes which have missing values will be estimated by these methods and will be checked by constraints for probabilistic rules. The proposed method was evaluated on medical databases, the experimental results of which show that induced rules correctly represented experts' knowledge.*

1 Introduction

Rule induction methods have been introduced in order to extract and discover useful patterns from databases[4, 5] by using heuristic search methods in which several kinds of measures or indices based on frequencies. One of the important problems is that these measures will be influenced by missing values, while this effect is lower than induction of decision trees[2]. In this paper, a new approach to missing values is introduced, called rough estimation of conditional probabilities. This technique uses three estimation strategies, ground mean, lower and upper estimation methods. The ground mean method assumes that a set of examples which have missing values reflects the frequency observed in a set of examples which do not have missing values. Lower estimation method assumes that all the cases having missing values will not belong to a target concept and upper estimation method assumes that all the cases with missing values will belong to a target concept. Attributes with missing values will be estimated by these methods and the estimated accuracy and coverage are used for induction of probabilistic rules.

The proposed method was evaluated on medical databases, the experimental results of which show that induced rules correctly represented experts' knowledge and several interesting patterns were discovered.

2 Rough Set Theory and Probabilistic Rules

In the following sections, we use the following notations of rough set theory[5]. First, a combination of attribute-value pairs, corresponding to a complex in AQ terminology[4], is denoted by a formula R. Secondly, a set of samples which satisfy R is denoted by $[x]_R$, corresponding to a star in AQ terminology. Finally, U, which stands for "Universe", denotes all training samples. Using these notations, we can define several characteristics of classification in the set-theoretic framework, such as classification accuracy and coverage. Classification accuracy and coverage(true positive rate) is defined as:

$$\alpha_R(D) = \frac{|[x]_R \cap D|}{|[x]_R|} (= P(D|R)), \text{ and}$$

$$\kappa_R(D) = \frac{|[x]_R \cap D|}{|D|} (= P(R|D)),$$

where $|A|$ denotes the cardinality of a set A, $\alpha_R(D)$ denotes a classification accuracy of R as to classification of D, and $\kappa_R(D)$ denotes a coverage, or a true positive rate of R to D, respectively.[1] It is notable that these two measures are equal to conditional probabilities: accuracy is a probability of D under the condition of R, coverage is one of R under the condition of D.

Probabilistic Rules

According to the definitions, probabilistic rules with high accuracy and coverage are defined as:

$$R \xrightarrow{\alpha,\kappa} d \text{ s.t. } \quad R = \vee_i R_i = \vee \wedge_j [a_j = v_k],$$
$$\alpha_{R_i}(D) \geq \delta_\alpha \text{ and } \kappa_{R_i}(D) \geq \delta_\kappa,$$

where δ_α and δ_κ denote given thresholds for accuracy and coverage, respectively.

3 Estimation of Accuracy and Coverage

3.1 Problems about Missing Values

According to the definitions of accuracy and coverage, it is easy to see that both measures are influenced by missing values, although coverage is more influenced than accuracy. Whereas accuracy is a function of $[x]_R$ and $[x]_R \cap D$, coverage is a function of $[x]_R \cap D$. If an attribute in R has a missing value, then $[x]_R \cap D$ will be smaller than the case when R does not have. In the case of accuracy, this effect will be smaller because $[x]_R \cap D$ is divided by $[x]_R$. However, coverage will suffer from this effect because the intersection is divided by D.

3.2 Missing Value Problems from the viewpoint of Sets

Let R and M denote an elementary attribute-value-pair $[a_i = v_j]$ and a set of examples missing the value of a_i. Also, let M_D denote a set of examples which belongs to a class D and which also belongs to M (i.e., $D \cap M$.) For simplicity,

---

[1] Those measures are equivalent to confidence and support defined by Agrawal[1].

we consider a_i to be a categorical variable, although the discussion below can be extended to continuous variables. Then, ordinary accuracy and coverage are defined as:

$$\alpha_R(D) = \frac{|[x]_R \cap (D - M_D)|}{|[x]_R|} = \frac{|[x]_R \cap (D \cap (U - M))|}{|[x]_R \cap (U - M) + [x]_R \cap M|}.$$

$$\kappa_R(D) = \frac{|[x]_R \cap (D - M_D)|}{|D|} = \frac{|[x]_R \cap (D \cap (U - M))|}{|D \cap (U - M) + D \cap M|}.$$

Estimation methods for accuracy and coverage can be viewed as interpretation of M_D by using some assumptions on D.

3.3 Ground Mean Measures

Simple assumption, based on statistical methods, is that M_D reflects the frequency observed in $U - M$. For example, if the frequency of D in $U - M$ is 50%, then the frequency of D in M can be assumed to be 50%. In this case, the formula above is modified into:

$$\alpha'_R(D) = \frac{|[x]_R \cap (D - M_D)|}{|[x]_R|} = \frac{|[x]_R \cap (D \cap (U - M))|}{|[x]_R|}.$$

$$\kappa'_R(D) = \frac{|[x]_R \cap (D - M_D)|}{|D - M|} = \frac{|[x]_R \cap (D \cap (U - M))|}{|D \cap (U - M)|}.$$

This estimation will be referred to as the ground coverage.

3.4 Lower Measures

Another assumption is that all the cases having missing values will not belong to a target concept, which is the most pessimistic strategy. Two measures modified by this assumption, called *lower accuracy* and *coverage* are defined as:

$$\alpha_R^L(D) = \frac{|[x]_R \cap D - M_D)|}{|[x]_R|} = \frac{|[x]_R \cap (D \cap (U - M))|}{|[x]_R|} = \alpha'_R(D).$$

$$\kappa_R^L(D) = \frac{|[x]_R \cap D - M_D)|}{|D|} = \frac{|[x]_R \cap (D \cap (U - M))|}{|D|}.$$

3.5 Upper Measures

The final assumption is that all the cases with missing values will belong to a target concept, which is the most optimistic strategy. The coverage modified by this assumption, called *upper coverage* is defined as:

$$\alpha_R^U(D) = \frac{|[x]_R \cap (D - M_D)| + |M_D|}{|[x]_R|} = \frac{|[x]_R \cap (D \cap (U - M))| + |M_D|}{|[x]_R|}.$$

$$\kappa_R^U(D) = \frac{|[x]_R \cap (D - M_D)| + |M_D|}{|D|} = \frac{|[x]_R \cap (D \cap (U - M))| + |M_D|}{|D|}.$$

These results are from univariate analysis, but it is notable that since the definition above is based on an assumption about relations between M and M_D, the extension of estimation into multivariate missing values is very easy: to apply the corresponding strategy to other attributes which have missing values.

4 Rule Induction

According to the definition of probabilistic rules and the characteristics of accuracy and coverage, an algorithm for induction of classification rules is defined as Figure 1.

procedure *Induction of Probabilistic Rules*;
  var
    i : *integer*; M, L_i : *List*;
  begin
    $L_1 := L_{er}$; /* L_{er}: List of Elementary Relations */
    $i := 1$; $M := \{\}$;
    for $i := 1$ **to** n **do**   /* n: Total number of attributes */
      begin
        while ($L_i \neq \{\}$) **do**
          begin
            Calculate and Estimate Accuracy and Coverage;
            Sort L_i with respect to the value of coverage;
            Select one pair $R = \wedge[a_i = v_j]$ from L_i, which have the largest value on coverage;
            $L_i := L_i - \{R\}$;
            if $(\kappa_R(D) \geq \delta_\kappa)$
              then do
                  if $(\alpha_R(D) \geq \delta_\alpha)$
                    then do $S_{ir} := S_{ir} + \{R\}$; /* Include R as Classification Rule */
                    $M := M + \{R\}$;
        end
        $L_{i+1} := $ (A list of the whole combination of the conjunction formulae in M);
      end
  end {*Induction of Probabilistic Rules* };

Fig. 1. An Algorithm for Probabilistic Rules

5 Experimental Results and Discussion

5.1 Performance of Rules Obtained

For experimental evaluation, a new system, called PRIMEROSE-REX3 (Probabilistic Rule Induction Method for Rules of Expert System ver 3.0), is developed, where the algorithms discussed in Section 4 are implemented. PRIMEROSE-REX3 was applied to the following medical domain: headache(RHINOS domain), whose training samples consist of 2175 samples, 10 classes and 41 attributes (5 attributes have missing values). The experiments were performed by the following three procedures. First, these samples were randomly splits into new training samples and new test samples. Second, using the new training samples, PRIMEROSE-REX3 induced rules with three estimation procedures. Third, the induced results were tested by the new test samples. These procedures were repeated for 100 times and average all the estimators over 100 trials.

Experimental results are shown in Table 1. There results suggest that this new approach performs as well as experts' rules.[2]

Table 1. Experimental Results (Accuracy: Averaged)

Method	Headache	CVD	Meningitis
Lower	78.1%	72.9%	81.7%
Groud Mean	89.3%	73.3%	75.5%
Upper	86.6%	75.4%	77.2%
Experts	91.7%	83.9%	89.2%

Acknowledgements

The author would like to thank reviewers for insightful comments.

References

1. Agrawal, R., Imielinski, T., and Swami, A., Mining association rules between sets of items in large databases, in *Proceedings of the 1993 International Conference on Management of Data (SIGMOD 93)*, pp. 207-216, 1993.
2. Breiman, L., Freidman, J., Olshen, R., and Stone, C., *Classification And Regression Trees*, Wadsworth International Group, Belmont, 1984.
3. Kryszkiewicz, M.and Rybinski, H. Incompleteness Aspects in Rough Set Approach. *Proceedings of Sixth International Workshop on Rough Sets, Data Mining and Granular Computing*, Duke, N.C., 1998.
4. Michalski, R. S., Mozetic, I., Hong, J., and Lavrac, N., The Multi-Purpose Incremental Learning System AQ15 and its Testing Application to Three Medical Domains, in *Proceedings of the fifth National Conference on Artificial Intelligence*, 1041-1045, AAAI Press, Menlo Park, 1986.
5. Pawlak, Z., *Rough Sets*. Kluwer Academic Publishers, Dordrecht, 1991.

---

[2] Recently, Kryszkiewicz and Rybinski propose a new approach to missing values by using an incomplete decision table in rough sets[3]. It will be our future work to compare our work with their approach.

Sustainability Knowledge Mining from Human Development Database

Xuefei WANG[1], Rusong WANG[2], Jue WANG[3]

[1]Department of Electronic Engineering & Information Science, University of Science and Technology of China, Hefei 230027, China, wangxf@eastmail.com
[2]Research Center for Eco-Environmental Sciences, Chinese Academy of Sciences, Beijing 100080, China, wangrs@sun.ihep.ac.cn
[3]Institute of Automation, Chinese Academy of Sciences, Beijing 100080, China, wangj@sunserver.ia.ac.cn

Abstract. This paper is to expose the concealed sustainability information to users from UNDP annual report of human development database. Different from the "understanding database by computer", the task is to tell user what meaning of the database is, and called "understanding database by human". The decernibility matrix (DM) in rough sets is used to get a qualitative description of the database. Domain knowledge is embedded in DM, and the set of its attribute reduction is employed to develop the sustainable development indicators (SDI) and its applications to the world's sustainability assessment.

1 Introduction

The data in the UNDP's reports of human development database (HDD) have been annually investigated, collected and analyzed by thousands of persons all over the world since 1990[1][2]. The database includes hundreds kinds of social, economic and natural data. It is used for comparison of the human sustainability of different countries through the human development indicators (HDI) induced from HDD.

However, the information abstracted from the HDD for construction of HDI is only concerned with life expectancy, education and GDP. While plenty of useful data about population, resource, environment and system context has not been used. As we may know, the sustainability of a country is connected with not only population quality and economic level, but also social and economic structure, resource and environmental state, and economic and ecological function. This paper is to excavate additional information from HDD for sustainability assessment, and to refine a new sustainability indicator after further reduction, which is more intuitive, easier to explain and more operable.

The task is to refine a set of reduction attributes from HDD, so those domain experts can understand the database. Different from the method based on machine learning, called "database understanding by computer" in this paper, it transforms the plain database language into human comprehendible language according to human demand, which is called "database understanding by human" [9]. It is one of the most significant tasks in KDD. The task can be divided into two related steps. The first is to find attributes reduction with domain knowledge. The second is to develop a sustainable development indicators (SDI) function and give its explanation according to the reduction attribute set [4].

Except the ordinary statistic methods for data analysis, we need some priori expertise to identify the key factors of different countries' SDI. According to the characteristics of sustainability study, decernibility matrix (DM)[8] in rough sets (RS)[6] is employed to get a qualitative description of the database [7]. This is firstly due to human development is a relative concept and only determined by development discrepancy among different countries, whereas DM method could just describe this discrepancy. Secondly, in order to evaluate differentiate countries' SDI, we need only to choose a representative set from piles of the discrepancy data. This is just in accordance with DM's reduction principles. This paper presents a modified DM with domain knowledge on SDI and uses it to solve the problems on data mining of HDD.

2 HDD Data and Pre-processing

HDD includes more than 300 attributes and 175 countries' data from 1990 to 1997, which can be classified as social, economic and environmental data, or structural and functional data. The first task is to reduce them into a succinct format so those users could easily understand and compare the human development state of different countries.

Because of the roughness, unevenness and incompleteness of the database, it is necessary to pre-process irregular and vacant data. The internal renewable water resource per capita of most countries' value, for example, is below 20, while in Iceland it is 624.5, 50 times higher than the average. It would wipe out the differentiation among most countries' water resource if we use the real value directly. A threshold set by experts to adjust the scaling for each of this irregular data in order to enlarge the differentiation.

The simplified attribute set is not enough for a better understanding of HDD. We need a new kind of language for refining of the sustainability indicator, which should be more understandable by common sense. An appropriate variation of the simplified attribute set has been carried out. For each of the nine attributes, we created a new SDI attribute table with different years' and countries' data, made statistical analyses and time series analyses for each table. Special attention was given to those irregular data and a revised attribute table, after irregular date filtering, error correction and vacancy substitution was obtained. Based on the revised attribute table, each year's revised HDD was reassembled. Finally, the annual SDI value of each country were calculated and ranked based on the revised HDD. The average SDI of every country in 90's and their tendency were got through statistical and regression analyses.

The limiting factors and promoting factors of each countries' human development could be identified according to whether the SDI value is less than 0.15 or larger than

0.85. Based on these factors, risk and opportunity assessment for each country can be carried out. The tendency of each country's SDI could be identified according to the results of regression analysis of each SDI during 1991-1997. When the slope is larger than +0.15%, the SDI is ascending, when the slope is less than -0.15%, the SDI is descending, when the slope is between +0.15% and -0.15%, the SDI is stabilizing.

3 A Modified DM Principle with Domain Knowledge

There are two steps in DM: finding DM and reduction. Domain knowledge is needed in both processes. As rough sets will result in a too fine division in the case of continuous variable and therefore affect the feasibility of reduction, a mapping of continuous variable set to discrete one is made firstly in the permission of domain knowledge. In addition, due to sustainability is a systematic concept concerned with efficiency, equity and vitality in all aspects of social, economic and ecological development, the final result of HDD reduction should cover all of these areas [3].

According to RS[7], the table can be defined as: S=<U, A, V, f>, where U is the universe. A is the set of attributes on U, V=$\cup$V$_a$, where V$_a$ is the value set of the attribute a, f is an information function. To embed domain knowledge to DM, its item t$_{ij}$ is defined as: t$_{ij}$ = {a: h$_a$ (i, V$_a$)$\neq$h$_a$ (j, V$_a$), $\forall$a, a$\in$A} where h$_a$ (.) is called human develop function, defined as a mapping: R$\rightarrow$\{0,1,2,3,4,5,6,7,8,9\}. A measurement of attribute significance is used in attribute reduction. The roughness based attribute significance is not a good index to discriminate different attributes in dealing with non-conflictive and non-overlapping database, such as HDD. We define the attribute significance γ(a) as the ratio of the attribute appearance frequency Frq(a)[5][6] to the total number K of items in DM. γ(a)=Frq(a)/K, α= ATTR(Max \{γ(x), $\forall$x, x$\in$A\}), where α is the most important attribute. It is selected as a reduction attribute.

Obviously, this frequency can be directly found from U/a or acquired from counting the number of attributes appeared in DM. The attribute with maximum value will be as a reduction attribute. However, it is not enough, the domain requires keeping balance in all of the social, economic and environmental aspects, an alternate strategy is developed as follows:

Let A=\{S, P, E\}. S, P, E represents social, economic and environmental attribute subsets respectively. When reduction, The most important attributes s, p, e for S, P, E respectively will be selected as reduction attributes. HDD attributes reduction algorithm can be described as:

1. M is a DM of HDD, and C$_0$ is the set of core in M. Let R=C$_0$.
2. Q=\{A$_{ij}$:A$_{ij}$$\cap$R$\neq$$\varnothing$, i$\neq$j, i,j=1,2,...,n\}, M=M-Q, B=A-R;
3. To all s$_k$, p$_k$, e$_k$$\in$B in S, P, E respectively, finding p(s$_k$), p(p$_k$), p(e$_k$) and let p(s$_q$)=max\{p(s$_k$)\}, p(p$_q$)=max\{p(p$_k$)\}, p(e$_q$)=max(p(e$_k$));
4. R$\Leftarrow$R$\cup$\{s$_q$, p$_q$, e$_q$\};
5. Repeat the above processes, until M=$\varnothing$.

Set R is a set of reduction attribute of above information table S (HDD). Because there was no core in HDD, the initiate R is empty.

4   Formulating SDI from HDD Data Mining

One objective of HDD data mining is to identify a more succinct attribute set SDI. The index system would not be rationale and applicable if the reduction process was going on independently year by year. To make efficient use of every year's HDD information, we firstly reduce the attributes year by year, then select those common attributes as the candidate index in SDI that appeared in most years' result. According to the DM principles, these attributes must be the most suitable attributes in HDD that represent the counties' characteristics, because the number of these discrepancy items in DM is biggest.

But only depending on the countries' discrepancy in certain attributes can not appropriately determine the SDI index system. Some key attribute may not be chosen in domain knowledge-independent process. The appearance frequency of GDP attribute, for example, is only 50% and can not meet our reduction rules, though it is a very important attribute in construction SDI. According to experts' knowledge, some most important attributes were labeled fade kernel and will have the priority to enter in the final reduction. In our work, Life expectancy at birth and GDP per capita were the fade kernels suggested by experts and entered into the reduction result.

5   Application of SDI and Database Understanding by Human

The visible results of the sustainability knowledge mining from HDD are:

1. Through statistical analyses, we got the SDI Tendency of different counties in the world. The average value of SDI all over the world is 0.45 from 1991-1997. The SDI value of strongest country is 5 times higher than that of weakest country.
2. The regional SDI rank from high to low is: North America, West Europe, East Europe, South America, Middle America, Pacific and Oceanic, East Asia, West Asia, South Asia and Africa. With the highest SDI is in North America (0.6274), and lowest is in Africa (0.3007), less than half of the North America.
3. The SDI values in 29% countries of the world are stronger. Three strongest countries are Canada, Sweden and Norway with SDI value of 0.740, 0.711 and 0.708 respectively.
4. The SDI values in 42% countries of the world are in middle level. In these countries, 52% are above the world's average, while 48% are below it.
5. The SDI values in 29% countries of the world are weaker. 82% of these countries locate at African. The three weakest countries are Afghanistan, Somali and Mali with SDI value of 0.117, 0.128 and 0.152 respectively. They are all less developing countries with poor resource and heavy social and natural disaster.
6. In the past eight years, the SDI value in 58.6% countries of the world are ascending, 16.1% countries are relatively stabilizing, and 25.3% are descending. While the SDI value of all former-USSR countries are declining.
7. The SDI values in 75% of the less sustainable developing countries (below average) are ascending, 12% are stabilizing and only 13% are descending.

8. The above result was calculated from UNDP's HDD (1991-1997), based on data before 1994. The conclusions only reflect the world's condition before 1994.

6 Conclusion

This paper exposes the concealed sustainability information to users from the UNDP annual report of Human Development Database via KDD. As users are mainly concerned with the dynamics and differences of various countries' development, and the experts' knowledge is critical in refining sustainability index, a modified decernibility matrix (DM) with domain knowledge is developed and used to acquire a succinct attribute reduction.

The results of data mining for HDD are as fellows:

1. Expansion of HDI into SDI, which includes more sustainability information from the same database of KDD.
2. Mining dynamic information from different year's HDD, and ascertaining the SDI change tendency.
3. Identification of limiting factors and promoting factors in each country.
4. Ascertained some data errors and uncertainties in some countries' data.
5. Comparison of the sustainability of different countries and regions in the world.
6. Providing a spatial and temporal map of world's sustainability based on the HDD data from 1991 to 1997.

References

1. United Nations Development Program (UNDP), *Human Development Report* 1990-1997, Oxford University Press, New York, 1990-1997.
2. R. Wang, *Country Case Study on Social Integration in China: Its Past, Present and Prospect*, Background paper for Human Development Report, New York, 1994.
3. R. Wang, Q. Zhao and Z. Ouyang, *Wealth, Health and Faith --- Sustainability Study in China*, China Environmental Science Press, Beijing, 1996.
4. B. Suzanne, Bedrich M. (eds.), *Proc. Scientific Workshop on Indicators of Sustainable Development*, SCOPE, 1995.
5. J. Wang, D. Miao, Y. Zhou, Introduction of Rough Sets and Application, *Pattern Recognition and Artificial Intelligence* 9(4), 337-344, 1996.
6. J. Wang., Rough Set Reduction and Data Enriching, *Hi-Tech Newsletter*, 7 (11), 1997.
7. Z. Pawlak, Rough Set, *Theoretical Aspects of Reasoning about Data*, Kluwer Academic Pub, 1991.
8. A. Skowrou, C. Rauszer, The Discernibility Matrices and Functions in Information Systems, In: R. Slowinski (ed.), *Intelligent Decision Support—Handbook of Applications and Advances of the Rough Sets Theory*, 1991.
9. U. Fayyad, G. Piatetsky-Shapiro, and R. Smyth, From Datamining to Knowledge Discovery: An Overview, *Advances in Knowledge Discovery and Data Mining*, AAAI Press/ The MIT Press, 1996.

Characterization of Default Knowledge in Ripple Down Rules Method

Takuya Wada, Tadashi Horiuchi, Hiroshi Motoda and Takashi Washio

Institute of Scientific and Industrial Research,
Osaka University
Mihogaoka, Ibaraki, Osaka 567-0047, JAPAN
{wada,horiuchi,motoda,washio}@ar.sanken.osaka-u.ac.jp

Abstract. "Ripple Down Rules (RDR)" Method is one of the promising approaches to directly acquire and encode knowledge from human experts. It requires data to be supplied incrementally to the knowledge-base being constructed and new piece of knowledge is added as an exception to the existing knowledge. Because of this patching principle, the knowledge acquired strongly depends on what is given as the default knowledge. Further, data are often noisy and we want the RDR noise resistant. This paper reports experimental results about the effect of the selection of default knowledge and the amount of noise in data on the performance of RDR using a simulated expert. The best default knowledge is characterized as the class knowledge that maximizes the minimum description length to encode rules and misclassified cases. This criterion also holds even when the data are noisy.

1 Introduction

Implicit assumption of the development of knowledge-based systems is that the knowledge of expertise is stable and it is worth investing much on knowledge acquisition from human experts. However, the rapid innovation of technology in recent years makes the existing knowledge out-of-date so soon and requests frequent update. In other words, we should now think that the knowledge of expertise is not static but dynamic in real world problems. In addition, the advancement of worldwide networks such as Internet has changed the computer usage practice drastically. It is now possible that many users have access to a single knowledge-based system through a network [9], and further, the needs arise that multiple experts supply the new knowledge continuously through the same network.

Under these circumstances, a new methodology to construct knowledge-based systems for continuous changes is in great demand. Knowledge is value-added data and includes such things as experience, insight and skill. "(Multiple Class) Ripple Down Rules ((MC)RDR)" [1,8][1] is one of the promising approaches to realize such knowledge-based systems and to directly acquire and encode knowledge from human experts. (MC)RDR is a performance system that does not

---

[1] In this paper, we limit our analysis to RDR.

require high level models of knowledge as a prerequisite to knowledge acquisition, and has been shown very effective in knowledge maintenance as well as acquisition of reflexive knowledge. Recent advancement shows that MCRDR can be applied to a configuration task [15]. Handling multiple sources by MCRDR has not yet been resolved.

RDR exclusively relies the knowledge to acquire on human experts and one of the advantages is that it does not require any data statistics as machine learning techniques do. Use of this knowledge, if available, may enhance RDR's performance. Default knowledge is one such knowledge that requires statistics to characterize itself. In this paper we try to identify what characterizes good default knowledge when the data available have noise, and show that selection of good default knowledge contributes to building a noise-resistant compact knowledge base.

2 Ripple Down Rules Revisited

Ripple Down Rules (RDR) is a knowledge acquisition technique that challenges the *KA bottleneck* problem by allowing rapid development of knowledge bases by human experts without the need of analysis or intervention of a knowledge engineer (KE). From long experience of knowledge-based systems development [1], it was made clear that human experts are not good at providing information on how they reach the conclusions, rather they can justify that their conclusions are correct [2,4]. Its basis is the maintenance and retrieval of cases. It tries to use the historical way in which the expert provides his/her expertise to justify the system's judgements [7]. The cases and associated justifications (rules) are added incrementally when a case is misclassified in the retrieval process. This is similar to "failure-driven memory" which was introduced by Schank [16]. Experts are very good at justifying their conclusions about a case in terms of differences from other cases [10]. When a case is incorrectly retrieved by an RDR system, the knowledge acquisition (maintenance) process requires the expert to identify how the case differs from the present case. This has a similar motivation to work on personal construct psychology where identifying differences is a key strategy [6]. The notion of on-going refinement by differentiating cases is a useful model of human episodic memory. Thus, RDR has reduced knowledge acquisition to a simple task of assigning a conclusion to a case and choosing the differentiating features between the current misclassified case and previously correctly classified case.

Each time a rule is added incrementally when a case is misclassified, the case that prompted the rule is stored (called the "cornerstone case"). Dependening on whether the last satisfied node is the same as the end node, the new rule and its cornerstone case are added at the end of YES or No branch of the end node. Knowledge is never removed or changed, simply modified by the addition of exception rules. The tree structure of the knowledge and the keeping of cornerstone cases ensure that the knowledge is used always in the same context when it was added.

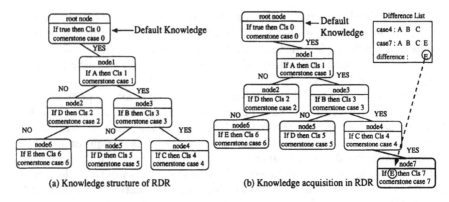

Fig. 1. Knowledge structure of Ripple Down Rules

The tree structure of RDR Knowledge Base is shown in Figure 1.(a). Each node in the binary tree is a rule with desired conclusions. Each node has a cornerstone case associated with it, the case that prompted the inclusion of the rule. The classification (conclusion) comes from the last rule that was satisfied by the current data. The knowledge acquisition process in RDR is illustrated in Figure 1.(b). To add a new rule into the tree structure, it is necessary to identify the location and the condition of the rule. When the expert wants to add a new rule, there must be a case that is misclassified by a rule which was applicable to the current case. The system asks the expert to select conditions from the difference list between these two cases: misclassfied case and the cornerstone case. Then the misclassified case is stored as the refinement case (new cornerstone case) with the new rule whose condition part distinguishes these cases.

3 Default Knowledge in Ripple Down Rules

The rule at the root node in RDR Knowledge Base, which is represented by a binary tree, is special. Its condition part is empty (it means that it is always satisfied) and its consequent part is a special conclusion called "default class". Here, the default class means a tacit conclusion for the current case when no other conclusion of the case is derived from the knowledge base.

Suppose that a conclusion A is set as the default class in RDR and a training case which has the conclusion A is supplied to the system. Even if no rule in the knowledge base fires for the case, the system correctly classifies the case using the default class A. Although the classification is correct, no explicit knowledge that characterizes the conclusion A is acquired. It is simply saying that since there is no conflicting knowledge, the conclusion must be A. Therefore, a different setting of the default class yields a different knowledge base with different performance (accuracy and size) even for the same problem domain.

The root node has only YES branch (Figure 1.(a) and (b)), while all the other nodes have both YES and NO branches. All rules below the root node are the exception rules of the root node. More generally, all rules below the YES branch of a certain node is the exception rules of that node. In the previous research it was common that the majority class in the domain was assumed as the default class [8]. Majority class in the domain means the class of the most frequent cases in the data set. This looks natural because we only need to acquire rules (knowledge) for the other (minority) classes as the exceptions of the default class and some subsequent refinement rules for the default class. The size of the knowledge base is expected to be compact. The majority class does not necessarily mean that it is easy to describe and characterize that class. The same is true for non-majority classes.

It is worth investigating how differently an RDR system behaves in terms of accuracy and size when a different setting of the default class is made. There are the same number of settings of the default class as are the number of classes in the domain. We discuss the reason why and how different performance of an RDR system is obtained with reference to the knowledge characterization of an expert. In this study a simulated expert is used as a replacement of human expert [5].

Another important aspect which the study of RDR so far has not addressed much is noise handling of data. It is always assumed that an human expert is available and judges the quality of data. In real world problems, noise is abound and we cannot get rid of it. We have to admit that human experts make mistakes.

It is known that one of the merits of RDR is that it can acquire the majority of knowledge at an early stage of knowledge acquisition compared by a standard empirical machine learning approach [11]. Intervention of human expert is the source of this high performance. How will these good properties be affected or not affected with the introduction of noise and the selection of default class is the main focus of the current study.

4 Experiments

4.1 Data Sets

We have selected 15 data sets (7 data sets with all nominal attributes, 7 data sets with all numerical attributes and 1 data set with mixed attributes, see Table 1) from University of California Irvine Data Repository [12].

4.2 Experimental method

We have conducted parametric studies using a simulated expert [5] for the above data sets. For each default class used, we have evaluated the classification accuracy and knowledge base size with different noise levels and different training data size. The results are compared with respect to these parameters and with other machine learning method.

Table 1. Summary of 15 data sets

Name	Case	Class	Attributes	Name	Case	Class	Attributes
Car	1728	4	Nom.* 6	Pendigits	10992	10	Num.** 16
Tic-Tac-Toe	958	2	Nom. 9	Iris	150	3	Num. 4
Nursery	12960	5	Nom. 8	Page-block	5473	5	Num. 10
Connect-4	16889	3	Nom. 42	Optdigits	5620	10	Num. 64
Mushroom	8124	2	Nom. 22	Yeast	1484	10	Num. 8
Monk	1711	2	Nom. 6	Waveform	5000	3	Num. 21
Splice	3190	3	Nom. 60	Image	2310	7	Num. 19
				Ann-thyroid	7200	3	Mixed 15/6***

*nominal attribute,**numerical attribute,***15 nominal/6 numerical

Simulated expert   As a simulated expert, we use C4.5 [13]. We run C4.5 with the default setting over an entire data for each noise level and for each data set. This is the maximum attainable performance that can be induced from the given data and we use this as the knowledge (expertise) of an expert. Here, we use the induction rule set which is generated from the decision tree derived by C4.5.

While a human expert checks the output of the RDR system, and when the conclusion is wrong, generates a new rule by selecting conditions from the difference list, a simulated expert similarly selects conditions from the difference list based on machine learning techniques. All conditions from the intersection of C4.5 rule conditions for the case and the difference list for the case are selected in this study. It should not be expected that the simulated expert will perform better than a real human expert. For noisy data, the simulated expert may misclassify some of the cases. Though a human expert may perform better than a simulated expert in this case, we adopt the classification by the simulated expert as the conclusion made by the expert. It is also noted that the simulated expert has small error rate even when the data is noise-free. This is because pruning is automatically made in C4.5.

Data preparation   Since RDR accepts data sequentially, the order of incoming data affects the performance. The whole data for each domain was reordered by random sampling and ten different data sets are generated to cancel out this ordering effect. For each data set of a fixed order, the first 75% of the data is taken as training data and the remaining 25% of the data as test data. To see the effect of how rapidly RDR can acquire the correct knowledge, the predicted error rate of test data is periodically evaluated at the points where 1%, 2%, 4%, 5%, 7%, 10%, 15%, 20%, 30% 45%, 50%, 60% and 75% (all) of the data are used.

Accuracy   The predicted error rate is used as a measure of accuracy. It is the average of the error rates of the remaining 25% data of the ten data sets, each with a different ordering.

Noise handling   Noise handling is different for nominal attributes and numerical attributes. For nominal attributes, the feature values were changed randomly to other alternatives with a specified fraction (noise level). For numerical attributes, noise of standard deviation equal to the specified fraction (noise level) of each attribute value range was randomly added assuming Gaussian distribution. The noise was added only to the attribute values and not to the class information with a fraction of 0%(without noise) 2%, 4%, 6%, 8%, 10%, 12%, 14%, 16%, 18% and 20%. The evaluation was performed at two points where 20% and 50% of the data were seen for both kinds of attributes. This is to see the effect of noise both at an earlier stage of knowledge acquisition where the system has not yet seen enough data and a later stage where the system's performance is approaching to an equilibrium.

Machine learning method   The RDR knowledge base is compared with the knowledge base built using a standard machine learning method C4.5 [13]. Since the learning by C4.5 is not incremental, we run C4.5 at the same data point where we check the accuracy of RDR knowledge base. This means that at an early stage, C4.5 must learn with small data set. The test data set is the same as the one used for RDR testing (the last 25% data).

Size of knowledge base   The size of the knowledge base is defined respectively to be the sum of the decision node in RDR binary tree and the number of induction rules in C4.5. This is because a decision node in RDR corresponds to an if-then rule.

4.3 Results

Due to the space limitation, we only show the detailed results of Car data set out of the 15 data sets, and the summary results of the whole data sets.

Table 2 summarizes the data characteristics and the main results. This data set has 6 nominal attributes and 4 classifications which are *unacc* (unacceptable), *acc* (acceptable), *good* and *vgood* (very good). The first three rows are 1) the number of cases for each class (a total of 1728 cases showing *unacc* is the majority class), 2) the number of induction rules for each class that was derived from the C4.5 decision tree, and 3) the error rate of the simulated expert C4.5 (as calculated by the command *C4.5rules*) for each class.

Figures 2 and 3 show the results of the machine learning method C4.5 and the four kinds of RDR each with different default class when trained by various data size in Car data set. The graphs respectively show the improving performance (error rate) and the increasing size of the knowledge base as the more data are available. From Figure 2, it is seen that the learning speed of RDRs are faster than that of C4.5. This is because RDR acquires the knowledge from the simulated expert who has enough knowledge of all cases in the problem domain. This is consistent with the results given in [11].

Among the four kinds of RDR, the learning speed of RDR(*acc*) whose default class is *acc* is fastest, and the size of the knowledge base of RDR(*acc*) is smallest as can be seen in the corresponding learning curves. It should be noted that RDR which has the majority class as the default class does not necessarily show the best performance. The majority class in this data set is *unacc*. This is also summarized in Table 2. Since it is not necessary to acquire the knowledge about the default class in RDR, RDR(*acc*) does not acquire the knowledge about the class *acc* but acquires the knowledge about the other classes, more precisely the knowledge to differentiate these classes from the class *acc*. The fifth, sixth and seventh rows show the ranking of the accuracy, the learning speed and the size of knowledge base for each default class. Note that the error rate of the simulated expert is lowest and the number of rules that are required to describe the class is largest for the class *acc*, which ranks the first. It means that RDR(*acc*) quickly acquires the knowledge about the other classes which happens to have higher error rates and do not require large description length. It does not acquire the explicit knowledge about the default class *acc* which has low error rate. The curves for the other defaults (*unacc, good, vgood*) are nearly the same, *vgood* being the worst. In Table 2 these are ranked either 2 or 3. The default class *vgood* has the highest error rate of the simulated expert and has the second smallest rule size to describe the class.

Table 2. Car Evaluation Database

Class	*unacc*	*acc*	*good*	*vgood*
Number of cases	1210	384	69	65
Number of induction rules	11	53	15	15
Error rate of simulated expert (%)	2.7	1.3	7.7	15.4
Minimum description length (bits)	261.4	638.2	271.3	232.1
Accuracy(ranking *)	2	1	3	3
Acquisition speed (ranking*)	3	1	2	3
Size of knowledge base (ranking*)	2	1	2	2

* Smaller, the better. Both the accuracy and the size are evaluated at 75% of the total data seen. The learning speed is evaluated at 20% of the total data seen. When the difference is small, the rank is rated the same.

From this observation, we can conjecture that the more induction rules are required to describe the class and the lower the error rate of the simulated expert for the default class is, the faster the learning speed of RDR is and the smaller the size of RDR knowledge base is. By having a class that requires more induction rules to describe itself as the default we can avoid adding these many rules later in the knowledge acquisition process. Likewise by having a class for which the predicted error is smaller, the refinement rule for the default class can be more error free and the probability of recursive exception taking place would be less.

In order to quantify the above observation, we introduce a new index to consider both the number of rules and the error (misclassification) rate of the

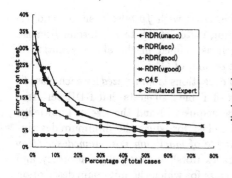

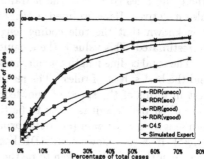

Fig. 2. Error rate for various sized training sets in Car data set. RDR(*unacc*), for example, means RDR whose default class is *unacc*.

Fig. 3. Size of the knowledge base for various sized training sets in Car data set

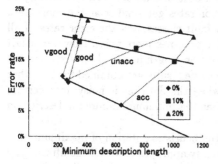

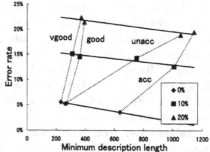

Fig. 4. Error rates vs. minimum description lengths of the four RDRs for three different noise levels: 0%,10% and 20% at the point where the first 20% of data are seen in Car data set.

Fig. 5. Error rates vs. minimum description lengths of the four RDRs for three different noise levels: 0%,10% and 20% at the point where the first 50% of data are seen in Car data set.

simulated expert for each default class, namely *"minimum description length"* as shown in the fourth row in Tables 2.

This index is calculated as the sum of the coding costs for induction rules and misclassified cases. The number of bits required to encode the induction rules is

$$\sum_{i=1}^{N} \{ \sum_{j=1}^{M_i} (-\log_2 p_{ij}) - \log_2(M_i!) \} - \log_2(N!)$$

where N is the number of rules, M_i is the number of conditions in the rule R_i, p_{ij} is the probability for which the j-th condition is satisfied in the rule R_i for all training cases. The number of bits required to encode the misclassified cases is

$$\log_2 \left(\binom{r}{fp} \right) + \log_2 \left(\binom{n-r}{fn} \right)$$

where the rules cover r of the n training cases with fp false positives and fn false negatives. Here, we used a weighting factor of 0.5 to the former because it is known that the rule coding length as defined in the above equation is overestimated. This value is the default setting of C4.5.

The total coding length for rules and exceptions is *minimized* for each class to find the best subset of rules[2]. The result of Table 2 suggests that RDR performs best in terms of the speed of knowledge acquisition and the size of knowledge base when the default is taken to be the class for which the minimum description length is *maximum* (*heuristic principle of maximum minimum description length*). It is also shown that RDR behaves worst in terms of its accuracy and size when the default is taken to be the class for which the minimum description length is minimum. This relation holds for noisy data as discussed below.

Figures 4 and 5 show the relation between the accuracies and the minimum description lengths of the four RDRs for three different noise levels: 0%,10% and 20% at the point where the first 20% and 50% of data are seen respectively in Car data set. It is observed that the error rates get smaller as the more data are seen for all noise levels and for all default classes, and the error rates of all four RDRs become higher as the data set becomes more noisy. However, RDR which has the maximum minimum description length has the best accuracy out of four RDRs on for all noise levels. The same results are obtained for the other data sets. We can conclude thet even when the data set is noisy, it is certain that RDR with the default class which has the maximum minimum description length has good accuracy.

Tables 3 and 4 summarize whether the heuristic criterion of maximum minimum description length (MMDL) is actually appropriate for all the fifteen data sets. From Table 3, it is seen that MMDL class is the best for 14 (including the data sets with Yes*) out of 15 data sets with respect to accuracy, for 13 out of 15 data sets with respect to acquisition speed and for 10 out of 15 data sets with respect to knowledge base size. If we relax the MMDL to be within the top 30%, we see that 12 out of 15 data sets are explained for all aspects (accuracy, speed, size) by this measure. In Table 4, the effect of noise on accuracy is shown for two situations where 20% and 50% of the data are seen. The level of noise added is 10% for both. Similar results are obtained for speed and KB size. We can conclude that the MMDL principle hold ever for noisy data.

We have conducted additional evaluation where we used the description length as calculated by C4.5 when only the first 10% of the data is seen. The result indicates that the relative values of the description lengh can well be estimated by using a small fraction of data. This means that we only need wait until a small amount of data is accumulated before initiating knowledge acquisition using the RDR method.

As RDR is a methodology to acquire the useful knowledge from vague and disordered knowledge of a human expert by forcing him/her to place in a specific context, it may not be the case that the expert knows clearly the error rate for each class in advance. However, there must be some difference in certainty or

---

[2] This is what C4.5 does in inducing rules from the decision tree.

Table 3. Summary (without noise)

Name	Accuracy		Speed		KB size		summary
	MMDL	≤30%	MMDL	≤30%	MMDL	≤30%	
Car	Yes		Yes		Yes		Yes
Tic-Tac-Toe	Yes		Yes		Yes		Yes
Nursery	Yes*		Yes		Yes		Yes
Connect-4	Yes		Yes		Yes		Yes
Mushroom	Yes*		Yes		Yes		Yes
Monk	Yes		Yes*		Yes		Yes
Splice	Yes*		No	No	No	No	No
Ann-thyroid	Yes		Yes		Yes		Yes
Pendigits	Yes*		Yes*		No	Yes	Yes
Iris	Yes*		Yes*		No	No	No
Page-block	Yes		Yes		Yes		Yes
Optdigits	Yes		Yes*		Yes		Yes
Yeast	Yes		Yes		Yes		Yes
Waveform	No	No	No	No	No	No	No
Image	Yes		Yes		No	Yes	Yes
	14/15		13/15		10/15	12/15	12/15

* means that there is very little difference between the best default class and the MMDL default class, and ≤ 30% means to check whether the MMDL class ranks within the top 30%.

confidence for the knowledge which the expert has for each class, and the result in this section shows that it is better to use the most informative (confident) class for the expert as the default class in RDR. This dose not necessarily mean to use the majority class. The proposed measure is based on the qualitative analysis of the RDR tree, and is certainly heuristic, but it appears that this can be a useful measure to characterize the goodness of default class.

5 Conclusion

This paper demonstrated experimental results about the effect of the selection of default knowledge and the amount of noise in data on the performance of RDR which is a knowledge acquisition technique without the need of analysis or intervention of a knowledge engineer. Because of the patching principle in RDR, the knowledge acquired strongly depends on what is given as the default knowledge.

It is clearly shown that RDR shows good performance in terms of its accuracy and size when the default is taken to be the class for which the minimum description length of induction rules and error cases is maximum (*heuristic principle of maximum minimum description length*). This is the situation where the default class in RDR is taken to be the class for which the number of rules

Table 4. Summary (with 10%noise)

Name	Accuracy(training20%)		Accuracy(training50%)		summary
	MMDL	≤30%	MMDL	≤30%	
Car	Yes		Yes		Yes
Tic-Tac-Toe	Yes		Yes		Yes
Nursery	Yes		Yes		Yes
Connect-4	Yes		Yes		Yes
Mushroom	Yes		Yes*		Yes
Monk	Yes*		Yes*		Yes
Splice	Yes		Yes		Yes
Ann-thyroid	Yes		Yes		Yes
Pendigits	No	Yes	No	No	No
Iris	Yes*		Yes*		Yes
Page-block	Yes		Yes		Yes
Optdigits	No	Yes	Yes*		Yes
Yeast	Yes		Yes		Yes
Waveform	No	No	No	No	No
Image	No	No	No	No	No
	11/15	13/15	12/15		12/15

* means that there is very little difference between the best default class and the MMDL default class, and ≤ 30% means to check whether the MMDL class ranks within the top 30%.

to describe is largest and the error rate of the simulated expert is lowest. This property also holds even when the data are noisy.

The experiments also show that the good properties of RDR that it can acquire the majority of knowledge at an early stage of knowledge acquisition faster than a standard empirical machine learning approach also holds for noisy data.

The above characteristics of RDR will be favorable to build a knowledge-bases system which assumes a network environment, where multiple users and experts interact with each other through the computer network. Acquiring or updating knowledge from multiple experts in a network environment is a new challenge.

Acknowledgement

Authors benefited much through the discussions with Dr. B. H. Kang in Hoseo University (Korea).

References

1. P. Compton, K. Horn, J. R. Quinlan and L. Lazarus. Maintaining an Expert System. In *Application of Expert Systems*, ed. J. R. Quinlan, pp. 366–385, Addison Wesley, 1989.

2. P. Compton and R. Jansen. A Philosophical Basis for Knowledge Acquisition. *Knowledge Acquisition*, Vol. 2, pp. 241–257, 1990.

3. P. Compton, G. Edwards, B. H. Kang, et al. Ripple Down Rules: Possibilities and Limitations. *Proc. of the 5th Knowledge Acquisition for Knowledge-Based Systems Workshop*, 1991.

4. P. Compton, G. Edwards, et al. Ripple Down Rules: Turning Knowledge Acquisition into Knowledge Maintenance. *Artificial Intelligence in Medicine*, Vol. 4, pp. 47–59, 1992.

5. P. Compton, P. Preston, B. H. Kang. The Use of Simulated Experts in Evaluating Knowledge Acquisition. *Proc. of the 9th Knowledge Acquisition for Knowledge-Based Systems Workshop*, 1995.

6. B. Gaines and M. Shaw. Cognitive and Logical Foundations of Knowledge Acquisition. *Proc. of the 5th Knowledge Acquisition for Knowledge-Based Systems Workshop*, 1990.

7. B. H. Kang and P. Compton. Knowledge Acquisition in Context: Multiple Classification Problem. *Proc. of PRICAI'92*, Vol. 2, pp. 847–853, 1992.

8. B. H. Kang. Validating Knowledge Acquisition: Multiple Classification Ripple Down Rules. *Ph.D Thesis, University of New South Wales*, 1996.

9. B. H. Kang, K. Yosida, H. Motoda, P. Compton Help Desk System with Intelligent Interface. *Applied Artificial Intelligence, Vol. 11, pp. 611–631*, 1997.

10. J. L. Kolodner. A Process Model of Case-Based Reasoning in Problem Solving. *Proc. of IJCAI'85*, Vol. 1, pp. 284–290, 1985.

11. Y. Mansuri, J. G. Kim, P. Compton, C. Sammut. An Evaluation of Ripple Down Rules. *Proc. of AKAW'91*, 1991.

12. P. M. Murphy and D. W. Aha. UCI Repository of Machine Learning Databases. ftp://ftp.ics.uci.edu/pub/machine-learning-databases/, 1994.

13. J. R. Quinlan. *C4.5: Programs for Machine Learning*, Morgan Kaufmann, 1993.

14. J. R. Quinlan. Induction of decision trees. *Machine Learning*, Vol. 1, pp. 81–106, 1986.

15. Z. Ramadan, P. Compton, P. Preston, T. Le-Gia, V. Chellen, M. Mulholland, D. B. Hibbert, P. R. Haddad, and B. Kang. From Multiple Classification RDR to Configuration RDR. *Proc. of the 10th Knowledge Acquition for Knowledge-Based System Workshop*, 1997.

16. R. C. Schank. *Dynamic Memory: A Theory of Reminding and Learning in Computers and People*, Cambridge University Press, 1982

Improving the Performance of Boosting for Naive Bayesian Classification

Kai Ming Ting and Zijian Zheng

School of Computing and Mathematics
Deakin University,
Australia.
{kmting,zijian}@deakin.edu.au

Abstract. This paper investigates boosting naive Bayesian classification. It first shows that boosting cannot improve the accuracy of the naive Bayesian classifier on average in a set of natural domains. By analyzing the reasons of boosting's failures, we propose to introduce tree structures into naive Bayesian classification to improve the performance of boosting when working with naive Bayesian classification. The experimental results show that although introducing tree structures into naive Bayesian classification increases the average error of naive Bayesian classification for individual models, boosting naive Bayesian classifiers with tree structures can achieve significantly lower average error than the naive Bayesian classifier, providing a method of successfully applying the boosting technique to naive Bayesian classification.

1 Introduction

For many KDD applications, the prediction (classification) accuracy is the primary concern. Recent studies on the boosting technique have brought a great success for increasing prediction accuracy of classifier learning algorithms [1, 9, 15, 16]. Boosting induces multiple classifiers in sequential trials by adaptively changing the distribution of the training set based on the performance of previously created classifiers. At the end of each trial, instance weights are adjusted to reflect the importance of each training example for the next induction trial. The objective of the adjustment is to increase the weights of misclassified training examples. Change of instance weights causes the learner to concentrate on different training examples in different trials, thus resulting in different classifiers. Finally, the individual classifiers are combined through voting to form a composite classifier. Bauer and Kohavi [1] report that boosting for decision tree learning achieves a relative error reduction of 27% in a set of domains. Although boosting occasionally increases the error of decision tree learning in some domains, all previous studies showed that it can significantly reduce the error of decision tree learning in the majority of domains [1, 3, 15].

On the other hand, Naive Bayesian classifier learning [7] is simple and fast. It has been shown that in many domains the prediction accuracy of the naive Bayesian classifier compares surprisingly well with that of other more complex learning algorithms such as decision tree learning, rule learning, and instance-based learning algorithms [5, 6, 12]. In addition, naive Bayesian classifier learning is robust to noise and irrelevant attributes. Therefore, it is interesting to explore how boosting affects Naive Bayesian classification.

In sharp contrast to boosting decision trees, our experiments show that boosting gets only 1% of relative error reduction over the naive Bayesian classifier on average in a set of domains from UCI [2]. The average error rate of the boosted naive Bayesian classifier over these domains is even higher than that of the naive Bayesian classifier. In quite a number of domains, boosting cannot increase, or even decreases, the accuracy of naive Bayesian classifier learning. We are interested in investigating the reason(s) why boosting performs poorly with naive Bayesian classifiers and the ways to improve its performance.

One key difference between naive Bayesian classifiers and decision trees, with respect to boosting, is the stability of the classifiers—naive Bayesian classifier learning is relatively stable with respect to small changes to training data, but decision tree learning is not. Combining these two techniques will result in a learning method that produces more unstable classifiers than naive Bayesian classifiers. We expect it will improve the performance of boosting for naive Bayesian classification.

The hybrid approach generates naive Bayesian trees. Kohavi [10] proposes such a hybrid approach, called NBTREE. The purpose is to improve the accuracy of the naive Bayesian classifier by alleviating the attribute inter-dependence problem of naive Bayesian classification.

Here, we want to explore whether and how the introduction of tree structures into naive Bayesian classification affects the performance of boosting for naive Bayesian classification. For this purpose, we use levelled naive Bayesian trees, which generates tree structures to a pre-defined maximum depth. The following section briefly presents the boosting technique including the details in our implementation. Section 3 describes the naive Bayesian classifier learning algorithm and the levelled naive Bayesian tree learning algorithm that are used as the base learners for boosting in this study. Section 4 empirically studies the effects of introducing tree structures into naive Bayesian classification on the performance of boosting for naive Bayesian classification. We conclude in the final section. The complete version of this paper can be found in Ting and Zheng [17].

2 Boosting

The basic idea of boosting has been briefly described at the very beginning of this paper. In our implementation, boosting uses reweighting rather than resampling [9, 15]. The boosting procedure is as follows. The weight adjustment formulas in step (iii) below are from a new version of boosting [16].

Boosting procedure: Given a base learner and a training set $\mathcal{T}$ containing N examples, $w_k(n)$ denotes the weight of the nth example at the kth trial, where $w_1(n) = 1/N$ for every n. At each trial $k = 1, \ldots, K$, the following three steps are carried out.

(i) A model M_k is constructed using the base learner from the training set under the weight distribution w_k.

(ii) $\mathcal{T}$ is classified using the model M_k. Let $\delta(n) = 1$ if the nth example in $\mathcal{T}$ is classified incorrectly; $\delta(n) = 0$ otherwise. The error rate of this model, ϵ_k, is defined as

$$\epsilon_k = \sum_n w_k(n)\delta(n). \tag{1}$$

If $\epsilon_k \geq 0.5$ or $\epsilon_k = 0$, then $w_k(n)$ is re-initialized using bootstrap sampling and continue the boosting process from step (i).

(iii) The weight vector $w_{(k+1)}$ for the next trial is created from w_k as follows:

$$w_{(k+1)}(n) = w_k(n)\frac{exp(-\alpha_k(-1)^{\delta(n)})}{z_k}, \tag{2}$$

where the normalizing term z_k and α_k are defined as

$$z_k = 2\sqrt{(1-\epsilon_k)\epsilon_k}, \qquad \alpha_k = \frac{ln((1-\epsilon_k)/\epsilon_k)}{2}. \tag{3}$$

After K trials, the models $M_1, \ldots, M_K$ are combined to form a single composite classifier. Given an example, the final classification of the composite classifier relies on the votes of all the individual models. The vote of the model M_k is worth α_k units. The voting scheme is simply summing up the vote for the predicted class of every individual model.

3 Naive Bayesian Classifier Learning and Levelled Naive Bayesian Tree Learning

In this section, we describe two base learning algorithms. One is the naive Bayesian classifier [7, 11, 12]. We will show that boosting does not significantly improve the performance of the naive Bayesian classifier. The other base learning algorithm is for generating levelled naive Bayesian trees. The objective of this algorithm is to investigate whether and how we can make boosting perform better for naive Bayesian classification.

3.1 Naive Bayesian Classifiers

The Bayesian approach to classification estimates the (posterior) probability that an instance belongs to a class, given the observed attribute values for the instance. When making a categorical rather than probabilistic classification, the class with the highest estimated posterior probability is selected.

The posterior probability, $P(C_j|V)$, of an instance being class C_j, given the observed attribute values $V = < v_1, v_2, \ldots, v_n >$, can be computed using the a priori probability of an instance being class C_j, $P(C_j)$; the probability of an instance of class C_j having the observed attribute values, $P(V|C_j)$; and the prior probability of observing the attribute values, $P(V)$. In the naive Bayesian approach, the likelihoods of the observed attribute values are assumed to be mutually independent for each class. With this attribute independence assumption, the probability $P(C_j|V)$ can be re-expressed as:

$$P(C_j|V) = \frac{P(C_j)}{P(V)} \prod_{i=1}^{n} P(v_i|C_j) \propto P(C_j) \prod_{i=1}^{n} P(v_i|C_j). \tag{4}$$

Note that since $P(V)$ is the same for all classes, its value does not affect the final classification, thus can be ignored. In our implementation of the naive Bayesian classifier, probabilities are estimated using frequency counts with an m-estimate correction [4]. Continuous attributes are pre-processed using an entropy based discretization method [8].

3.2 Levelled Naive Bayesian Trees

Our motivation for designing the levelled naive Bayesian tree learning algorithm is to introduce instability to naive Bayesian classification. We use the maximum depth of a tree, as a parameter of the algorithm, to control the level of tree structures incorporated into naive Bayesian classification.

The Levelled Naive Bayesian Tree learning algorithm, called LNBT, has the same tree growing procedure as in a Top-Down Decision Tree induction algorithm. Like C4.5 [14], LNBT also uses the information gain ratio criterion to select the best test at each decision node during the growth of a tree. The differences between LNBT and C4.5 are: (i) LNBT grows a tree up to a pre-defined maximum depth (d); (ii) LNBT does not perform pruning; (iii) LNBT generates one local naive Bayesian classifier at each leaf using all training examples at that leaf and all attributes that do not appear on the path from the root to the leaf; and (iv) LNBT stops splitting a node, if it contains less than 30 training examples, to ensure reasonably accurate estimates for local naive Bayesian classifiers. When the maximum tree depth d is set at 0, LNBT is identical to a naive Bayesian classifier generator. Therefore, the naive Bayesian classifier is referred to as LNBT(0) later on in this paper.

4 Experiments

In this section, we first empirically show the failure of boosting the naive Bayesian classifier. Then, we incorporate tree structures into naive Bayesian classification, and show that this will improve the performance of boosting for naive Bayesian classification. We refer BLNBT($d \geq 1$) to boosted levelled naive Bayesian classifier, and BLNBT($d=0$) to boosted naive Bayesian classifier. The parameter K controlling the number of models generated in boosting is set at 100 for all experiments.

Table 1. Description of the domains used in the experiments.

Dataset	Training Data size	Testing Method/Size	# Classes	# Attr		
Waveform	300	10 runs/5000	3			40C
Led24	500	10 runs/5000	10	24B		
Euthyroid	3163	2 x 5cv	2	18B		7C
Hypothyroid	3163	2 x 5cv	2	18B		7C
Splice	3177	2 x 5cv	3		60N	
Abalone	4177	2 x 5cv	3		1N	7C
Nettalk(stress)	5438	2 x 5cv	5		7N	
Nursery	15960	2 x 5cv	5			8C
Coding	20000	2 x 5cv	2		15N	
Adult	32561	1 run/16281	2	1B	7N	6C
DNA	2000	1 run/1186	3		60N	
Satellite	4435	1 run/2000	6			36C
Letter	15000	1 run/5000	26			16C
Shuttle	43500	1 run/14500	7			9C

N: nominal; B: binary; C: Continuous

It is interesting to see the performance improvement that can be gained by two orders of magnitude increase in computation.

Fourteen domains of moderate to large data sizes from the UCI machine learning repository [2] are used in the experiments. These data sizes provide a more reliable assessment of the algorithms than small ones. Table 1 gives a description of these domains and the testing methods and data sizes used in the experiments. DNA, Satellite, Letters and Shuttle are four datasets used in the Statlog project [13].

The main concern of this study is the accuracy performance of learning algorithms. Therefore, we report the *error rate* of each algorithm under consideration on the test set in each domain. To compare two algorithms, A vs B for example, we provide the error rate ratio of A over B: ϵ_A/ϵ_B in each domain, where ϵ_A is the test error rate of A and ϵ_B is the test error rate of B. If multiple runs are conducted in a domain, the reported value is an average value over the runs. To compare two algorithms, A vs B, across the 14 domains, the w/t/l record is reported, which is the numbers of wins, ties, and losses between the error rates of A vs B in the 14 domains. A one-tailed pairwise sign-test is applied on this w/t/l record to examine whether A performs better than B significantly more often than the reverse at a level better than 0.05. The significance level p will be provided for the sign-test on each w/t/l record.

4.1 Boosting Naive Bayesian Classifiers

Table 2 shows the error rates of the naive Bayesian classifier and the boosted naive Bayesian classifier as well as their error ratios. From this table, we can see that although boosting can improve the accuracy of the naive Bayesian classifier in 9 out of the 14 domains, it does decrease the accuracy of the naive

Table 2. Error rates (%) of the naive Bayesian classifier and the boosted naive Bayesian classifier as well as their error ratios.

Dataset	Error rate (%)		Error ratio
	LNBT(0)	BLNBT(0)	BLNBT(0)/LNBT(0)
Wave	20.20	26.72	1.32
Led24	27.48	28.39	1.03
Euthyroid	4.14	3.21	.77
Hypothyroid	1.49	1.31	.88
Abalone	41.19	40.73	.99
Nettalk(s)	16.03	15.04	.94
Splice	4.63	7.29	1.57
Coding	28.75	28.72	1.00
Nursery	9.80	7.73	.79
Adult	16.49	15.03	.91
DNA	5.48	7.08	1.29
Satellite	17.70	16.60	.94
Letter	25.26	24.12	.95
Shuttle	0.18	0.09	.50
mean	15.63	15.86	.99
w/t/l			9/1/4
p			.1334

Bayesian classifier in 4 other domains. A one-tailed pairwise sign-test fails to show that boosting reduces the error of the naive bayesian classifier significantly more often than the reverse across the 14 domains at a level of 0.05. When boosting decreases the error of the naive Bayesian classifier, the error reduction is often small: Only in one domain does boosting reduce the error of the naive Bayesian classifier by more than 25%. The mean relative error reduction of boosting over the naive Bayesian classifier in the 14 domains is only 1%, indicating very marginal improvement due to boosting. In terms of the mean error rate, boosted naive Bayesian classifier is worse than the naive Bayesian classifier by 0.23 percentage points across the 14 domains, indicating the poor average performance of boosting.

In short, boosting does not work well with naive Bayesian classification. This is in sharp contrast to the success of boosting decision trees. There are two possible explanations for this observation. First, the naive Bayesian classifier could be optimal in some domains. In such a case, we cannot expect boosting to further improve its accuracy. For example, all the attributes are independent for each class in the Led24 domain. Thus, the naive Bayesian classifier is optimal in this domain. Consequently, a relative increase of 3% error due to boosting in the Led24 domain is not surprising. The other explanation is that the naive Bayesian classifier is quite stable with respect to small changes to training data, since these changes will not result in big changes to the estimated probabilities. Therefore,

Table 3. Error rates (%) of LNBT(d) and error ratios of BLNBT(d) vs LNBT(d) for $d = 0, 1, 3, 5,$ and 10.

Dataset	BLNBT(d) vs LNBT(d)									
	$d = 0$		$d = 1$		$d = 3$		$d = 5$		$d = 10$	
	err(%)	ratio	err(%)	ratio	err(%)	ratio	err(%)	ratio	err(%)	ratio
Wave	20.20	1.32	24.78	.95	29.34	.73	29.34	.73	29.34	.73
Led24	27.48	1.03	29.28	1.03	31.14	1.11	30.04	1.17	30.04	1.16
Euthyroid	4.14	.77	3.59	.82	2.88	1.18	2.88	1.15	2.88	1.11
Hypothyroid	1.49	.88	1.50	.98	1.56	.96	1.56	.90	1.56	.91
Abalone	41.19	.99	37.31	.99	38.11	1.00	38.34	1.02	38.34	1.02
Nettalk(s)	16.03	.94	13.41	1.11	16.28	.74	16.28	.74	16.28	.74
Splice	4.63	1.57	4.91	1.35	8.06	.61	9.21	.50	9.22	.46
Coding	28.75	1.00	27.92	.97	26.33	.70	26.42	.66	26.42	.66
Nursery	9.80	.79	8.16	.82	5.56	.11	3.55	.05	3.55	.08
Adult	16.49	.91	16.43	.92	15.92	.97	15.78	1.00	16.21	.98
DNA	5.48	1.29	6.24	.95	8.09	.55	8.85	.54	9.70	.44
Satellite	17.70	.94	15.95	.87	17.30	.66	17.60	.64	17.60	.62
Letter	25.26	.95	20.64	.74	21.12	.51	22.80	.39	22.78	.37
Shuttle	0.18	.50	0.09	.69	0.09	.53	0.08	.49	0.08	.49
mean	15.63	.99	15.02	.94	15.84	.74	15.91	.71	16.00	.70
w/t/l		9/1/4		11/0/3		11/1/2		10/1/3		11/0/3
p		.1334		.0287		.0112		.0461		.0287

boosting naive Bayesian classifiers may not be able to generate multiple models with sufficient diversity. These models cannot effectively correct each other's errors during classification by voting. In such a situation, boosting cannot greatly reduce the error of naive Bayesian classification. The experiments in the following subsection are designed to provide support to this argument.

4.2 Boosting Levelled Naive Bayesian Trees

Decision tree learning is not stable in the sense that small changes to training data may result in different decision trees. We expect that introducing tree structures into naive Bayesian classifiers can increase the instability of naive Bayesian classification, thus improving the effectiveness of boosting for naive Bayesian classification. To investigate this issue, we compare levelled naive Bayesian Trees with its boosted version by gradually increasing the maximum depth of the trees. The results are shown in Table 3, which indicates the error rates of LNBT(d) and error ratios of BLNBT(d) over LNBT(d) for $d = 1, 3, 5,$ and 10. As a base line for comparison, the results of LNBT(0) and BLNBT(0) are also included in the table. From this table, we have the following observations:

- Comparing BLNBT(d) with LNBT(d), boosting continues to improve the average accuracy of the levelled naive Bayesian tree as we increase the depth

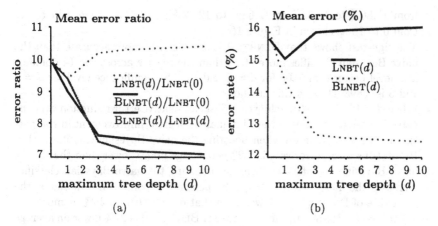

Fig. 1. Error ratio and mean error rate in the 14 domains as functions of d

of the tree. Similarly, the error ratio of BLNBT(d) over LNBT(d) continues to decrease from .99 to .70 as d increases from 0 to 10. Note that the results for $d = 10$ are very close to those for $d = 5$, since LNBT(d) does not build trees with a depth more than 5 in many domains.

- In all cases, boosting reduces the error of the levelled naive Bayesian tree significantly more often than the reverse at a level better than 0.05.
- Introducing tree structures into the naive Bayesian classification increases the error on average. After a small decrease in error resulted from introducing 1-level tree structures into the naive Bayesian classification, introducing more tree structures consistently increases the error on average: from 15.02 to 16.00 when d increases from 1 to 10.

The last observation above indicates that the relative accuracy improvement of boosting for naive Bayesian classification when tree structures are added which is shown in Table 3 might not be interesting, since the algorithms being compared to have higher error than the naive Bayesian classifier. To clarify this issue, we use the naive Bayesian classifier LNBT(0) as the base classifier for comparison. We analyze the error ratio of LNBT(d) over LNBT(0), and the error ratio of BLNBT(d) over LNBT(0) for $d = 1, 3, 5$, and 10, and present them in Figure 1(a). The mean error rates of LNBT(d) and BLNBT(d) in the 14 domains are depicted in Figure 1(b). From this analysis, we obtain the following observations:

- As expected from the last observation, the mean error ratio of LNBT(d) over the naive Bayesian classifier in the 14 domains consistently increases when d increases from 1, indicating that introducing tree structures into naive Bayesian classification decreases its accuracy while increasing its instability.
- The mean error ratio of BLNBT(d) over the naive Bayesian classifier in the 14 domains keeps decreasing when d increases from 1 to 10. In addition, we find that the mean error rate of BLNBT(d) in the 14 domains consistently reduces

from 15.86% to 14.32% to 12.63% to 12.52% to 12.41%, when d increases from 0 to 10 as shown in Figure 1(b).

- The sign-test shows that $\text{BLNBT}(d)$ is significantly more accurate than the naive Bayesian classifier more often than the reverse across the 14 domains at a level better than 0.05 for $d = 5$ and 10. The significance level for $d = 1$ and 3 is .0898, close to this cut point.

- When $d = 10$, $\text{BLNBT}(d)$ achieves 27% mean relative error reduction over the naive Bayesian classifier in the 14 domains—a great improvement in comparison to the 1% reduction when boosting the naive Bayesian classifier. Also, $\text{BLNBT}(d)$'s mean error rate is 3.22 percentage points lower than that of the naive Bayesian classifier. In contrast, boosting the naive Bayesian classifier increases the mean error rate by 0.23 percentage points. In 6 domains, the error rate of $\text{BLNBT}(10)$ is lower than that of $\text{LNBT}(0)$ by 25% or more.

- Compared to $\text{BLNBT}(0)$, the error rate of $\text{BLNBT}(10)$ is 27% lower on average over the 14 domains, although the base learning algorithm of $\text{BLNBT}(10)$ has an mean error 4% higher than the base learning algorithm of $\text{BLNBT}(0)$. A sign-test shows that $\text{BLNBT}(10)$ has lower error than $\text{BLNBT}(0)$ significantly more often than the reverse at a level .0287 across the 14 domains.

In summary, all the experimental results show that introducing tree structures into the naive Bayesian classification can lead to the success of boosting for naive Bayesian classification. Introducing tree structures seems to increase the instability of naive Bayesian classification. Although the levelled naive Bayesian tree learner is less accurate than the naive Bayesian classifier on average, boosting levelled naive Bayesian trees can produce significantly higher accuracy than the naive Bayesian classifier, performing much better than directly boosting the naive Bayesian classifier.

5   Conclusions

Although boosting achieves great success with decision tree learning, we experimentally show that boosting does not work well for naive Bayesian classification. There are two possible reasons for this: (i) The naive Bayesian classifier is optimal in some domains; (ii) The naive Bayesian classifier is relatively stable with respect to small changes to training data. We cannot expect to further increase the accuracy of the naive Bayesian classifier in the first situation. For the second situation, we proposed to introduce tree structures into naive Bayesian classification to increase its instability, and expect that this can improve the success of boosting for naive Bayesian classification.

We have conducted a set of experiments on boosting naive Bayesian classification with tree structures in 14 natural domains. The experimental results show that although introducing tree structures into naive Bayesian classification increases the average error of naive Bayesian classification for individual models, boosting naive Bayesian classifiers with tree structures can achieve significantly lower average error than the naive Bayesian classifier, providing a method of successfully applying the boosting technique to naive Bayesian classification.

References

1. Bauer, E. & Kohavi, R.: An empirical comparison of voting classification algorithms: Bagging, boosting, and variants. To appear in *Machine Learning*, (1999).
2. Blake, C., Keogh, E. & Merz, C.J.: UCI Repository of Machine Learning Databases [http://www.ics.uci.edu/~mlearn/MLRepository.html]. Irvine, CA: University of California, Department of Information and Computer Science. (1998).
3. Breiman, L.: Bias, variance, and arcing classifiers. *Technical Report 460*, Department of Statistics, University of California, Berkeley, CA. (1996).
4. Cestnik, B.: Estimating probabilities: A crucial task in machine learning. *Proceedings of European Conference on Artificial Intelligence*. (1990) 147–149.
5. Cestnik, B., Kononenko, I., & Bratko, I.: ASSISTANT 86: A knowledge-elicitation tool for sophisticated users. In I. Bratko & N. Lavrač (eds.), *Progress in Machine Learning – Proceedings of the Second European Working Session on Learning*. (1987) 31–45. Wilmslow, UK: Sigma Press.
6. Domingos, P. & Pazzani, M.: Beyond independence: Conditions for the optimality of the simple Bayesian classifier. *Proceedings of the Thirteenth International Conference on Machine Learning*. (1996) 105–112. San Francisco, CA: Morgan Kaufmann.
7. Duda, R.O. & Hart, P.E.: *Pattern Classification and Scene Analysis*. New York: John Wiley. (1973).
8. Fayyad, U.M. & Irani, K.B.: Multi-interval discretization of continuous-valued attributes for classification learning. *Proceedings of the Thirteenth International Joint Conference on Artificial Intelligence*. (1993) 1022–1027. Morgan Kaufmann.
9. Freund, Y. & Schapire, R.E.: Experiments with a new boosting algorithm. *Proceedings of the Thirteenth International Conference on Machine Learning*. (1996) 148–156. Morgan Kaufmann.
10. Kohavi, R.: Scaling up the accuracy of naive-Bayes classifiers: A decision-tree hybrid. *Proceedings of the Second International Conference on Knowledge Discovery and Data Mining*. (1996) 202–207. The AAAI Press.
11. Kononenko, I.: Comparison of inductive and naive Bayesian learning approaches to automatic knowledge acquisition. In B. Wielinga *et al.* (eds.), *Current Trends in Knowledge Acquisition*. Amsterdam: IOS Press. (1990).
12. Langley, P., Iba, W.F., & Thompson, K.: An analysis of Bayesian classifiers. *Proceedings of the Tenth National Conference on Artificial Intelligence*. (1992) 223–228. The AAAI Press.
13. Michie, D., Spiegelhalter, D.J., & Taylor, C.C.: *Machine Learning, Neural and Statistical Classification*, Ellis Horwood Limited. (1994).
14. Quinlan, J.R.: *C4.5: Program for Machine Learning* (1993) Morgan Kaufmann.
15. Quinlan, J.R.: Bagging, boosting, and C4.5. *Proceedings of the 13th National Conference on Artificial Intelligence*. (1996) 725–730. The AAAI Press.
16. Schapire, R.E., Freund, Y., Bartlett, P. & Lee, W.S.: Boosting the margin: A new explanation for the effectiveness of voting methods. *Proceedings of the Fourteenth International Conference on Machine Learning*. (1997) 322–330. Morgan Kaufmann.
17. Ting, K.M. & Zheng, Z.: Improving the performance of boosting for naive Bayesian classification. *TR C99/01*, School of Computing and Mathematics, Deakin University. (1999). [http://www3.cm.deakin.edu.au/~kmting].

Convex Hulls in Concept Induction

D.A. Newlands and G.I. Webb

School of Computing and Mathematics, Deakin University, Geelong, Victoria, 3217, Australia.
doug@deakin.edu.au, webb@deakin.edu.au

Abstract. This paper investigates modelling concepts as a few, large convex hulls rather than as many, small, axis-orthogonal divisions as is done by systems which currently dominate classification learning. It is argued that this approach produces classifiers which have less strong hypothesis language bias and which, because of the fewness of the concepts induced, are more understandable. The design of such a system is described and its performance is investigated. Convex hulls are shown to be a useful inductive generalisation technique offering rather different biases than well-known systems such as C4.5 and CN2. The types of domains where convex hulls can be usefully employed are described.

Keywords: convex hulls, induction, classification learning.

1 Introduction

Classification learning has been dominated by the induction of axis-orthogonal decision surfaces in the form of rule-based systems and decision trees. While the induction of alternate forms of decision surface has received some attention, in the context of non-axis orthogonal decision trees, statistical clustering algorithms, instance based learning and regression techniques [8, 9, 1, 23, 11, 4, 3, 20, 7], this issue has received little attention in the context of decision rules. This paper is concerned with the construction of convex polytopes in N-space and the interpretation of these as rule-like structures.

Typically, machine learning systems produce many rules per class and, although each rule may be individually comprehensible, not all will be and holistic appreciation of concepts modeled may be impossible due to their fragmentary presentation. Each concept, constructed as a large convex polytope, is expected to correspond closely to a single underlying concept of the domain. The form of these concepts also gives access to work on extracting mathematical descriptions via the techniques of computational geometry including diameters of polytopes, intersections and equations for the surfaces of polytopes [14].

Concept representation using regions, which are less strongly constrained in their shape than hyperrectangles, will reduce the hypothesis language bias, which might be expected to be particularly strong in axis orthogonal systems. The performance of a prototype system [13] indicates that the technique of using geometrically minimal enclosing hyperpolygons to represent concepts is sound and has the potential to infer more accurate classifiers than Straight Axis Parallel (SAP) and Straight Non-Axis Parallel (SNAP) systems in Curved Edge (CE) domains. The main problem uncovered in the prototype was *spiking* which is the inappropriate association of points from separated regions of the same class causing misclassification of points in the intervening region. Insisting on the convexity of the polytopes eliminates this possibility. A tight-fitting polytope offers generalisations which are of much smaller volume than generalisations which are minimal in terms of axis orthogonally biased hypothesis languages. This offers a much more conservative induction process and might be expected to make fewer errors in making positive predictions. The classification performance of a convex hull based system is compared to other well-understood systems.

When a classifier produces concepts of a different shape from the underlying concept, there will always be error in the representation. This is expected from the Law of Conservation of Generalisation Performance [17] or the No Free Lunch Theorem [22], notwithstanding the caveats of Rao et al. [16], but is still a problem as limited data limits the accuracy of the representation. Since the geometric approach is considerably less limited in the orientation and placement of decision surfaces, one might expect better performance than axis orthogonal systems can provide over a range of domains where the underlying decision surfaces are not axis orthogonal.

2 Implementation of CH1

The perceived problem with SAP biased induction systems is that they will represent SNAP concepts by a possibly large number of small regions. More comprehensible concept descriptions will be obtained if single concepts can be represented by single induced structures so CH1, will construct large aggregates of instances. Instances of other classes within such large structures will be treated as exceptions and will be modeled separately subsequently. It is not possible to use an incremental approach to building convex hulls, such as that employed in the prototype system, PIGS [13], because of the problems with *spiking* [12]. In the CH1 algorithm, construct-next-rule() constructs a convex hull, using the quickhull software [19] which is an implementation of the quickhull algorithm [2] using a variant of Grünbaum's Beneath-Beyond Theorem [6], around all points of the most frequent class in the misclassified points set and prepends [21] it to the decision list of hulls. Each hull is defined by the intersection of a set of planes each of which is defined by the components of an outward-pointing, unit normal to the plane and its perpendicular distance from the origin. Thus each facet in N dimensional space is described by N+1 real numbers. Techniques for rule placement other than simple prepending were investigated [12] but simple hill-climbing heuristics were found to frequently get trapped in local minima and so were abandoned. The algorithm handles categorical values by having, associated with each hull, a set of valid values for each categorical attribute. To be covered by a rule, the categorical attribute values must be in the set and the continuous attributes must be covered by the hull. The current approach is oriented towards ordinal attributes and is not intended for use in domains with many categorical attributes. The algorithm will construct convex hulls where possible but will resort to an Axis Orthogonal hull (i.e. hyperrectangle) if necessary. The algorithm continues until all training points are classified correctly or the algorithm cannot reduce the number of unclassified points.

The CH1 algorithm is stated as

CH1
   Rule-list = empty
   FOR all classes
      EXTRACT unclassified-points[this_class] from training-set
      prev-num-misclassified-pts[this_class] = ∞
   ENDFOR
   construct-next-rule and update num-misclassified-pts
   WHILE num-misclassified-pts > 0
   AND num-misclassified-pts < prev-num-misclassified-pts[this_class]
      prev-num-misclassified-pts[this_class] = num-misclassified-pts
      misclassified-points = all points in training-set not correctly
            classified by Rule-list
      construct-next-rule and update num-misclassified-pts
   ENDWHILE
END.

CONSTRUCT-NEXT-RULE
   SET best rule to empty
   COUNT number of each class in misclassified points
   FOR all classes
      IF number in this class is zero
         continue to next class
      ENDIF
      extract-next-rule
      EVALUATE DL with this new rule prepended
      IF this rule is best so far
         SAVE rule to best rule
      ENDIF
   ENDFOR
   INSERT best rule in DL in appropriate position
   CONSTRUCT new misclassified points list
END.

EXTRACT-NEXT-RULE
   FOR all points of this class in misclassified points list
      FOR all attributes
         IF categorical
            SET array entry in rule
         ELSE
            PUT in continuous attribute file
         ENDIF
      ENDFOR
      IF not enough points to construct hull OR forcing AO_HULL

```
            construct AO_HULL
      ELSE
            construct convex hull
            IF qhull fails due to degenerate geometry
                  construct AO_HULL
            ENDIF
      ENDIF
   ENDFOR
END.
```

For an initial comparison of CH1 and C4.5 [15], artificial data sets [12] with mostly curved edges (2, 3 & 4 dimensional spheres and pairs of concentric spheres and one set of mixed shapes) were used so that the density of data points, the dimensionality of the data set and the complexity of the data set could be controlled. C4.5 was chosen as a well-known exemplar of an SAP-biased system. All experiments in this paper use a randomly selected and randomly ordered 80% of the data for training and 20% for testing. The resulting accuracies are presented in Table 1, the first result in each box is that for C4.5, the second is CH1 and an "*" shows where there was superiority at p = 0.05 in a matched pairs t-test. For small data sets, C4.5 tends to have better accuracy. As the

Data size	1000	2000	4000	8000	15000
Circle	96.28/96.55	97.46/97.25	97.73/98.20*	98.54/98.86*	98.89/99.29*
Sphere	90.66/90.69	92.84/93.36*	94.57/95.19*	95.31/96.57*	95.97/97.47*
Hyp-sphr	*90.42/89.63	*92.41/90.70	*94.04/93.50	*94.87/94.10	95.81/95.83*
CnCrcl	92.16/92.89*	93.97/94.52*	95.57/96.83*	96.84/98.80*	97.65/98.7*
CnSphr	*88.95/88.32	85.01/86.29*	87.89/90.50*	90.54/92.92*	92.13/94.71*
CnHySp	*81.36/78.12	*84.21/81.92	*87.21/86.24	*89.88/89.49	90.78/91.62*
RCC	*95.06/93.80	*96.75/95.97	97.45/97.62*	98.10/98.42*	98.74/99.01*

Table 1. C4.5 and CH1 Accuracy on Artificial Data Sets

size of the data set rises, CH1 always becomes significantly better. The point at which the change takes place becomes higher as the dimensionality increases. It is possible that CH1's need for large numbers of data points is a consequence of its less stringent geometric bias. It chooses between a greater number of classifiers because it has more options in terms of position and orientation of each decision surface and, thus, it needs more data to make good choices. If it has sufficient data then its greater flexibility should enable it to make better classifiers.

2.1 Time Complexity of CH1

If a learning domain contains n points with c classes in a space of dimension d, it is expected from design criteria that there will be approximately c groups of unclassified points to be processed and the expected number of facets per hull is $\log^{d-1} \frac{n}{c}$ [14]. Since a linear search is used for the c hulls, the time complexity for classifying n points is $O(nc \log^{d-1} \frac{n}{c})$. The time complexity of the hull creating algorithm can be shown [12] to be

$$O(c^3 * \log^{d-1} n * n^{\lfloor (d+1)/2 \rfloor})$$

3 Modification of Convex Hulls

A convex hull based system will tend to construct enclosures which are a subset of the underlying concept. It can be shown [12] that a hull can be simply inflated like a balloon and that this will produce a statistically significant improvement in its classification accuracy. Another technique for generalising convex hulls is to remove facets which do not contribute to its resubstitution classification accuracy. Two techniques for this are explored in [12]. Typically, hulls are pruned from around 100 facets to between 1 and 5 facets.

4 Evaluation of CH1

4.1 Evaluation on Selected Domains

This learning system will initially be evaluated on domains for which there is reasonable expectation that the decision surfaces are either curved or are straight but not axis orthogonal. The performance of CH1 will be compared with that of C4.5, CN2 and OC1. The former two are presented as exemplars of SAP learning systems and the latter is included as an example of SNAP learning.

Body Fat The BMI data set [23] has attributes of height and weight of persons and they are classified according to their Body Mass Index (BMI) [18] which is the weight(kg) divided by the square of the height(metres). In this experiment, the height and the weight will be used as the attributes and the decision surfaces are known, from a consideration of the fact that $BMI \propto \frac{1}{h^2}$, to be distinctly curved. Thus, in this domain, it is expected that C4.5, CN2 [5] and OC1 [11], with their preference for long straight lines, will be poorly biased whereas CH1 will be neutrally biased. The data set, derived from frequency tables for height and weight in [18], can be viewed as a realistic simulation of a real-world classification problem.

This experiment was carried out, with a range of data set sizes, 20 times as this was sufficient to obtain statistically significant results. The results are plotted in Figure 1. The win-loss ratio for CH1 against CN2 is 20:0 and this is significant at p = 0.01 using a sign test. Similarly, the win-loss ratio for CH1 versus C4.5 is also 20:0 and is significant at the same level. Comparing CH1 with OC1, the win-loss ratio is 12:3 which is significant at p = 0.05 using a sign test. On all data sets of size less than 1500, CH1 provides a better model of the data.

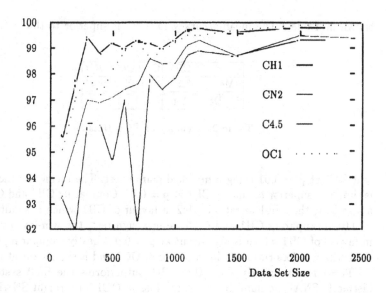

Fig. 1. Learning Curves for Body Fat

With larger amounts of data, the performance of OC1 is slightly superior. A possible explanation is that with low data densities, OC1 generates unsuitably large decision surfaces which do not match the underlying concepts closely but which are not invalidated in the training set. At high data densities, OC1 is constrained from constructing overly large decision surfaces and its performance becomes very close to that of CH1 since its biases happen to suit the class distributions in this domain marginally better than those of CH1.

POL Parallel oblique lines (POL) is an artificial data set which suits the inductive biases of OC1 [11]. Since the decision surfaces are known to be straight lines at 45 degrees, the strong SAP bias of C4.5 and CN2 should reduce their performance but the performance of CH1 should be superior since it can provide decision surfaces close to the correct orientation. OC1 uses all of the neighbouring points to orient a single large surface where CH1 has to place and orient, possibly, several surfaces from the same amount of information. Therefore, OC1 should provide the best performance of the methods being compared. Twenty repetitions of comparisons with matched data sets of various sizes were sufficient to obtain statistically significant results. The set for 500 points is typical and is shown in Table 2 The mean accuracy for CH1 is superior to that of both CN2

	CH1	CN2	C4.5	OC1
Mean	97.3[2,3]	95.1	95.2	99.2[1]
Std.Dev.	1.4	1.1	1.1	0.4

Table 2. Accuracy on POL Data Set

and C4.5 at p = 0.01 using a matched pairs t-test. The mean accuracy of OC1 is similarly superior to that of CH1 at p = 0.01. Comparing CH1 and CN2 using a sign test, the win-loss ratio is 18:2 in favour of CH1 which is significant at p = 0.01. Comparing CH1 and C4.5 using a sign test, the win-loss ratio is 17:3 in favour of CH1 which is significant at p = 0.01. Lastly, comparing CH1 with OC1, the win-loss ratio is 1:19 in favour of OC1 and is significant at p = 0.01.

These results clearly show that CH1 outperforms the SAP systems on a distinctly SNAP domain. However, the bias of OC1 for straight SNAP decision surfaces exactly suits this domain and OC1 is far superior to CH1, CN2 and C4.5.

These two experiments suggest that CH1 will provide significantly superior performance to axis orthogonally biased classifier systems on strongly SNAP or curved concepts. Particularly, on curved concepts, it provides superior performance to SAP systems and better performance than OC1 at low and medium data densities. At high data densities, the performance of OC1 may overtake that of CH1.

4.2 Evaluation on a Variety of Domains

The evaluation was extended to include a cross-section of well-known, mainly continuous, domains from the UCI Repository [10]. An experiment, using matched pairs comparisons, was run 100 times on each domain using CH1, C4.5 and CN2 and the results are shown in Table 3. Because the quickhull software has infeasible run-times on some datasets, only randomly selected subsets of the available data were used. Sizes of data sets used are shown in the result table. Comparing CH1 with C4.5, a win-loss ratio of 3:22 is significant at p = 0.01. Similarly comparing CH1 and CN2, a win-loss ratio of 4:21 is also significant at p = 0.01. There is no significant difference between C4.5 and CN2 with a win-loss ratio of 14:10. Worse is the fact that when CH1 is superior, it is never markedly superior but when it is worse, it can be considerably worse.

This is a disappointing result and CH1 is only superior on balance-scale, echocardiogram and ionosphere. This raises the possibility that, since most UCI Repository data sets may have been collected and defined in the context of SAP-based systems, the Repository may have a preponderance of data sets suited to such systems. If our understanding of how the performance of various sytems depends on their language bias and the shapes of the underlying concepts is

Domain (Size)	Accuracy			No. Concepts	No. CH1 Hulls	No. C4.5 Regions
	CH1	C4.5	CN2			
balance-scale(625)	$83.26^{2,3}$	76.67	81.30^{2}	3	5.6	108.2
B.canc.Wisc.(699)	99.06^{3}	$99.42^{1,3}$	97.75	2	2.8	33.2
bupa(345)	58.77	63.49^{1}	$64.42^{1,2}$	2	3.7	95.8
cleveland(30)	55.54	$87.73^{1,3}$	87.64^{1}	2	3.7	66.8
echocardiogram(62)	$70.81^{2,3}$	69.11^{3}	67.90	2	2.6	13.5
german(135)	50.71	$60.66^{1,3}$	57.13^{1}	2	7.3	76.4
glass(214)	64.14	73.31^{1}	$76.28^{1,2}$	3	5.9	43.5
glass7(214)	55.21	66.18^{1}	$66.34^{1,2}$	7	13.0	49.4
heart(34)	67.71	80.29^{1}	$81.53^{1,2}$	2	3.7	11.4
hepatitis(35)	40.51	$41.57^{1,3}$	41.27^{1}	2	2.0	4.4
horse-colic(40)	62.01	77.03^{1}	$87.78^{1,2}$	2	2.3	9.6
hungarian (70)	62.48	$88.55^{1,3}$	86.07^{1}	2	3.6	55.2
ionosphere(351)	$90.83^{2,3}$	87.71	89.69^{2}	2	5.0	29.4
iris(150)	69.85	$94.74^{1,3}$	94.13^{1}	3	3	8.6
new-thyroid(215)	75.78	91.83^{1}	$95.30^{1,2}$	3	3.0	14.5
page-blocks(140)	57.47	87.20^{1}	$90.34^{1,2}$	5	7.6	14.8
pid(150)	80.30	82.34^{1}	$82.95^{1,2}$	2	5.1	39.0
satimage (225)	72.36	$91.33^{1,3}$	90.16^{1}	6	5.8	19.4
segment(1200)	91.94	$94.41^{1,3}$	94.32^{1}	7	22.0	63.0
shuttle(100)	66.32	$93.84^{1,3}$	92.05^{1}	7	4.8	9.0
sonar(208)	56.64	$74.12^{1,3}$	70.50^{1}	2	2.5	31.6
soybean(200)	81.01	$90.68^{1,3}$	84.60^{1}	19	19.7	70.2
vehicle(30)	45.03	$80.61^{1,3}$	79.36^{1}	4	4.5	20.2
waveform(30)	35.80	$72.76^{1,3}$	65.70^{1}	3	3.3	17.2
wine(35)	84.04	$87.01^{1,3}$	85.45^{1}	3	3.0	39.5

Table 3. Comparison of CH1, C4.5 and CN2

correct, it would be expected that OC1 would have worse predictive accuracy than CH1 on the three data sets identified above.

This will be examined experimentally with 20 runs of the comparison experiment. The results are shown in Table 4. The results show that CH1 is signifi-

Accuracy	CH1	OC1.
balance-scale	78.7	91.5^{1}
echocardiogram	73.0^{2}	65.5
ionosphere	91.2^{2}	76.8

Table 4. Accuracy of CH1 and OC1 on Selected Domains

cantly superior to OC1 for the echocardiogram and ionosphere data sets, using a matched pairs t-test at p = 0.05. However, OC1 is similarly superior to CH1 on the balance-scale data set which was unexpected. Closer examination of the data sets shows that the attribute values are essentially continuous for echocardiogram and ionosphere but that those of the balance-scale are entirely integer values. These will make the decision surfaces consist of flat surfaces between integer values and thus OC1, which favours flat surfaces, will be suitably biased and the result is understandable. The continuous attributes of the other domains suggest that flat surfaces are an unsuitable bias and that OC1 will perform poorly as found.

The interaction between the underlying concept geometry and the induced structures can be explained thus. If the data sets are SAP biased, then SAP classifiers have the correct orientation of the decision surface automatically and only have to position the surface from the evidence. A SNAP system has to decide both the orientation and the position of the decision surface from the same amount of evidence so it has a bigger space of theories to explore with the same evidence.

5 Complexity of Domain Representations

One advantage advanced for the use of convex hulls is that, from a human comprehension viewpoint, the number of structures induced is similar to the number of underlying concepts. For CH1, the number of structures is the number of convex hulls which are constructed and for C4.5 the number of structures is the number of hyperrectangular regions which are identified. The number of actual concepts in each domain and the number of concepts induced by CH1 and C4.5, averaged over 100 runs, are shown in columns 4–6 of Table 3. The average number of concepts for satimage and shuttle are lower than one might expect because the sample used contains effectively only 5 classes for satimage rather than 6 and, for shuttle, contains about 3 classes rather than 7. The smallness of the number of concepts induced by CH1 can be seen in comparison with C4.5. The number of hulls induced by CH1 is always very close to the number of actual concepts in each domain. Using a sign test, the number of hulls produced by CH1 is superior to C4.5 at p=0.01.

6 Conclusions

Convex hulls have been shown to be a simple, satisfactory method for constructing useful polytopes offering smaller generalisations than techniques which use hypothesis language based generalisation. The use of facet deletion and inflation have been noted as improving the performance of the classifier.

The performances of differing systems has been shown to depend on the orientation of the surfaces which can be induced and those of the actual underlying concept. If the SAP classifier has the same orientation for its decision surfaces as the underlying concepts of the domain then it will always outperform CH1 because it is well biased.

It has been demonstrated that the advantages offered by the use of convex hulls, rather than SAP-based classifiers are:-

- a classifier with less bias in terms of the geometry of induced concepts.
- a classifier which induces one large structure per concept rather than many small structures is philosophically appealing and affords an economy of representation which SAP systems cannot provide.
- CH1 with fewer, larger hulls offers classification accuracy which is superior to well known systems on data sets where the underlying concepts are known to be curved or SNAP. On data sets with SAP underlying concepts, CH1 needs higher data densities to be competititve.
- convex hulls offer access to mathematical descriptions of modeled concepts.

The disadvantages of CH1 are that after the effort to create the convex hull, it is immediately deconstructed using facet deletion and inflation and that many commonly used data sets may have underlying SAP concepts. CH1 needs more data than an SAP system since it has to position and orient line segments rather than just place them as an SAP system does. On all domains examined with known curved or SNAP concepts, CH1 outperforms both C4.5 and CN2.

References

1. D.W. Aha, D. Kibler, and M.K. Albert. Instance-based learning algorithms. *Machine Learning*, 6:37–66, 1991.
2. C.B. Barber, D.P. Dobkin, and H. Huhdanpaa. The quickhull algorithm for convex hulls. Submitted to ACM Trans. Mathematical Software, May 1995.
3. L. Breiman, J.H. Friedman, R.A. Olshen, and C.J. Stone. *Classification and Regression Trees*. Wadsworth Int. Group, Belmont, California, 1984.
4. C.E. Brodley and P.E. Utgoff. Multivariate decision trees. *Machine Learning*, 19:45–77, 1995.
5. P. Clark and Tim Niblett. The cn2 induction algorithm. *Machine learning*, 3:261–284, 1989.
6. B. Grünbaum. Measures of symmetry for convex sets. In *Proc. 7th Symposium in Pure Mathematics of the AMS*, pages 233–270, 1961.
7. D. Heath, S. Kasif, and S. Salzberg. Learning oblique decision trees. In *Proc. 13th IJCAI*, pages 1002–1007. Morgan Kaufmann, 1993.
8. C. Matheus and L.A. Rendell. Constructive induction on decision trees. In *Proceedings of IJCAI*, pages 645–650, 1989.
9. Michalski, R.S., Mozetic, I., Hong, and N. J. Lavrac. The multi-purpose incremental learning system aq15 and its testing and application to three medical domains. In *Proceedings of the Fifth National Conference on Artificial Intelligence*, pages 1041–1045. Morgan Kaufman, 1986.
10. P.M. Murphy and D.W. Aha. The uci repository of machine learning databases, http://www.ics.uci.edu/ mlearn/mlrepository.html.
11. S.K. Murthy, S. Kasif, and S. Salzberg. A system for induction of oblique decision trees. *Journal of Artificial Intelligence Research*, 2:1–32, 1994.
12. D.A. Newlands. *Convex Hulls in Concept Induction*. PhD thesis, School of Computing and Mathematics, Deakin University, Geelong 3217, Victoria, Australia, 1997. Available from http://www3.cm.deakin.edu.au/doug.

13. D.A. Newlands and G.I. Webb. Polygonal inductive generalisation system. In *Industrial and Engineering Applications of Artificial Intelligence and Expert Systems*, pages 587–592, 1995.

14. F.P. Preparata and M.I. Shamos. *Computational Geometry*. Texts and Monographs in Computer Science. Springer-Verlag, New York, 1985.

15. J.R. Quinlan. *C4.5 programs for Machine Learning*. Morgan Kaufmann, San Mateo, California, 1995.

16. R.B. Rao, D. Gordon, and W. Spears. For every generalisation action, is there really an equal and opposite reaction? analysis of the conservation law for generalisation performance. In *The 12th International Conference on Machine Learning*, pages 471–479, 1995.

17. C. Schaffer. A conservation law for generalisation performance. In *Machine Learning: Proc. of the 11th International Conference*. Morgan Kaufmann, San Francisco, 1993.

18. J. Schell and B. Leelarthaepin. *Physical Fitness Assessment*. Leelar Biomediscience Services, Box 283, Matraville 2036, NSW, Australia, 1994.

19. Software Development Group, Geometry Center, 1300 South Second Street, Suite 500, Minneapolis, MN 55454, USA. *Geomview Manual*.

20. P.E. Utgoff and C.E. Brodley. Linear machine decision trees. Technical report, U. Mass. at Amherst, 1991.

21. G.I. Webb. Recent progress in learning decision lists by prepending inferred rules. In *Second Singapore International Conference on Intelligent Systems*, pages B280–B285, 1994.

22. D.H. Wolpert. Off-training set error and a priori distinctions between learning algorithms. Technical Report SFI TR 95-01-00, Santa Fe Institute, 1995.

23. S.P. Yip. *Empirical Attribute Space Refinement in Classification Learning*. PhD thesis, Deakin University, Geelong, Victoria 3217, Australia, 1995.

Mining Classification Knowledge Based on Cloud Models*

Jianhua Fan[1] and Deyi Li[2]

[1]Nanjing Communications Engineering Institute, Nanjing, China, 210016
Jianhuaf@hotmail.com
[2]The Institute of Electronic System Engineering, No. 307, Zhengchang Zhuang,
Fengtai District, Beijing, China, 100039
ziqin@public2.bta.net.cn

Abstract. Data classification is an important research topic in the field of data mining and knowledge discovery. There have been many data classification methods studied, including decision-tree method, statistical methods, neural networks, rough sets, etc. In this paper, we present a new mathematical representation of qualitative concepts—Cloud Models. With the new models, mapping between quantities and qualities becomes much easier and interchangeable. Based on the cloud models, a novel qualitative strategy for data classification in large relational databases is proposed. Then, the algorithms for classification are developed, such as cloud generation, complexity reduction, identifying interacting attributes, etc. Finally, we perform experiments on a challenging medical diagnosis domain, acute abdominal pain. The results show the advantages of the model in the process of knowledge discovery.

1 Introduction

Data classification is an important research topic in the field of data mining and knowledge discovery. It finds the common properties among a set of objects in a database and classifies them into different classes. There have been many data classification methods studied, including decision-tree method, statistical methods, neural networks, rough sets, etc.

In machine learning studies, a decision-tree classification method, developed by Quinlan[1], has been influential. A typical decision tree learning system is ID-3[1], which adopts a top-down irrevocable strategy that searches only part of the search space. It guarantees that a simple, but not necessarily the simplest, tree is found. An extension to ID-3, C4.5[2],extends the domain of classification from categorical attributes to numerical ones. In [3], Shan. et. al. proposed an novel approach, which uses rough sets to ensuring the completeness of the classification and the reliability of

---
* Research was supported in part by Chinese National Advanced Technology Development Projects(No.863-306-ZT06-07-2).

the probability estimate prior to rule induction. There are many other approaches on data classification, such as [4, 5, 6].

In this paper, we present a new mathematical representation of qualitative concepts — Cloud Models. With the new models, a novel approach for data classification in large relational databases is proposed.

2 The Qualitative Strategy

The laboriousness of the development of realistic DMKD applications, previously reported examples of knowledge discovery in the literature and our experience in real-world knowledge discovery situations all lead us to believe that knowledge discovery is a representation-sensitive, human-oriented task consisting of friendly interactions between a human and a discovery system. Current work in DMKD uses some form of (extended or modified) SQL as the data mining query language and some variant of predicate calculus for the discovered results. The variants frequently contain some form of quantitative modifier, such as confidence, support, threshold, and so forth. This tends to lead to discovered rules such as :

With 37.8% of support and 15.7% of confidence, patients whose age are between 20 and 30 and have acute pain on the low-right side of the abdomen more than 6.24 hours can be classified as appendicitis.

Rather than the qualitative representation:

Generally speaking, young patients who have acute low-right abdominal pain for a relative long time may get appendicitis.

This is, however, more than a simple issue of semantics and friendliness. The former rules are not robust under change to the underlying database, while the latter ones are. In a real, very large database, data are often infected with errors due to the nature of collection. In addition, an on-line discovery system supporting a real database must keep up with changing data. It does not make much sense if a very precisely quantitative assertion is made about the behavior of an application domain based on such a database. It may be necessary, to some extent, to abandon the high standards of rigor and precision used in conventional quantitative techniques. At this moment, a piece of qualitative knowledge extracted may be more tolerant and robust. Clearly, quantitative results such as confidence and support cannot remain constant under conditions of any change. By contrast, qualitative representation will remain true until there is a substantial change in the database.

On the other hand, quantitative knowledge discovered at some lower levels of generalization in DMKD may still be suitable, but the number of the extracted rules increases. In contrast, as the generalization goes up to a higher level of abstraction, the discovered knowledge is more strategic. The ability to discovery quantitative and yet significant knowledge about the behavior of an application domain from a very large database diminishes until a threshold may be reached beyond which precision and significance (or relevance) become almost mutually exclusive characteristics. That is to say that, if the generalization to a very large database system exceeds a limit, the reality and exactness of its description become incompatible. This has been described as the principle of incompatibility. To describe phenomena qualitatively, we take linguistic variables and linguistic terms and show how quantitative and qualitative inference complement and interact with each other in a simple mechanism.

Our point of departure in this paper is to represent linguistic terms in logical sentences or rules. We imagine a linguistic variable that is semantically associated with a list of all the linguistic terms within a universe of discourse. For example, "age" is a linguistic variable if its values are "young", "middle-age", "old", "very old" and so forth, rather than the real ages which are considered as the universe of discourse of the linguistic variable "age," say from 0 to 100. In the more general case, a linguistic variable is a tri-tuple {X, T(x), Cx(u)} in which X is the name of the variable, T(x) is the term-set of X; that is, the collection of its linguistic values, U is a universe of discourse, Cx (u) is a compatibility function showing the relationship between a term x in T(x) and U. More precisely, the compatibility function maps the universe of discourse into the interval [0,1] for each u in U.

It is important to understand the notion of compatibility functions. Consider a set of linguistic terms. T. in a universe of discourse, U, — for example, the linguistic term, "young" in the interval [0,100]. T is characterized by its compatibility function Cx : u [0,1]. The statement that the compatibility of, say, "28 years old" with "young" is about 0.7, has a relationship both to fuzzy logic and probability.

In relation to fuzzy logic, the correct interpretation of the compatibility value "0.7" is that it is an indication of the partial membership to which the element "age-value 28" belongs to the fuzzy concept of the label "young". To understand the relationship with probability on the other hand, the correct interpretation of the compatibility value "0.92" is that it is merely subjective indication. Human knowledge does not conform to such a fixed crisp membership degree "0.7" at the "28 years old". There do not exist any unique partial membership values, which could be universally accepted by human beings to the universe of discourse U. But there is a random variable showing that the membership degree at "28 years old" takes a random value, behind which a subjective probability distribution is obeyed. The degree of compatibility takes on random value itself. This type of randomness is adhered to the fuzziness.

3 Qualitative Representation Based on Cloud Models

3.1 Cloud Models

Following the important characteristics of linguistic variables and terms, we define a new concept of cloud models to represent linguistic terms. Let U be the set, U = {u}, as the universe of discourse, and T, a linguistic term associated with U. The membership degree of u in U to the linguistic term T, C_T (u), is a random variable with a probability distribution. $C_T(u)$ takes values in [0,1]. A cloud is a mapping from the universe of discourse U to the unit interval [0,1].

The bell-shaped clouds, called normal clouds are most fundamental and useful in representing linguistic terms, see Fig.1. A normal cloud is described with only three digital characteristics, expected value (Ex), entropy (En) and hyper entropy (He).[7]

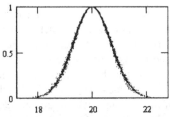

Fig. 1. Normal Cloud with digital characteristic E_x=20 E_n=0.7 H_e=0.025

The expected value Ex of a cloud is the position at the universe of discourse, corresponding to the center of gravity of the cloud. In other words, the element Ex in the universe of discourse fully belongs to the linguistic term represented by the cloud model. The entropy, En, is a measure of the fuzziness of the concept over the universe of discourse showing how many elements in the universe of discourse could be accepted to the linguistic term. It should be noticed that the entropy defined here is a generic notion, and it need not be probabilistic. The hyper entropy, He, is a measure of the uncertainty of the entropy En. Close to the waist of the cloud, corresponding to the center of gravity, cloud drops are most dispersed, while at the top and bottom the focusing is much better. The discrete degree of cloud drops depends on He.[6,7]

3.2 Cloud Generators

Given three digital characteristics E_x, E_n, and H_e, to represent a linguistic term, a set of cloud drops may be generated by the following algorithm[8]:

Algorithm 1: Normal Cloud Generation

Input: the expected value of cloud E_x, the entropy of cloud E_n,
the hyper entropy of cloud H_e, the number of drops N.
Output: a normal cloud with digital characteristics E_x, E_n, and H_e.

1) *Produce a random value x which satisfies with the normal distribution probability of mean = E_x, and standard error = E_n;*
2) *Produce a random value E_n' which satisfies with the normal distribution probability of mean = E_n, and standard error = H_e;*
3) *Calculate* $y = e^{\frac{-(x-E_x)^2}{2(E_n')^2}}$;
4) *Let (x, y) be a cloud drop in the universe of discourse;*
5) *Repeat 1-4 until the number of drops required all generated.*

The idea of using only three digital characteristics to generate a cloud is creative. The generator could produce as many drops of the cloud as you like (Fig. 1). This kind of generators is called a forward cloud generator. All the drops obey the properties described above. Cloud-drops may also be generated upon conditions. It is easy to set up a half-up or half-down normal cloud generator with the similar strategy, if there is a need to represent such a linguistic term.

It is natural to think about the generator mechanism in an inverse way. Given a number of drops, as samples of a normal cloud, the three digital characteristics Ex, En, and He could be obtained to represent the corresponding linguistic term. This kind of cloud generators may be called backward cloud generators. Since the cloud model represents linguistic terms, the forward and backward cloud generators can be served interchangeably to bridge the gap between quantitative and qualitative knowledge.

4 Classification with Cloud Models

4.1 Concept Generalization based on Synthesized Cloud

Suppose we have two linguistic atoms, $A_1(Ex_1,En_1,He_1)$ and $A_2(Ex_2,En_2,He_2)$ over the same universe of discourse U. A *virtual linguistic atom*, $A_3(Ex_3,En_3,He_3)$ may be create by synthesizing the two using the following definition:

$$Ex_3 = \frac{Ex_1 \times En_1 + Ex_2 \times En_2}{En_1 + En_2} \tag{1}$$

$$En_3 = En_1 + En_2 \tag{2}$$

$$He_3 = \frac{He_1 \times En_1 + He_2 \times En_2}{En_1 + En_2} \tag{3}$$

This kind of virtual cloud is called *Synthesized Cloud.*

From the geometrical point of view, this definition satisfies the property that the torques of A_3 (which are the products of the center of gravity of $A_3$and the perpendicular distances to the horizontal and vertical axes repectively) are equal to the sum of torques of A_1 and A_2. The lingustic atom A_3 can be considered as the generalization of A_1 and A_2.

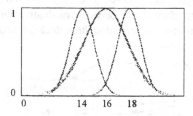

Fig. 2. Generalizing "*about 14*" and "*about 18*" to "*teenager*"

To make this concrete. Fig.2 shows how the conceptes "*about 14*" and "*about 18*" may be generalized to that of "*teenager*".This definition can be conveniently extended to the synthesis of many linguistic atoms. The price paid is that the entropy of the generalized linguistic atom increases, which reflects the more general information coverage.

4.2 Reduction of Classification Complexity and Softening Thresholds

In KDD-related problems, the universe U is finite and is highly desirable for it to be small. Only finite classifications are "learnable," i.e., we can potentially acquire complete knowledge about such classifications. Unfortunately, most finite classifications are not learnable due to the excessively large number of possible equivalence classes. Only a small fraction of all possible classifications expressible in terms of the indiscernibility relation are learnable.

To evaluate the computational tractability of the finite classification learning problem, we adopt the notion proposed by Ning Shan in [3]—classification complexity, defined as the number of equivalence classes in the classification. In practice, this number is usually not known in advance. Instead, a crude upper bound on the classification complexity for a subset of attributes $B \subseteq C$, can be computed "a priori" by the following fomula:

$$TC(B,V) = \prod_{p \in B} card(V_p) \tag{4}$$

The quantity TC(B,V) is called the theoretical complexity of the set of attributes B given the set of values V of the attributes B. If the number of attributes and the size of the domain Vp for each attribute is large, then TC(B,V) grows exponentially large. It is very difficult to find a credible classification based on a large number of attributes unless the attributes are strongly dependent (e.g., functionally dependent) on each other (limiting the number of equivalence classes).

Complexity reduction increases the credibility of the classification by generalizing condition attributes. The information generalization procedure applies attribute-oriented concept tree ascension [9,10] to reduce the complexity of an information system. It generalizes a condition attribute to a certain level based on the attribute's concept tree, which is provided by knowledge engineers or domain experts. Trivially, the values for any attribute can be represented as a one-level concept tree where the root is the most general value "ANY" and the leaves are the distinct values of the attribute. The medium level nodes in the concept tree with more than two levels are qualitative terms, which are expressed in cloud models (see Fig. 3). The data corresponds to higher level nodes must cover the data corresponds to all the descendant nodes. The transformations between qualitative terms and quantitative values of condition attributes are implemented through cloud models.

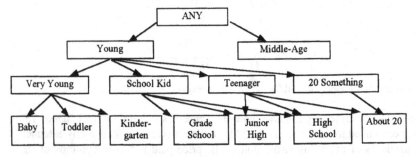

Fig. 3. Concept Tree with Qualitative Terms

We modified the algorithm proposed by Shan et al. In [3], which extracts a generalized information system. In this algorithm, there are two important concepts — the attribute threshold and the theoretical complexity threshold, which constrain the generalization process. Since the exact values of the thresholds are very hard to determine, we apply the linguistic terms to soften them in our modified algorithm. The two linguistic terms are represented with cloud models. Since the thresholds are not exact values, we call them *soft thresholds*. The entropy of soft thresholds can effectively control cycle numbers. This is a novel contribution of this paper.

Condition attributes are generalized by ascending their concept trees until the number of values for each attribute is less than or equal to the user-specified soft attribute threshold for that attribute and the theoretical complexity of all generalized attributes is less than or equal to the user-specified soft theoretical complexity threshold. For each iteration, one attribute is selected for generalization (this selection can be made in many ways). Lower level concepts of this attribute are replaced by the concepts of the next higher level. The number of possible values at a higher level of an attribute is always smaller than at a lower level, so the theoretical complexity is reduced.

Algorithm 2: Reduction of Classification Complexity

Input: (1) The original system S with a set of condition attributes C_i $(1 \leq i \leq n)$;
(2) a set of H of concept trees, where each H_i $\in H$ is a concept hierarchy for the attribute C_i.
(3) S_{ti} is a soft threshold for attribute C_i with digital characteristic $(Ex_{ti}, En_{ti}, He_{ti})$ and d_i is the number of distinct values of attribute C_i;
(4) S_{TC} defined by user is a soft theoretical complexity threshold with digital characteristic $(Ex_{tc}, En_{tc}, He_{tc})$.
Output: The generalized information system S'

$S' \leftarrow S$

$$TC_1 = \prod_{i=1}^{n} d_i$$

Generate soft threshold values S_{TC} and S_{ti}
while $TC_1 > S_{TC}$ and $\exists d_i > S_{ti}$ do
  Select an attribute $C_i \in C$ such that d_i / S_{ti} is maximal
  Ascend tree H_i one level and make appropriate substitutions in S'
  Remove duplicates from S'
  Recalculate d_i
  Recalculate $TC_1 = \prod_{i=1}^{n} d_i$
  Regenerate soft threshold values S_{TC} and S_{ti}
Endwhile

4.3 Identifying Interacting Attributes

The local discovery of interacting attributes has been reported in [11]. All condition attributes are grouped into disjoint clusters without considering the decision attribute(s). Each cluster contains attributes that are directly or indirectly dependent upon each other. The global discovery method selects a subset of condition attributes that are based on their relevance to the decision attribute(s). Here, we adopt the global generalization algorithm for attribute clusters in[3].

4.4 Search for Classifications

After reduction of complexity and identifying interacting attributes, we search for credible classifications of the database tuples based on some selected interacting attributes. A classification is credible if it is complete or almost complete with respect to the domain from which the database was collected. Here, we adopt the SLIQ(Supervised Learning In Quest) method, which was developed by Mehta et al.[4]. It is a supervised learning method that constructs decision trees from a set of examples. It uses a novel pre-sorting technique in the tree growing phase. This sorting procedure is integrated with a breadth-first tree growing strategy to enable classification of disk-resident datasets. SLIQ also uses a new tree-pruning algorithm that is inexpensive, and results in compact and accurate trees. Since we can interchange between qualitative and quantitative representation, the supervising process is much easier, and the results are robust. The combination of these techniques enables it to scale for data sets with many attributes and classify data sets irrespective of the number of classes, attributes, and examples.

4.5 Experiments and Results

In this section, we discuss the domain of acute abdominal pain, focusing on the models used for the diagnosis, which will test and verify our model and algorithms. The most serious common cause of acute abdominal pain is appendicitis, and in many cases a clear diagnosis of appendicitis is difficult, since other diseases such as Non-Specific Abdominal Pain (NSAP) can present similar signs and symptoms (findings). The tradeoff is between the possibility of an unnecessary appendectomy and a perforated appendix, which increases mortality rates five-fold. The high incidence of acute abdominal pain coupled with the poor diagnosis accuracy, make any improvements in diagnostic accuracy significant.

The abdominal pain data used for this study consists of 10270 cases, each with 169 attributes. The class variable, final diagnosis, has 19 possible values, and the variables have a number of values ranging from 2 to 32 values. The resulting database addresses acute abdominal pain of gynaecological origin, based on case-notes for patients of reproductive age admitted to hospital, with no recent history of abdominal or back pain. In compiling the database, the first 202 cases were used in the design of the database itself; thus, they cannot be used for the purpose of testing any model. Moreover, out of the 10270 cases, the diagnosis of only 8950 cases was definitely known (definite diagnoses); the remaining 1320 cases were assigned the best possible diagnosis, as a presumed diagnosis. Finally, 120 patients occur more than once in the database.

Table 1. Classification Results for Acute Abdominal Pain

Class Variable	Cloud Models Method	C4.5	Expert Diagnosis
Appendicitis	3707	3269	3770
Stomach disease	3025	2750	3108
Liver diseases	636	567	669
Spleen diseases	304	288	310
Gallbladder diseases	247	243	235
Small intestine diseases	236	235	240
Large intestine diseases	225	229	224
Uterus diseases	221	220	212
Kidney diseases	211	199	214
Gallstone	163	167	180
Duodenitis	118	139	145
Colonitis	159	168	165
Caecitis	138	150	156
Rectitis	166	184	187
Alimentary intoxication	134	141	145
Acid intoxication	77	84	87
Parcreatitis	54	61	68
Intimitis	69	82	83
Other diseases	380	1094	72

Our results show that 2 of 19 classes accounted for almost 67% of the cases, whereas each of the other classes accounted for 7% or less of the cases. For each of the 2 most common classes, since the probability distribution was induced from many cases, our model was significantly better than C4.5 methods (shown as table 1), correctly classifying about 89% of the cases.

On the other hand, on the cases involving the other 17 classes, C4.5 classifier performed better than the cloud models approach (not significantly better). This because the cloud models could not accurately estimate the complicated distributions from so few cases, leading to poor predictive accuracy.

These results offer some insights into the cloud models. In complex domains with many attributes, such as the abdominal pain domain, feature selection may play a very important part in classifiers for diagnosis; this is especially true when the data set is relatively small. In such cases, it is difficult to accurately acquire classification rules for the larger data set. Moreover, in domains where there are sufficient cases (as for the two main classes in the abdominal pain data set), cloud models method plays very well since they can easily model attribute dependencies. However, if the number of cases is small, then the simple decision tree method may perform better.

5 Conclusion

Data classification is a well-recognized operation in data mining and knowledge discovery research field and it has been studied extensively in statistics and machine learning literature. We described a novel approach to search for domain classification. The goal of the search is to find a classification or classifications that jointly provide a good, in the qualitative terms' sense, approximation of the interest. We presented a new mathematical representation of qualitative concepts—Cloud Models. With the models, mapping between quantities and qualities becomes much easier and interchangeable. Based on them, we introduced the concept of soft threshold and concept tree with qualitative terms. We also developed algorithms for clouds generation, complexity reduction, and identifying interacting attributes, etc. After classification search, further steps in the qualitative approach to knowledge discovery involve classification analysis and simplification, rule induction and prediction, if required by any application. These aspects will require a lot of work, and have been omitted here, as they will be presented in detail in other publications.

References

1. J.R. Quinlan , "Induction of decision trees," Machine Learning, Vol. 1, 1986, pp81-106.
2. J.R. Quinlan, "C4.5: Programs for Machine Learning," Morgan Kaufmann,1993.
3. Shan,N., Ziarko, W., Hamilton, H.J., and Cercone, "Discovery Classification Knowledge in Databases Using Rough Sets", In Proceedings of KDD-96: Second International Conference on Knowledge Discovery & Data Mining, Menlo Park, CA: AAAI Press, 1996.
4. M. Mehta, R. Agrawal, and J. Rissanen, "A fast scaleable classifier for data mining," In Proc. of the Fifth Int'l Conference on Extending Database Technology, 1996.
5. A.Agrawal, S.ghosh, T. Imielinkski, B. Iyer, and A. Swami, "An Interval Classifier for Database Mining Applications," Proceedings of the 18th International Conference on Very Large Data Bases, August 1992, p.560-573.
6. Li Deyi, Shi Xuemei, Meng Haijun. "Membership clouds and clouds generators", The Research and Development of Computers,1995,42(8):32-41.
7. D.Li, X.Shi,P.Ward and M.M.Gupta, "Soft Inference Mechanism Based on Cloud Models," in Proceedings of the First International Workshop on Logic Programming and Soft Computing, Edited by Francesca Arcelli Fontana, Ferrante Formato and Trevor P. Martin, Bonn, Germany, Sept 6, 1996, p.38-62.
8. Deyi Li, Jiawei Han, Xuemei Shi, and Man Chung Chan, "Knowledge representation and discovery based on linguistic atoms", Knowledge-Based Systems, Elsevier Science B.V. 10(1998):431-440.
9. J. Han, Y. Cai, and N. Cercone, "Data-driven discovery of quantitative rules in relational databases", IEEE Trans. Knowledge and Data Engineering, Vol. 3, 1993, p.29-40.
10. Y. Cai, N. Cercone, and J. Han, "Attribute-Oriented Induction in Relational Databases," In Knowledge Discovery in Database, 1991, p.213-228.
11. Ziarko, W. And Shan, N. "On Discovery of Attribute Interactions and Domain Classifications", In Lin.T.Y eds., Special Issue in Journal of Intelligent Automation and Soft Computing, 1995.

Robust Clustering of Large Geo-referenced Data Sets

Vladimir Estivill-Castro and Michael E. Houle

Department of Computer Science & Software Engineering,
The University of Newcastle, Callaghan, NSW 2308, Australia.

Abstract. Clustering geo-referenced data with the medoid method is related to k-MEANS, with the restriction that cluster representatives are chosen from the data. Although the medoid method in general produces clusters of high quality, it is often criticised for the $\Omega(n^2)$ time that it requires. Our method incorporates both proximity and density information to achieve high-quality clusters in $O(n \log n)$ expected time. This is achieved by fast approximation to the medoid objective function using proximity information from Delaunay triangulations.

1 Introduction

Geographic data and associated data sets are now being generated faster than they can be meaningfully analysed. Spatial Data Mining [7,9,10,13,15,16] aims at benefiting from this information explosion. It provides automated and semi-automated analysis of large volumes of spatial information associated with a GIS and the discovery of interesting, implicit knowledge in spatial databases.

Central to spatial data mining is clustering, which seeks to identify subsets of the data having similar characteristics. Clustering allows for generalisation analyses of the spatial component of the data associated with a GIS [20]. Clustering of large geo-referenced data sets has many applications, and has recently attracted the attention of many researchers [6,8,10,20,26–28]. The volume of the data forces clustering algorithms for spatial data mining to be as fast as possible at no expense to the quality of the clustering. They must be especially fast if the knowledge discovery process is to be an exploratory type of analysis [22], where many potential hypotheses must be constructed and tested.

In spatial settings, the clustering criteria almost invariably make use of some notion of proximity, as it captures the essence of spatial autocorrelation and spatial association. Proximity is of crucial importance, and is usually evaluated by geo-referenced distances. Bottom-up approaches, in which clusters are formed by composition of items which are 'close' together, accord with the view that in geographical application areas, nearby items have more influence upon each other. An examples of such an agglomerative approach is DBSCAN [8].

However, top-down approaches to clustering are also of interest. The top-down perspective defines clustering as partitioning a heterogeneous data set into smaller, more homogeneous groups. This amounts to identifying regions of elements which are very different from others in the set. The classical example of this is k-MEANS, which partitions the data by assigning each data point to a representative. The partition optimises a statistical homogeneity criterion — namely, the total expected dissimilarity between an item and its representative.

We present a *medoid*-based clustering method that incorporates both proximity and density information. Medoid-based clustering [10, 11, 14, 20] is similar to mean-based clustering, except in that it considers only data points as representative points. The medoid-based approach was introduced to spatial data mining [20] with CLARANS (a random hill-climber strategy). CLARANS required quadratic time per iteration [20, 8] and produced poor partitions [11, 19]. Since then, medoid-based methods have been introduced which generally produce clusters of higher quality than k-MEANS, and which are robust to outliers, robust to noise and work well with random initialisation [11]. Nevertheless, there are two main criticisms of medoid-based clustering: if the number n of data points is large, it typically requires $\Theta(n^2)$ for some hill-climbing iterations, whereas k-MEANS requires only $O(n)$ time; also, as with k-MEANS, the number of clusters k must be specified in advance. Recently, more efficient and effective hill-climbers have been developed for the medoids approach in the context of spatial data mining [10]. We present further improvements upon these methods.

The medoid-based clustering algorithm that we present requires only expected $O(n \log n)$ time, and does not require specification of the number of clusters in advance. Moreover, we achieve this by incorporating proximity information using the Voronoi diagram [21] of the data points. The end result is a partitioning method for clustering that incorporates density and proximity information as in the agglomerative approaches. To our knowledge, this is the first time the bottom-up and top-down philosophies have been combined in this way for clustering. The algorithm is competitive with recently developed proximity methods for clustering, but improves in several aspects: in particular, there is no need to specify parameters such as the number or density of clusters.

The organisation of this paper is as follows. The details of the medoid-based approach are presented in Section 2. Section 3 discusses the use of Voronoi diagrams in developing a fast algorithm. We also show how the method can automatically determine the number of clusters into which the data should be grouped. Section 4 is devoted to experimental results, in which our method is compared to several others. We conclude with some final remarks in Section 5.

2   The k-MEDOIDS problem

By starting with a random clustering and iteratively improving it via hill-climbing, the k-MEANS method approximately optimises the following problem:

$$\text{minimise} \ \ M(C) = \sum_{i=1}^{n} w_i \, d(s_i, rep[s_i, C]), \tag{1}$$

where

- $S = \{s_1, \ldots, s_n\} \subset \Re^m$; is a set of n data items in m-dimensional real space;

- the weight w_u may reflect the relevance of the observation s_u, and the distance $d(s_u, s_v)$ may be a metric such as one of the Minkowski distances.
- $C = \{c_1, \ldots, c_k\}$ is a set of k *centres*, or representative points of $\Re^m$; and
- $rep[s_i, C]$ is the closest point in C to s_i.

The partition into clusters is defined by assigning each s_i to its representative $rep[s_i, C]$. Those data items assigned to the same representative are deemed to be in the same cluster; thus, the k centres encode the partition of the data. Typically, $m = 2$ (the points are two-dimensional coordinates of GIS data), and the Euclidean distance metric (or its squared value) is used.

The k-MEDOIDS approach [14, 20] attempts to solve the centres problem shown in Equation (1), but with the added restriction that $C \subset S$. This version of the combinatorial problem is well known to the operations research community as the *p-median problem* (the operations research literature uses p instead of k for the number of groups). The p-median problem cannot be expected to be solved optimally for the large number of observations that knowledge discovery applications typically involve. The problem is NP-hard, and many heuristic approaches have been attempted to obtain approximate solutions for moderately large n [4, 19]. A heuristic by Teitz and Bart [24] has been remarkably successful in finding local optima of high quality, in applications to facility location problems [4, 18, 23], and (after some improvements) very accurate for the clustering of large sets of low-dimensional spatial data [10], even in the presence of noise or outliers. We will refer to this heuristic as TAB.

TAB starts at a randomly-chosen solution C_0. Letting C_t be the current node at time step t, the TAB search is organised in such a way that, in an amortised sense, only a constant number of neighbours of C_t are examined for the next interchange [10]. When searching for a profitable interchange, it considers the points in turn, according to a fixed circular ordering $(s_1, s_2, \ldots, s_n)$ of the points. If point s_i already belongs to the medoid set, the point is ignored, and the turn passes to the next point in the circular list, s_{i+1} (or s_1 if $i = n$). If s_i is not a medoid point, then it is considered for inclusion in the medoid set. The most advantageous interchange C^j of non-medoid s_i and medoid s_j is determined, over all possible choices of $s_j \in C_t$. If $C^j = \{s_j\} \cup C_t \setminus \{s_i\}$ is better than C_t, then C^j becomes the new current solution C_{t+1}; otherwise, $C_{t+1} = C_t$. In either case, the turn then passes to the next point in the circular list. If a full cycle through the set of points yields no improvement, a local optimum has been reached, and the search halts. To compute $M(C')$ on a solution C' requires $O(n)$ time — $O(n)$ steps to find $rep[s, C'], \forall s \in S$ ($rep[s, C']$ is either unchanged or the new medoid s_i), and $O(n)$ to compute $M(C')$ as defined in Equation (1). Therefore, the time required to test medoids of C_t for replacement by s_i is $O(kn)$ time. In most situations, $k \ll n$, and thus the test can be considered to take linear time.

3 Incorporating proximity and improving efficiency

Although the TAB heuristic is faster than all other known hill-climbers [4], it requires at least $\Omega(n^2)$ time to locate a local optima for the k-MEDOIDS problem with n data points. To terminate, TAB requires a pass through the data set in which each potential exchange is shown not to improve the value of $M(C)$ [4]. In this section, we present a variant of the k-MEDOIDS approach that requires only $O(n \log n)$ time to terminate. The fundamental idea is that the clustering measure $M(C)$ for k-MEDOIDS is a guide to clustering only — its optimisation is only the means towards that goal. Although evaluating $M(C)$ exactly requires $\Theta(kn)$ time for any given C, we could reduce the complexity of TAB from $\Omega(n^2)$ to $O(un)$ time, if $M(C)$ can be well approximated in $O(un)$ time for some u.

How can $M(C)$ be approximated in time sublinear in n if it is a sum of n terms? The idea is to consider only the most important contributions to the sum, according to what $M(C)$ is meant to measure about a clustering. For each cluster, $M(C)$ totals the weighted discrepancies between the points in the cluster and their representative. Minimising $M(C)$ is equivalent to minimising $M(C)/W$, where $W = \sum_{i=1}^{n} w_i$ is the sum of all weights. The relative importance w_i/W of point s_i can be interpreted as a probability, perhaps as that of a query for the representative of point s_i. The minimisation of $M(C)$ can be viewed as an attempt to minimise the expected distance between a point and its representative. Note also that if K_j is the cluster represented by a medoid $rep[K_j]$, then

$$\frac{M(C)}{W} = \sum_{i=1}^{n} \frac{w_i}{W} d(s_i, rep[s_i, C]) = \sum_{j=1}^{k} \sum_{s_i \in K_j} \frac{w_i}{W} d(s_i, rep[K_j]).$$

Here, $M(C)/W$ consists of k terms, each measuring the expected discrepancy (lack of homogeneity) within a cluster.

The purpose of clustering is to identify subsets, each of whose points are highly similar to one another. However, the greatest individual contributions to that portion of $M(C)$ associated with a cluster K_j are made by outliers assigned to K_j, points which exhibit the least similarities to other points, and which generally should not be considered to be part of any cluster. To eliminate the contributions of outliers towards the expected discrepancy within clusters, we estimate the expected discrepancy amongst non-outlier points only. To do this, we limit the contributions to $M(C)$ to those points which lie amongst the closest to the medoids of C. Instead of finding a medoid set which best represents the entire set of points S, we propose that a medoid set be found which best represents the set of points *in its own vicinity*.

In order to be able to efficiently determine the set of those points in the vicinity of a set of medoids, we preprocess the full set of n points as follows:

1. For each point $s_i \in S$, we find u points that rank highly amongst the nearest neighbours of s_i.

2. Using this information, we construct a *proximity directed graph* $G = (S, E)$ of regular out-degree u and with the set of n points $s_1, \ldots, s_n$ as nodes. The edge set E consists of those pairs of nodes (s_i, s_j) for which s_j is one of the u points found to be close to s_i in the previous step.

The adjacency representation of this regular graph has $O(un)$ size. The value of u will be chosen so that $uk \ll n$.

During the hill-climbing process, whenever TAB evaluates a candidate set C_t of medoids, only uk data points will be examined. First, only those points that are adjacent in the proximity digraph to some medoid $c_j \in C_t$ are ordinarily allowed to contribute to the evaluation of $M(C_t)$. We call this set $P(C)$ of points the *party* of C. Namely, $P(C) = \{s_i \in S | (c_j, s_i) \in E$ and $c_j \in C\}$. However, since two medoids in C_t may share neighbours in the proximity graph, the situation may arise where fewer than uk points are evaluated, (i.e. $\|P(C_t)\| < uk$). In order for the hill-climbing process not to be attracted to medoid sets where fewer than uk points are evaluated, two strategies can be applied to pad the number of evaluations out to exactly uk.

The first strategy fills the quota of uk points by randomly selecting from among the remaining points. The second strategy fills the quota from among the points of the proximity graph by repeatedly adding the contribution of the point which is farthest from its representative medoid, as many times as necessary to bring the total number of contributions to $M(C)$ up to exactly uk. More precisely, the point chosen is the one that maximises the following expression:

$$\max_{\{j | 1 \leq j \leq k \ \& \ c_j \in C_t\}} \max_{\{s_i \in P(C_t) | \ rep[C_t, s_i] = c_j\}} d(s_i, c_j).$$

In our implementations, we have opted for the latter strategy to assure convergence. Unlike the former strategy, the latter is deterministic, and preserves the hill-climbing nature of TAB.

Using the proximity digraph allows us to obtain an approximation $M'(C)$ to $M(C)$ in $O(uk)$ time. Note that our approach does not restrict the candidates for a swap in the search by TAB, but rather it achieves its time savings by effectively simplifying the graph for the p-median problem that TAB must solve. Restricting swaps in TAB on the basis of their distance is common in the statistical literature, but has been shown to result in solutions of poor quality [19].

We complete the description of our approach with the details of the proposed preprocessing. Given a set of data points $S = \{s_1, \ldots, s_n\}$ in the plane, the Voronoi region of $s_i \in S$ is the set of points (not necessarily data points) which have s_i as a nearest neighbour; that is, $\{x \in \Re^2 | \forall j \neq i, d(x, s_i) \leq d(x, s_j)\}$. Taken together, the n Voronoi regions of S form the Voronoi diagram of S (also called the Dirichlet tessellation or the proximity map).

The Delaunay triangulation $\mathcal{D}(S)$ of S is a planar graph embedding defined as follows: the nodes of $\mathcal{D}(S)$ consist of the data points of S, and two nodes s_i, s_j are joined by an edge if the boundaries of the corresponding Voronoi regions share a line segment. Delaunay triangulations capture in a very compact form the proximity relationships among the points of S. Fig. 1 (a) shows the Delaunay triangulation of a set of 100 data points. They have many useful properties [21], the most relevant to our goals being the following:

1. If s_i is the nearest neighbour of s_j from among the data points of S, then (s_i, s_j) is an edge in $D(S)$.
2. The number of edges in $\mathcal{D}(S)$ is at most $3n - 6$.
3. The average number of neighbours of a site s_i in $\mathcal{D}(S)$ is less than 6.
4. The circumcircle of a triangle in $\mathcal{D}(S)$ contains no other point of S.

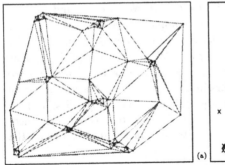 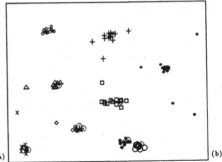

Fig. 1. (a) A data set and its Delaunay triangulation. (b) Clustering produced using a proximity graph derived from the Delauney triangulation.

For each data point $s_i \in S$, consider the ordering of the points of $S \setminus \{s_i\}$ according to the lengths of their shortest paths to s_i within $\mathcal{D}(S)$, from smallest to largest. Here, the length of the path is taken to be the sum of the lengths of its constituent edges in the planar embedding, according to the distance metric d. We claim that the first u sites in this ordering rank very highly amongst the u-nearest neighbours of s_i. When $u = 1$, this is certainly true, due to the first property of Delaunay triangulations stated above. But even for larger values of u, the orderings are still strongly correlated.

Since the triangulation $\mathcal{D}(S)$ can be robustly computed in $O(n \log n)$ time, this structure offers us a way to compute a proximity graph of high quality in subquadratic time. For each medoid point $s_i \in S$, we choose for inclusion in the party $P(C)$ its u-nearest neighbours, according to shortest-path distance within $\mathcal{D}(S)$. The adjacency list for each s_i can be found by means of a modified single-source shortest-path search from s_i, stopping when u distinct neighbours are discovered. The total time required to find u neighbours for all s_i is in $O(un)$. Setting $u = \Theta(\log n)$ allows the proximity graph to be constructed in $O(n \log n)$ total time. Thereafter, each evaluation of $M(C)$ will take $\Theta(\log n)$ time. Although in theory, intermediate hill-climbing steps can involve a linear number evaluations of $M(C)$, they typically involve only about four full TAB cycles through the set of medoid candidates, each cycle taking $\Theta(n \log n)$ time. The termination step itself will take only $\Theta(n \log n)$ time.

Fig. 1 (b) shows the clustering obtained with our algorithm using $k = 10$. The positions of the 10 medoids are indicated with the $\odot$ symbol. We have found that our approach does not sacrifice the quality of the clustering. As with k-MEANS, medoid-based clustering uses the number k of groups as a parameter supplied by the user. Arguably k is an easier parameter to estimate than the density parameters of DBSCAN and STING, and slightly overestimating k is usually not a problem with medoid approaches: whenever k is increased by one, it usually splits one cluster into two subclusters, or places the extra medoid at an outlier. In contrast, k-MEANS typically adjusts many clusters.

Nevertheless, the knowledge discovery process should obtain a robust suggestion for k. Algorithms minimising $M(C)$ do not search for k for two fundamental reasons: (1) The motivation of solving the p-median problem seems to come from a facility location application to locate $p = k$ given facilities (and not to find clusters) and (2) As k increases, $M(C)$ monotonically decreases. Minimising $M(C)$ while allowing k to vary results in $k = n$ — every point is a cluster.

However, the use of $\mathcal{D}(S)$ can rapidly suggest an initial value for k. In fact, the proximity information of its dual, the Voronoi diagram, is implicitly encoded in the Delaunay triangulation, making $\mathcal{D}(S)$ a useful structure for clustering in space [5]. Consider the Delaunay triangulation in Fig. 1. Note that the perimeter lengths of the Delaunay triangles seem either large or small, with few in between. If three points s_i, s_j, s_k form a Delaunay triangle, the circle passing through them is empty of other points of S — and is therefore likely to be small whenever the points belong to a common cluster [21]. The bounding circle in turn limits the perimeter of the triangle, and therefore triangles spanning three points in a common cluster are likely to have smaller perimeter (but not necessarily smaller area) than those spanning points from different clusters. We examine the distribution of perimeter lengths among the $2n - 4$ triangles, and find a value to discriminate between large and small perimeter lengths. We then classify triangles as either large or small. All triangles of small perimeter are selected, and those selected triangles sharing bounding edges are aggregated. The number of contiguous 'patches' or aggregations is the suggestion for k. We have found that a very large range of discriminant values partition into small and large triangles leading to high-quality suggestions for the number k of groups.

4 Comparison and Discussion

The first agglomerative algorithm to require $\Theta(n \log n)$ expected time is DB-SCAN [8]. The algorithm is regulated by two parameters, which specify the density of the clusters. The algorithm places the data points in an R^*-tree, and uses the tree to perform u-nearest-neighbour queries (usually $u = 4$) to achieve the claimed performance in an amortised sense. An extra $\Theta(n \log n)$ expected time is taken in helping the users determine the density parameters, by sorting all distances between a point and its 4-nearest neighbours, and finding a valley in the distribution of these distances. It has been found [26, 27] that determining the parameters of DBSCAN is difficult for large spatial databases. An alternative that does not require input parameters is DBCLASD [27]. Like DBSCAN, DBCLASD can find clusters of arbitrary shape, not necessarily convex; however, DBCLASD is significantly slower than DBSCAN. The clusters produced by DBSCAN and our approach seem to be of equal quality. Our approach shares with DBSCAN the interesting feature that it does not require any assumptions or declarations concerning the distribution of the data. We have also found that the both require roughly the same computational time, once the parameters of DBSCAN have been discovered. Otherwise, DBSCAN must continually ask for assistance from the user. The reliance of DBSCAN on user input can be eliminated using our approach, by using the density of the patches formed by small Delauney triangles as the density parameter for DBSCAN. This ultimately improves DBSCAN, which originally was intended to use a density parameter for each cluster, and not a global user-supplied parameter [8].

Imposing a grid on the data results in another approach [3, 26, 28]. Intuitively, when a grid is imposed on the data, those grid boxes containing a large number of data points would indicate good candidates for clusters. The difficulty for the user is in determining the granularity of the grid. Maximum entropy discretization [3] allows for the automatic determination of the grid granularity, but the size of the grid grows quadratically in the number of points. Later, the BIRCH method saw the introduction of a hierarchical structure for the economical storage of grid information [28]. The recent STING method [26] combines aspects of these two approaches. In two dimensions, STING constructs a hierarchical data structure whose root covers the region of analysis.

In a fashion similar to that of a quadtree, each region has 4 children representing 4 sub-regions. However, in STING, all leaves are at equal depth in the structure, and all leaves represent areas of equal size in the data domain. The structure is built by finding information at the leaves and propagating it to the parents according to arithmetic formulae; for example, the total number of points under a parent node is obtaining by summing the total number of points under each of its children. When used for clustering, the query proceeds from the root down, eliminating branches from consideration because of distribution criteria. As only those leaves that are reached are relevant, the data points under these leaves can be agglomerated. It is claimed that once the search structure is in place, the time taken by STING to produce a clustering will be sublinear. As we indicated earlier, determining the depth of the structure (or the granularity of the grid) is a challenge. STING is a statistical parametric method. It assumes the data is a mixture model and works best with knowledge of the distributions involved. These conditions favour methods such as Expectation Maximisation, Autoclass [2], Minimum Message Length (MML) [25] and Gibb's sampling. Recall that DBSCAN and our approach are non-parametric.

A second problem with STING is that the grid to be imposed on the data grows very rapidly with the number of dimensions. Thus, with bidimensional points, this limits the number of slabs to $O(n^{1/2})$, if linear time and storage is desired. This in turn imposes limitations upon the granularity of the cells in the grid. The construction of the hierarchical data structure requires $\Omega(n \log n)$ time if there are $\Omega(n)$ leaves. Note that if an insertion algorithm works with a tree with nodes and pointers, then the construction time is proportional to the external path length of the tree. If a linearisation of space is used, then the arithmetic to summarise from offspring to parents demands operations with the bit patterns of the indices of slabs. This costs $\Omega(\log n)$ per point. STING construction works in linear time if the depth is of the structure is restricted to 4 levels [26]. Our implementation of STING uses $O(n)$ space, as it limits the number of cells at the bottom level to $g = 4^c$, where c is the first integer such that $4^c > n$. STING finds clusters that are restricted to orthogonal polygons, and its result is a choropletic (two-colour) map where disjoint regions are assumed to indicate different clusters. A statistical test on density is made on bottom level cells to decide if they are in a cluster or not. In the example of Fig. 1, STING accepts only cells with a count of 4 or larger. Thus, only 6 groups are found by STING, although the data set has at least 8 obvious clusters. Many points that are clearly members of clusters are not labelled as such, because they have been separated from their clusters, lying in cells with a low count. This poor clustering reflects many of the problems with this type of statistical approach when attempting to keep the algorithmic time requirements close to $O(n \log n)$.

STING is very well suited for an OLAP environment and SQL-type queries specifying several characteristics on the attributes on geo-referenced records. In such settings, an indexing hierarchical structure such as STING's allows for the elimination of many sub-nodes on the basis of attributes values, thereby arriving at a relatively small number of cells at the bottom level where the statistical density tests are performed. In fact, it may be the SQL query itself which specifies the minimum density threshold.

Construction of a *dendogram*, a type of proximity tree, allows another hierarchical approach for clustering two-dimensional points in $O(n \log n)$ time [17]. Initially, each data point is associated with its own leaf, and each leaf constitutes a cluster with only one member. Iteratively, the pair of nodes representing the two closest clusters are joined under a new parent node, and their data points together form a new cluster associated with that parent node. The two clusters are deleted from the pool of available clusters, and the new merged cluster is added to the pool. The process terminates when only one cluster remains. Unfortunately, it is unclear how to use the proximity tree to obtain associations from distinct data layers in a GIS [8].

There are two classical approaches to finding the number k of groups: AUTOCLASS [2] and Minimum Message Length(MML) [25]. Both demand a declaration of a probabilistic mixture model. AUTOCLASS [2] searches for the classes using a Bayesian statistical technique. It requires an explicit declaration of how members of class are distributed in the data in order to form a probabilistic class model. AUTOCLASS uses a variant of Expectation Maximisation, and thus, it is a randomised hill-climber similar to k-MEANS or TaB, with additional techniques for avoiding local maxima. Similarly, MML methods [25] require the declaration of a model for which to describe the data, in two parts. The first part is an encoding of parameters of the mixture model; the second is an encoding of the data given the parameters. There is a trade-off between the complexity of the model and the quality of fit. Also hard optimisation problems must be solved heuristically when encoding parameters in the fewest number of bits.

For an approach that does not assume a predefined mixture model, Ng and Han [20] proposed to run CLARANS once for each k, from 2 to n. For each of the discovered clusterings, the *silhouette coefficient* [14] is calculated. The clustering of maximum silhouette coefficient is chosen, determining the number of classes. This is prohibitively expensive for large values of n.

5 Final remarks

We have presented a clustering method which both exhibits the characteristics of density-based clustering (like DBSCAN) and is fully autonomous. It does not demand the declaration of a density model from the user, and because it uses a medoid-based approach is robust to outliers and noise. All this is achieved within $O(n \log n)$ expected time.

Recently, the Knowledge Discovery and Data Mining perspective on clustering has generally been that of scaling algorithms for a density estimation problem solved through k-MEANS [1] or Expectation Maximisation [12]. In particular, much effort has been focused on the sensitivity of k-MEANS and Expectation Maximisation on the set of representatives used to initialise the search [1].

The medoids approach is robust with respect to random initialisation. However, researchers have recently identified a set of desiderata for clustering methods [1, 12] with which our medoid approach complies. Namely, the clustering method should be stoppable and resumable, with the capacity to obtain a clustering solution at any time, and to be able to improve on the quality of the solution given more computational resources. Also, since clustering is central to spatial generalisation, it has been suggested [26] that clustering methods should find groups directly from the data; this favours medoids over k-MEANS.

References

1. P.S. Bradley, U. Fayyad, and C. Reina. Scaling clustering algorithms to large databases. R. Agrawal and P. Stolorz, eds., *Proc. of the 4th Int. Conf. on Knowledge Discovery and Data Mining*, 9–15. AAAI Press, 1998.
2. P. Cheeseman, M. Self, J. Kelly, W. Taylor, D. Freeman, and J. Stutz. Bayesian classification. *Proc. of the Seventh National Conf. on Artificial Intelligence*, 607–611, Palo Alto, CA, 1988. AAAI, Morgan Kaufmann.
3. D.K.Y. Chiu, A.K.C. Wong, and B. Cheung. Information discovery through hierarchical maximum entropy discretization and synthesis. G. Piatetsky-Shapiro et al., eds., *Knowledge Discovery in Databases*, 125–140, 1991. AAAI Press.
4. P. Densham and G. Rushton. A more efficient heuristic for solving large p-median problems. *Papers in Regional Science*, 71:307–329, 1992.
5. C. Eldershaw and M. Hegland. Cluster analysis using triangulation. B.J. Noye, M.D. Teibner, and A.W. Gill, eds., *Proc. of Computational Techniques with Applications CTAC97*, 201–208. World Scientific Singapore, 1997.
6. M. Ester, A. Frommelt, H.P. Kriegel, and J. Sander. Algorithms for characterization of trend detection in spatial databases. R. Agrawal et al., eds., *Proc. of the Fourth Int. Conf. KDD-98*, 44–50. AAAI Press, 1998.
7. M. Ester, H.P. Kriegel, and J. Sander. Spatial data mining: A database approach. A. School and A. Voisard, eds., *Advances in Spatial Databases, 5th Int. Symp., SDD-97*, 47–66, Berlin, Germany, 1997. Springer-Verlag LNCS 1262.
8. M. Ester, H.P. Kriegel, S. Sander, and X. Xu. A density-based algorithm for discovering clusters in large spatial databases with noise. E. Simoudis, et al. eds., *Proc. of the 2nd Int. Conf. KDD-96*, 226–231, Menlo Park, CA, 1996. AAAI Press.

337

9. M. Ester, H.P. Kriegel, and X. Xu. Knowledge discovery in large spatial databases: Focusing techniques for efficient class identification. M.J. Egenhofer et al. eds., *Advances in Spatial Databases SDD-95*, 70–82, 1995. Springer-Verlag LNCS 951.

10. V. Estivill-Castro and A.T. Murray. Discovering associations in spatial data - an efficient medoid based approach. X. Wu et al., eds., *Proc. of the 2nd Pacific-Asia Conf. PAKDD-98*, 110–121, 1998. Springer-Verlag LNAI 1394.

11. V. Estivill-Castro and A.T. Murray. Mining spatial data via clustering. T.K. Poiker and N. Chrisman, eds., *Proc. of the 8th Int. Symp. on Spatial Data Handling (SDH-98)*, 522–532. Int. Geographical Union, 1998.

12. U. Fayyad, C. Reina, and P.S. Bradley. Initialization of iterative refinement clustering algorithms. R. Agrawal and P. Stolorz, eds., *Proc. of the Fourth Int. Conf. on Knowledge Discovery and Data Mining*, 194–198. AAAI Press, 1998.

13. K. Han, J. Koperski and N. Stefanovic. GeoMiner: A system prototype for spatial data mining. *SIGMOD Record*, 26(2):553–556, 1997.

14. L. Kaufman and P.J. Rousseuw. *Finding Groups in Data: An Introduction to Cluster Analysis*. John Wiley & Sons, NY, USA, 1990.

15. E.M. Knorr, R.T. Ng, and D.L. Shilvock. Finding boundary shape matching relations in spatial data. A. School et al., eds., *Advances in Spatial Databases, 5th Int. Symp., SDD-97*, 29–46, Berlin, Germany, 1997. Springer-Verlag LNCS 1262.

16. K. Koperski and J. Han. Discovery of spatial association in geographic information databases. M.J. Egenhofer et al., eds., *Advances in Spatial Databases — Proc. of the 4th Int. Symp. SDD-95*, 47–66, 1995. Springer-Verlag LNCS 951.

17. D. Krznaric and C. Levcopoulos. Fast algorithms for complete linkage clustering. *Discrete & Computational Geometry*, 19:131–145, 1998.

18. A.T. Murray and R.L. Church. Applying simulated annealing to location-planning models. *J. of Heuristics*, 2:31–53, 1996.

19. A.T. Murray and V. Estivill-Castro. Cluster discovery techniques for exploratory spatial data analysis. *Int. J. of GIS*, 12(5):431–443, 1998.

20. R.T. Ng and J. Han. Efficient and effective clustering methods for spatial data mining. J. Bocca, et al., eds., *Proc. of the 20th Conf. on Very Large Data Bases (VLDB)*, 144–155, San Francisco, CA, 1994. Santiago, Chile, Morgan Kaufmann.

21. A. Okabe, B. Boots, and K. Sugihara. *Spatial Tesselations - Concepts and applications of Voronoi diagrams*. John Wiley & Sons, NY, USA, 1992.

22. S. Openshaw. Two exploratory space-time-attribute pattern analysers relevant to GIS. S. Fotheringham and P. Rogerson, eds., *Spatial Analysis and GIS*, 83–104, London, UK, 1994. Taylor and Francis.

23. D. Rolland, E. Schilling and J. Current. An efficient tabu search procedure for the p-median problem. *European J. of Operations Research*, 96:329–342, 1996.

24. M.B. Teitz and P. Bart. Heuristic methods for estimating the generalized vertex median of a weighted graph. *Operations Research*, 16:955–961, 1968.

25. C.S. Wallace and P.R. Freeman. Estimation and inference by compact coding. *J. of the Royal Statistical Society, Series B*, 49(3):223–265, 1987.

26. W. Wang, J. Yang, and R. Muntz. STING: a statistical information grid approach to spatial data mining. M. Jarke, ed., *Proc. of the 23rd Int. Conf. on Very Large Data Bases*, 186–195, Athens, Greece, August 1997. VLDB, Morgan Kaufmann.

27. X. Xu, M. Ester, H.P. Kriegel, and J. Sander. A distribution-based clustering algorithm for mining large spatial databases. *Proc. of the 14th Int. Conf. on Data Engineering*, 324–33, Orlando, FL, February 1998. IEEE, IEEE Computer Society.

28. T. Zhang, R. Ramakrishnan, and M. Livny. BIRCH: an efficient data clustering method for very large databases. *SIGMOD Record*, 25(2):103–114, June 1996.

A Fast Algorithm for Density-Based Clustering in Large Database

Bo Zhou[1], David W. Cheung[2], and Ben Kao[2]

[1] Department of Computer Science and Engineering
The Zhejiang University, Hangzhou, China
bzhou@csis.hku.hk
[2] Department of Computer Science and Information Systems
The University of Hong Kong, Hong Kong
{dcheung, kao}@csis.hku.hk

Abstract. Clustering in large database is an important and useful data mining activity. It expects to find out meaningful patterns among the data set. Some new requirements of clustering have been raised : good efficiency for large database; easy to determine the input parameters; separate noise from the clusters [1]. However, conventional clustering algorithms seldom can fulfill all these requirements. The notion of density-based clustering has been proposed which satisfies all these requirements [1]. In this paper, we present a new and more efficient density-based clustering algorithm called FDC. The clustering in this algorithm is defined by an equivalence relationship on the objects in the database. The complexity of FDC is linear to the size of the database, which is much faster than that of the algorithm DBSCAN proposed in [1]. Extensive performance studies have been carried out on both synthetic and real data which show that FDC is the fastest density-based clustering algorithm proposed as far.

Keywords: Clustering, Density-base method, Spatial Database

1 Introduction

Both the number of databases and the amount of data stored in a database are increasing rapidly in recent years. There are lots of useful information hidden in the data. Therefore, automatic knowledge discovery in database becomes more and more important. Clustering — the grouping of objects into meaningful classes — is one of the important data mining tasks.

Data mining has raised new requirements for clustering [1]:

- Good efficiency for large database : there may be millions of objects inside the database. Clustering algorithm should scale up well against large database, and hence should not be memory-based.
- Reduce dependence on input parameters : because appropriate values for the parameters are often difficult to determine. For example, we usually do not know apriori the number of clusters.

- Able to separate noise from the data : there may exist some points in the database that do not belong to any meaningful cluster — the algorithm should be able to separate these *noise points* from the clusters.

None of the conventional clustering algorithms can fulfill all these requirements. Recently, some new algorithms have been developed to improve the efficiency of clustering in large database : these include algorithms such as CLARANS [2,3], BIRCH [4] and CURE [5]. However, these algorithms are not designed to handle noise, and many of them need to assume the number of clusters before starting the clustering.

A density-based algorithm DBSCAN is proposed in [1,6]. It requires the user to specify two parameters to define the density threshold for clustering: *Eps*, the radius of the neighborhood of a point; *MinPts*, the minimum number of points in the neighborhood. Clusters are then found by starting from an arbitrary point, if its *Eps*-neighborhood contains more than *MinPts* points, then all the points in the *Eps*-neighborhood belong to the same cluster. The process is repeated on the newly added points until all points have been processed. Points that cannot be absorbed into any cluster are noise points. The notion of density-based cluster can fulfill the aforementioned requirements on clustering for mining useful patterns in large databases [1]. DBSCAN uses an R*-tree to manage all the points and to compute neighborhood of a data point. Its complexity is at least on the order of $N \log N$, where N is the size of the database. In this paper, we introduce a new density-based notion of clustering in which the clusters are equivalent classes of a binary relationship defined between objects in the database. This notion gives a more precise definition than that in [1]. We also propose an algorithm called FDC to compute density-based clusters. The complexity of FDC is linear to N and hence is much faster than DBSCAN.

The rest of the paper is organized as follows. In Section 2 , we present our notion of density-based clustering. Section 3 introduces the algorithm FDC. The performance studies of FDC are presented in Section 4, the results are compared with DBSCAN. We use synthetic data as well as real data in our studies. Finally, we conclude our paper in Section 5.

2 A Density-Based Notion of Clusters

We first give a brief overview of the notion of density-based clustering as defined in [1]. Given a set of objects (or points) in a database D, a distance function *dist* on the objects, a neighborhood radius *Eps*, and a threshold *MinPts* on the minimum number of objects in the neighborhood, the notion of clustering in [1] is defined as the following:

Definition 1. (directly density-reachable) An object p is *directly density-reachable* from an object q if

- $p \in N_{Eps}(q)$, where $N_{Eps}(q) = \{t | t \in D, dist(q,t) \leq Eps\}$,
- $|N_{Eps}(q)| \geq MinPts$ (*core point condition*).

Definition 2.(density-reachable) An object p is *density-reachable* from an object q if there is a chain of objects $p_1 = q$, p_2, $\cdots$, $p_n = p$, such that p_{i+1} is directly density-reachable from p_i, $\forall i = 1, \cdots, n-1$.

Definition 3. (density-connected) An object p is *density-connected* to an object q if $\exists o \in D$ such that both p and q are density-reachable from o.

A *cluster* is defined as a set of density-connected objects which is maximal with respect to density-reachability. The objects not contained in any cluster are the *noise*.

Definition 4: (cluster) A *cluster* C with respect to *Eps* and *MinPts* in D is a non-empty subset of D satisfying the following conditions:

- Maximality: $\forall p, q \in D$, if $q \in C$ and p is density-reachable from q, then $p \in C$.
- Connectivity: $\forall p, q \in C$, p is density-connected to q.

Based on the above notion of cluster, it can be concluded that a cluster C in D can be grown from an arbitrary core point in C by absorbing the points in its *Eps*-neighborhood into C recursively. DBSCAN is developed based on this idea.

The density-connected relationship is symmetric but not transitive, while density-reachable is transitive but not symmetric. The notion of clustering in Definition 4 is a partitioning on objects in D with respect to the relationships *density-connected* and *density-reachable*. However, these two relationships are not compatible with each other. In some case, there is a contradiction between the *Maximality* and *Connectivity* conditions. In Fig. 1, there are two clusters of points C_1 and C_2 touching at their boundary. There exists some point p in the boundary area, which is density-reachable from a core point q_1 in C_1 and from another core point q_2 in the second cluster C_2. However, p itself is not a core point because of not enough neighborhood points. Let us assume that there is no chain connecting the points in C_1 to C_2, i.e., they are not density-connected. With respect to this situation, we would expect p to belong to both clusters C_1 and C_2. If the Maximality condition holds, then C_1 and C_2 should be merged into one cluster. On the other hand, the points in C_1 are not density-connected to those in C_2, hence they shouldn't be together in one cluster. This anomaly shows that the two relationships density-reachable and density-connected are not quite compatible with each other. Algorithmically, DBSCAN would assign the point p to the cluster which is generated first, and the two clusters are hence separated at the boundary near p.

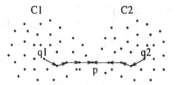

p density-reachable from q1

p also density-reachable from q2

q1 and q2 are not density-connected

Fig. 1. Clustering Anomaly

We found that the above anomaly can be resolved by defining a new "connectivity" notion called "density-linked" which is an equivalent relationship. More importantly, we found out that density-based clusters can than be defined as equivalent classes with respect to this equivalent relationship. This enhanced notion of connectivity has given density-based clustering a simple and sound theoretical base.

To simplify the representation, we denote the relationship that *object p is directly density-reachable from q* by $p \Leftarrow q$. We redefine the notion of connectivity by the *density-linked* relationship.

Definition 5(density-linked) The binary relationship *density-linked* $\Leftrightarrow$ (with respect to $Eps > 0$ and $MinPts > 1$ in set D) is defined as the following:

- $\forall o \in D, o \Leftrightarrow o$;
- $\forall p, q \in D, p \neq q$, then $p \Leftrightarrow q$ iff $\exists p = o_1, o_2, \cdots, o_n = q \in D$ such that $\forall i = 1, \cdots, n-1$, either $o_i \Leftarrow o_{i+1}$ or $o_{i+1} \Leftarrow o_i$.

From the definition, we can directly deduce the following important lemma:
Lemma 1: The relationship *density-linked* $\Leftrightarrow$ with respect to given Eps and $MinPts$ in set D is an equivalent relationship.

For a non-empty set D, the equivalent relationship $\Leftrightarrow$ can be used to determine an unique partitioning of D. In fact, we can define density-based clustering by this partitioning.

Definition 6 (cluster & noise) Suppose $\pi = C_1, C_2, \cdots, C_m$ are the equivalent classes on D defined by the relationship $\Leftrightarrow$ with respect to Eps and $MinPts$.

- if $|C_i| > 1$, then C_i is a **cluster**;
- if $|C_i| = 1$ and $o \in C_i$, then o is a **noise**.

A cluster C defined above will contain at least $MinPts$ points. Because C will contain at least two points p and q. By definition, either $p \Leftarrow q$ or $q \Leftarrow p$. Hence one of them must be a core point and its Eps-neighborhood will contain at least $MinPts$ points, which will all be in the cluster C.

Besides the merit that the clustering is defined by a simple equivalent relationship, we also have resolved the above mentioned anomaly : our definition allow a cluster to include two (or more) disjoint (not density-connected) sets of core points which share a thin layer of border points.

Before introducing our clustering algorithm, we present a theorem which characterises the basic computation in the algorithm. It provides a criteria to determine the *clustering property* of every object in D. (The clustering property of an object is the information of whether it is a noise or which cluster does it belongs to.)

Theorem 1 Given a data set D and the relationship *density* $-$ *linked* $\Leftrightarrow$ with Eps and $MinPts$. $\forall o \in D$, its clustering property can be determined by the following rule:

- if $|N_{Eps}(o)| = 1$, o is a noise;
- if $|N_{Eps}(o)| \geq MinPts$, o is a core point of a cluster, and all objects in $N_{Eps}(o)$ belong to the same cluster;
- otherwise, let $T = \{p | p \in N_{Eps}(o), |N_{Eps}(p)| \geq MinPts\}$, if $T \neq \emptyset$ than o and all objects in T belong to the same cluster; else, o is a noise.

Following Theorem 1, we need to compute the $N_{Eps}(o)$ for every point o in the database to determine its clustering property. If either condition 1 or 2 is true, then the point's clustering property has been determined; otherwise, we can skip the point temporary. Eventually one of the two possibilities in case 3 will become true : either it is found in the Eps-neighborhood of some other core point, or it is a noise. Note that, unlike DBSCAN, in Theorem 1 no recursion is required to compute the clustering property of the objects. We will show in the next section that a linear algorithm can be developed to compute all the clusters based on this theorem.

3 The FDC Algorithm for Density-Based Clustering

In this section we present the efficient algorithm FDC (Fast Density-Based Clustering) for density-based clustering defined by the density-linked relationship. The main task is to compute efficiently the Eps-neighborhood for **every point** in the database. We assume that the total size of the objects are too large to be processed together in the memory.

FDC is a multi-stage algorithm. It first stores all the data points in a k-d tree. This partitions the whole data space into a set of rectangular subspaces, each represented by a leaf node on the tree. We assume that the subspaces on the k-d tree are small enough to be processed in the memory. Secondly, we search the Eps-neighborhoods for the points in each subspace (leaf node) separately. Those points whose clustering property can be determined entirely within the subspace are first identified and removed from the memory. The remaining points are those that are near the split boundary of the node. In order to find out all the neighboring points for these boundary points, cross boundary searching is performed across the split boundary at the internal nodes of the k-d tree. Note that after a leaf node is processed, only a smaller number of boundary points need to be maintained in the memory to support cross boundary searching.

The first step of FDC is to build a k-d tree on the database. As an example, in Fig. 2, a 2-dimensional data space is partitioned into 7 subspaces representing by the leaf nodes $n_1, \cdots, n_7$ in the corresponding k-d tree.

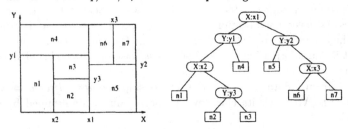

Fig. 2. K-d tree from FDC

After building the k-d tree structure, FDC performs a postorder bottom-up traversal on the tree. At a leaf node, FDC performs a cell-based procedure **NodeClustering** to determine the clustering property for all the points in the node except those that are near the split boundary (boundary points). When FDC traverses to a non-leaf node, it uses the cross boundary searching procedure **CrossClustering** to compute the *Eps*-neighborhoods for the boundary points found previously in its two child nodes. Cross boundary searching at an internal node is performed on the split boundary in the k-d tree. Once FDC reaches the root node of k-d tree, the clustering property of all the points can be determined.

In order to manage the cross boundary searching, we define the *cross clustering order(CCO)* of a node. It is an ordering of the boundaries of a node which determines the order of performing cross boundary searching at the node. For example, the *CCO* of node n_3 in Fig. 2 is $< L_y, L_x, U_y, U_x >$. (We use L_x and U_x to denote the lower and upper X-axis boundaries respectively.) In fact, the *CCO* of a node is the reverse of the split order when the node is being generated. For example, node n_1 has two split boundaries, and U_y is generated before U_x. Therefore, the *CCO* of node n_1 is $< U_x, U_y >$.

We present the algorithm FDC in Fig. 3 and explain some details in the following subsections.

/* Input: D: database ; *Eps, MinPts*: thresholds; Output: Clusters of D. */
1)   scan the database D once to build a k-d tree Tr ;
     for each point $p \in D$, $p.CID = UNCLASSIFIED$;
2)   initialize the global variable $CidSet$;
3)   traverse Tr in a postorder and for each node *Node* do {
4)   if *Node* is a leaf node then $NodeClustering(Node, Eps, MinPts)$;
5)   if *Node* is an internal node then
             $CrossClustering(Node, Lbps, Rbps, Eps, MinPts)$;
                 /* Lbps, Rbps are the boundary points found in the two child nodes */
6)   }
7)   scan D and re-label all the points with cluster ids determined in $CidSet$;

Fig. 3. Algorithm **FDC**

3.1   NodeClustering : a cell-based clustering procedure

NodeClustering is used to perform clustering in each leaf node. The most time consuming task is to find out the neighbors for all points inside the subspace of the node. The simplest way is to compute the distance between any pair of points in the node and this would require an $O(N_n^2)$ computation, where N_n is the number of the points inside the node. FDC has developed a cell-based approach whose time complexity is linear to the number of points.

NodeClustering (see Fig. 4) first divides the subspace into equal sized rectangular cells whose length on each dimension is equal to *Eps*. All data points in the subspace are mapped into these cells. Since we can control the size of the leaf node, it is reasonable to assume that both the data set of the node and the multi-dimensional cell array can be fit into the main memory.

Let $C(c_1, c_2, \cdots, c_d)$ be a cell where $c_i, i = 1, \cdots, d$ are the cell coordinates and i is dimension index. We use $NC(C(c_1, c_2, \cdots, c_d)) = \{C(a_1, a_2, \cdots, a_d) | a_i = c_i \pm 1, i = 1, \cdots, d;$ and $C(a_1, \cdots, a_d)$ does not exceed the boundary of the node$\}$

to denote the set of immediate neighboring cells of C. A typical non-boundary cell C (those that does not touch the boundary of the node) has 3^d immediate neighboring cells in $NC(C)$. For any points in C, their Eps-neighboring points must be located within the cells in $NC(C)$. Therefore, we only need to check the 3^d cells in $NC(C)$ in order to find out all neighboring points for any point in C. Note that $NodeClustering$ needs to maintain the boundary points for future cross boundary searching.

```
/*   Input: Node: a leaf node on the k-d tree; Node.D is the set of data points;
             Node.S is the subspace; and Node.CCO is the cross clustering order.
        Eps, MinPts: the clustering parameters.
     Output: RCS: the points whose clustering property have been determined;
             BPS[]: the boundary points on each split boundary */
        /* prepare for clustering */
1)      quantize Node.S by mapping all the points in Node.D into a cell array CS
        determined by Eps;
        /* clustering */
2)      for each non-empty cell c in CS do{
3)         for each point p in c do {
4)            calculate N_Eps(p) in NC(c);
5)            if |N_Eps(p)| ≥ MinPts then
6)               AssignClusterID(N_Eps(p));
7)         }
8)      }
        /* dispatch points */
9)      for each point p in Node.D do {
10)        for each boundary b_i in Node.CCO =< b_1, · · · , b_m > do
11)           if p is close to boundary b_i then
12)              { add p to BPS[b_i]; goto 9) };
13)        if p is not close to any boundary in Node.CCO then
14)           if p.CID ≠ UNCLASSIFIED then save p.CID on disk
                 /* the cluster id of p has been identified */
15)           else report p as a noise;
16)     }
```

Fig. 4. Procedure NodeClustering

At step 5, if $|N_{Eps}(p)|$ is less than $MinPts$, according to Theorem 1, if $\exists q \in N_{Eps}(p)$ such that q is a core point, then p, q would belong to the same cluster, otherwise, p is a noise. In fact, if the condition is true, q will be identified as a core point when it is being processed at step 5 and p will be assigned to the same cluster as q. If not, p will not be assigned to any cluster, and will be maintained as a boundary point at step 12 or reported as a noise at step 15.

Assign cluster id. At step 6, we need to assign a set of points P (points in the neighborhod of a core point) to a unique cluster, but some of the points in the set may have been assigned different cluster ids already. However, these points are in fact density-linked, even though there cluster ids are different. Therefore, FDC needs to mark these different cluster ids as equivalent. It uses a global object $CidSet$ to generate and maintain cluster ids. Any two cluster ids which are assigned to density-linked points will be marked equivalent in *CidSet*. Once all points are processed, all equivalent cluster ids in *CidSet* can be identified. At the end, FDC scan the database again and re-assign unique cluster ids to all the points according to the equivalent ids in *CidSet* (step 7 in FDC in Fig. 3).

Identify boundary points. At step 11 of procedure *NodeClustering*, we need to determine the boundary points. There are two types of boundary points. Given a split boundary b_i of a node, the *type one boundary points* are those whose distance from b_i is less than *Eps*. For this type of boundary points, we need to perform cross boundary searching to find out points on the other side of the boundary that fall in their *Eps*-neighborhoods. *Type two boundary points* are those in the set $\{p|p.CID = UNCLASSFIED$, and $\exists q \in N_{Eps}(p), q$ is a type one boundary point$\}$. These are points which have not been assigned to any cluster but are close to a type one boundary point. If a type one boundary point turns out to be a core point after a cross boundary searching, then the type two boundary points close to it will be absorbed into the same cluster.

We can find out type two boundary points by the following procedure: (1) the distance from the point to the boundary is between *Eps* and 2*Eps*; (2) the point is not a core point (otherwise, it would have been assigned to a cluster); (3) none of the points in its *Eps*-neighborhood has been identified as a core point. A type two boundary point will become a noise unless a type one boundary point close to it becomes a core point in a cross boundary searching.

A boundary point is dispatched only to one boundary for the purpose of cross boundary searching. If a point is close to more than one boundaries, the boundary appears first in the *CCO* of the node will be selected for cross boundary searching. For example, the *CCO* of the node n_2 in Fig. 2 is $< U_y, L_x, U_x >$. If a points in n_2 is close to both U_x and U_y, it will be dispatched to U_y for cross boundary searching.

3.2 CrossClustering : cross boundary searching at an internal node

The procedure *CrossClustering* is applied on internal nodes to compute the *Eps*-neighborhoods of the boundary points founded in its child nodes (step 5 of FDC in Fig. 3). It combines the type one boundary points on the two sides of a split boundary from the child nodes. *CrossClustering* again uses the cell-based method to identify the area of searching for the boundary points.

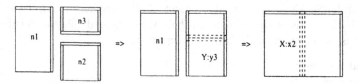

Fig. 5. The procedure *CrossClustering*

An example is presented in Fig. 5 to illustrate the procedure *CrossClustering*. The procedure is first applied to the internal node $Y : y_3$ in Fig. 2. The cross boundary searching is done between its two child nodes n_2 and n_3. The cells containing boundary points at L_y of n_3 and U_y of n_2 are involved in the searching. In the next level up, the procedure is applied to the internal node $X : x_2$, boundary points at U_x of n_1 and those at L_x of $Y : y_3$ are involved in the cross boundary searching at $X : x_2$. During the process, any type one boundary point whose *Eps*-neighborhood has enough points will be promoted to a core point. In addition, all type two boundary points in its immediate neighboring cells will be assigned the same cluster id. At the end of the process, all remaining unassigned boundary points become noise.

3.3 Complexity of FDC

In this section we analyse the complexity of FDC. Since k-d tree is very common, we skip the analysis of the cost of building the tree. However, we would like to note that it is cheaper to build a k-d tree than a R*-tree. Also, according to our performance study, the time spent in building the k-d tree is only a small part of the total cost in the clustering.

I/O cost: FDC needs to perform two passes on the k-d tree. The first is to perform *NodeClustering* in the leaf nodes and *CrossClustering* in the internal nodes. The second pass is to re-label all the points with their unique cluster ids. Therefore, the I/O cost is on the order of scanning the database twice.

CPU cost: For every point $p \in D$, no matter whether it is a boundary point or a non-boundary point, it only needs to compute its distances from the points in its 3^d immediate neighboring cells. Since *Eps* would be rather small, it is reasonable to assume that the number of points in each cell are bounded by a constant. Therefore, the complexity of computing the *Eps*-neighborhoods for all the points is on the order of $3^d \times N$, where N is the number of points in the database. Since d is in general a small integer, the time complexity of FDC is linear to the size of the database.

4 Performance Studies

We have carried out extensive performance studies to investigate FDC on a Sun Enterprise 4000 share-memory computer. The machine has twelve 250 MHz Ultra Sparc processors, running Solaris 2.6, and 1G main memory. We use both synthetic data and real database in the experiments. Our goal is to compare FDC with DBSCAN in various environment. FDC is implemented in C, and the code of DBSCAN is provided by its author. We compared efficiency of the two algorithms with respect to the following parameters:

- database size
- number of clusters
- number of dimensions
- percentage of noise points in the database

The efficiency is measured by response time. Since building the R*-tree in DBSCAN is more complicated than the k-d tree in FDC, in order to make a fair comparison, we have excluded the time to build the trees in the two algorithms. Also, our results have shown that the cost of building the k-d tree is only a small fraction of the total cost of FDC. However, the cost of building the R*-tree is a substantial part of the total cost in DBSCAN.

4.1 Synthetic data generation

The synthetic data are generated by a 2-step procedure controlled by the parameters listed in Table 1. In the first step, pre-defined (size and shape) non-overlapping clusters are randomly generated in the data space. In the second step, points are generated within each cluster with a uniform distribution. The total number of points generated in the clusters is $N \times (1 - p_s)$. An additional $N \times p_s$ points are randomly added to the data space as noise points. In all the studies, except otherwise mentioned explicitly, the percentage of noise p_s is set to 10%.

Table 1. Data generation parameters

d	number of dimensions in the data space
L_i	length of each dimension of the data space, $i = 1, \cdots, d$
N_c	number of clusters
$Shape_j$	shape and size of each cluster, $j = 1, \cdots, N_c$
N	number of data points
p_s	percentage of noise points

4.2 Results on the synthetic data sets

Database size: Our first experiment examines the effect of the database size. We fix the size of a 3-dimensional data space and the number of clusters is set to 10. The number of data points varies from 0.5 million to 3 million. Fig. 6 shows the result : FDC is significantly faster than DBSCAN by a factor between 55 and 70. As predicted, the response time of FDC is linear to the database size. In contrast, the response time of DBSCAN increases much faster than the database size. This shows that the linear growth of the complexity of FDC guarantees that it is a more efficient algorithm than DBSCAN.

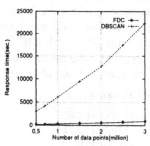
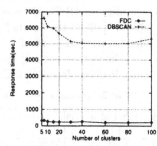

<table>
<tr><td align="center">Fig. 6. Effect of N</td><td align="center">Fig. 7. Effect of N_c</td></tr>
</table>

Number of clusters: Fig. 7 shows the result of varying the number of clusters from 1 to 100. One million data points are generated in a 3-dimensional data space. The results shows that FDC consistently outperforms DBSCAN. As the number of clusters increases, the number of core points decreases, and the total cost of searching would decrease. Therefore, the response time of both algorithms go down slightly when the number of cluster increases.

Number of dimensions: To examine the scalability of FDC against the number of dimensions, we vary the number of dimensions from 2 to 6. The number of data points are fixed to 1 million with 10 clusters. Fig. 8 shows that, even though the response time of FDC does increase exponentially against the increase in the dimension, it increases much slower than DBSCAN.

Percentage of noise points: In this experiment, we study the effect of the percentage of noise points. We vary the percentage from 1% to 25%. The data space has 1 million points and 10 clusters. Fig. 9 again shows that FDC is consistently better than DBSCAN. The response time of both algorithms decrease when the percentage increases — when the number of noise points increases, the number of data points in clusters decreases, and it is cheaper to identify a noise point than a point in a cluster.

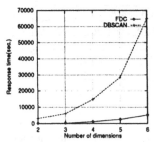 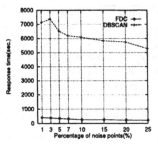

Fig. 8. Effect of d **Fig. 9.** Effect of p_s

4.3 Real data results

We also have studied the efficiency of FDC on a real data set, the SEQUOIA 2000 benchmark data [7]. This benchmark uses real data sets that are representative of Earth Science tasks. We use the point data in the database in our experiment. The performance studies on DBSCAN was also done on the same benchmark [1]. We extract 20% to 100% of the points from the database to compile a series of data sets of different sizes. The result of comparing FDC with DBSCAN is shown in Table 2. It shows that the response time of FDC increases linearly to the size of data base. It outperforms DBSCAN by a factor from 42 to 50.

Table 2. Response times on real database (sec.)

Number of points	12511	25022	37533	50044	62555
FDC	2.23	5.04	7.77	10.18	12.72
DBSCAN	94.09	217.57	348.81	476.07	632.21

In summary, the performance studies clearly demonstrates that FDC is superior than DBSCAN. In particular, its response time increases linearly to the size of the database while that of DBSCAN increases much faster.

5 Discussion and Conclusion

We believe that clustering in large database to identify interesting patterns is an important and useful data mining activity. However, conventional algorithms suffer from severe drawbacks when applied to large database. The density-based notion of cluster is useful in extracting meaningful patterns in large database. In particular, it can separate noises from the meaningful clusters.

In this paper, we have made the following contributions:

- We have defined a new density-based notion of cluster which is derived from an equivalence relationship.
- We have developed a linear algorithm FDC for computing density-based clusters in large database.
- We have performed an in-depth performance study on both synthetic and real data. The result clearly demonstrates that FDC is significantly more efficient than the previously proposed algorithm DBSCAN.

Future research will consider the following issues. The effectiveness of the algorithm is sensitive to the parameters *Eps* and *MinPts*. A mechanism to determine the parameters would be very useful. Enhance the scalability of FDC in high dimensional database is also a challenging problem.

Acknowledgment: We would like to thank Martin Ester for providing the code of DBSCAN and the SEQUIOA 2000 point data set.

References

1. M. Ester, H. Kriegel, J. Sander, and X. Xu. A Density-Based Algorithm for Discovering Clusters in Large Spatial Databases with Noise. In *Proc. of 2nd International Conf. on Knowledge Discovery and Data Mining*, pages 226-231, Portland, Oregon, Aug. 1996.
2. R. T. Ng, J. Han. Efficient and Effective Clustering Methods for Spatial Data Mining. In *Proc. of the 20th VLDB Conf.*, pages 144-155, Santiago,Chile, Sept. 1994.
3. M. Ester, H. Kriegel, and X. Xu. A Database Interface for Clustering in Large Spatial Databases. In *Proc. of the First International Conf. on Knowledge Discovery in Databases and Data Mining*, pages 94-99, Montreal,Canada, Aug. 1995.
4. T. Zhang, R. Ramakrishnan, and M. Livny. BIRCH : An Efficient Data Clustering Method for Very Large Databases. In *Proc. of the ACM SIGMOD Conf. on Management of Data*, pages 103-114, Montreal, Quebec, June 1996.
5. S. Guha, R. Ratogi, and K. Shim. CURE: An Efficient Clustering Algorithm for Large Databases. In *Proc. of the ACM SIGMOD Conf. on Management of Data*, pages 73-84, Seattle, Washington, June 1998.
6. M. Ester, H. Kriegel, J. Sander, M. Wimmer and Xiaowei Xu. Incremental Clustering for Mining in a Data Warehousing Environment. In *Proc. of the 24th VLDB Conf.*, pages 323-333, New York city, New York, Aug. 1998.
7. M. Stonebraker, J. Frew, K. Gardels, J. Meredith. The Sequoia 2000 Benchmark. In *Proc. of the ACM SIGMOD Conf. on Management of Data*, pages 2-11, Washington,D.C., May, 1993.

A Lazy Model-Based Algorithm
for On-Line Classification

Gabor Melli

DataSage, Inc. www.datasage.com
gmelli@datasage.com

Abstract. This paper presents a *lazy model-based* algorithm, named DBPredictor, for on-line classification tasks. The algorithm proposes a local discretization process to avoid the need for a lengthy preprocess stage. Another advantage of this approach is the ability to implement the algorithm with tightly-coupled SQL relational database queries. To test the algorithm's performance in the presence of continuous attributes an empirical test is reported against both an *eager model-based* algorithm (C4.5) and a *lazy instance-based* algorithm (*k*-NN).

1 Introduction

The large number of structured observations now stored in relational databases has created an opportunity for classification tasks that require a prediction for only a single event. This type of prediction will be referred to as on-line classification, to differentiate it from classification tasks that allow for batch style model induction. This paper proposes an algorithm, called DBPredictor, for such on-line classification tasks. The algorithm performs a top-down heuristic search through the IF *antecedent* THEN *consequent* rule space of the specific event to be classified. The two challenges addressed in this paper are the local discretization of numerical attributes and a tightly-coupled implementation against SQL based databases.

Section 2 contrasts the lazy model-based approach to classification form other well known approaches. Section 3 describes DBPredictor with a focus on the support for numerical attributes and an SQL interface. Section 4 presents the results of an empirical investigation into DBPredictor's accuracy with respect to the number of numerical attributes. Finally, Section 5 concludes with a paper summary.

2 Previous Work

An algorithm for on-line classification tasks must decide whether to use an *eager* or *lazy* approach, and whether it should be *model-based* or *instance-based*. Eager algorithms induce a complete classification structure (classifier) before they can process any classification requests. Lazy algorithms, on the other hand, commence to work immediately on classifying the given event [3]. Model-based algorithms, represent their result in a language that is richer than the language used to describe the dataset, while instance-based algorithms represent their result in the same language that is used to described the dataset [11].

Based on these descriptions, on-line classification tasks would likely benefit from a *lazy model-based* algorithm. Such an algorithm would focus its effort on classifying the particular event in question, and would also return a rationale that may help the person interpret the validity of the prediction. Two recent proposals that do make use of a lazy model-based approach include of former version of DBPredictor [8] and the LazyDT [6] (Lazy Decision Tree) algorithms. The main difference between these algorithms is the use of a rules in one and the use of decision tree paths in the other.

These two algorithms however, cannot be tightly-coupled with a SQL based relational database [2, 7] because they require datasets to be both discretized and stored in memory. The version of DBPredictor presented in this paper addresses both these issues and presents a *tightly-coupled* implementation of the SQL Interface Protocol (SIP) proposal [2, 7]. Other details of this algorithm are presented in [9].

3 Algorithm

DBPredictor requires three input parameters: a partially instantiated event e; the attribute whose value is to be predicted A_c; and a dataset D from the same domain as e. With this information, DBPredictor performs a search through a constrained space of all the applicable IF *antecedent* THEN *consequent* classification rules. The search starts from a general *seed rule* that covers e. The algorithm then generates several candidate rules that are more specialized than the previous rule. To determine which rule to further specialize on, the candidate rules are tested with a heuristic function F(). The rule that achieves the highest value at each specialization step is the one selected for the next round of specialization. The search proceeds until a stopping criterion is encountered.

3.1 top_down_search()

Once the seed rule r_0 has been composed, DBPredictor simply outputs the rule returned by a call to top_down_search with parameters $(r_0, (D, e, A_c))$. This procedure performs a greedy top-down search through a constrained rule space. Procedure 3.1 presents a pseudo-code overview of top_down_search(). Only two of its four sub-procedures are described in detail in the coming sections: generate_antecedents(), and get_consequent(). The heuristic function F() can be any impurity measure. Several heuristics, such as entropy and Euclidean distance have been successfully tested in [9]. Finally, best_rule() selects the rule with the highest estimated predictive value.

3.2 generate_antecedents()

The generate_antecedents() procedure returns the set of rules to be tested by the heuristic function. To constrain the search space from the 2^n possible attribute-value combinations, the procedure returns only the, up to $n - 1$ rules possible by specializing on each of the n attributes.

Procedure 3.1 top_down_search()

Input: (r, P): rule r and algorithm parameters $P \Leftarrow (D, e, c)$.
Output: A rule r' that covers e but which cannot be further specialized.
Method:
1: R $\Leftarrow$ generate_antecedents(r, P)
2: **for all** rule $r' \in R$ **do**
3:   $r'_{conseq.} \Leftarrow$ get_consequent(r', P)
4:   $r'_{value} \Leftarrow F(r', r)$
5: **end for**
6:
7: $best\_r' \Leftarrow$ best_rule(R)
8: **if** ($best\_r' \neq \emptyset$) **then**
9:   **return**(top_down_search($best\_r', P$))
10: **else**
11:   **return**(r)
12: **end if**

Symbolic Attributes The first time a specialization is attempted on a proposition that refers to a symbolic attribute A_i, the proposition is simply updated from $(A_i = ANY)$ to $(A_i = e_i)$. If the proposition on this attribute has already been specialized, then no further specialization is attempted.

Numerical Attributes The method described above for symbolic attributes cannot be successfully applied to continuous attributes. If, for example, $e_2 = 6.5$ and the range on attribute A_2 is [0.5, 9.0], then generating the proposition $(A_2 = 6.5)$ would likely result in a rule that covers few, if any, records in the dataset. One way to overcome this situation is by discretizing all continuous attributes in the dataset before using the classification algorithm. This approach could be thought of as eager discretization because many of the regions that are made discrete are not necessary for the single classification task at hand. DBPredictor instead uses a two sided test $(A_i \in [e_i - \delta, e_i + \delta])$, where $\delta > 0$, on continuous attributes. After a scan through the dataset to locate the min, max range for each attribute, he δ for each proposition in the seed rule is set to the larger of $(max - e_i)$ and $(e_i - min)$. The proposition in the example above would be initialized to $(A_2 \in [6.5 - 6, 6.5 + 6)$.

At each specialization DBPredictor makes δ' strictly smaller than the previous δ used by the parent's proposition. The decrease in δ between iterations is determined by an internally set fraction named num_ratio (numerical partitioning ratio):

$$\delta' \Leftarrow \frac{\delta}{\text{num\_ratio}}$$
$$P'_i \Leftarrow \left(A_i \in [e_i - \delta', e_i + \delta'] \right)$$

An empirically determined default value for num_ratio is presented in Section 4.

3.3 get_consequent()

Once a set of rule antecedents have been generated, the get_consequent() procedure is used to construct each rule's consequent. For a given rule's antecedent ($r.antecedent$), the procedure executes the following SQL query to return a summary of attribute A_c for all the dataset records that match the antecedent: SELECT A_c, COUNT(*) FROM D WHERE $r.antecedent$ GROUP BY A_c. This implementation has the advantage that it does not require the usage of temporary tables nor the existence of a key attribute in the dataset.

4 Empirical Results

An empirical study was conducted to test DBPredictor's accuracy with respect to the proportion of continuous attributes in the dataset.[1] Twenty three datasets from the UCI repository [10] were used in this study: anneal, heart-h, audiology, hepatitis*, breast-w, horse-colic, chess, iris*, credit-a, letter, credit-g, liver-disease, diabetes, mushroom, echocardiogram*, segment, glass, soybean-small, hayes-roth*, tic-tac-toe*, heart, vote, and heart-c. An attempt was made to include previously studied datasets [6, 5, 12] with a wide variety of sizes and proportions of continuous attributes[2]. The benchmark algorithms for this study were the C4.5 r8 decision tree algorithm [11, 12] and the IB1 k-nearest neighbor algorithm [4]. Finally, each algorithm's true error rate on each dataset was estimated with the use of multiple ten-fold stratified cross-validation tests.

4.1 Tuning num_ratio

The first portion of the empirical study determined an appropriate value for DBPredictor's num_ratio internal parameter. All three algorithm's were tuned on five datasets marked with a * beside its name. The value for num_ratio that achieve the lowest average error rate on these five datasets was 1.5. This value was passed on to the next study. Similarly, the IB1 algorithm's k was set to 5 after being tuned on the same five datasets as DBPredictor.

4.2 Continuous Domains

To test for bias with respect to the proportion of numerical attributes in a dataset the three pairwise combinations between DBPredictor, C4.5 and IB1 were contrasted. For each pair, the datasets in which one algorithm performed significantly better[3] than the other were identified. Table 1 summarizes the results of the three pairwise tests. Rather than being skewed to a strong bias for or against continuous attribute, the results suggest that DBPredictor's bias is instead situated between that of IB1 and C4.5.

---

[1] An ANSI-C implementation of the algorithm can be downloaded from the www.cs.sfu.ca/~melli/DBPredictor Web site.
[2] the 23 datasets possessed on average 48% numerical attributes and ranged from 0% to 100%
[3] based on a two-tailed t-test with 99.5% confidence

Table 1. Average percentage of numerical attributes in the datasets that each algorithm performed significantly more accurately than another algorithm. The datasets that DBPredictor was more accurate than IB1 had 39% numerical attributes on average.

DBP/C4.5	DBP/IB1	C4.5/IB1
54%/55%	39%/52%	20%/57%

5 Conclusion

This paper presents an algorithm, named DBPredictor, that is targeted to on-line classification tasks. These tasks require the prediction of a single event's class, based on the records stored in a relational database. DBPredictor uses a lazy model-based approach in that it performs only the work it requires to classify the single event. The opportunity presented in this paper is the use of proposition specialization. A tightly-coupled SQL based implementation of the algorithm is presented, along with the results of an empirical study into the relative bias for or against datasets with numerical attributes.

References

1. AAAI. *Thirteenth National Conference on Artificial Intelligence*. AAAI Press, 1996.
2. R. Agrawal and J. C. Shafer. Parallel mining of association rules: Design, implementation, and experience. *IEEE Trans. Knowledge and Data Engineering*, 8:962–969, 1996.
3. D. W. Aha, editor. *Lazy Learning*. Kluwer Academic, May 1997.
4. D. W. Aha, D. Kibler, and M. K. Albert. Instance-based learning algorithms. *Machine Learning*, 6(1):37–66, 1991.
5. P. Domingos. Unifying instance-based and rule-based induction. *Machine Learning*, 24(2):141–168, August 1996.
6. J. H. Friedman, R. Kohavi, and Y. Yun. Lazy decision trees. [1], pages 717–724.
7. G. H. John and B. Lent. SIPping from the data firehose. In *Proceedings, Third International Conference on Knowledge Discovery and Data Mining*, pages 199–202. AAAI Press, 1997.
8. G. Melli. Ad hoc attribute-value prediction. [1], page 1396.
9. G. Melli. Knowledge based on-line classification. Master's thesis, Simon Fraser University, School of Computing Science, April 1998.
10. P. M. Murphy and D. W. Aha. UCI repository of machine learning databases. Irvine, CA: University of California, Department of Information and Computer Science, 1995. ftp://ics.uci.edu/pub/machine-learning-databases.
11. J. R. Quinlan. *C4.5: Programs for Machine Learning*. Morgan Kaufmann, 1993.
12. J. R. Quinlan. Improved use of continuous attributes in C4.5. *Journal of Artificial Intelligence Research*, 4:77–90, March 1996.

An Efficient Space-Partitioning Based Algorithm for the K-Means Clustering [*]

Khaled AlSabti[1], Sanjay Ranka[2], and Vineet Singh[3]

[1] Department of CS, King Saud University, alsabti@ccis.ksu.edu.sa
[2] Department of CISE, University of Florida, ranka@cise.ufl.edu
[3] Hitachi America Ltd., vineet.singh@alumni.stanford.org

Abstract. k-means clustering is a popular clustering method. Its core task of finding the *closest* prototype for every input pattern involves expensive distance calculations. We present a novel algorithm for performing this task. This and other optimizations are shown to significantly improve the performance of the k-means algorithm. The resultant algorithm produces the same (except for round-off errors) results as those of the direct algorithm.

1 Introduction

Clustering has been a widely studied problem in a variety of application domains including data mining. Several algorithms have been proposed in the literature. The partitioning based clustering algorithms partition a dataset into a set of k clusters. Each cluster is represented either by the center of gravity of the cluster (as in k-means) or by one of the objects of the cluster located near its center [2]. Two competing clustering algorithms are compared based on the quality of clustering achieved, and the time and space requirements for the computation. Depending on the application requirements, one or more of the above features may be relevant.

The k-means clustering algorithm has been shown to be effective for many practical applications. However, its direct implementation is computationally very expensive, especially for large datasets. We propose a novel algorithm for performing k-means clustering. The new algorithm uses a space-partitioning based technique that deals with subsets of patterns collectively in determining the *cluster membership*. Each subset of patterns represent a subspace in the patterns space. It organizes the patterns in a partitioned-based structure (e.g., k-d tree). This can then be used to find all the patterns which are closest to a given prototype efficiently. The new algorithm has a significantly superior performance than the direct algorithm. Further, it produces the same (except for round-off errors due to limited precision arithmetic) clustering results. It is also competitive to other state-of-the art methods for improving the performance of k-means clustering.

---

[*] A large part of this work was done while the authors at the Information Technology Lab (ITL) of Hitachi America, Ltd.

2 The k-means Clustering Method

Several forms of k-means have been studied in the literature [4, 2]. In this paper we adapt Forgey's method [2]. k-means is an iterative technique which starts with an initial clustering (e.g., generated randomly), and improves the quality of the clustering as it iterates. This process is halted when a *stopping criterion* is met; e.g., the cluster membership no longer changes or the quality of the clustering is not changed significantly. Clustering partitions the input patterns into k (user-defined) disjoint subsets. Each cluster is represented by a prototype pattern such as its centroid. The quality of the clustering is improved by updating the assignment of patterns to clusters (i.e., cluster membership). Each iteration of the direct algorithm consists of three steps:

- **Step 1:** Updating the cluster membership to improve the overall quality. A pattern is assigned to a cluster when its prototype is the *nearest* prototype for the given pattern. This involves calculating the distance between every pattern to every prototype. In this paper we use Euclidean distance as the distance function. This step is the computationally intensive part of the algorithm; it requires $\Theta(nkd)$ time, where n is the number of patterns, and d is the dimensionality of the pattern.
- **Step 2:** Computing the new set of prototypes by finding the centroid of each cluster, and it takes $\Theta(nd)$ time.
- **Step 3:** Evaluating the stopping criteria. Using the standard mean squared error for the stopping criterion requires $\Theta(nd)$ time.

The number of iterations required can vary from a few to several thousands depending on the problem instance. The appropriate choice of k is a problem and domain dependent. Generally, the user has to try several values [2]. The partitioning based clustering algorithms, such as k-means, are generally very sensitive to the initial clustering, and the user generally tries several initializations [1]. Thus, a direct implementation of k-means can be computationally very intensive, especially for applications with large datasets.

Two main approaches, described in the literature, can be used to reduce the computational requirements of k-means: prototype-based, and membership-based. In the former, the prototypes are organized in a suitable structure so that finding the closest prototype for a given pattern becomes more efficient [1]. This approach is best used when the prototypes are fixed. However, in this paper we are assuming that the prototypes will change dynamically. Hence, many of these optimizations are not directly applicable. The latter technique uses the information of the cluster membership from the previous iteration to reduce the number of distance calculations. P-CLUSTER is a k-means algorithm which exploits the fact that the change of cluster membership is relatively few after the first few iterations [3]. It also uses the fact that the movement of the cluster centroids is small for consecutive iterations (especially after a few iterations). These optimizations are orthogonal to our approach (see Section 4).

3 The New Algorithm

Our algorithm partitions the patterns space into disjoint, smaller subspaces for collectively finding the closest prototype for a subset of patterns representing a subspace. The main intuition behind our approach is as follows. All the prototypes are potential *candidates* for the closest prototype for *all* the patterns. However, we may be able to *prune* the candidate set by: (1) partitioning the space into a number of disjoint, smaller subspaces, and (2) using simple geometrical constraints. Clearly, each subspace will potentially have different candidate sets. Further, a prototype may belong to the candidate sets of several subspaces. This approach can be applied recursively until the size of the candidate set is one for each subspace. At this stage, all the patterns in the subspace have the sole candidate as their closest prototype. As a result of using the above approach, we expect to significantly reduce the computational requirements of the three steps of the k-means algorithm. This is because the computation has to be performed only with subspaces (representing many patterns) and not the patterns themselves in most cases. The improvements obtained using our approach are crucially dependent on obtaining a good pruning method.

In the first phase of the new algorithm, we build a k-d tree to organize the patterns (detailed implementations are presented elsewhere [1]). The root of such a tree represents all the patterns, while the children of the root represent subsets of the patterns completely contained in smaller subspaces. For each node of the tree, we keep the number of patterns, the linear sum of the patterns, and the square sum of the patterns. In the second phase, the initial prototypes are derived (as in the direct algorithm). In the third phase, the algorithm performs a number of iterations (as in the direct algorithm) until a stopping criteria is met. For each cluster i, we maintain the number of patterns, the linear sum of the patterns, and the square sum of the patterns. In each iteration, we start from the root node with all k candidate prototypes. At each node, we apply a pruning function (described below) on the candidate prototypes. If the number of candidate prototypes is equal to one, the traversal below that internal node is not pursued. All the patterns belonging to this node have the surviving candidate as the closest prototype. The patterns-clusters assignment can be guaranteed to be the same to those of the direct algorithm by avoiding *overpruning* the candidate prototypes. The cluster statistics are updated based on the information stored in that internal node.

One iteration of the direct algorithm (or any other algorithm) is applied on a leaf node with more than one candidate prototype. This process uses the candidate prototypes and the patterns of the leaf node. At the end of each iteration, the new set of prototypes is derived and the error function is computed. These computations can efficiently be performed while deriving the exact (or similar due to the round-off error) results as those of the direct algorithm [1].

The cost of the pruning is the extra overhead in the above process. However, effective pruning may decrease the overall number of the distance calculations which decreases the overall time requirement. Clearly, there is a trade-off between the cost of the pruning technique, and its effectiveness. We used the following pruning strategy at each internal node of the tree:
- For each candidate prototype, find the minimum and maximum distances to any point in the subspace
- Find the minimum of maximum distances, call it $MinMax$

– Prune out all candidates with minimum distance greater than $MinMax$

The above strategy *guarantees* that no candidate is pruned if it can potentially be closer than any other candidate prototype to a given subspace. Thus, our algorithm produces the same (except for round-off errors) clustering results to those of the direct algorithm. Our pruning approach is a *conservative* approach and may miss some of the pruning opportunities. However, it is relatively inexpensive, and can be shown to require a constant time per a candidate prototype [1]. Choosing a more expensive pruning algorithm may decrease the overall number of distance calculations. This may, however, be at the expense of higher overall computation time due to an offsetting increase in cost of pruning.

4 Experimental Results

Since the clustering quality of the new algorithm is the same (except for round-off errors) clustering results to those of the direct algorithm, we have measured the performance of the new algorithm in terms of the distance calculations and the total execution time. We also compare our algorithm with P-Cluster. We have designed a hybrid algorithm in which the new algorithm is applied for the top levels of the tree, and P-CLUSTER is applied to the leaf nodes. All the experiments are conducted on an IBM RS/6000 running AIX version 4, with a clock speed of 66 MHz and a memory size of 128 MByte. We present representative results. For more details, the reader is referred to [1]. Our performance evaluation of the algorithms is based on the following measures:

– FRD: the factor of reduction in distance calculations with respect to those of the direct algorithm
– ADC: Average number of the distance calculations performed per pattern in each iteration
– FRT: the factor of reduction in overall execution time with respect to those of the direct algorithm

FRD and ADC reflect on the intrinsic quality of the algorithm and are relatively architecture and platform independent.

Table 1. Description of the datasets; range along each dimension is the same unless explicitly stated

Dataset	Size	Dimensionality	No. of Clusters	Characteristic	Range
DS1	100,000	2	100	Grid	[-3,41]
DS2	100,000	2	100	Sine	[2,632],[-29,29]
DS3	100,000	2	100	Random	[-3,109],[-15,111]
R4	256k	2	128	Random	[0,1]
R8	256k	4	128	Random	[0,1]
R12	256k	6	128	Random	[0,1]

We used several synthetic datasets (see Table 1). The three datasets DS1, DS2 and DS3 are described in [5]. For the datasets R1 through R12, we generated k (16 or 128) points randomly in a cube of appropriate dimensionality. For the ith point we generated $i\frac{2n}{(k+1)k}$ points around it, using uniform distribution. These resulted in clusters with a non-uniform number of points [1].

Table 2 and other results (in [1]) show that our algorithm can improve the overall performance of k-means by an order to two orders of magnitude. The average number of distance calculations required is very small and can

Table 2. The overall results for 10 iterations

Dataset	k	The time of the Direct Algorithm (in seconds)	Our Algorithm			
			Total Time (in seconds)	FRT	FRD	ADC
DS1	64	23.020	2.240	10.27	54.72	1.19
DS2	64	22.880	2.330	9.81	43.25	1.50
DS3	64	23.180	2.340	9.90	52.90	1.23
R4	64	64.730	3.090	20.94	139.80	0.46
R8	64	89.750	8.810	10.18	24.15	2.69
R12	64	117.060	29.180	4.01	5.85	11.10

vary anywhere from 0.46 to 11.10, depending on the dataset and the number of clusters required.

Table 3 compares our algorithm to P-CLUSTER and the hybrid algorithm. We can draw the following conclusions from this table and other results (in [1]): (1) The performance of our algorithm is better than P-CLUSTER for almost all cases for small number of iterations. For larger number of iterations and larger dimensional data, the performance of P-Cluster is better. This behavior is partially attributed to the heuristics used by P-CLUSTER, which are more effective after the first few iterations. The performance improvements of our algorithm do not change significantly for larger number of iterations since our pruning strategy does not optimize across iterations, and (2) The hybrid algorithm captures the best qualities of both the algorithms. It outperforms or is comparable to the two algorithms.

Table 3. The ADC produced by the three algorithms for 10 iterations

Dataset	k								
	16			64			128		
	P-CLUSTER	Our Alg.	Hybrid	P-CLUSTER	Our Alg.	Hybrid	P-CLUSTER	Our Alg.	Hybrid
DS1	4.66	0.51	0.51	6.59	0.96	0.99	7.80	1.39	1.49
DS2	3.51	0.25	0.25	5.55	0.64	0.66	8.28	1.48	1.56
DS3	4.02	0.41	0.42	7.83	1.08	1.12	7.99	1.87	1.98
R4	5.39	0.32	0.32	4.04	0.46	.0.49	5.78	1.27	1.22
R8	5.73	1.87	2.13	7.62	2.68	3.19	8.57	3.92	3.85
R12	7.12	7.68	6.58	10.70	11.10	8.63	12.00	15.92	9.56

5 Conclusion

We have presented a novel technique for improving the performance of the k-means algorithm. It can improve the performance of the direct algorithm by an order to two orders of magnitude, while producing the same (except for round-off errors) results. Further, the new algorithm is very competitive to P-CLUSTER. The performance of our algorithm is better than P-CLUSTER for almost all cases for small number of iterations. For larger number of iterations, we have developed and presented a hybrid algorithm (using P-CLUSTER). This hybrid algorithm is empirically shown to require less (or comparable) number of distance calculations as compared to P-CLUSTER.

References

1. K. AlSabti. *Efficient Algorithms for Data Mining*. Ph.D. Thesis, Syracuse University, 1998.
2. R. C. Dubes and A. K. Jain. *Algorithms for Clustering Data*. Prentice Hall, 1988.
3. D. Judd, P. McKinley, and A. Jain. Large-Scale Parallel Data Clustering. *Proc. Int'l Conference on Pattern Recognition*, August 1996.
4. K. Mehrotra, C.K. Mohan, and S. Ranka. *Elements of Artificial Neural Networks*. MIT Press, 1996.
5. T. Zhang, R. Ramakrishnan, and M. Livny. BIRCH: An Efficient Data Clustering Method for Very Large Databases. *Proc. of the ACM SIGMOD'96*.

A Fast Clustering Process for Outliers and Remainder Clusters

Chih-Ming Su, Shian-Shyong Tseng*, Mon-Fong Jiang, Joe C.S. Chen

Department of Computer and Information Science
National Chiao Tung University
Hsinchu, Taiwan
E-mail: sstseng@cis.nctu.edu.tw

Abstract. Identifying outliers and remainder clusters which are used to designate few patterns that much different from other clusters is a fundamental step in many application domain. However, current outliers diagnostics are often inadequate when in a large amount of data. In this paper, we propose a two-phase clustering algorithm for outliers. In Phase 1 we modified k-means algorithm by using the heuristic "if one new input pattern is far enough away from all clusters' centers, then assign it as a new cluster center". So that the number of clusters found in this phase is more than that originally set in k-means algorithm. And then we propose a clusters-merging process in the second phase to merge the resulting clusters obtained in Phase 1 into the same number of clusters originally set by the user. The results of three experiments show that the outliers or remainder clusters can be easily identified by our method.

1 Introduction

Cluster analysis could be defined as the process of separating a set of patterns(objects) into clusters such that members of one cluster are similar. The definition of the term "remainder cluster"[2] is used to designate few patterns that much different from other clusters. They are often to be seemed as noises like outliers. Therefore, in most traditional clustering algorithms, the patterns are either neglected or given a lower weight to avoid the data being clustered.

However, in some specific applications we have to find out the abnormal patterns from a large amount of data. For example, in the medicine domain, we may want to find extraordinary cases of patient data; in network problem domain, we may want to find the abnormal behaviors from log data. The above problems would not be easily solved by traditional clustering algorithms, because the data often have more than ten thousand records. So using traditional clustering algorithm to cluster the minor and abnormal patterns will either cost much time or not work well. Even data mining approaches can find potential relations in large amount of data, but few for this goal.

In this paper, a two-phase clustering algorithm for outliers is proposed. In the first phase, we propose a modified k-means algorithm by using a heuristic

---

* Corresponding author.

"if one new input pattern is far enough away from all clusters' centers, then assign it as a new cluster center". It results that the number of clusters found in this phase is more than that originally set in k-means algorithm. And then we propose a clusters-merging algorithm in the second phase to merge the resulting clusters obtained in Phase 1 into the same number of clusters as that originally set by the user.

The merging algorithm first constructs a minimum spanning tree for these clusters and set it as a member of a forest. Then remove the longest edge of a tree from the forest and replace the tree with two newly generated subtrees. And repeatedly remove the longest edge from the forest until the number of trees is sufficient enough. Finally the smallest clusters are selected and regarded as outliers base upon our heuristic "the smaller the cluster is, the more probability the outlier has".

The structure of this paper is as follows. Section 2 presents the related work of outlier detection, and clustering methods. Section 3 gives a detailed description of our algorithm in order to find outlier data. Finally, we present some experimental results on different data to show the performance of our algorithm and conclusion in section 4.

2 Related Work

For the selection of variables and identification of outliers, several robust algorithms have been proposed for detecting multiple outliers[3][4] which can produce estimates by giving up the outliers for the purpose of inference. Among the methods suggested for detecting outliers, three popular models will be briefly introduced as follows.

- Bayesian model[5][8]: Bayesian model averagingly provides optimal predictive ability. Its discriminant analysis compares certain linear combinations of posterior densities of feature vector with respect to the classes considered. However, this approach will not be practical in many applications due to large number of models for which posteriors need to be computed.
- Hierarchical clustering model[6]: In hierarchical clustering model, single linkage merges clusters based on the distance between the two closest observations in each cluster, and the results of the clustering can be seen as "cluster tree". The clusters which are added later can be seen as outliers or remainder clusters. However, since the time complexity is $O(n^3)$, it is not suitable for large amount of data.
- Nearest neighbor model[1]: Nearest neighbor model, like hierarchical classification, is a simpler pattern classification method. Its computational expensiveness requires a reduction in the number of reference patterns. The algorithm is very simple with satisfactorily high learning speed while its convergence is only local; hence precise arrangement of initial position of prototypes is needed for its convergence.

In data-mining applications where data tends to be very large, e.g., 100 thousand records, an important factor is the computing resources required (CPU time and memory space). Resource consumption varies considerably between the different methods, and some methods become impractical for all but small data sets, e.g., hierarchical clustering methods are in $O(n^2)$ for memory space, and $O(n^3)$ for CPU time[7]. However, our modified k-means algorithms generally have a time and space complexity of order n, where n is number of records in the data set.

3 Our Method

We first use the modified k-means algorithm to cluster a large quantity in a coarse manner and also to allow the amount of clusters more than k. The noise data may be clustered into an independent cluster with higher probability rather than using traditional algorithm. In the second phase, a minimum spanning tree is built according to the distance of edges where each node of the tree represents the center of each cluster obtained in Phase 1. Then we remove the longest k-1 edges and the left k clusters are not much balance partitioned as other algorithm does. The algorithm of our clustering method is divided into two phases:

- Phase 1. Modified k-means process
- Phase 2. Clusters-merging process

3.1 Modified k-means (MKM)

We use a heuristic of "jump", which is splitting the outlier as another cluster center in cluster iteration process. This heuristic is permitting to adjust the number of clusters. Like ISODATA algorithm[9], adding more clusters will help us to find out potential outliers or remainder cluster which is not conspicuous. Let k' be the number of adjustable clusters. Initially, set k' = k, and randomly choose k' patterns as cluster centers, $C=\{z_1, z_2, ..., z_{k'}\}$ in R_n. In the period of iteration, when adding one pattern to its nearest cluster, we compute not only the new cluster's center but also the minimum distance min(C) between any two clusters' centers. So, for any pattern x_i, the minimum distance $min(x_i, C)$ of its nearest cluster's center is computed by

$$min(x_i, C) = min\|x_i - z_j\|^2 \ for j = 1, ..., k',\tag{1}$$

$$min(C) = min\|z_j - z_h\|^2 \ for j = 1, ..., k', j \neq h.\tag{2}$$

According to the above heuristic, more clusters can be found after the splitting of data. In some extreme case, each pattern is put into its own cluster, i.e., k' = m. This will result in too many clusters. So the number k_{max} is defined as the maximum number of cluster we may afford. In the modified k-means algorithm, when the patterns are split into $k_{max}+1$ clusters, two closest clusters will be merged to be one. The Modified k-means Algorithm is as follows:

Step 1:Randomly choose k' (k' = k) initial seeds as cluster centers.

Step 2:For i ← 1 to m do :

If $\min(x_i, C) > \min(C)$ then go to Step 3. Else go to Step 5.

Step 3:Assign x_i to be the center of a new cluster $C_{k'}$ and set k' ← k'+1.

Step 4:If k' > k_{max}, merge the closest two clusters into one and set k'=k_{max}.

Step 5:Assign xi to its nearest cluster.

Step 6:Go to Step 2 until the cluster membership stabilizes.

From Step 2 to Step 4, we compare the distance with "the minimum distance between pattern to nearest cluster" and "the minimum distance among clusters". We use the heuristic "if one pattern is far enough, then assign it as a new cluster". It is important to note that the splitting and merging operation employed here are quite similar to the splitting and merging operations proposed in ISO-DATA[9]. However, ISODATA sets parameters by user to determine splitting or merging. Thus, it is not suitable when user do not know both the property and the scatter of the patterns. So in our scheme splitting performs due to the condition at that time, and merging performs when too many clusters occur. So it is not necessary to thoroughly know the distribution of the data before clustering.

3.2 Clusters-Merging Process

Most cluster techniques use density as criteria to determine the result of clustering is good or not. But there is no need in our method to split a large cluster into several partitions to reduce the density. So the criteria of our method to project outlier data, like the criteria of hierarchical techniques, depends on distances. In Phase 2 we propose a clusters-merging process to merge the resulting clusters obtained in Phase 1. We first construct a minimum spanning tree for these clusters and set it as a member of a forest F. Then remove the longest edge of a tree from the forest and replace the tree with two newly generated subtrees. And repeatedly remove the longest edge from the forest until the number of trees in F equals to k.

Finally, we select the smallest clusters from F, which may be regarded as outliers, according to our heuristic "the smaller the cluster is, the more probability the outlier has". We like to note here that a cluster would be regarded as outliers which can be further improved by the help of some domain experts. The algorithm is as follows:

Step 1:Step1. Construct an MST by the centroids of set C and add it to F.

Step 1:For i ← 1 to k-1 do

Find and remove a tree with the longest edge among all the edges in F.

Step 1:Select the smallest clusters from F, which can be regarded as outliers.

4 Experiments and Conclusion

To compare the clustering performance obtained by our outliers clustering process and k-means algorithm, two different experiments have been implemented

364

on Iris data and e-mail log. The Iris data set is a well-known benchmark which has some noises.

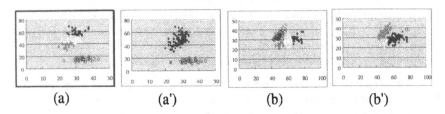

(a)   (a')   (b)   (b')

Fig. 1. The result of first experiment. Fig.1(a)(b) are obtained by k-means algorithm while 1(a')(b') are obtained by our outliers clustering process.

In Figs. 1(a)(a') we choose 1st and 2nd attributes of Iris data as two input parameters. Fig.1(a) is the results of k-means algorithm while (a') is by our process and so as Fig.1(b)(b'). In e-mail log, there are 25511 entries are analyzed. We can find that our process can obvious cluster ourliers as independent clusters. The outliers or remainder clusters not only can be easily identified but also can be computed more quickly.

References

1. Brito M. R., Chavez E. L., Quiroz A. J. and Yukich J. E., 'Connectivity of the mutual k-nearest-neighbor graph in clustering and outlier detection,' *Statistics and Probability Letters.* , Vol 35, 33-42, 1997.
2. Cedno A. A. and Suer G. A., 'The use of a similarity codefficient-based method to perform clustering analysis to a large set of data with dissimilar parts,' *Computers ind. Engng.*,Vol. 33, Nos 1-2, 225-228, 1997.
3. Hadi, A. S. , Simonoff, J. S. ,' Procedures for the identification of multiple outliers in linear models.' *J. Amer. Statist. Assoc.* 88(424) 1264-1272, 1993.
4. Kianifard, F., Swallow, W., 'A Monte Carlo comparison of five procedures for identifying outliers in linear regression.' *Comm. Statist.*, Part A, 1913-1938. 1990.
5. Mardia, K. V., Kent J. T. and Bibby J. M. *Multivariate Analysis.* Academic Press, London. 1979.
6. Mojena, R., 'Hierarchical grouping methods and stopping rules: an evaluation.' *Comput. J.* Vol20, 359-363, 1977.
7. Murtagh, F., *Multidimensional clustering Algorithms.* Physica-Verlag,Vienna, 1985.
8. Ritter, G., Gallegos M. T. and Gaggermeier K., 'Automatic context-sensitive karyotyping of human chromosomes based elliptically symmetric statistical distributions,' *Pattern Recognition* Vol 23, 823-831, 1995.
9. Tou, J., Gonzalez, R., *Pattern Recognition Principles.* Addison-Wesley, Reading ,MA, 1974.

Optimising the Distance Metric in the Nearest Neighbour Algorithm on a Real-World Patient Classification Problem

Hongxing He[1] and Simon Hawkins[2]

[1] Health Insurance Commission,
134 Reed Street, PO Box 1001, Tuggeranong, ACT 2900, Australia,
hongxing.he@hic.gov.au
[2] CRC for Advanced Computational Systems,
CSIRO Mathematical and Information Sciences,
GPO Box 664, Canberra, ACT 2601, Australia,
Simon.Hawkins@cmis.csiro.au

Abstract. The study develops a new method for finding the optimal non-Euclidean distance metric in the nearest neighbour algorithm. The data used to develop this method is a real world doctor shopper classification problem. A statistical measure derived from Shannon's information theory – known as mutual information – is used to weight attributes in the distance metric. This weighted distance metric produced a much better agreement rate on a five-class classification task than the Euclidean distance metric (63% versus 51%). The agreement rate increased to 77% and 73% respectively when a genetic algorithm and simulated annealing were used to further optimise the weights. This excellent performance paves the way for the development of a highly accurate system for detecting high risk doctor-shoppers both automatically and efficiently.

1 Background

Established in 1974, the Health Insurance Commission of Australia (HIC) administers Australia's universal health insurance programs. The HIC has a fiducial responsibility to protect the public purse and to ensure that taxpayer's funds are spent wisely on health care. A major problem, in recent times, are the large number of patients who consult many different doctors ('doctor-shop') in order to obtain high volumes of prescription drugs. These patients are at risk of obtaining volumes of medicine far in excess of their own current therapeutic need, either for sale or to support their own drug habit.

2 Methodology

Three general rules were used to screen the entire Australian population of 18 million people in order to identify patients who may be doctor-shoppers. Of the 13,000 people identified as possible doctor-shoppers using these rules, a random sample of 1,199 people was carefully scrutinised by an expert clinical pharmacologist. Using 15 features to profile each patient's behaviour over a year-long period, the expert classified these patients on a 5-point scale according to the likelihood that they were doctor-shoppers. This scale ranged from class 1 (patients most likely to be doctor-shoppers) to class 5 (patients least likely to be doctor-shoppers). This classified sample of 1199 patients was then divided randomly into two groups: a training set of 800 patients and a test set of 399 patients. The training set was used to set the parameters of a nearest neighbour (NN) algorithm. The performance of the NN algorithm was then measured on the test set. The aim of the present study was to achieve the best possible agreement rate on the test set. Once this is achieved, the NN algorithm can be applied to the unclassified samples of 13,000 patients who were identified as possible doctor-shoppers using simple rules.

3 Nearest Neighbour (NN) algorithm

The NN algorithm (Dasarathy 1991) is a class of learning algorithms that uses a simple form of table look-up to classify examples. In the nearest neighbour algorithm used in the current study, a new case is assigned the classification of its nearest neighbour. The distance (squared) between x_{j_1} (a new case) and x_{j_2} (a known case) is defined by equation (1):

$$d(x_{j_1}, x_{j_2}) = \sum_{i=1}^{k} [w_i(x_{j_1}^1 - x_{j_2}^i)]^2, \tag{1}$$

where $x_{j_1}^i$ is the ith feature of case x_{j_1} and w_i is the weight assigned to the ith feature. The following approach was used to evaluate the performance of various methods for optimising the feature weights, w_i. First, each case in the training set is assigned a 'predicted classification' using the 'leave-one-out' method. Weights in the NN distance metric are then set in order to minimise the number of misclassifications in the training set. The 399 cases in the test set are then assigned the 'predicted classifications' of their nearest neighbour in the training set. The agreement rate is calculated from the confusion matrices in the training and test set. The agreement rate represents the percentage of patients in all five classes who are correctly classified by the NN algorithm.

4 Mutual information

Using this approach, the weights $w_i (i = 1, 2, 3, ...)$ are assigned the value of the mutual information between each feature in a patient's profile and the classification of the patient. The mutual information of two variables (Linsker 1990; Shannon and Weaver 1949) is a measure of the common information or entropy that is shared between the two variables. In the present study, the mutual information between the patient's classification and a particular feature is used to judge if the feature could, of itself, contribute usefully to the classification scheme. Setting weights to the mutual information value of their associated feature provides a heuristic way of heavily weighting the most discriminatory features. The mutual information between two variables, a feature x and the patient classification y, is defined in equation (2):

$$I(x,y) = \int_{-\infty}^{+\infty} \sum_{i=1}^{n} f(x,y_i) log \frac{f(x|y_i)}{f(x)} dx, \tag{2}$$

where $f(x,y_i)$ is the joint probability density function of x and y being in class i; $f(x|y_i)$ is the conditional probability density function of x given y being in class i; and n is the number of classes. In our study, class y is a categorical variable taking five discrete values ranging from class 1 through to class 5. Since the mutual information is defined on the basis of the prior and conditional probability distribution of random variables, accurate estimates can only be obtained using very large samples. Although such large samples are rarely available in real-world applications, approximate estimates can be obtained from the small number of pre-classified profiles that are usually available. In the present study, the mutual information value of each of the 15 patient features was estimated from the 800 samples in the training set.

5 Optimising weights in the NN distance metric

The cost function to be minimised is defined in equation (3):

$$F = \frac{N_{mix}}{N_{tot}} + \alpha \sum_{i=1}^{n} w_i^2. \tag{3}$$

The first term is the fraction of cases that are mis-classified. The second term is designed to control the inflation of weight values with α as the regularisation coefficient.

5.1 Genetic algorithm

Genetic algorithms (Holland 1992) are loosely based on Darwinian principles of evolution: reproduction, genetic recombination and the survival-of-the-fittest. In the present study, each individual in the total population (N) contains 15 floating numbers representing the set of 15 weights associated with the 15 features. The values of all weights in the population are initially generated using a random number lying between 0 and 1. The values of the cost function are calculated for each generation and rank ordered in ascending order. The following three operations are used to create two new individuals at each generation who replace the two least optimal individuals.

Selection: At each iteration, two individuals in the population are selected as parents to produce two offspring for the next generation. In the steady state approach to generating offspring, the population is kept static with most individuals being retained in the next generation. The selection of parent individuals is random with more optimal ones having a higher probability of being selected.

CrossOver: In the crossover operation, two new individuals are formed using both parents selected in the selection process. The n_1 weight values from one individual (father individual) and $n - n_1$ from another individual (mother individual) are selected. n_1 is chosen randomly.

Mutation: After two offspring are formed, the weight value for each feature has a certain probability of being increased or decreased by a small amount. The extent of this change is decided by a normally distributed random number.

5.2 Simulated Annealing (SA)

Developed by Kirkpatrick *et al* (Kirkpatrick 1983; Kirkpatrick 1984; Haykin 1994), SA is designed to avoid sub-optimal solutions that can result when a complex system with many parameters is trapped by local minima in parameter space. This is achieved by occasionally using solutions that result in an increase to the cost function. This helps the system find the global minimum by allowing it to jump out of local minima.

In our study, the Metropolis algorithm is applied to simulate the cooling of a physical system in a heat bath as its temperature moves toward thermal equilibrium. At each step in this cooling process, the weight of a randomly selected feature is changed by a small random amount. The change is always accepted if this results in a lower cost function. Even when the cost function is increased by the change, the change is still accepted with a small probability given by equation (4)

$$P(\Delta E) = exp(-\frac{\Delta E}{T}), \qquad (4)$$

where ΔE is the change in the energy E of the system (i.e., the cost function) and T is the temperature of the system. The probability of acceptance is initially set sufficiently high to ensure that nearly all changes are accepted. The probability of acceptance is gradually lowered as the system is cooled until the only changes accepted are those resulting in a lower cost function.

6 Results

Table 1 compares the agreement rates obtained using different weight optimisation methods with results obtained using an unweighted NNalgorithm based on Euclidean distance and a multi-layer perceptron. The performance of the unweighted NN algorithm was poor with an agreement rate of just 51% on the test

Table 1. Agreement rate (%) obtained using various weight optimisation methods.

	Training Set	Test Set
Euclidean Distance	53.13	51.13
Random+SA	72.00	68.67
Mutual Info	63.13	62.91
MutInfo+SA	77.13	73.43
Genetic Algorithm	80.38	76.69
Multi-layer Perceptron	70.63	71.43

set. This compared to the excellent agreement rate of 71% obtained using a multi-layer perceptron. The performance of the NN algorithm improved markedly to a 63% agreement rate when features are assigned weights equal to their mutual information values. Performance is improved further (73% agreement rate) by applying simulated annealing to these mutual information values. Performance is improved to its highest level (77% agreement rate) when a genetic algorithm is used to optimise weights set to random initial values.

7 Conclusion

The appropriate weighting for each feature in the NN algorithm is reasonably well approximated by the mutual information between each feature in a patient's profile and the patient's classification. Performance is improved further by refining the mutual information values using either simulated annealing or a genetic algorithm. When optimised weights are used, the NN algorithm is able to achieve an agreement rate on a real-world dataset that is at least as good as that obtained using a multi-layer perceptron. As long as an appropriately weighted distance metric is used, this study demonstrates the feasibility of applying the NN algorithm to a large scale real world application.

References

Dasarathy, B. V.: 1991, *NN (Nearest Neighbour) Norms: NN pattern Classification Techniques*, IEEE CS Press, Los Alamitos, Calif.
Haykin, S.: 1994, *Neural Networks: A Comprehensive Foundation*, McMillan, New York.
Holland, J. H.: 1992, *Adaptation in Natural and Artificial Systems*, MIT Press, Cambridge, MA.
Kirkpatrick, S.: 1983, Optimisation by simulated annealing, *Science* **220**, 671–680.
Kirkpatrick, S.: 1984, Optimisation by simulated annealing: Quantitative studies, *Journal of Statistical Physics* **34**, 975–986.
Linsker, R.: 1990, Connectionist modelling and brain function: The developing interface, MIT Press, Cambridge, MA, pp. 351–392.
Shannon, C. E. and Weaver, W.: 1949, *The Mathematical Theory of Communication*, University of Illinois Press, Urbana, IL.

Classifying Unseen Cases with Many Missing Values

Zijian Zheng[1] and Boon Toh Low[2]

[1] School of Computing and Mathematics
Deakin University, Geelong, Victoria 3217, Australia
zijian@deakin.edu.au
[2] Department of Systems Engineering and Engineering Management
The Chinese University of Hong Kong, Shatin, N.T., Hong Kong
btlow@se.cuhk.edu.hk

Abstract. Handling missing attribute values is an important issue for classifier learning, since missing attribute values in either training data or test (unseen) data affect the prediction accuracy of learned classifiers. In many real KDD applications, attributes with missing values are very common. This paper studies the robustness of four recently developed committee learning techniques, including Boosting, Bagging, SASC, and SASCMB, relative to C4.5 for tolerating missing values in test data. Boosting is found to have a similar level of robustness to C4.5 for tolerating missing values in test data in terms of average error in a representative collection of natural domains under investigation. Bagging performs slightly better than Boosting, while SASC and SASCMB perform better than them in this regard, with SASCMB performing best.

1 Introduction

One primary concern of classifier learning is the prediction accuracy. Recent research has shown that committee (or ensemble) learning techniques [1] can significantly increase the accuracy of base learning algorithms, especially decision tree learning [2, 3, 4]. Committee learning induces multiple individual classifiers to form a committee by repeated application of a single base learning algorithm. At the classification stage, the committee members vote to decide the final classification. Decision tree learning [5] is one of the most well studied classifier learning techniques. It has been widely used in many KDD applications.

On the other hand, handling missing attribute values is an important issue for classifier learning, since missing attribute values in either training data or test (unseen) data affect the prediction accuracy of learned classifiers. Most currently available decision tree learning algorithms including C4.5 [5] can handle missing attribute values in training data and test data. The committee learning techniques with these decision tree learning algorithms as their base learners can also do this through the decision tree learning algorithms. Quinlan [6] experimentally compares effectiveness of several approaches to dealing with missing values for single decision tree learning, and shows that combining all possible outcomes of a test with a missing value on the test example at the classification stage gives better overall prediction accuracy than other approaches. C4.5

adopts this approach [5]. For other approaches to dealing with missing attribute values at the tree generation stage and classification stage, see [6].

To the best of the authors' knowledge, no study has been carried out on the effect of missing attribute values on the accuracy performance of committee learning techniques. In this paper, we study the robustness of four recently developed committee learning techniques including Boosting [4, 7], Bagging [3], SASC [8], and SASCMB [9] relative to C4.5 for tolerating missing values in test data. The motivation for this research is as follows. These four committee learning techniques can dramatically reduce the error of C4.5. This observation was obtained from experiments in domains containing no or a small amount of missing attribute values. It is interesting to know how the accuracy of the committee learning methods changes relative to that of C4.5, as test sets contain more and more missing attribute values. In some real world applications, unseen (test) examples do contain many missing attribute values, while training set contains relatively complete attribute information. For example, in medical diagnosis, the training data from historical records of patients could contain almost all attribute values. However, when a new patient presents, it is desirable to perform a preliminary diagnosis before the results of some time-consuming medical examinations become available if time is crucial, or before conducting some very expensive medical examinations if cost is important. In this situation, classification needs to be performed on unseen examples (new patients) with many missing attribute values. We expect this classification to be as accurate as possible, although we cannot expect that it reaches the accuracy level when these attribute values are not missing.

In the following section, we briefly describe the ideas of the four committee learning techniques. Section 3 empirically explores the robustness of C4.5 and the four committee learning algorithms for tolerating missing attribute values in test data. The last section summaries conclusions and outlines some directions for future research. The full version of this paper is available from [10], which also contains an approach to improving the robustness of the committee learning techniques for tolerating missing attribute values in test data.

2 Boosting, Bagging, SASC, and SASCMB

Bagging [3] generates different classifiers using different bootstrap samples. Boosting [2, 4, 7] builds different classifiers sequentially. The weights of training examples used for creating each classifier are modified based on the performance of the previous classifiers. The objective is to make the generation of the next classifier concentrate on the training examples that are misclassified by the previous classifiers. BOOST and BAG are our implementations of Boosting and Bagging respectively. SASC [8] builds different classifiers by modifying the set of attributes considered at each node, while the distribution of the training set is kept unchanged. Each attribute set is selected stochastically. SASCMB is a combination of Boosting, Bagging, and SASC. It generates N subcommittees. Each subcommittee contains S decision trees built from a bootstrap sample of the training data using a procedure that combines Boosting and SASC by both stochastically selecting attribute subsets and adaptively modifying the distribution of the training set. Brief descriptions of BOOST, BAG, and SASC as well as a full description of SASCMB can be found from [9] in the same proceedings. Readers may refer to the references mentioned above for further details about these algorithms.

3 Effects of Missing Values on Accuracy

In this section, we use experiments to explore how the accuracy of the committee learning methods changes relative to that of C4.5, as test sets contain more and more missing attribute values. Thirty-seven natural domains from the UCI machine learning repository [11] are used.[3]

In every domain, two stratified 10-fold cross-validations were carried out for each algorithm. Some of these 37 domains contain missing attribute values, but some not. To simulate the situation where unseen examples contain certain amount of missing attribute values, we randomly introduce missing attribute values into test sets at a given level L. For each fold of the cross-validations, each learning algorithm is applied to the training set. To get a reliable test accuracy estimate of each learned classifier, it is evaluated using ten different corrupted versions of the original test set of the fold with the same level of missing attribute values, L, and the evaluation results are averaged. Each of the corrupted versions is derived by replacing, with the probability L, each attribute value in the original test set with the missing value "?". In each domain, all the algorithms are run on the same training and test set partitions with the same ten corrupted versions of each test set. The result reported for each algorithm in each domain is an average value over 20 trails. We investigate 10%, 20%, 30%, 40%, and 50% for L in this study. Pruned trees are used for all the algorithms. All BOOST, BAG, SASC, and SASCMB use probabilistic predictions (without voting weights) for voting to decide the final classification. The committee size is set at 100 in the experiments for BOOST, BAG, and SASC. The subcommittee size and the number of subcommittees are set at 5 and 20 respectively, resulting in 100 trees in total for SASCMB. The probability of each attribute being selected into the subset is set at the default, 33%, for SASC and SASCMB.

Figure 1 shows the average error rates of the five learning algorithms over the 37 domains as a function of the missing attribute value level L. The detailed error rates of these algorithms and error ratios of each committee learning algorithm over C4.5 and more discussions can be found in [10]. From these experimental results, we have the following observations.

(1). All the four committee learning algorithms can significantly reduce the average error of C4.5 at all missing attribute value level from 0 to 50% across the 37 domains. Among them, SASCMB always has the lowest average error. These are clearly shown in Figure 1.

---

[3] In [9], We use 40 domains. To reduce the computational requirements of the experiments for this study, we exclude three largest domains from the test suite. The partial results in these 3 domains that we have got are consistent with our claims in this paper.

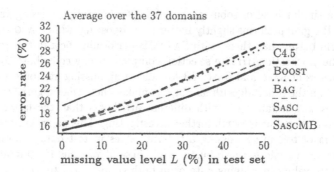

Fig. 1. Effects of missing values in test data on the error of the five learning algorithms

(2). The average error of C4.5 in the 37 domains increases linearly to the growth of the missing attribute value level.

(3). When $L = 0$, BOOST performs better than BAG and SASC in terms of either lower average error rate or lower average error ratio to C4.5. However, SASC is superior, on average, to BOOST when test sets contain 10% missing attribute values or more, while BAG is superior, on average, to BOOST when test sets contain 30% missing attribute values or more. This indicates that BAG and SASC perform better than BOOST for tolerating missing attribute values in test data.

(4). The average error difference between BOOST and C4.5 grows slightly when L increases from 0 to 20%. It, then, starts to drop. When L reaches 50%, the average error difference becomes smaller than the corresponding value for $L = 0$. However, since the average error difference changes not much for different L, BOOST can be considered as at a similar level of robustness to C4.5 for tolerating missing values in test data.

(5). In terms of the robustness for tolerating missing attribute values in test data, BAG performs better than BOOST. The average error difference between BAG and C4.5 grows (faster than that for BOOST) when L increases from 0 to 30%. After that, the average difference decreases slightly, but the average difference for $L = 50\%$ is higher than that for $L = 0$ and $L = 10\%$.

(6). In the same regard, SASC and SASCMB perform better than BOOST and BAG, with SASCMB performing best. The average error difference relative to C4.5 for either SASC or SASCMB keeps growing when L changes from 0 to 40%. At the end of the curves, that is at the point $L = 50\%$, the difference reduces only very slightly for either SASC or SASCMB.

4 Conclusions and Future Work

In this paper, we have empirically explored the robustness of four recently developed committee learning algorithms relative to C4.5 for tolerating missing attribute values in test data using a representative collection of natural domains. The four committee learning algorithms are Boosting, Bagging, SASC, and SASCMB with C4.5 as their base learner. It has been found that Boosting is at a similar level of robustness to C4.5 for tolerating missing values in test data. Bagging performs slightly better than Boosting, while SASC and SASCMB perform better than them, with SASCMB performing best in this regard.

The stochastic attribute selection component may contribute to the greater robustness of SASC and SASCMB for tolerating missing attribute values in test data than the other algorithms, since it makes the former algorithms have more chances to generate trees with different attributes than the latter algorithms. However, this issue is worth further investigating. This paper only addresses the problem of tolerating missing attribute values in test data. Another interesting research topic is the robustness of these algorithms for tolerating missing attribute values in training data or in both training and test data.

Acknowledgments

Many thanks to Geoffrey Webb and Kai Ming Ting for their helpful comments on this research. The authors are grateful to Ross Quinlan for providing C4.5. Much of this research was carried out when the first named author was visiting Dept of Systems Engineering and Engineering Management at the Chinese University of Hong Kong. He is grateful to the dept for its support during this visit.

References

1. Dieterich, T.G.: Machine learning research. *AI Magazine* **18** (1997) 97-136.
2. Quinlan, J.R.: Bagging, Boosting, and C4.5. *Proceedings of the 13th National Conference on Artificial Intelligence.* Menlo Park, CA: AAAI Press (1996) 725-730.
3. Breiman, L.: Bagging predictors. *Machine Learning* **24** (1996) 123-140.
4. Schapire, R.E., Freund, Y., Bartlett, P., and Lee, W.S.: Boosting the margin: A new explanation for the effectiveness of voting methods. *Proceedings of the 14th International Conference on Machine Learning.* Morgan Kaufmann (1997) 322-330.
5. Quinlan, J.R.: *C4.5: Program for Machine Learning.* Morgan Kaufmann (1993).
6. Quinlan, J.R.: Unknown attribute values in induction. *Proceedings of the 6th International Workshop on Machine Learning.* Morgan Kaufmann (1989) 164-168.
7. Schapire, R.E.: The strength of weak learnability. *Machine Learning* **5** (1990) 197-227.
8. Zheng, Z. and Webb, G.I.: Stochastic attribute selection committees. *Proceedings of the 10th Australian Joint Conference on Artificial Intelligence.* Berlin: Springer-Verlag (1998).
9. Zheng, Z. and Webb, G.I.: Stochastic attribute selection committees with multiple boosting: Learning more accurate and more stable classifier committees. *Proceedings of the 3rd Pacific-Asia Conference on Knowledge Discovery and Data Mining.* Berlin: Springer-Verlag (1999).
10. Zheng, Z. and Low, B.T.: Classifying unseen cases with many missing values. Tech Report (TR C99/02) (available at http://www3.cm.deakin.edu.au/~zijian/Papers/comm-missing-trC99-02.ps.gz), School of Computing and Mathematics, Deakin University, Australia (1999).
11. Blake, C., Keogh, E. and Merz, C.J.: UCI Repository of Machine Learning Databases (http://www.ics.uci.edu/~mlearn/MLRepository.html). Irvine, CA: University of California, Dept of Information and Computer Science (1998).

Study of a Mixed Similarity Measure for Classification and Clustering

Tu Bao Ho, Ngoc Binh Nguyen, Takafumi Morita

Japan Advanced Institute of Science and Technology (JAIST)
Tatsunokuchi, Ishikawa, 923-1292 JAPAN

Abstract. This paper presents a study on mixed similarity measures (MSM) that allows doing classification and clustering in many situations without discretization. For supervised classification we do experimental comparative studies of classifiers built by decision tree induction system C4.5 and k nearest neighbor rule using MSM. For unsupervised clustering we first introduce an extension of k-means algorithm for mixed numeric and symbolic data, then evaluate clusters obtained by this algorithm with natural classes. Experimental studies allow us to draw conclusions (meta-knowledge) that are significant in practice about the mutual use of discretization techniques and MSM.

1 Introduction

Similarity measures between objects play an essential role in many fields of computing such as pattern recognition (PR), machine learning (ML) or knowledge discovery in databases (KDD) - a rapidly growing interdisciplinary field that merges together techniques of databases, statistics, machine learning and others in order to extract useful knowledge from large databases. Initially, pattern recognition techniques have been developed mainly to deal with numerical datasets. However, most real-world databases in KDD contain heterogeneously numeric and symbolic attributes (mixed data) that require efficient techniques in these situations.

This paper focuses on finding an answer to a question: whether or not MSM are beneficial for KDD and if so when they are more appropriate than discretization techniques? We limit ourselves on a study of the MSM developed in [5] from a similarity measure in biological taxonomy [2].

2 A Mixed Similarity Measure

In [5], the authors present a similarity measure for data with mixed numeric and nominal attributes where its core is a similarity measure developed for biological taxonomy [2]. The key idea of this MSM is uncommon feature values make greater contribution to the overall similarity between two objects.

Two objects i and j are considered more similar than two other objects l and m if i and j exhibit a greater match in attribute values that are more uncommon in the population. The similarity measure between $(S_{ij})_k$ and $(S_{lm})_k$ can be expressed as follows for *symbolic attributes*:

$$\left.\begin{array}{c}((V_i)_k = (V_j)_k) \wedge ((V_l)_k = (V_m)_k) \\ ((p_i)_k = (p_j)_k) \geq ((p_l)_k = (p_m)_k)\end{array}\right\} \implies (S_{ij})_k \leq (S_{lm})_k \quad (1)$$

where $(p_i)_k, (p_j)_k, (p_l)_k$, and $(p_m)_k$ define the probabilities of occurrence of the respective attribute values $(V_i)_k, (V_j)_k, (V_l)_k$ and $(V_m)_k$ in the population.

When comparing similarity for pairs of *numeric attribute values*, the measure takes both the magnitude of the attribute value difference and the uniqueness of the attribute values pair into account. Given two pairs of objects (i, j) and (l, m). When the magnitude of difference for two pairs of values are equal, then the uniqueness of segment defined by the values weights the similarity index. The uniqueness of the segment is computed by summing up the frequency of occurrences of all values encompassed by the pair of values, i.e., $\sum_{t=(V_i)_k}^{(V_j)_k} p_t$ and $\sum_{t=(V_i)_k}^{(V_m)_k} p_t$ for object value pairs $((V_i)_k, (V_j)_k)$, and $((V_l)_k, (V_m)_k)$, respectively.

$$(|(V_i)_k - (V_j)_k| > |(V_l)_k - (V_m)_k|) \implies (S_{ij})_k < (S_{lm})_k \quad (2)$$

$$\left.\begin{array}{c}|(V_i)_k - (V_j)_k| = |(V_l)_k - (V_m)_k| \\ \sum_{t=(V_i)_k}^{(V_j)_k} p_t \geq \sum_{t=(V_i)_k}^{(V_m)_k} p_t\end{array}\right\} \implies (S_{ij})_k < (S_{lm})_k \quad (3)$$

Using the dissimilarity score of the pair as $(D_{ij})_k = 1 - (S_{ij})_k$, the similarity test scores for numeric attributes is combined by Fisher's χ^2 transformation:

$$(\chi_c)^2_{ij} = -2 \sum_{k=1}^{t_c} ln((D_{ij})_k) \quad (4)$$

where t_c is the number of numeric attributes in the data. The similarity test scores from nominal attributes are combined using Lancaster's *mean value* χ^2 transformation [4]:

$$(\chi_d)^2_{ij} = 2 \sum_{k=1}^{t_d} \left(1 - \frac{(D_{ij})_k ln(D_{ij})_k - (D_{ij})'_k ln(D_{ij})'_k}{(D_{ij})_k - (D_{ij})'_k} \right) \quad (5)$$

where t_d is the number of nominal attributes in the data, $(D_{ij})_k$ is the dissimilarity score for nominal attribute value pair $((V_i)_k, (V_j)_k)$, $(D_{ij})'_k$ is the next smaller dissimilarity score in the nominal set. The significance value of this χ^2 distribution can be looked up in standard tables or approximated from the expression:

$$D_{ij} = e^{-\frac{\chi^2_{ij}}{2}} \sum_{k=0}^{(t_d + t_c - 1)} \frac{(\frac{1}{2}\chi^2_{ij})^k}{k!} \quad (6)$$

where $\chi^2_{ij} = (\chi_c)^2_{ij} + (\chi_d)^2_{ij}$. The overall similarity score representing the set of $(t_c + t_d)$ independent similarity measures is $S_{ij} = 1 - D_{ij}$. The similarity measures obtained from individual attributes are combined to give the overall similarity between pairs of objects. For details and illustrations of this MSM, see [5].

3 Classification with Mixed Similarity Measures

We compare the performance of two classifiers, one is built by the decision tree induction system C4.5 [7] that does discretization of numeric data, and another is the k-nearest neighbor rule [1]. From the obtained results we draw some conclusions on the mutual use of these two techniques in practice. The experiments are done as follows: (1) Construct a classifier by k-NNR using this MSM without discretization. To classify an unknown instance, its k nearest neighbors are determined by this MSM and the instance will be assigned to the most common class among k nearest neighbors. We varied different values of k and fixed $k = 7$ as it gives stable results in these experiments; (2) Construct a classifier by decision tree system C4.5 with discretization; and (3) Carry out experimental comparative studies of these classifiers on databases from the UCI repository which contain both symbolic and numeric attributes by a 10-fold stratified cross validation. The predictive accuracy is estimated with a 95 % confidence interval estimate.

From the UCI repository of databases we select 18 datasets that contain mixed symbolic and numeric data. Table 1 presents results of predictive accuracy (%) of C4.5 and k-NNR with this MSM when databases contain more numeric attributes than symbolic ones. Table 2 presents results when databases contain more symbolic attributes than numeric ones. These results allow us to formulate some hypotheses (meta-knowledge) about the mutual use of this MSM and discretization for a given task of classification: (1) When a database contains more numeric attributes than symbolic ones, it maybe better to use MSM than discretization. The experimental results reconfirm an intuition as in this case we do not have to discretize many numerical attributes: (1a) The predictive accuracy of k-NNR with this MSM is often higher than that of C4.5 using discretization; (1b) However, k-NNR requires much more time than C4.5 to calculate MSM in these cases; (2) When a database contains more symbolic attributes than numeric ones, it maybe better to do discretization and use classifiers with symbolic data, vice-versa: (2a) The predictive accuracy of of k-NNR with this MSM is often lower than that of C4.5 using discretization; (2b) However, the computational time for this MSM is much lower than that of cases of many numeric attributes.

Table 1. Accuracy of two classifiers (when more numeric than symbolic attributes)

Database	Instances	Attributes	% of Attributes (Num : Sym)	Class	C4.5	k-NNR
imports-85	205	25	62 : 38	7	33.3 ± 6.4	61.9 ± 6.4
machine	209	8	78 : 28	8	63.2 ± 6.7	66.8 ± 5.4
echocardiogram	132	12	69 : 31	2	55.4 ± 8.5	63.5 ± 7.0
ecoli	336	7	88 : 12	10	76.1 ± 4.8	79.5 ± 4.0
heart	270	13	54 : 46	2	77.1 ± 5.0	82.1 ± 4.6
meta-data	528	21	91 : 9	2	90.6 ± 2.6	100
yeast	1484	9	88 : 12	10	37.6 ± 4.2	55.4 ± 2.5

Table 2. Accuracy of two classifiers (when more symbolic than numeric attributes)

Database	Instances	Attributes	% of Attributes (Num : Sym)	Class	C4.5	k-NNR
adult	1000	14	43 : 53	7	86.8 ± 2.3	74.7 ± 2.7
anneal	898	38	24 : 76	6	92.0 ± 1.7	70.3 ± 2.9
ann-thyroid	460	21	29 : 71	3	95.8 ± 1.7	94.6 ± 2.4
australian	690	14	43 : 57	3	86.8 ± 2.5	63.9 ± 3.4
crx	690	15	40 : 60	2	83.8 ± 2.7	61.0 ± 3.4
german	1000	20	35 : 65	2	69.2 ± 2.9	64.1 ± 3.0
hepatitis	155	19	32 : 68	2	57.3 ± 7.9	54.0 ± 7.3
horse-colic	368	28	32 : 68	2	68.9 ± 4.8	61.6 ± 4.5
solar-flare	1389	12	23 : 77	2	87.4 ± 1.7	72.6 ± 2.4
allbp	517	29	24 : 76	3	97.4 ± 1.8	45.1 ± 10.3
zoo	109	18	12 : 88	7	91.0 ± 1.8	45.1 ± 10.3

4 Clustering with Mixed Similarity Measures

The well-known k-means algorithm [6], [3] is very simple and powerful. k-means algorithm and its variants are efficient in clustering large datasets and thus very suitable for knowledge discovery and data mining. Given a set X of n objects and an integer $k > 1$, k-means algorithm produces a partition of X into k clusters. This algorithm can be briefly summarized in the four following steps: (1) Select arbitrarily k centers of k clusters from X; (2) Generate a new partition by assigning each object to its nearest cluster center; (3) Compute k new cluster centers; and (4) Repeat steps 2 and 3 until the stopping condition satisfies.

However, the use of this algorithm is limited to numeric data as it requires computing new centers of clusters and a cost function that all based on the similarity measure between instances. In [8], the author presented an extension of k-means algorithm for symbolic data. Using MSM we present here another extension of k-means algorithm for mixed symbolic and numeric data. The key point in this extension is in step 3: how to compute new cluster centers for mixed data? In fact, we determine the center of each cluster as a vector containing mixed symbolic and numeric components according to the original attributes in the dataset. The components of this center are calculated as follows: (1) For each numeric attribute, its value for the new center is the mean of values of the cluster's instances at this attribute; and (2) For each symbolic attribute, its value for the new center is the value with highest frequency among values of the cluster's instances at this attribute.

We have implemented this extension of k-means algorithm with MSM and carried out experiments with several UCI datasets containing mixed data. To investigate the performance of clustering by k-means algorithm with MSM, experiments are done as follows: (1) Choose the value k as the number of natural classes in the given dataset; (2) Choose k initial centers by one of two ways: (2a) selecting arbitrarily k first instances in the dataset; (2b) selecting k representatives of clusters as k instances from original classes in the dataset (if possible); (3) For each generated class we determine its instances, then compare them to

Table 3. Prediction accuracy by k-means algorithm with MSM for mixed datasets

Database	Instances	Attributes	% of Attributes (Num : Sym)	Class	Prediction accuracy (%) Centers by (2a)	Centers by (2b)
allbp	517	29	24 : 76	3	68.20	59.49
ann-thyroid	460	21	29 : 71	3	75.30	82.20
australian	690	14	43 : 57	3	79.12	86.10
cleve	303	13	50 : 50	5	56.61	83.67
crx	690	15	40 : 60	2	76.44	79.92
hepatitis	155	19	32 : 68	2	53.40	70.18
solar-flare	1389	12	23 : 77	2	56.22	51.11
zoo	109	18	12 : 88	7	79.71	96.54

those of the original class to find how they match each other; (4) Run 20 iterations for each dataset and determine the best prediction accuracy for (2a) and (2b). The experimental results are shown in Table 3.

The following observations can be made from these experiments: (1) The MSM is a quite good measure for clustering datasets with both numeric and symbolic data. In some cases the prediction accuracy is very high, such as 96% for the dataset 'zoo' (in comparing with the class of original data); (2) The highest prediction accuracy of partitions were often found within 10 iterations of the k-means algorithm for arbitrarily centers by (2a), and within 5 iterations for arbitrarily centers by (2b); (3) It is better to choose initially cluster centers by their representatives from original classes if some background knowledge or class labels are available; (4) Most computation time is for calculating MSM.

To develop another MSM that preserves good properties of the considered MSM but much faster, and to design efficient KDD algorithms using new MSM are our objectives of further work.

References

1. Duda, R. and Hart, P., *Pattern Classification and Scene Analysis*, Wiley, 1973.
2. Goodall, D.W., "A New Similarity Index Based On Probability" in *Biometrics*, Vol.22, pp. 882-907, 1966.
3. Jain, A.K. and Dubes, R.C., *Algorithms for Clustering Data* Prentice Hall, Englewood Cliffs, 1988.
4. Lancaster, H.O., "The Combining of Probabilities Arising from Data in Discrete Distributions" in *Biometrika*, Vol. 36, pp. 370-382, 1949.
5. Li, C. and Biswas, G., "Unsupervised Clustering with Mixed Numeric and Nominal Data - A New Similarity Based Agglomerative System" *KDD: Techniques and Application*, World Scientific, pp. 33–48, 1997.
6. MacQueen, J.B., "Some Methods for Classification and Analysis of Multivariate Observations", *Proc. 5th Berkeley Symposium on Mathematical Statistics and Probability*, pp. 281-297, 1967.
7. Quinlan, J.R. *C4.5: Programs for Machine Learning*, Morgan Kaufmann, 1993.
8. Ralambondrainy, H., "A Conceptual Version of the K-means Algorithms", *Pattern Recognition Letters*, Vol.16, pp.1147–1157, 1995.

Visually Aided Exploration of Interesting Association Rules

Bing Liu, Wynne Hsu, Ke Wang, and Shu Chen

School of Computing
National University of Singapore
Lower Kent Ridge Road, Singapore 119260
{liub, whsu, wangk, chens} @comp.nus.edu.sg
http://www.comp.nus.edu.sg/{~liub, ~whsu, ~wangk}

Abstract. Association rules are a class of important regularities in databases. They are found to be very useful in practical applications. However, the number of association rules discovered in a database can be huge, thus making manual inspection and analysis of the rules difficult. In this paper, we propose a new framework to allow the user to explore the discovered rules to identify those interesting ones. This framework has two components, an interestingness analysis component, and a visualization component. The interestingness analysis component analyzes and organizes the discovered rules according to various interestingness criteria with respect to the user's existing knowledge. The visualization component enables the user to visually explore those potentially interesting rules. The key strength of the visualization component is that from a single screen, the user is able to obtain a global and yet detailed picture of various interesting aspects of the discovered rules. Enhanced with color effects, the user can easily and quickly focus his/her attention on the more interesting/useful rules.

1. Introduction

Association rules, introduced in [2], have received considerable attention in data mining research and applications. The main strengths of association rule mining are that the target of discovery is not pre-determined, and that it is able to find all association rules that exist in the database. Thus, association rules can reveal valuable and unexpected information in the database. However, these strengths are also its weakness, i.e., the number of discovered rules can be huge, in thousands or even tens of thousands, which makes manual inspection of the rules to identify the interesting ones an almost impossible task. Automated assistance is thus needed.

Determining the interestingness of a rule is not a simple task. A rule can be interesting to one person but not interesting to another. The interestingness of a rule is essentially subjective. It depends on the user's existing knowledge about the domain and his/her current interests.

This paper proposes a new interactive and iterative framework to help the user find interesting association rules. The proposed framework consists of two components, an interestingness analysis component and a visualization component. The interestingness analysis component allows the user to specify his/her existing knowledge. It then uses this input knowledge to analyze the discovered rules according to various interestingness criteria, and through such analysis to identify those potentially interesting rules for the user. The visualization component makes it easy for the user to visually ex-

plore the potentially interesting rules. The key strength of the visualization component is that from a single screen, the user is able to obtain a global and yet detailed picture of various interesting aspects of the discovered rules. This enables him/her to visually detect any unusual pattern without the need to browse through a large number of rules. Three main types of information are shown on the screen:
(1) different kinds of potentially interesting rules.
(2) different degrees of rule interestingness and the number of rules in each kind.
(3) interesting items in the conditional part or the consequent part of the rules.
Enhanced with color effects, these types of information can lead the user to easily and quickly explore various aspects of the discovered rules and to focus his/her attention on those truly interesting/useful ones. The whole system works as follows:

Repeat until the user decides to stop
1 the user specifies some existing knowledge or modifies the knowledge specified previously;
2 the system analyzes the discovered rules according to some interestingness criteria;
3 the user inspects the analysis results through the visualization component, saves the interesting rules, and removes those unwanted rules.

2. Association Rules and Subjective Rule Interestingness

2.1 Generalized association rules

Let $I = \{i_1, ..., i_w\}$ be a set of items, T be a set of transactions, and G be a set of *taxonomies* or *class hierarchies*. A taxonomy is a directed acyclic graph on the items in I, where an edge represents an *is-a* relationship. A taxonomy example is shown in Fig 1. A *generalized association rule* [15] is an implication of the form $X \rightarrow Y$, where $X \subset I$, $Y \subset I$, and $X \cap Y = \varnothing$. The rule $X \rightarrow Y$ holds in the transaction set T with confidence c if $c\%$ of transactions in T that support X also support Y. The rule has support s in T if $s\%$ of the transactions in T contains $X \cup Y$. A transaction t that supports an item in I also supports all its ancestors in I. For example, an association rule could be:

cheese, milk $\rightarrow$ Fruit   [support = 5%, confidence = 70%],

which says that 5% of people buy cheese, milk and Fruit together, and 70% of the people who buy cheese and milk also buy Fruit (of any kind).

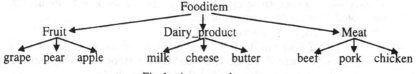

Fig 1. An example taxonomy

2.2 Subjective rule interestingness

Past research has identified two main subjective rule interestingness measures:
Unexpectedness [14, 7]: Rules are interesting if they "surprise" the user.
Actionability [11]: Rules are interesting if the user can do something with them to his/her advantage.

The two measures of interestingness are not mutually exclusive. Interesting rules can be classified into three categories [14]:
1: rules that are both unexpected and actionable,
2: rules that are unexpected but not actionable, and
3: rules that are actionable but expected.
Category 1 and 2 can be handled by finding unexpected rules, and category 3 can be

handled by finding the rules that conform to the user's knowledge. This paper proposes a new framework to help the user find these two types of rules, i.e., unexpected rules, and expected rules (or conforming rules).

3. The Interestingness Analysis Component

This component uses the user's existing knowledge to analyze and identify various types of potentially interesting rules from the discovered association rules.

3.1. The specification language

A specification language is designed to enable the user to express his/her existing knowledge. This language focuses on representing the user's existing knowledge about associative relations on items in the database. The basic syntax of the language takes the same format as association rules.

This language has three levels of specifications. Each represents knowledge of a different degree of preciseness. They are: *general impressions, reasonably precise concepts,* and *precise knowledge.* The first two levels represent the user's vague feelings. The last level represents his/her precise knowledge. This division is important because a user typically has a mixture of vague and precise knowledge.

The proposed language also uses the idea of class hierarchy (or taxonomy) as in generalized association rules. The hierarchy in Fig 1 can also be represented by:

{grape, pear, apple} ⊂ Fruit ⊂ Fooditem
{milk, cheese, butter} ⊂ Dairy_product ⊂ Fooditem
{beef, pork, chicken} ⊂ Meat ⊂ Fooditem

Fruit, Dairy_product, Meat and Fooditems are classes (or class names). grape, pear, apple, milk, cheese, beef, pork, chicken, #Fruit, #Dairy_product, #Meat and #Fooditems are items. Note that in generalized association rules, class names can also be treated as items, in which case, we append a "#" in front of a class name. Note also that in the proposed language, a class hierarchy does not need to be constructed beforehand. A class can be created any time when needed by using a set of items (see the examples below).

General Impression (GI): It represents the user's vague feeling that there should be some associations among some classes of items, but he/she is not sure how they are associated. This can be expressed with:

$$gi(<S_1, ..., S_m>) \ [support, confidence]$$

where (1) Each S_i is one of the following: an item, a class, or an expression C+ or C*, where C is a class. C+ and C* correspond to one or more, and zero or more instances of the class C, respectively.

(2) A discovered rule: $a_1, ..., a_n \rightarrow b_1, ..., b_k$, *conforms* to the GI if $<a_1, ..., a_n, b_1, ..., b_k>$ can be considered to be an instance of $<S_1, ..., S_m>$, otherwise it is *unexpected* with respect to the GI.

(3) *Support* and *confidence* are optional. The user can specify the minimum *support* and the minimum *confidence* of the rules that he/she wants to see.

Example 1: The user believes that there exist some associations among {milk, cheese}, Fruit items, and beef (assume we use the class hierarchy in Fig 1). He/she specifies this as:

$$gi(<\{milk, cheese\}*, Fruit+, beef>)$$

{milk, cheese} here represents a class constructed on the fly unlike Fruit. The following are examples of association rules that conform to the specification:

apple → beef

grape, pear, beef → milk

The following two rules are unexpected with respect to this specification:

    (1)   milk → beef   (2)   milk, cheese, pear → clothes

(1) is unexpected because Fruit+ is not satisfied. (2) is unexpected because beef is not present in the rule, and clothes is not from any of the elements in the GI.

Reasonably Precise Concept (RPC): It represents the user's concept that there should be some associations among some classes of items, and he/she also knows the direction of the associations. This can be expressed with:

$$rpc(<S_1, ..., S_m \rightarrow V_1, ..., V_g>) \quad [support, confidence]$$

where (1) Each S_i or V_j is the same as S_i in the GI specification.

          (2) A discovered rule, $a_1, ..., a_n \rightarrow b_1, ..., b_k$, *conforms* to the RPC, if the rule can be considered to be an instance of the RPC, otherwise it is considered as *unexpected* with respect to the RPC.

          (3) *Support* and *confidence* are again optional.

Example 2: Suppose the user believes the following:

    $rpc(<\text{Meat, Meat, \#Dairy\_product} \rightarrow \{\text{grape, apple}\}+>)$

The following are examples of association rules that conform to the specification:

    beef, pork, Dairy_product → grape

    beef, chicken, Dairy_product → grape, apple

The following two rules are unexpected with respect to the specification:

    (1)   pork, Dairy_product → grape   (2)   beef, pork → grape

(1) is unexpected because it has only one Meat item, but two Meat items are needed as we have two Meat's in the specification. (2) is unexpected because Dairy_product is not in the conditional part of the rule.

Precise knowledge (PK): The user believes in a precise association. This is expressed with:

$$pk(<S_1, ..., S_m \rightarrow V_1, ..., V_g>) \quad [support, confidence]$$

where (1) Each S_i or V_j is an item in I.

          (2) A discovered rule: $a_1, ..., a_n \rightarrow b_1, ..., b_k$ [*sup, confid*], is *equal* to the PK, if the rule part is the same as $S_1, ..., S_m \rightarrow V_1, ..., V_g$. Whether it *conforms* to the PK or is *unexpected* depends on the support and confidence specifications.

          (3) *Support* and *confidence* need to be specified (they are not optional).

Example 3: Suppose the user believes the following:

    $pk(<\#\text{Meat, milk} \rightarrow \text{apple}>)$ [10%, 50%]

The discovered rule below conforms to the PK quite well because the supports and confidences of the rule and the PK are quite close.

    Meat, milk → apple [8%, 53%]

However, if the discovered rule is the following:

    Meat, milk → apple [4%, 30%]

then it is less conforming, but more unexpected, because its support and confidence are quite far from those of the PK.

3.2. Analyzing the discovered rules using user's existing knowledge

We now present how to use the user's specifications to analyze the discovered rules. For GIs and RPCs, we only perform syntax-based analysis, i.e., comparing the syntactic structure of the discovered rules with GIs and RPCs. It does not make sense to do semantics-based analysis because the user does not have precise associations in mind. Using PKs, we can perform semantics-based analysis (based on support and confidence) on the discovered rules. Due to space limitations, we could not present this in the paper (see [9] for details).

Let U be the set of user's specifications representing his/her knowledge space. Let A be the set of discovered association rules. The proposed technique analyzes the discovered rules by "matching" and ranking the rules in A in a number of ways for finding different kinds of interesting rules, *conforming rules, unexpected consequent rules, unexpected condition rules* and *both-side unexpected rules.*

Conforming rules: A discovered rule $A_i \in A$ conforms to a piece of user's knowledge $U_j \in U$ if both the conditional and consequent parts of A_i match $U_j \in U$ well. We use $confm_{ij}$ to denote the degree of *conforming match.*

Purpose: conforming rules show us those discovered rules that conform to or are consistent with our existing knowledge fully or partially.

Unexpected consequent rules: A discovered rule $A_i \in A$ has unexpected consequents with respect to a $U_j \in U$ if the conditional part of A_i matches U_j well, but not the consequent part. We use $unexpConseq_{ij}$ to denote the degree of *unexpected consequent match.*

Purpose: unexpected consequent rules show us those discovered rules that may be contrary to our existing knowledge. These rules are often very interesting.

Unexpected condition rules: A discovered rule $A_i \in A$ has unexpected conditions with respect to a $U_j \in U$ if the consequent part of A_i matches U_j well, but not the conditional part. We use $unexpCond_{ij}$ to denote the degree of *unexpected condition match.*

Purpose: unexpected condition rules show us that there are other conditions that can lead to the consequent of the specification. We are thus guided to explore unfamiliar territories.

Both-side unexpected rules: A discovered rule $A_i \in A$ is both-side unexpected with respect to a $U_j \in U$ if both the conditional and consequent parts of the rule A_i do not match U_j well. We use $bsUnexp_{ij}$ to denote the degree of *both-side unexpected match.*

Purpose: both-side unexpected rules remind us that there are other rules whose conditions and consequents are not mentioned in our specification. It helps us to go beyond our existing concept space.

The values for $confm_{ij}$, $unexpConseq_{ij}$, $unexpCond_{ij}$, and $bsUnexp_{ij}$ are between 1.00 and 0. 1.00 represents the complete match, either the complete conforming or the complete unexpectedness match, and 0 represents no match. Let L_{ij} and R_{ij} be the degrees of condition and consequent match of rule A_i against U_j respectively. We have (for both GIs and RPCs),

$$confm_{ij} = L_{ij} * R_{ij}; \qquad unexpConseq_{ij} = \begin{cases} 0 & L_{ij} - R_{ij} \leq 0 \\ L_{ij} - R_{ij} & L_{ij} - R_{ij} > 0 \end{cases};$$

$$unexpCond_{ij} = \begin{cases} 0 & R_{ij} - L_{ij} \leq 0 \\ R_{ij} - L_{ij} & R_{ij} - L_{ij} > 0 \end{cases};$$

$$bsUnexp_{ij} = 1 - max(confm_{ij}, unexpConseq_{ij}, unexpCond_{ij});$$

We use $L_{ij} - R_{ij}$ to compute the unexpected consequent match degree because we wish to rank those rules with high L_{ij} but low R_{ij} higher. Similar idea applies to $unexpCond_{ij}$. The formula for $bsUnexp_{ij}$ ensures that those rules with high values in any other three categories should have low values here, and vice versa.

Due to the space limitation, we are unable to give the detailed computation methods for L_{ij} and R_{ij}, which depend on whether U_j is a GI or a RPC. The computations can all be done efficiently. See [9] for full details. After $confm_{ij}$, $unexpConseq_{ij}$, $unexpCond_{ij}$, and $bsUnexp_{ij}$ have been computed, we can rank the discovered rules with respect to a U_j. It is also possible to rank the rules with respect to the whole set of specifications U. However, in our applications, we find that such rankings can be quite confusing, and are thus omitted.

4. The Visualization Component

After the discovered rules are analyzed with the method presented in the last section, we want to display those different types of potentially interesting rules to the user. The issue here is how to show the essential aspects of the rules such that we can take advantage of the human visual capabilities to allow the user to identify the truly interesting rules easily and quickly. Let us discuss what the essential aspects are:

1. Types of potentially interesting rules: We should separate them because different types of interesting rules give the user different information.
2. Degrees of interestingness ("match" values): We should group rules according to their degrees of interestingness. This enables the user to focus his/her attention on the most unexpected (or conforming) rules first and to decide whether to view those rules with low degrees of interestingness.
3. Interesting items: We focus on showing the interesting items rather than the rules. This is perhaps the most crucial decision that we have made. In our applications, we find that it is those unexpected items that are most important to the user because due to 1 above, the user already knows what kind of interesting rules he/she is looking. For example, when the user is looking at unexpected consequent rules, it is natural that the first thing he/she wants to know is what are the unexpected items in the consequent parts. Even if we show the rules, the user still needs to look for the unexpected items in the rules.

The main screen in the visualization system contains all the above information. Below, we use an example to describe the visualization system.

The visualization system consists of 4 main modules:
1. *Class hierarchy builder*: it allows the user to build class hierarchies as in Fig 1.
2. *GI viewer*: it allows the user to specify GIs and to visualize the results produced by the interestingness analysis system.
3. *RPC viewer*: it allows the user to specify RPCs and to visualize the results produced by the interestingness analysis system.
4. *PK viewer*: it allows the user to specify PKs and to visualize the results produced by the interestingness analysis system.

Here, we only focus on presenting the *RPC viewer*. Due to space limitations, we are unable to show the others. They are similar in concept to the *RPC viewer*. We will also not discuss the *Class hierarchy builder* since it is straightforward.

4.1. The example setting

Our example uses a RPC specification. The rules in the example are a small subset of rules (857 rules) discovered in an exam results database. This application tries to discover the associations between the exam results of a set of 7 specialized courses (called GA courses) and the exam results of a set of 7 basic courses (called GB courses). A course together with an exam result form an item, e.g., GA6-1, where GA6 is the course code and "1" represents a bad exam grade ("2" represents an average grade and "3" a good grade). The discovered rules and our existing concept specification are listed below.

- **Discovered association rules:** The rules below have only GA course grades on left-hand-side and GB course grades on right-hand-side (we omit their support and confidence).

R1:	GA1-3 → GB2-3	R7:	GA4-1 → GB7-2
R2:	GA4-3 → GB4-3	R8:	GA6-2 → GB7-2
R3:	GA2-3 → GB2-3	R9:	GA5-1, GA2-2 → GB2-2
R4:	GA2-3 → GB5-1	R10:	GA5-2, GA1-2 → GB3-2
R5:	GA6-1 → GB1-3	R11:	GA6-1, GA3-3 → GB6-3
R6:	GA4-2 → GB3-3	R12:	GA7-2, GA3-3 → GB4-3

- Our existing concept specification

Assume we have the common belief that students good in GA courses are likely to be good in GB courses. This can be expressed as a RPC (also see it in Fig 2):

Spec1: rpc(GA-good → GB-good)

where the classes, GA-good and GB-good, are defined as follows:

GA-good ⊃ {GA1-3, GA2-3, GA3-3, GA4-3, GA5-3, GA6-3, GA7-3}
GB-good ⊃ {GB1-3, GB2-3, GB3-3, GB4-3, GB5-3, GB6-3, GB7-3}

4.2. Viewing the results

After running the system with the above RPC specification, we obtain the screen in Fig 2 (the main screen). We see "RPC" in the middle. To the bottom of "RPC", we have the *conforming rules visualization unit*. To the left of "RPC", we have the *unexpected condition rules visualization unit*. To the right, we have the *unexpected consequent rules visualization unit*. To the top, we have *both-side unexpected rules visualization unit*. Below, we briefly discuss these units in turn with the example.

Conforming rules visualization unit: Clicking on **Conform**, we will see the complete conforming rules ranking in a pop-up window:

Rank 1:	1.00	R1	GA1-3 → GB2-3
Rank 1:	1.00	R2	GA4-3 → GB4-3
Rank 1:	1.00	R3	GA2-3 → GB2-3
Rank 2:	0.50	R11	GA6-1, GA3-3 → GB6-3
Rank 2:	0.50	R12	GA7-2, GA3-3 → GB4-3

The number (e.g., 1.00, and 0.50) after each rank number is the conforming match value, $confm_{i1}$. The first three rules conform to our belief completely. The last two only conform to our belief partially because GA6-1 and GA7-2 are unexpected. This list of rules can be long in a real-life application. The following mechanisms help the user focus his/her attention, i.e., enabling him/her to view rules with different degrees of interestingess ("match" values) and to view the interesting items.

- On both sides of **Conform** we can see 4 pairs of boxes, which represent sets of rules with different conforming match values. If a pair of boxes is colored, it means that there are rules there, otherwise there is no rule. The line connecting "RPC" and a pair of colored boxes also indicates that there are rules under them. The number of rules is shown on the line. Clicking on the box with a value will give all the rules with the corresponding match value and above. For example, clicking on 0.50 shows the rules with $0.50 \leq confm_{i1} < 0.75$. Below each colored box with a value, we have two small windows. The one on the top has all the rules' condition items from our RPC specification, and the one at the bottom has all the consequent items. Clicking on each item gives us the rules that use this item as a condition item (or a consequent item).
- Clicking on the colored box without a value (below the valued box) brings us to a new screen (not shown here). From this, the user sees all the items in different classes involved, and also conforming and unexpected items.

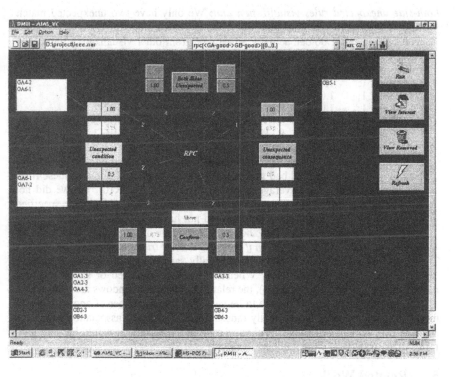

Fig 2. RPC main visualization screen

Unexpected condition rules visualization unit: The boxes here have similar meanings as the ones for conforming rules. From Fig 2, we see that there are 4 unexpected condition rules. Two have the unexpected match value of 1.00 and two have 0.50. The window (on the far left) connected to the box with a match value gives all the unexpected condition items. Clicking on each item reveals the relevant rules. Similarly, clicking on the colored box next to the one with a value shows both the unexpected condition items and the items used in the consequent part of the rules. To obtain all the rules in the category, we can click **Unexpected Conditions**.

Rank 1:	1.00	R5	GA6-1 → GB1-3
Rank 1:	1.00	R6	GA4-2 → GB3-3
Rank 2:	0.50	R11	GA6-1, GA3-3 → GB6-3
Rank 2:	0.50	R12	GA7-2, GA3-3 → GB4-3

1.00 and 0.50 are the $unexpCond_{i1}$ values. Here, we see something quite unexpected. For example, many students with bad grades in GA6 actually have good grades in GB1.

Unexpected consequent rules visualization unit: This is also similar to the conforming rules visualization unit. From Fig 2, we see that there is only one unexpected consequent rule and the unexpected consequent match value is 1.00. Clicking on the colored box with 1.00, we will obtain the unexpected consequent rule:

Rank 1:	1.00	R4	GA2-3 → GB5-1

This rule is very interesting because it contradicts our belief. Many students with good grades in GA2 actually have bad grades in GB5.

Both-side unexpected rules visualization unit: We only have two unexpected match value boxes here, i.e., 1.00 and 0.50. Due to the formulas in Section 3.2, rules with $bsUnexp_{ij} < 1.00$ can actually all be seen from other visualization units. The unexpected items can be obtained by clicking on the box above the one with a value. All the ranked rules can be obtained by clicking **Both Sides Unexpected**.

Rank 1:	1.00	R7	GA4-1 → GB7-2
Rank 1:	1.00	R8	GA6-2 → GB7-2
Rank 1:	1.00	R9	GA5-1, GA2-2 → GB2-2
Rank 1:	1.00	R10	GA5-2, GA1-2 → GB3-2
Rank 2:	0.50	R11	GA6-1, GA3-3 → GB6-3
Rank 2:	0.50	R12	GA7-2, GA3-3 → GB4-3

From this ranking, we also see something quite interesting, i.e., average grades lead to average grades and bad grades lead to average grades. Some of these rules are common sense, e.g., average to average rules (R8 and R10), but we did not specify them as our existing knowledge (if "average to average" had been specified as our knowledge earlier, these rules would not have appeared here because they would have been removed). This shows the advantage of our technique, i.e., *it can remind us what we have forgotten if the rules are not truly unexpected.*

The system also allows the user to incrementally save interesting rules and remove unwanted rules, and to view them. Whenever a rule is removed or saved (also removed from the original set of rules), the related pictures and windows are updated.

The proposed system has proven to be very useful in a number of applications. In these applications, there are typically thousands of discovered association rules (the smallest rule set has 770 rules). Without the proposed system, it would be very hard for us to analyze these large numbers of rules.

5. Related Work

Traditionally, a query-based approach is used to help the user identify or generate interesting rules. The approach takes many forms, e.g., templates [6], M-SQL [5], DMQL [4], and action hierarchy [1]. Although query languages can be quite different, a query basically defines a set of rules of a certain type (or constraints on the rules to be found). To "execute" a query means to find all rules that satisfy the query. We believe that the query-based approach is insufficient for two main reasons:

1. It is hard to find the truly unexpected rules. It only finds those anticipated rules because what the user's queries are still within his/her existing knowledge space.
2. The user often does not know or is unable to specify completely what interest him/her. He/she needs to be stimulated. The query-based approach does not actively perform this task because it only returns those rules that satisfy the queries.

Our technique not only finds those conforming rules like query-based methods, but also provides three types of unexpected rules. Our approach also helps the user to provide more knowledge to the system by reminding him/her what he/she might have forgotten. If the top ranking rules are not unexpected, then they serve to remind the user what he/she has forgotten. Our visualization component allows the user to easily and quickly explore those interesting rules.

[7, 8] report a related technique for analyzing classification rules [13] using user's existing concepts. However, the technique there cannot be used for analyzing association rules. Association rules require a different specification language and different ways of analyzing and ranking the rules. [7, 8] also do not have visualization systems.

[12] proposes a method of discovering unexpected rules in the rule generation

phase by taking into consideration the user's expectations. This method is, however, not as efficient and flexible as our post-analysis method because the user is normally unable to specify his/her expectations about the domain completely. User interaction with the system is needed in order for him/her to provide a more complete set of expectations and to find more interesting rules. However, user interaction is difficult for the approach in [12] because it is not efficient to run a rule miner whenever the user remembers another piece of knowledge. The association rule mining is typically very time consuming. Post-analysis facilitates user interaction due to its efficiency.

6. Conclusion

This paper proposes an integrated framework for exploration of discovered rules in order to find those interesting ones. The interestingness analysis system uses three types of user's existing knowledge to analyze the discovered rules and to organize them in various ways to expose the user to many interesting aspects of the discovered rules. A simple but powerful visualization system enables the user to view and identify interesting rules easily and quickly.

References

[1]   Adomavicius, G. and Tuzhilin, A. "Discovery of actionable patterns in data-bases: the action hierarchy approach." *KDD-97*, 1997, pp. 111-114.
[2]   Agrawal, R., Imielinski, T. and Swami, A. Mining association rules between sets of items in large databases. *SIGMOD-1993*, 1993, pp. 207-216.
[3]   Fayyad, U., Piatesky-Shapiro, G. and Smyth, P. "From data mining to knowledge discovery: an overview," In: *Advances in knowledge discovery and data mining*, U. Fayyad, G. Piatesky-Shapiro, P. Smyth and R. Uthurusamy, (eds.), AAAI/MIT Press, 1996, pp. 1-34.
[4]   Han, J., Fu, Y., Wang, W., Koperski, K. and Zaiane, O. "DMQL: a data mining query language for relational databases." *SIGMOD Workshop on KDD*, 1996.
[5]   Imielinski, T., Virmani, A. and Abdulghani, A. "DataMine: application programming interface and query language for database mining." *KDD-96*, 1996.
[6]   Klemetinen, M., Mannila, H., Ronkainen, P., Toivonen, H., and Verkamo, A.I. "Finding interesting rules from large sets of discovered association rules." *CIKM-94*, 1994, pp. 401-407.
[7]   Liu, B., and Hsu, W. "Post-analysis of learned rules." *AAAI-96*, 1996.
[8]   Liu, B., Hsu, W., and Chen, S. "Using general impressions to analyze discovered classification rules." *KDD-97*, 1997, pp. 31-36.
[9]   Liu, B., Hsu, W., and Wang, K. "Helping user identifying interesting association rules" *Technical Report*, 1998.
[10] Liu, B., Hsu, W. and Ma, Y. M. "Integrating classification and association rule mining." *KDD-98*, 1998, pp. 80-86.
[11] Piatesky-Shapiro, G., and Matheus, C. "The interestingness of deviations." *KDD-94*, 1994.
[12] Padmanabhan, B., and Tuzhilin, A. "A belief-driven method for discovering unexpected patterns." *KDD-98*, 1998, pp. 94-110.
[13] Quinlan, J. R. *C4.5: program for machine learning.* Morgan Kaufmann, 1992.
[14] Silberschatz, A., and Tuzhilin, A. "What makes patterns interesting in knowledge discovery systems." *IEEE Trans. on Know. and Data Eng.* 8(6), 1996.
[15] Srikant, R. and Agrawal, R. "Mining Generalized association rules." *VLDB-1995*, 1995.
[16] Srikant, R., Vu, Q. and Agrawal, R. "Mining association rules with item constraints." *KDD-97*, 1997, pp. 67-73.

DVIZ: A System for Visualizing Data Mining

Jianchao Han and Nick Cercone

Department of Computer Science, University of Waterloo
Waterloo, Ontario N2L 3G1 Canada
Email: {ncercone@math, j2han@neumann}.uwaterloo.ca

Abstract. We introduce an interactive system which visualizes the knowledge in data mining processes, including attribute values, evolutionary attributes, associations of attributes, classifications and hierarchical concepts. The basic framework of knowledge visualization in data mining is discussed and the algorithms for visualizing different forms of knowledge are presented. The application of our initial prototype system, DVIZ, to *Canada Education Statistics* is described and some preliminary results presented.

Keywords: Data mining, data visualization, knowledge discovery.

1 Introduction

Visualizing data mining should prove useful to various applications, e.g., stock market trends, oil streak patterns and smoke in fluid dynamics, multiple needle strip charts in seismology, factor analysis, etc. Data mining is popularly recognized as an important and difficult stage of knowledge discovery in databases[3], which is defined as the extraction of interesting knowledge (rules, regularities, patterns, constraints) from data in large databases. It is a process of searching and analyzing data in order to find implicit but potentially useful information, knowledge, regularities, overviews and even to automatically construct knowledge-bases[6].

Generally speaking, the knowledge discovered in databases is represented as various rules, e.g., generalization rules, characterization rules, classification rules, association rules, evolution rules, etc. These rules are always static. In most cases, users are often impatient to understand and use the results of data mining as quickly as possible, and they prefer to visualize the process and results rather than analyzing an abstract logical form.

Recent research on data visualization techniques encompasses the effective portrayal of data with the additional goal of providing insights about the data[2]. Data visualization is a process of transforming the generated abstract data into a meaningful visual form so that users can understand the data more easily. Effective visualization makes a data mining system's nature apparent at a glance.

We briefly introduce visualization techniques and their applications to data mining. The visualization techniques employed in this paper include:

- *Individual attribute visualization*, which is used to visualize the data of an individual attribute in time series. Color intensity and brightness are functions of date.
- *Evolutionary attribute visualization*, which is used to show the evolution of a specified attribute in the form of a curve with a background that is colored according to the attribute values in the time series.
- *Classification visualization*, which uses a constraint slider to set the maximal number of classes to be classified; as long as the classifying attribute is specified, the objects will be classified and rendered in terms of the classifying attribute.
- *Attributes association visualization*, which is used to show the association between two or three attributes. The associations are represented as a colored tube that is drawn at the specified point for each tuple of attributes values and colored according to the R, G and B values based on attributes values.
- *Hierarchical concepts visualization*, which is used to visualize hierarchical data. Sliders are used to control the levels of hierarchical data.

These techniques are discussed in greater detail below and illustrated in Figure 3 and Figure 4.

These methods have been used to visualize *Canadian Statistics Data of Education* according to the analysis of various data for each province, e.g., the number and the amount of full time student loans, secondary school graduates, full time (part time) and male (female) enrollment in colleges or universities, university undergraduate or graduate degrees granted, etc. By visualizing these data, we can directly and straightforwardly characterize, summarize, associate, and classify different types of data, and predict the trend of some events in terms of past data.

We first summarize the data visualization techniques, and introduce the structure of our system, DVIZ, in Section 2. The principle and rendering of each subsystem are discussed individually in Section 3. The application of DVIZ to *Canadian Education Statistics* is presented in Section 4. Finally, in Section 5, we give conclusions and discuss our future work.

2 System Structure

2.1 Basic Framework for Visualization

Among various data visualization techniques, there is a basic common framework which are an extension of Abowd and Beale's model of human-computer interaction [9]. This basic framework consists of four main components: User, Database, Visualization and Interaction, as shown in Figure 1.

The **User** component describes the human user of the system, providing a description of his sophistication (e.g., expertise with the data visualized or with the system itself), the tasks which he wishes to perform (e.g., discovering associations between data, classifying data into categories, etc.), and his level of authority to view or modify data.

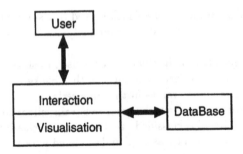

Fig. 1. Basic Framework for Visualization

The **Database** component represents the actual database to be "mined" and visualized, encompassing the data model used, the schema and the instances which populate the database.

The **Visualization** component presents the data to the user by using the different predefined metaphors such as color, shape, shadow, texture, etc. to represent different items of data and arranging the physical layout on the screen. Generally, this component contains a subcomponent that extracts relevant information from the database , processes the extracted information and transfers the results into metaphors. In our system, this subcomponent is the data mining process.

The **Interaction** component addresses how the user may alter the presentation of the data, or the data itself. This component interprets the user's intention, the medium selected to realize the intention, and the effect of the action selected. Interaction effects may change the data, the visualization, or both.

In our interpretation and implementation of this model, we have integrated the algorithms for mining data with the techniques used to visualize theses results. This seamless integration is most apparent in the interaction component where the effect of an interaction (action at the user, e.g., moving a slider or picking an attribute) forces a recomputation of results for subsequent and simultaneous display.

Figure 1 shows this framework, where the interaction and the visualization components are combined together to form the user-friendly interface, which is usually implemented as an interactive visualization.

This basic framework provides an integrated model, coordinating the subcomponents. This point is particularly important to ensure that the resulting system is open and able to cooperate with other software systems. This framework facilitates incorporation of interactive components from various sources and provides for multiple visualization of the same data.

2.2 System Architecture

In our system, we use sliders and an attributes list for choices as an interactive method to set visualization parameters, and color, curve and square as a visualization metaphor. The system consists of six subsystems, shown in Figure 2, each of which can be used to visualize different data characteristics and/or the relationships among data. To implement our prototype, we adopt different visualization techniques to design the different subsystems. These visualization techniques primarily include geometric techniques, graph-based techniques, three-dimensional techniques, dynamic techniques, and simplified pixel-oriented techniques.

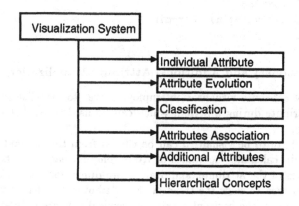

Fig. 2. System Architecture

The characteristics of this system can be described as follows:

- The basic technique used among all subsystems is a dynamic technique, which permits visualization of the data by the dynamic interaction.
- All subsystems use one or two sliders as the interactive method to control the visualization of data.
- All subsystems can visualize the data of more attributes (higher dimensional data), but some can do so simultaneously, and others only do so sequentially. By choosing different attribute(s) from the attribute list, the user can visualize the data of a specified attribute(s).
- The method of rendering is based on the maximum and minimum data of given attribute(s). Generally speaking, the object with maximum data is rendered more red (greater R value and less G value of RGB color), the object with minimum data is rendered more green (less R value and greater G value), and the object with intermediate data is rendered more yellow.

3 Algorithms of Visualization

3.1 Individual Attribute Data Visualization

When the attribute to be visualized is specified, as the date slider is moved, the color of each object area will be recalculated with respect to the attribute values in time series. The algorithm for RGB color calculation follows.

```
For specified attribute and date (time)
  Find the maximum and minimum values among all provinces
  For each province
    Find the value(val) of the specified attribute in the
        specified date
    Calculate the R, G, B corresponding to this value:
    r=val/max*256
    g=256*(1-(val-min)/(max-min))
    b=0
```

3.2   Evolutionary and Additional Attribute Visualization

Evolutionary attribute visualization employs curves to visualize the data of a specified attribute during a period, which can be used to predict the trend of the attribute.

The attribute to be visualized can be chosen from the attributes list. This subsystem will calculate the values of RGB color for each area based on the average values of the attribute, and draw a two-dimensional coordinate with a curve in each area to show the trend of the attribute for different years. In the coordinates shown, the horizontal axis and vertical axis are date and attribute values respectively. The curve is a polyline, the points of which are calculated as follows, suppose (X, Y):

```
For each area and each year
  X=(current_year-min_year)/(max_year-min_year)*X_len
  Y=(current_value-min_value)/(max_value-min_value)*Y_len
```

The RGB color calculation of each area is computed by the following algorithm.

```
For the specified attribute
  Find the maximum and minimum average values during the period
  For each area
    Find value of the specified attribute in the specified year
    Calculate the R, G, B corresponding to this area:
    r=val/max*256
    g=256*(1-(val-min)/(max-min))
    b=0
```

Additional attributes evolutionary visualization employs the same method as above but for values of more than one attribute during a period, which can be used to predict the trends of attributes, and compare among the additional attributes. This method is different from evolutionary attribute visualization in that only one object area is visualized with respect to additional attributes at a time.

3.3 Classification Visualization

Classification visualization is used to classify areas like provinces and territories based on the specified classifying attribute, and to visualize each class with different colors that are calculated in terms of the values of the classifying attributes of those classes.

This subsystem finds the corresponding values for all areas, and partitions the interval *[minimum value, maximum value]* into subintervals, the number of which is specified by the class number slider. Based on this partition, the sum of the classifying attribute values in the same class will be found and used as the classifying attribute value for this class. Finally, the classifying attribute values are used to calculate the colors of classes in the same way as that of individual attribute visualization. The rendering algorithm is as follows:

```
Find the maximum and minimum values of the classifying attribute
for all classes
For each class
  Find the sum of attribute values
  Calculate the R, G, B:
    r=sum/max*256
    g=(1-(sum-min)/(max-min))*256
    b=0
```

3.4 Attributes Association Visualization

Attributes association visualization is used to visualize the relationships among associated attributes [1, 5]. For two or three specified associated attributes, a cube will be drawn in the corresponding area for each year. All cubes have the same size, but each cube's color is calculated based on the values of associated attributes in different years. For two associated attributes, only R- and G-values of RGB color are calculated and the B-value default 0. For three associated attributes, R-, G-, and B-values will all be calculated, where each attribute corresponds to one value of R, G, and B. Thus, this method can visualize five dimensional data.

After two or three associated attributes are specified, the rendering algorithm works as follows:

```
Find max and min of the first attribute, R_max and R_min
Find max and min of the second attribute, G_max and G_min
Find max and min of the third attribute, B_max and B_min
For each area (object) and each year
  Find the values R_val, G_val, and B_val of three attributes
  Calculate color:
    r=(R_val-R_min)/(R_max-R_min)*256
    g=(G_val-G_min)/(G_max-G_min)*256
    b=(B_val-B_min)/(B_max-B_min)*256
  Draw a cube at the origin with RGB
```

```
Rotate around X and Z axes,respectively
Translate to the corresponding position
```

3.5 Hierarchical Concepts Visualization

Hierarchical concepts (in the sense of [3, 10]) visualization is used to visualize the hierarchical data (concepts) of a specified attribute. When the highest level concept is chosen, all objects will be rendered in the same color. While the lowest level concept is chosen, all objects will be rendered in the same way as that in individual attribute visualization. While an attribute to be visualized is chosen and the level of concepts is specified by moving sliders, the system will find the maximum and minimum attribute values for the concepts in the current level, calculate the color, and then draw the objects that the concepts cover. The following is the rendering algorithm.

```
Find max and min attribute values among all current concepts
For each current concept
  Find its attribute value
  Calculate the color
    r=val/max*256
    g=(1-(val-min)/(max-min))*256
    b=0
```

4 DVIZ Implementation and Application to the Canada Education Statistics

We have used DVIZ to visualize the data set that are excerpted from "The 1997 year book"[11] published by the Canadian government. We chose 21 statistics indices from among them. The collection of data to be visualized is from the time period 1990 to 1995. If there do not exist statistics data in some year for some province, we use zero to represent these statistics and render them in black (that is, RGB color = (0, 0, 0)). Due to space limitations, we simply introduce two subsystems of our DVIZ implementation, evolutionary attributes and hierarchical concepts. Other attributes which our implementation considers from *the Canada Education Statistics* data set include individual attributes, classification attributes, association attributes and hierarchical attributes.

In Figure 3 we show the application of DVIZ in visualizing the trend of attribute *Per Capital Health Expenditure*. Each province area is rendered according to the average attribute value during the period, and its corresponding curve is drawn in that area.

In Figure 4 we visualize the third level concepts in a hierarchy of geographic concepts. We divide the geography of Canada into hierarchical concepts. The highest level concept is the entire country–*Canada*, which consists of two second level concepts–*Eastern Canada* and *Western Canada*. *Eastern Canada* is composed of *Atlantic Region* and *Central Canada*, and *Western Canada* is composed

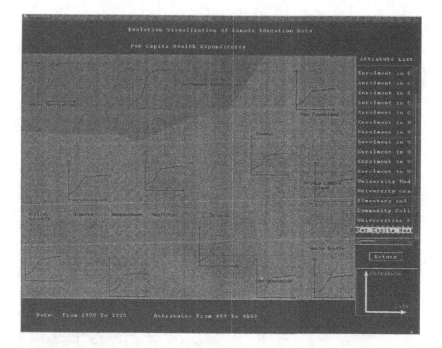

Fig. 3. Evolutionary Attribute–Per Capital Health Expenditure

of *The Prairies*, *British Columbia*, and *The North*. At the lowest level are each province and territory. In Figure 4, the attribute *Secondary School Graduates in 1995* is chosen.

DVIZ is implemented under X windows on an SGI IRIS workstation with Motif and GL(Graphics Library), where Motif is used to control the interactive interface, and GL is used to draw layout on the draw window. The source program consists of about 12600 lines of C code.

5 Conclusions and Future Work

We briefly introduced the system structure of knowledge visualization in data mining that we implemented and its application to the visualization of *the Canadian Education Statistics*. We discussed the basic ideas and algorithms of six visualization methods developed for our system. In these visualization methods, we utilized several important visualization techniques, including geometric projection techniques[7], dynamic techniques[8], hierarchical techniques, etc. These visualization methods cover almost all data mining rules which may be discovered so that our methods should prove useful to visualize the results and the processes of data mining. In our implementation, we emphasize the interaction between the computer and the human, since we believe that interactive visualization[4]

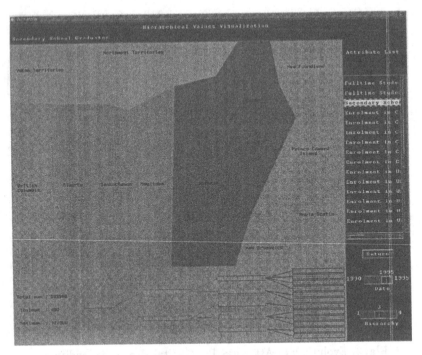

Fig. 4. the concepts in level 3 visualization in 1995

plays the most important role in data mining to guide the process interactively of discovering knowledge. Our system has demonstrated that it is useful for users, by visualizing a large data set, to understand the relationships among data and to concentrate on the meaningful data to discover knowledge.

Our next task is to improve this system and we will focus on the representation of geometries and the combination of visualization techniques and data mining algorithms.

The capability of this system will be expanded to visualize not only the static results of data mining but also the dynamic processes of discovering knowledge in large data set. Combining the visualization and data mining algorithms will produce a much more efficient method of knowledge discovery. Our primary thinking is first to use visualization techniques to limit the domain of data by interacting with user and then to mine the data to discover rules, and finally to visualize the resulting knowledge.

The geometries representing different knowledge will be developed to ensure the graphics have clearer meaning and are more easily understood. The correspondence between the knowledge and these geometries should be direct and straightforward. There is a contradiction between the straightforwardness and the expressiveness of the geometries, however, so how to make the trade-off between them is being considered. The arrow icon or fluid flow can be used to represent the evolutionary rule, the association rule can be visualized as an animation in which the decision attribute geometry varies in shape and/or color with the condition attributes geometries, the classification rule can be represented as the ranges of 3D-dimensional space, and so on.

We realize that what we have presented is an initial step toward the specification of an integrated data mining and visualization system and we expect significant further developments exploiting these humble beginnings shortly.

Acknowledgments: The authors are members of the Institute for Robotics and Intelligent Systems (IRIS) and wish to acknowledge the support of the Networks of Centers of Excellence Program of the Government of Canada, the Natural Sciences and Engineering Research Council, and the participation of PRECARN Associates Inc.

References

1. R. Agrawal, T. Imielinski, A. Swami, Mining association rules between sets of items in large databases, Proc. of the ACM SIGMOD Conf. of Management of Data, 1993.
2. S. Card, S. G. Eick, N. Gersho, Information Visualization, ACM Siggraph'96 Course No.8 News, ACM, New York, 1996.
3. N. Cercone, H. Hamilton, Database Mining, Encyclopedia of Electrical and Electronics Engineering, John Wiley & Sons, 1998.
4. J. X. Chen, D. Rine, H. D. Simon, Advancing Interactive Visualization and Computational Steering, IEEE Computational Science and Engineering, Winter 1996.
5. T. Fukuda, Y. Morimoto, S. Morishita, T. Tokuyama, Data Mining Using Two-Dimensional Optimised Association Rules: Scheme, Algorithms, and Visualization. Proc. of ACM SIGMOD Internal Conf. on Management of Data, 1996.
6. J. Han, Data Mining Techniques. Proc. of the ACM SIGMOD Internal Conf. on Management of Data, 1996.
7. A. Inslberg, B. Dimsdale, Parallel Coordinates: A Tool for Visualizing Multi-Dimensional Geometry, Visualization'90, 1990.
8. D. A. Keim, H. P. Kriegel, Visualization Techniques for Mining Large Databases: A Comparison, Transaction on Knowledge and Data Engineering, Dec.,1996.
9. J. B. Kennedy, K. J. Mitchell, P. J. Barchay, A framework for information visualization, SIGMORD Record, Vol.25, No.4, Dec., 1996.
10. R. Srikant, R. Agrawal, Mining generalized association rules, Proc. of the 21th International Conference on VLDB, pp.407-419, 1995.
11. The 1997 Year Book, The Canadian Government, 1997.

A Minimal Causal Model Learner

Honghua Dai

School of Computing and Mathematics, Deakin University
662 Blackburn Road, Vic 3168 , Australia
Tel: (613) 9244 7323 (O), Fax: (613) 9244 7460.
Email: hdai@deakin.edu.au

Abstract

The minimal-model semantics of causation is an essential concept for the identification of a best fitting model in the sense of satisfactory consistent with the given data and be the simpler, less expressive model. Therefore to develop an algorithm being able to derive a minimal model is an interesting topic in the area of causal model discovery. various causal induction algorithms and tools developed so far can not guarantee that the derived model is a minimal model. This paper proves that the MML induction approach introduced by Wallace et al is a minimal causal model learner. The experimental results obtained from the tests on a number of both artificial and real models provided in this paper confirm this theoretical result.

Keywords: Minimal model, causal discovery, data mining, machine learning, knowledge acquisition, artificial intelligence.

1   Introduction

Given a data set D with m instances $\{I_i, 1 \leq i \leq m\}$ and n variables $\{x_j, 1 \leq j \leq n\}$, the central task of causal discovery is to find a causal model M which provides a satisfactory explanation to the data D. In the model space, there are a great number of possible models which may fit the data. If the causal variable is represented by a from node and the effect variable is represented by a to node, then a causal model can be represented by a directed acyclic graph. So the number of causal models for a given data set of n variables is the number of directed graphs with n nodes. It is known that the number of directed graph with n nodes is $4^{\binom{n}{2}}$[6, p182]. To search for a right model within this large number of possible models is extremely difficult. Naturally, we could consider the problem in two major aspects. The first one is how to find a causal model from the model space which explains the data well.

It is obvious that there are many such models. The second question is that among all the possible models which provides a satisfactory explanation to the given data set, which is the best model and how can we find it? A widely adopted general strategy is to choose the simpler, less expressive model. The reason might be that scientists prefer simpler models. This idea well fit the idea of MML principle in choosing a model with less descriptive complexity.

2 Preliminary

We view a causal model as a representation of a set of regularities which explain the given data. Among all the possible models there are some relations and special features which are interesting and are important to the implementation of our central task of causal discovery.

Equivalent Model. The basic relation between two models is the equivalent relation. Given a model space Ω, and two models $M_1, M_2 \in \Omega$, M_1 and M_2 are said to be equivalent if they represent the same set of probability distributions, denoted as $M_1 \equiv M_2$. In other words, two causal models are equivalent if the set of probability distributions, corresponding to the causal structure, that can be represented using one of the DAGs is identical to the set of probability distributions that can be represented using the other.

Lemma 2.1 Equivalent Model 1. *Let Ω be a model space, two causal models $M_1, M_2 \in Omega$ are equivalent iff $M_1 \preceq M_2$ and $M_1 \succeq M_2$.*

Lemma 2.2 Equivalent Model 2.. *Two causal models are equivalent if they define the same probability distributions.*

Lemma 2.3 Equivalent Model 3. *Two DAGs are equivalent iff they have the same skeleton and the same V-structure.*

Equivalent Class. A set of models A is said to be an equivalent class of a model M, if the set is composed of and only of the models which are equivalent to M.

Definition 2.1 Consistency. *Let D be a data set, P is a distribution over D and M is a structure induced from D. We say the structure is consistent with the data D, if the D can accommodate M by which D can be generated with the distribution P.*

Minimal Model. Scientists prefer simpler models because such models are more constrained, thus more falsifiable; they provide scientists less opportunity to overfit the data hindsightedly and, therefore attain greater credibility[4, 5]. Following Judea Pearl's explanation, a minimal model can be defined as below,

Definition 2.2 Minimal Model. *Let D be a given data set, M be a model derived from D by a causal model learner A. M is said to be a minimal model, iff M ⊂ [M'], where M' is the simplest model consistent with D, and [M'] is the equivalent class of the model M'.*

In other words, a causal model M discovered from a given data set D is said to be a minimal model *iff* we can not find a simpler, less expressive model, eqally consistent with the data.

3 MML Induction

Given a data set D of m instances. Each instance has n values of the n variables, our task is to induce the causal model with the highest posterior probability from this given data set. In [7], Chris Wallace and his fellows give a causal model discovery approach based on Minimum Message Length (MML) principle. The basic idea of the MML induction approach is to measure a causal model with message length and choose the model with minimum message length. The algorithm can be described as follows,

Algorithm 3.1 MML-Induction.

Step 1: *Describe the causal model Give a general description of a causal model which fits the given data set.*

Step 2: *Encode the causal model Give a general formula of the cost for encoding the causal model.*

Step 3: *Minimize the cost To choose the unknown parameters of the general formula so that the cost for encoding the causal model being minimized.*

Step 4: *Search for the causal model To search the causal model in the model space so that the model being selected has the minimum message length.*

Encoding causal models. The total message length for encoding the causal mode is

$$L = -lnP(M) - lnP(D|M) = L(M) + L(D|M) \tag{1}$$

where $L(M) = -log_2 P(M)$ is the cost (in bits) of encoding the causal model M, and $L(D|M) = -log_2 P(D|M)$ is the cost of encoding the sample data D given the model M.

$$L(M) = L^{(s)} + L^{(p)} \tag{2}$$

$$L^{(s)} = \log n! + \frac{n(n-1)}{2} - \log \rho \tag{3}$$

where ρ is the total orderings consistent with the DAG.

$$L^{(p)} = \sum_{i=1}^{} [\frac{n_i}{2} \log 2\pi + n_i \log \alpha_i + \frac{1}{2\alpha_i^2 \sigma_i^2} \sum_{k=1}^{n_i} a_{ik}^2 + \frac{1}{2}\log(2m) + \frac{1}{2}\log|A|] \quad (4)$$

And the message length for encoding the data given the model is given by

$$L(D|M) = \frac{N}{2}log2\pi + Nlog\sigma + \sum_{i=1}^{N} \frac{r_i^2}{2\sigma^2} \quad (5)$$

The combined message length for encoding the parameters and the data given the model is

$$L^{(p)} + L(D|H) = \frac{N+K}{2}log2\pi + Klog\alpha + Nlog\sigma + \quad (6)$$

$$\frac{1}{2\sigma^2}(\sum_{i=1}^{N} r_i^2 + \sum_{k=1}^{K} \frac{a_k^2}{\alpha^2}) + \frac{1}{2}log(2N) + \frac{1}{2}log|A| \quad (7)$$

Minimizing the Costs To choose the unknown parameters oe and aj; (1 j n) so that the combined message length be minimized, we examine the partial derivatives with respect to the unknown parameters σ and the a_j ($1 \leq j \leq n$):

$$\frac{\partial(L^{(p)} + L(D|H))}{\partial \sigma} = \frac{N}{\sigma} - \frac{1}{\sigma^3}(\sum_{i=1}^{N} r_i^2 + \sum_{k=1}^{K} \frac{a_k^2}{\alpha^2}) = 0 \quad (8)$$

And for $j = 1, 2, \ldots, K$,

$$\frac{\partial(L^{(p)} + L(D|H))}{\partial a_j} = \frac{1}{2\sigma^2}(2\sum_{i=1}^{} r_i(-x_{ij}) + 2\frac{a_j}{\alpha^2}) = \frac{1}{\sigma^2}(-\sum_{i=1}^{N} r_i x_{ij} + \frac{a_j}{\alpha^2}) = 0 \quad (9)$$

Letting $\alpha = 1$, we have

$$(A + I)a = b \quad (10)$$

where

$$a = \begin{pmatrix} a_1 \\ a_2 \\ \cdots \\ a_K \end{pmatrix} \quad b = \begin{pmatrix} y \cdot x_1 \\ y \cdot x_2 \\ \cdots \\ y \cdot x_K \end{pmatrix} \quad (11)$$

and $x_j = (x_{1j}, x_{2j}, \ldots, x_{Nj})$ for $j = 1, 2, \ldots, K$ and $y = (y_1, y_2, \ldots, y_N)$. A is the $K \times K$ square matrix $A = (a_{ij})_{K \times K} = (x_i \cdot x_j)_{K \times K}$ and I is a $K \times K$ unit matrix. From (8) and (10), we can get the final solution

$$\begin{cases} \hat{a} = (A+I)^{-1}b \\ \hat{\sigma}^2 = \frac{1}{N}(\sum_{i=1}^{N} r_i^2 + \sum_{k=1}^{K} \frac{a_k^2}{\alpha^2}) \end{cases} \quad (12)$$

where $\alpha^2 \approx 1, r_i = y_i - \sum_{k=1}^{K} a_k x_{ik}$. Adding these values to $L_1^{(s)}$ produces the total MML cost for a given model relative to the input data. The $\{a_j, (1 \leq j \leq n)\}$ is the path coefficients of the derived causal model.

4 Minimal Model Theorem

From the derivation of the MML-CI algorithm, we can get the following theorem. The theorem states that the model derived by MML-CI algorithm is a simpler and less expressive model among all the models which are consistent with the given data set.

Theorem 4.1 Minimal Model Theorem.
Let D be a training data set with sufficient large sample size. A causal model discovered via MML principle from the given data set D is a minimal model.

Proof:
The pre-condition that given a training data set with sufficient large sample size is a condition which ensure that the data set provides enough information so a learner is able to find a right model from it. It does nothing with if the MML induction is minimal model learner. So in the following proof we will avoid dealing with this condition.

Let D be a given data set with m samples and each sample has n values of attributes; M be the derived model from D via MML. To simplify the problem we assume that the model contains one dependent variable only, i.e.,

$$\hat{y}_i = \sum_{j=1}^{n} a_j x_{ij} + r_i \qquad (13)$$

With $i = 1, 2, \ldots, m$, where variable means are assumed to be zero, $r_i \sim N(0, \sigma^2)$, x_{ij} are the ith observation of the independent variable x_j and $sigma, \{a_j | 1 \leq j \leq n\}$ unknown.

The second part of the message length $L(D|M)$, the message length for encoding the data D given the model M is given by

$$L(D|H) = \frac{N}{2} log 2\pi + N log \sigma + \sum_{i=1}^{N} \frac{r_i^2}{2\sigma^2} \qquad (14)$$

As the unknown parameters are selected so that

$$\frac{\partial(L^{(p)} + L(D|H))}{\partial a_j} = 0 \qquad (15)$$

i.e.,

$$\frac{a_j}{\alpha^2} - \sum_{i=1}^{m} r_i x_{ij} = 0 \qquad (16)$$

This optimization procedure ensure that the derived model M consists with the data D.

Secondly, in MML induction the model is selected from the model space using the criterion

$$\min L = \min[L(M) + L(D|M)] \qquad (17)$$

This means that,

The length of M is the length of M′.

where M' is the model which is consistent with the given data.

This proves that the MML induction derived model M is a simpler, less expressive model.

Therefore the model discovered via MML induction from a given data set D is a minimal model. □

5 Experimental results

Three groups of experiments have been conducted to show that the causal models derived form a given data set applying MML induction are (1) consistent with the given dat a set; (2) the derived models are the simpler, less expressive ones. In the first two experiments, each one use a group of artificial models. The experiment 3 uses real models from literatures

Experiment 1:

The first experiment we performed was for the given four artificial models as shown in Figure 1 (a)(b)(c)(d), we generate a sample data set with 5000 samples for each one of the four models, and then derives a model from each one of the generated data sets. The induced models are shown in Figure 1(a')(b')(c') and (d'). From the results, we can easily find that derived models have the exactly the same structure as the original models. We can also find that the models (a'), (b'), (c') and (d') are consistent with (a), (b), (c) and (d) respectively as the data sets were generated from the original model. That is to say, the derived models are consistent with the data sets generated from (a), (b), (c) and (d) respectively. It also can be verified that we can not find a model simpler, less expressive model than (a'), (b'), (c') or (d') which is not belongs to [(a')], [(b')], [(c')] or [(d')]. These results confirm that the derived models are minimal models.

Experiment 2:

In the experiment 2, we again give four artificial models as shown in Figure 2(a)(b)(c)(d). This time, we generate a data set with 1000 samples for models (1) and (2); and generate a data set with 5000 samples from models (3) and (4) respectively. Because the models (1) and (2) are less complexity in term of the number of nodes and the number of links. As we can see from the derived models illustrated in Figure 2(a')(b')(c') and (d'), the models (a'), (b') and (c') has the exactly the same structure as the original models (a), (b) and (c) which we applied to generate the data sets. The derived model (d') has the exact the same structure as the original

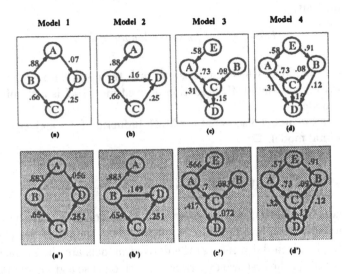

Model 1   Model 2   Model 3   Model 4

(a)   (b)   (c)   (d)

(a')   (b')   (c')   (d')

Figure 1: MML-CI Test Results on Artificial Models 1

model (d) except that the orientation of the arc in between the variables A and C is reversed. However the model (d') is statistically equivalent to (d).

Experiment 3:

Figure 3 illustrates the test results of the MML-CI systems on four real models. Model (a) in Figure 3 is the Blau's stratification process model of occupation [2]. Model (b) in Figure 3 is the Retherford and Choe's model of the fertility of Fijian women. Model (c) in Figure 3 is the Goldberg's mediation model [1, p43] of vote performances. Model (d) in Figure 3 is the model of Verbal and Mechanical Ability described in [3, pp162-185]. In Figure 3, the models (a'), (b'), (c') and (d') are the derived models. The derived models (c') and (d') have the exactly the same structures and the same orientations as the original models (c) and (d) respectively. Model (a') and its original model (a) has the exactly the same structure except one link in between D and F with the reversed orientations. It is obvious that model

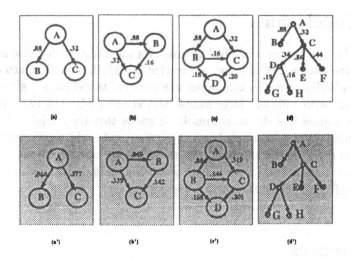

Figure 2: MML-CI Test Results on Artificial Models 2

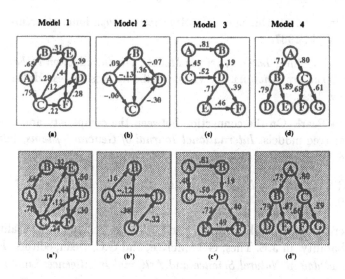

Figure 3: MML-CI Test Results on Real Applications

(a) is equivalent to model (d). So (a') is consistent with the data generated from model (a). The interesting thing is that the derived model (b') has a simpler structure than the original model (b). It dropped two weak links. It has smaller message length as it is simpler. The expected log likelihood of the model (a) and the model (a') is almost the same, of course, the model (a) is consistent with the generated data so does the model (a').

6 Conclusions

Minimal model learner is an ideal approach for the discovery of causal models from given data set. This paper proves that the MML induction introduced by Chris Wallace and his companies is a minimal model learner given that a data set with sufficient large sample size is provided. The experimental results confirms this theoretical result. It shows that the model derived by MML induction is the simpler, less expressive model which consistent with the given data. This result is significant because it indicates that the MML induction is a minimal model learner which is able to derive the best model in term of the descriptive complexity and accuracy.

References

[1] H. B. Asher83. *Causal modeling.* Sage Publications, Beverly Hills, 1983.

[2] P. Blau and O. Duncan. *The American occupational structure.* Wiley, New York, 1967.

[3] John C. leohlin. *Latent Variable Models: An Introduction to Factor Path and Structure Analysis.* Lawrence Erlbaum Associates, Hillsdale, New Jersey, 1992.

[4] Judea Pearl. On the connection between the complexity and credibility of inferred models. *International Journal of General Systems*, 4:255–264, 1978.

[5] K. R. Popper. *The Logic of Scientific Discovery.* Basic Books, New York, 1959.

[6] Peter Spirtes, Clark Glymour, and Richard Scheines. Causality from probability. In J.E. Tiles, G.T. McKee, and G.C. Dean, editors, *Evolving Knowledge in Natural Science and Artificial Intelligence*, London, 1990. Pitman.

[7] Chris Wallace, Kevin Korb, and Honghua Dai. Causal discovery via MML. Technical report, Department of Computer Science, Monash University, 1996.

Efficient Graph-Based Algorithm for Discovering and Maintaining Knowledge in Large Databases

K. L. Lee, Guanling Lee and Arbee L. P. Chen

Department of Computer Science
National Tsing Hua University
Hsinchu, Taiwan 300
Email: alpchen@cs.nthu.edu.tw

Abstract. In this paper, we study the issues of mining and maintaining association rules in a large database of customer transactions. The problem of mining association rules can be mapped into the problems of finding *large itemsets* which are sets of items bought together in a sufficient number of transactions. We revise a graph-based algorithm to further speed up the process of itemset generation. In addition, we extend our revised algorithm to maintain discovered association rules when incremental or decremental updates are made to the databases. Experimental results show the efficiency of our algorithms. The revised algorithm significantly improves over the original one on mining association rules. The algorithms for maintaining association rules are more efficient than re-running the mining algorithms for the whole updated database and outperform previously proposed algorithms that need multiple passes over the database.

1 Introduction

Data Mining has been considered as a new area in database research [5]. When a huge amount of data has been collected in large databases, it is quite important to extract potentially useful knowledge embedded in it. To extract such previously unknown knowledge from large databases is the task of data mining. Various types of knowledge can be mined from large databases, such as mining characteristic and classification rules [8,9], association rules [1,2,10], and sequential patterns [6,10].

Data mining has been widely applied in retail industry to improve market strategies. Each customer transaction stored in the database typically consists of customer identifier, transaction time, and the set of items bought in this transaction. It is important to analyze the customer transactions to discover customer purchasing behaviors. The problem of mining association rules over customer transactions was introduced in [1]. While new transactions are added to a database or old ones are removed, rules or patterns previously discovered should be updated. The problem of maintaining discovered association rules was first studied in [3], which proposed the FUP algorithm to discover new association rules when incremental updates are made to the database. The algorithm proposed in [4] improve FUP by generating and counting fewer candidates.

The graph-based algorithm DLG proposed in [10] can efficiently solve the problems of mining association rules. In [10], DLG is shown to outperform other algorithms which need to make multiple passes over the database. In this paper, we first propose the revised algorithms DLG* to achieve higher performance. Then we develop two algorithms DIUP (DLG* for Incremental Updates) and DDUP (DLG* for Decremental Updates), which are based on the framework of DLG*, to handle the problem of maintaining discovered association rules in the cases of insertion and deletion of transaction data.

This paper is organized as follows. Section 2 gives detailed descriptions of the above two problems. The algorithms DLG* is described in Section 3. The algorithms DIUP and DDUP for maintaining association rules are described in Section 4. Experimental Results are discussed in Section 5, and Section 6 concludes our study.

2 Problem Descriptions

2.1 Mining association rules

The following definitions refer to [2]. Let $I = \{i_1, i_2, ..., i_m\}$ be a set of literals, called *items*. A set of items is called an *itemset*. The number of items in an itemset is called the *length* of an itemset. Itemsets of length k are referred to as k-*itemsets*. Let D be a database of transactions, a transaction T *contains* itemset X if and only if $X \subseteq T$. An association rule is an implication of the form $X \Rightarrow Y$, where $X \subseteq I$, $Y \subseteq I$, and $X \cap Y = \phi$. The *support count* of itemset X, sup_X, is the number of transactions in D containing X. The association rule $X \Rightarrow Y$ has *support* $s\%$ if $s\%$ of transactions in D contain $X \cup Y$, i.e. $sup_{X \cup Y} / |D| = s\%$. The association rule $X \Rightarrow Y$ has a confidence $c\%$ if $c\%$ of transactions in D that contain X also contain Y, i.e. $sup_{X \cup Y} / sup_X = c\%$.

The problem of mining association rules is to generate all rules that have support and confidence greater than the user specified thresholds, *minimum support* and *minimum confidence*. As mentioned before, the problem of mining association rules can be divided into the following steps:

1. Find out all frequent itemsets that have support above the user specified minimum support. Each such itemset is referred to as a *large* itemset. The set of all large itemsets in D is L, and L_k is the set of large k-itemsets.
2. Generate the association rules from the large itemsets with respect to another threshold, minimum confidence.

The second step is relatively straightforward. However, the first step is not trivial if the total number of items $|I|$ and the maximum number of items in each transaction $|MT|$ are large. For example, if $|I| = 1000$, $|MT| = 10$, there are 2^{1000} possible itemsets. We need to identify large itemsets among $\sum_{i=1}^{10} C_i^{1000} \cong 2.66 \times 10^{23}$ potentially large itemsets. Therefore, finding all large itemsets satisfying a minimum support is the main problem of mining association rules.

2.2 Update of association rules

The following definitions refer to [4]. Let L be the set of large itemsets in the original database D, and $s\%$ be the minimum support. Assume the support count of each large itemset X, sup_X, is available. Let d^+ (d^-) be the set of added (deleted) transactions, and the support count of itemset X in d^+ (d^-) is denoted as sup^+_X (sup^-_X). With respect to the same minimum support $s\%$, an itemset X is large in the updated database D' if and only if the support count of X in D', sup'_X, is not less than $|D'| \times s\%$, i.e. $(sup_X - sup^-_X + sup^+_X) \geq (|D| - |d^-| + |d^+|) \times s\%$.

Thus the problem of updating associations rules is to find the set of new large itemsets L' in D'. Note that a large itemset in L may not appear in L'. On the other hand, an itemset not in L may become a large itemset in L'.

3 The Revised Algorithm DLG*

DLG is a three-phase algorithm. The *large 1-itemset generation phase* finds large items and records related information. The *graph construction phase* constructs an *association graph* between large items, and at the same time generates large 2-itemsets. The *large itemset generation phase* generates large k-itemsets ($k>2$) based on this association graph. The DLG* algorithm reduces the execution time during the *large itemset generation phase* by recording additional information in the *graph construction phase*.

3.1 Large 1-itemset generation phase

The DLG algorithm scans the database to count the support and builds a bit vector for each item. The length of a bit vector is the number of transactions in the database. The bit vector associated with item i is denoted as BV_i. The jth bit of BV_i is set to 1 if item i appears in the jth transaction. Otherwise, the jth bit of BV_i is set to 0. The number of 1's in BV_i is equal to the support count of the item i.

For example, Table 1 records a database of transactions, where **TID** is the transaction identifier, and **itemset** records the items purchased in the transaction. Assume the minimum support count is 2 transactions ($|D| \times$ minimum support). The large items and the associated bit vectors are shown in Table 2.

TID	Itemset
100	2 3 4 5 6
200	1 3 7
300	3 6
400	1 2 3 4
500	1 4
600	1 2 3
700	2 4 5

Large item	Bit vector
1	010111
2	1001011
3	1111010
4	1001101
5	1000001
6	1010000

Table 1. A database of transactions

Table 2. The bit vectors of large items in Table 1

3.2 Graph construction phase

The support count for the itemset $\{i_1,i_2,...,i_k\}$ is the number of 1's in $BV_{i1} \wedge BV_{i2} \wedge ... \wedge BV_{ik}$, where the notation "$\wedge$" is a logical AND operation. Hence, the support count of the itemset $\{i_1,i_2,...,i_k\}$ can be found directly by applying logical AND operations on the bit vectors of the k itemsets instead of scanning the database. If the number of 1's in $BV_i \wedge BV_j$ ($i<j$) is not less than the minimum support count, a directed edge from item i to item j is constructed in the association graph. Also, $\{i,j\}$ is a large 2-itemset. Take the database in Table 1 for example, the association graph is shown in Figure 1, and $L_2=\{\{1,2\},\{1,3\},\{1,4\},\{2,3\},\{2,4\},\{2,5\},\{3,4\},\{3,6\},\{4,5\}\}$.

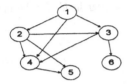

	2	3	4	5	6	Item	total
1	1	1	1	0	0	1	3
2		1	1	1	0	2	4
3			1	0	1	3	4
4				1	0	4	4
5					0	5	2
6						6	1

Fig. 1. The association graph for Table 1

Table 3. The related information recorded by DLG* for Figure 1

3.3 Large itemset generation phase

For each large k-itemset $\{i_1,i_2,...,i_k\}$ in L_k ($k>1$), the last item i_k is used to extend the itemset into $(k+1)$-itemsets. If there is a directed edge from i_k to item j, the itemset $\{i_1,i_2,...,i_k,j\}$ is a candidate $(k+1)$-itemset. If the number of 1's in $BV_{i1} \wedge BV_{i2} \wedge ... \wedge BV_{ik} \wedge BV_j$ is not less than the minimum support count, $\{i_1,i_2,...,i_k,j\}$ is a large $(k+1)$-itemset in L_{k+1}. If no large k-itemset is generated in the k-th iteration, the algorithm terminates.

Consider the above example, candidate large 3-itemsets can be generated based on L_2. The candidate 3-itemsets are $\{\{1,2,3\}, \{1,2,4\}, \{1,2,5\}, \{1,3,4\}, \{1,3,6\}, \{1,4,5\}, \{2,3,4\}, \{2,3,6\}, \{2,4,5\}, \{3,4,5\}\}$. After applying the logical AND operations on the bit vectors of the three items in each candidate, the large 3-itemset $L_3=\{\{1,2,3\}, \{2,3,4\}, \{2,4,5\}\}$ is generated. The candidate 4-itemsets are $\{\{1,2,3,4\}, \{1,2,3,6\}, \{2,3,4,5\}\}$. After applying the logical AND operations on the bit vectors of the four items in each candidate, no large 4-itemset is generated. Thus, the algorithm terminates.

3.4 Improvements over DLG

In the k-th ($k>2$) iteration, DLG generates candidate k-itemsets by extending each large $(k-1)$-itemset according to the association graph. Suppose on the average, the out-degree of each node in the association graph is q. The number of candidate itemsets is $|L_{k-1}| \times q$, and DLG must perform $|L_{k-1}| \times q \times (k-1)$ logical AND operations on bit vectors to determine all large k-itemsets. The key issue of the DLG* algorithm is to reduce the number of candidate itemsets. The following properties are used by DLG* to reduce the number of candidates.

Lemma 1   If a $(k+1)$-itemset $X=\{i_1,...,i_k,i_{k+1}\} \in L_{k+1}$ ($k \geq 2$), then $\{i_j,i_{k+1}\} \in L_2$ for $1 \leq j \leq k$, that is, item i_{k+1} is contained in at least k large 2-itemsets.

In the large itemset generation phase, DLG* extends each large k-itemset in L_k ($k \geq 2$) into $(k+1)$-itemsets like the original DLG algorithm. Suppose $\{i_1,i_2,...,i_k\}$ is a large k-itemset, and there is a directed edge from item i_k to item i. From Lemma 1, if the $(k+1)$-itemset $\{i_1,i_2,...,i_k,i\}$ is large, it must satisfy the following two conditions (Otherwise, it cannot be large and is excluded from the set of candidate $(k+1)$-itemsets).

1. Item i must be contained in at least k large 2-itemsets. In other words, the total number of in-degrees and out-degrees of the node associated with item i must be at least k.

2. Any $\{i_j,i\}$ ($1 \leq j \leq k$) must be large. A directed edge from i_k to item i means that $\{i_k,i\}$ is also a large 2-itemset. Therefore, we only need to check if all $\{i_j,i\}$ ($1 \leq j \leq k-1$) are large.

These simple checks significantly reduce the number of candidate itemsets. In order to speed up these checks, we record some information during the graph construction phase. For the first condition, for each large item, we count the number of large 2-itemsets containing this item. For the second condition, a bitmap with $|L_1| \times |L_1|$ bits is built to record related information about the association graph. If there is a directed edge from item i to item j, the bit associated with $\{i,j\}$ is set to 1. Otherwise, the bit is set to 0. DLG* requires extra memory space of size quadratic to $|I|$, but speeds up the performance significantly.

Let's illustrate the DLG* algorithm with the example in Table 1. The extra information recorded by DLG* is shown in Table 3. For large 2-itemset $\{1,2\}$, it can be extended into $\{1,2,3\}$, $\{1,2,4\}$, and $\{1,2,5\}$. Consider $\{1,2,3\}$, item 3 is contained in 4 (≥ 2) large 2-itemsets, and the bit associated with $\{1,3\}$ in the bitmap is 1. Therefore, $\{1,2,3\}$ is a candidate. Consider $\{1,2,5\}$, item 5 is contained in 2 (≥ 2) large 2-itemsets, but the bit associated with $\{1,5\}$ in the bitmap is 0. Therefore, $\{1,2,5\}$ is not a candidate. In the third iteration, DLG generates 10 candidates, but DLG* only generates 5 candidates ($\{1,2,3\}$, $\{1,2,4\}$, $\{1,3,4\}$, $\{2,3,4\}$, $\{2,4,5\}$). For large 3-itemset $\{1,2,3\}$, it can be extended into $\{1,2,3,4\}$, $\{1,2,3,6\}$. Consider $\{1,2,3,4\}$, item 4 is contained in 4 (≥ 3) large 2-itemsets, and the bits associated with $\{1,4\}$ and $\{2,4\}$ in the bitmap are both 1. Therefore, $\{1,2,3,4\}$ is a candidate. Consider $\{1,2,3,6\}$, item 6 is contained in 1 (<3) large 2-itemsets. Therefore, $\{1,2,3,6\}$ is not a candidate. In the fourth iteration, DLG generates 3 candidates, but DLG* generates only 1 candidate $\{1,2,3,4\}$. In this example, DLG* has reduced the number of candidate k-itemsets ($k>2$) by $\frac{13-6}{13} \times 100\% \approx 54\%$.

4   Efficient Update Algorithms based on DLG*

In this section, we introduce two update algorithms for transaction insertion and deletion. The algorithms DIUP and DDUP are based on the framework of DLG* , which can be split into three phases. As in [3], we assume the support counts of all large itemsets found in the previous mining operations are available. If a candidate itemset X is large in the original database, we can directly get the support count sup_x in the original database D. Otherwise, we must apply logical AND operations on the bit vectors associated with D to find the support count sup_x. However, we can use the following properties to reduce the cost of performing logical AND operations. As defined in section 2, sup_x^+ is the support count of itemset x in the set of inserted transactions d^+ and sup_x^- is the support count in the set of deleted transactions d^-. The following lemma is similar to Lemma 4 in [4].

Lemma 2   If an itemset X is not large in the original database, then X is large in the updated database only if $sup_x^+ - sup_x^- > (|d^+|-|d^-|) \times s\%$.

For each k-itemset X not in L_k, we first apply logical AND operations on the bit vectors associated with the changed part of the database (d^+ and d^-). For the itemsets X satisfying $sup_x^+ - sup_x^- \le (|d^+|-|d^-|) \times s\%$, we can determine they will not be large in L' without applying logical AND operations on the bit vectors associated with the unchanged part of the database ($D- d^-$). In the following, we describe the DIUP and DDUP algorithms for the cases of insertion ($|d^-|=0$) and deletion ($|d^+|=0$) in detail.

4.1 Large 1-itemset generation phase

The DIUP algorithm scans the set of inserted database d^+ and builds a bit vector BV_i^+ for each item i. The number of 1's in BV_i^+ is equal to the support count of the item i in d^+. In order to determine which item is large in the updated database D' more efficiently, DIUP requires the support count of each item in the original database D be stored in the previous mining operation. Hence, we can directly calculate the new support count $sup'_{(i)} = sup_{(i)} + sup'^+_{(i)}$. If an item i is large in D', DIUP scans the original database and builds a bit vector BV_i. After completing the phase, the bit vectors BV_i and BV_i^+ for each large item i are available. This requires extra storage space of size linear to $|I|$ to store $sup_{(i)}$ for each item i, but reduces the cost of building bit vectors and counting supports for those items not large in the updated database. For each large item i, we allocate two bits $i.\Delta$ and $i.\delta$. We set the bit $i.\Delta$ ($i.\delta$) to 1 if item i is large in (D) (d^+). Otherwise, the bit is set to 0. The usage of these two bits is explained in the following two phases.

For example, consider the database in Table 4, which is updated from the original database in Table 1. Assume the minimum support is 25%, that is, an itemset is in L' if the support count is not less than $9 \times 0.25 = 2.25$. The bit vectors and two associated bits (Δ and δ) for each large item is shown in Table 5. The large items in the updated database are items 1, 2, 3, 4, and 5. Since they are all large in L_1, their associated Δ bits are all set to 1. If the support count of any item is not less than $|d^+| \times 0.25 = 0.5$, this item is large in d^+. Since $sup^+_{(2)} = sup^+_{(4)} = 1$ (>0.5), $sup^+_{(5)} = 2$ (>0.5), $sup^+_{(1)} = sup^+_{(3)} = 0$, we set $2.\delta = 4.\delta = 5.\delta = 1$, $1.\delta = 3.\delta = 0$.

TID	Itemset
100	2 3 4 5 6
200	1 3 7
300	3 6
400	1 2 3 4
500	1 4
600	1 2 3
700	2 4 5
800	4 5
900	2 5

Large item	BV	BV⁺	Δ δ
1	0101110	00	1 0
2	1001011	01	1 1
3	1111010	00	1 0
4	1001101	10	1 1
5	1000001	11	1 1

Table 4. An example of the insertion case

Table 5. The bit vectors and associated bits of large items in Table 4

4..2 Graph construction phase

Each 2-itemset $X=\{i,j\}$ ($i<j$), where i, j are large items in D', is a candidate 2-itemset. The $sup^{+}_{\{i,j\}}$ can be found by counting the number of 1's in $BV_i^{+} \wedge BV_j^{+}$. For $X \in L_2$, sup_x is available from the previous mining result, we can calculate $sup'_x = sup_x + sup^{+}_x$. If sup'_x is not less than $|D'| \times s\%$, then X is added into L'_2. For $X \notin L_2$, according to Lemma 2, $X \in L'_2$ only if $sup^{+}_x > | d^{+}| \times s\%$. If $sup^{+}_x > | d^{+}| \times s\%$, we perform $BV_i \wedge BV_j$ and count the number of 1's to find sup_x, then add this count to get sup'_x. If sup'_x is not less than $|D'| \times s\%$, X is added into L'_2.

The two bits $i.\Delta$ and $i.\delta$ of each large item i can be used to further improve the performance. If any subset of an itemset X is not large, X cannot be large, either. Before we check whether $\{i,j\} \in L_2$, we can check if both $i.\Delta$ and $j.\Delta$ are equal to 1. If either $i.\Delta$ or $j.\Delta$ is 0, X cannot be large in L_2. Thus, we save the cost of the membership check, which is costly when $|L_2|$ is large. For $X \notin L_2$, if either $i.\delta$ or $j.\delta$ is 0, sup^{+}_x cannot be greater than $|d^{+}| \times s\%$. Thus, we know $X \notin L'_2$ without performing $BV_i^{+} \wedge BV_j^{+}$, which is costly when the number of transactions in d^{+} is large.

For each large 2-itemset $\{i,j\}$, a directed edge from item i to item j is constructed in the association graph. We also set two bits $X.\Delta$ and $X.\delta$ for each large 2-itemset X.

Continue the above example, there are 10 candidate 2-itemsets. These candidates are all in L_2, except $\{1,5\}$ and $\{3,5\}$. Consider $\{1,2\} \in L_2$, $sup^{+}_{\{1,2\}}$=the number of 1's in $BV_1^{+} \wedge BV_2^{-}$ (i.e., (00))=0, then $sup'_{\{1,2\}}$=2+0=2 (<2.25). Therefore, $\{1,2\} \notin L'_2$. Consider $\{1,5\} \notin L_2$, $\{1,5\} \notin L'_2$ since $1.\delta$=0. After checking these 10 candidates, L'_2={{1,3}, {2,3}, {2,4}, {2,5}, {4,5}}. The association graph is shown in Figure 2, and Table 6 shows the associated bits of the large 2-itemsets.

L'₂	Δ	δ
{1,3}	1	0
{2,3}	1	0
{2,4}	1	0
{2,5}	1	1
{4,5}	1	1

Fig. 2. The association graph constructed by DIUP

Table 6. The associated bits of the large 2-itemsets

4..3 Large itemset generation phase

Candidate itemset C_k is extended from L'_{k-1} by the way used in DLG*. Suppose $X=\{i_1,i_2,...,i_k\}$ is a large k-itemset, and a candidate $Y=\{i_1,i_2,...,i_k,i_{k+1}\}$ can be generated successfully based on X. Similar to the above phase, we get sup_Y^+ by performing $BV_1^+ \wedge BV_2^+ \wedge ... \wedge BV_{k+1}^+$, and then check whether $Y \in L_{k+1}$. The bits $X.\Delta$ and $i_{k+1}.\Delta$ are used to save the cost of the membership check. For $Y \notin L_{k+1}$, if either $X.\delta$ or $i_{k+1}.\delta$ is 0, we know $Y \notin L'_{k+1}$ without performing $BV_1^+ \wedge BV_2^+ \wedge ... \wedge BV_{k+1}^+$. Two bits $X.\Delta$ and $X.\delta$ are set for each large itemset X, which can be used in the next iteration.

Continue the above example. There is only one candidate 3-itemset {2,4,5} extended from large 2-itemset {2,4}. Since {2,4,5} $\in L_3$, $sup'_{(2,4,5)} = sup_{(2,4,5)} + sup^+_{(2,4,5)} = 2+0 = 2$ (<2.25). Therefore, {2,4,5} $\notin L'_3$. Table 7 compares the number of candidates of DLG* with that of DIUP. DLG* performs logical AND operations on bit vectors associated with the whole updated database ($D \cup d^+$), with a total of 11 candidates. DIUP performs logical AND operations on bit vectors associated with d^+, with a total of 9 candidates, and performs no operation on those associated with D.

In the k-th iteration, $N \times (k-1)$ logical AND operations are performed to determine all large k-itemsets, where N is the candidate number. While DLG* performs $10 \times 1+1 \times 2=12$ operations on the bit vectors of length 9, DIUP performs $8 \times 1+1 \times 2=10$ operations on the bit vectors of length 2. Therefore, DIUP reduces the cost of performing logical AND operations by $1-\frac{10 \times 2}{12 \times 9} \approx 81\%$.

Iteration	DLG*	DIUP	
	$D \cup d^+$	D	D^+
2	10	0	8
3	1	0	1

Table 7. Number of candidate itemsets

4.4 The deletion algorithm DDUP

The DDUP algorithm is similar to the DIUP algorithm. As DIUP, we allocate two bits X.Δ and X.δ to indicate if the large itemset X is large in D and d⁻. The bit X.Δ is used to reduce the cost of the membership check. The usage of X.δ is different from that in DIUP, i.e., we need not to check whether X is large if X.δ is equal to 0. Due to space limitation, the complete description of DDUP is omitted.

5. Experimental Results

To assess the performance of our graph-based algorithms for discovering and maintaining large itemsets, the algorithms DLG [10], DLG*, FUP$_2$ [4], DIUP, and DDUP are implemented on a Sun SPARC/20 workstation. We first show the improvement of DLG* over DLG, and then demonstrate the performance of DIUP and DDUP by comparing with DLG* and FUP$_2$, which is the most efficient update algorithm so far developed.

5.1 Synthetic data generation

In each experiment, we use synthetic data as the input dataset to evaluate the performance of the algorithms. The method to generate synthetic transactions is the same as the one used in [10]. The parameters used are similar to those in [10] except the size of the changed part of the database (d^+ or d^-). The parameters used to generate our synthetic database is listed in Table 8. The readers can refer to [10] for a detailed explanation of these parameters.

$|D|$	Number of transactions
$|d|$	Number of inserted/deleted transactions
$|I|$	Average size of the potentially large itemsets
$|MI|$	Maximum size of potentially large itemsets
$|L|$	Number of the potentially large itemsets
$|T|$	Average size of the transactions
$|MT|$	Maximum size of the transactions
N	Number of items

Table 8. The parameters

We generate datasets by setting $N=1000$ and $|L|=1000$. We choose two values for $|T|=10$ and 20, and the corresponding $|MT|=20$ and 40, respectively. We choose two values for $|I|=3$ and 5, and the corresponding $|MI|=5$ and 10, respectively. We use Tx.Iy.Dm.dn, adopted from [8], to mean that $|T|=x$, $|I|=y$, $|D|=m$ thousands, and $|d|=n$ thousands. Notice that a positive value n means the size of inserted transactions $|d^+|$, and a negative one means the size of deleted transactions $|d^-|$.

5.2 Effects of the minimum support on the update algorithms

The value of minimum support is varied between 0.5% to 2 %. We use the setting T10.I5.D100.d+1 for the insertion case, and T10.I5.D100.d-1 for the deletion case.

Figure 3 shows the experimental results in the insertion case. As shown, DIUP is 1.8 to 3.5 times faster than DLG*, and 1.9 to 3.8 times faster than FUP$_2$. Figure 4 shows in the deletion case, DDUP is 1.8 to 3.7 times faster than DLG*, and 2.7 to 6.6 times faster than FUP$_2$.

The results show that DIUP and DDUP always have a better performance than re-running DLG* and FUP$_2$. The speed-up ratio over DLG* decreases as the minimum support increases, because the number of large itemsets becomes smaller and re-running DLG* is less costly. In general, the smaller the minimum support is, the larger the speed-up ratio over FUP$_2$ is, since FUP$_2$ makes more database scans. However, in the range $0.5 \leq s \leq 1.25$ in Figure 3 and $0.75 \leq s \leq 1.25$ in Figure 4, the speed-up ratio becomes smaller. This is because in these cases, the number of candidate itemsets increases with a smaller minimum support, but the number of database scans does not increase much for FUP$_2$.

5.3 Effects of the update size on the update algorithms

Next, we examine how the size of the changed part of the database affects the performance of the algorithms. When the amount of changes becomes large, the performance of update algorithms degrades. There are two major reasons for it. First, the previous mining results become less useful when the updated database is much different from the original one. Second, the number of transactions which need to be handled increases. Two series of experiments showed in Figure 5 and Figure 6 are conducted to support the analysis. In the insertion case, we increase the number of inserted transactions from 20k to 120k to evaluate the performance ratio. The results shows that DIUP is 3.4 to 3.7 times faster than FUP_2, and 1.4 to 1.9 times faster than DLG*. Although the execution time of DLG* also increases as $|d^+|$ does, the speed-up ratio decreases. However, DIUP still has a better performance even when $|d^+|=120k$, which is larger than the size of the original database.

6. Conclusion and Future Work

We study efficient graph-based algorithms for discovering and maintaining knowledge in the database. The revised algorithm DLG* is developed to efficiently solve the problem of mining association rules. DLG* improves DLG [10] by reducing the number of candidates and the cost of performing logical AND operations on bit vectors. Two update algorithms DIUP and DDUP, which are based on the framework of DLG*, are further developed to solve the problem of maintaining association rules in the cases of insertion and deletion. The experimental results show that both of them significantly outperform FUP_2 [10], which is the most efficient update algorithm developed so far. DIUP always performs faster than re-running DLG* even when $|d^+|$ is larger than the size of the original database $|D|$, and DDUP keeps a better performance when $|d^-|$ is not greater than 30% of $|D|$.

Currently, we are also developing graph-based algorithms for mining and maintaining different kinds of knowledge, such as sequential patterns and generalized association rules.

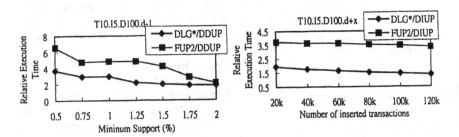

Fig. 3. Effects of the minimum support in the deletion case

Fig. 4. Effects of the number of inserted transactions

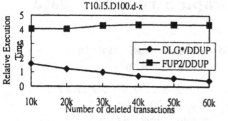

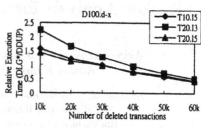

Fig. 5. Effects of the number of deleted transactions

Fig. 6. The comparison of DDUP with DLG*.

Reference

[1]   R. Agrawal, T. Imielinski, and A. Swami Mining Association Rules between Sets of Items in Large Databases. In *Proc. of ACM SIGMOD*, pages 207-216, 1993.

[2]   R. Agrawal and R. Srikant. Fast Algorithm for Mining Association Rules. In *Proc. of the International Conference on Very Large Data Bases*, pages 487-499, 1994.

[3]   D. W. Cheung, J. Han, V. T. Ng, and C. Y. Wong. Maintenance of Discovered Association Rules in Large Databases: An Incremental Updating Technique. In *Proc. of the International Conference on Data Engineering*, pages 106-114, 1996.

[4]   D. W. Cheung, S.D. Lee, and Benjamin Kao. A General Incremental Technique for Maintaining Discovered Association Rules. In *Proc. of International Conference on Database Systems for Advanced Applications*, April 1-4, pages 185-194, 1997.

[5]   E. Simoudis, J. Han and U. Fayyad. Proc. of the 2nd International Conference on Knowledge Discovery and Data Mining (KDD96), 1996.

[6]   R. Srikant and R. Agrawal. Mining Sequential Patterns: Generalizations and Performance Improvements. In *Proc. of the Fifth International Conference on Extending Database Technology (EDBT)*, Avignon, France, March 1996.

[7]   J. T.-L. Wang, G.-W. Chirn, T. G. Marr, B. Shapiro, D. Shasha, and K. Zhang, Combinatorial Pattern Discovery for Scientific Data: Some Preliminary Results. In *Proc. of ACM SIGMOD*, pages 115-125, 1994.

[8]   S. J. Yen and A. L. P. Chen. An Efficient Algorithm for Deriving Compact Rules from Databases. In *Proc. of International Conference on Database Systems for Advanced Applications*, pages 364-371, 1995.

[9]   S. J. Yen and A. L. P. Chen. The Analysis of Relationships in Databases for Rule Derivation. In *Journal of Intelligent Information Systems*, Vol.7, pages 1-24, 1996.

[10]   S. J. Yen and A. L. P. Chen. An Efficient Approach to Discovering Knowledge from Large Databases, In *Proc. of the IEEE/ACM International Conference on Parallel and Distributed Information Systems*, pages 8-18, 1996.

Basket Analysis for Graph Structured Data

Akihiro Inokuchi, Takashi Washio and Hiroshi Motoda[1]
Kouhei Kumasawa and Naohide Arai[2]

[1] Institute of Scientific and Industrial Research, Osaka University
8-1 Mihogaoka, Ibaraki, Osaka, 567-0047, Japan
{inokuchi,washio,motoda}@ar.sanken.osaka-u.ac.jp
[2] Recruit Co., Ltd
8-4-14 Ginza Chuo-ku, Tokyo, 104-8001, Japan

Abstract. The Basket Analysis derives frequent itemsets and association rules having support and confidence levels greater than their thresholds from massive transaction data. Though some recent research tries to discover wider classes of knowledge on the regularities contained in the data, the regularities in form of the graph structure has not been explored in the field of the Basket Analysis. The work reported in this paper proposes a new method to mine frequent graph structure appearing in the massive amount of transactions. A specific procedure to preprocess graph structured transactions is introduced to enable the application of the Basket Analysis to extract frequently appearing graph patterns. The basic performance of our proposing approach has been evaluated by a set of graph structured transactions generated by an artificial simulation. Moreover, its practicality has been confirmed through the appliaction to discover popular browsing patterns of clients in WWW URL network.

1 Introduction

The Basket Analysis derives frequent itemsets and association rules having support and confidence levels greater than their thresholds from massive transaction data [1],[2]. Some recent research of the Basket Analysis tries to discover wider classes of knowledge on the regularities contained in the data. One representative work is to introduce taxonomy of items and Boolean constraints among items under the taxonomy [3]. The association rules among items satisfying the specified constraints are efficiently derived from massive data in their approach. Another extension of the Basket Analysis on the class of the knowledge discovery is to derive association rules among continuously ordered items, i.e., sequential item patterns [4]. The taxonomy and Boolean constraints are one of the most commonly used constraints in various data analyses. The sequential data of items are also frequently observed in practical applications.

Another familiar structure and constraint of data which have not been explored in the field of the Basket Analysis are the graph structure, i.e., constraints on the uni-directional and/or bi-directional relations among nodes. The data having the graph structure are widely seen in various problem domains such as the network flow phenomena in information stream of internet, that of car traffic stream in urban areas, the parallel process streams in computer operating systems, the structure of URLs and their links in the WWW service and causality among physical states. The discovery of frequently observed graph structure from a set of given data has been researched in the machine learning area, and the most representative approach is called "GBI (Graph Based Induction)" [5],[6]. Given a set of transactions where each transaction represents a graph consisting of some nodes and links, GBI searches typical graph structures observed more than a threshold frequency in the transaction data. Another version of GBI program can discover some specific graph structures which characterize the features of nodes and/or links contained in the graph. Though GBI provides a powerful measure to figure out important graph structures from a set of given data, its basic algorithm requires a thorough search in the data to find links contained in the objective structures. Accordingly, the state of the art to mine the graph structures is not satisfactory for the really massive data.

The work reported in this paper proposes a new method to mine frequent graph structures appearing in the massive transactions. A specific procedure to preprocess graph structured transactions is introduced to enable the application of the Basket Analysis to extract frequently appearing graph patterns.

2 Transaction having Graph Structure

The transaction analyzed by the conventional Basket Analysis is a set of items. For example, the transactions for customers buying items in a grocery store are represented as follows.

$$customer_1 : \{milk, bread, butter, - - -\},$$

$$- - - - -$$

$$customer_n : \{milk, bread, apple, - - -\}.$$

On the other hand, a transaction of graph structure contains nodes and links as depicted in Figure 1. Given the graph structured massive transactions, if a subgraph pattern of $\{A \to B \to C \to A\}$ appears more than a certain frequency level, then this subgraph can be called a *"frequent subgraph"* similar to the *"frequent itemset"*. Furthermore, if the transactions containing the subgraph of $\{A \to B\}$ also contains $\{A \to B \to C \to A\}$ more than a certain fraction of the transactions, then an *"association rule among subgraph structures"* of $\{A \to B\} \Rightarrow \{A \to B \to C \to A\}$ is mined from the transactions. Though the basic content of this problem is similar to the data mining of association rules among items, the conventional Basket Analysis can only discover the frequent itemsets and the association rules among the itemsets but not those of graph structures. To apply the Basket Analysis to the graph structured data, the data representation of each graph structured transaction is transformed into the form of the itemset transactions in our approch. Thus, the devivation of association rules among graph structured transactions is enable by this transformation within the framwork of the coventional Basket Analysis.

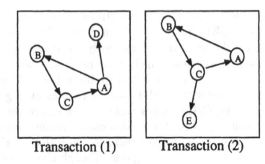

Transaction (1)   Transaction (2)

Fig. 1. Transactions containing graph structures.

The basic principle of the transformation of the graph structured transactions into the itemset transactions is as follows. Given a set of all nodes $V_{all} = \{v_1, v_2, ..., v_p\}$ and a set of all links among them $L_{all} = \{v_i \to v_j | v_i, v_j \in V_{all}\}$, then the transaction T_k having a graph structure is represented as a subset of L_{all}, i.e., $T_k \subseteq L_{all}$. As a transaction to be analyzed in the conventional Basket Analysis is a subset of all items in the data excluding the null set, the transactions having graph structures can also be analyzed in the same framework by handling each link $v_i \to v_j$ in T_k as an item.

For example, the two graph structured transactions depicted in Figure 1 can be represented as the itemset transactions as

$$\{A \to B, B \to C, C \to A, A \to D\}, \tag{1}$$
$$\{A \to B, B \to C, C \to A, C \to E\}. \tag{2}$$

By regarding each different link as a corresponding different item, the standard Basket Analysis is applicable to mine frequent subgraph structures and the association rules among the structures.

3 Implementation of Basket Analysis

3.1 Preprocessing graph structured transactions

The transactions containing graph structured data are given in various forms in practical fields. For example, the data of the network flow phenomena are usually represented as a collection of the series of nodes and links where the objects such as information packets and cars go through. In case of parallel process streams in computer operating systems, the streams of the processes and the data exchanged among the processes are represented in form of the list of the names of the processes and data together with the list of the pointers connecting these processes and the data. However, any graph data contained in a transaction can be generally transformed without much computational effort into the form of an adjaency matrix which is a very well known representation of a graph in the mathematical graph theory [7]. Each row and column of the matrix correspond to a node that appears in the graph respectively, and if a link from the i-th node to the j-th node appears in the transaction, the value "1" is assigned to the ij-element of the matrix, otherwise the value "0" is assigned.

For the first example in Figgre 1, the adjaency matrix becomes as follows. For the second, it is similarly represented.

$$
\begin{array}{c}
\quad A\ B\ C\ D \\
\begin{array}{c} A \\ B \\ C \\ D \end{array}
\left[
\begin{array}{cccc}
0 & 1 & 0 & 1 \\
0 & 0 & 1 & 0 \\
1 & 0 & 0 & 0 \\
0 & 0 & 0 & 0
\end{array}
\right]
\end{array}
\quad \text{for the transaction (1)}
$$

Once the adjaency matrix of each transaction is derived, the transaction in form of an itemset representing the graph structure is obtained by choosing each pair of nodes (i, j) having the value "1" in the ij-element and adding the arrow "$\rightarrow$" from the node i to the node j in each pair. When the transaction data contain only non-directed graph structure where the direction of each link between any two nodes is not specified, the adjaency matrix of each transaction becomes diagonally symmetric. In this case, the bar "$-$" is added between the nodes i and j, and $i - j$ and $j - i$ become an identical link.

After the data transform of the transactions have been conducted, all links appearing in all transaction are sorted and numbered in a lexicographical order for the efficient item processing similarly to the conventional Basket Analysis. In the example of Figure 1, all links are numbered as follows.

$$ A \rightarrow B \equiv 1, \quad B \rightarrow C \equiv 2, \quad C \rightarrow A \equiv 3, \quad A \rightarrow D \equiv 4, \quad C \rightarrow E \equiv 5. $$

Then, the expression (1) is rewritten as

$$ \{1, 2, 3, 4\}, \tag{3} $$

The frequent subgraphs and the association rules among the subgraph structures directly obtained by the Basket Analysis are also represented by the number labels of the links. For the comprehensiveness of the results, their representations are transformed back to the original links at the final stage of the analysis.

3.2 Deriving representative association rules

The standard Basket Analysis derives all frequent itemsets and all association rules having support and confidence levels greater than their thresholds, and filters out trivial rules by applying statistical heuristics [1],[2]. However, some researches have pointed out that this standard approach can not get rid of redundant rules and also misses some essential rules because of the incompleteness of the statistical heuristics used for the rule filtering [8], [9]. To alleviate this difficulty, the authors have proposed a complete logical rule filter which can retain only "representative association rules" [8]. The identical idea has also been provided by the other researcher [9]. The representative association rule has the characteristic to derive maximal consequences from minimal facts while maintaining their support and confidence greater than or equal to the given threshold levels. We apply this principle to derive "association rules among subgraph structures"

The principle to derive the representative association rules is briefly explained in this subsection. An association rule has the following form where "*Body*": B stands for an itemset and "*Head*": H another itemset (a superset of B). [1]

$$B \Rightarrow H, \text{ where } B \subset H.$$

The "*support*" values of B and H, i.e., $sup(B)$ and $sup(H)$, are ratios of the number of transactions including each set to the total number of transactions respectively. The "*confidence*" value, $conf(B \Rightarrow H)$, stands for the credibility of the rule, and is defined as a ratio of the number of transactions including H to the number of transactions including B. The Basket Analysis generates all frequent itemset having its support value greater than a threshold $l - sup$, and derives all association rules where its head is a frequent itemset and its confidence value is greater than another threshold value $s - conf$.

The association rules derived by these procedures have many redundancies that derive identical consequences from identical given facts. These redundancies reduce the comprehensiveness of the regularities discovered in the data and the efficiency of the use of those rules for some specific purposes. Instead of using statistical heuristics to remove the redundancies, we apply the following criteria.

Support threshold: The head of every association rule must have the support greater than a threshold "*lowest support*": $l - sup$.

Uniform confidence: Every association rule must have a confidence close to but not less than a level "*specified confidence*": $s - conf$.

Maximal consequence: Every association rule must derive a maximally specific consequence from a minimal fact.

The following definitions are introduced to implement these criteria.

Minimal bodysetF For a specified confidence $s - conf$, if a rule $B \Rightarrow H$ satisfies the following condition, B is said to be a "*minimal bodyset*" of $Head : H$ under $s - conf$.

$$conf(B \Rightarrow H) \geq s - conf \text{ and } conf(B' \Rightarrow H) < s - conf \quad \forall B' \subset B$$

Maximal headsetF For a specified confidence $s - conf$, if a rule $B \Rightarrow H$ satisfies the following condition, H is said to be a "*maximal headset*" of $Body : B$ under $s - conf$.

$$conf(B \Rightarrow H) \geq s - conf \text{ and } conf(B \Rightarrow H') < s - conf \quad \forall H' \supset H$$

Representative association ruleF For a specified confidence $s - conf$ and a lowest support $l - sup$, if $Body : B$ and $Head : H$ of a rule $B \Rightarrow H$ are the minimal bodyset and the maximal headset respectively, $B \Rightarrow H$ is said to be a "*representative association rule*".

This rule satisfies the aforementioned three criteria.

The representative association rules still contain some redundancy in terms of the inference ability. We apply a logical "*rule-filter*" where the rule $AB \Rightarrow ABR$ is removed, when two maximal estimation rules

$$AB \Rightarrow ABR \text{ and } B \Rightarrow BCR$$

---

[1] This representation of association rules is different from the standard notion $B \Rightarrow R$ where $R = H - B$. We use H instead of R for ease of our explanation.

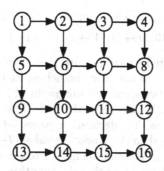

Fig. 2. A 4×4 path array.

are obtained. Here, every intersection among A, B, C, R is empty, and $AB = A + B, ABR = A + B + R$ and $BCR = B + C + R$. This rule-filtering does not violate the aforementioned criteria.

4 Performance Evaluation

4.1 Validation through simulation data

The basic performance of our proposed method to discover frequent graph structures and the association rules among the structures has been validated through the graph structured transaction data having clear characteristics. The data have been artificially generated through a Monte-Carlo simulation on a path array shown in Figure 2. This is a 4×4 link array, and vehicles starts from the node 1 to arrive at the node 16 by following directed (one way) links. Each vehicle chooses one of the links to proceed with an equivalent probability (50% each) at every binary branch of the links. A run of a vehicle from the start node 1 to the final goal node 16 corresponds to a transaction consisting of the intermediate links along the path that the vehicle passes through. The total number of the links between the adjacent nodes in this path array is 24, and the number of the items (links) involved in each transaction is 6. Furthermore, the total number of path sequences from the node 1 to 16 is 20, and the total number of the possible frequent itemsets in this example are theoretically known to be 847. The probability of each path that vehicles go through can also be theoretically evaluated. Totally, 10000 transactions, i.e., the 10000 history simulations of vehicle operations, are generated to ensure sufficient statistical accuracy of the validation. Multiple combinations of support and confidence thresholds of the Basket Analysis are applied in the validation analysis. The algorithm of a priori [1] has been used to derive frequent subgraphs. The effect of the support threshold $l - sup$ has been assessed in the range of $[0\%, 35\%]$, and that of the confidence threshold $s - conf$ has been changed in the range of $[30\%, 90\%]$.

Three examples of the frequent subgraphs discovered by the analysis are shown bellow.

$$\{1 \rightarrow 2, 2 \rightarrow 3\} \qquad (support = 25.3\%),$$

$$\{1 \rightarrow 2, 8 \rightarrow 12, 12 \rightarrow 16\} \qquad (support = 25.4\%),$$
$$\{1 \rightarrow 5, 5 \rightarrow 9, 9 \rightarrow 10, 10 \rightarrow 11, 11 \rightarrow 15, 15 \rightarrow 16, \} \ (support = 3.1\%).$$

The first example is a trivial case that its theoretical support value is easily known to be 25% because of the twice branching at the nodes 1 and 2. The second example contains two separated subgraphs of $1 \rightarrow 2$ and $8 \rightarrow 12 \rightarrow 16$. This is because many path ways from the node 2 to the node 8 exists, and the frequencies that each of the intermediate paths between the nodes 2 and 8 appear in the data are less than the support threshold $l-sup = 25\%$ in this case. The expected probability to go from the node 2 to the node 8 is 50%, and thus the total expected probability to go though these three paths are 25% which is consistent with the support value obtained in the simulation. The last example contains a full path ways from node 1 to node 16. The vehicle chooses one of the binary branching paths at the node $1, 5, 9, 10$ and 11 with equivalent probability. Thus, the expected probability to occur this path way is $(1/2)^5 = 1/32$ which is also consistent with its support value.

The followings are two examples of the association rules among subgraph structures.

$$\{1 \rightarrow 2\} \Rightarrow \{1 \rightarrow 2, 2 \rightarrow 3\} \ (support = 25.3\%, confidence = 50.9\%),$$
$$\{2 \rightarrow 3\} \Rightarrow \{1 \rightarrow 2, 2 \rightarrow 3\} \ (support = 25.3\%, confidence = 100.0\%).$$

Both of them represent the fact that a vehicle goes through the path way $1 \rightarrow 2 \rightarrow 3$ with the support value of about 25%. However, the difference of their confidence reflects the geometrical configuration of the paths $1 \rightarrow 2$ and $2 \rightarrow 3$. When a vehicle goes to the node 2 from the node 1, there are two choices to go forward at the node 2. In contrast, in the case that a vehicle goes through the path $2 \rightarrow 3$, it always should have passed the path $1 \rightarrow 2$. More complex examples reflecting the geometry of the paths are shown below where the confidence threshold $s - conf$ is set at 30%.

$$\{2 \rightarrow 6, 11 \rightarrow 15\} \Rightarrow \{1 \rightarrow 2, 2 \rightarrow 6, 6 \rightarrow 7, 7 \rightarrow 11, 11 \rightarrow 15, 15 \rightarrow 16\}$$
$$(suppoprt = 2.9\%, confidence = 50.6\%),$$
$$\{2 \rightarrow 6, 11 \rightarrow 15\} \Rightarrow \{1 \rightarrow 2, 2 \rightarrow 6, 6 \rightarrow 10, 10 \rightarrow 11, 11 \rightarrow 15, 15 \rightarrow 16\}$$
$$(suppoprt = 2.9\%, confidence = 49.4\%).$$

As easily understood by viewing Figure 2, when a vehicle goes though the paths $2 \rightarrow 6$ and $11 \rightarrow 15$, it necessarily goes though $1 \rightarrow 2$ and $15 \rightarrow 16$, and there are only the two choices $6 \rightarrow 7 \rightarrow 11$ and $6 \rightarrow 10 \rightarrow 11$ to go from the node 6 to the node 11. Accordingly, the confidence of each rule becomes around 50%. These observations indicate that the Basket Analysis for graph structured transactions in our proposed framework can properly derive the frequent subgraphs and the association rules among subgraph structures in a quantitative sense. Table 1 shows the effect of the condition of support and confidence thresholds on the computational complexity required. The level of the support threshold has a significant influence to the number of the frequent subgraphs. The computation time of "*Apriori*" is the time required to derive all frequent subgraphs, and that of "*Rulegen*" is the time to derive all representative association rules from the

Table 1. Computational complexity for support and confidence thresholds.

l-sup	s-conf	Num. of freq. subgraphs	Max. size of freq. subgraphs	Num. of rules	Comp. time[sec] Apriori	Rulegen
35	90	5	2	0	0.07	0.06
	70			0		0.05
	50			2		0.05
	30			4		0.06
25	90	18	3	4	0.13	0.06
	70			6		0.05
	50			12		0.05
	30			12		0.05
15	90	54	4	12	0.24	0.06
	70			17		0.07
	50			22		0.07
	30			22		0.07
5	90	523	6	68	0.55	0.42
	70			86		0.42
	50			120		0.44
	30			130		0.45
0	90	847	6	134	0.58	0.89
	70			152		0.88
	50			179		0.89
	30			226		0.97

frequent subgraphs. The task to derive all frequent subgraphs faces the combinatorial explosion of the items for a low support threshold, while the *"Apriori"* maintains its significant efficiency due to its well organized algorithm. The computation time required by *"Rulegen"* also does not show very drastic increase. These observations are consistent with the complexity analysis for the conventional Basket Analysis [1], [8]. The increase of the maximum size of the frequent subgraphs saturates under the condition of $l - sup$ less than 15%, where the length of the full path way from the node 1 to the node 16 is 6. This is because the support of some full path ways such as $1 \to 2 \to 3 \to 4 \to 8 \to 12 \to 16$ has the maximum value of $(1/2)^3 = 1/8$ which is slightly less than 15%.

4.2 Application to WWW browsing histories

The practical performance of the proposed method has been examined through a real scale application. The data analyzed is the log file of the commercial WWW server of Recruit Co., Ltd. in Japan. The URLs on WWW form a huge graph, where URLs are nodes mutually connected by many links. When a client visits the commercial WWW site, he or she browses only a small part of the huge graph at an access session as depicted in Figure 4, and the browsing history of the session becomes a graph structured transaction. The total number of the URLs involved in this commercial WWW site is more than 100000, and it is one

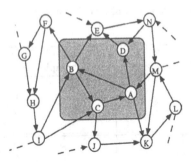

Fig. 3. A subgraph transaction in a huge URL graph.

of the largest site in Japan. Its total number of hit by the nation wide internet users always remains within the third place from the top in every month in Japanese internet record, and the typical size of the log file of the WWW server for a day is over $400MB$.

The basic format of an access record to a URL by a client in the log file is indicated in Figure 4. As the log file consists of the sequence of the access records, they are initially sorted by the IP addresses, and each subsequence having an identical IP address corresponding to the browsing access history in a session of an individual client is extracted. Then, those subsequences are transformed into adjaency matrix, and each graph structured transaction for a session of the individual IP client address are generated as explained in the earlier section.

Table 2 summarizes the statistical result of the analysis of this data by our approach varying the support threshold $l - sup$ and the confidence threshold $s - conf$. This table also shows the similar tendencies on the number of frequent subgraphs and the computation time with Table 1 that their increases are observed when $l - sup$ is decreased. In contrast, the number of the derived association rules are decreased, when $s - conf$ is decreased for low $l - sup$. This tendency is contradictory to the case of Table 1. This tendency is attributed to the feature of the WWW accesses that only the limited number of the URL access patterns are commonly shared among many clients while the access patterns of an individual client are slightly different from those common patterns. In other words, the transaction data involve many common subgraphs and the associations among them in the WWW case. For example, if the following two association rules involving common subgraphs of $A \to B$ on the lhs and $E \to F$ on the rhs are derived under a high confidence threshold $s - conf_H$,

$$\{A \to B, B \to C\} \Rightarrow \{A \to B, B \to C, E \to F\},$$
$$\{A \to B, B \to D\} \Rightarrow \{A \to B, B \to D, E \to F\},$$

then these two rules are subsumed into the following rule under a lower confidence threshold $s - conf_L$, and the above two rules are filtered out by the

| IP address of a client | $\triangle$ | Time stamp of the access | $\triangle$ | URL address |

$\triangle$:space character

Fig. 4. Basic format of an access record.

Table 2. Statistics of analysis on WWW access transactions.

1-sup [%]	s-conf [%]	Num. of freq. subgraphs	Num. of rules	Comp. time[sec] Apriori	Comp. time[sec] Rulegen
0.6	90.0	132	5	151	1
	70.0		8		2
	50.0		18		2
	30.0		30		2
0.4	90.0	625	251	392	24
	70.0		186		25
	50.0		216		24
	30.0		241		25
0.3	90.0	4,568	2,292	629	486
	70.0		773		441
	50.0		107		419
	30.0		101		420

aforementioned maximal consequence principle.

$$\{A \to B\} \Rightarrow \{A \to B, E \to F\}.$$

On the other hand, the transactions generated in the path array example do not share very much common association patterns among subgraphs, since the motion of the vehicles along the directed paths are randomly determined. This feature induces the monotonic increase of the rules under the decease of $s - conf$.

Finally, we show two examples of the association rules among subgraph structures obtained in this application. Figure 5 depicts a rule representing that more than 50% of the clients who pass the link from the URL titled as "Sports" to another "Ball Game" also pass the link from the "Ball Game" to that of "Baseball". Another example shown in Figure 6 says that nearly 60% of the clients who go though the link from "Travel" to "Restaurant" also go through the path of "Restaurant" $\to$ "Hobby" $\to$ "Arts" $\to$ "Society and Culture" $\to$ "Entertainment" $\to$ "News" $\to$ "Sports". Though the lhs and the rhs of these example rules just represent the node sequences, the association rules among various types of subgraphs including branching and cyclic structures are derived. Figure 7 shows such an example including loops in the pattern. This type of knowledge derived by the proposed approach can be used to investigate the associations among the interest topics of clients of the WWW site which provides important insights for marketing on necessary services.

5 Related Work and Discussion

R. Feldman et al. applied the conventional Basket Analysis to mine associations rules among keyword subsets involved in text files such as document files and HTML files, and they proposed a method to generate keyword graphs from the association rules [10]. The graphs are generated by merging the pairwise associations among keywords involved in the rules. Though this approach can represent

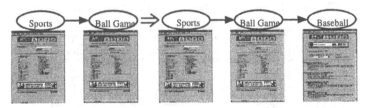

Fig. 5. Rule example (1) ($support = 0.4\%, confidence = 52.1\%$)

Fig. 6. Rule example (2) ($support = 0.4\%, confidence = 59.7\%$)

the associations among multiple nodes in form of graphs, it is to derive associations among sets of items and not for the applications where the transactions contain graph structured data. On the other hand, Chen et al. proposed to derive the longest access sequence patterns among URLs. Their work is close to our approch. However, knowledge representation discoverd by their framwork is limited to the access sequence patterns, whereas our apporch can discover graph structured patterns which cover wider classes of knowledge.

As shown in the previous section, the ability of our method to mine frequent subgraph structures and the associations among them are valid, and it is efficient for some practical and large scale applications. However, one weakness of our current approach is the requirement that all nodes must be mutually distinct in the object which produces the transactions. For instance, a common graph structure such as memory cell circuits contained in an LSI chip can not be discovered from the transactions representing fragments of the chip, because all nodes (devices) must be labeled by mutually different numbers, and the memory cells having an identical structure are represented by the transactions containing different links in this situation. To overcome this limitation, our approach must be extended to handle the types(colors) or attributes of nodes and links in graphs.

Fig. 7. Rule example (3) ($support = 0.3\%, confidence = 47.7\%$)

6 Conclusion

The work reported in this paper proposed an approach to mine frequent graph structures and the association rules among them embedded in massive transaction data. The approach consists of a preprocessing stage of the transaction data and the Basket Analysis. The validity of the principle we proposed has been confirmed by adopting to an artificially simulated graph structured data, and its practicality has been also demonstrated through a large scale real world problem to mine frequent browsing patterns of URLs and the associations among those patterns.

References

1. R.Agrwal and R.Srikant.: Fast algorithms for mining association rules. In *Proc. of the 20th VLDB Conference,* (1994) 487–499
2. G. Piatestsky-Shapiro.: Discovery, analysis, and presentation of strong rules. Knowledge Discovery in Databases. AAAI/MIT Press (1991)
3. R.Srikant, Q.Vu and R.Agrwal.: Mining Association Rules with Item Constraints. In *Proc. of 3rd Conference on Knowledge Discovery and Data Mining,* (1997) 67–73
4. T.Shintani and M.Kitsuregawa.: Mining Algorithms for Sequential Patters in Parallel: Hash Based Approach. In *Research and Development in Knowledge Discovery and Data Mining (Proc. of 3rd Conference on Knowledge Discovery and Data Mining),* (1998) 283–294
5. K.Yoshida and H.Motoda.: Clip: Concept Learning from Inference Pattern. In *Artificial Intelligence,* Vol.75, No.1 (1995) 63–92
6. H.Motoda and K.Yoshida.: Machine Learning Techniques to Make Computers Easier to Use. in *Proc. IJCAI97: Fifteenth International Joint Conference on Artificial Intelligence,* Vol.2 (1997) 1622–1631
7. N.Biggs.: Algebraic Graph Theory. Cambridge Univ. Press. (1973)
8. T.Washio and H.Motoda.: Mining Association Rules for Estimation and Prediction. in *Proc. PAKDD98: Research and Development in Knowledge Discovery and Data Mining,* (1998) 417–419
9. M.Kryszkiewicz.: Representative Association Rules. in *Proc. PAKDD98: Research and Development in Knowledge Discovery and Data Mining,* (1998) 198–209
10. R.Feldman, W.Klosgen and A.Zilberstein.: Visualization Techniques to Explore Data Mining Results for Document Collections. in *Proc. KDD97: Third International Conference on Knowledge Discovery and Data Mining,* (1997) 16–23
11. M.-S. Chen, J.S. Park and P.S Yu.: Efficient Data Mining for Path Traversal Patterns. In *IEEE Transaction on Knowledge and Data Engineering,* Vol.10, No.2 (1998) 209–221

The Evolution of Causal Models: A Comparison of Bayesian Metrics and Structure Priors

Julian R. Neil and Kevin B. Korb

School of Computer Science and Software Engineering

Monash University, Clayton, Vic., 3168, Australia

{jrn,korb}@csse.monash.edu.au

Abstract. We report the use genetic algorithms (GAs) as a search mechanism for the discovery of linear causal models when using two Bayesian metrics for linear causal models, a Minimum Message Length (MML) metric [10] and a full posterior analysis (BGe) [3]. We also consider two structure priors over causal models, one giving all variable orderings for models with the same arc density equal prior probability (P1) and one assigning all causal structures with the same arc density equal priors (P2). Evaluated with Kullback-Leibler distance prior P2 tended to produce models closer to the true model than P1 for both metrics, with MML performing slightly better than BGe. By contrast, when using an evaluation metric that better reflects the nature of the causal discovery task, namely a metric that compares the results of predictive performance on the *effect nodes* in the discovered model P1 outperformed P2 in general, with MML and BGe discovering models of similar predictive performance at various sample sizes. This supports our conjecture that the P1 prior is more appropriate for causal discovery.

With the rise of probabilistic networks for data analysis and prediction, there has been steady progress on automating their discovery [1,4,10,9]. Many processes described for learning such networks give them a causal interpretation, raising a question fundamental to the problem of scientific discovery itself — how to discover causal relationships from observed data. We focus on a particular type of probabilistic network, linear causal models, which are widely employed in the social sciences, as in structural equation models (SEMs). Using evolutionary search [6] we compare two Bayesian metrics for linear causal models, one based on Wallace's Minimum Message Length (MML) Principle [10] and the other by Geiger and Heckerman [3]. We then examine the implications of the assumed prior over causal structures on the accuracy and relevance of the discovered models. We consider two structure priors, one in which models of a given arc density are considered equally likely *a priori*, and one in which each total ordering for models of the same arc density has equal prior probability.

1 Linear Causal Models

In this paper we limit our attention to models that can be represented as directed acyclic graphs (DAGs). Each vertex in the graph is a random variable, and arcs in the graph corresponds to a direct causal connection. For linear causal models, every variable is a weighted linear sum of its parents. We assume variable $X_i, 1 \leq i \leq K$ have independently normal residuals $r_{in} \sim N(0, \sigma_i^2)$. X_i is then given by:

$$x_{in} = \sum_{X_k \in \Pi_i^S} a_{ki} x_{kn} + r_{in} \tag{1}$$

where $\mathbf{\Pi}_i^S$ is the set of parents of X_i in DAG S, x_{in} is the nth instance of X_i in a joint sample D of $\mathbf{X}$. The parameter set of X_i is $\boldsymbol{\theta}_i = \langle \sigma_i, \{a_{ki} : X_k \in \mathbf{\Pi}_i^S\} \rangle$.

An important property of causal models arises from the conditional independence relations that can be inferred from a model's structure. Pearl [7] defines *d-separation*, which identifies all implied independencies of a DAG model. If we assume that our DAG models of causality satisfy the Markov property – i.e., every d-separation in the model implies a conditional independency in the population under study – then distinct DAGs can entail identical conditional independencies and thus represent identical joint probability distributions. Because such models are indistinguishable by examining their implied distributions alone (and, hence, by examining observational data alone), they are said to be *statistically equivalent*. In particular, two DAGs are statistically equivalent just in case they have identical undirected adjacencies and have identical *v-structures* — triples $\{X, W, Y\}$, where X and Y are not adjacent, but are both parents of W. Such models then differ only in the orientation of one or more arcs. In contrast, a causal interpretation of these models necessarily distinguishes any two models that differ even just in the orientation of a single arc, say that between X and Y. In one model X is a cause of Y, while in the other Y is a cause of X. At the practical level of employing these two causal models, there can be radically different implications upon intervention (e.g., medical intervention).

1.1 The BGe Metric

Geiger and Heckerman [3] (and with Chickering in [4]) derive a Bayesian metric for scoring linear causal models. They evaluate the posterior probability of a hypothesis H given some sample data D. Although it is difficult to normalize the posterior, for model selection it suffices to calculate the joint probability of the hypothesis H and the data D $P(H, D) = P(H)f(D|H)$. For non-causal linear models Geiger and Heckerman define H to be the hypothesis that the sample distribution can be represented by the structure S. Under this definition, if H is true for some structure S, then H is true for all structures that are statistically equivalent to S. Heckerman and Geiger [3] call this property *hypothesis equivalence*. Although they restrict their analysis to individual structures, Heckerman and Geiger note that according to hypothesis equivalence, statistical equivalence classes of models should be scored collectively rather than individual models themselves. However, if a model is considered causal, the hypothesis must include the assertion that each node in S is a direct cause of each of its children. This interpretation invalidates hypothesis equivalence, and thus statistically equivalent *causal* networks need not be assigned equal scores. Nevertheless, Heckerman and Geiger surmise that equivalent scores are often appropriate even when models are causally interpreted [2]. Our interest is exclusively with causal models. We have argued elsewhere against non-causal interpretations [9]; here we provide a Bayesian metric that distinguishes between equivalent causal models.

Using hypothesis equivalence Heckerman and Geiger derive the following metric for scoring linear causal models:

$$\text{BGe}(S, D) = P(S) \prod_{i=1}^{K} \frac{f(D^{\{X_i, \Pi_i\}} | S_C)}{f(D^{\{\Pi_i\}} | S_C)} \tag{2}$$

where $D^{\mathbf{Y}}$ is the data D restricted to $\mathbf{Y}$ and S_C is a fully connected network. To calculate $f(D^{\mathbf{Y}} | S_C)$ for an arbitrary structure S, they require that the user supply a *prior* parameterized model, as well as two parameters reflecting strength of belief in its accuracy, N'_μ and N'_T. For this paper we have assumed the least informative parameter priors possible. We set the prior network to contain no arcs and use equivalent sample sizes $N'_\mu = 1$ and $N'_T = K + 2$.

1.2 MML Induction

Minimum Message Length induction [8] applies Bayesian conditionalization in information-theoretic form. A two-part message is constructed hypothetically: first, the hypothesis itself is encoded, including any parameters, and second, the data are encoded given the hypothesis. That hypothesis giving the shortest total message is then preferred. Wallace *et al.* [10] derive the length of the message needed to transmit a single variable X_i of a linear causal model (cf. also [6]).

The MML and BGe metrics differ in two main ways . First, BGe integrates the parameters out of the posterior, whereas MML considers parameter estimation an important part of model discovery. Second, Geiger and Heckerman assume that statistically equivalent models satisfy hypothesis equivalence and prove that this requires a normal-Wishart prior over the parameters. In contrast, the MML metric adopts an independently normal prior for path coefficients and a uniform prior over the residual variances. Statistically equivalent structures then have identical likelihoods only using maximum likelihood parameter estimates.

1.3 Structure Priors

To find structure priors for networks, some researchers assume a prior ordering of the variables; many use a uniform distributions over structures. Geiger and Heckerman use a prior that penalizes deviations from a user supplied prior network. We prefer to follow Wallace *et al.* [10] in suggesting that in the absence of any knowledge of the causal ordering of the variables, the most sensible prior over total orderings is uniform, which prior we dub (P1). We consider this to be the best uninformed structure prior for a causal interpretation of the inferred models. In an effort to demonstrate this, we contrast (P1) with (P2) which takes all causal structures with the same arc density to be equally likely.

2 Evolutionary Search

Various search methods have been applied for discovering causal models. For this study we employed a non-standard genetic algorithm (cf. [5]), using DAGs directly as the genetic representation, with genetic operators designed for DAGs. These operators are described in detail in [5] and are extended in [6]. To find linear causal models using the MML measure, we use use the negative message length as our fitness function. Similarly, we use the log of (2) for the BGe measure. We will simply refer to the GAs with the respective fitness function and structure prior combination as MML-P1, MML-P2, BGe-P1 and BGe-P2.

3 Results

We compared these four methods on seven small datasets (of 2–7 nodes) from the social sciences, and on several stochastically generated models.[1]

---

[1] For details of the experimental parameters see [6].

3.1 Comparison of MML and BGe with priors P1 and P2

We calculated the Kullback-Leibler (KL) distances between the inferred and the true distributions in order to measure the relation between the implied distribution of the true and learned models, using maximum likelihood estimates for each model's parameters. Because KL distance only measures the difference in implied distributions, it does not distinguish between statistically equivalent models, and so it should prefer models found when prior P2 is used.

Table 1 compares the KL distance averaged over 50 datasets. The reported KL distances are multiplied by 100 to reflect the sample size. Boldface results indicate the metric with the smallest average KL for each dataset. To measure sampling error, the last column of Table 1 gives average KL distances between the true model with maximum likelihood parameter estimates for each dataset and the true model with its original estimates, and so is an optimal value for KL distances. As expected, the P2 prior dominates the results for both metrics, with MML-P2 clearly outperforming the other metrics on average.

Table 1. Average KL distances over 50 datasets of 100 cases for various test models. Annotations reported paired t-test significance at a level of 0.05 (e.g., for dataset 15.2 MML-P2 is significantly better than BGe-P1).

Dataset	MML-P1	MML-P2	BGe-P1	BGe-P2	True
15.1	**41.95**	44.05	43.50	42.19	17.89
15.2	37.71	**36.31** $_{B_1}$	39.50	37.30 $_{B_1}$	12.11
15.3	39.93 $_{B_1}$	**39.74**	43.63	41.74	17.73
15.4	33.23	**31.19** $_{M_1}$	31.58	32.56	14.41
15.5	26.69	**24.48** $_{B_1 B_2 M_1}$	27.80	26.37 $_{B_1}$	9.33
12.1	20.97	20.92	21.24	**20.28**	8.55
12.2	31.11	**28.96** $_{B_1}$	33.18	30.27 $_{B_1}$	11.46
12.3	10.41	10.45	11.26	**9.83** $_{B_1}$	5.69
12.4	31.99	**30.45**	32.65	31.34	13.28
12.5	25.63	**23.63**	25.43	23.69 $_{M_1}$	15.68
10.1	24.77	24.64	25.10	**24.52**	11.03
10.2	**21.59**	22.09	22.06	21.61	9.94
10.3	23.52	22.80	23.61	**22.66**	10.80
10.4	7.01	7.28	**6.26**	6.83	5.41
10.5	18.39	**16.72** $_{B_1 M_1}$	19.99	17.72 $_{B_1}$	6.55
Loehlin	9.11 $_{M_2}$	10.88	**8.98** $_{M_2}$	9.41 $_{M_2}$	8.06
Rodgers	25.32 $_{B_1}$	**22.99** $_{B_1 B_2 M_1}$	28.57	23.93 $_{M_1 B_1}$	10.17
Miller	6.83	6.91	**6.76**	**6.76**	6.54
Goldberg	12.95	**12.34**	13.87 $_{M_2}$	13.17	7.26
Fiji	7.27 $_{B_1}$	**6.96** $_{B_1}$	9.05	7.55 $_{B_1}$	4.59
Evans	7.69	7.53	**7.28** $_{M_1}$	7.30 $_{M_1 M_2}$	6.65
Blau	19.06 $_{B_1 B_2}$	**17.44** $_{B_1 B_2 M_1}$	21.53	21.06	8.99

If our goal in discovering models is to predict endogenous variables, to intervene in or explain the relationships between variables, then we are most interested in how well the discovered models represent the true causal system. KL distance, however, fails to distinguish between statistically equivalent models. To overcome this limitation, we evaluated learned models by how well they predicted values in the set of *effect nodes*, i.e., nodes with no descendents. Predictive accuracy in effect nodes was measured by summing their expected negative log likelihood $E[-LL]$. This measure discriminates between two structures in which a causal arc into an effect node is reversed even if the two models are statistically equivalent. Table 2 gives average $E[-LL]$ results for our experimental models. The results clearly show that P1 gives better predictive performance over the effect nodes than P2. This supports our conjecture that for learning causal struc-

Table 2. Average expected negative log likelihood of the effect nodes over 50 datasets of 100 cases for various test models.

Dataset	MML-P1	MML-P2	BGe-P1	BGe-P2	True
15.1	9.760	9.794	**9.748** M_2	9.789	9.541
15.2	15.702	15.661	15.751	**15.638** B_1	15.070
15.3	11.663 B_2M_2	11.825	**11.639** M_2B_2	11.899	11.418
15.4	11.415	11.423	**11.379** $M_1M_2B_2$	11.435	11.242
15.5	13.799	**13.724**	13.852	13.845	13.148
12.1	12.035	12.023	12.018	**11.969**	11.718
12.2	9.688	**9.660**	9.685	9.668	9.399
12.3	**13.763** M_2	13.797	13.765 M_2	13.770 M_2	13.702
12.4	6.863 B_2M_2	7.145	**6.829** M_2B_2	7.166	6.708
12.5	**10.598** B_2M_2	10.847	10.625 M_2B_2	10.768	10.390
10.1	**5.216**	5.235	5.220	5.256	5.077
10.2	9.233	9.249	9.279	**9.214**	8.683
10.3	**5.443** $B_1B_2M_2$	5.622	5.481 M_2B_2	5.646	5.330
10.4	11.417 B_2M_2	11.652	**11.405** M_2B_2	11.691	11.289
10.5	11.543	11.498	11.473 M_1	**11.456** M_1	11.200
Loehlin	5.648 B_2M_2	6.055	**5.625** M_2B_2	6.082	5.621
Rodgers	1.917	1.867 B_1M_1	1.911	**1.863** M_1B_1	1.717
Miller	1.523	**1.499**	1.501	1.526	1.100
Goldberg	1.483 M_2	1.554	**1.469** M_2	1.500	1.357
Fiji	**1.996** B_2	2.002	2.005	2.009	1.965
Evans	1.678	1.705	**1.660**	1.695	1.620
Blau	1.820	1.828	**1.798**	1.812	1.661

ture a structure prior that considers variable orderings equally likely is more appropriate than one that treats statistically equivalent models as equally likely.

4 Conclusion

Using genetic algorithms to search for linear causal models, we compared two Bayesian metrics (MML and BGe), each with two structure priors (P1 and P2). On KL-distance the structure prior that considers equivalent structures equally likely (P2) on average finds models closer to the true model than the prior that treats variable orderings as equally likely (P1), with MML finding more models of shorter KL-distances than BGe on average. However, when the correctness of the discovered causal structure is measured more directly, via predictive performance over the effect nodes, P1 clearly outperforms P2 for both measures, with BGe and MML showing similar performance. This supports our conjecture that a structure prior treating orderings as equally probable is more suited to causal discovery than one that assigns statistically equivalent models equal prior probabilities.

References

1. G.F. Cooper and E. Herskovits. A Bayesian method for the induction of probabilistic networks from data. *Machine Learning*, 9:309-347, 1992.
2. D. Heckerman. A Bayesian approach to learning causal networks. *Proc of the 11th Conf on Uncertainty in AI*, pp. 285-295, 1995. Morgan Kaufmann.
3. D. Heckerman and D. Geiger. Learning Bayesian networks: A unification for discrete and Gaussian domains. *Proc of the 11th Conf on Uncertainty in AI*, pp. 274-284, San Francisco, California, 1995. Morgan Kaufmann.
4. D. Heckerman, D. Geiger, and D.M. Chickering. Learning Bayesian networks. *Machine Learning*, 20:197-243, 1995.

5. J.R. Neil and K.B. Korb. The MML evolution of causal models. Technical Report 98/17, School of Computer Science, Monash University, 1998.
6. J.R. Neil and K.B. Korb. The evolution of causal models: A comparison of bayesian metrics and structure priors. Technical Report 1999/27, School of Computer Science, Monash University, 1999.
7. J. Pearl. *Probabilistic Reasoning in Intelligent Systems.* Morgan Kaufmann, 1988.
8. C.S. Wallace and P.R. Freeman. Estimation and inference by compact coding. *Jrn Royal Stat Soc (Series B)*, 49:240-252, 1987.
9. C.S. Wallace and K.B. Korb. Learning linear causal models by MML sampling. Thompson (ed.) *Causal Models and Intelligent Data Management*, Springer, 1999.
10. C.S. Wallace, K.B. Korb, and H. Dai. Causal discovery via MML. L. Saitta, editor, *Proc of the 13th Int Conf on Machine Learning*, pp. 516-524, 1996.

KD-FGS: A Knowledge Discovery System from Graph Data Using Formal Graph System

Tetsuhiro Miyahara[1], Tomoyuki Uchida[1], Tetsuji Kuboyama[2],
Tatsuya Yamamoto[3], Kenichi Takahashi[1], and Hiroaki Ueda[1]

[1] Faculty of Information Sciences,
Hiroshima City University, Hiroshima 731-3194, Japan
{miyahara@its, uchida@cs, takahasi@its, ueda@its}.hiroshima-cu.ac.jp
[2] Center for Collaborative Research, University of Tokyo, Tokyo 153-0041, Japan
kuboyama@ccr.u-tokyo.ac.jp
[3] Graduate School of Information Sciences,
Hiroshima City University, Hiroshima 731-3194, Japan
yamamoto@rea.its.hiroshima-cu.ac.jp

Abstract. A graph is one of the most common abstract structures and is suitable for representing relations between various objects. The analyzing system directly manipulating graphs is useful for knowledge discovery. Formal Graph System (FGS) is a kind of logic programming system which directly deals with graphs just like first order terms. We have designed and implemented a knowledge discovery system KD-FGS, which receives the graph data and produces a hypothesis by using FGS as a knowledge representation language. The system consists of an FGS interpreter and a refutably inductive inference algorithm for FGSs. We report some experiments of running KD-FGS and confirm that the system is useful for knowledge discovery from graph data.

1 Introduction

Machine learning and data mining technology have been used for knowledge discovery and prediction in many fields [1]. The aim of knowledge discovery is to find a small and understandable hypothesis which explains data nicely. A graph is one of the most common abstract structures and is suitable for representing relations between various objects [6]. We believe that the analyzing system directly dealing with graphs is useful for knowledge discovery.

Formal Graph System (FGS, [5]) is a kind of logic programming system which directly deals with graphs just like first order terms. So FGS is suitable to represent logical knowledge explaining the given graph data. In this paper, we propose a knowledge discovery system KD-FGS (see Fig. 1). As inputs, the system receives positive and negative examples of graph data. As an output, the system produces an FGS program which is consistent with the positive and negative examples if such a hypothesis exists. Otherwise, the system refutes the hypothesis space. KD-FGS consists of an FGS interpreter and a refutably

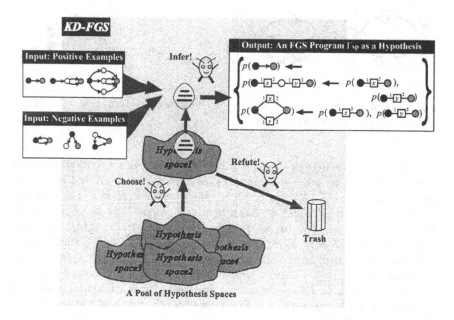

Fig. 1. KD-FGS: a knowledge discovery system from graph data using FGS

inductive inference algorithm of FGS programs. The FGS interpreter is used to check whether a hypothesis is consistent with the given graph data or not.

A *refutably inductive inference algorithm*, proposed by Mukouchi and Arikawa [2], is a special type of inductive inference algorithm with refutability of hypothesis spaces. Suppose that a hypothesis space is refutably inferable and data are successively given to the algorithm for the hypothesis space. If there exists a hypothesis describing the data in the hypothesis space, then the algorithm will *infer the hypothesis*, that is, it will eventually identify the hypothesis. If not, then the algorithm will *refute the hypothesis space*, that is, it will tell us that no hypothesis in the hypothesis space explains the data and stop. When the hypothesis space is refuted, the algorithm chooses another hypothesis space and tries to make a discovery in the new hypothesis space. By refuting the hypothesis space, the algorithm gives important suggestions to achieve the goal of knowledge discovery. Thus, KD-FGS is useful for knowledge discovery from graph data.

2 FGS as a New Knowledge Representation Language

Formal Graph System (FGS, [5]) is a kind of logic programming system which directly deals with graphs just like first order terms.

Let Σ and Λ be finite alphabets, and let X be an alphabet, whose element is called a *variable label*. Assume that $(\Sigma \cup \Lambda) \cap X = \emptyset$. A *term graph* $g = (V, E, H)$ consists of a vertex set V, an edge set E and a multi-set H whose element is

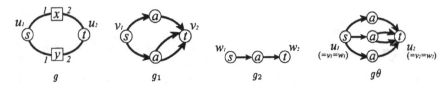

Fig. 2. Term graphs g and $g\theta$ obtained by applying a substitution $\theta = \{x :=$ $[g_1, (v_1, v_2)], y := [g_2, (w_1, w_2)]\}$ to g.

a list of distinct vertices in V and is called a *variable*. And a term graph g has a vertex labeling $\varphi_g : V \to \Sigma$, an edge labeling $\psi_g : E \to \Lambda$ and a variable labeling $\lambda_g : H \to X$. A term graph is called *ground* if $H = \emptyset$. For example, a term graph $g = (V, E, H)$ is shown in Fig. 2, where $V = \{u_1, u_2\}$, $E = \emptyset$, $H = \{e_1 = (u_1, u_2), e_2 = (u_1, u_2)\}$, $\varphi_g(u_1) = s$, $\varphi_g(u_2) = t$, $\lambda_g(e_1) = x$, and $\lambda_g(e_2) = y$. An *atom* is an expression of the form $p(g_1, \ldots, g_n)$, where p is a predicate symbol with arity n and $g_1, \ldots, g_n$ are term graphs. Let $A, B_1, \ldots, B_m$ be atoms with $m \geq 0$. Then, a *graph rewriting rule* is a clause of the form $A \leftarrow B_1, \ldots, B_m$. An *FGS program* is a finite set of graph rewriting rules. For example, the FGS program Γ_{SP} in Fig. 1 generates the family of all two-terminal series parallel (TTSP) graphs.

Let g be a term graph and σ be a list of distinct vertices in g. We call the form $x := [g, \sigma]$ a *binding* for a variable label $x \in X$. A *substitution* θ is a finite collection of bindings $\{x_1 := [g_1, \sigma_1], \ldots, x_n := [g_n, \sigma_n]\}$, where x_i's are mutually distinct variable labels in X and each g_i $(1 \leq i \leq n)$ has no variable labeled with an element in $\{x_1, \ldots, x_n\}$. For a set or a list S, the number of elements in S is denoted by $|S|$. In the same way as logic programming system, we obtain a new term graph f by applying a substitution $\theta = \{x_1 := [g_1, \sigma_1], \cdots, x_n := [g_n, \sigma_n]\}$ to a term graph $g = (V, E, H)$ in the following way. For each binding $x_i := [g_i, \sigma_i] \in \theta$ $(1 \leq i \leq n)$ in parallel, we attach g_i to g by removing the all variables $t_1, \cdots, t_k$ labeled with x_i from H, and by identifying the m-th element of t_j and the m-th element of σ_i for each $1 \leq j \leq k$ and each $1 \leq m \leq |t_j| = |\sigma_i|$, respectively. The resulting term graph f is denoted by $g\theta$. In Fig. 2, for example, we draw the term graph $g\theta$ which is obtained by applying a substitution $\theta = \{x := [g_1, (v_1, v_2)], y := [g_2, (w_1, w_2)]\}$ to the term graph g. A graph rewriting rule C is *provable from* an FGS program Γ if C is obtained from Γ by finitely many applications of graph rewriting rules and modus ponens.

3   Refutably Inductive Inference of FGS Programs

In this section, we show that sufficiently large hypothesis spaces of FGS programs are refutably inferable and thus give a theoretical foundation of the KD-FGS system. We give our framework of refutably inductive inference of FGS programs according to [2, 4]. Let $g = (V, E, H)$ be a term graph. We denote the *size* of g by $|g|$ and define $|g| = |V| + |E| + |H|$. For example, $|g| = |V| + |E| + |H| = 2 + 0 + 2 = 4$

for the term graph $g = (V, E, H)$ in Fig. 2. For an atom $p(g_1, \ldots, g_n)$, we define $\|p(g_1, \ldots, g_n)\| = |g_1| + \cdots + |g_n|$.

Definition 1. A graph rewriting rule $A \leftarrow B_1, \ldots, B_m$ is said to be *weakly reducing* (resp., *size-bounded*) if $\|A\theta\| \geq \|B_i\theta\|$ for any $i = 1, \ldots, m$ and any substitution θ (resp., $\|A\theta\| \geq \|B_1\theta\| + \cdots + \|B_m\theta\|$ for any substitution θ). An FGS program Γ is *weakly-reducing* (resp., *size-bounded*) if every graph rewriting rule in Γ is weakly reducing (resp., size-bounded).

For example, the FGS program Γ_{SP} in Fig. 1 is weakly reducing but not size-bounded. The set of all ground atoms (i.e., ground facts) is called the *Herbrand base*, denoted by $\mathcal{HB}$, and is considered as the set of all training examples. A subset I of $\mathcal{HB}$ is called an *interpretation*, and is considered as a set of positive training examples. An FGS program Γ is called a *correct program* for an interpretation I if the least Herbrand model of Γ, which is the set of all ground atoms proved from Γ, is equal to I. A *complete presentation* of an interpretation I is an infinite sequence $(w_1, t_1), (w_2, t_2), \cdots$ of elements in $I \times \{+, -\}$ such that $\{w_i \mid t_i = +, i \geq 1\} = I$ and $\{w_i \mid t_i = -, i \geq 1\} = \mathcal{HB} \setminus I$. A refutably inductive inference algorithm is said to *converge* to an FGS program Γ for a presentation, if it produces the same FGS program Γ after some finitely many times of hypothesis changes. We can construct a machine discovery system for a refutably inferable hypothesis space. Thus the following Theorem 1 gives a theoretical foundation of KD-FGS.

Definition 2 ([2]). A refutably inductive inference algorithm is said to *refutably infer a hypothesis space $\mathcal{C}$ from complete data*, if it satisfies the following condition: For any interpretation $I \subseteq \mathcal{HB}$ and any complete presentation δ of I, (1) if there exists a correct program in $\mathcal{C}$ for I then the algorithm converges to a correct program in $\mathcal{C}$ for I from δ, (2) otherwise the algorithm refutes $\mathcal{C}$ from δ.

Theorem 1 (Based on [2]). *For any $n \geq 0$, the hypothesis space $\mathcal{WR}^{[\leq n]}$ (resp., $\mathcal{SB}^{[\leq n]}$) of all weakly reducing (resp., size-bounded) FGS programs with at most n graph rewriting rules is refutably inferable from complete data.*

4 Implementation and Experimental Results

We have implemented a prototype of the KD-FGS system by constructing an FGS interpreter and a refutably inductive inference algorithm in Common Lisp. The FGS interpreter is an extension of the Prolog interpreter (P. Norvig[3], Chap. 11). In Table 1, we summarize 6 experiments of running KD-FGS on a DEC-Alpha compatible workstation (clock 500 MHz) with GCL2.2. In Exp. 1 and 2, input data are positive and negative examples of TTSP graph (see Fig. 1). In Exp. 1 (resp., 2), the hypothesis space $\mathcal{C}_1$ (resp., $\mathcal{C}_2$) is the set of all restricted weakly reducing FGS programs with at most 2 (resp., 2) atoms in each body and at most 2 (resp., 3) rules in each program, which is denoted by "#atom$\leq$ 2, #rule$\leq$ 2" (resp., "#atom$\leq$ 2, #rule$\leq$ 3"). After the system receives 3 positive

Table 1. Experimental results on the KD-FGS system

No.	Examples	Hypothesis Space	Received Examples	Result
1	TTSP	#atom$\leq$ 2, #rule$\leq$ 2	#pos=3, #neg=5	refute
2	graph	#atom$\leq$ 2, #rule$\leq$ 3	#pos=3, #neg=5	infer
3	undirected	#atom$\leq$ 1, #rule$\leq$ 2	#pos=3, #neg=6	refute
4	tree	#atom$\leq$ 1, #rule$\leq$ 3	#pos=3, #neg=6	infer
5	directed	#atom$\leq$ 1, #rule$\leq$ 2	#pos=3, #neg=10	refute
6	tree	#atom$\leq$ 1, #rule$\leq$ 3	#pos=4, #neg=10	refute

and 5 negative examples, which is denoted by "#pos=3, #neg=5", it refutes C_1 in Exp. 1 (resp., it converges to a correct FGS program in C_2 for TTSP graphs in Exp. 2). We confirm that the system is useful for knowledge discovery from graph data.

5 Conclusion

We have designed and implemented a knowledge discovery system KD-FGS which produces an FGS program as logical knowledge for graph data. In order to achieve practical speedup of KD-FGS, we are implementing another FGS interpreter, which is based on a bottom-up theorem proving method, in a parallel logic programming language KLIC.

Acknowledgments

The first and second authors would like to thank Prof. Setsuo Arikawa and Prof. Yasuhito Mukouchi for helpful advices and suggestions. This work is partly supported by Grant-in-Aid for Scientific Research (08680378, 09780356) from the Ministry of Education, Science, Sports and Culture, Japan and Grant for Special Academic Research (9763, 9778) from Hiroshima City University.

References

1. S. Muggleton and D. Page. Special issue on inductive logic programming. *Machine Learning*, 26(2–3):97–252, 1997.
2. Y. Mukouchi and S. Arikawa. Towards a mathematical theory of machine discovery from facts. *Theoretical Computer Science*, 137:53–84, 1995.
3. P. Norvig. *Paradigms of Artificial Intelligence Programming: Case Studies in Common Lisp.* Morgan Kaufmann, 1992.
4. T. Shinohara. Rich class inferable from positive data: length-bounded elementary formal systems. *Information and Computation*, 108:175–186, 1994.
5. T. Uchida, T. Shoudai, and S. Miyano. Parallel algorithm for refutation tree problem on formal graph systems. *IEICE Transactions on Information and Systems*, E78-D(2):99–112, 1995.
6. K. Yoshida and H. Motoda. Inductive inference by stepwise pair expansion. *Journal of Jpn. Soc. Artif. Intell.*, 12(1):58–67, 1997.

Probing Knowledge in Distributed Data Mining

Yike Guo and Janjao Sutiwaraphun

Department of Computing, Imperial College
180 Queen's Gate, London SW7 2BZ, UK
{Y.Guo, J.Sutiwaraphun}@doc.ic.ac.uk

Abstract. In this paper, we propose a new approach to apply meta-learning concept to distributed data mining. We name this approach *Knowledge Probing* where a supervised learning process is organised into two learning stages. In the first learning phase, a set of base classifiers are learned in parallel from a distributed data set. In the second learning phase, meta-learning is applied to induce the relationship between an attribute vector and the class predictions from all the base classifiers. By applying this approach to an environment where base classifiers are produced from distributed data sources, the output of *Knowledge Probing* process can be viewed as the assimilated knowledge of that distributed learning system. Some initial experimental results on the quality of the assimilated knowledge are presented. We believe that an integration of *Knowledge Probing* technique and the available data mining algorithms can provide a practical framework for distributed data mining applications.

Keywords: Distributed data mining, Committee Learning, Classification data mining.

1 Introduction

The vast quantities of commercial and scientific data being stored worldwide currently are increasingly being seen as the source of hidden knowledge. In the past decade a significant amount of researches in the field of data mining have been done, resulting in a variety of algorithms and techniques for automatically extracting this hidden information from data. However, there are some important challenges in using data mining technologies to real world applications:

- data can be large: the execution time of the learning processes can be prohibitive when applying the algorithms to volumes of data generated in real world applications
- data can be distributed: data can be physically distributed at remote sites

Distributed data mining provides a promising solution to these challenges. The idea is to use data mining algorithms to extract knowledge from several (normally disjointed) distributed data sets and then use the knowledge from these individual learned models to create a unified body of knowledge that well represents the whole data. Thus, distributed data mining can be characterised as an integration of multiple distributed learned models. Such an integration can be done by learning the results of multiple base-learning processes. We can therefore relate distributed data mining with two important research fields of machine learning : *committee learning*, where multiple models are learned for making accurate predictions by avoiding various kinds of learning bias and *meta-learning*, where models are re-learned and integrated. The following advantages of distributed data mining stem directly from the combination of these two learning approaches:

- *Learning Accuracy :* Using different learning algorithms to learn models from distributed data sources increases the possibility of achieving higher accuracy especially on a large-size domain. This is because the integration of such models can represent an integration of different learning biases which possibly compensate one another in their inefficient characteristics. Through statistical reasoning, the average of independent estimators (i.e. base models learned from distributed data set) will have less variance than one individual estimator (i.e. a single model learned from a whole data set). If variance is defined as a quantity that measures the sensitivity of a model to an unseen data item, then learning multiple models can be an effective way to overcome the over-fitting problem or the problem of a model being trained to the point where it is highly accurate on the training set, but not on unseen data items. Hansen & Salamon [11] have shown that, for an ensemble of neural networks, if all base models have the same probability of making error of less than 0.5 and if all of them make errors independently, then the overall error must decrease as a function of the number of models. Some current researches have also shown that, for learning algorithms such as CART and C4.5 which have a high variance [3], a framework of multiple learning from partitioned learning spaces would reduce error caused by the variance of the algorithms [2, 3].

- *Execution Time and Memory Limitation:* Distributed data mining provides a natural solution for large scale data mining where algorithm complexity and memory limitation are always the main obstacles. If there is a multicomputer system available, then each processor can work on a different partition of data in order to independently derive a model. Some minor communication overhead is expected to incur in this process. A clever model combination technique then can benefit from the set of derived models. Hence, a distributed architecture such as distributed memory parallel computer systems or workstation clusters will be an ideal platform for distributed data mining. This approach is scalable, as an increasing amount of data can be compensated by a linear increase of number of processors or workstations.

So far, many researches on distributed data mining have been concentrated on committee learning [1, 4] where the emphasis is put on making accurate predictions based on multiple models. Another key technology for distributed data mining is *knowledge assimilation*. That is, after knowledge is induced from subsets of data, the key step of the distributed data mining process is to integrate pieces of knowledge into a comprehensive model which represents the whole data set. To achieve that goal, meta-learning is required to learn the relationship of all the knowledge learned from the base learning phase. Applying meta learning technology to knowledge assimilation is still a very new research field.

One pioneer work on applying meta-learning to distributed data mining is done by Chan and Stolfo [6]. They concentrate on learning from the output of concept learning systems. Although Chan's approach of meta-learning provides an interesting and potentially useful solution to the distributed learning and data mining, there are some fundamental limitations. The first one is the problem of knowledge representation. In Chan's approach, the final classifier produced can be regarded as a black box. It does not provide any understanding of the data. It therefore can serve the purpose of prediction, but lacks in the descriptive function because the meta-classifier is not the integration of the knowledge from the base classifiers, but instead the statistical combination of predictions from base classifiers. Moreover, the algorithm seems to be susceptible to the distribution of initial data sets. It is noted in [7] that a bias introduced by a particular distribution formed by a data reduction method has to be taken into consideration. It appears that, in Chan's approach, the quality of the classifier depends on the distribution of the initial data set. In addition, the distribution of the unseen (test) data set is also likely to have an effect on the accuracy of the classifier. Thus, the accuracy of a meta-classifier tends to vary if there is a difference in the distribution of the training set and the unseen data set.

In our opinion, one of the most important goals of meta-learning is to assimilate knowledge learned by base learning systems. This is particularly important to the application of data mining since the descriptive power of the model learned by a meta-learning system determines the value of the model. In order to derive a descriptive model, we propose the idea of *Knowledge Probing (KP)* as a new meta-learning approach for assimilating the knowledge learned by base learning systems in a distributed data mining environment. The paper is organised as follows : in the following section, we present the basic concept of the knowledge probing framework. The design of the experiments is presented Section 3. The experimental results and analysis are in Section 4. The conclusion and further work are discussed in the last section.

2 Knowledge Probing Framework

Knowledge Probing (*KP*) is first proposed in [9] as a technique to probe descriptive knowledge from a black box model. In classification data mining term, a black box model, for example, a neural network, is a model which takes an unclassified data set as an input and gives a set of class predictions as an output. The key idea underlying *KP* is to derive a descriptive model from a black box model by learning from the un-classified data set and the corresponding set of predictions made by the black box. The basic principle of *KP* can be presented as follows:

```
Input: A set S of n unseen data items,
       a black box model B,
       a learning algorithm D which provides descriptive output.
```

```
Prediction phase: creating the class values of data items in S
```

$$C \ = \ B(\ \{s\_i \ | \ s\_i \ \in \ S, \ i \ = \ 1,\ldots,n\} \ )$$

```
Learning phase: learning from the new training set
                constructed from S using the predicted class
                values C
```

$$B^* \ = \ D(\ \{(s\_i, \ c\_i) \ | \ s\_i \ \in \ S, \ c\_i \ \in \ C, \ i \ = \ 1,\ldots,n\} \ )$$

```
Output: Descriptive model B*
```

This idea can be easily extended for model integration in distributed learning environment. In distributed data mining, a set of distributed learned base models are used collaboratively to make predictions based on a *prediction scheme* such as a simple voting or the arbiter-combiner model of Chan and Stolfo [5]. We can therefore regard such a set of base models together with its prediction scheme as a black box. *Knowledge Probing* approach can then be employed to derive a descriptive model which assimilates the knowledge of all base models.

Given a set of models (classifiers) $\mathcal{M} = \{M_j | j = 1, \ldots, k\}$, a prediction scheme $\mathcal{P}$ which uses the model set $\mathcal{M}$ to assign class values to unseen data items and a learning algorithm $\mathcal{L}$ which is capable of producing a descriptive model. A knowledge probing procedure can be extended as follows:

```
Input: A set S of n unseen data items,
       A set  M of k base models,
       A prediction scheme  P,
       A learning algorithm  L which provides descriptive output.
```

```
Prediction phase: creating the class values of data
                  items in S using the prediction scheme P
```

```
for i = 1 to n {
    for j = 1 to k {
        {c_ij = M_j(s_i) | M_j ∈ M, s_i ∈ S}
    }
    C_i = P(c_i1,...,c_ik)
}
```

```
Learning phase: learning from the new training set constructed
                from S together with the combined prediction values
```

$$B^* = \mathcal{L}(\ \{(s\_i,\ C\_i)\ |\ s\_i \in S,\ i = 1,\dots,n\}\ )$$

`Output: Descriptive model` B^*

The key step of the *KP* approach is to use an independent data set[1] to probe knowledge from all base models. Since the final model is learned from a data set whose class values are assigned by a prediction scheme, which integrates a set of predictions made by all base models, it then can be regarded as an approximation of the integration of the base models. Therefore, if the model B^* which is learned from the learning algorithm $\mathcal{L}$ has a descriptive representation, then the model in fact assimilates the knowledge of all base models in $\mathcal{M}$.

Implementing a high quality *KP* framework is a challenging research since the rich choices in implementing each component result in a high dimensional design space. Empirical studies is therefore crucial to understand the issues of constructing a high quality *KP* framework for distributed data mining. In the next section, we present the design of the experiments performed to study behaviours of *KP* framework.

3 Experimental Design

To investigate the behaviours of *KP* framework in comparison with the traditional learning approach[2], two corresponding sets of experiments are designed to be executed in parallel.

The detail of the design is as follow.

3.1 Data Preparation

The set of experiments are done on fifteen data sets from the UCI Repository of Machine Learning Databases [14]. We simulate distributed environment by partitioning training sets. Some part of the data set is used as a probing set. In order to provide a reasonable amount of data for the base model learning phase and probing phase, we chose the data sets which are relatively large in size (at least 1,000 instances). Another concern about data preparation is the size of the evaluation or test set. To make a reliable comparison between the two approaches, the result should have a small deviation. This requires the test set size to be relatively large. Bauer and Kohavi [2] observe that in some data sets,

---

[1] An approach to prepare this independent data set is expected to be a crucial further research issue of *KP*. Meanwhile, to avoid additional bias, the probing data set used in this study is independent from all data used to learn any base model. That is all data items in the probing set are separated from data used in the first learning phase.

[2] In this paper, we refer to the traditional learning approach as a learning process which takes a complete data set as an input and generates a single model as an output.

a learning algorithm can generate a high accuracy model by using only a small part of the training set. For example, in the MUSHROOM data set, training with 2/3rd of data usually results in 0% error. For this purpose, we have used the *Learning Curve* feature of $\mathcal{MLC}$++ [12] to generate learning curves of different training and test set sizes on chosen data sets. In selecting the training set size of each data set, we chose the size where the error is relatively low and there is a reasonable amount of data left to use as a test set. In this experiment, at least 60% of the data set is used as a test set. In addition, we also chose the point where the standard deviation of the estimation was not large in order to avoid the variability of learning from small training sets.

Details of all data sets and the percentage of data used as in training are described in Table 1.

Data Set	Size	Attribute		Missing value(%)	#Class	Data Density	Entropy	training size (%)
		Discrete	Cont.					
Real World Data Set								
ABALONE	4,177	1	7	0	29	6.12×10^{-16}	1.00	20
ADULT	48,842	8	6	0.95	2	4.01×10^{-17}	0.79	30
GERMAN	1,000	13	7	0	2	1.02×10^{-13}	0.88	40
HYPOTHYROID	3,163	18	7	6.74	2	1.29×10^{-17}	0.28	40
CHESS	3,196	36	0	0	2	3.10×10^{-08}	1.00	20
LETTER	20,000	0	16	0	26	1.08×10^{-15}	4.70	20
MUSHROOM	8,124	22	0	1.39	2	4.96×10^{-12}	1.00	20
NURSERY	12,960	8	0	0	5	1.00	1.72	30
SATELLITE	6,435	0	36	0	7	1.58×10^{-64}	-	20
SEGMENT	2,310	0	19	0	7	1.57×10^{-44}	2.81	30
SHUTTLE	58,000	0	9	0	7	4.03×10^{-14}	0.96	20
SICK	3,162	18	7	6.74	2	8.60×10^{-18}	0.45	40
THYROID	3,772	22	7	5.54	5	Inf	-	40
Artificial Data Set								
LED7	2,000	7	0	0	10	15.60	3.32	30
WAVEFORM	5,000	0	40	0	3	1.55×10^{-108}	1.58	20

Table 1. Details of all data sets used in the experiments.

3.2 Overall Design

To ensure the fairness of the comparison, each experiment is separated into three phases: data preparation phase, distributed committee learning phase and Knowledge Probing phase. The data preparation is done once for each data set. The same training and evaluation sets are then used in the later phases for both sequential and distributed approaches, which are executed parallelly. In each of those experiments, given a data set, a learning algorithm L, a prediction scheme

P and some parameters, i.e. number of partitions, the experiments are designed as follows.

Data Preparation Phase

1. According to our previous studies [15, 10], we randomly divide the data set into two parts, T and PS with the proportion of 90 % and 10% respectively. PS is used as a probing set in the second phase of the framework. T is kept to be further divided in the next phase.
2. T is randomly divided into D and E. D is used as a data set from which we further sample training sets. According to the suggestion of Kohavi and Wolpert [13], D is made twice the size of the desired training set size which is chosen from points in the *Learning Curve*. E is use as an evaluation set. The size of E is designed to be at least 40% of T.
3. Ten sample sets (training sets) x are generated from D by using uniform random sampling without replacement.

First Phase: Distributed Committee Learning

1. In each sample set x from the previous phase, we perform a mutually exclusive partitioning of the data into n roughly equal subsets. (Here, we used n equals to four.)
2. With a given learning algorithm L, we learn a model from each subset and call it a *base model*.
3. A set of n *base models* together with the prediction scheme P are then evaluated on the evaluation set E.

Parallelly, the sequential learning is done as follows:

1. A learning algorithm L is used to learn a single model M_s from a sample set x.
2. M_s is then evaluated on the evaluation set E.

Second Phase: Knowledge Probing

1. The set of n *base models* from the first phase is used to generate n sets of predictions on the probing set PS.
2. A prediction scheme P is then used to combine those n sets of predictions into a set of combined prediction C_{d2}.
3. A probing set PS with new class values from C_{d2} is then learned by L and output a final model F_d.
4. Model F_d is then evaluated on the evaluation set E.

Parallelly, the sequential learning is done as follows:

1. Model M_s is used to give a set of predictions C_{s2} on the probing set PR.
2. The probing set PR with the new assigned class value from C_{s2} is then learned by L and output the final model F_s.
3. F_s is evaluated on the evaluation set E.

In this study, we use C4.5 as a learning algorithm (L), a probabilistic prediction[3] as a prediction scheme (P) and we use number of partitions equal to four.

4 Experimental Results and Analysis

The results of the experiments on fifteen data sets of the *Distributed Committee Learning* phase (first phase) and the *Knowledge Probing* phase (second phase) are listed in table 2. The results of each experiment (on one data set) were average over ten trials of samples.

Data Set	Accuracy				Tree size	
	First phase		Second phase			
	Sequential	Distributed	Sequential	Distributed	Sequential	Distributed
ABALONE	20.7672	22.4479	20.5410	22.2749	146.10	123.30
ADULT	84.1456	84.5841	83.9809	84.3332	196.30	158.50
GERMAN	66.0167	68.3565	65.7103	66.3788	18.10	13.50
HYPOTHYROID	98.4622	97.6889	97.6274	97.3374	5.20	4.80
CHESS	94.3221	94.0498	94.3105	94.0614	18.20	11.60
LED7	70.0000	70.4729	68.2337	68.4979	28.20	26.20
LETTER	67.1896	63.8235	64.2143	59.0777	414.20	483.40
MUSHROOM	99.3959	98.5480	99.1224	98.5183	17.70	11.20
NURSERY	91.8028	89.8842	90.3773	89.4555	87.90	52.00
SATELLITE	79.4363	80.3299	78.1628	77.7704	47.80	47.80
SEGMENT	90.8063	87.3406	87.9061	84.5728	23.40	21.60
SHUTTLE	99.6539	99.5176	99.5755	99.4840	19.60	8.60
SICK	97.0650	96.7838	96.9684	96.6608	9.60	9.70
THYROID	98.5856	97.5691	98.1547	97.0718	7.00	6.20
WAVEFORM	69.2108	73.3160	68.5698	68.6439	74.20	84.20

Table 2. The average accuracy and tree size (over 10 trials) of both learning phases.

Comparison between Phases The average accuracy in Table 2 showed that in the aspect of accuracy, the probed models of both distributed and sequential approaches appear to have lower accuracy than the model from the first phase, which is what we expected. Because this framework comprises of two phases of learning and it is the fact that in each learning phase, an inductive bias has to be introduced to cut down the search space, which can also introduce additional

---

[3] In probabilistic prediction, each base model gives a prediction as a set of probabilities of each class. The probabilities from all base models are then summed according to the class. The final prediction is the class of the highest probability.

error to the final result. The difference in accuracy between both phases can be viewed as an additional error introduced by *KP*, which the average additional error over all data sets is 0.89 % in sequential case and 1.37 % in distributed case.

Comparison between Sequential and Distributed Approaches In the first phase, six data sets in distributed approach have shown an improvement in accuracy between 0.44 - 4.11 % while there is such an improvement between 0.07 - 1.73 % in five data sets in the second phase. Nonetheless, the accuracy of the distributed approach is still relatively comparable to the sequential one. The difference in accuracy between these two approaches in the first phase can be considered as the error introduced by distributed committee learning. In this study, the average additional error is 0.14 %. In the aspect of size of the probed tree, the results from Table 2 showed that eleven out of fifteen data sets have shown an decrease in tree size.

Therefore, in general, the accuracy of the models from the distributed approach of both steps have shown to be comparable to the ones of the sequential approach while the probed trees of the first approach have shown to be relatively smaller.

5 Conclusion and Further Work

In this paper, we have presented our ongoing research on *Knowledge Probing* as a new approach towards distributed data mining. Preliminary experiments have shown that the framework can be an effective approach in producing a model of comparable quality to the traditional approach by assimilating knowledge from distributed learned models. We are now investigating various issues of building up a distributed data mining framework based on the knowledge probing approach. In particular, currently we are studying an impact of properties of a probing set to the quality of the final model. It is also a very interesting research to studying the theoretical performance model of the framework. Some interesting researches on applying Bayesian learning theory for estimating performance of distributed learning, such as the work of Yamanishi [16], has an influence on our research on this subject.

KP framework provides a general method for knowledge assimilation in various scenarios of data mining including extracting knowledge from neural networks, integrating different data mining tasks (e.g. combing a regression procedure with classification) and incremental learning. A range of applications of the knowledge probing methodology will be investigated in our future work.

References

1. K. M. Ali and M. J. Pazzani. Error reduction through learning multiple descriptions. *Machine Learning*, 24(3):173–202, September 1996.

2. E. Bauer and R. Kohavi. An empirical comparison of voting classification algorithms: Bagging, boosting and variants. *Machine Learning*, Submitted:1–33, 1998.
3. L. Breiman. Heuristics of instability in model selection. Technical report, Statistics Department, University of California at Berkeley, California, 1994.
4. L. Breiman. Bagging predictors. *Machine Learning*, 24:123–140, 1996.
5. P. Chan and S. Stolfo. Meta-learning for multistrategy and parallel learning. In *Proceeding of the Second International Work on Multistrategy Learning*, pages 150–165, 1993.
6. P. Chan and S. Stolfo. Toward parallel and distributed learning by meta-learning. In *In Working Notes AAAI Work. Knowledge Discovery in Databases*, pages 227–240. AAAI, 1993.
7. P. Chan and S. Stolfo. On the accuracy of meta-learning for scalable data mining. *Journal of Intelligent Information System*, 8:5–28, 1996.
8. Y. Freund and R. E. Schapire. A decision-theoretic generalization of on-line learning and an application to boosting. In *Proceedings of the Second European Conference on Computational Learning Theory*, pages 23–37. Springer Verlag, 1995.
9. Y. Guo, S. Rüeger, J. Sutiwaraphun, and J. Forbes-Millott. Meta-learning for parallel data mining. In *Proceedings of the Seventh Parallel Computing Workshop*, pages 1–2. Fujitsu Laboratories Ltd., November 1997.
10. Y. Guo and J. Sutiwaraphun. Knowledge probing in distributed data mining. Technical report, Department of Computing, Imperial College, September 1998.
11. L. K. Hansen and P. Salamon. Neural network ensembles. *IEEE Transactions on Pattern Analysis and Machine Intelligence*, 12(10):993–1001, 1990.
12. R. Kohavi, D. Sommerfield, and J. Dougherty. Data mining using MLC++: A machine learning library in C++. In *Tools With Artificial Intelligence 1996*, pages 234–245. IEEE Computer Society Press, November 1996. http://www.sgi.com/Technology/mlc.
13. R. Kohavi and D. Wolpert. Bias plus variance decomposition for zero-one loss functions. In L. Saitta, editor, *Machine Learning: Proceedings of the Thirteenth International Conference*, pages 275–283. Morgan Kaufmann, 1996.
14. C. J. Merz and P. M. Murphy. UCI repository of machine learning databases. University of California, Department of Information and Computer Science, http://www.ics.uci.edu/~mlearn/MLRepository.html, 1996.
15. J. Sutiwaraphun. Investigating into distributed data mining. Technical report, Department of Computing, Imperial College, May 1998.
16. K. Yamanishi. Distributed cooperative bayesian learning strategies. In *Proceedings of the 1997 10th Annual Conference on Computational Learning Theory*, pages 250–262, Nashville, TN, July 1997. ACM, New York.

Discovery of Equations and the Shared Operational Semantics in Distributed Autonomous Databases

Zbigniew W. Raś and Jan M. Żytkow

Computer Science Dept. University of North Carolina, Charlotte, N.C. 28223
e-mail: ras@uncc.edu & zytkow@uncc.edu
also Institute of Computer Science, Polish Academy of Sciences

Abstract. Empirical equations are an important class of regularities that can be discovered in databases. In this paper we concentrate on the role of equations as definitions of attribute values. Such definitions can be used in many ways that we briefly describe. We present a discovery mechanism that specializes in finding equations that can be used as definitions. We introduce the notion of shared operational semantics. It consists of an equation-based system of partial definitions and it is used as a tool for knowledge exchange between independently built databases. This semantics augments the earlier developed semantics for rules used as attribute definitions. To put the shared operational semantics on a firm theoretical foundation we developed a formal interpretation which justifies empirical equations in their definitional role.

1 Shared semantics for distributed autonomous DB

In many fields, such as medical, manufacturing, banking, military and educational, similar databases are kept at many sites. Each database stores information about local events and uses attributes suitable for a local task, but since the local situations are similar, the majority of attributes are compatible among databases. Yet, an attribute may be missing in one database, while it occurs in many others. For instance, different military units may apply the same battery of personality tests, but some tests may be not used in one unit or another. Similar irregularities are common with medical data. Different tests may be applied in different hospitals.

Missing attributes lead to problems. A recruiter new at a given unit may query a local database S_1 to find candidates who match a desired description, only to realize that one component a_1 of that description is missing in S_1 so that the query cannot be answered. The same query would work in other databases but the recruiter is interested in identifying suitable candidates in S_1.

In this paper we introduce operational semantics that provides definitions of missing attributes. Definitions are discovered by an automated process. They are used for knowledge exchange between databases and jointly form an integrated semantics of our Distributed Autonomous Knowledge System.

The task of integrating established database systems is complicated not only by the differences between the sets of attributes but also by differences in structure and semantics of data, for instance, between the relational, hierarchical and network data models. We call such systems heterogeneous. The notion of an intermediate model, proposed by Wiederhold, is very useful in dealing with the heterogeneity problem, because it describes the database content at a relatively high abstract level, sufficient to guarantee homogeneous representation of all databases. In this paper we propose a discovery layer to be an intermediate model for networked databases. Our discovery layer contains rules and equations extracted from a database.

To eliminate the heterogeneity problem D. Maluf and G. Wiederhold [5] proposed to use an ontology algebra which provides the capability for interrogating many knowledge resources, which are largely semantically disjoint, but where *articulations* have been established that enable knowledge interoperability. The main difference between our approaches is that they do not use the intermediate model for communication, and they did not consider automated discovery systems as knowledge sources.

Navathe and Donahoo [6] proposed that the database designers develop a metadata description (an intermediate model) of their database schema. A collection of metadata descriptions can then be automatically processed by a schema builder to create a partially integrated global schema of a heterogeneous distributed database. In contrast, our intermediate model (a discovery layer) is built without any help from database designers. Its content is created through the automated knowledge extraction from databases.

1.1 Methods that can construct operational definition

Many computational mechanisms can be used to define values of an attribute. Ras et al. [4], [11] (1989-1990) introduced a mechanism which first seeks and then applies as definitions rules in the form "If Boolean-expression(x) then a(x)=w" which are partial definitions of attribute a. Recently, Prodromidis & Stolfo [8] mentioned attribute definitions as a useful task. In this paper we expand attribute definitions from rules to equations. We call them operational definitions because each is a mechanism by which the values of a defined attribute can be computed. Many are partial definitions, as they apply to subsets of records that match the "if" part of a definition.

1.2 Shared semantics in action: query answering

Many real-world situations fit the following generic scenario. A query q that uses attribute a is "unreachable" at database S_1 because a is missing in S_1. A request for a definition of a is issued to other sites in the distributed autonomous database systems. The request specifies attributes $a_1, ..., a_n$ available at S_1. When attribute a and a subset $\{a_{i_1}, ..., a_{i_k}\}$ of $\{a_1, ..., a_n\}$ are available in another database S_2, a discovery mechanism is invoked to search for knowledge at S_2. A computational mechanism can be discovered by which values of a can be computed from values of some of $a_{i_1}, ..., a_{i_k}$. If discovered, such a mechanism is returned to site s_1 and used to compute the unknown values of a that occur in query q.

The same mechanism can apply if attribute a is available at site s_1, but some values of a are missing. In that case, the discovery mechanism can be applied at s_1, if the number of the available values of a is sufficiently large.

2 Other applications

Functional dependencies in the form of equations are a succinct, convenient form of knowledge. They can be used in making predictions, explanations and inference. $a = r_m(a_1, a_2, ..., a_m)$ can be directly used to predict values $a(x)$ of a for object x by substituting the values of $a_1(x), a_2(x), ..., a_m(x)$ if all are available. If some are not directly available, they may be predicted by other equations.

When we suspect that some values of a may be wrong, an equation imported from another database may be used to verify them. An equation acquired at the same database may be used, too, if the discovery mechanism is able to distinguish the wrong values as the outliers. For instance, patterns discovered in clean data can be applied to discovery of wrong values in the raw data.

Equations that are used to compute missing values are empirical generalizations. Although they may be reliable, we cannot trust them unconditionally, and it is a good practice to seek their further verification, especially if they are applied to the expanded range of values of a. The verification may come from additional knowledge that can be used as alternative definitions. Ras [9], [10] (1997-1998) used rules coming from various sites and verified their consistency. His system can use many strategies which find rules describing decision attributes in terms of classification attributes. It has been used in conjunction with such systems like $LERS$ (developed by J. Grzymala-Busse) or $AQ15$ (developed by R. Michalski).

Equations that are generated at different sites can be used, too, to cross-check the consistency of knowledge and data coming from different databases. If the values of a computed by two independent equations are approximately equal, each of the equations receives further confirmation as a computational method for a.

All equations by which values of a can be computed expand the understanding of a. Attribute understanding is often initially inadequate when we receive a new dataset for the purpose of data mining. We may know the domain of values of a, but we do not understand a's detailed meaning, so that we cannot apply background knowledge and we cannot interpret the knowledge discovered about a. In such cases, an equation that links a poorly understood attribute a with attributes $a_1, ..., a_n$, the meaning of which is known, explains the meaning of a in terms of $a_1, ..., a_n$.

3 Request (Quest) for a definition

For the purpose of inducing equations from data we could adapt various discovery systems [7][2]. We have chosen the 49er system (Zytkow and Zembowicz, 1993) because it applies to data available in databases and because it searches for equations that apply to subsets of data, in addition to equations that apply to all data. The system allows to describe one attribute as a function of other attributes and it seeks equations when attributes are numerical. It has demonstrated successful applications in many databases coming from various domains.

Special requirements are needed for an equation that can be used as a definition of a given numerical attribute. One of the main problems with the search for equations is that the best fit can be always found for any dataset in any class of models (equations). But is the best fit good enough? How good is good enough? Equations often provide rough estimates of patterns, but those estimates may be not good for definitions. How good must be a fit of an equation so that this equation can be used as a definition?

When we know the desired accuracy of fit, we know how to evaluate equations against data. In database applications there is a "natural" limit on the accuracy for those common attributes whose values are numerical and discrete. Consider an attribute whose values are integers, such as weight in pounds or age in years. The error (accuracy) of fit can be derived from the granularity of the domain. For any three adjacent values v_1, v_2, v_3 in the ascending order, the acceptable accuracy of determination of v_2 is $(v_3 - v_1)/4$. For instance, for the age in years, the accuracy is half a year. That error rate is entirely satisfactory, but sometime even a worse fit is still acceptable from a definition.

Consider the situations when the required accuracy of fit ε_i is provided for all data $(x_i, y_1, \varepsilon_i)$, $i = 1, ..., n$. For each candidate equation the probability can be estimated that $(x_i, y_1, \varepsilon_i)$, $i = 1, ..., n$ could have been generated by $f(x_i) + r_i$, where r_i is generated from normal distribution $N(0, \varepsilon)$. A demanding probability threshold such as $Q \geq 0.01$ is also needed.

In summary, the quest for a definition in the form of an equation includes:

- the attribute a for which a definition is sought in the form of an equation;
- the accuracy of attribute a for each value in the domain V_a of a;
- a set of attributes $\{a_1, ..., a_n\}$ which can be used in the definition;

The resultant equations, if any, have the form $a(x) = f(a_{i_1}, ..., a_{i_k})$, and they fit the data within a demanding probability threshold $Q = 0.01$, which is the default value for definitions.

3.1 Functionality Test

Plenty of time can be saved if equations are not sought in data which do not satisfy the mathematical definition of functional relationship.

Definition: Given a set D of value pairs (v_i, w_i), $i = 1, ..., N$ of two attributes a and b, and the range V_a of a; b **is a function of** a in V_a iff for each v_0 in V_a, there is exactly one value w_0 of b, such that (v_0, w_0) is in D.

The following algorithm approximates this definition. It determines whether it is worthwhile to search for an equation that fits the data.

Algorithm: Test approximate functional relationship between a and b
  given the contingency table of actual record counts and set V_a of values of a
  AV ← average number of records per cell
  for each value in V_a
    find all groups of cells with adjacent values of b and counts > AV
    if # of groups > α then return NO-FUNC
  if average # of groups > β then return NO-FUNC else return FUNCTION

This algorithm is controlled by two modifiable parameters, α and β, which measure local (α) and global (β) uniqueness of b; that is, the number of values of b for the same value of a. The default values used by 49er is $\alpha = 2$ for data from databases, and $\beta \approx 1.5$. For $\alpha = 3$ the functionality test fails when for a value in V_a there are more than 3 adjacent groups of cells with above average density of points. This higher value 3 of α solves the problem of rare outliers, allowing up to 2 outliers if they happen rarely. However, many outliers or frequent multiple values in y should fail the test, therefore the value of β is much smaller and close to 1. Note that both parameters set to 1 corresponds to the strict mathematical definition of functionality given above. Presence of error, noise, and other data imperfections force values of α and β to be larger than 1. The noise handling by varying the number of cells in the table is treated in detail by Żytkow & Zembowicz (1993).

The same mechanism applies when we want to determine a functional relation in a set of data tuples D of the size $1 + k$ for $k \geq 2$. If the test is successful, equations in the form $b(x) = r(b_1, ..., b_k)$ are sought. If the test fails, it will be applied to subsets of data when they are generated by 49er.

3.2 Equation Finder's search

The task of equation finding can be formally defined by the input of n datapoints which come from projection of attributes a and b from data table S, and the computation of required accuracy of b: $(v_i, w_i, \varepsilon_i)$, $i = 1, ..., n$. The output is the list of acceptable equations. Since the equations are initially 2-d and can be subsequently refined, the acceptance threshold is at this stage less demanding $(Q \geq 0.0001)$

Equation Finder's search can be decomposed into (1) generation of new terms, (2) selection of pairs of terms, (3) generation and evaluation of equations for each pair of terms. The combination of these three searches can be summarized by the following algorithm:

Algorithm: Find Equation
  T ← (A B)   ; the initial list of terms for search #1
  old-T ← NIL   ; the list of terms already used
  E ← a set of polynomial equation models   ; list of models for search #3
  loop until new terms in T exceed threshold of complexity

```
2T ← list of new pairs of terms created from T and old-T
        ; the list generated by search #2, initially (A B)
for each pair in 2T and for each model in E
    find and evaluate the best equation
if at least one equation accepted, then
    return all accepted equations and HALT the search
old-T ← old-T augmented with T
T ← list of new terms created from old-T
```

For each pair of terms (either original attributes a and b or terms x and y) generated by search #1, and for each polynomial up to the maximum pre-specified degree, search # 3 proposes polynomial models $y = f(x, a_0, \ldots, a_q)$, which are then solved for b, if possible, and compared with the models considered earlier. For each equation which comes out as a new one, the best values are found for the parameters (coefficients) a_0, ..., a_q, and error values ε_{a_0}, ..., ε_{a_q} for each parameter. Each polynomial coefficient for which $|a_i| < \varepsilon_{a_i}$ is removed. The equation is accepted as a definition of b by a if the significance measure exceeds a threshold, set to 0.01. If that threshold is not met, a refinement process (not treated in this paper) applies to the equation if the significance measure exceeds a threshold, set by default at 0.0001. The significance is based on χ^2 test and the number of degrees of freedom, that is on the number of data points minus the number of parameters in the equation.

Correlation analysis is often used as a measure of linearity of a relation. Our approach offers a far broader search for equations. Many textbook examples show that correlation values are close to zero (that means, no correlation) even though a sharp functional dependency occurs in the data. Our Equation Finder returns well-fitted equations in many such cases.

3.3 Efficiency

The functionality test operates on contingency tables. Since the size of the table is typically small compared to the size of data, and the test requires one pass through the table, it is extremely efficient. It also saves large amount of time because it prevents a far more costly equation finding search, when it cannot be successful. Generation of a contingency table is linear in the number of records. The number of contingency tables is linear in the number of attributes considered. If the number of original attributes is very large, various techniques of feature selection can be used to reduce their number. For a comprehensive treatment of feature selection, see [3]. Sampling, in turn, can reduce the number of records. Equation finding is linear in the number of records and is proportional to the number of models considered. The space of Equation Finder search can be limited in different ways by setting the parameter values for each search, such as depth of search and the list of operators. The potentially most costly is search in the subsets of data, but it can be also adjusted to the available resources, by limiting the depth of search.

4 A shared semantics of equations in a Distributed Autonomous Knowledge System

In this section each *database* in Distributed Autonomous Database Systems will be extended to a *knowledge system*. We first recall the notions of an information system and a distributed information system. Next we define the shared meaning of attributes in a Distributed Autonomous Knowledge System $DAKS$.

By an **information system** we mean a structure $S = (X, A, V)$, where X is a finite set of objects, A is a finite set of attributes, and $V = \bigcup\{V_a : a \in A\}$ is a set of their values. We assume that:

- V_a, V_b are disjoint for any $a, b \in A$ such that $a \neq b$,
- $a : X \longrightarrow V_a$ is a function for every $a \in A$.

Instead of a, we will often write $a_{[S]}$ to denote that a in an attribute in S.

By a **distributed information system** [9] we mean a pair $DS = (\{S_i\}_{i \in I}, L)$ where:

- I is a set of sites.
- $S_i = (X_i, A_i, V_i)$ is an information system for any $i \in I$,
- L is a symmetric, binary relation on the set I,

In this paper we assume a distributed information system $DS = (\{S_i\}_{i \in I}, L)$ which is consistent, that is,

$$(\forall i)(\forall j)(\forall x \in X_i \cap X_j)(\forall a \in A_i \cap A_j)\ (a_{[S_i]}(x) = (a_{[S_j]})(x).$$

In the remainder of this paper we assume that $DS = (\{S_i\}_{i \in I}, L)$ is a distributed information system which is consistent. Also, we assume that $S_j = (X_j, A_j, V_j)$ and $V_j = \bigcup\{V_{ja} : a \in A_j\}$, for any $j \in I$.

We will use A to name the set of all attributes in DS, $A = \bigcup\{A_j : j \in I\}$.

4.1 Shared operational semantics

The shared semantics (see [12]) is defined for the set A of all attributes in all information systems in DS. For each attribute a in A, the operational meaning of a is defined by:

1. the set of (pointers to) information systems in which a is available: $\{S_i : a \in A_i\}$;
2. the set of information systems in which a definition of a has been derived, jointly with the set of definitions in each information system. Definitions can be equations, boolean forms, etc.
3. the set of information systems in which a definition of a can be used, because the defining attributes are available there. An attribute a is a defined attribute in an information system S if:
   (a) a definition DEF of a has been discovered in an S_i in DS;
   (b) all other attributes in the definition DEF are present in S; in such cases they can be put together in a JOIN table and DEF can be directly applied.

4.2 Equations as partial definitions: the syntax

We will now define the syntax of definitions in the form of equations. Partial definitions are included, as they are often useful. In the next subsection we give an interpretation of partial definitions.

Functors are the building blocks from which equations and inequalities can be formed. Those in turn are the building blocks for partial definitions. Assume that x is a variable over X_i and $r_1, r_2, ..., r_k$ are functors. Also, we assume here that m_j is the number of arguments of the functor r_j, $j = 1, 2, .., k$. The number of arguments can be zero. A zero argument functor is treated as a constant.

By a set of $s(i)$-atomic-terms we mean the least set $T0_i$ such that:

- $0, 1 \in T0_i$,

for any symbolic attribute $a \in A_j$,

- $[a(x) = w] \in T0_i$ for any $a \in A_i$ and $w \in V_{ia}$,
- $\sim [a(x) = w] \in T0_i$ for any $a \in A_i$ and $w \in V_{ia}$,

for any numerical attributes $a, a_1, a_2, ..., a_{m_j}$ in A_i,

- $[a \; \rho \; r_j(a_1, a_2, ..., a_{m_j})](x) \in T0_i$, where $\rho \in \{=, \leq, \geq\}$

$s(i)$-atomic-terms of the form $[a(x) = w]$ and $[a = r_j(a_1, a_2, ..., a_{m_j})](x)$ are called equations.

By a set of $s(i)$-partial-definitions (it s(i)-p-defs in short) we mean the least set T_i such that:

- if $t(x) \in T0_i$ is an equation, then $t(x) \in T_i$,
- if $t(x)$ is a conjunction of $s(i)$-atomic-terms and $s(x)$ is an equation, then $[t(x) \longrightarrow s(x)] \in T_i$,
- if $t_1(x), t_2(x) \in T_i$, then $(t_1(x) \vee t_2(x)), (t_1(x) \wedge t_2(x)) \in T_i$.

For simplicity we often write t instead of $t(x)$.

The set $s(I)$-p-defs represent all possible candidate definitions built from attributes that can come from different information systems in DS. $s(I)$-p-defs is defined in a similar way to $s(i)$-p-defs: the set V_i is replaced by $\bigcup\{V_j : j \in I\}$ and the set A_i is replaced by $\bigcup\{A_j : j \in I\}$.

4.3 Equations as partial definitions: the interpretation

By a standard interpretation of $s(i)$-p-defs in $S_i = (X_i, A_i, V_i)$ of a distributed information system DS we mean a function M_i such that:

- $M_i(0) = \emptyset$, $M_i(1) = X_i$
- $M_i(a(x) = w) = \{x \in X_i : a_{[S_i]}(x) = w\}$,
- $M_i(\sim (a(x) = w)) = \{x \in X_i : a_{[S_i]}(x) \neq w\}$,
- for any $\rho \in \{=, \leq, \geq\}$,
  $M_i((a \; \rho \; r_j(a_1, a_2, ..., a_{m_j}))(x)) =$
  $\{x \in X_i : a_{[S_i]}(x) \; \rho \; r_j(a_{1[S_i]}(x), a_{2[S_i]}(x), ..., a_{m_j[S_i]}(x))\}$,

- $M_i([t \longrightarrow s]) = \{x \in X_i : \text{if } [x \in M_i(t)] \text{ then } x \in M_i(s)]\}$,
- if t_1, t_2 are $s(i)$-p-$defs$, then
  $M_i(t_1 \vee t_2) = M_i(t_1) \cup M_i(t_2), \ M_i(t_1 \wedge t_2) = M_i(t_1) \cap M_i(t_2)$,
  $M_i(t_1 = t_2) = (\text{if } M_i(t_1) = M_i(t_2) \text{ then } True \text{ else } False)$.

Let us assume that $[t1 \longrightarrow (a_1(x) = w1)], [t2 \longrightarrow (a_2(x) = w2)]$ are $s(i)$-p-$defs$. We say that they are S_i-consistent, if either $a_1 \neq a_2$ or $M_i(t_1 \wedge t_2) = \emptyset$ or $w1 = w2$. Otherwise, these two $s(i)$-p-$defs$ are called S_i-inconsistent.

Similar definitions apply when $w1$ and $w2$ in those partial definitions are replaced by $r_1(a_1, a_2, ..., a_{m_j})(x)$ and $r_2(a_1, a_2, ..., a_{m_j})(x)$.

5 Discovery layer

In this section, we introduce the notions of a discovery layer and a distributed autonomous knowledge system. Also, we introduce the concept of a dynamic operational semantics to reflect the dynamics of constantly changing discovery layers.

Notice that while in the previous sections $s(i)-p-defs$ have been interpreted at the sites at which all relevant attributes have been present, we now consider $s(I) - defs$ imported from site k to site i.

By a discovery layer D_{ki} we mean any $s(i)$-consistent set of $s(k)-p-defs$, of the two types specified below, which are satisfied, by means of the interpretation M_k, by most of the objects in S_k:

- $[t \longrightarrow [(a = r_m(a_1, a_2, ..., a_m))(x)]]$, where $a_1, a_2, ..., a_m \in A_i$ and $a \in A_k$ and t is a conjunction of atomic terms that contain attributes that occur both in A_i and in A_k
- $[t \longrightarrow (a(x) = w)]$, where $a \in A_k$ and t satisfies the same conditions as above.

Suppose that a number of partial definitions have been imported to site i from a set of sites K_i. All those definitions can be used at site i.

Thus, the discovery layer for site $i \in I$ is defined as a subset of the set $D_i = \bigcup\{D_{ki} : k \in K_i\}$.

By Distributed Autonomous Knowledge System $(DAKS)$ we mean $DS = (\{(S_i, D_i)\}_{i \in I}, L)$ where $(\{S_i\}_{i \in I}, L)$ is a distributed information system and D_i is a discovery layer for a site $i \in I$.

Figure 1 shows the basic architecture of $DAKS$ (WWW interface and a query answering system $kdQAS$ that can request and use $s(I)$-p-$defs$ are also added to each site of $DAKS$).

Predicate logic and i-operational semantics are used to represent knowledge in $DAKS$. Many other representations are, of course, possible. We have chosen predicate logic because of the need to manipulate $s(I) - defs$ syntactically without changing their meaning. This syntactical manipulation of $s(I)$-$defs$ will be handled by $IQAS$. By designing an axiomatic system which is sound we are certain that the transformation process for $s(I)$-p-$defs$ based on these axioms

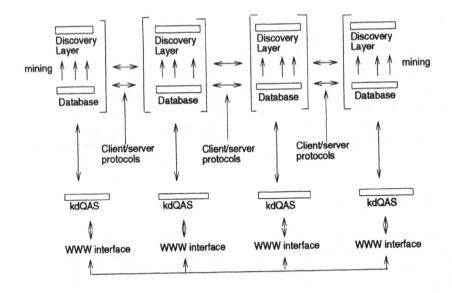

Fig. 1. Distributed Autonomous Knowledge System

either will not change their meaning or will change it in a controlled way. It will produce $s(i)$-p-$defs$ approximating the initial $s(I)$-p-$defs$.

Clearly, if for each non-local attribute we collect rules and equations from many sites of $DAKS$ and then resolve all inconsistencies among them, the resulting rules and equations in the local discovery layer have more chance to be locally true.

Let M_i be a standard interpretation of $s(i)$-p-$defs$ in S_i and $C_i = \bigcup\{V_k : k \in I\} - V_i$. By i-operational semantics of $s(I)$-p-$defs$ in $DS = (\{(S_i, D_i)\}_{i \in I}, L)$ where $S_i = (X_i, A_i, V_i)$ and $V_i = \bigcup\{V_{ia} : a \in A_i\}$, we mean the interpretation N_i such that:

- $N_i(0) = \emptyset$, $N_i(1) = X_i$
- for any $w \in V_{ia}$,
  $N_i(a(x) = w) = M_i(a(x) = w)$, $N_i(\sim (a(x) = w)) = M_i(\sim (a(x) = w))$
- for any $w \in C_i \cap V_{ka}$ where $k \neq i$,
  $N_i(a(x) = w) = \{x \in X_i : ([t \longrightarrow [a(x) = w]] \in D_i \wedge x \in M_i(t))\}$
  $N_i(\sim (a(x) = w)) = \{x \in X_i : (\exists v \in V_a)[(v \neq w) \wedge ([t \longrightarrow [a(x) = v]] \in D_i) \wedge (x \in M_i(t))]\}$
- for any $w \in C_i \cap V_{ka}$ where $k \neq i$ and a is a numeric attribute,
  $N_i((a(x) = w)) = \bigcup\{x \in X_i : (\exists y \in M_k[a(y) = w = r_m(a_1, a_2, ..., a_m)])$
  $[M_i([a_{1[S_i]}(x) = a_{1[s_k]}(y)] \wedge [a_{2[S_i]}(x) = a_{2[s_k]}(y)] \wedge ... \wedge [a_{m[S_i]}(x) = a_{1[s_k]}(y)])$
  $\wedge [a(y) = w = r_m(a_1, a_2, ..., a_m)] \in D_i\}$
  $N_i(\sim (a(x) = w)) = X_i - N_i(a(x) = w)$
- for any $s(I)$-terms t_1, t_2
  $N_i(t_1 \vee t_2) = N_i(t_1) \cup N_i(t_2)$, $N_i(\sim (t_1 \vee t_2)) = (N_i(\sim t_1)) \cap (N_i(\sim t_2))$,

$N_i(t_1 \wedge t_2) = N_i(t_1) \cap N_i(t_2)$, $N_i(\sim (t_1 \wedge t_2)) = (N_i(\sim t_1)) \cup (N_i(\sim t_2))$, $N_i(\sim\sim t) = N_i(t)$.

- for any $s(I)$-terms t_1, t_2

$N_i(t_1 = t_2) = ($ if $N_i(t_1) = N_i(t_2)$ then $True$ else $False)$

The i-operational semantics N_i represents a pessimistic approach to evaluation of $s(I)$-p-$defs$ because of the way the non-local $s(I)$-$atomic$-$terms$ are interpreted (their lower approximation is taken).

References

1. Batini, C., Lenzerini, M., Navathe, S., "A comparative analysis of methodologies for database schema integration", in *ACM Computing Surveys*, Vol 18, No. 4, 1986, 325-364

2. Dzeroski, S. & Todorovski, L. 1993. Discovering Dynamics, *Proc. of 10th International Conference on Machine Learning*, 97-103.

3. Liu, H. & Motoda, H. 1998. *Feature selection for knowledge discovery and data mining*, Kluwer.

4. Maitan, J., Ras, Z., Zemankova, M., "Query handling and learning in a distributed intelligent system", in *Methodologies for Intelligent Systems, IV*, (Ed. Z.W. Ras), North Holland, 1989, 118-127

5. Maluf, D., Wiederhold, G., "Abstraction of representation for interoperation", in *Proceedings of Tenth International Symposium on Methodologies for Intelligent Systems*, LNCS/LNAI, Springer-Verlag, No. 1325, 1997, 441-455

6. Navathe, S., Donahoo, M., "Towards intelligent integration of heterogeneous information sources", in *Proceedings of the Sixth International Workshop on Database Re-engineering and Interoperability*, 1995

7. Nordhausen, B. & Langley, P. 1993. An Integrated Framework for Empirical Discovery, *Machine Learning*, *12*, 17-47.

8. Prodromidis, A.L. & Stolfo, S., "Mining databases with different schemas: Integrating incompatible classifiers", in *Proceedings of The Fourth Intern. Conf. onn Knowledge Discovery and Data Mining*, AAAI Press, 1998, 314-318

9. Ras, Z., "Resolving queries through cooperation in multi-agent systems", in *Rough Sets and Data Mining* (Eds. T.Y. Lin, N. Cercone), Kluwer Academic Publishers, 1997, 239-258

10. Ras, Z., Joshi, S., "Query approximate answering system for an incomplete DKBS", in *Fundamenta Informaticae Journal*, IOS Press, Vol. 30, No. 3/4, 1997, 313-324

11. Ras, Z., Zemankova, M, "Intelligent query processing in distributed information systems", in *Intelligent Systems: State of the Art and Future Directions*, Z.W. Ras, M. Zemankova (Eds), Ellis Horwood Series in Artificial Intelligence, London, England, November, 1990, 357-370

12. Żytkow, J. An interpretation of a concept in science by a set of operational procedures, in: *Polish Essays in the Philosophy of the Natural Sciences*, Krajewski W. ed. Boston Studies in the Philosophy of Science, Vol.68, Reidel 1982, p.169–185.

13. Żytkow, J. & Zembowicz, R., "Database Exploration in Search of Regularities", in *Journal of Intelligent Information Systems*, No. 2, 39-81

14. Żytkow, J.M., Zhu, J., and Zembowicz R. Operational Definition Refinement: a Discovery Process, *Proceedings of the Tenth National Conference on Artificial Intelligence*, The AAAI Press, 1992, p.76–81.

The Data-Mining and the Technology of Agents to Fight the Illicit Electronic Messages

A. Zighed[1], M. Côté[2], N. Troudi[2]

[1] ERIC, Université Lumière Lyon 2, France
zighed@univ-lyon2.fr
[2] Computer Science Department, Université Laval, Canada
{mcote, troudi}@iad.ift.ulaval.ca

Abstract. The SPAMS are these undesirable messages that we receive by the slant of the electronic mail and that promise us glory and fortune or stun us of political slogans or violent or pornographic contents. The following article shows how to use techniques of data mining, like methods of supervised learning based on induction graphs, to analyse these Spams in order to be able to eliminate them from our electronic mail.

1 Introduction

We now find, in our electronic mails, so much messages, the Spams, that goes from advertising to pornographic pictures and any kind of propaganda.

USENET is strongly used by the Spamers[1] to reach a thousands of subscribers quickly. Internet suppliers appraise that 30% of the received messages are illicit messages. We see better the size of this problem by remembering that between 1995 and 1998, the data volume transmitted every day via USENET [3] passed from 586 MB to more than 5 go. That doesn't include messages directly sent in our electronic mailboxes. That is why we must try to reduce the volume of infiltration of these messages.

2 Anti-Spams techniques

Numerous computer companies try to find tools to fight the Spams. Software proposed up to now are relatively simple. Most of anti-Spams softwares use only the messages header to filter them. Seeing that the Spammers were able to bypass the rules of anti-Spams softwares, programmers decided to also analyse the content of messages. Techniques to fight Spams using rules that combine keywords are not always adapted to the users reality. Other anti-spams figthing techniques have been tested [5], [1]

One of tracks that appeared us promising is the one proposed by [4] that introduces the concept of auto-training. This paper is in keeping this perspective.

---

[1] By this name, we designate the Spams authors.

3 Data-mining and learning

The limits of the classical approaches mentionned above incite us therefore to find an intelligent system capable to adjust itself to Spammers inventions and ingenuity. One solutions offers to us is to use Data-Mining techniques and more especially supervised training techniques.

In this reasearch, we set oneself two hierarchical target:

- The first is to create a software able to automaticly learn how to recognize Spams.
- The second aims to make this training incremental in order to allow the software to adjust to the new techniques of the Spammers.

There is a spam message archives available on Internet *ftp.spam-archive.org*. The idea is to donwload these undesirable messages and to attach them messages that we could qualify of legal. These last could be all our stocked messages. At the end, we get a training basis and test for training algorithms.

4 Learning data

We downloaded on the FTP site *ftp.spam-archive.org*, 10 000 English Spams. Training techniques that we consider to use work on table of data attribute-value, i.e. table of two dimensions in which rows represent messages and columns the attributes of each messages.

The Messages are in a natural state, i.e. in a variable length text whose format doesn't distinguish itself of others electronic messages that we receive everyday.

The first question is therefore to know how to transform these texts in a vector of descriptors "attribute=value". We use an approach based on n-grams that we are going now to describe.

The trigrams technique uses the frequency of three letter sequences in a big sample of a given language. The idea is to capture the intuition according to which it is, for example, more likely for a word that ends by "-ed " to be a English word, as well as it is more likely for a word ending by "-ez " to be French [6]. A trigram is a following of three characters in a text. For example, the word "dollar" include the trigrams "dol", "oll ", "lla " and "lar ". Trigrams are used in research on the natural language for grammatical analysis [2], for the orthographic spell checkers, for automatic character recognition systems, etc.

If we code every available message in the examples basis according to the frequency of a trigramme and that we wish an universal program, we risk to generate vectors that would reach 300 trillions of attributes. Theoretically we could certainly work on such descriptions but, in fact, few machines would support such volume of data. Actually some trigrams are not present whereas others are too frequent in all types of messages to be revealing of something. The idea is to study the manner to select informative trigrams for the training.

The least frequent trigrams can not be most applicable, because they are too specific. To determine this subset of trigrammes, we made a compilation of trigrams in 200 messages judged Spams that we took on the FTP site: ftp.spam-archive.org. Then, we ordered these trigrams according to their number of occurence in the 200 messages.

On the basis of the 200 analyzed Spams , we found 15889 different trigrams of which some have been observed more than 18000 times.

We selected arbitrarily 225 trigrams[2] having a frequency of apparition that appeared us reasonable: present at least 15 times. Currently, we study other strategies for selection.

The training file Ω_a is composed with 400 messages from which 200 are Spams messages and 200 messages non-spams[3]. For each message, ω we calculated the frequency of each 225 trigrams selected and added an attribute C indicating the class of adherence of the message. If the ω message is a Spam, we have $C(\omega) = 1$ otherwise, $C(\omega) = 2$.

All other available messages have been used subsequently as sample of validation.

5 Training method

We used the SIPINA method [7]. This method generalizes the notion of decision tree since it drives to graphs of induction no arborescent.

In the case of our study, all attributes are quantitative, the procedure of discretization rely upon a method called Fusbin [7] [8] that aims to determine, according to the criteria indicated higher, the best cutting point producing a bi-partition.

We have to specify that we used several strategies like CART [11], C4.5 [10], Chaid, etc. The goal of this paper is not to compare different methods but to show the feasibility of a anti-spams system combining the concept of trigram and techniques of data-mining.

6 Results

The graph generated by SIPINA in the learning phase is given by the figure 1 :

We note therefore that there are only two trigrams, the number 72 "Ts!" and the number 184 "Sgr", which almost separate the totality of two messages class. We can note that the rate of good recognition is 97 %. We can observe that on the 200 Spams only three have been classified in the second class and for the non-spams seven have only been classified in the first class.

---

[2] We choose 255 trigrams to reduce the computation time. Theoricaly, there is no limits.

[3] Non-spams have been provided by the Dr., Jacques Gélinas, PhD from the Decision Support Technologies team in Defence Research Establishment Val-Cartier (Canada) that we want to thank.

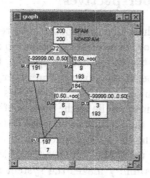

Fig. 1. Learning phase induction graph.

The validation file, that doesn't contain message of the training sample, is composed of 321 Spams and 279 Non-spams. The rate of recognition gotten on this validation sample is 97%, what confirms the training result.

7 Spam Miner

Spam Miner is an intelligent software agent which is capable:

- To find trigramms in a text,
- To compile these trigramms,
- To find the 225 necessary trigrams for the construction of a data base,
- To do the data mining (with SIPINA or another algorithm),
- To construct classification rules of messages from results of the knowledge extraction,
- To apply rules of classification found.

During an initial phase of intensive training, the user sorts out messages for the agent indicating which messages are Spams and which are not. The agent compiles the Spams and builds the list of the 225 necessary trigrams for the construction of the data base then constructs it. Applying the algorithm of data mining chosen, the agent finds a first set of rules to classify messages. Then comes a phase of validation and adjustment. The agent sorts out messages that enter in the mail and classify then in two groups via a system of flag: the group of Spams and the group of Non-spams. The user verifies that the agent classifies messages well and indicates him its mistakes. The agent will use these corrections to modify its 225 trigrams and to improve its data base and its classification rules. Days after days, the agent will become more effective, the user will trust him more and more and will have nearly no need to be preoccupied with the classification of its messages.

Spam Miner is endowed with a convivial graphic user interface, working under Windows. A user guide is presented in appendix. A copy of the software can be gotten freely by sending an e-mail to authors.

8 Conclusion and perspectives

In this work, we tried to show that it is possible to recognize a certain type of message as soon as we dispose of a set of examples. Some messages that we used for the training phase and the validation are specific, like the notion of Spams. Indeed, this concept can be, from a user to an other, variously discerned and go to lead to different results because training bases and validation would be different. The interest of our study lie in the quality of the step used rather than the general reach or not of the identification rules of the Spams.

The recommended methodology is applicable on other languages using the UNICODES characters by using the software Spam Miner directly. And more, the automatic training possibility makes the system more universal and more robust to change because it tris to constantly improve itself. Evidently there is always a space for the improvement of the concept and the performances. This technique could also be used for other purposes. For example, the process could be used by the available search bots on Internet [12]. We could also use this process to filter WEB pages accessed by our children and refuse their access if their content isn't suitable.

References

[1]   Email Remover, "anti-spams" component
       http://home.pacific.net.sg/~thantom/eremove.htm
[2]   Grammatical Trigrams description of statistic approaches for the modelization
       of the language.
       http://www.rxrc.xerox.com/publis/mltt/jadt/node2.html
[3]   Hobbes Internet Timeline,
       http://www.isoc.org/guest/zakon/Internet/History/HIT.html
[4]   Mail Jail,
       http://hotfiles.zdnet.com/cgi-bin/texis/swlib/hotfiles/info.html?fcode=000G3C
[5]   Spam Hater,
       http://www.cix.co.uk/~net-services/spam/spam_hater.htm
[6]   Trigram Technique,
       http://www.rxrc.xerox.com/publis/mltt/jadt/node2.html
[7]   Zighed, A., Rakotomalala, R.: Graphes d'induction et apprentissage machine.
       Hermès Paris. (1998) (to appear)
[8]   Zighed, A., Rabaseda, S., Rakotomalala, R., Feschet, F.: Discretization Methods
       in Supervised Learning. Encyclopedia Of Computer Science and Technology.
       Marcel Dekker. (1998) (to appear)
[9]   Rakotomalala, R.: Graphes d'induction. PhD Thesis, Université Claude Bernard
       - Lyon I. (1997)
[10]   Quinlan, J.R.: C4.5 Program for machine learning., Morgan Kaufman, San Mateo
       California, (1993)
[11]   Breiman, L., Friedman, J.H., Olshen, R.A., Stone, C.J.: Classification and re-
       gression trees, Belmont, CA, Wadsworth (1984)
[12]   Côté, M., Troudi, N.: NetSA : Une architecture multiagent pour la recherche sur
       Internet. L'EXPERTISE informatique, vol. 4, bfseries 1, (1999), 25-29

Knowledge Discovery in SportsFinder: An Agent to Extract Sports Results from the Web

Hongen Lu, Leon Sterling, Alex Wyatt

Intelligent Agent Laboratory
Department of Computer Science and Software Engineering
University of Melbourne, Parkville, VIC 3052, AUSTRALIA
{helu, leon}@cs.mu.oz.au

Abstract. There is a wealth of information to be mined from the World Wide Web. Unfortunately, standard natural language processing (NLP) extraction techniques perform poorly on the choppy, semi-structured information fragments, such as sports results, which are popular to be published on the Web pages nowadays. In this paper, we present an information agent: SportsFinder, an agent to extract sports scores from the World Wide Web, as well as the knowledge discovering method to learn new express patterns to improve the agent's performance.

1 Introduction

A wealth of on-line information can be made available to automatic processing by information extraction (IE) systems. Each IE application needs a separate set of rules tuned to the domain and writing style, which creates a knowledge engineering bottleneck [8].

This paper examines an alternative: learning the express patterns of on-line information and using these patterns to improve the IE system's performance. The domain of sports results was chosen for this research because of the fact that it highlights the contrast between the uniformity and diversity of information on the Web. The great popularity and appeal mean that very few generalisations can be made about people who publish sports results on-line. Consequently, there is a wide variety of different formats, languages and conventions used on sporting Web sites world-wide. It can be seen that the uniformity provided by conventions and the unambiguous nature of the results make the domain a plausible test bed for information extraction.

2 Agent Architecture

We present an information agent called SportsFinder, an agent to extract sports scores from the Web. The overall agent architecture is shown in Fig. 1. The agent is comprised of Knowledge Bases, Web Page Retriever, Game Unit Isolator, Score Expert and User Interface. All these components are implemented in Java.

User Interface. It is the interface between the user and the agent. User Interface gets the user's query and provides SportsFinder's result to the user. If

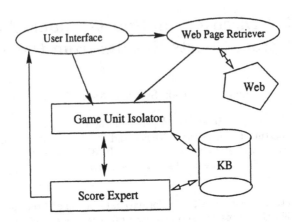

Fig. 1. SportsFinder's Architecture

the user's desired sport or competition is not in SportsFinder's knowledge bases, it will provide the dialog for users to add new knowledge to the system. The acquired knowledge from the user is added to relevant knowledge bases.

Knowledge Bases. They store the information needed to extract sports scores. There are two knowledge bases in this system: the world knowledge base and the domain knowledge base. The world knowledge base contains the information about where the sports results Web site is, and the protocol to contact them; the domain knowledge base contains the knowledge of a certain sport result, such as the biggest score one team can get in a soccer match.

Web Page Retriever. The task of the Web Page Retriever is to take the URL of the page where the results are stored and connect to that URL. If the URL is invalid, an error message is returned to the user. Otherwise, the Web Page Retriever fetches the content of that URL and passes it to the Game Unit Isolator.

Definition 1. Information Source: The content of the URL which stores sports scores SportsFinder extract from is an Information Source, denoted as $\mathcal{IS}$.

Definition 2. Game Unit : Let $S_t = <D_1, D_2, \ldots, D_n>$. If $\exists\, D_i \approx$ Name Given $\wedge\ \exists\, j$, k that $D_j, D_k \in$ Number then S_t is a Game Unit.

Game Unit Isolator. Game Unit Isolator segments information source into game units, which are the candidates to be extracted for sports scores, we formalise this process as: $\mathcal{IS} \longrightarrow S_1, S_2, \ldots, S_m$. Game Unit Isolator first looks for the user's selected name. It then finds the nearest HTML tag couples closing the given name, and if this segment is a Game Unit, then extracts its express pattern. When the user wants to know the standing of a player, Game Unit Isolator segments the information source into game units according the extracted express pattern. Once a Game Unit is identified, it is passed to the Score Expert.

Score Expert. Score Expert extracts and validates the sports scores from a Game Unit based on domain knowledge. In a Game Unit, there maybe several numbers to be the game score, score expert heuristically guesses which is mostly to be the game score based on the domain knowledge of a given sport.

3 Algorithm

3.1 Pattern Scanner

Instead of a fully natural language understanding method, we use the express patterns to recognise and extract the sports scores. It is just like semi understanding of the text. Although the sports results are very simple, their expressions in HTML vary wildly. We use HTML tags and some special characters to present the score patterns. For example, the HTML source for a soccer result is:

```
<TR> <TD WIDTH=180> ARSENAL </TD>
     <TD WIDTH=50> 5 - 0 </TD>
     <TD WIDTH=180> BARNSLEY </TD>
</TR>
```

and we define its express pattern as:

```
Pattern:: <TR> <TD *> TeamA </TD>
               <TD *> ScoreA - ScoreB </TD>
               <TD *> TeamB </TD>
          </TR>
```

the wild card '*' means to skip any number of characters until the next occurrence of the following term in the pattern, and '-' is a special character. Pattern scanner extracts the express patterns of a game unit.

3.2 Fuzzy Pattern Comparison

This algorithm calculates the similarity of two patterns. The similarity measure used here allows for arbitrary length deletions and insertions, that is to say the algorithm measures the biggest possible similarity of two patterns under certain allowed mismatches and internal deletions.

Let the two express patterns be $\tilde{A} = a_1 a_2 \cdots a_n$ and $\tilde{B} = b_1 b_2 \cdots b_m$. A similarity $s(a, b)$ is given between pattern elements a and b. Deletions of length k are given weight W_k. To find the high degrees of similarity, we set up a matrix H. H_{ij} is the maximum similarity of two segments ending in a_i and b_j, respectively.

First set $H_{k0} = H_{0l} = 0$ for $0 \le k \le n$ and $0 \le l \le m$.

$$H_{ij} = \max\{H_{i-1,j-1} + s(a_i, b_j), \max_{k \ge 1}\{H_{i-k,j} - W_k\}, \max_{l \ge 1}\{H_{i,j-l} - W_l\}, 0\}$$

for $1 \le i \le n$ and $l \le j \le m$.

The formula for H_{ij} is calculated as fellows:

1. If a_i and b_j are associated, the similarity is $H_{i-1,j-1} + s(a_i, b_j)$.
2. If a_i is at the end of a deletion of length k, the similarity is $H_{i-k,j} - W_k$.
3. If b_j is at the end of a deletion of length l, the similarity is $H_{i,j-l} - W_l$.
4. Finally, a zero is included to prevent calculated negative similarity, indicating no similarity up to a_i and b_j.

Definition 3. Possible Similarity: We define a function: $PosSim(\tilde{A}, \tilde{B}) \rightarrow [0, 1]$ to measure the biggest possible similarity of express patterns $\tilde{A}$ and $\tilde{B}$.

$$PosSim(\tilde{A}, \tilde{B}) = \max_{0 \leq i \leq n, 0 \leq j \leq m} \{H_{ij}\} / (\sum_{i=0}^{n} \sum_{j=0}^{m} s(a_i, b_j) - W_{|m-n|})$$

If $PosSim(\tilde{A}, \tilde{B})$ is greater than a threshold, then we consider $\tilde{A}$ and $\tilde{B}$ as the same express pattern. The algorithm for express pattern learning is summarised in Fig. 2.

---

1. Segment the $\mathcal{IS}$ into Game Units.
2. Scan the Game Unit's express pattern.
3. Match the Game Unit's express pattern with *known* patterns. If the value of $PosSim(\tilde{A}, \tilde{B})$ is greater than a threshold, success; Otherwise try another *known* pattern. If no pattern matched, back to step 2, select another Game Unit.
4. Validation. Validate the likely Team Name, query it to the *known* $\mathcal{IS}$.
5. Feedback. Present the user the result, if it is wrong try again or learn the pattern interactively. Add the recently learned pattern to the base.

Fig. 2. Algorithm for Learning New Express Patterns

4 Empirical Results

Our preliminary testing indicated that SportsFinder is able to successfully extract sports scores for a variety of sports with a high success rate. One test was on five randomly selected teams in each of nine competitions. In this 45 trials, SportsFinder was able to extract the correct results in 43 of them. The result is encouraging. And most impressively started with limited known express patterns, SportsFinder can improve its performance by learning new express patterns. This makes SportsFinder able to deal with the dynamic change of sports sites. Using the fuzzy pattern comparison algorithm, SportsFinder can calculate the position of a given team or player in a sports result ladder, like the results of golf and cycling. For example, in Fig. 3, by comparing the express patterns between lines, SportsFinder can give that Vijay Singh's position in 1997 NEC World Series of Golf Tournament is No. 6.

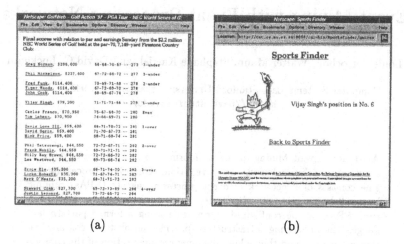

(a)   (b)

Fig. 3. (a) A Golf Tournament Web Page. (b) SportsFinder's Result.

5 Conclusion

As the Web grows dramatically, more and more new contents and express patterns will be available. SportsFinder is a step towards quick and easy extraction of needed information from the Web without having to rely on specialised programmers. In our test, SportsFinder can extract an ever-widening diversity of types of sports scores by learning new express patterns.

References

1. O. Etzioni, D. Weld, and R. Doorenbos. A Scalable Comparison-Shopping Agent for the World-Wide Web. In *Proceedings of the First International Conference on Autonomous Agents*, Feb. 1997.
2. D. Freitag. Toward Genaral-Purpose Learning for Information Extraction. In *Proceedings of COLING/ACL*, Jan. 1998.
3. D. Freitag. Information Extraction from HTML: Application of a General Machine Learning Approach. *AAAI-98*.
4. K. Hammond, R. Burke, C. Martin, and S. Lytinen. FAQ Finder: A Case-Based Approach to Knowledge Navigation. In *Working Notes of the AAAI Symposium on Information Gathering from Heterogeneous Distributed Environment*, 69-73, 1995
5. S. Huffman. Learning Information Extraction Patterns from Examples. *Connectionist, Statistical, and Symbolic Approaches to Learning for Natural Language Processing*, Springer, 246-260, 1996.
6. N. Kushmerick, D. Weld, and R. Doorenbos. Wrapper Induction for Information Extraction. *IJCAI-97*.
7. M. Perkowitz, O. Etzioni. Category Translation: Learning to Understand Information on the Internet. *IJCAI-95*.
8. S. Soderland. Learning Information Extraction Rules for Semi-structured and Free Text. *Technical Report, Department of Computer Science and Engineering, University of Washington*, Dec. 1997.

Event Mining with Event Processing Networks

Louis Perrochon, Walter Mann, Stephane Kasriel, and David C. Luckham

Computer Systems Lab, Stanford University, Stanford, CA 94306, USA
http://pavg.stanford.edu/

Abstract. Event Mining discovers information in a stream of data, or events, and delivers knowledge in real-time. Our event processing engine consists of a network of event processing agents (EPAs) running in parallel that interact using a dedicated event processing infrastructure. EPAs can be configured at run-time using a formal pattern language. The underlying infrastructure provides an abstract communication mechanism and thus allows dynamic reconfiguration of the communication topology between agents at run-time and provides transparent, location-independent access to all data. These features support dynamic allocation of EPAs to machines in a local area network at run time.

1 Introduction

Event mining (EM) delivers knowledge about a complex system in real-time based on events that denote the system's activities. A system can be anything from a single semiconductor fabrication line to the interconnected check-out registers of a nation-wide retailer. Such systems may be probed to produce events as the system operates. Events are then mined in a multitude of ways: Unwanted events are filtered out, patterns of logically corresponding events are aggregated into one new complex event, repetitive events are counted and aggregated into a new single event with a count of how often the original event occurred, etc. This mining process of producing fewer "better" events out of many "lesser" events can be iterated. The presentation of the mined events to the user is virtually unlimited. EM is particularly well suited for event based systems, but is applicable to other systems as well, e.g. updates in a database can be interpreted as events. The following two applications are typical examples of EM:

Business applications: EM based real-time decision support systems constantly gather information from throughout the enterprise and immediately respond to changes in information. These systems are business event driven, where a business event represents any significant change in business data or conditions.

Enterprise network and systems management: Event patterns that may lead to a failure (e.g. an important disk filling up) or that could signal break-in attempts (i.e. connect requests to multiple targets from a single source over a short time) are detected as they occur. EM provides immediate notification of such conditions to the managers of large, mission critical networks. Automatic prioritizing of alerts and quick root cause analysis leads to reduced response time, higher up-time and allows network managers to quickly respond to critical situations.

In order to understand complex systems and efficiently deal with complex patterns of events, logging with just a time stamp is often not enough. The two following features greatly increase the power of EM:

Complex event structures: Events should be stored as complex objects together with relationships among them instead of just tuples in a relational sense. EM should support event relationships beyond time, e.g. causality: one event causes another. In today's networked real-time environments events come from multiple independent sources and not all events are ordered in respect to each other. If such a natural partial order of events is implicitly reduced to a total order in logging, information is lost and non-determinism is introduced [1].

Flexibility: Because EM happens in real-time, queries need not be hard coded, but be must be flexible, and configurable at runtime. It should be possible at any time to start a new query against an ongoing event stream, that either considers only new events, only old events, or both.

EM supporting these two features is part of Stanford University's RAPIDE project. We developed an extensive set of tools that supports logging, mining, storing, and viewing of events in real-time. RAPIDE events are related by time and cause. Each relation builds a partial order on all the events. A formal pattern language [2] supports the construction of filters and maps, constructs that aggregate simple events to complex events on a higher level of abstraction [3]. The same process can be used to query complex events, thus building a more and more abstract view of the system. Our tools are implemented and available for Sun/Solaris 2.6 and Linux and can process several hundred events per second on an Ultra 1. We are currently negotiating with pilot users in industry.

2 Event Processing Networks

The RAPIDE EM technology is based on the concept of Event Processing Networks (EPNs). Such networks consist of any number of Event Processing Agents (EPAs), namely event sources, event processors and event viewers. Fig. 1 shows an overview over the three categories, with thin arrows indicating the (logical) flow of events from sources through processors to viewers.

Event sources in our applications are typically middleware sniffers. The system middleware can be pure TCP/IP, an event communication service based on a proprietary protocol like TIBCO Inc.'s TIB or Vitria, Inc.'s Communicator, or a military standard like the MIL STD 1553. We also automatically instrument the source code of system written in Java to intercept events within the Java engine [4]. Typical examples for event processors are filters and maps. Filters pass on only a subset of their input, maps aggregate multiple events in the input to

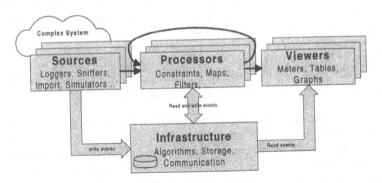

Fig. 1. Event Mining (EM)

output events thus generating events on a higher level of abstraction. Any third party event processor can be inserted into an EPN allowing for the integration with other approaches. Typical event viewers are a graphical viewer for partially ordered sets of events, a tabular viewer of event frequency or a simple gauge metering the value of an important parameter.

Data needs to be stored persistently because agents may want to access past events, even long after they have happened. Also the number of objects currently under consideration may easily exceed the size of the available main memory, thus EM requires some way of storing objects temporarily to disk. RAPIDE EM includes a shared data store that keeps track of all the objects. New objects are written into the data store from where agents and viewers read them. A communication service notifies other EPAs when new objects are added.

Events flow through the EPN in real-time and are displayed in viewers as soon as they are created, limited only by the speed of the underlying infrastructure. Processed events are displayed in viewers shortly after the underlying events have been created by the event source. EPNs are dynamic in that all EPAs can be added and removed at runtime. Newly added agents can either ignore all previous events and just start with the current event at the time they are added, or they can try to catch up all events from the beginning. As EPNs are distributed, EPAs can reside on machines distributed across a network.

3 Real Time Pattern Queries

The RAPIDE pattern language allows the user to describe patterns of events. A RAPIDE pattern matcher searches for all occurrences of a pattern of events in a partially ordered set. A typical example would search for all A events that cause both a B and a C event, with B and C independent of each other. In RAPIDE this pattern could be specified as: $A \to (B \sim C)$. In OQL, clumsily enhanced with a * operator denoting one or several repetitions of the path expression, this query would look like:

```
select tuple(e.ID, f.ID, g.ID)
from event e, e.(successor)* f, e.(successor)* g
where e.type='A' and f.type='B' and g.type='C' and
(NOT f.(successor)*=g) OR (NOT f.(successor)*=g) OR f=g)
```

Executing this query from scratch whenever a new event is added to the set is very inefficient, as potentially the whole set has to be traversed. Also, computing the complete transitive closure of the successor relation as a derived relationship is not feasible in a real-time setting. The algorithms we use instead were originally inspired by [5]. Our pattern matching algorithm searches whatever it can on the available data and keeps partially completed results around if possible. When new data arrives, only the partial results which might possibly benefit from the new event need to be reinvestigated.

We call this process incremental query execution or *incremental queries*. Incremental queries return new hits as new records are inserted and optimize re-execution of an ongoing query when new objects are inserted. This optimization is a trade off between storing all partial results on the one hand and rebuilding all partial results on the other hand. Incremental queries are similar to materialized views with real-time constraints. For our purpose, we can think of incremental queries as a repository of ongoing queries, along with some state information on these queries. Every time a new event is added, the queries of this repository would be allowed to run on that element only and the requesting client would be notified if there are new hits. Incremental queries require two interdependent modules:

Notification (call-backs, triggers) that notifies interested clients of insertions and updates on specific objects in the database, and

Dynamic Adaptation that modifies the current query execution plan depending on the newly inserted object and runs the query. This must be done efficiently, e.g. the query tree should be executed in such a way that a minimal amount of work is redone. We believe that these two elements are useful even beyond implementing pattern matching for EM: e. g. for rule processing in real time expert systems [6].

The commercial OODBMS that we looked at had very limited support for notification: most of them require polling the database for new events. With polling, throughput does not scale with the size of the database because searching time for any new object is not constant. One way out is to partition the database. However, big partitions do not help much, and small partitions increase the number of partitions which adds the overhead of keeping track of them. Worse, references between partitions are slower than references within a partition, reducing throughput. In addition, polling has to be done by all readers individually, increasing the load in an event processing network. Overall, our experiments with polling lead to a throughput of only a few objects per second. Hence having readers poll the database for new events is completely unrealistic for our purposes. Only one of the commercial OODBMS we looked at offered call-backs (triggers) on certain changes in the database, but so slow that we could only hope to notify a few objects per second. But clearly, efficient call-backs with minimal delay is critical. To support our requirements, we added our own notification mechanism.

4 Mining Event Patterns

Given an infrastructure for building large databases of events and their temporal, causal, and data attributes, along with a formal pattern language for expressing relationships between events in a compact and expressive way, then event mining is the process of extracting patterns from large sets of events in real time.

Our initial experiments in this area focus on using statistical analysis of stored relationships between events (causality, equivalent data parameters) to identify common yet complex behaviors implied by the events.

The patterns extracted via event mining may then be used to initiate further event processing. For example, they may be used to filter out normal event behavior of a system, so that variations of it may be examined. Or, the patterns extracted may be aggregated into higher level events, to allow views of the event activity at a more abstract level.

A critical factor for real-time event mining is the need to process each new event in constant time. Otherwise incoming events will eventually start to queue up and lead to a big back log. Heuristic methods that are effective and efficient enough are one area of future research.

References

[1] Pratt, V. R. Modeling concurrency with partial orders. Int. J. of Parallel Programming, 1986. 15(1): p. 33–71.

[2] RAPIDE, Rapide 1.0 Pattern Language Reference Manual. Stanford University, Stanford, 1997.

[3] Luckham, D. C. and Frasca, B., Complex Event Processing in Distributed Systems. Computer Systems Laboratory Technical Report CSL–TR–98–754. Stanford University, Stanford, 1998.

[4] Santoro, A., et al., eJava - Extending Java with Causality. In Proceedings of 10th International Conference on Software Engineering and Knowledge Engineering (SEKE'98). 1998. Redwood City, CA, USA.

[5] Fidge, C. J., Timestamps in message-passing systems that preserve the partial ordering. Australian Computer Science Communications, 1988. 10(1): p. 55–66.

[6] Wolfson, O., et al., Incremental Evaluation of Rules and its Relationship to Parallelism. In Proceedings of SIGMOD'91 Conference on the Management of Data. 1991. Boulder, CO: ACM Press.

An Analysis of Quantitative Measures Associated with Rules

Y.Y. Yao[1] and Ning Zhong[2]

[1] Department of Computer Science, University of Regina
Regina, Saskatchewan, Canada S4S 0A2
E-mail: yyao@cs.uregina.ca

[2] Department of Computer Science and Systems Engineering, Faculty of Engineering
Yamaguchi University, Tokiwa-Dai, 2557, Ube 755, Japan
E-mail: zhong@ai.csse.yamaguchi-u.ac.jp

Abstract. In this paper, we analyze quantitative measures associated with if-then type rules. Basic quantities are identified and many existing measures are examined using the basic quantities. The main objective is to provide a synthesis of existing results in a simple and unified framework. The quantitative measure is viewed as a multi-facet concept, representing the confidence, uncertainty, applicability, quality, accuracy, and interestingness of rules. Roughly, they may be classified as representing one-way and two-way supports.

1 Introduction

In machine learning and data mining, the discovered knowledge from a large data set is often expressed in terms of a set of if-then type rules [7, 21]. They represent relationships, such as correlation, association, and causation, among concepts. Typically, the number of potential rules observable in a large data set may be very large, and only a small portion of them is actually useful. In order to filter out useless rules, certain criteria must be established for rule selection. A common solution is the use of quantitative measures. One may select the rules which have the highest values. Alternatively, one may choose a threshold value and select rules whose measures are above the threshold value. The well known ID3 inductive learning algorithm [23] is an example of the former, and the approach for mining association rules in transaction databases [1] is an example of the latter. The use of quantitative measures also play a very important role in the interpretation of discovered rules, which provides guidelines for the proper uses of the rules.

Many quantitative measures have been proposed and studied, each of them captures different characteristics of rules. However, several important issues need more attention. Different names have been used for essentially the same measure, or a positive monotonic transformation of the same measure (called order preserving transformation [15]). Additional measures are being proposed, without realizing that the same measures have been studied in related fields such as expert systems, pattern recognition, information retrieval, and statistical data analysis. The relationships between various measures have not been fully investigated. There is clearly a need for a systematic study on the interpretation, classification, and axiomatization of quantitative measures associated with rules. Important initial studies have been reported by Piatetsky-Shapiro [25], and Major and Mangano [17] on the axiomatic characterization of quantitative measures, and by Klösgen [15] on the study of special classes of quantitative measures.

This paper may be viewed as a first step in the study of quantitative measures. A simple set-theoretic framework is suggested for interpreting if-then type rules. Basic quantities are identified and many existing measures are examined using the basic quantities. The results may lay down the groundwork for further systematic studies.

2 The Basic Framework and Basic Quantities

Consider an if-then type rule of the form:

$$\text{IF } E \text{ THEN } H \quad \text{with } \alpha_1, \ldots, \alpha_m, \tag{1}$$

which relates two concepts E and H. For clarity, we also simply write $E \longrightarrow H$. A rule does not necessarily represent a strict logical implication, with logical implication as the degenerate case. The values $\alpha_1, \ldots, \alpha_m$ quantifies different types of uncertainty and properties associated with the rule. In principle, one may connect any two concepts in the above rule form. The quantities $\alpha_1, \ldots, \alpha_m$ measures the degree or strength of relationships [34]. Examples of quantitative measures include confidence, uncertainty, applicability, quality, accuracy, and interestingness of rules.

We use the following set-theoretic interpretation of rules. It relates a rule to the data sets from which the rule is discovered. Let U denote a finite universe consisting of objects. Each object may be considered as one instance of a data set. If each object is described by a set of attribute-value pairs, the concepts E and H can be formally defined using certain languages, such as propositional and predicate languages [15]. We are not interested in the exact representation of the concepts. Instead, we focus on the set-theoretic interpretations of concepts [13, 18, 22]. For a concept E, let $m(E)$ denote the set of elements of U that satisfy the condition expressed by E. We also say that $m(E)$ is the set of elements satisfying E. Similarly, the set $m(H)$ consists of elements satisfying H. One may interpret m as a meaning function that associates each concept with a subset of U. The meaning function should obey the following conditions:

$$m(\neg E) = U - m(E),$$
$$m(E \wedge H) = m(E) \cap m(H),$$
$$m(E \vee H) = m(E) \cup m(H), \tag{2}$$

representing the sets of elements not satisfying E, satisfying both E and H, and satisfying at least one of E and H, respectively. With the meaning function m, a rule $E \longrightarrow H$ may be paraphrased as saying that "IF an element of the universe satisfies E, THEN the element satisfies H".

Using the cardinalities of sets, we obtain the following contingency table representing the quantitative information about the rule $E \longrightarrow H$:

	H	$\neg H$	Totals
E	$\|m(E) \cap m(H)\|$	$\|m(E) \cap m(\neg H)\|$	$\|m(E)\|$
$\neg E$	$\|m(\neg E) \cap m(H)\|$	$\|m(\neg E) \cap m(\neg H)\|$	$\|m(\neg E)\|$
Totals	$\|m(H)\|$	$\|m(\neg H)\|$	$\|U\|$

where $| \cdot |$ denotes the cardinality of a set. For clarity, we rewrite the table as follows:

	H	$\neg H$	Totals
E	a	b	$a + b$
$\neg E$	c	d	$c + d$
Totals	$a + c$	$b + d$	$a + b + c + d = n$

The values in the four cells are not independent. They are linked by the constraint $a + b + c + d = n$. The 2×2 contingency table has been used by many authors for representing information of rules [9, 11, 27, 29, 33]. From the contingency table, we can define some basic quantities.

The *generality* of E is defined by:

$$G(E) = \frac{|m(E)|}{|U|} = \frac{a + b}{n}, \tag{3}$$

which indicates the relative size of the concept E. A concept is more general if it covers more instances of the universe. If $G(E) = \alpha$, then $(100\alpha)\%$ of objects in U satisfy E. The quantity may be viewed as the probability of a randomly selected element satisfying E. Obviously, we have $0 \le G(E) \le 1$.

The *absolute support* of H provided by E is the quantity:

$$AS(H|E) = \frac{|m(H) \cap m(E)|}{|m(E)|} = \frac{a}{a + b}. \tag{4}$$

The quantity, $0 \le AS(H|E) \le 1$, shows the degree to which E implies H. If $AS(H|E) = \alpha$, then $(100\alpha)\%$ of objects satisfying E also satisfy H. It may be viewed as the conditional probability of a randomly selected element satisfying H given that the element satisfies E. In set-theoretic terms, it is the degree to which $m(E)$ is included in $m(H)$. Clearly, $AS(H|E) = 1$, if and only if $m(E) \subseteq m(H)$. The *change of support* of H provided by E is defined by:

$$CS(H|E) = AS(H|E) - G(H) = \frac{an - (a + b)(a + c)}{(a + b)n}. \tag{5}$$

Unlike the absolute support, the change of support varies from -1 to 1. One may consider $G(H)$ to be the prior probability of H and $AS(H|E)$ the posterior probability of H after knowing E. The difference of posterior and prior probabilities represents the change of our confidence regarding whether E actually causes H. For a positive value, one may say that E causes H; for a negative value, one may say that E does not cause H. The *mutual support* of H and E is defined by:

$$MS(E,H) = \frac{|m(E) \cap m(H)|}{|m(E) \cup m(H)|} = \frac{a}{a+b+c}. \tag{6}$$

One may interpret the mutual support, $0 \leq MS(E,H) \leq 1$, as a measure of the strength of the double implication $E \longleftrightarrow H$. It measures the degree to which E causes, and only causes, H. The mutual support can be reexpressed by:

$$MS(E,H) = 1 - \frac{|m(E) \Delta m(H)|}{|m(E) \cup m(H)|}, \tag{7}$$

where $A \Delta B = (A \cup B) - (A \cap B)$ is the symmetric difference between two sets. The measure $|A \Delta B|/|A \cup B|$ is commonly known as the MZ metric for measuring distance between two sets [19]. Thus, MS may be viewed as a similarity measure of E and H.

The degree of *independence* of E and H is measured by:

$$IND(E,H) = \frac{G(E \wedge H)}{G(E)G(H)} = \frac{an}{(a+b)(a+c)}. \tag{8}$$

It is the ratio of the joint probability of $E \wedge H$ and the probability obtained if E and H are assumed to be independent. One may rewrite the measure of independence as [10]:

$$IND(E,H) = \frac{AS(H|E)}{G(H)}. \tag{9}$$

It shows the degree of the deviation of the probability of H in the subpopulation constrained by E from the probability of H in the entire data set [16, 31]. With this expression, the relationship to the change of support becomes clear. Instead of using the ratio, the latter is defined by the difference of $AS(H|E)$ and $G(H)$. When E and H are probabilistic independent, we have $CS(H|E) = 0$ and $IND(E,H) = 1$. Moreover, $CS(H|E) \geq 0$ if and only if $IND(E,H) \geq 1$, and $CS(H|E) \leq 0$ if and only if $IND(E,H) \leq 1$. This provides further support for use of CS as a measure of confidence that E causes H. However, CS is not a symmetric measure, while IND is symmetric. The difference of $G(H \wedge E)$ and $G(H)G(E)$:

$$D(H,E) = G(H \wedge E) - G(H)G(E), \tag{10}$$

is a symmetric measure. Compared with $D(H,E)$, the measure $CS(H|E)$ may be viewed as a relative difference.

The generality of a concept is related to the probability that a randomly selected element will be an instance of the concept. It is the basic quantity from which all other quantities can be expressed as follows:

$$AS(H|E) = \frac{G(H \wedge E)}{G(E)},$$

$$CS(H|E) = \frac{G(H \wedge E) - G(H)G(E)}{G(E)},$$

$$MS(E,H) = \frac{G(E \wedge H)}{G(E \vee H)},$$

$$IND(E,H) = \frac{G(E \wedge H)}{G(E)G(H)},$$

$$D(H,E) = G(H \wedge E) - G(H)G(E). \tag{11}$$

From the above definitions, we can establish the following relationships:

$$G(E) = AS(E|U),$$

$$CS(H|E) = (IND(E,H) - 1)G(H),$$

$$AS(H|E) = \frac{G(H)}{G(E)}AS(E|H),$$

$$MS(E,H) = \frac{1}{\frac{1}{AS(E|H)} + \frac{1}{AS(H|E)} - 1},$$

$$D(H,E) = CS(H|E)G(E). \tag{12}$$

In summary, all measures introduced in this section have a probability related interpretation. They can be roughly divided into three classes:

generality:	G,
one-way association (single implication):	$AS, CS,$
two-way association (double implication):	$MS, IND, D.$

Each type of association measures can be further divided into absolute support and change of support. The measure of absolute one-way support is AS, and the measure of absolute two-way support is MS. The measures of change of support are CS for one-way, and IND and D for two-way. It is interesting to note that all measures of change of support are related to the *deviation* of joint probability of $E \wedge H$ from the probability obtained if E and H are assumed to be independent. In other words, a stronger association is presented if the joint probability is further away from the probability under independence. The association can be either positive or negative.

3 A Review of Existing Measures

This section is not intended to be an exhaustive survey of quantitative measures associated with rules. We will only review some of the measures that fit in the framework established in the last section.

3.1 Generality

The generality is one of the two standard measures used for mining association rules [1]. For rule $E \longrightarrow H$, the generality:

$$G(E \wedge H) = \frac{a}{n} \tag{13}$$

is commonly known as the *support* of the rule. It represents the percentage of positive instances of E that support the rule. On the other hand, the generality $G(E)$ is the percentage of instances to which the rule can be applied. Iglesia *et al.* [13] called the quantity $G(E)$ the *applicability* of the rule. Klösgen [15] referred to it as a measure of *coverage* of the concept E.

3.2 One-way support

The absolute support $AS(H|E)$ is the other standard measure used for mining association rules [1], called *confidence* of the rule $E \longrightarrow H$. Different names were given to this measure, including the *accuracy* [13, 29], *strength* [8, 15, 26], and *certainty factor* [15]. In the context of information retrieval, the same measure is referred to as the measure of *precision* [32]. Tsumoto and Tanaka [29] used the quantity $AS(E|H)$ for measuring the *coverage* or *true positive rate*. It is regarded as a measure of sensitivity by Klösgen [15]. The same measure was also used by Choubey *et al.* [5]. In the context of information retrieval, the measure is referred to as the measure of *recall* [32]. The use of change of support $CS(H|E)$ was discussed by some authors [4, 25].

Additional measures of one-way support can be obtained by combining basic quantities introduced in the last section. Yao and Liu [31] used the following quantity for measuring the significance of a rule $E \longrightarrow H$:

$$S_1(H|E) = AS(H|E) \log IND(E,H) = \frac{a}{a+b} \log \frac{an}{(a+b)(a+c)}. \tag{14}$$

The measure is a product of a measure of one-way support $AS(S|E)$ and the logarithm of a measure of two-way support $IND(E,H)$. Since logarithm is a monotonic increasing function, it reflects the properties of $IND(E,H)$. Gray and Orlowska [10] proposed a measure of one-way support, called measure of rule interestingness, by combining generality and absolute support:

$$i(H|E) = \left(IND(E,H)^l - 1\right) G(E \wedge H)^m = \left(\left(\frac{an}{(a+b)(a+c)}\right)^l - 1\right)\left(\frac{a}{n}\right)^m. \tag{15}$$

where l and m are parameters to weigh the relative importance of the two measures. Klösgen [15] studied another class of measures:

$$K(H|E) = G(E)^\alpha (AS(H|E) - G(H)). \tag{16}$$

It is a combination of generality and change of support. When $\alpha = 0$, the measure reduced to the change of support.

Following Duda, Gasching, and Hart [6], Kamber and Shinghal [14], Schlimmer and Granger [24] used the measure of *logical sufficiency*:

$$LS(H|E) = \frac{AS(E|H)}{AS(E|\neg H)} = \frac{a(b+d)}{b(a+c)}. \tag{17}$$

and the measure of *logical necessity*:

$$LN(H|E) = \frac{AS(\neg E|H)}{AS(\neg E|\neg H)} = \frac{c(b+d)}{d(a+c)}. \tag{18}$$

McLeish *et al.* [20] viewed LS as the weight of evidence if one treats E as a piece of evidence. A highly negative weight implies that there is significant reason to belief in $\neg H$, and a positive weight supports H. It should pointed out that weight of evidence plans an important rule in Bayesian inference. Ali, Manganaris and Srikant [2] defined the relative risk of a rule $E \longrightarrow H$ as follows:

$$r(H|E) = \frac{AS(H|E)}{AS(H|\neg E)} = \frac{a(c+d)}{c(a+b)}. \tag{19}$$

It is fact related to the measure LS, if one change the places of E and H.

Based on the probability related interpretation of $AS(H|E)$, Smyth and Goodman [28] defined the *information content* of rules. For $E \longrightarrow H$, we have:

$$
\begin{aligned}
J(H\|E) &= G(E) \left(AS(H|E) \log \frac{AS(H|E)}{G(H)} + AS(\neg H|E) \log \frac{AS(\neg H|E)}{G(\neg H)} \right) \\
&= G(E) \left(AS(H|E) \log IND(E, H) + AS(\neg H|E) \log IND(\neg H, E) \right) \\
&= \frac{1}{n} \left(a \log \frac{an}{(a+b)(a+c)} + b \log \frac{bn}{(a+b)(b+d)} \right). \tag{20}
\end{aligned}
$$

This measure is closely related to the *divergence* measure proposed by Kullback and Leibler [12].

3.3 Two-way support

The measure of independence IND has been used by many authors. Silverstein *et al.* [27] referred to it as a measure of interest. Büchter and Wirth [3] regarded it as a measure of dependence. Gray and Orlowska [10] used the same measure, and provided the interpretation given by equation (9).

The measure of two-way support corresponding to equation (14) is given by Yao and Liu [31] as:

$$S_2(E, H) = G(E \wedge H) \log IND(E, H) = \frac{a}{n} \log \frac{an}{(a+b)(a+c)}. \tag{21}$$

By setting $l = m = 1$ in equation (15), we have:

$$i(H|E) = IND(E, H)D(E, H), \tag{22}$$

which is a multiplication of two basic measures of two-way support. By setting $\alpha = 1$ in equation (16), we immediately obtain the measure D.

The measure of two support corresponding to the measure of divergence (20) is given by the measure of mutual information. For rule $E \longrightarrow H$, we have:

$$
\begin{aligned}
M(E; H) &= G(E \wedge H) \log \frac{G(E \wedge H)}{G(E)G(H)} + G(E \wedge \neg H) \log \frac{G(E \wedge \neg H)}{G(E)G(\neg H)} + \\
&\quad G(\neg E \wedge H) \log \frac{G(\neg E \wedge H)}{G(\neg E)G(H)} + G(\neg E \wedge \neg H) \log \frac{G(\neg E \wedge \neg H)}{G(\neg E)G(\neg H)} \\
&= \frac{1}{n} \left(a \log \frac{an}{(a+c)(a+b)} + b \log \frac{bn}{(b+d)(a+b)} + \right. \\
&\quad \left. c \log \frac{cn}{(a+c)(c+d)} + d \log \frac{dn}{(b+d)(c+d)} \right)
\end{aligned}
\tag{23}
$$

The relationship between J and M can be established as:

$$
M(E; H) = J(H\|E) + J(H\|\neg E).
\tag{24}
$$

By extending the above relationship, in general one may obtain measures of two-way support by combining measures of one-way support. For example, both $AS(H|E) + AS(E|H)$ and $AS(H|E)AS(E|H)$ are measures of two-way support.

3.4 Axioms for quantitative measures of rules

Piatetsky-Shapiro [25] suggested that a quantitative measure of rule $E \longrightarrow H$ may be computed as a function of $G(E)$, $G(H)$, $G(E \wedge H)$, rule complexity, and possibly other parameters such as the mutual distribution of E and H or the domain size of E and H. For the evaluation of rules, Piatetsky-Shapiro [25] introduced three axioms. Major and Mangano [17] added a fourth axioms. Klösgen [15] studied a special class of measures that are characterized by two quantities, the absolute one-way support $AS(H|E)$ and the generality $G(E)$. The generality $G(H \wedge E)$ is obtained by $AS(H|E)G(E)$. Suppose $Q(E, H)$ is a measure associated with rule $E \longrightarrow H$. The version of the four axioms given by Klösgen [15] is:

(i). $Q(E, H) = 0$ if E and H are statistically independent,
(ii). $Q(E, H)$ monotonically increases in $AS(H|E)$ for fixed $G(E)$,
(iii). $Q(E, H)$ monotonically decreases in $G(E)$ for fixed $G(E \wedge H)$,
(iv). $Q(E, H)$ monotonically increases in $G(E)$ for fixed $AS(H|E) > G(H)$.

Axiom (i) implies that only measures of change of support are considered. Other axioms states that all measures must have the property of monotonicity. Many of the measures discussed in this paper fall into this class.

4 Conclusion

We have presented a simple and unified framework for the study of quantitative measures associated with rules. Some basic measures have been proposed and studied. Many existing measures have been investigated in terms of these basic measures.

This paper is a preliminary step towards a systematic study on quantitative measures associated with rules. Further investigations on the topic are planed. We will examine the semantics and implications of various measures, and study axioms for distinct types of measures.

References

1. Agrawal, R., Imielinski, T., and Swami, A. Mining association rules between sets of items in large databases, *Proceedings of the ACM SIGMOD International Conference on the Management of Data*, 207-216, 1993.
2. Ali, K., Manganaris, S., and Srikant, R. Partial classification using association rules, *Proceedings of KDD-97*, 115-118, 1997.
3. Büchter, O. and Wirth R. Discovery of association rules over ordinal data: a new and faster algorithm and its application to basket analysis, in [30], 36-47, 1998.
4. Chen, M., Han, J. and Yu, P.S. Data mining, an overview from a databases perspective, *IEEE Transactions on Knowledge and Data Engineering*, 8, 866-883, 1996.
5. Choubey, S.K., Deogun, J.S., Raghavan, V.V., and Sever, H. Comparison of classification methods, *Proceedings of 1997 Joint Conference in Information Sciences*, 371-374, 1997.
6. Duda, R.O., Gasching, J., and Hart, P.E. Model design in the Prospector consultant system for mineral exploration, in: Webber, B.L. and Nilsson, N.J. (Eds.), *Readings in Artificial Intelligence*, Tioga, Palo Atlto, CA, 334-348, 1981.
7. Fayyad, U.M, Piatetsky-Shapiro, G., Smyth, P., and Uthurusamy, R. (Eds.), *Advances in Knowledge Discovery and Data Mining*, AAAI Press / MIT Press, California, 1996.
8. Fhar, V. and Tuzhilin, A. Abstract-driven pattern discovery in databases, *IEEE Transactions on Knowledge and Data Engineering*, 5, 926-938, 1993.
9. Gaines, B.R. The trade-off between knowledge and data in knowledge acquisition, in: Piatetsky-Shapiro, G. and Frawley, W.J. (Eds.), *Knowledge Discovery in Databases*, AAAI/MIT Press, 491-505, 1991.
10. Gray, B. and Orlowska, M.E. CCAIIA: clustering categorical attributes into interesting association rules, in [30], 132-143, 1998.
11. Ho, K.M. and Scott, P.D. Zeta: a global method for discretization of continuous variables, *Proceedings of KDD-97*, 191-194, 1997.
12. Kullback, S. and Leibler, R.A. On information and sufficiency, *Annals of Mathematical Statistics*, 22, 79-86, 1951.
13. Iglesia, B. Debuse, J.C.W. and Rayward-Smith V.J. Discovering knowledge in commercial databases using modern heuristic techniques, *Proceedings of KDD-96*, 44-49, 1996.
14. Kamber, M. and Shinghal, R. Evaluating the interestingness of characteristic rules, *Proceedings of KDD-96*, 263-266, 1996.

15. Klösgen, W. Explora: a multipattern and multistrategy discovery assistant, in [7], 249-271, 1996.
16. Liu, H., Lu, H., and Yao, J. Identifying relevant databases for multidatabase mining, in [30], 211-221, 1998.
17. Major, J. and Mangano, J. Selecting among rules induced from a hurricane database, The Journal of Intelligent Information Systems, 4, 1995.
18. Mannila, H. and Toivonen, H. Multiple uses of frequent sets and condensed representations, Proceedings of KDD-96, 189-194, 1996.
19. Marczewski, E. and Steinhaus, H. On a certain distance of sets and the corresponding distance of functions, Colloquium Mathemmaticum, 6, 319-327, 1958.
20. McLeish, M., Yao, P., Garg, M., and Stirtzinger, T. Discovery of medical diagnostic information: an overview of methods and results, in: Piatetsky-Shapiro, G. and Frawley, W.J. (Eds.), Knowledge Discovery in Databases, AAAI/MIT Press, 477-490, 1991.
21. Michalski, R.S., Carbonell, J.G., and Mitchell, T.M. (Eds.), Machine Learning, Tioga, 1983.
22. Pawlak, Z. Rough Sets: Theoretical Aspects of Reasoning about Data, Kluwer Academic Publishers, Boston, 1991.
23. Quinlan, J.R. Induction of decision trees, Machine Learning, 1, 81-106, 1986.
24. Schlimmer, J.C. and Granger, Jr. R.H. Incremental learning from noisy data, Machine Learning, 1, 317-354, 1986.
25. Piatetsky-Shapiro, G. Discovery, analysis, and presentation of strong rules, in: Piatetsky-Shapiro, G. and Frawley, W.J. (Eds.), Knowledge Discovery in Databases, AAAI/MIT Press, 229-238, 1991.
26. Shen, W. and Leng, B. Metapattern generation for integrated data mining, Proceedings of KDD-96, 152-157, 1996.
27. Silverstein, C., Brin, S., and Motwani, R. Beyond market baskets: generalizing association rules to dependence rules, Data Mining and Knowledge Discovery, 2, 39-68, 1998.
28. Smyth, P. and Goodman, R.M. Rule induction using information theory, in: Piatetsky-Shapiro, G. and Frawley, W.J. (Eds.), Knowledge Discovery in Databases, AAAI/MIT Press, 159-176, 1991.
29. Tsumoto, S. and Tanaka, H. Automated discovery of functional components of proteins from amino-acid sequences based on rough sets and change of representation, Proceedings of KDD-95, 318-324, 1995.
30. Wu, X., Kotagiri, R,. and Bork, K.B. (Eds.), Research and Development in Knowledge Discovery and Data Mining, Springer, Berlin, 1998.
31. Yao, J. and Liu, H. Searching multiple databases for interesting complexes, in: Lu, H., Motoda, H., and Liu, H. (Eds.), KDD: Techniques and Applications, World Scientific, Singapore, 1997.
32. Yao, Y.Y. Measuring retrieval performance based on user preference of documents, Journal of the American Society for Information Science, 46, 133-145, 1995.
33. Zembowicz, R. and Żytkow, J.M. From contingency tables to various forms of knowledge in database, in [7], 39-81, 1996.
34. Zhong, N., Dong, J., Fujitsu, S., and Ohsuga, S. Soft techniques for rule discovery in data, Transactions of Information Processing Society of Japan, 39, 2581-2592, 1998.

A Strong Relevant Logic Model of Epistemic Processes in Scientific Discovery

(Extended Abstract)

Jingde Cheng

Department of Computer Science and Communication Engineering
Kyushu University, 6-10-1 Hakozaki, Fukuoka, 812-8581, Japan
cheng@csce.kyushu-u.ac.jp

Abstract. This paper presents some significant fundamental observations and/or assumptions on scientific discovery processes and their automation, shows why classical mathematical logic, its various classical conservative extensions, and traditional (weak) relevant logics cannot satisfactorily underlie epistemic processes in scientific discovery, and presents a strong relevant logic model of epistemic processes in scientific discovery.

1 Introduction

Any scientific discovery must include an epistemic process to gain knowledge of or to ascertain the existence of some empirical and/or logical conditionals previously unknown or unrecognized. As an applied and/or technical science, Computer Science should provide scientists with some epistemic representation, description, reasoning, and computing tools for supporting the scientists to suppose, verify, and then ultimately discover new conditionals in their research fields. However, no programming paradigm in the current computer science focuses its attention on this issue. In order to provide scientists with a computational method to program their epistemic processes in scientific discovery, we are establishing a novel programming paradigm, named '*Epistemic Programming*', which regards conditionals as the subject of computing, takes primary epistemic operations as basic operations of computing, and regards epistemic processes as the subject of programming.

Modeling epistemic processes in scientific discovery satisfactorily is an indispensable step to automating scientific discovery processes. This paper presents some significant fundamental observations and/or assumptions, which underlie our research direction, on scientific discovery processes and their automation, shows why classical mathematical logic, its various classical conservative extensions, and traditional (weak) relevant logics cannot satisfactorily underlie epistemic processes in scientific discovery, presents a strong relevant logic model of epistemic processes in scientific discovery as the logical foundation to underlie epistemic programming.

2   Fundamental Observations and/or Assumptions

First of all, we present here some significant fundamental observations and/or assumptions, which underlie our research direction, on scientific discovery processes and their automation as follows:

(1) Specific knowledge is the power of a scientist: Any scientist who made a scientific discovery must have worked in some particular scientific field and more specifically on some problem in a particular domain within the field. There is no universal scientist who can make scientific discoveries in every field.

(2) Any scientific discovery has an ordered epistemic process: Any scientific discovery must have, among other things, a process that consists of a number of ordered epistemic activities that may be contributed by many scientists in a long duration. Any scientific discovery is nether an event occurs in a moment nor an accumulation of disorderly and disorganized inquisitions.

(3) New conditionals are epistemic goals of any scientific discovery: Any scientific discovery process must include an epistemic process to gain knowledge of or to ascertain the existence of some empirical and/or logical conditionals previously unknown or unrecognized. Finding some new data or some new fact is just an initial step in a scientific discovery but not the scientific discovery itself.

(4) Scientific reasoning is indispensable to any scientific discovery: Any discovery must be unknown or unrecognized before the completion of discovery process. Reasoning is the sole way to draw new conclusions from some premises that are known facts and/or assumed hypothesis. There is no scientific discovery that does not invoke scientific reasoning.

(5) Scientific reasoning must be justified based on some sound logical criterion: The most intrinsic difference between discovery and proof is that discovery has no explicitly defined target as its goal. Since any epistemic process in any scientific discovery has no explicitly defined target, the sole criterion the epistemic process must act according to is to reason correct conclusions from the premises. It is logic that can underlie valid scientific reasoning.

(6) Scientific reasoning must be relevant: For any correct argument in scientific reasoning as well as our everyday reasoning, the premises of the argument must be in some way relevant to the conclusion of that argument, and vice versa. A reasoning including some irrelevant arguments cannot be said to be valid in general.

(7) Scientific reasoning must be ampliative: A scientific reasoning is intrinsically different from a scientific proving in that the purpose of reasoning is to find out some facts and conditionals previously unknown or unrecognized, while the purpose of proving is to find out a justification for some fact previously known or assumed. A reasoning in any scientific discovery must be ampliative such that it enlarges or increases the reasoning agent's knowledge in some way.

(8) Scientific reasoning must be paracomplete: Any scientific theory may be incomplete in many ways, i.e., for some sentence 'A' neither it nor its negation can be true in the theory. Therefore, a reasoning in any scientific discovery must be paracomplete such that it does not reason out a sentence even if it cannot reason out the negation of that sentence.

(9) Scientific reasoning must be paraconsistent: Any scientific theory may be inconsistent in many ways, i.e., it may directly or indirectly include some contradiction such that for some sentence 'A' both it and its negation can be true together in the theory. Therefore, a reasoning in any scientific discovery must be paraconsistent such that from a contradiction it does not reason out an arbitrary sentence.

(10) Epistemic activities in any scientific discovery process are distinguishable: Epistemic activities in any scientific discovery process can be distinguished from other activities, e.g., experimental activities, as explicitly described thoughts.

(11) Normal scientific discovery processes are possible: Any scientific discovery process can be described and modeled in a normal way, and therefore, it can be simulated by computer programs automatically.

(12) Specific knowledge is the power of a program: Even if scientific discovery processes can be simulated by computer programs automatically in general, a particular computational process which can certainly perform a particular scientific discovery must take sufficient knowledge specific to the subject under investigation into account. There is no generally organized order of scientific discovery processes that can be applied to every problem in every field.

(13) Any automated scientific discovery process must be valid: Any automated process of scientific discovery must be able to assure us of the truth, in the sense of not only fact but also conditional, of the final result produced by the process if it starts from an epistemic state where all facts, hypotheses, and conditionals are regarded to be true and/or valid.

(14) Any automated scientific discovery process need an autonomous forward reasoning mechanism: Any backward and/or refutation deduction system cannot serve as an autonomous reasoning mechanism to form and/or discover some completely new things. What we need in automating scientific discovery is an autonomous forward reasoning system.

3 The Fundamental Logic to Underlie Epistemic Processes

Based on the fundamental observations and/or assumptions presented in Section 2, the fundamental logic that can underlie epistemic processes has to satisfy some essential requirements. First, as a criterion for validity of reasoning, the logic underlying scientific reasoning in epistemic processes must take the relevance between the premises and conclusion of an argument into account. Second, the logic must be able to underlie paracomplete and paraconsistent reasoning; in particular, the *principle of Explosion* that everything follows from a contradiction cannot be accepted by the logic as a valid principle. Third, for any set of facts and conditionals, which are considered as true and/or valid, given as premises of a reasoning based on the logic, any conditional reasoned out as a conclusion of the reasoning must be true and/or valid in the sense of conditional.

Almost all the logic-based works on modeling epistemic processes are based on classical mathematical logic (CML for short) or its some classical conservative extensions [6], keeping as much as fundamental characteristics of CML. However, CML cannot satisfy all the above three essential requirements for the fundamental logic. First, because of the classical account of validity that an argument is valid if and only if it is impossible for all its premises to be true while its conclusion is false, a reasoning based on CML may be irrelevant, i.e., the conclusion reasoned out from the premises of that reasoning may be irrelevant at all, in the sense of meaning, to the premises. Second, CML is of no use for reasoning with inconsistency, since the principle of Explosion is a fundamental characteristic of CML. Third, as a result of representing the notion of conditional, which is intrinsically intensional, by the extensional notion of material implication, CML has a great number of implicational paradoxes as its logical axioms or theorems which cannot be regarded as entailments from the viewpoint of scientific reasoning as well as our everyday reasoning.

Traditional (weak) relevant logics [1, 2] have rejected those implicational paradoxes in CML, but still have some 'conjunction-implicational paradoxes' and 'disjunction-implicational paradoxes' [4] as their logical axioms or theorems, which cannot be regarded as entailments from the viewpoint of scientific reasoning as well as our everyday reasoning.

In order to establish a satisfactory logic calculus of conditional to underlie relevant reasoning, the present author has proposed some strong relevant logics and shown their applications [4, 5]. Since the strong relevant logics are free not only implicational paradoxes but also conjunction-implicational and disjunction-implicational paradoxes, we can use them to model epistemic processes in scientific discovery without those problems in modeling epistemic processes by CML, various classical conservative extensions of CML, and traditional (weak) relevant logics.

4   A Strong Relevant Logic Model of Epistemic Processes

For a given L-theory with premises P, denoted by $T_L(P)$, and any formula 'A' of L, A is said to be explicitly accepted by $T_L(P)$ if and only if $A \in P$ and $\neg A \notin P$; A is said to be explicitly rejected by $T_L(P)$ if and only if $A \notin P$ and $\neg A \in P$; A is said to be explicitly inconsistent with $T_L(P)$ if and only if both $A \in P$ and $\neg A \in P$; A is said to be explicitly independent of $T_L(P)$ and is called a explicitly possible new premise for $T_L(P)$ if and only if both $A \notin P$ and $\neg A \notin P$. For any given formal theory $T_L(P)$ and any formula $A \notin P$, A is said to be implicitly accepted by $T_L(P)$, if and only if $A \in T_L(P)$ and $\neg A \notin T_L(P)$; A is said to be implicitly rejected by $T_L(P)$ if and only if $A \notin T_L(P)$ and $\neg A \in T_L(P)$; A is said to be implicitly inconsistent with $T_L(P)$ if and only if both $A \in T_L(P)$ and $\neg A \in T_L(P)$; A is said to be implicitly independent of $T_L(P)$ and is called a implicitly possible new premise for $T_L(P)$ if and only if both $A \notin T_L(P)$ and $\neg A \notin T_L(P)$.

Let $K \subseteq F(EcQ)$, where $F(EcQ)$ is the set of formulas of predicate relevant logic EcQ, be a set of sentences to represent known knowledge and/or current beliefs of an agent. For any $A \in T_{EcQ}(K)-K$ where $T_{EcQ}(K) \neq K$, an epistemic deduction of A from K, denoted by K^{d+A}, by the agent is defined as $K^{d+A} =_{df} K \cup \{A\}$; for any $A \notin T_{EcQ}(K)$, an explicitly epistemic expansion of K by A, denoted by K^{e+A}, by the agent is defined as $K^{e+A} =_{df} K \cup \{A\}$; for any $A \in K$, an explicitly epistemic contraction of K by A, denoted by K^{-A}, by the agent is defined as $K^{-A} =_{df} K-\{A\}$; for any $A \notin T_{EcQ}(K)$, an *implicitly epistemic expansion* of K by A, denoted by $T_{EcQ}(K)^{e+A}$, is defined as $T_{EcQ}(K)^{e+A} =_{df} T_{EcQ}(K \cup N)$ where $N \subseteq F(EcQ)$ such that $A \notin K \cup N$ but $A \in T_{EcQ}(K \cup N)$; for any $A \in T_{EcQ}(K)$, an *implicitly epistemic contraction* of K by A, denoted by $T_{EcQ}(K)^{-A}$, is defined as $T_{EcQ}(K)^{-A} =_{df} T_{EcQ}(K-N)$ where $N \subseteq F(EcQ)$ such that $A \notin T_{EcQ}(K-N)$; a *simple induction* by the agent is an epistemic expansion such that for $\exists x(A) \in K$ and $\forall x(A) \notin T_{EcQ}(K)$, do $K^{e+\forall x(A)}$; a *simple abduction* by the agent is an epistemic expansion such that for $B \in K$, $(A \Rightarrow B) \in K$, and $A \notin T_{EcQ}(K)$, do K^{e+A}. The basic properties of these epistemic operations can be found in [5].

An *epistemic process* of an agent is a sequence $K_0, o_1, K_1, o_2, K_2, ..., K_{n-1}, o_n, K_n$ where $K_i \subseteq F(EcQ)$ ($n \geq i \geq 0$), called an *epistemic state* of the epistemic process, is a set of sentences to represent known knowledge and/or current beliefs of the agent, and o_{i+1} ($n > i \geq 0$), is any of primary epistemic operations, and K_{i+1} is the result of applying o_{i+1} to K_i. An epistemic process $K_0, o_1, K_1, ..., o_n, K_n$ is said to be *consistent* if and only if $T_{EcQ}(K_i)$ is consistent for any i ($n \geq i \geq 0$); an epistemic process $K_0, o_1, K_1, ..., o_n, K_n$ is said to be *inconsistent* if and only if $T_{EcQ}(K_i)$ is consistent but $T_{EcQ}(K_j)$ is inconsistent for all j>i; an epistemic process $K_0, o_1, K_1, ..., o_n, K_n$ is said to be *paraconsistent* if and only if $T_{EcQ}(K_i)$ is inconsistent but $T_{EcQ}(K_j)$ is consistent for some j>i; an epistemic process $K_0, o_1, K_1, ..., o_n, K_n$ is said to be *monotonic* if $K_i \subseteq K_j$ for any i<j; an epistemic process $K_0, o_1, K_1, ..., o_n, K_n$ is said to be *nonmonotonic* if $K_j \subset K_i$ for some i<j. Any epistemic process $K_0, o_1, K_1, ..., o_n, K_n$ including an epistemic contraction must be nonmonotonic.

The idea to model epistemic processes in scientific discovery using relevant logic rather than classical mathematical logic was first proposed in 1994 by the present author [3]. Other work by the author on this direction and a comparison with related work can be found in [5].

References

1. Anderson, A. R., Belnap Jr., N. D.: Entailment: The Logic of Relevance and Necessity. Vol. I. Princeton University Press (1975)
2. Anderson, A. R., Belnap Jr., N. D., Dunn, J. M.: Entailment: The Logic of Relevance and Necessity. Vol. II. Princeton University Press (1992)
3. Cheng, J.: A Relevant Logic Approach to Modeling Epistemic Processes in Scientific Discovery. Proc. 3rd Pacific Rim International Conference on Artificial Intelligence. Vol. 1. (1994) 444-450
4. Cheng, J.: The Fundamental Role of Entailment in Knowledge Representation and Reasoning. Journal of Computing and Information. Vol. 2. No. 1 (1996) 853-873
5. Cheng, J.: A Strong Relevant Logic Model of Epistemic Processes in Scientific Discovery. Working Notes of ECAI-98 Workshop on Machine Discovery (1998) 20-29
6. Gärdenfors, P., Rott, H.: Belief Revision. In: Gabbay, D. M., Hogger, C. J., Robinson, J. A. (eds.): Handbook of Logic in Artificial Intelligence and Logic Programming. Vol.4. Epistemic and Temporal Reasoning. Oxford University Press (1995) 35-132

Discovering Conceptual Differences among Different People via Diverse Structures

Tetsuya Yoshida[1] Teruyuki Kondo[1] Shogo Nishida[1]

Dept. of Systems and Human Science, Grad. School of Eng. Science, Osaka Univ.,
1-3 Machikaneyama-cho, Toyonaka, Osaka 560-8531, Japan

Abstract. We extend a method for discovering conceptual differences among people by introducing diverse structures utilizing Genetic Algorithm (GA). In general different people seem to have different ways of conception and thus can have different concepts even on the same thing. Removing conceptual differences seems especially important when people with different backgrounds and knowledge carry out collaborative works as a group; otherwise they cannot communicate ideas and establish mutual understanding even on the same thing. In our approach knowledge from users is structured into decision trees so that differences in concepts can be discovered as the differences in the structure of trees. In our previous approach ID3 algorithm is utilized to construct a single decision tree based on the information theory. However, it has a problem that conceptual differences which are not represented in the tree due to the low information gain cannot be dealt with. To solve this problem, this paper proposes a new method for discovering conceptual differences which utilizes diverse structures via GA. Experiments were carried out on motor diagnosis cases with artificially encoded conceptual differences and the result shows the superiority of introducing diverse structures with GA to a single decision tree which is constructed with ID3.

1 Introduction: Discovering Conceptual Difference

It is required to support collaborative works with the participation of various people by extending conventional information processing technologies in accordance with the need for dealing with large-scale accummulated cases. In addition, the importance of facilitating interdisciplinary collaboration among people with different backgrounds has been recognized these days. As for supporting collaborative works among people, various researches have been carried out in the field of CSCW (Computer Supported Cooperative Work) [1].

We aim at supporting mutual understanding among people when they collaboratively work as a group. In this paper we focus on dealing with "Conceptual Difference" at the symbol level. Usually different symbols are used to denote different concepts, however, the same symbol can be used to denote different concepts depending on the viewpoint of people and the context in which the symbol is used. In contrast, different symbols can be used to represent the same concept. These can occur especially among people with different backgrounds and knowledge. Conceptual differences dealt with in this paper are defined as follows:

– Type 1: different symbols are used to denote the same concept.
– Type 2: the same symbol is used to denote different concepts.

We have proposed a system for discovering conceptual differences among people based on the cases provided by users [3, 6]. In that system concepts held by users are structured into a concrete representation of decision trees and the system points out the possibility of conceptual differences based on the structure of decision tree. By representing the knowledge of each user as a single decision tree, the system could discover conceptual differences with high probability, however, several problems are found due to the usage of single decision tree for each user.

ID3 algorithm [4] has been utilized to construct decision trees since it is fast and thus is suitable for interactive systems. The system architecture which incorporates the descovering method is shown in Fig 1. By accepting the cases as input the system constructs decision trees for them and tries to discover conceptual differences in attributes, values and classes based on the structural differences in trees. Since there are 2 types of conceptual differences for 3 entities, the system tries to discover 6 kinds of conceptual differences and shows the candidates for them in the descending order of the possibility to users. Based on the result from the system users discuss each other to change their concepts toward reducing conceptual differences and modify input data to the system. The above processes are repeated interactively to remove CD gradually. In future we plan to extend the system so that it be applicable to more than two users.

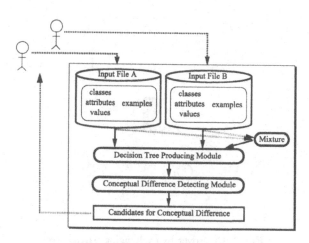

Fig. 1. System Architecture

2 Discovery Method based on Diverse Structures

ID3 algorithm constructs only one fixed structure for an input file. Thus, it sometimes occurs that the attributes and the values with conceptual difference do not appear in decision trees. Since conceptual difference is discovered based on the structure of trees, the system with ID3 algorithm cannot discover conceptual difference which does not appear in decision trees explicitly. If decision trees with diverse structures for an input file are constructed, the possibility of discovering conceptual difference increases and thus the above problem might be solved. Since GA (Genetic Algorithm) can carry out efficient or convinient search by keeping or improving the quality of decision trees [5], we apply GA to construct various types of decision trees and to increase the possibility of finding out the appropriate conceptual difference by keeping diverse structures.

The tree structure is used to represent the genetic information in order to reflect the structure of decision trees in our approach. The nodes except the leaves in the representation contain the position in the decision tree and the attribute to judge the branch in the decision tree. The branch in the genetic representation contains the value, which indicates the branch to follow in the decision tree.

In our approach, three operators, crossover, mutation and selection, are used in GA. Crossover is used to exchange the partial trees as in Figure 2. The same attribute might appear more than once on the path from the root to the leaf as the result of crossover. Since the nodes with the same attribute except the first one is meaningless, these are removed as in Figure 3. Moreover, leaf nodes with no case data are removed since they do not contribute to the classification.

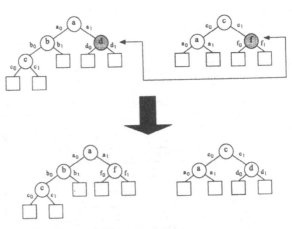

Fig. 2. Crossover by exchanging partial trees.

The set of decision trees which should survive to the next generation needs to have the ability to classify examples efficiently and to have diverse structures as described above. Therefore, selection is carried out under the following two indexes; error rate and mutual distance. When examples are classified into a single class efficiently in each leaf, error rate gets larger. Smaller value in this index is better. When each structure in one set of decision trees is more diverse,

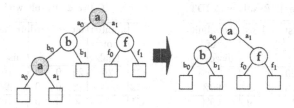

Fig. 3. Remove redundant nodes on one path

mutual distance among decision trees gets larger, and larger value in this index is judged as better. Decision trees with smaller error rate survive in the first stage, and mutual distance is calculated for each set of decision trees which are constructed as the combination of the trees. Finally the set of decision trees with the largest mutual distance becomes the initial population in the next generation. For further details on our algorithm, please refer to [2].

2.1 Experiment and Evaluation

A prototype system has been developed on the UNIX workstation with C language. As an example, the motor diagnosis case was evaluated. In this case, two persons gave their knowledge in the form of thirty examples, which were composed of six attributes, two or three values and five classes, respectively. The artificial conceptual difference, including what could not be discovered by the system with ID3 algorithm alone, were given to the system to evaluate the ability to discover conceptual difference. GA was carried out until the hundredth generation.

Experiments were carried out in the condition that two kinds of conceptual differences occured at the same time in the test cases. As the quantitative ealuation, the number of discovery and its probability of discovery up to the third candidate were collected in the experiments both for the system with ID3 and that with GA. The experiments showed that the candidates which had higher possibility of expressing conceptual difference were intensified and that noisy candidates were restrained by employing diverse structures. It was confirmed by these results that the performance improves by adopting GA as the decision tree construction algorithm. is shown in Table 2.1 and Table 2.1.

3 Conclusion

This paper has proposed a method to improve the discovery of conceptual differences among people from cases by utilizing multiple decision trees with diverse structures. Experiments were carried out for our previous system with ID3 algorithm and for the system with the proposed method and the result on motor diagnosis cases showed that the peformance on discovery was improved compared with our previous approach. Further experiments are to be carried out to

Table 1. Result with ID3.

	number of trials	1st	2nd	3rd	probability of discovery
C1	20	20	0	0	100%
C2		18	0	0	90%
C1	30	17	1	0	60%
A2		5	3	7	50%
C1	30	30	0	0	100%
V2		52	0	0	87%
C2	30	22	0	1	77%
V1		24	4	0	93%
A1	30	12	13	3	93%
A2		6	3	7	53%
A1	30	12	11	7	100%
V2		45	2	6	88%

Table 2. Result with GA.

	number of trials	1st	2nd	3rd	probability of discovery
C1	20	20	0	0	100%
C2		18	0	0	90%
C1	30	30	0	0	100%
A2		19	6	2	90%
C1	30	30	0	0	100%
V2		52	8	0	100%
C2	30	23	1	0	80%
V1		30	0	0	100%
A1	30	14	10	4	93%
A2		20	8	2	100%
A1	30	20	9	1	100%
V2		38	22	0	100%

clarify the characteristics of our approach as well as to tune the parameters used in Genetic Algorithm toward improving the performance of the system.

Acknowledgments

This research is partially supported by Grant in Aid for Scientific Research from the Japanese Ministry of Education, Science and Culture (10875080, 09450159, 10143211).

References

1. R. Baecker, editor. *Readings in Groupware and Computer-Supported Cooperative Work - Assisting Human-Human Collaboration.* Morgan Kaufmann, 1993.
2. T. Kondo, N. Saiwaki, H. Tsujimoto, and S. Nishida. A Method of Detecting Conceptual Difference among Different People on the basis of Diverse Structures. In *9th SICE Symposium on Decentralized Autonomous Systems*, pages 125–130, 1997. in Japanese.
3. T. Kondo, T. Yoshida, and S. Nishida. Design of the Interfaces to Detect Conceptual Difference among Different People. *Information Processing Society of Japan*, 39(5):1195–1202, May 1998. in Japanese.
4. J. R. Quinlan. Induction of decision trees. *Machine Learning*, 1:81–106, 1986.
5. John R.Koza. *Genetic programming II: automatic discovery of reusable programs.* MIT Press, 2nd edition, 1994.
6. T. Yoshida, T. Kondo, and S. Nishida. Discovering Conceptual Differences among People from Cases. In *The First International Conference on Discovery Science*, pages 162 – 173, December 1998.

Ordered Estimation of Missing Values

Oscar Ortega Lobo and Masayuki Numao

Department of Computer Science
Tokyo Institute of Technology
2-12-1 Ookayama, Meguro-ku
Tokyo 152-8552, Japan
e-mail: {beatriz,numao}@cs.titech.ac.jp

Abstract. When attempting to discover by learning concepts embedded in data, it is not uncommon to find that information is missing from the data. Such missing information can diminish the confidence on the concepts learned from the data. This paper describes a new approach to fill missing values in examples provided to a learning algorithm. A decision tree is constructed to determine the missing values of each attribute by using the information contained in other attributes. Also, an ordering for the construction of the decision trees for the attributes is formulated. Experimental results on three datasets show that completing the data by using decision trees leads to final concepts with less error under different rates of random missing values. The approach should be suitable for domains with strong relations among the attributes, and for which improving accuracy is desirable even if computational cost increases.

1 Introduction

Machine learning techniques have been successfully employed to extract concepts embedded in data describing instances from a particular domain. When the instances are described by attributes and propositions on attribute values for each instance, this type of learning is called *propositional learning*. Algorithms already exist that manage to build concepts from the above type of data [8, 2].

One troublesome aspect of data sets used in machine learning is the occurrence of unknown attribute values for some instances in the available data. Missing values phenomenon is likely to occur after generating by-products on different data collections, which is an operation commonly carried out during the process of knowledge discovery [5]. When missing values occur in the data, the learning algorithm fails to find an accurate representation of the concept (e.g., decision trees or rules). Properly filling missing values in data can help in reducing the error rate of the learned concepts. Thus, the purpose of this paper is to introduce and evaluate a mechanism to fill missing values in the data employed by a propositional learning algorithm.

This paper is organized as follows. First, the approach for estimating missing values is explained, then experimental results on several datasets are discussed, followed by a survey of related work. Finally, suitable domains, restrictions, and further improvements are discussed.

2 Estimating Missing Values

Having established the need to fill missing values in the data of a particular domain, it is advisable to make the most efficient use of information already available in the data. That is to say, it seems worthwhile to design a method that uses the maximum amount of information derivable from the data, while at the same time holding computational demands to a sustainable level. In this section, a new method for filling missing values is described in terms of how these two requirements have been met.

In order to fulfill the first requirement, decision trees are constructed for each attribute by using a reduced training set with only those examples that have known values for the attribute. The reason for using decision trees is that they are suitable for representing relations among the most important attributes when determining the value of a target attribute. In addition, decision tree learning algorithms are fast on formulating accurate concepts.

After constructing a decision tree for filling the missing values of an attribute, it makes sense to use the data with filled values in order to construct a decision tree for filling the missing values of other attributes. Therefore, the order followed when constructing attribute trees and filling the missing values per attribute becomes important. The ordering proposed here is based on the concept in Information Theory called *mutual information*, which has been successfully used as a criteria for attribute selection in decision tree learning [8].

Mutual Information between two ensembles X and Y is defined by:

$$H(X;Y) \equiv \sum_{x \in A_x} P(x) \ log \frac{1}{P(x)} - \sum_{y \in A_y} P(y) \left[\sum_{x \in A_x} P(x|y) \ log \frac{1}{P(x|y)} \right] \quad (1)$$

Mutual information measures the average reduction in uncertainty about X that results from learning the value of Y, or vice versa. If the attributes and the class are assumed as ensembles, then, by measuring mutual information among attributes and class, inferences can be done about the strength of the relations between them.

In propositional learning, attributes that have low mutual information with respect to the class have less chance to participate in the final concept, so that properly filling the missing values for such attributes will have very low impact on the accuracy of the final concept. In contrast, attributes having high mutual information with respect to the class have a higher chance of being incorporated into the final concept, making it worthwhile trying to obtain a finer filling of their missing values.

Considering previous discussion and the requirement of holding computational demands to a sustainable level, the ordering proposed in this approach can be expressed as follows. Let C to be the class variable. At first, construct decision trees and fill the missing values for attributes which have low mutual information with respect to C. When constructing the decision tree for any particular attribute A_i discard from the training set those attributes A_k for which $H(A_i;C) < H(A_k;C)$.

3 Experiments and Discussion

The experimental focus of this paper is to compare the accuracy of decision tree learning from data sets whose missing values have been filled by different methods. In the experiments, the proposed *attribute trees method* is compared with two other methods used in machine learning for dealing with missing values: the *majority method* [4] and the *probabilistic method* [3].

Ten-fold cross validation experiments were carried out for each of the three methods. Each experiment was conducted for rates of artificial missing values ranging from 10% to 70%. Artificial missing values were generated in identical proportions and following the same distribution for each attribute. Figure 1 shows a summary of the characteristics of the three datasets used for the evaluations.

name	instances	attr	class
Soybean	307	35 cat	19
BreastCW	699	9 num	2
Mushroom	8124	21 cat	2

Fig. 1. Summary of Datasets

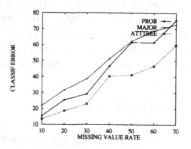

Fig. 2. Results on Soybean

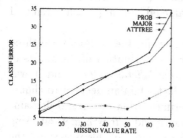

Fig. 3. Results on BreastCW

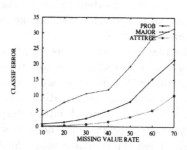

Fig. 4. Results on Mushroom

When looking at the effects of missing data, the most reasonable assumption is that future data will contain the same proportion and kinds of missing values as the present data [2]. Accordingly, the experiments conducted in this study included artificial missing values in identical proportion and distribution in both training and test data.

Figures 2, 3, and 4 plot the average classification error for concepts learned on each of the target domains, depending on each of the three methods. The difference in error performance between the *attribute trees* method and the other two methods was found to be significant at the 95% confidence level for all tested rates of missing values in all data sets. These results indicate that when missing values occur in both the training and test instances, the *attribute trees* method is superior on modeling the missing values in the three domains tested.

The worst performance was obtained with the *majority method*, as was expected, since this method can not be used for filling missing values in the test data. In contrast, the *probabilistic* and *attribute trees* methods are more complete in the sense that they can deal with missing values in both training and test data.

The *probabilistic method* constructs a model of the missing values, which depends only on the prior distribution of the attribute values for each attribute being tested in a node of the tree. This approach is adequate when most of the attributes are independent, so that the model can rely on the values of each attribute, without regard of the other attributes. Attribute trees are more complete models because they can represent complex relations among the attributes, which appear when there is high dependency among the attributes.

4 Related Work

In propositional learning, one of the first approaches for dealing with missing values was to ignore instances with missing data [8]. This approach was soon found to be weak in the sense of not-profiting of useful information present in instances with some missing attribute values. Thus, a method that considered the most frequent attribute value as a good candidate for filling the missing value was proposed and extended later to take the most frequent attribute value for the class of the instance that has the missing value [4].This approach is referred as *majority method*.

Another approach is to assign all possible values for the attribute, weighted by its prior probability estimated from the known distribution of the values of the attribute[3]. This approach is referred as *probabilistic method*, and it was borrowed for the implementation of C4.5[7]. In fact, Quinlan decided to choose the probabilistic approach after extensive experimentation on several domains [6], comparing the three methods mentioned above and a fourth method using decision trees per each attribute. The approach presented in this paper and the latest tested by Quinlan have two differences. First, here the attribute trees are constructed following an ordering, and second, only the attributes with less mutual information with respect to the class are taken as input for the construction of a tree for a particular attribute.

On the statistics side of research on decision tree learning, the *surrogate splits method* was formulated by Breiman[2] on his work on binary regression trees. This method always keeps secondary attributes to be tested at each node of the decision tree when it happens that the value of the primary attribute is missing. In fact, this method can be viewed as an specific case of the more general approach of using decision trees to fill the missing values of the attributes[6].

5 Concluding Remarks

A method for obtaining missing values has been proposed and successfully tested on several data sets. On the tested domains, the new method is seen to provide significantly better performance than the two methods currently used to deal with missing values in propositional learning. Domains with high dependency among the attributes are thought to be the most suitable for application of the approach introduced in this paper.

All the datasets tested here have discrete values for their attributes. This restriction follows from the nature of the decision tree learner used to construct the attribute trees. Further experimentation on using a decision tree learner that can deal with continuous classes is advisable.

The increase in computational cost was not evaluated here. Indeed, the approach is thought to be suitable for domains for which an increase in computational cost is worth to the benefit obtained by lowering the classification error.

6 Acknowledgments

This research has been done under a grant from Japanese Ministry of Education. The experimental data sets are from UCI Machine Learning Repository [1]

References

1. C. Blake, E. Keogh, and C.J. Merz. UCI repository of machine learning databases. In [http://www.ics.uci.edu/~mlearn/MLRepository.html]. University of California, Department of Information and Computer Science, Irvine, CA, 1998.
2. Leo Breiman, Jerome H. Friedman, Richard A. Olshen, and Charles J. Stone. Classification and Regression Trees. Chapman & Hall, 1993.
3. B. Cestnik, I. Kononenko, and I. Bratko. Assistant-86: A knowledge-elicitation tool for sophisticated users. In Ivan Bratko and Nada Lavrac, editors, Progress in Machine Learning. Sigma Press, Wilmslow, UK, 1987.
4. I. Kononenko and E. Roscar. Experiments in automatic learning of medical diagnostic rules. Technical report, Jozef Stefan Institute, Ljubjana, Yugoslavia, 1984.
5. W.Z. Liu, A.P. White, S.G. Thompson, and M.A. Bramer. Techniques for dealing with missing values in classification. In Proc of Advances in Intelligent Data Analysis (IDA '97), volume 1280 of Lecture notes in computer science, pages 527-536. Springer, 1997.
6. J. R. Quinlan. Unknown attribute values in induction. In Proceedings of the sixth international Machine Learning workshop, pages 164-168. Morgan Kaufmann, 1989.
7. J. Ross Quinlan. Unknown attribute values. In C4.5 Programs for Machine Learning, pages 27-32. Morgan Kaufmann, 1993.
8. J.R. Quinlan. Induction of decision trees. Machine Learning, 1:81-106, 1986.

Prediction Rule Discovery Based on Dynamic Bias Selection

Einoshin Suzuki and Toru Ohno

Electrical and Computer Engineering, Yokohama National University,
79-5 Tokiwadai, Hodogaya, Yokohama 240-8501, Japan
suzuki@dnj.ynu.ac.jp

Abstract. This paper presents an algorithm for discovering prediction rules with dynamic bias selection. A prediction rule, which is aimed at predicting the class of an unseen example, deserves special attention due to its usefulness. However, little attention has been paid to the dynamic selection of biases in prediction rule discovery. A dynamic selection of biases is useful since it reduces humans' burden of choosing and adjusting multiple mining algorithms. In this paper, we propose a novel rule discovery algorithm D^3BiS, which is based on a data-driven criterion. Our approach has been validated using 17 data sets.

1 Introduction

Currently, most of the methods for prediction rule discovery have a fixed combination of biases. A constructive induction algorithm such as [4] is not always appropriate in prediction rule discovery, since the applicability of the hypothesis is not considered in learning from examples. Morik proposed a multistrategy rule discovery system [6], but his goal is characterization of a data set rather than the discovery of prediction rules. In order to cope with this problem, we propose D^3BiS, a rule discovery system based on dynamic bias selection. This selection is based on an evaluation criterion of class-attributes dependency. Preliminary results with 15 data sets from the UCI repository [5] and 2 real-world data sets [7] are promising.

2 Discovery of Prediction Rules

2.1 Problem Description

Consider a **training data set** D_{L0} with examples each of which is expressed with m attributes. First, every continuous attribute, if any, is converted to a nominal attribute using a discretization method [1], and we obtain a **discretized training data set** D_L. An event representing, in propositional form, a single value assignment to an attribute will be called an **atom**. We define a **prediction rule** $y \rightarrow x$ as the production rule of which **premise** y is represented by a logical expression of atoms and **conclusion** x is a single atom.

In D^3BiS, we consider the problem of finding a set of K rules $R = \{r_1, r_2, \cdots, r_K\}$ with a fixed conclusion x from D_L. In this problem, an algorithm is evaluated according to the set of rules it discovers in terms of a **test data set** D_{T0}. A **discretized test data set** D_T is defined as the output of the algorithm which is employed in the discretization of the training data set. The proportions of examples that an atom z covers in the discretized training data set and the discretized test data set are represented by $\widehat{\Pr}(z)$ and $\Pr(z)$ respectively.

In evaluating the goodness of a rule set R, we consider two indices: the **applicability** $\Pr(Y)$ **of a rule set**, which is the proportion of examples that the premises of a rule set R covers in D_T, and the **accuracy** $\Pr(x|Y)$ **of a rule set**, which is the the proportion of the correct predictions for these examples. When an example in D_T is covered by more than two rules in R, we define that the rule with the smallest subscript is selected for its prediction.

J-measure [8] is a single criterion which evaluates both applicability and accuracy with various desirable properties. In this paper, we employ **J-measure** $J_T(R)$ **of a rule set** R in a discretized test data set D_T as the evaluation criterion of R, where $\overline{x}$ represents the negation of x.

$$J_T(R) \equiv \Pr(x, Y) \log_2 \frac{\Pr(x|Y)}{\Pr(x)} + \Pr(\overline{x}, Y) \log_2 \frac{\Pr(\overline{x}|Y)}{\Pr(\overline{x})} \qquad (1)$$

2.2 Biases in Rule Discovery

In this paper, a discovery task is viewed as a search problem, in which a node of a search tree represents a rule r. We define that the premise of a rule contains no atoms in a node of depth 1, and as the depth increases by 1, an atom is added to the premise of the rule. The rules which have the K highest values of an evaluation criterion are outputted as a rule set. D^3BiS employs depth-first search until a fixed depth, and beam search for further depth.

First, for the evaluation criterion, we consider predictiveness and J-measure of a rule. **Predictiveness** of a rule $y \to x$ is defined as the conditional probability $\widehat{\Pr}(x|y)$ in the discretized training data set. When more than two rules have the same predictiveness, they are evaluated according to their $\widehat{\Pr}(y)$. **J-measure [8]** $J_L(r)$ **of a rule** $r : y \to x$ is defined as follows.

$$J_L(r) \equiv \widehat{\Pr}(x, y) \log_2 \left(\frac{\widehat{\Pr}(x|y)}{\widehat{\Pr}(x)} \right) + \widehat{\Pr}(\overline{x}, y) \log_2 \frac{\widehat{\Pr}(\overline{x}|y)}{\widehat{\Pr}(\overline{x})} \qquad (2)$$

Second, for the rule representation, we consider a conjunction rule and an M-of-N rule. A conjunction rule is a production rule whose premise is a conjunction of atoms. On the other hand, an M-of-N rule is a production rule whose premise becomes true when more than M of its N atoms become true.

Third, for the discretization method, we consider the equal frequency method [1] and the minimum entropy method of [2]. The equal frequency method, when the number of bins is k, divides n examples so that each bin contains n/k (possibly duplicated) adjacent values. The minimum entropy method discretizes examples so that the class entropy is minimized. In [2], the number of bins is automatically determined.

3 Data-driven Selection of Biases

The biases presented in the previous section can be divided into two groups: simple biases and complex biases. Predictiveness, an M-of-N rule and the equal frequency method belong to simple biases, while other biases are complex biases. If the class can be easily predicted, a simple bias would be more effective than a complex one. Therefore, we select simple biases when the data set is easy.

Now the problem is to evaluate the difficulty of a data set. We have modified the dependency between the class and the other attributes in COBWEB [3]. The following **modified dependency** Dep' is employed in D^3BiS, where A_i and V_{ij} represent an attribute and an attribute value respectively.

$$Dep' \equiv \frac{1}{m} \left[\sum_{i=1}^{m} \sum_{j} \widehat{\Pr}(A_i = V_{ij})^2 \left(\widehat{\Pr}(x|A_i = V_{ij})^2 - \widehat{\Pr}(x)^2 \right.\right.$$

$$\left.\left. + \widehat{\Pr}(\bar{x}|A_i = V_{ij})^2 - \widehat{\Pr}(\bar{x})^2 \right) \right] \tag{3}$$

First, consider the selection of the evaluation criterion. Generally, predictiveness is superior in finding rules with large $\widehat{\Pr}(x|y)$, and J-measure of a rule in finding rules with large $\widehat{\Pr}(y)$. When the modified dependency Dep' is large, predictiveness is considered to be a good criterion since it is relatively easy to find rules with large $\widehat{\Pr}(y)$. When the modified dependency is small, predictiveness tends to find rules each of which premise covers a small number of examples. Therefore, D^3BiS employs predictiveness when the modified dependency is smaller than a given **evaluation threshold** θ_E, and J-measure of a rule otherwise.

Second, consider the selection of the rule representation. With respect to the applicability $\Pr(Y)$ of a rule set, an M-of-N rule usually beats a conjunction rule since each rule has large $\widehat{\Pr}(y)$. On the other hand, a conjunction rule is superior to an M-of-N rule in the accuracy $\Pr(x|Y)$ of a rule set since each rule has large $\widehat{\Pr}(x|y)$. When the modified dependency Dep' is large, this superiority seems to decrease since each rule has large $\widehat{\Pr}(y)$. Therefore, D^3BiS employs an M-of-N rule when the modified dependency is large, and a conjunction rule otherwise. For this judgement, we have found that the attribute which has the largest dependency to the class plays an important role. We introduce the **modified dependency** $Dep(A_i)'$ for an attribute A_i.

$$Dep(A_i)' \equiv \frac{1}{m} \left[\sum_{j} \widehat{\Pr}(A_i = V_{ij})^2 \left(\widehat{\Pr}(x|A_i = V_{ij})^2 - \widehat{\Pr}(x)^2 \right.\right.$$

$$+\widehat{\Pr}(\overline{x}|A_i = V_{ij})^2 - \widehat{\Pr}(\overline{x})^2 \Big) \Bigg] \tag{4}$$

D^3BiS employs an M-of-N rule if $MAX(dep(A_i)) > \theta_{R1}Dep'$, where θ_{R1} is a **representation threshold 1**, or if Dep' is larger than a given **representation threshold 2** θ_{R2}. Otherwise, a conjunction rule is employed unless predictiveness is employed as evaluation criterion. This constraint is due to the fact that the combination of these 2 biases tends to produce rules each of which $\widehat{\Pr}(y)$ is small.

Third, consider the selection of the discretization method. D^3BiS tries the equal frequency method with 2 to 10 bins and the minimum entropy method, then selects the method with the maximum Dep'. Here, the equal frequency method tends to have a large number of bins since it does not consider class information. For a similar reason as above, D^3BiS always employs the minimum entropy method when predictiveness is employed as the evaluation criterion.

4 Experimental Evaluation

The effectiveness of D^3BiS has been evaluated with 17 data sets from which 47 discovery tasks were settled. Data sets used in the experiments are: hepatitis, servo, wine, imports-85, heart, housing, australian, diabetes, vehicle, tic-tac-toe, segmentation, allbp, allhyper, allhypo and mushroom from UCI repository [5]; kiosk and horse from [7]. For a data set with a discrete class, we have chosen, as a conclusion, every class which covers more than 1% of the whole examples. For "housing" and "servo", their continuous class attributes are first discretized with the equal frequency method into 5 bins, and the bins with the largest and the smallest values are chosen as a conclusion. Same method was used for "imports-85", where "price" and "city-mpg" attributes are considered as a class attribute.

We employed a combination of depth-first search until depth 3, and beam search with beam width 5 for further depth in the experiments. A 5 fold cross validation was used in estimating the J-measure of the rule sets. Concerning the parameters in section 3, we used $K = 5$, $\theta_E = 0.04$, $\theta_{R1} = 0.9$ and $\theta_{R2} = 0.008$.

In the experiments, we observed that the combinations of biases selected by D^3BiS were frequently almost as good as their respective best combination. In terms of J-measure of a rule set, 30 combinations selected by D^3BiS were more than 90 % of their respective best combination. Therefore, D^3BiS selected the best or a nearly best combination of biases in 2/3 of the cases.

We investigated this performance of D^3BiS in terms of the number of examples covered by the conclusion, and the results are shown in table 1. In the table, the second column represents the ratio of the J-measure of the rule set discovered by D^3BiS to the J-measure of the rule set discovered with the best combination. The third column represents average performance of biases combinations.

From the table, D^3BiS is as good as the best method, and far outperforms the average performance. D^3BiS's performance, unlike the average case, increases as the number of examples increases. We attribute this to its analysis of biases in terms of the dependency between the class and the other attributes.

Table 1. Relative performance $J_T(R)$ of D^3BiS and the average case to the best case with respect to the number of examples in the conclusion

# of examples (tasks)	0 - 99 (16)	100 - 199 (8)	200 - 299 (5)	300 - 399 (10)	500 - (8)
D^3BiS	0.79	0.94	0.92	0.92	1.00
Average	0.67	0.68	0.65	0.73	0.67

5 Conclusions

This paper has described a novel approach for discovering prediction rules using dynamic selection of biases. The selection is based on the analysis of the dependency between the class and the other attributes. An evaluation criterion, which is a modification of class-attributes dependency [3], is employed for this purpose. Experimental results with 47 discovery tasks show that our system is effective for the discovery of prediction rules.

Acknowledgement

This work was partially supported by the Grant-in-Aid for Scientific Research (C) from the Japanese Ministry of Education, Science, Sports and Culture.

References

1. Dougherty, J., Kohavi, R. and Sahami, M.: "Supervised and Unsupervised Discretization of Continuous Features", *Proc. ICML-95*, pp. 194–202(1995).
2. Fayyad, U. M. and Irani, K. B.: "Multi-Interval Discretization of Continuous-Valued Attributes for Classification Learning", *Proc. IJCAI-93*, pp. 1022–1027 (1993).
3. Fisher, D. H.: "Knowledge Acquisition Via Incremental Conceptual Clustering", *Machine Learning*, Vol. 2, pp. 139–172 (1987).
4. Giordana, A., Neri, F., Saitta, L. et al.: "Integrating Multiple Learning Strategies in First Order Logics", *Machine Learning*, Vol. 27, No. 3, pp. 209–240 (1997).
5. Merz, C. J. and Murphy, P. M.: "UCI Repository of Machine Learning Databases", *http://www.ics.uci.edu/~mlearn/MLRepository.html*, Dept. of Information and Computer Sci., Univ. of California Irvine (1996).
6. Morik, K. and Brockhausen, P.: "A Multistrategy Approach to Relational Knowledge Discovery in Databases", *Machine Learning*, Vol. 27, No. 3, pp. 287–312 (1997).
7. Ohno, T.: *Study on Rule Induction with Dynamic Bias Selection*, Master thesis, Elec. and Computer Eng., Yokohama Nat'l Univ., Japan (1998).
8. Smyth, P. and Goodman, R. M.: "An Information Theoretic Approach to Rule Induction from Databases", *IEEE Trans. Knowledge and Data Eng.*, Vol. 4, No. 4, pp. 301–316 (1992).

Discretization of Continuous Attributes for Learning Classification Rules

Aijun An and Nick Cercone

Department of Computer Science, University of Waterloo
Waterloo, Ontario N2L 3G1 Canada

Abstract. We present a comparison of three entropy-based discretization methods in a context of learning classification rules. We compare the binary recursive discretization with a stopping criterion based on the Minimum Description Length Principle (MDLP)[3], a non-recursive method which simply chooses a number of cut-points with the highest entropy gains, and a non-recursive method that selects cut-points according to both information entropy and distribution of potential cut-points over the instance space. Our empirical results show that the third method gives the best predictive performance among the three methods tested.

1 Introduction

Recent work on entropy-based discretization of continuous attributes has produced positive results [2, 6] . One promising method is Fayyad and Irani's binary recursive discretization with a stopping criterion based on the Minimum Description Length Principle (MDLP) [3]. The MDLP method is reported as a successful method for discretization in the decision tree learning and Naive-Bayes learning environments [2, 6]. However, little research has been done to investigate whether the method works well with other rule induction methods. We report our performance findings of the MDLP discretization in a context of learning classification rules. The learning system we use for experiments is ELEM2 [1], which learns classification rules from a set of training data by selecting the most relevant attribute-value pairs. We first compare the MDLP method with an entropy-based method that simply selects a number of entropy-lowest cut-points. The results show that the MDLP method fails to find sufficient useful cut-points, especially on small data sets. The experiments also discover that the other method tends to select cut-points from a small local area of the entire value space, especially on large data sets. To overcome these problems, we introduce a new entropy-based discretization method that selects cut-points based on both information entropy and distribution of potential cut-points. Our conclusion is that MDLP does not give the best results in most tested datasets. The proposed method performs better than MDLP in the ELEM2 learning environment.

2 The MDLP Discretization Method

Given a set S of instances, an attribute A, and a cut-point T, the class information entropy of the partition induced by T, denoted as $E(A, T; S)$, is defined as

$$E(A, T; S) = \frac{|S_1|}{|S|} Ent(S_1) + \frac{|S_2|}{|S|} Ent(S_2),$$

where $Ent(S_i)$ is the class entropy of the subset S_i, defined as

$$Ent(S_i) = -\sum_{j=1}^{k} P(C_j, S_i) log(P(C_j, S_i)),$$

where there are k classes $C_1, \cdots, C_k$ and $P(C_j, S_i)$ is the proportion of examples in S_i that have class C_j. For an attribute A, the MDLP method selects a cut point T_A for which $E(A, T_A; S)$ is minimal among all the boundary points[1]. The training set is then split into two subsets by the cut point. Subsequent cut points are selected by recursively applying the same binary discretization method to each of the newly generated subsets until the following condition is achieved:

$$Gain(A, T; S) <= \frac{log_2(N-1)}{N} + \frac{\Delta(A, T; S)}{N}$$

where N is the number of examples in S, $Gain(A, T; S) = Ent(S) - E(A, T; S)$, $\Delta(A, T; S) = log_2(3^k - 2) - [kEnt(S) - k_1 Ent(S_1) - k_2 Ent(S_2)]$, and k, k_1 and k_2 are the number of classes represented in the sets S, S_1 and S_2, respectively. Empirical results, presented in [3], show that the MDLP stopping criterion leads to construction of better decision trees. Dougherty *et al.* [2] also show that a global variant of the MDLP method significantly improved a Naive-Bayes classifier and it also performs best among several discretization methods in the context of C4.5 decision tree learning.

3 Experiments with MDLP Discretization and ELEM2

We conducted experiments with two versions of ELEM2. Both versions employ the entropy-based discretization method, but with different stopping criteria. One version uses the global variant of the MDLP discretization method, i.e., it discretizes continuous attributes using the recursive entropy-based method with the MDLP stopping criterion applied before rule induction begins. The other version uses the same entropy criterion for selecting cut-points before rule induction, but it simply chooses a maximal number of m entropy-lowest cut-points without recursive application of the method. m is set to be $max\{2, k * log_2 l\}$ where l is the number of distinct observed values for the attribute being discretized and k is the number of classes. We refer to this method as Max-m. Both versions first sort the examples according to their values of the attribute and then evaluate only the boundary points in their search for cut-points.

We first conduct the experiments on an artificial data set. Each example in the data set has two continuous attributes and a symbolic attribute. The

---

[1] Fayyad and Irani proved that the value T_A that minimizes the class entropy $E(A, T_A; S)$ must always be a value between two examples of different classes in the sequence of sorted examples. These kinds of values are called boundary points.

Training	Predictive accuracy		No. of cut-points		No. of rules		No. of Boun-
Set Size	MDLP	Max-m	MDLP	Max-m	MDLP	Max-m	dary Points
47	56.71%	95.20%	0	14	3	6	58
188	90.41%	100%	2	21	4	6	96
470	100%	100%	5	22	6	6	97
1877	100%	100%	29	22	6	6	97
4692	100%	100%	73	22	6	6	97

Table 1. Results on the Artificial Domain.

two continuous attributes, named $A1$ and $A2$, have value ranges of $[0, 90]$ and $[0, 5]$, respectively. The symbolic attribute, *color*, takes one of the four values: *red, blue, yellow* and *green*. An example belongs to class "1", if the following condition holds: $(30 < A1 \leq 60) \wedge (1.5 < A2 \leq 3.5) \wedge (color = blue \ or \ green)$; otherwise, it belongs to class "0". The data set has a total of 9384 examples. We randomly chose 6 training sets from these examples. The sizes of the training sets range from 47 examples (0.5%) to 4692 examples (50%). We run the two versions of ELEM2 on each of the 6 training sets to generate a set of decision rules. The rules are then tested on the original data set of 9384 examples. Table 1 depicts, for all the training sets, the predictive accuracy, the total number of cut-points selected for both continuous attributes, the total number of rules generated for both classes, and the number of boundary points for both continuous attributes. The results indicate that, when the number of training examples is small, the MDLP method stops too early and fails to find enough useful cut-points, which causes ELEM2 to generate rules that have poor predictive performance on the testing set. When the size of the training set increases, MDLP generates more cut-points and its predictive performance improves. For the middle-sized training set (470 examples), MDLP works perfectly because it finds only 5 cut-points from 97 boundary points, which include all of the four right cut-points that the learning system needs to generate correct rules. However, when the training set becomes larger, the number of cut-points MDLP finds increases greatly. In the last training set (4692 examples), it selects 73 cut-points out of 97 potential points, which slows down the learning system. In contrast, the Max-m method is more stable. The number of cut-points it produces ranges from 14 to 22 and its predictive performance is better than MDLP when the training set is small. We also run the two versions of ELEM2 on a number of actual data sets obtained from the UCI repository [4], each of which has at least one continuous attribute. Table 2 reports the ten-fold evaluation results on 6 of these data sets.

4 Discussion

The empirical results presented above indicate that MDLP is not superior to Max-m in most of tested data sets. One possible reason is that, when the training set is small, the examples are not sufficient to make the MDLP criterion valid and meaningful so that the criterion causes the discretization process to stop too

Data	Number of	Predictive accuracy		Average no. of rules	
Set	Examples	MDLP	Max-m	MDLP	Max-m
bupa	345	57.65%	66.93%	4	65
german	1000	68.30%	68.50%	107	100
glass	214	63.14%	68.23%	31	30
heart	270	81.85%	82.59%	48	30
iris	150	95.33%	96.67%	8	7
segment	2310	95.76%	90.65%	67	99

Table 2. Results on the Actual Data Sets.

early before producing useful cut-points. Another possible reason is that, even if the recursive MDLP method is applied to the entire instance space to find the first cut-point, it is applied "locally" in finding subsequent cut-points due to the recursive nature of the method. Local regions represent smaller samples of the instance space and the estimation based on small samples using the MDLP criterion may not be reliable.

Now that MDLP does not seem to be a good discretization method for ELEM2, is Max-m a reliable method? A close examination of the cut-points produced by Max-m for the *segment* data set uncovers that, for several attributes, the selected cut-points concentrate on a small local area of the entire value space. For example, for an attribute that ranges from 0 to 43.33, Max-m picks up 64 cut-points all of which fall between 0.44 and 4, even if there are many boundary cut-points lying out of this small area. This problem is caused by the way the Max-m method selects cut-points. Max-m first selects the cut-point that has the lowest entropy value and then selects as the next point the point with the second lowest entropy, and so on. This strategy may result in a large number of cut-points being selected near the first cut-point because their entropy values are closer to the entropy value of the first cut-point than the entropy values of the cut-points located far from the first cut-point. The cut-points located on a small area around the first cut-point offer very little additional discriminating power because the difference between them and the first cut-point involves only a few examples. In addition, since only the first m cut-pints are selected by Max-m, selecting too many cut-points in a small area may prohibit the algorithm from choosing the promising points in other regions.

5 A Revised Max-m Discretization Method

To overcome the weakness of the Max-m method, we propose a new entropy-based discretization method by revising Max-m. The new method avoids selecting cut-points within only one or two small areas. The new method chooses cut-points according to both information entropy and the distribution of boundary points over the instance space. The method is referred to as EDA-DB (Entropy-based Discretization According to Distribution of Boundary points). Similar to Max-m, EDA-DB selects a maximal number of m cut-points, where m is defined as in the Max-m method. However, rather than taking the first m entropy-lowest cut-points, EDA-DB divides the value range of the attribute into intervals and selects in each interval m_i number of cut-points based on the entropy calculated over the entire instance space. m_i is determined by estimating the probability distribution of the boundary points over the instance space. The EDA-DB discretization algorithm is described as follows. Let l be the number of distinct observed values for a continuous attribute A, b be the total number of boundary points for A, and k be the number of classes in the data set. To discretize A,

1. Calculate m as $max\{2, k * log_2(l)\}$.
2. Estimate the probability distribution of boundary points:
   (a) Divide the value range of A into d intervals, where $d = max\{1, log(l)\}$.
   (b) Calculate the number b_i of boundary points in each interval iv_i, where $i = 1, 2, \cdots, d$ and $\sum_{i=1}^{d} b_i = b$.
   (c) Estimate the probability of boundary points in each interval iv_i $(i = 1, 2, \cdots, d)$ as $p_i = \frac{b_i}{b}$.
3. Calculate the quota q_i of cut-points for each interval iv_i $(i = 1, 2, \cdots, d)$ according to m and the distribution of boundary points as follows: $q_i = p_i * m$
4. Rank the boundary points in each interval iv_i $(i = 1, 2, \cdots, d)$ by increasing order of the class information entropy of the partition induced by the boundary point. The entropy for each point is calculated globally over the entire instance space.
5. For each interval iv_i $(i = 1, 2, \cdots, d)$, select the first q_i points in the above ordered sequence. A total of m cut-points are selected.

6 Experiments with EDA-DB

We conducted experiments with EDA-DB coupled with ELEM2. We first conducted ten-fold evaluation on the *segment* data set to see whether EDA-DB improves over Max-m on this data set which has a large number of boundary points for several attributes. The result is that the predictive accuracy is increased to 95.11% and the average number of rules drops to 69. Figure 1 shows the ten-fold evaluation results on 14 UCI data sets. In the figure, the solid line represents the difference between EDA-DB's predictive accuracy and Max-m's, and the dashed line represents the accuracy difference between EDA-DB and MDLP. The results indicate that EDA-DB outperforms both Max-m and MDLP on most of the tested data sets.

7 Conclusions

We have presented an empirical comparison of three entropy-based discretization methods in a context of learning decision rules. We found that the MDLP method stops two early when the number of training examples is small and thus it fails to detect sufficient cut-points on small data sets. Our empirical results also indicate that Max-m and EDA-DB are better discretization methods for ELEM2 on most of the tested data sets. We conjecture that the recursive nature of the MDLP method may cause most of the cut-points to be selected based on small

514

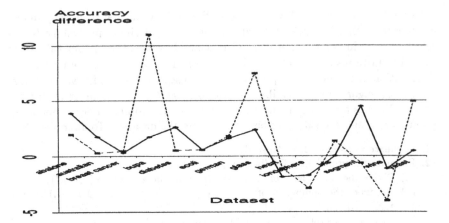

Fig. 1. Ten-fold Evaluation Results on Actual Data Sets.

samples of the instance space, which leads to generation of unreliable cut-points. The experiment with Max-m on the *segment* data set reveals that the strategy of simply selecting the first m entropy-lowest cut-points does not work well on large data sets with large number of boundary points. The reason for this is that entropy-lowest cut-points tend to concentrate on a small region of the instance space, which leads to the algorithm failing to pick up useful cut-points in other regions. Our proposed EDA-DB method alleviates the Max-m's problem by considering the distribution of boundary points over the instance space. Our test of EDA-DB on the *segment* data set shows that EDA-DB improves over Max-m on both the predictive accuracy and the number of rules generated. The experiments with EDA-DB on other tested data sets also confirm that EDA-DB is a better method than both Max-m and MDLP.

References

1. An, A. and Cercone, N. 1998. ELEM2: A Learning System for More Accurate Classifications. *Lecture Notes in Artificial Intelligence 1418.*
2. Dougherty, J., Kohavi, R. and Sahami, M. 1995. Supervised and Unsupervised Discretization of Continuous Features. *Proceedings of the Twelfth International Conference on Machine Learning.* Morgan Kaufmann Publishers, San Francisco, CA.
3. Fayyad, U.M. and Irani, K.B. 1993. Multi-Interval Discretization of Continuous-Valued Attributes for Classification Learning. *IJCAI-93.* pp. 1022-1027.
4. Murphy, P.M. and Aha, D.W. 1994. *UCI Repository of Machine Learning Databases.* URL: http://www.ics.uci.edu/AI/ML/MLDBRepository.html.
5. Quinlan, J.R. 1993. *C4.5: Programs for Machine Learning.* Morgan Kaufmann Publishers. San Mateo, CA.
6. Rabaseda-Loudcher, S., Sebban, M. and Rakotomalala, R. 1995. Discretization of Continuous Attributes: a Survey of Methods. *Proceedings of the 2nd Annual Joint Conference on Information Sciences,* pp.164-166.

BRRA: A Based Relevant Rectangles Algorithm for Mining Relationships in Databases

Sadok BEN YAHIA[1] and Ali JAOUA[2]

[1] Sciences Faculty of Tunis, Comp. Sci. Dept., Campus Universitaire, 1060 Le Belvedère,Tunis, Tunisia sadok.benyahia@fst.rnu.tn
[2] King Fahd University, Info. and Comp. Sci. Dept. Dahran 31261, Saoudi Arabia

Abstract. Data mining is the discovery of previously unknown or hidden and potentially useful knowledge in databases. In this paper, we present an algorithm, called BRRA, that mines relationships in a database in order to derive compact rules set. This algorithm is based on a mathematical concept called relevant rectangles representing full association between a set of i arguments and a set of j images in a binary relation. **Key words:** Knowledge discovery algorithm, relevant rectangle, inference rules

1 Introduction

Over the past two decades there has been a huge increase in the amount of data being stored in databases. Knowledge discovery (KD) aiming to delve in this data that has been largely ignored by bringing to surface previously unknown, potentially useful and hidden knowledge in a database.

In this paper, we propose an algorithm, called BRRA: Based relevant rectangles algorithm, that mines relationships in database in order to derive rules. The derived rules are a description of the dependencies between a target attribute and a conjunction of the condition attributes. In order to have an efficient use, the derived rule set must be compact (i.e., minimal cardinality of rules and minimal number of condition attributes in each rule).

This paper is organized as follows. In section 2, we present the mathematical background of the rectangle concept. Section 3, is devoted to the presentation of the KD algorithm in order to derive compact rules set. Section 4, presents the evaluation model assessing the compactness of the derived rule set and discusses the computational complexity of the KD algorithm. Finally, section 5 concludes this paper and points out future issues.

2 Basic definitions

In our proposal, we use the concept of *relevant rectangle* (RR). A RR reflects interesting semantic and structural properties. Roughly speaking, a "rectangle", of a binary relation R, is a couple of two sets (A, B) such that $A \times B \subseteq R$.

Searching for RRs of a finite binary relation is a problem which has been previously studied by pure mathematicians within the framework of lattice theory and which has been later proved relevant in several practical fields of computer science[2].

Definition 1. A binary relation R on a set E in a set F, is a subset of the Cartesian product $E \times F$. We define the domain of R, denoted dom(R), as $dom(R) = \{x \mid \exists y : (x, y) \in R\}$, and the range of R, denoted ran(R), as $ran(R) = \{y \mid \exists x : (x, y) \in R\}$.

Definition 2. Let R be a binary relation defined on E in F. A rectangle of R is a couple of two sets such that $A \subseteq E, B \subseteq F$ and $A \times B \subseteq R$ where A denotes dom(R) and B ran(R).

Definition 3. Let R be a binary relation defined on E in F. A rectangle (A, B) of R is said maximal if and only if: $A \times B \subseteq A' \times B' \subseteq R \Rightarrow A = A'$ and $B = B'$.

Example 1. Let us consider the binary relation defined on E in F where E={1, 2, 3, 4} and F={A, B, C}. The rectangle $RE1$ from R given in figure 1 is said to be maximal where the rectangle $RE2$ is not maximal since $RE2 \subseteq RE1$.

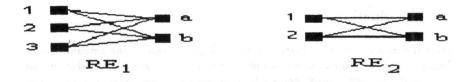

Fig. 1. Example of maximal rectangle.

In the following, we present an heuristic to choose the RR between different maximal ones. Let us consider $(RE_1, RE_2, \ldots, RE_p)$, p maximal rectangles of a binary relation R. The rectangle RE is said to be relevant if and only if it verifies the following condition:

$|dom(RE)| = \max_{i=1,\ldots,p} |dom(RE_i)|$. In case of equality of the cardinality of two or more rectangles domain, then the rectangle RE is elected as relevant if $|ran(RE)| = \min_{i=1,\ldots,p} |ran(RE_i)|$.

Example 2. In figure 2, given that $|dom(RE_1)| = |dom(RE_2)|$, the rectangle RE_1 is elected as relevant, since $|Ran(RE_1)| < |Ran(RE_2)|$.

3 KD algorithm

In order of easy data characterization by means of rules and avoiding complex rules derivation, one must diminish the number of distinct values in each

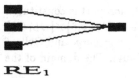
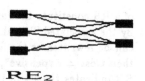

RE₁   **RE₂**

Fig. 2. Example of relevant rectangle.

attribute by performing a conceptual abstraction (or generalization) on the database. This abstraction step ascends specific values to higher-level concepts. For example, suppose that the domain of the attribute "Age" is the range $[0-60]$. Therefore, the distinct age values ranging from $0-5$ and from $6-12$ can be replaced by the user-defined concepts "infant" and "youngster", respectively.

Since the KD algorithm is based on the research of RRs, the n-ary generalized relation is then transformed into a binary relation called BR. BR is defined between a set of tuple numbers (N) and a set of properties P, as a subset of the Cartesian product N×P, by: BR(N, P)= 1, if the tuple has the property 'P'; BR(N, P)= 0 otherwise.

The binary relation BR is the entry to the KD algorithm given in the following.

KD algorithm
Input: A binary relation BR and a target attribute.
Output: A set of compact If-Then rules.
Begin

1. For all distinct values of the target attribute (TA) Do
2. **Decomposition step**: the original base BR is decomposed in two sub-bases B_1 and B_0. B_1 contains the tuples such that $t_i.TA=1$, and B_0 contains the tuples such that $t_i.TA=0$, $i = 1, \ldots, n$, where n is the number of tuples.
3. **Generation step**: Generate the RRs covering the tuples of the sub-base B_1. Theoretically, each generated RR corresponds to a rule of the form "If X is A then Y is B". Where X is a set of attributes X_i, $i = 1, \ldots, k$, and A is the set of its associated values v_i, $i = 1, \ldots, k$. Y is the target attribute and B is its associated value. The semantics of such kind of rules is when 'X is A' is satisfied, we can imply that 'Y is B' is also satisfied. At this step, All the generated rules are stated as possible rules until the verification step is performed.
4. **Verification step**: This step consists in checking if it exists counter-examples to the generated rules. In fact, we consider the condition attributes of each rule $(A_1, A_2, \ldots, A_k)$ and check in B_0 if it exists a tuple t_j such that $(t_j.A_1 = 1$ and $t_j.A_2 = 1$ and ... and $t_j.A_k = 1)$, then this rule is discarded.

End.

A RR, represents the full association between a set of i arguments and a set of j images in a binary relation. Hence, we assume that the properties of the range of a RR constitute the rule condition part and the conclusion part is constituted by the associated TA value. For example, the following RR: $\{1,2,5,6\}\times\{DL, C6\}$ can be rewritten as the following If-Then rule: "If Displace = *Large* and Cyl= *6* then Cost = Expensive", where *Cost* is the target attribute. The domain of the RR indicates the set of tuples covered by this rule.

Example 3. In the following table, we present the generalized base GBC storing cars characteristics yielded by the step of abstraction[5].

N	Displace	Fuelcap	Mass	Speed	Cyl	Cost
1	large	high	medium	medium	6	expensive
2	large	low	heavy	fast	6	expensive
3	medium	medium	light	fast	6	medium
4	small	low	light	slow	6	cheap
5	large	medium	medium	medium	6	expensive
6	large	medium	light	medium	6	expensive
7	small	low	light	medium	6	cheap
8	small	medium	light	slow	4	cheap
9	medium	low	medium	medium	6	medium
10	medium	high	medium	fast	6	expensive
11	medium	high	light	fast	6	expensive
12	small	high	heavy	medium	4	expensive
13	small	high	light	medium	4	cheap
14	medium	low	heavy	medium	4	expensive
15	medium	medium	medium	medium	4	medium
16	medium	high	medium	medium	4	medium
17	small	medium	medium	fast	4	medium
18	medium	medium	heavy	slow	4	expensive

Choosing the attribute "Cost" as a target attribute and applying the BRRA algorithm to the binary relation derived from the relation GBC, the following compact If-Then rule set is derived (with indication of the set of the covered tuples by each rule):

R1: If **Displace** = *Large* and **Cyl**= *6* then **Cost** = Expensive $\{1, 2, 5, 6\}$,

R2: If **Mass** = *Heavy* then **Cost** = Expensive $\{2, 12, 14, 18\}$,

R3: If **Fuelcap** = *High* and **Cyl** = *6* then **Cost** = Expensive $\{1, 10, 11\}$,

R4: If **Mass** = *Medium* and **Cyl** = *4* then **Cost**= Medium $\{15, 16, 17\}$,

R5: If **Displace** = *Medium* and **Cyl** = *6* then **Cost**=Medium $\{3, 9\}$,

R6: If **Displace** = *Small* and **Mass** = *Light* then **Cost**=Cheap $\{4, 7, 8, 13\}$.

4   Evaluation model

Yen et al [5] proposed an evaluation model in order to evaluate the compactness of a rule set. This model, denoted E, the larger is, the more compact the rule set is, and is equal to $\mathbb{E} = \frac{1}{r}\sum_{i}^{r}(\frac{t_i}{n_i}\times\frac{1}{C_i})$, where : r: the cardinality of the rule set; t_i: the number of tuples covered by rule i in the rule set; n_i: the number of tuples in which the target attribute value involved in the consequent of the rule i appears; C_i: the number of the condition attributes in the antecedent of rule $i, 1 \leq i \leq r$.

A comparative table between BRRA and other approaches is given in the following table.

Approach	Rule set cardinality	E
BRRA	6	0.31
LCR[5]	6	0.33
ID3 [3]	9	0.172
Cai et al [4]	18	0.033

In terms of data access, the complexity of the BRRA is linear and needs to scan the base only once which is not the case for other approaches[1, 6] where we may need to scan the relation repeatedly. It is easy to show that the computational complexity is $O(m \times |R|)$ where $m =$ number of attributes and $|R| =$ relation cardinality, given that, the complexity of the second step is equal to $\min(n, m)^2 \times \max(n, m)$.

5 Conclusion

In this paper, we have proposed a new algorithm, based on the discovery of the RRs, to mine relationships or dependencies between attributes in database. The presented algorithm is under implementation and the issue of the paralellization of the generation step (the most costly one) is under study. Another issue to which the present work shall be extended is the handling of uncertain data.

References

1. R. Agrawal, T. Imielinski and A. Swami. Mining Association Rules between sets of items in large Databases. *ACM SIGMOD Records* , pages 207-216, 1993.
2. N. Belkhiter, C. Bourhfir and A. Jaoua. Décomposition rectangulaire optimale d'une relation binaire: Application aux bases de données documentaires. *INFOR*, 32(1):33–54, 1994.
3. J. R. Quinlan. Induction of decision trees. *Machine learning*, (1):81–106, 1986.
4. Y.cai, N. cercone and J. Han. Attribute-oriented Induction in relational databases. In *Knowledge Discovery in Databases. Menlo Park, CA: AAAI/MIT*, pages 213-228, 1991.
5. S.J. Yen and Arbee L.P. Chen. The analysis of relationships in databases for rule derivation. In *Journal of Intelligent Information Systems*, 7(3):235–260,1996.
6. W. Ziarko. The discovery, Analysis, and representation of data dependencies. In *Knowledge Discovery in Databases. Menlo Park, CA: AAAI/MIT*, pages 195-209, 1991.

Mining Functional Dependency Rule of Relational Database[1]

Xiaopeng Tao, Ning Wang, Shuigeng Zhou, Aoying Zhou, Yunfa Hu

xptao@fudan.edu.cn
Computer Science Department of Fudan University, Shanghai, P. R. China, 200433

Abstract. This paper defines a kind of rule, functional dependency rule. The functional dependency degree of relational database can be depicted by this kind of rule. We give a algorithm to mine this kind of rule and prove some theorem to ensure the high efficiency and the correction of the algorithm. At last, we point some experiment result to support our conclusion.

1 Introduction

Now most of real-world data are stored in relational databases, such as bank data, marketing data, etc. So it is significant to research the mining technology oriented relational database.

In relational database theory, the functional dependency relationship (called FD in the following) among relation's attributes is a very important and basic concept. We usually confirm that the function dependency relations when designing the database tables. But frequently we just get the data of table and don't know the relationship among attributes. And some times there are some FDs beyond our consciousness. So we need sophisticated methods to find the FDs from the data of a table.

The remainder of this paper is organized as follows. In section 2, we first give the definition of functional dependency rule (It is called FDR in the following) of relations. Then we give some extension definitions and prove some theorems so as to design and analyze mining algorithm in section 3. In the last section, the conclusions and future work are presented

2 The Definition of FDR

There is noise in the practice data, so finding absolute FD is meaningless. We need methods to evaluate the FD degree, which is called FDR, among attributes of a table.

Definition 1 Data distribution is a function, its parameters are table and table's attribute set, its value is a set, whose element is a 2-tuple. In each 2-tuple, the first part

[1]Project supported by the National Natural Science Foundation of China and the National Doctoral Subject Foundation

is the value of attribute set, the second part is the number of the value appearing in the table. We denote function, data distribution, as $dd(T, A)=\{(v_1, n_1), (v_2, n_2), ... (v_p, n_p)\}$.

Definition 2 Value Distribution is a function, its parameters are the same as the function of definition 1, and its value is a set of distinct value of the appointed attributes. We denote this function as $ddval\ (T, A)=\{v_1, v_2,..., v_p\}$.

Definition 3 Number Distribution is a function, its parameters the same as the function of definition 1, its value is a set of natural numbers which record the times each value of attributes appearing in table. We denote this function as $ddnum\{T, A\}=\{n_1, n_2, ..., n_p\}$.

Definition 4 This function computes the times of one special value of attributes. We denote it as $getnum(T,A=v_i,B)=n_i$.

The value of function ddval is composed of the first part of the value of function dd. The value of function ddnum is composed of the second part of value of function dd. The value of function getnum is the number whose value equals the appointed value.

We add the condition to extend the function dd, $cdd(T, C, B)=dd(T', B)$, the T' is composed with the tuples which accord with the condition C. The extension is the same to the other two functions.

We suppose A, B are table's attributes, the total number of table's tuples is n. The data distribution of attribute A is $\{(a_1, n_1), (a_2. n_2), ..., (a_p, n_p)\}$, that means a_i existing in attribute A n_i times. The max number of each data distribution of attribute B corresponding to every value of attribute A $(a_1, a_2, ..., a_p)$ is $m_1, m_2, ..., m_p$.

Obviously, the expression, $\sum_{i=1}^{p} n_i = n$, is established.

The string "*fdd* " stand for the functional dependency agree in the following part

Definition 5 $fdd(A,B) = \dfrac{\sum\limits_{i=1}^{p} m_i}{\sum\limits_{i=1}^{p} n_i} = \dfrac{\sum\limits_{i=1}^{p} m_i}{n} = \dfrac{\sum\limits_{i=1}^{p} \max(cddnum(T, A = a_i, B)}{n}$.

w_i is the weight of different value of attribute A, usually the greater the number of the value is ,the greater the w_i is.

Definition 6 Given confindence threshold is minc, if $fdd(A, B)>=minc$, then we say there exists the functional dependency rule (FDR), denoted or B=f(A) (For distingishing with the concept of FD in relational database theory, not using the mark, A->B). The A is called determining term, B depending term.

Remark 1: According to the definition 6, we can easily get the conclusion: $fdd((A, B), A)=1$ and $fdd(A, (A, B))=fdd(A, B)$, so it is no significance when the intersection set of determining term and depending term is not empty. In this paper, we just discuss the rule whose intersection set of determining term and depending term is empty.

Remark 2: Symbol A and B express attribute set, such as $\{A_1, A_2, ...,A_n\}$. In this paper, we can omit the set symbol '{' and '}' for writting conveniently. For example,.we write (B, C)=f(A) instead of $(\{B, C\})=f(\{A\})$, A=f(B, C) instead of $\{A\}=f(\{B, C\})$.

3 The Algorithm of Mining Function Dependency Rule

3.1 The Related Theorems

Theorem 1 If FDR, B=f(A), is established, then the FDR B=f(A, C) is established.
Proof: We just need to proof fdd({A, C}, B)>=fdd(A, B).
Suppose dd(T, A)={(a$_1$, an$_1$), (a$_2$. an$_2$), ..., (a$_p$, an$_p$)}, dd(T, {A, C})={(ac$_1$, acn$_1$), (ac$_2$. acn$_2$), ..., (ac$_p$, acn$_p$). Obviously, the data distribution of A and C is a partition of data distribution of A. Suppose (ac$_1$, acn$_1$), (ac$_2$. acn$_2$), ..., (ac$_q$, acn$_q$) is the partition of (a$_1$, an$_1$), then

$$\sum_i \sum cdd(T, A = a_i, B) = \sum_i \sum_j \sum cdd(T, (A = a_i, C = c_j), B)$$

$$\max(cdd(T, A = a_i, B)) <= \sum_j \max(cdd(T, (A = a_i, C = c_j), B))$$

$$fdd(\{A, C\}, B) = \frac{\sum_i \sum_j \max(cdd(T, (A = a_i, C = c_j), B))}{n} >=$$

$$\frac{\sum_i \max(cdd(T, A = a_i, B))}{n} = fdd(A, B) >= \min c$$

So, rule B=f(A, C) is established.
Corollary 1 If B=f(A), then B=f(A, C, ...)
Theorem 2 If B=f(A), is not established, then the {B, C}=f(A) is not established.
Proof: We just need to proof fdd(A, {B, C})<=fdd(A, B).
Because the data distribute of (B, C) according to every value of attribute A is a partition of the data distribute of B, the expression below is established.

$$\max(cdd(T, A = a_i, (B, C))) <= \max(cdd(T, A = a_i, B))$$

$$fdd(A, \{B, C\}) \frac{\sum_i \max(cdd(T, A = a_i, (B, C)))}{n} <=$$

$$\frac{\sum_i \max(cdd(T, A = a_i, B))}{n} = fdd(A, B) < \min c$$

So, rule (B, C)=f(A) is not established.
Corollary 2 If not B=f(A), then not (B, C, ...)=f(A).
Corollary 3 If (B, C)=f(A), then B=f(A) and C=f(A).

Definition 7 One FDR is called basic FDR, if any one attribute is deleted from its determining term or any one attribute is added into its depending term, then the rule is not established.

Theorem 3 All the FDRs can be deduced from basic FDRs by the Theorem 1 and Theorem 2.

Proof: We use mathematics induction to proof this theorem.

1) The induction step: If the rule is not basic FDR.

Supposing the rule's determining term has n attributes, the rule's depending term has m attributes, then it can be denoted to C=f(A, B). A is a attribute. B and C are attribute sets with n-1 elements and m elements specially.

Supposing the rules, whose determining term has n-1 attributes and depending term has m+1 attributes, can be deduced from basic FDR.

By theorem 1, (C, D)=f(B) => C=f(A, B), D is a attribute.

So the conclusion is established.

2) The induction base: If the rule is basic FDR, then it is clear that the conclusion is established.

3.2 The Idea of Algorithm

We use a DAG figure to organize all of the rules. Each rule is one node in the figure. If there are two rules, r1 and r2, r2 is the directly reducing rule of r1, then there is a direct line from r1 to r2 in the figure., the node of r1 is called father of node of r2. The task of finding all the basic FDRs is to search all the nodes who is establish, but whose father is not established.

The root of the DAG is the searching starting point. If the father is established, this searching branch is wiped out, else searching all the sons. Obviously, all the rules found by this method are basic FDR, and all the FDRs will be deduced from the basic FDR by the Theorem 3.

3.3 Mining All the FDR in Relational Database Table

Algorithm Mining all the basic FDR in relational database table.

Input: Table T={A_1, A_2, ..., A_m}, confidence threshold minc.

Output: Table fdrTab=(ruleID, DeterTerm, DepenTermr)

Data Structure: Queue qWaitJudgeRules, Set sFDR, sNonFDR

1) variable initializing. fdrTab=empty, adding rules T=f(NULL) into sNonFDR

2) cycle, until sNonFDR is empty

    2.1) producing qWaitJudgeRules by the directly reducing rules of sNonFDR taking out the directly reducing rules of sFDR,

    2.2) inserting all the rules of sFDR into fdrTab

    2.3) cycle, until qWaitJudgeRules is empty

        2.3.1) take the head rule of qWaitJudgeRules, called r

        2.3.2) if the rule r is established,

                then insert rule r into table sFDR

                else insert rule r into table sNonFDR

3) output the result

3.4 The Analysis of Time Complexity

There are two layer cycle, the first cycle's max length is the number of table's attributes m-1, the second cycle's max length is a function of the time of the first layer cycle. If the time of the first layer cycle is i $(1<=i<=m-1)$, then the second cycle's max length is $C_m^i(2^{m-i}-1)$, so the time complexity of algorithm 5 is

$$\sum_{i=1}^{m-1} C_m^i(2^{m-i}-1)n = O((1.5)^m n).$$

If we use the most brutal method, the pure enumerating method. All the terms are the element of the power set of attributes of table. If table has m attributes, then the power set's cardinal number is 2^m. If we judge the rule between two terms one by one, and there are two directions. The time complexity is $O(2^m(2^m-1)n) = O((2^{2m}-2^m)n) = O(2^{2m}n)$. So our algorithm is much faster than the naive algorithm.

There is a symmetrical algorithm of the above algorithm. We could define the negative concept of reducing relation of two rule, that is called denying relation. Then we organize the DAG by denying relation. The symmetrical algorithm searches the DAG from the root to find all the nodes that can not be denied. The result is the deepest nodes that are established. If the confidence value, minc, is very big, the symmetrical algorithm is faster than the above algorithm.

4 Discussion and Conclusion

This paper puts forward the definition of functional dependency rule of relational table and gives the efficient algorithm for mining the rules. Our experimental results prove our argumentation.

At last, it should be indicated that the relation between our FDR and the famous association rule is very close. The FDR can be regarded as a summery of a group of association rules. Further, we can use association rule to define and mine FDR.

References

1. M.S. Chen, J. Han, and P.S. Yu, `` Data Mining: An Overview from a Database Perspective'', *IEEE Transactions on Knowledge and Data Engineering*, 8(6): 866-883, 1996.
2. R. Agrawal, K. Shim: ``Developing Tightly-Coupled Data Mining Applications on a Relational Database System'', Proc. of the 2nd Int'l Conference on Knowledge Discovery in Databases and Data Mining, Portland, Oregon, August, 1996.
3. D. Fisher. *Improving inference through conceptual clustering*. In Proc. 1987 AAAI Conf., pages 461--465, Seattle, Washington, July 1987.

Time-Series Prediction with Cloud Models in DMKD [1]

Rong Jiang[1], Deyi Li[2] and Hui Chen[1]

[1] Institute of Communication Engineering, No.2 Biaoyin, Nanjing, China, 210016
rongjiang@yahoo.com   huic@263.net
[2] Institute of Electronic System Engineering, No.6, Wanshou Road, Beijing, China, 100036
ziqin@public2.bta.net.cn

Abstract. A growing attention has been paid to mining time-series knowledge, while time-series prediction becomes one of the important aspects of data mining and knowledge discovery (DMKD). This paper presents a new mechanism of time-series prediction with cloud models. This mechanism not only synthesizes different predictive knowledge with different granularities, but also combines two kinds of predictive strategy: local prediction and overall prediction. We focus this paper on the application of cloud models to transform between quantitative and qualitative knowledge, synthesize different kinds of knowledge and realize the soft inference.

1. Introduction

Data mining and knowledge discovery (DMKD) has become an active and growing research area. And recently, mining qualitative predictive knowledge for time-series prediction has been listed as one of the challenges for DMKD. Time-series prediction is to forecast future values from a temporal sequence of data. Such prediction is required in many fields, such as the prediction of weather, network load, future sales, stock market and so on.

There are many kinds of time-series predictive approaches. The most common "classical" approaches include: Autoregressive(AR), Moving Average(MA) and combined approaches: ARMA, ARIMA, and ARCH. Neural network models are an alternative to the classical methods [4, 7]. Recently, some interesting work has also been done on applying machine learning to temporal domains [6, 8]. Although these approaches all have their own advantages, there exist common shortcomings among them. Firstly, these methods usually give one or a sequence of numbers as predictive results. The quantitative results are difficult for the users to understand and usually crisp, while qualitative knowledge may be more robust and easier to understand, but difficult to express and calculate in computers. So representation of predictive knowledge is a challenging and inescapable subject. Secondly, in most of these methods, little attention has been paid to the time granularity, although it is a very important element as we analyze the time-series data.

---

[1] Research was supported by the National Advanced Technology Development Projects (No.863-306-ZT06-07-2).

In the rest paper, a new mechanism of time-series prediction based on cloud models will be proposed. Representation of predictive knowledge with cloud models is presented in section 2. Then, section 3 expounds the new mechanism of time-series prediction, and section 4 gives the results of experiment and the conclusion.

2. Representation of predictive knowledge with cloud models

Suppose we have a set of time-series data D: $\{(a_i, b_i) \mid 0 \leq i < t\}$, meanwhile a_i is a value of time attribute A, and b_i is a value of numerical attribute B. The task of prediction is to forecast the value b_t of the future time a_t. To complete the predictive task, the first problem we meet with is the representation of predictive knowledge. Usually people represent their predictive knowledge as linguistic rules such as, if it is the mid-season then the sales may be high, which include uncertain concepts "mid-season" and "high", as well as uncertain inference "if... then ...may...". So predictive knowledge is a kind of qualitative knowledge, which is always indeterminate and uncertain. In this section, a randomized method—cloud model will be introduced to represent the predictive knowledge.

Let U be the set $U=\{u\}$, as the universe of discourse, and T a term associated with U. The membership degree of u in U to the term T, $C_T(u) \in [0,1]$, is a random number with a stable tendency. The cloud of T is a mapping from the universe of discourse U to the unit interval $[0,1]$. That is:

$$C_T(u):U \rightarrow [0,1] \quad \forall u \in U \quad u \rightarrow C_T(u) \tag{1}$$

The normal cloud (NC) is based on normal distributions. It can be characterized by three digital parameters: A(Ex, En, He). The expected value Ex points out the center of gravity of a cloud. The entropy En is a measure of the fuzziness of the concept over the universe of discourse, showing how many elements could be accepted by the term A. The hype-entropy He is a measure of the uncertainty of the entropy En. The larger the value of He, the more random the set of membership degrees is distributed. Figure 1 shows the appropriate NC for the term "young". Instead of a membership curve, the mapping from $\forall u \in U$ to the interval $[0,1]$ is a one-point to multi-point transition, which shows the uncertainty: fuzziness and randomness of an element belonging to the term. So, the degree of membership of u to T is a probability distribution rather than a fixed value.

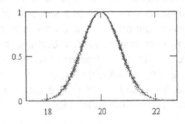

Fig. 1. The Normal Cloud of the Term "young"(20, 0.7, 0.025)

Based on cloud models, a linguistic variable can be defined as a set of linguistic terms, represented as $A\{A_1(Ex_1, En_1, He_1)...A_2(Ex_2, En_2, He_2)...A_m(Ex_m, En_m, He_m)\}$. To realize the transform between quantitative values and qualitative concepts, four kinds of cloud generators are introduced as basic cloud generator, u-condition cloud generator, μ-condition cloud generator and backward cloud generator.[1, 3]

In the daily life of our society, most of the social behaviors carry out according to the nature time: year, month, or day. Thus their varying regularity is periodical in some degree. However, there are too many uncertain factors influencing those behaviors, and we couldn't catch every factors well and truly. So we take them as quasi-periodical regularity and represent them as predictive linguistic rules. To realize the linguistic rules, it is difficult but important to maintain the uncertainty of inference. Here we use linguistic rule based on cloud models to carry on the soft inference "A→B", meanwhile A and B are linguistic concepts represented by cloud models. Two cloud generators, u-condition cloud generator and μ-condition cloud generator, are connected to construct the rule, which is shown in figure 2. See [1, 2, 3, and 9] for details.

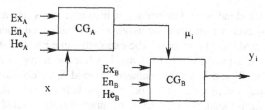

Fig. 2. the Implement of Predictive Linguistic Rule A→B

Although the knowledge of quasi-periodical regularity grasps the time-series in a whole, it is not precise and fresh enough to forecast. For the time-series data take on stability in a short time, we can discover predictive knowledge of current tendency from the current data. It should be uncertain, obeying the distribution of current data, and be represented as a qualitative tendency instead of a quantitative value. We introduce a new concept based on cloud model—Current Cloud $I_t(Ex, En, He)$ to represent the predictive knowledge of current tendency. Meanwhile, Ex points out the center of current tendency as the expected predictive value, En is a measure of the fuzziness of current tendency, showing how many values could be accepted by the tendency, and He gives a measure of the uncertainty of the entropy En.

3. Mechanism of time-series prediction with cloud models

Now, two kinds of predictive knowledge have been described. The predictive linguistic rules emphasize the overall regularity of the time-series data, while the current cloud focuses on the temporary tendency of current data. Their knowledge granularities are also different. The predictive linguistic rules are the summary of the time-series data in many historical periods, so its granularity is higher than that of current cloud, which only sums up the current data in the recent period. The following algorithm is to realize time-series prediction with cloud models by synthesizing these two kinds of predictive knowledge.

Algorithm: Time-series Prediction with Cloud Models

1. Dividing the time series data set D into the set of historical data HD and the set of current data CD;
2. Mining quasi-periodical regularity as set of predictive linguistic rules: PLR={$A_i \rightarrow B_i$, i=1,...,m} from HD;
3. Mining current tendency as current cloud I_t from CD;
4. Activating a linguistic rule $A_i \rightarrow B_i$ in PLR, through judging which antecedent linguistic term the time value a_t belongs to;
5. Synthesizing the historical cloud B_i and the current cloud I_t into a new cloud S_t;
6. Realizing the soft inference $A_i \rightarrow S_t$ to forecast.

We can use the following equations to synthesize the cloud B_i (Ex_1, En_1, He_1) and I_t (Ex_2, En_2, He_2) to S_t (Ex, En, He):

$$Ex = \frac{Ex_1 En_1 + Ex_2 En_2}{En_1 + En_2} \quad En = En_1 + En_2 \quad He = \frac{He_1 En_1 + He_2 En_2}{En_1 + En_2} \quad (2)$$

The synthesized cloud is used to synthesize linguistic terms into a generalized one. In this paper, however, we give another usage of the synthesized cloud. That is to sum up two kinds of predictive knowledge. The expected value Ex of synthesized cloud S_t ranges between the expected values of B_i and I_t, while the entropy En of S_t is the sum of the entropies of B_i and I_t. So the synthesized cloud S_t covers more values than B_i and I_t, which means it provides more possible predictive results than any of them. Through synthesized cloud, the knowledge of quasi-periodical regularity and current tendency are blent together. They can not be distinguished in the cloud S_t any more.

The soft inference $A_i \rightarrow S_t$ can be realized directly by the connection of two cloud generators as described in section 2. Different from other predictive methods, this mechanism can provide the predictive results in many forms instead of just a dull digital value. Firstly, we can get the two drops (a_t, μ) and (μ, y) respectively on the two mathematically expected curves of the antecedent cloud A_i and consequent cloud S_t, and provide y as the expected predictive result. Secondly, we can get two drops (a_t, μ_i) and (μ_i, y_i) randomly, and output y_i as an uncertain predictive result. Lastly, we can activate the rule for many times, and get as many drops as we like. The set of y_i can be provided to the user for further analysis. It is clear that the predictive results is uncertain, which exactly reflects our thought of randomization and soft inference.

4. Experiment and Conclusion

Sales prediction has important significant in commercial behaviors, while production sales always have quasi-period regularity according to the period year. We used the auto sales in dollar nominal plotted alongside the CPI from 1989 to 1995 as our experimental data. Five predictive linguistic rules were discovered from them. Figure 3 shows the predictive results of short rang and long rang horizon from the 20th week to the 52nd week of 1995 compared with the original time-series data of 1995.

529

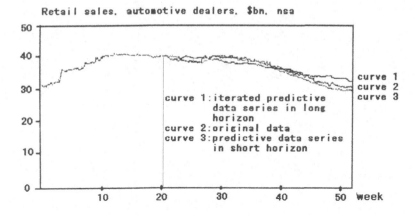

Fig. 3. the Forecasting Results of the Sales in 1995

This paper proposes a new mechanism of time-series prediction with cloud models. It can discover two kinds of qualitative predictive knowledge, quasi-periodical regularity and current tendency, which are respectively represented as predictive linguistic rules and current cloud based on cloud models. This mechanism not only synthesizes different predictive knowledge with different granularities, but also combines two kinds of predictive strategy: local prediction and overall prediction. We intend to focus our future efforts in the directions concerning the dimension of predictive factor and the concept drift.

References

1. Deyi Li, Jiawei Han, XuiMei Shi and Man-chung Chan, Knowledge Representation and Discovery Based on Linguistic Atoms, Knowledge-Based System, 10(1998), 431-440.
2. Deyi Li, Kaichang Di and Deren Li, Mining Association with Linguistic Cloud Models, Manuscript, 1998.
3. Deyi Li, XuiMei Shi, Paul Ward and m.M. Gupat, Soft inference Mechanism Based on Cloud Models, Logic Programming and Soft Computing, Reach Studies Press, 1997.
4. Francoise Fessant, Samy Bengio and Daniel Collobert, On the Prediction of Solar Activity Using Different Neural Network Models, from www.syntim.inria.fr/fractales.
5. Gautam Das and King-Ip Lin, Rule Discovery from Time Series, In Proceeding of KDD98, 16-22.
6. Laird P., Discrete Sequence Prediction and its Applications, AAAI-92 Proceedings of the Tenth National Conference on Artificial Intelligence, 1992.
7. Park D. C., M. A. El-Sharkawi, and R.J. Marks, Electric Load Forecasting Using an Artificial Neural Network, IEEE Transaction on Power Systems, 6:2, 442-449,1991.
8. Scott Mitchell, The Application of Machine Learning Techniques to Time-Series Data, 1995.
9. ZhaoHui Yang and Deyi Li, Planar Clouds and its Application in Prediction, the Journal of Computer Science, 1998, Vol.21, No.11, 961-969.

Author Index

Lecture Notes in Artificial Intelligence (LNAI)

Lecture Notes in Computer Science